People and Places in Colonial Venezuela

People and Places in Colonial Venezuela

JOHN V. LOMBARDI

Maps and Figures by Cathryn L. Lombardi

Indiana University Press

BLOOMINGTON & LONDON

Published in Canada by Fitzhenry and Whiteside Limited,
Don Mills, Ontario

Manufactured in the United States of America

Library of Congress Cataloging in Publication Data
Lombardi, John V
People and places in colonial Venezuela.
Bibliography.
Includes index.
1. Caracas (Archdiocese)--Population--History. I. Title.
HB3580.C3L65 1976 301.32'9'87 75-25433
ISBN 0-253-34330-5 1 2 3 4 5 80 79 78 77 76

For John Lombardi and Janice P. Lombardi

Contents

ILLUSTRATIONS

MAPS

FIGURES AND TABLES

PREFACE

This book marks the beginning of what promises to be a long-term inquiry into the number, distribution, and characteristics of Venezuela's people during the century of transition, 1750-1850. During those years, Spain's outpost colony in Tierra Firme became a mature colonial society, developed a major metropolitan city, led the South American independence movement, and created a republican government fully integrated into the North Atlantic commercial system. These activities have long drawn the attention of scholars with a wide range of interests, and historians--Venezuelan and foreign--have examined many aspects of these events. But before this work can be brought together into any satisfactory synthesis, we must have available some reliable estimates of Venezuela's human resources; we must know who lived where and when. How, for example, can the catastrophic impact of the Venezuelan wars for independence be evaluated without a secure knowledge of the changes they caused in the region's population base? Clearly, our ability to offer reasonable hypotheses about the dynamic processes of Venezuela's past has been severely limited by the absence of systematic surveys of the area's population.

This volume presents a first approximation of such a survey, through a hypothetical reconstruction of Venezuela's population landscape at a given point in time. It presents a new body of data on the people and places of late colonial Venezuela, and begins the task of analyzing and describing the characteristics of the people residing in the area. Venezuela has a remarkable collection of population data, but practically none of it is useable as it comes from the archives. It must be coded, processed, identified, compared, and evaluated before it can help us to write population history. By limiting the scope of this work to the Bishopric of Caracas--that is the parishes reporting to the Bishop and then Archbishop of Caracas between 1771 and 1838--it has been possible to use the largest body of internally consistent data. The resulting profile of Venezuela's people can serve as a standard for the evaluation and analysis of the less consistent data available for earlier and later time periods. The remaining data, less extensive in geographic and temporal coverage, will be organized, verified, and added to the population file in subsequent volumes. The hypotheses presented here can then be reevaluated, new estimates and corrections made, and more reliable adjustments proposed.

Part I of this volume contains three types of analysis. The first two chapters seek to establish the limits of the inquiry begun here. Chapter 1 outlines the principal features of the physical landscape and sketches the geopolitical formation of the area we call Venezuela. Chapter 2 surveys the population records available for the country in the period under study, evaluates their utility and accuracy, and sets priorities for their exploitation. This chapter also defines the subset of population records used in this volume.

The next two chapters trace the broad features of the population landscape of the Bishopric in two dimensions during the critical decade 1800-1809. First, in Chapter 3, the parishes of the Bishopric are analyzed in terms of structure, size, and regional distribution, which provides a starting point for an analysis of Venezuela's urban network. Second, Chapter 4 explores some of the characteristics of the Bishopric's population at the close of the colonial period: race, sex, marriage, and children are explored in the detail and specificity permitted by the data. Here, too, a series of preliminary hypotheses emerge as starting points for future work.

The final section, Chapter 5, examines the consequences of the wars for independence on one of Venezuela's important cities, San Carlos de Austria. Although some questions cannot be satisfactorily answered because of limitations in the data, the story of a city's response to the war suggests a host of fascinating hypotheses for investigation. All of these chapters are illustrated by series of figures--graphs, tables, plots--and carry in Appendix A a sizeable complement of descriptive tables.

Part II consists of reference material based on the subset of data described in Chapter 2 as Type III format data. The tables display the data from ecclesiastical censuses in a parish-by-parish format, with a number of simple combinations and calculations included to increase their utility. A machine-readable version of this file will be made available at the conclusion of the project, but many historians will find Part II adequate for their needs, especially if access to computers and computer technicians is difficult or inconvenient.

Foreign words and phrases have been italicized only the first time they appear in the book. All percentages reported have been rounded and therefore may not always add up to 100.0%.

Because this book mentions a large number of places, some system for finding and identifying them had to be devised. That has been accomplished through Appendix B and the Index to Parts I and II. Apendix B contains a series of lists of parish names. Readers interested in the location of any particular town or concerned about the version of a town's name used here would consult the name lists and location maps in Appendix B. All place names appearing in the text and notes, on the maps, and in the introductions to the Appendices and to Part II, are indexed. Place names appearing in alphabetized lists such as those in Appendix B and in the Tables in Part II are not indexed. All alphabetizing is done by the English alphabet; thus the Spanish letters _ll_ and _rr_ are alphabetized as separate rather than as single letters. The _ñ_ is treated as an _n_.

Throughout this work, I have made every effort to avoid the technical scholasticism that so tempts the practitioner of what has been called quantitative history. My own interest in these numbers comes from a fascination with the dynamics of Venezuelan social history and from a conviction that our analysis of these phenomena must begin with an understanding of the basic elements of the historical process: man and his material world. If the work reported on here informs demographers or sociologists, I will be delighted, though it was prepared for historians who share my interest and enthusiasm for the past.

* * *

Like most large projects, this book could only have been completed with the advice and assistance of a large number of people and institutions. Work on the data for this volume began in Caracas in 1967, when Trent M. Brady surveyed the extensive collection of census records in the Archivo Arquidiocesano, while working on a study of miscegenation in colonial Venezuela. At that time, Brady and I agreed to collaborate on the work of collection and analysis. I microfilmed the data collection during the spring of 1967. With the financial support of the Graduate School Research Committee, University of Wisconsin, Brady had the microfilm run onto Xerox sheets. Then Cathryn L. Lombardi and I spent parts of 1967-68 and 1968-69 coding and checking the data for the first pass through the census file. Brady prepared the basic list of parishes and parish locations. With the continued support of the University of Wisconsin, Brady arranged for the Social Systems Research Institute at Madison to punch and verify the coded data. During this first phase of the research, we received excellent advice from Eduard Glasser, Assistant Director of the Social Systems Research Institute, Madison, and Karl E. Tauber of the University of Wisconsin. Due to the press of other commitments, Trent Brady effectively withdrew from active participation in the project. However, without Brady's energetic and resourceful promotion of this enterprise in its early stages, this volume would never have been possible.

During this first stage of the project, Brady received substantial support from the University of Wisconsin and from the Canada Council, while I benefited from the aid of Indiana University's Office of Research and Advanced Studies and Latin American Studies Program. In Caracas, the support of the Fundación John Boulton and the Fundación Creole made the microfilm operation possible.

At the Fourth Congress of the International Economic History Association (Bloomington, Indiana, 1968), we received especially valuable comments and suggestions on a preliminary description of the project. I especially want to thank Woodrow W. Borah and Sherburne F. Cook for their advice and encouragement at that time.

David W. Davies (Claremont, California) initiated me into the mysteries of computer programming and showed me that no historian need feel inadequate when confronted with the simpleminded complexity of the computer.

While the present volume builds on the work mentioned above and could never have been completed without that preliminary effort, the data and analysis included here have been reworked from the original data file. Cathryn Lombardi and I recoded the entire data file from the microfilm and Xerox, in order to correct errors and misinterpretations made during the first pass through the file. I prepared the text in Part I, along with its supporting material in the Appendices, during the academic year 1974-75, thanks in part to a sabbatical leave from Indiana University. The material in Part II was worked up from the recoded data file during 1974-75, and processed at the Indiana University Marshal H. Wrubel Computing Center. I am greatly indebted to the staff of the WCC for their patience and technical assistance.

The preparation of this book was greatly facilitated by the support of the Mid-West Universities Consortium for International Activities (MUCIA). Under the joint direction of Professor Germán Carrera Damas (CENDES--Universidad Central de Venezuela) and myself, the project "Formation, Structure, and Dynamics of a Primate City: A Case Study of Caracas (1560-1960)", involving participants from Venezuela and the MUCIA universities, has been working on a variety of topics related to the history of Caracas as a central city. Because the notion of a central, primate, city requires a context and a scale of comparison to give it meaning, this book is designed to provide the setting within which the primacy of Caracas can be evaluated. The project, funded for the period 1974-1976, will produce a series of monographs on the city of Caracas. This is the first contribution to that series.

Throughout this project, I have been the grateful recipient of excellent advice from a variety of colleagues here and in Venezuela.

At every stage in this work Pedro Grases (Sociedad Bolivariana de Venezuela) and Manuel Pérez Vila (Fundación John Boulton) offered me their full support, their excellent advice, and their generous hospitality. In similar fashion the custodians of a variety of archives and institutions in Caracas made every effort to facilitate my work: Fray Cesáreo de Armellada at the Archivo Arquidiocesano de Caracas, Mario Briceño Perozo at the Archivo General de la Nación, Carlos Felice Cardot at the Academia Nacional de la Historia, Cosme Romero at the Dirección de Cartografía Nacional (Ministerio de Obras Públicas), and George Hall at the Fundación Creole.

From the beginning of this project I have counted on the expert counsel, enthusiastic encouragement, and firm friendship of Germán Carrera Damas (Universidad Central de Venezuela). I have also received valuable advice from José Antonio De Armas Chitty (Universidad Central de Venezuela).

A number of colleagues at Indiana University read this book in manuscript, made valuable suggestions for improvement, or helped in other ways. My thanks go to James R. Scobie, George I. Stolnitz, Paul R. Lucas, Edwin R. Coover, George M. Wilson, Robert E. Quirk, and

Martin Ridge. Kathy Waldron helped with the parish name file. I would like to thank the staff of the Indiana University Press for their excellent advice and assistance, and the staff of the Marshall H. Wrubel Computing Center, of whom Jean Nakhnikian and John Gerth were especially helpful. Roberta E. Adams prepared the text for processing, checked the notes, and in general made the production of this book possible.

I am also most grateful for the comments I received from colleagues at other institutions: John L. Phelan and Peter H. Smith at the University of Wisconsin, Dauril Alden at the University of Washington, Woodrow W. Borah at the University of California, David W. Davies in Claremont, California, Stanley J. Stein at Princeton University, Mary Lombardi in Davis, California, and James A. Hanson at Brown University. The illustrations are by Elisabeth S. Moe, to whom I am most grateful for the excellent renderings of some characteristic eighteenth-century scenes.

All of the maps, bar graphs, and figures are the work of Cathryn L. Lombardi. She is also responsible for much of the coding and verification of the population file. Without her support, encouragement, and understanding, the book would never have been completed.

To all of these individuals and institutions, and to countless others not specifically mentioned here whose contributions have been nevertheless important, I acknowledge a sizeable debt for making this book possible and for improving the final version.

October 1975
Bloomington, Indiana

Part I

The Population of the Bishopric of Caracas in the Late Colonial Period

Introduction

One of the remarkable achievements of Spain's colonial administrators in the New World was the information system they designed, modified, and manipulated throughout the centuries of Spanish America's colonial period. Starting with the first reports from Columbus on the discovery of the New World and continuing through the decline and collapse of the imperial system some three hundred years later, Spanish administrators at all levels of the bureaucracy collected, organized, summarized, transmitted, and stored information on every possible aspect of life in the Spanish domain. From the birth of the poorest slave child to the installation of viceroys, from the folklore of obscure and isolated native tribes to the rules of precedence in high colonial courts, and from the price of coffee beans in forgotten coastal towns to the movement of treasure fleets: everything interested the Crown's ministers and everything had to be recorded. No other European monarch seemed to comprehend so clearly the principle of all complex organizations and large-scale enterprises that knowledge is power. That commitment to the acquisition of reliable, complete, and comprehensive information is one of the few totally consistent and universally pursued objectives of Spain's three-century rule in America. Thanks to that compulsion to know everything, Spain's imperial mission must rank as the best-documented achievement of its kind before the advent of computerized information systems.

Ironically, much of the historian's frustration in attempting to analyze and interpret the development, organization, and operation of this empire comes from trying to deal with the immense volume of information available on any subject he might choose. After many generations of scholarship in the Americas and elsewhere, we are only beginning to achieve satisfying explanations of what the Spanish accomplished in the New World. Thanks to the efforts of countless scholars, we have come to understand the formal structure of the imperial system as reflected in the laws and in the institutions for political, religious and economic control. These advances in scholarship have given the Spanish imperial structure a surface and a context. Nevertheless, a complete understanding of many of the functions, mechanisms, and activities--in a word, the life--that existed beneath that surface, within that structure, still escapes us.[1]

Once the surface features of this structure were known well enough and the form relatively well established, scholars began to narrow the focus of their research in an effort to discover what lay beneath. But because of the incredibly rich archives, the massive files of information on every conceivable topic, and the inconsistent and idiosyncratic characteristics of many of those materials, scholars almost despaired of bringing enough order to the information for successful synthesis. Fortunately, historians have an amazing capacity to attempt the impossible. In spite of their well known disdain for cooperative, large-scale projects, and their penchant for investigating only those topics and subjects that amuse or interest, a long series of careful, patient, and imaginative historians have produced monographs that demonstrate in many cases what life in the Spanish American empire must have been like.

In this continual campaign to explain and analyze colonial Spanish American life, we have gradually come to understand and to some degree control the legacy of Spain's information system. The success in this enterprise follows a clear progression in the use of the documents. The trend in historical scholarship has been from the study of the most generalized documents towards the most specialized. We have moved, for example, from the rules governing empires to the rules governing the family and from the organization of imperial commerce to the study of local economies. Detailed microstudies--those sharply focused investigations that attempt to validate or replace our intuitive notions about the quality and content of Spanish colonial life--have allowed us to construct even better representations of Spain's empire in America.[2]

It is from within this context that _People and Places in Colonial Venezuela_ draws its inspiration. This book starts from the assumption that the better we understand the physical, material, and measurable aspects of a historical process, the better prepared we will be to evaluate and analyze what is neither material nor measurable. Although the precise definition of the measurable, material, world is difficult to establish, some fundamental relationships are obviously included. Because history concerns the interaction of man and his creations within a matrix of time and space, a reliable understanding of the characteristics and dimensions of that space would almost seem required. Similarly, a firm knowledge of where and in what number individuals have or have not been located within the space would also appear necessary. Because history demands an accounting of change over time, the student of material, measurable, things must show how the relationships of these people to their places have varied.

People do not, of course, inhabit places in the abstract. They live in structures, wear apparel, acquire possessions, build monuments, and in general manipulate and control their environment. Along with the study of the numbers and distribution of people, we must also catalog and analyze the things that surround their lives. For the historian, the purpose of counting, classifying, measuring, and evaluating material and human resources is not simply to know the quantities and magnitudes involved, although that is important, but to establish the sizes, shapes, and numbers of people and things in order to bring under systematic control the physical dimensions of the universe being analyzed.

In the case of the Spanish colonial empire, such a study will permit us to establish the scale or the orders of magnitude of the enterprise. To take an obvious example, when we speak of imperial or metropolitan capitals, we must be sure that we know whether we speak of towns on the order of 50,000 inhabitants or cities of 500,000 and be prepared to analyze the consequences of the difference in scale implied by those numbers. When we discuss the pursuit of wealth, we need to know on what scale the wealth is measured. For example, was the Mexican colonial worth 10,000 pesos wealthier, in relative terms, than the Venezuelan worth 5,000? What could he buy with that amount of wealth, and where, within the context of his universe, would that income have placed him? These matters of scale are not easily resolved and the research effort required to produce good scales over any appreciable geographic or temporal span is substantial. However, with the aid of a variety of technological devices, the project has become increasingly more manageable. We can hope that in a scholarly lifetime, individuals or research teams can make progress on the task of defining the limits, the orders of magnitude, of the measurable aspects of Spain's American empire.

Within this strategy of bringing the measurable characteristics of colonial Spanish America under systematic control, some tactical research decisions have to be made. The most rational and systematic tactic is to divide the materials and topics into semiautonomous blocks, units of study large enough to be helpful and interesting, but small enough to be studied in a reasonable amount of time. In this book that tactic has led to the selection of Venezuela, or more properly the Captaincy-General of Venezuela, as the geographical dimension, and the period 1750 to 1850 as the temporal dimension. Within that two-dimensional matrix, this book begins an attempt to determine the limits of Venezuela's population and to prepare for a continuing inquiry into the other measurable aspects of Venezuela's material world.

The choice of this place and time responds to a set of characteristics that make Venezuela an attractive focus. The core area of this colonial jurisdiction, the Bishopric of Caracas, produced a remarkable collection of population records for the last decades of Spanish rule. These documents are so rich and so extensive that, in theory, it should be possible to reconstruct the life histories of all the parishes in the Bishopric, at least in terms of birth, death, marriage, family, and residence patterns. In addition, Venezuela attracts the scholar because of its special position within the Spanish imperial structure. It was what we could call a late-blooming colony. Until the middle of the eighteenth century, Venezuela experienced modest economic growth and warranted a marginal place in the imperial organization. During the second half of the eighteenth century, however, the region matured and prospered. Its economic base in cacao and cattle expanded, its population grew rapidly, and its political institutions matured and consolidated. By 1777 the disparate provinces in the area of present-day Venezuela were joined under the jurisdiction of a captain general located in what had become a minor metropolitan center, Caracas. Because Venezuela matured late and because the scale of life--that is government, society, economics, and culture--remained relatively simple when compared to the major metropolitan centers of Mexico or Lima, its complexity is much more manageable. We can expect, for example, to disentangle the web of interrelationships that made up Venezuelan society through the use of a finite quantity of scholarly resources. And although the scale of Venezuelan activities is neither as large nor as complex as that found in Mexico or Peru, almost all the important elements of the Spanish colonial system appear. Thus conclusions, hypotheses, and relationships identified in the Venezuelan context may be expected to aid in the understanding of the social order in other Spanish American jurisdictions.

The time frame for the inquiry of which this study forms a part encloses what can be called the century of transition, 1750-1850. During those hundred years, Venezuela became a mature colony, consolidated power and authority in the central city of Caracas, waged a long disruptive war for independence, and by 1850 had established the major patterns of republican organization. From an economic, social, and political appendage of Spain, Venezuela became a peripheral dependent of the rapidly industrializing North Atlantic community. Because of its location and history, Venezuela provides an unusually promising place to test hypotheses about the structure and dynamic relationships of the North Atlantic hegemony. But before these relationships can be fully cataloged and explained, we must have a firm understanding of the material base of places like Venezuela that formed such an important part of that North Atlantic economic empire.[3]

Within this rather ambitious framework, the goals of the study begun in this volume are modest. While Venezuela's historical and geographical literature contains numerous contributions of very high quality, many works that might help provide a general background for this book are missing, excessively detailed, or too general. Before talking about Venezuela's population, for example, we need a short synthesis of Venezuelan geography that can provide a standardized geographical and regional nomenclature. Although Venezuela's geographical literature is remarkably well-developed, no single work brings together the information in a form most useful for this analysis. As a result, since an agreement on physical conditions and geographical nomenclature is required for subsequent discussion, the first chapter in the present volume sets out the major regions and subregions of Venezuela with an indication of their distinguishing characteristics. This chapter also indicates the major political subdivisions of the region during the last decades of colonial rule. Because this geographical survey must serve not only as a reference for this volume but also for the analysis in subsequent volumes, it is developed in somewhat greater detail and scope than would be required for this work alone.

Two major subdivisions can be identified within the organization of the broader inquiry of which this book forms a part. The first consists of the analysis of population characteristics; the second involves the analysis of material culture. Within the first subdivision, the range of concerns can be further divided into what I call the base line characteristics and the dynamic processes. Base line characteristics refer to a series of measures of Venezuela's population that give the scale and principal features of the regions' population landscape. They include such basic notions as the distribution of people, child/woman ratios, percentages of adults married, racial distribution, and the structure of the urban network. The dynamic processes include the traditional demographic concerns of mortality, fertility, migrations, and their effect upon age structure. By extension, the analysis of growth and the evaluation of the demographic consequences of historical or natural events are also included here. For practical reasons, it is impossible to deal with all these concerns at once, and as a result, a series of tactical decisions had to be made about how to proceed. These decisions, of course, depended to a great extent on an assessment of the scope, quality, and quantity of demographic material available for Venezuela's colonial period. The present volume contains that assessment of demographic resources which, like the geographic discussion, is also designed to serve the interests of subsequent volumes.

With an understanding of the materials available, the selection of topics and the limitations on the discussion here responded to the following rationale. Because it is usually difficult to interpret micro-level studies without a reasonably complete understanding of the macro-level context, I have given first priority to the establishment of a population profile for Venezuela at the end of the colonial period. Further, because of the way the data were prepared and stored, I have given first priority to the study of the largest body of internally consistent population records above the nominal level. Thus those documents from the parish level that show population aggregated by race, class, sex, civil category, and age, should be collected, organized, and analyzed before the parish level data that show lists of individuals by name, with indications of age, sex, occupation, race, and civil category. This hierarchy of document use presupposes a research methodology that will maximize the amount of useable information that can be extracted from the materials, with the minimum investment of scholarly resources.

In exploiting the aggregated data, all the available information can be processed and analyzed, at least for the Bishopric of Caracas, because the volume of material does not exceed what can be done with the resources available. The nominal level data, such as the household lists, municipal censuses, parish registers, and the like, pose a different problem and require a slightly different methodology. These materials, extraordinarily rich in detail, represent an enormous quantity of information that must be coded, organized, and processed to be useable for analysis. Because of the volume of information involved, a research strategy utilizing careful sampling techniques would appear to be the most efficient. But the design of these sampling techniques and the interpretation of the resulting data could prove difficult without a secure knowledge of the general population characteristics of Venezuela. Therefore, this volume focuses on the aggregated data, and especially on that subset of the data representing the largest group of internally consistent records for the Bishopric of Caracas. It is thus possible to establish a reasonably secure base line of population characteristics that can serve as a reference for more detailed examinations based on less complete or less tractable information.

Among the difficulties associated with this approach is the temptation to view the population profile prepared for the Bishopric of Caracas and the structure of urban centers described here as representing static and relatively unchanging arrangements. While the information provides a close approximation of the conditions characteristic of the decade 1800-1809, those conditions were apparently subject to considerable change both before and after the base line period. Although in its present stage of development the population file on

Venezuela does not permit an unambiguous analysis of the striking fluctuations in population typical of the Bishopric's parishes, the file is good enough for a case study of the kind of population effects brought about during the decades of the independence wars, 1810-1823. To remind us of the rapidly changing population totals of Venezuela's parishes, I have included in this first volume a case study of the impact of war on one of Venezuela's cities.

This effort, then, provies a base line description of the Bishopric's population in the decade 1800-1809. It focuses on those characteristics for which the data is reliable and for which the additional information still being processed promises little new insight. For example, the network of parishes classified into hamlets, villages, towns, and cities, may be marginally improved when the population file is complete, but it is unlikely that the analysis presented here will require major modification because of new data. In contrast, no effort has yet been made to fill the gaps in the population series for individual parishes, because the complete file, when finished, may make much of the estimation unnecessary.

An integral part of the philosophy guiding this project is the notion that any data gathered and processed through the assistance of public agencies should be open and available to all. None of the work begun here would have been possible without the cooperation and support of countless individuals and institutions in the United States and Venezuela. To repay this debt, the data and results must be made accessible as soon as possible. In this project that imperative has been met in two ways. First, the basic file on which this volume is based is published with the text in tables designed to be as helpful as possible without exceeding a manageable size. This procedure insures that anyone here, in Venezuela, or elsewhere, can use the population file prepared with the support of Venezuelan and United States entities, and guarantees that scholars unfamiliar with computer techniques can use the data easily. Second, when the Venezuelan population file is complete, the machine readable version of that file will be made available.

It is within the context of the research design described here, and subject to the limitations discussed above, that this volume has been written. Its purpose is to initiate a long term study of Venezuela's population and its goal is to aid the research of the many scholars working on that wide range of topics requiring a sound knowledge of Venezuela's population during the century of transition.

La Guaira-Caracas Road

ONE

Venezuela in Time and Space

That northernmost portion of South America known today as the Republic of Venezuela contains within its boundaries a remarkable variety of geographic features that have helped determine patterns of settlement and organization in the region since the beginning of European settlement. A glance at a relief map of Venezuela immediately reveals the country's major geographic features. Sweeping into the southwestern corner of Venezuela, a spur of South America's mightiest mountain chain, the Andes, curves northward, dividing east and west to form the basin of Lake Maracaibo, losing height until it broadens out into the Segovia Highlands on the west and the Goagira Peninsula on the east and then falling off gradually into the Caribbean. Directly east of the Segovia Highlands, a lesser range of mountains parallels the coast, effectively blocking off the interior of Venezuela from easy access via the Caribbean. These mountains run uninterrupted as far as Cape Codera, where they are broken by the Unare Basin only to reemerge again in the northeastern corner of the country. The remaining coast of Venezuela, lying south of Trinidad, is taken up by the magnificent Orinoco Delta. East and south of the Andes and the Coastal Range stretches a vast plain, descending very slowly from the foothills towards the Apure and Meta Rivers on the south and the Orinoco River on the east. Below the Meta, these plains or Llanos continue into Colombia until they meet the Andean foothills. In the east the Llanos reach to the Orinoco, which marks the beginning of the still undeveloped Guayana Highlands, a land dominated by low mountains and large mesas covered with rich grasslands and extensive tropical forests.[1]

Within this panorama, six major regions can be defined, whose boundaries are fixed according to physiographic criteria. Each region can in turn be divided into subregions, divisions useful in the analysis of the parishes of late colonial Venezuela (Map 1-1). First among these regions is the Coast, that band of low altitude beach, plain, and rock which, after looping around Lake Maracaibo, borders the entire east-west coast, and includes the fan of the Orinoco Delta. The second region, the Coastal Range, stands just behind the Coast in the central and eastern portion of Venezuela. Although representing only a small fraction of Venezuela's surface area, the Coastal Range, in its rich intermontane valleys, has held the principal economic and political centers of the country since at least the mid-eighteenth century. The Segovia Highlands, the third major region, displays a broken topography of low mountains, high plains, valleys, and semidesert, and forms a transitional area between the Andes and the Coastal Range. Surrounded by the coastal landscape around Coro, the Andean environment of Trujillo and Mérida, the Coastal Range of Caracas and Valencia, and the Llanos, this region early became a major transfer point for settlement and administration. The fourth region, the Andes, stretches south-southwest until joining the main

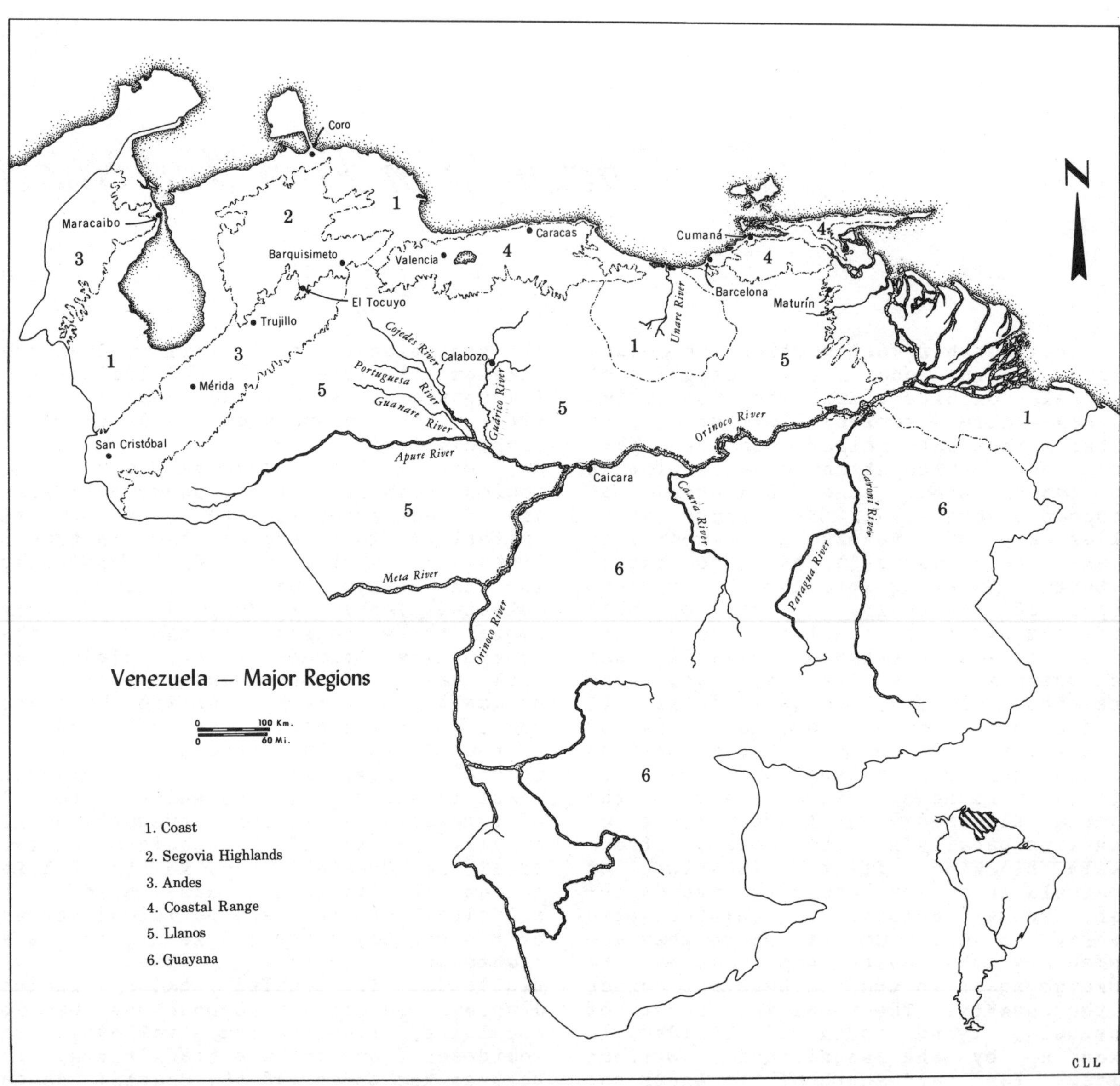
Coro
Maracaibo
Barquisimeto
Valencia
Caracas
Cumaná
Barcelona
Maturín
El Tocuyo
Trujillo
Mérida
San Cristóbal
Calabozo
Caicara
Cojedes River
Portuguesa River
Guanare River
Guárico River
Unare River
Apure River
Orinoco River
Caura River
Caroní River
Paragua River
Meta River
N
Venezuela — Major Regions
0 100 Km.
0 60 Mi.
1. Coast
2. Segovia Highlands
3. Andes
4. Coastal Range
5. Llanos
6. Guayana
CLL

Map 1-1

trunk of that mountain chain in Colombia and is formed of spectacular peaks and green valleys. As a highway between the Caribbean and the prosperous areas of Colombia, the Andes served as a difficult but frequently used communications route, and in the early years as a possible path to the mythical El Dorado. The fifth region, the vast plains or Llanos, forms the interior heartland of Venezuela and is made up of rolling land covered with grass, clumps of trees, and occasional palm forests. The area is dominated by its rivers and streams, and the inhabitants, who have lived off cattle and horses since the beginning of European settlement, have always regulated their lives by the rains that swell the rivers and flood parts of the plains. Beyond the Orinoco lies Guayana, an area that has received effective settlement only in recent decades. Today, as in colonial times, settlement hugs the edges of Guayana, and notions of the region's fabulous riches remain for the most part untested.[2]

Table 1-1. Surface Area of Venezuelan Regions

Region	Area (Km²)	% of Total Area
Coast	152,680	16.6
Segovia Highlands	24,200	2.6
Andes	53,880	5.9
Coastal Range	29,440	3.2
Llanos	237,280	25.8
Guayana	423,000	46.0
Total	920,480Km²	100.0%

Source: Atlas de Venezuela (Caracas, 1971), pp. 123-124.
Note: Coast does not include Continental Platform or Lake Maracaibo but does include the islands and the Orinoco Delta. Percentages may not total 100.0% because of rounding.

These, then, are the regions that will serve as the framework for this book: the Coast, the Coastal Range, the Segovia Highlands, the Andes, the Llanos, and Guayana; six regions, of which we will treat five. Guayana, for all of its fascination and mystery, has given us few statistics on population and none within the limits of this study. Due to the vagaries of ecclesiastical management, the information for this study is concentrated on the central and western area of Venezuela, from the Unare Basin on the east to the Apure River on the south. In the following discussion, then, the central and western coast will receive more attention than the east, and the analysis of the Coastal Range will necessarily be focused on that portion of the mountains west of Unare. Similarly, the Llanos north of Apure and west of Unare are our primary interest. Nevertheless, a general overview of the regions may be useful.

The Coast

Should an adventurous traveler care to sail along the entire coastline of Venezuela from east to west, his first contact with the country would be the Orinoco Delta. Spanning over 400 kilometers on the ocean side, it tapers back into the Orinoco River channel some 200 kilometers inland. The Delta, made up of low plains and swamp crisscrossed by streams and rivers, covers just under 60,000 square kilometers. From the earliest moments of Spanish interest in Venezuela, the Delta has served as one of five natural entries into the interior. Countless missionaries and explorers passed through the Delta and then along the Orinoco to the Apure, or farther still to the Meta, and from there into the Venezuelan Llanos or perhaps into Colombia, the Andes, and Bogotá. Because of the low-lying land and the humid, rainy climate, and because there were few exploitable resources in this region, settlements were mostly temporary and sparse. Where they did exist, along the major entry points into the Orinoco, as Tucupita and Barrancas or Curiapo and Santa Catalina, they survived mostly on the traffic carried in and out of the interior on the Orinoco. But this swampy, rainy, and hot subregion served primarily to announce the Orinoco, and to lure the unwary into heroic efforts to open all of South America to direct trade with Europe via this great river and her tributaries[3] (Map 1-2).

Following along the coast, it becomes necessary to cut across the Gulf of Paria, swing around the tip of the Paria peninsula, and sail due west to the tip of Point Araya. This double-ended

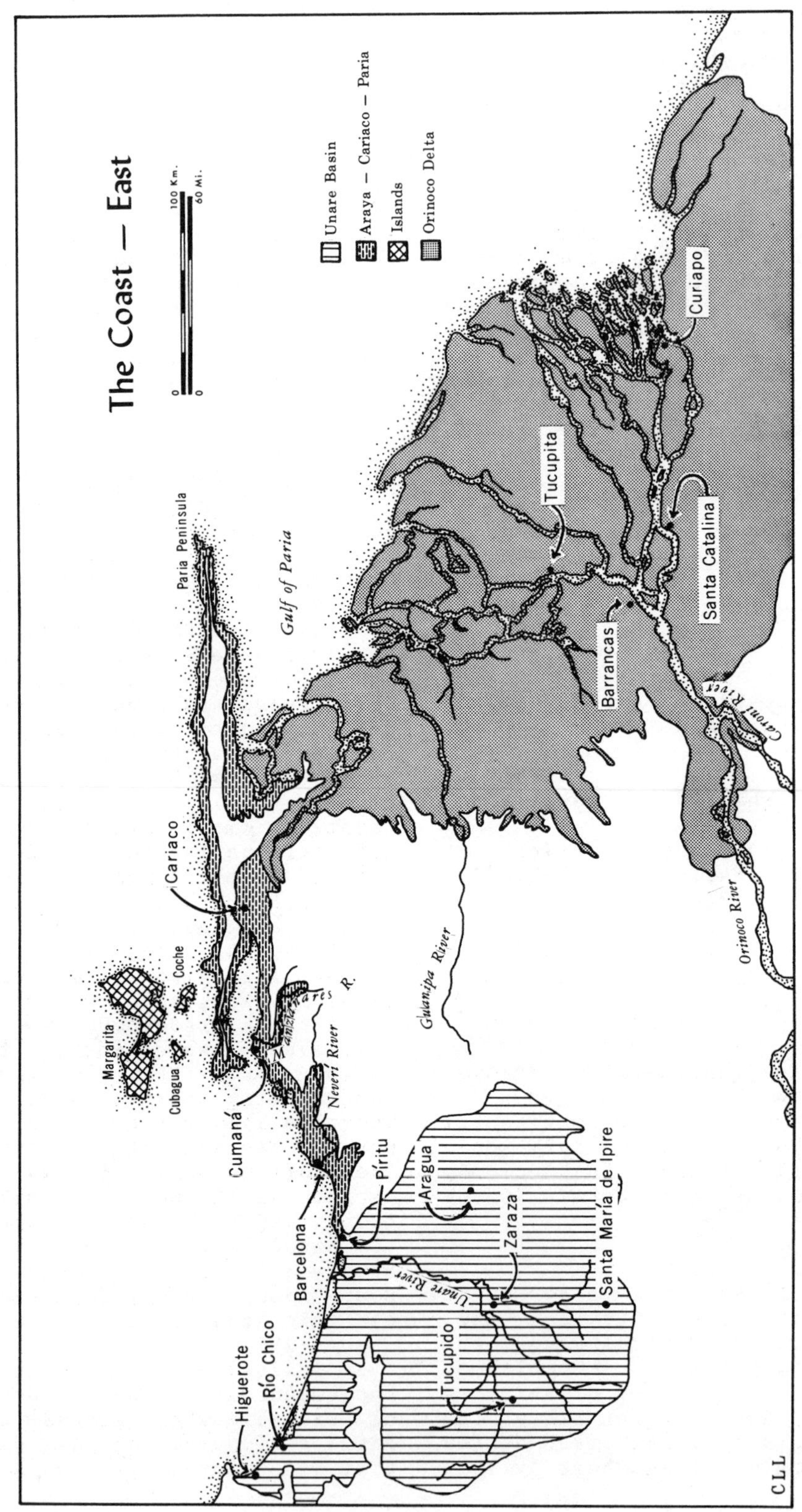
The Coast — East
0
100 Km.
0
60 Mi.
Unare Basin
Araya – Cariaco – Paria
Islands
Orinoco Delta
Paria Peninsula
Gulf of Paria
Curiapo
Tucupita
Santa Catalina
Barrancas
Caroní River
Orinoco River
Guanipa River
Cariaco
Margarita
Coche
Cubagua
Cumaná
Manzanares R.
Neverí River
Píritu
Aragua
Santa María de Ipire
Zaraza
Barcelona
Unare River
Tucupido
Higuerote
Río Chico
CLL

Map 1-2

peninsular formation stretches some 260 kilometers from tip to tip, and presents a narrow coastal beach with dry forests. The eastern peninsula is mostly arid desert; indeed, a major salt deposit, the Salinas de Araya, is located there and has been exploited since pre-Colombian times. By following the southern edge of Araya into the Gulf of Cariaco, our traveler enters one of the most beautiful portions of the subregion. Narrow beaches, green islands of semidry vegetation, and crystal blue water combine to make the coastline from Araya around the gulf to Cumaná one of the most impressive in the world. This same type of coastline extends from Cumaná southwestward about 100 kilometers past Barcelona to Píritu and the Unare River. Along this coast, our traveler will see but two major rivers until he reaches the Unare: the Manzanares near Cumaná, and the Neverí near Barcelona. And from the Gulf of Paria to beyond Barcelona, the section of the Cariaco-Araya-Paria Coast, he will have seen no easy way into the interior, since the coastline from Paria to Barcelona is backed up by the virtually unbroken mountains of the Coastal Range. But if the coast appears forbidding, it nevertheless provided a place for some of the earliest Spanish settlements on the mainland, settlements such as Cumaná, Barcelona, or Cariaco, which drew sustenance from the pearl fisheries of Cubagua and Margarita Islands some ten to fifteen kilometers off Point Araya. The coastline from Paria to Píritu, which forms the Cariaco-Araya-Paria subregion, contains just over 4,000 square kilometers of surface area and stretches almost 700 kilometers in length.[4]

As our traveler sails west from Barcelona, the terrain behind the beaches gradually declines, until when he reaches the mouth of the Unare River he can see a substantial break in the wall of hills, a coastal plain that seems to reach into the interior beyond the southern horizon. He is, of course, seeing the subregion of the Unare Basin and its associated coastline. Should he wish to follow the Unare into the interior, he would discover a basin formed mostly by a flat, low-lying plain cut by the series of small streams and rivers feeding the Unare. In the interior, the Unare Basin is defined on the east by the Eastern Llanos, an area of flat land broken by a system of mesas and drained by rivers and streams that flow into the Gulf of Paria and the Orinoco Delta, and on the south and east by the Calabozo Llanos, an area of savanna drained by rivers and streams of the Apure, Portuguesa, Guanare, and Orinoco systems. Along the coast lies a band of low ground, beaches, and narrow plains built up by the currents which sweep from east to west depositing sand all along the coast from Píritu to Higuerote. In all, the Unare Basin contains some 25,500 square kilometers of area and has long served as a principal entry into the cattle regions of the Venezuelan Llanos. Scattered throughout the subregion are hamlets, villages, and towns, whose existence in the eighteenth century depended on cattle, and whose founders frequently were missionaries in search of native souls to save in places such as Píritu, Tucupido, Zaraza, Santa María de Ipire, or Aragua de Barcelona.[5]

Leaving Higuerote and rounding Cape Codera, our traveler will sail along the Central Coast, a strip of inhospitable beach and rocky mountainside which runs for over 200 kilometers to just east of Puerto Cabello. The lack of any major attractions along this coast and the absence of outstanding harbors delayed the settlement of the subregion until the richness of the valleys in the Coastal Range made the effort worthwhile. In the hot oppressive climate only a few hamlets and villages emerged: Naiguatá, Caraballeda, and La Guaira. Here and there along the coast a small stream or river can be seen making a patch of green and providing the space and soil for the cultivation of cacao or bananas. By the late eighteenth century, this narrow subregion, covering only 1,240 square kilometers, housed the major port for Venezuela. The emergence of La Guaira as the premier harbor for the province stemmed, of course, not from its exceptional qualities, for it is an indifferent harbor exceeded by such locations as Puerto Cabello, Tucacas, or La Vela, but from its proximity to the richest agricultural regions of the country in the Caracas valley and the other valleys of the Central Coastal Range (Map 1-3).

As our traveler continues westward, he will notice the coastal plain widen out as he approaches Puerto Cabello. From Puerto Cabello to just east of Puerto Cumarebo, this wide Chichiriviche plain extends inland in a slow rising

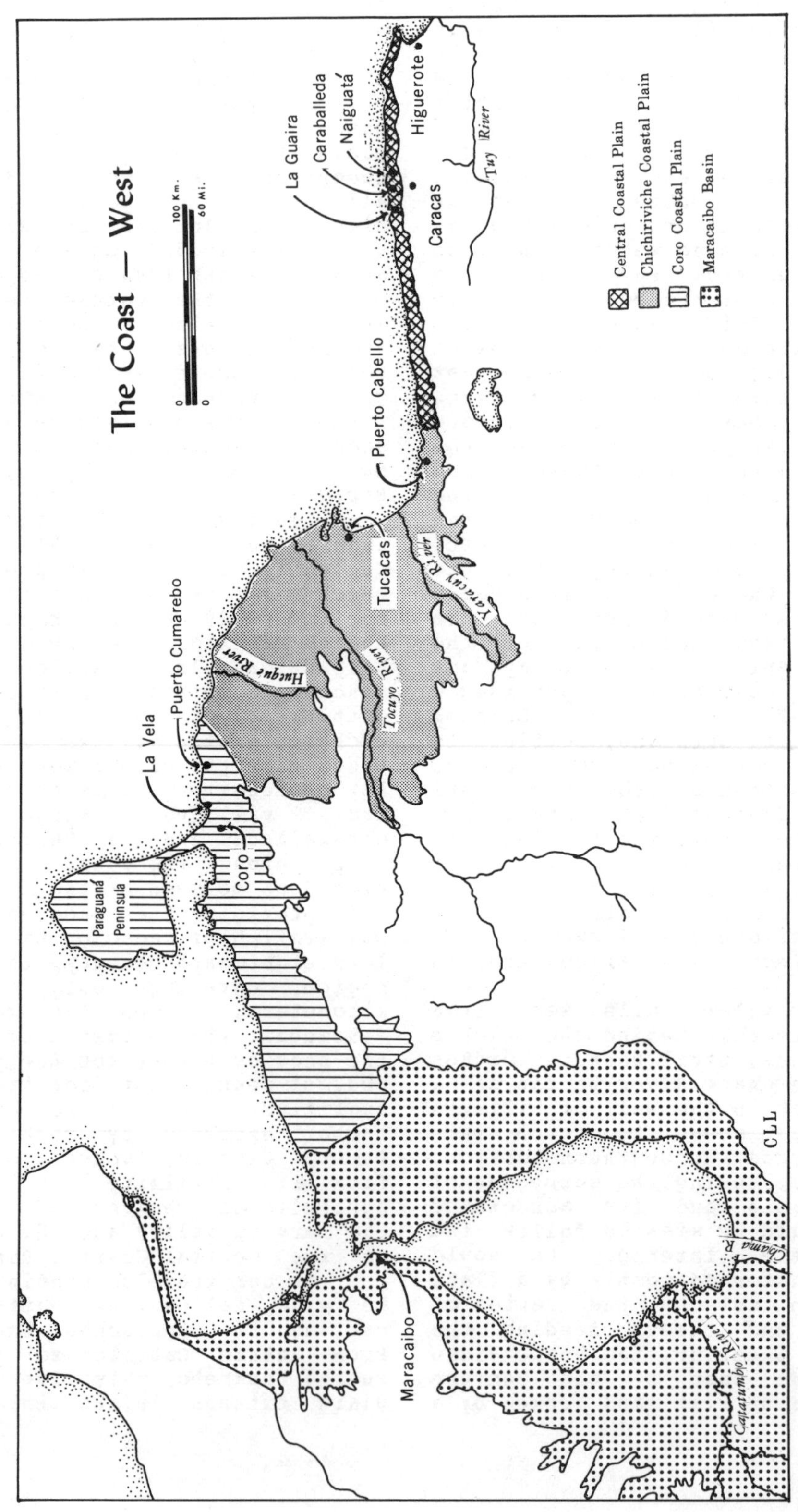
The Coast — West
0
100 Km.
0
60 Mi.
La Guaira
Caraballeda
Naiguatá
Higuerote
Caracas
Tuy River
Puerto Cabello
Tucacas
Yaracuy River
Puerto Cumarebo
Hueque River
Tocuyo River
La Vela
Coro
Paraguaná Peninsula
Maracaibo
Catatumbo River
Chama R.
Central Coastal Plain
Chichiriviche Coastal Plain
Coro Coastal Plain
Maracaibo Basin
CLL

Map 1-3

formation along the rivers flowing out of the Segovia Highlands. The first of these is the Yaracuy River, which separates the Coastal Range on the east from the Segovia Highlands on the west. This river provides another of the entryways into the interior plains, and because of its location and accessibility, served as an excellent highway for the smugglers of the eighteenth century to transport illicit goods and products. Passing the Yaracuy, our traveler will see Tucacas, an excellent port with no important hinterland. Sailing north and east from Tucacas, he will come to the Tocuyo River, which leads back inland some 140 kilometers to a hot dry plain that attracted few settlers. The last river plain of this subregion surrounds the course of the Hueque River, an equally dry and unattractive area. In all, the Chichiriviche Coastal Plain extends some 150 kilometers along the coast and covers about 16,000 square kilometers.

With the prevailing wind from the east, our traveler can push westward along the coast and enter the Coro Coastal Plain, a band of sand and low hills, interrupted by the Paraguaná Peninsula, reaching almost to the mouth of Lake Maracaibo. Although this desert and scrub brush terrain presents no obvious attractions, the area just east and directly south of the Paraguaná Peninsula became the site of one of Venezuela's earliest settlements. Through the port of La Vela and its town of Coro some kilometers inland, European adventurers entered the country to follow the southward-rising mountains in search of El Dorado, or to roam the Segovia Highlands, founding towns and establishing outposts that would serve as bases for the exploration and settlement of the rich valleys of the Central Coastal Range and the prairies of the Llanos. Although Coro survived as a major colonial center, serving as a gateway into the mountains and highlands and as an early colonial administrative center, the coastal plain of Coro has never been able to support in addition more than the port of La Vela and a minor fishing center at Puerto Cumarebo. West of the Paraguaná Peninsula, the coast becomes hotter and dryer, although the coastal plain widens out as it approaches the opening of the Maracaibo Basin. It is an inhospitable coast that urges the traveler on toward Maracaibo. The Coro Coastal Plain and Paraguaná Peninsula cover an east-west distance of about 250 kilometers and a surface area of just under 11,500 square kilometers.[6]

As our traveler crosses the sandbar blocking entry into Lake Maracaibo and sails into the great lake itself, he will begin to appreciate the dream of those Spanish colonists who envisioned the lake as a mighty passage into the heart of the Andes. The existence of several navigable rivers around the lake, such as the Catatumbo and the Chama, encouraged these dreams. Unfortunately, pirates, the impassibility of the Maracaibo Bar, the hot, humid climate, and the indifference of colonial officials prevented the realization of this vision. Sailing around the lake on the eastern shore, our traveler will find a band of low land, bordered on the east and south by the Segovia Highlands and the eastern spur of the Andes, and on the west by Colombia and the western spur of the Andes. The lake is some 200 kilometers from Maracaibo to the southern end and about 100 kilometers at the widest point. The Maracaibo Basin covers about 33,000 square kilometers, excluding the lake itself, which is about 13,000 square kilometers in area.[7]

During this long trip, our traveler has seen all of the coastal subregion except the islands. Excluding Trinidad, once part of the Spanish empire, these Venezuelan islands add up to 1800 square kilometers. For the purposes of our study, the only islands of significance lie off the eastern coast, just north of the Peninsula of Araya. Margarita is the largest, with a surface area of 1,280 square kilometers, followed by Coche and Cubagua. Vitally important during the early years of settlement because of the pearl trade, these islands rapidly declined in importance with the exhaustion of the pearl fisheries and the growth of mainland settlements.

This, then, is the nature of the Coast, an area stretching the width of Venezuela, some 1500 kilometers east and west, and covering some 153,000 square kilometers of surface. This is the subregion Europeans first encountered, and here they established their first settlements. From hamlets and villages on the coastal plain came the expeditions that opened up Venezuela to European discovery, settlement, and exploitation.

Table 1-2. Surface Area of Coast

Subregion	Area (Km²)	% of Region
Orinoco Delta	59,500	39.0
Cariaco-Araya-Paria	4,280	2.8
Unare Basin	25,500	16.7
Central Coast	1,240	0.8
Chichiriviche Coastal Plain	15,840	10.4
Coro Coastal Plain	11,420	7.5
Maracaibo Basin	33,100	21.7
Islands	1,800	1.2
Total	152,680Km²	100.0%

Source: Atlas de Venezuela (Caracas, 1971), pp. 123-124.
Note: Excludes Lake Maracaibo and Continental Platform but includes islands. Percentages may not total 100.0% because of rounding.

The Segovia Highlands

Should our traveler care to continue his journey through Venezuela, his next trip should take him through the Segovia Highlands. This region of high plains and low broken hills lies mostly between 500 and 800 meters altitude. In all, the Segovia Highlands cover some 24,000 square kilometers. The traveler leaving Coro for the south will encounter hot, dry, scrub brush countryside. By working his way through the hills and by staying on the plains, he can find the numerous small settlements scattered throughout the region. This Segovia Highland is made up of four mountainous formations which loosely surround two principal savannas or plains. Along the northern edge of the Highlands rise the low Northern Mountains, broken almost in the middle to give access to the interior Plains of Falcón. To the west, defining the border of the Segovia Highlands with the Maracaibo Basin, lies another mountain formation, the Barbacoas Mountains. Extending east from the northern end of the Barbacoas Mountains are the Baragua Mountains, a series of hills and mountains broken by valleys and small plains, which separate the northern Plains of Falcón from the southern Lara Depression. A fourth mountainous formation just south of the Baraguas and almost parallel to the Barbacoas Mountains separates the Lara Plains around Barquisimeto from the Urama and Tocuyo river valleys (Map 1-4).

Although cooler than the lower elevations of the coast, most of the Segovia Highlands region is hot and dry. The hamlets, villages, and towns established here can be found scattered along transportation routes, as is Pedregal; nestled against the hills, as is San Luis; located on important rivers or streams, as is Carora; or dominating a grassland, as does El Tocuyo or Barquisimeto.

These Segovia Highlands, formed by the Andes as they decline and spread before plunging into the sea, provided the locale for the second stage of Spain's expansion into western Venezuela. From Coro, the point of the first stage, Spanish captains moved to El Tocuyo and Barquisimeto, there to lay the base for the subsequent push into the Central Coastal Range. As a region with access to Indian labor and with the terrain to raise cattle and some food crops, the Segovia Highlands, and especially El Tocuyo, had the resources to support an exploration base.[8]

Table 1-3. Surface Area of the Segovia Highlands

Subregion	Area (Km²)	% of Region
Northern Mountains	2,720	11.2
Plains of Falcón	4,000	16.5
Barbacoas Mountains	5,200	21.5
Baragua Mountains	4,720	19.5
Lara Depression	4,000	16.5
Lara Mountains	3,560	14.7
Total	24,200Km²	100.0%

Source: Atlas de Venezuela (Caracas, 1971), pp. 123-124.
Note: Percentages may not total 100.0% because of rounding.

The Andes

From El Tocuyo in the Segovia Highlands, our traveler could proceed directly into the main branch of the Venezuelan Andes. Moving north and east,

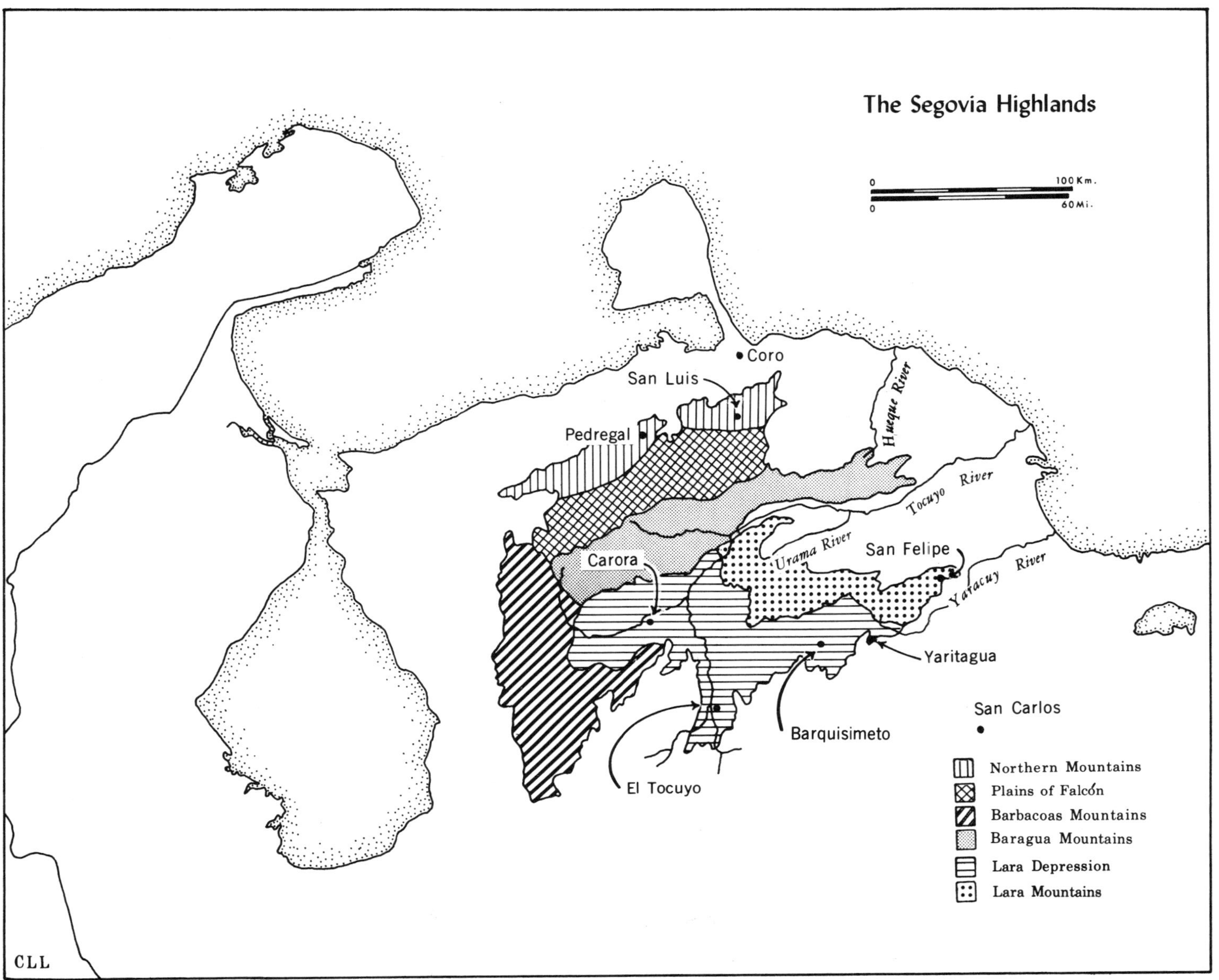

The Segovia Highlands
0
100 Km.
0
60 Mi.
Coro
San Luis
Pedregal
Hueque River
Tocuyo River
Urama River
San Felipe
Yaracuy River
Carora
Yaritagua
San Carlos
Barquisimeto
El Tocuyo
Northern Mountains
Plains of Falcón
Barbacoas Mountains
Baragua Mountains
Lara Depression
Lara Mountains
CLL

Map 1-4

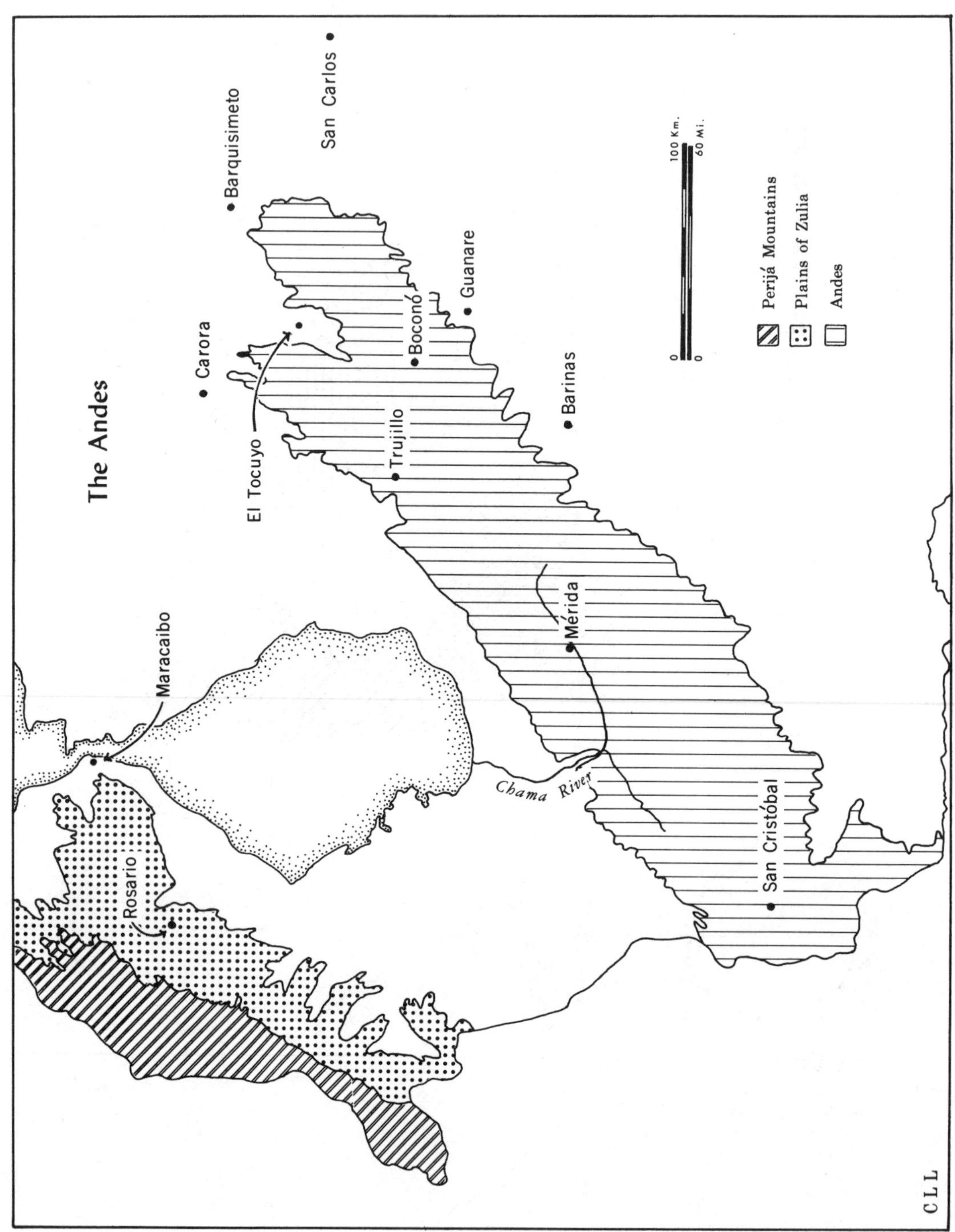
The Andes
San Carlos
Barquisimeto
Carora
El Tocuyo
Trujillo
Boconó
Guanare
Barinas
Mérida
Maracaibo
Rosario
Chama River
San Cristóbal
0
100 Km.
0
60 Mi.
Perijá Mountains
Plains of Zulia
Andes
CLL

Map 1-5

he could pass through Barquisimeto and by taking a southeasterly tack could enter the Llanos. Or he could turn east and north to reach the mountains and valleys of the Central Coastal Range. Since the first adventurers in Venezuela looked to the Andes for their discoveries and for possible enrichment, we will send our imaginary traveler southwest into the mountains. This branch of the Andes is composed of a double file of mountain ranges enclosing a series of intermontane valleys. As our traveler moves through this complex and spectacularly beautiful landscape, he will discover that the mountains reach their highest elevations around Mérida, which is surrounded by peaks right at the 5,000 meter mark. The principal towns established here nestle in the high valleys and depressions which break the mountains into their complicated subregions. Trujillo, one of the lowest Andean towns, lies in a valley at 800 meters; nearby Boconó lies at 1,225 meters; Mérida, midst the peaks, lies in a valley at 1,641 meters; and San Cristóbal, at 825 meters in the depression of Táchira, is almost on a par with Trujillo (Map 1-5).

In passing from one town to another along winding mountain roads, our traveler can easily appreciate the attractiveness of the rich valleys and understand the reasons for the early development of stable and self-sufficient population centers throughout the region. The difficulty of communication and trade between the Andean valleys and the rest of Venezuela becomes equally clear. Nevertheless, the presence of substantial Indian populations, of fertile land for pasture and crops, and of a cool and healthful climate brought settlers to the area long after the El Dorado dream had faded.

The western spur of the Venezuelan Andes, the Perijá Mountains, is considerably lower than the eastern spur, reaching a maximum of around 3,730 meters, and proved relatively unattractive to the early settlers because of the Indians' fierce resistance and a lack of suitable valleys. Nevertheless, some small population centers, such as Rosario, did emerge on the high Plains of Zulia, which rise from 500 to about 800 meters along the edge of the Perijá Mountains.[9]

Table 1-4. Surface Area of the Andes

Subregion	Area (Km²)	% of Region
Andes	36,080	67.0
Perijá Mountains	7,480	13.9
Plains of Zulia	10,320	19.2
Total	53,880Km²	100.0%

Source: Atlas de Venezuela (Caracas, 1971), pp. 123-124.
Note: Percentages may not total 100.0% because of rounding.

The Coastal Range

After returning to El Tocuyo and resting from his Andean trek, our traveler can strike out north and east, crossing the Yaracuy river valley to enter the Coastal Range. This extensive range of low mountains, more a Caribbean formation than an Andean extension, is broken into an eastern and a western section by the Unare Basin. From the mid-sixteenth century on, the eastern portion, known as the Central Coastal Range, came to contain Venezuela's principal villages, towns, and cities, and by the late eighteenth century, controlled the region's major political, judicial, commercial, and ecclesiastical institutions. Because of the area's critical importance in Venezuelan history, and because it is the focus of this study, we will spend some time acquainting ourselves with the physical characteristics of the place (Map 1-6).

As our traveler crosses the Yaracuy valley and enters the Nirgua-Tinaquillo Hills, he will find himself in a plain or valley which winds its way north and east for seventy or eighty kilometers. The Nirgua-Tinaquillo Hills that give their name to this subregion border the valley to the south, while a series of low hills separates it from the Yaracuy River and the coast. Going from the town of Nirgua through Montalbán, our traveler can then enter the Valencia Basin through the town of the same name.

The Valencia Basin, a lake surrounded by a fertile plain, forms a drainage area with no outlet to the sea. The town of Valencia itself lies at the western edge of the subregion at an altitude of almost 500 meters. Although rather hot, this valley constituted one

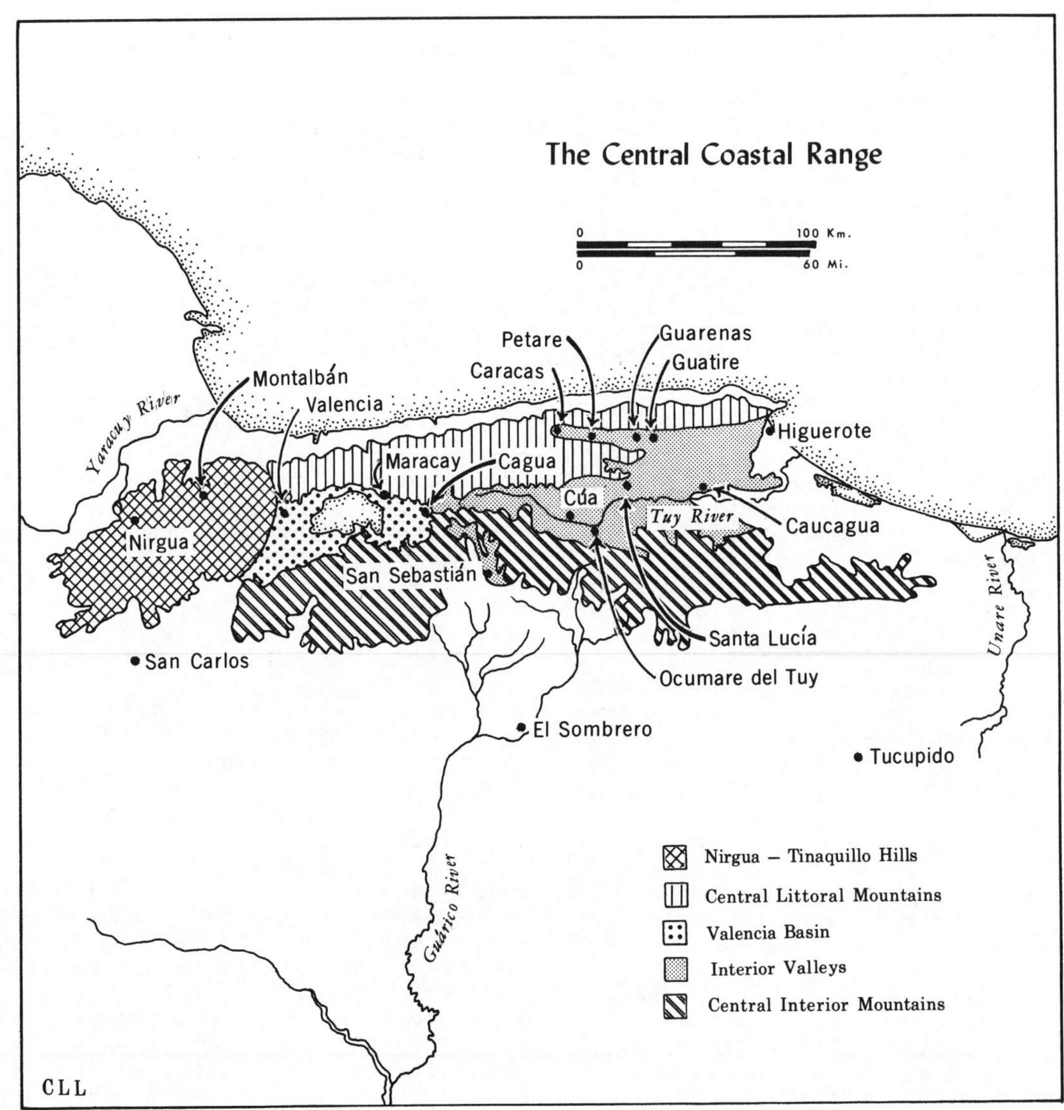
The Central Coastal Range
0
100 Km.
0
60 Mi.
Petare
Guarenas
Guatire
Caracas
Montalbán
Valencia
Yaracuy River
Higuerote
Maracay
Cagua
Cúa
Tuy River
Caucagua
Nirgua
San Sebastián
Santa Lucía
Unare River
San Carlos
Ocumare del Tuy
El Sombrero
Tucupido
Guárico River
Nirgua – Tinaquillo Hills
Central Littoral Mountains
Valencia Basin
Interior Valleys
Central Interior Mountains
CLL

Map 1-6

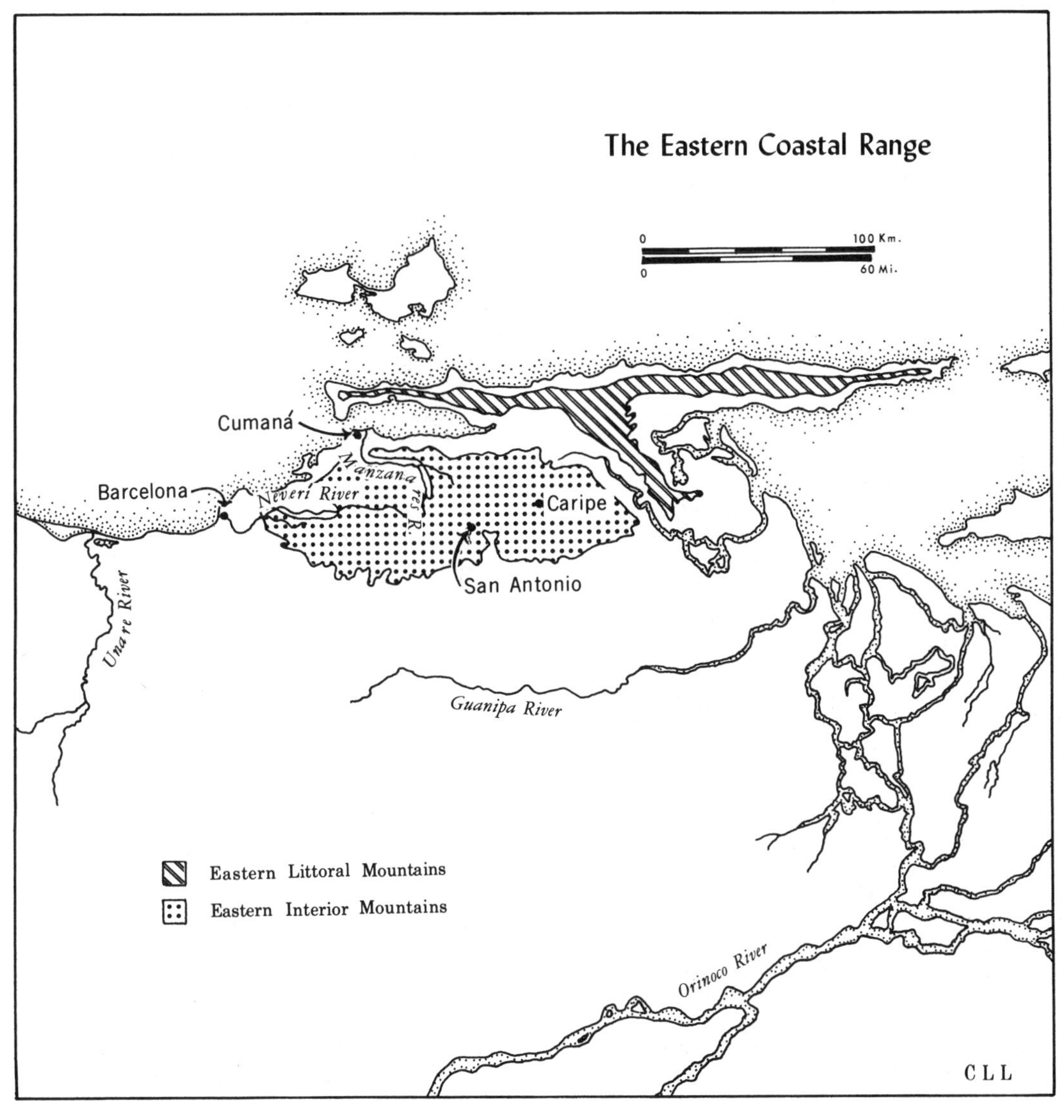
The Eastern Coastal Range
0
100 Km.
0
60 Mi.
Cumaná
Barcelona
Neverí River
Manzanares R.
Caripe
San Antonio
Unare River
Guanipa River
Orinoco River
Eastern Littoral Mountains
Eastern Interior Mountains
CLL

Map 1-7

of the major areas of agriculture even before the eighteenth century. Extending some sixty kilometers east and west, the Basin is bordered on the north by the Central Littoral Mountains and on the south by the Central Interior Mountains.

If our traveler leaves the Valencia Basin eastward, he will drop into a series of irregularly shaped valleys and plains that interconnect and broaden out towards the west until they reach the coastal lowlands. This subregion of the Interior Valleys can best be seen as a system of three major divisions. The traveler will first pass through the San Sebastián valley, a small formation of some 240 square kilometers drained by the upper reaches of the Guárico River. Continuing eastward over a dividing series of low hills, he will drop into the Aragua-Tuy valleys, almost 2,000 square kilometers of rich agricultural land along the Aragua and Tuy rivers. A major crop-producing region since at least the seventeenth century, this area is dominated by a series of agricultural towns and villages such as Cúa, Ocumare del Tuy, and Santa Lucía. This valley opens into the Caracas valleys at the northeast corner through the Tuy River channel.

The Caracas valleys take the shape of an irregular, narrow, isosceles triangle laid on its side, with the apex to the west and the base running north and south in the east. Covering an area of just under 1,500 square kilometers, the triangle's base lies at an altitude of about 50 meters where it meets the coast and rises at the apex deep in the Central Coastal Range to just over 1,000 meters. At the high point of the valley rests the major city of Venezuela, a primate city since at least the second half of the eighteenth century, Caracas. These Caracas valleys of rich agricultural land contain numerous hamlets, villages, and towns. Entering the valleys at the southeast corner, our traveler will encounter such centers as Caucagua, Guatire, Guarenas, and Petare, before reaching the head of the valley at Caracas.

The Central Littoral Mountains surrounding Caracas on three sides are a striking complex of green mountains that rise to a maximum elevation of almost 3,000 meters at the peak of Naiguatá north of Petare, and then fall precipitously to the rocky Central Coast of La Guaira and Caraballeda. The westernmost section of the mountains is populated primarily along the southern foothills, as at Maracay, or in the scattered narrow valleys along the northern face. This pattern holds for almost the entire seaward side of the chain. Due south and then west of Caracas in the Los Altos Hills are a number of towns and villages nestled in the small valleys or clinging to the hillsides, such as Los Teques. In all, the Central Littoral Mountain region occupies just under 5,000 square meters.

Table 1-5. Surface Area of the Coastal Mountains

Subregion	Area (Km²)	% of Region
Central Coastal Range	21,720(100.0%)	73.8
Nirgua-Tinaquillo Hills	3,760(17.3)	12.8
Central Littoral Mountains	4,800(22.1)	16.3
Valencia Basin	1,280(5.9)	4.3
Interior Valleys	3,560(16.4)	12.1
Central Interior Mountains	8,320(38.3)	28.3
Eastern Coastal Range	7,720(100.0%)	26.2
Eastern Littoral Mountains	2,120(27.5)	7.2
Eastern Interior Mountains	5,600(72.5)	19.0
Total	29,440Km²	100.0

Source: Atlas de Venezuela (Caracas, 1971), pp. 123-124.

Parallel to and almost the same length as the Central Littoral Mountains are the Central Interior Mountains, which run east and west, separating the interior valleys from the Llanos. These mountains, broken by numerous small valleys and openings to the plains, have two major formations of almost equal area. On the east are the Altos of Platillón and the Calza Hills, and on the west is the Fila Maestra. The major corridor to the Llanos lies between these two, which helps explain the existence of

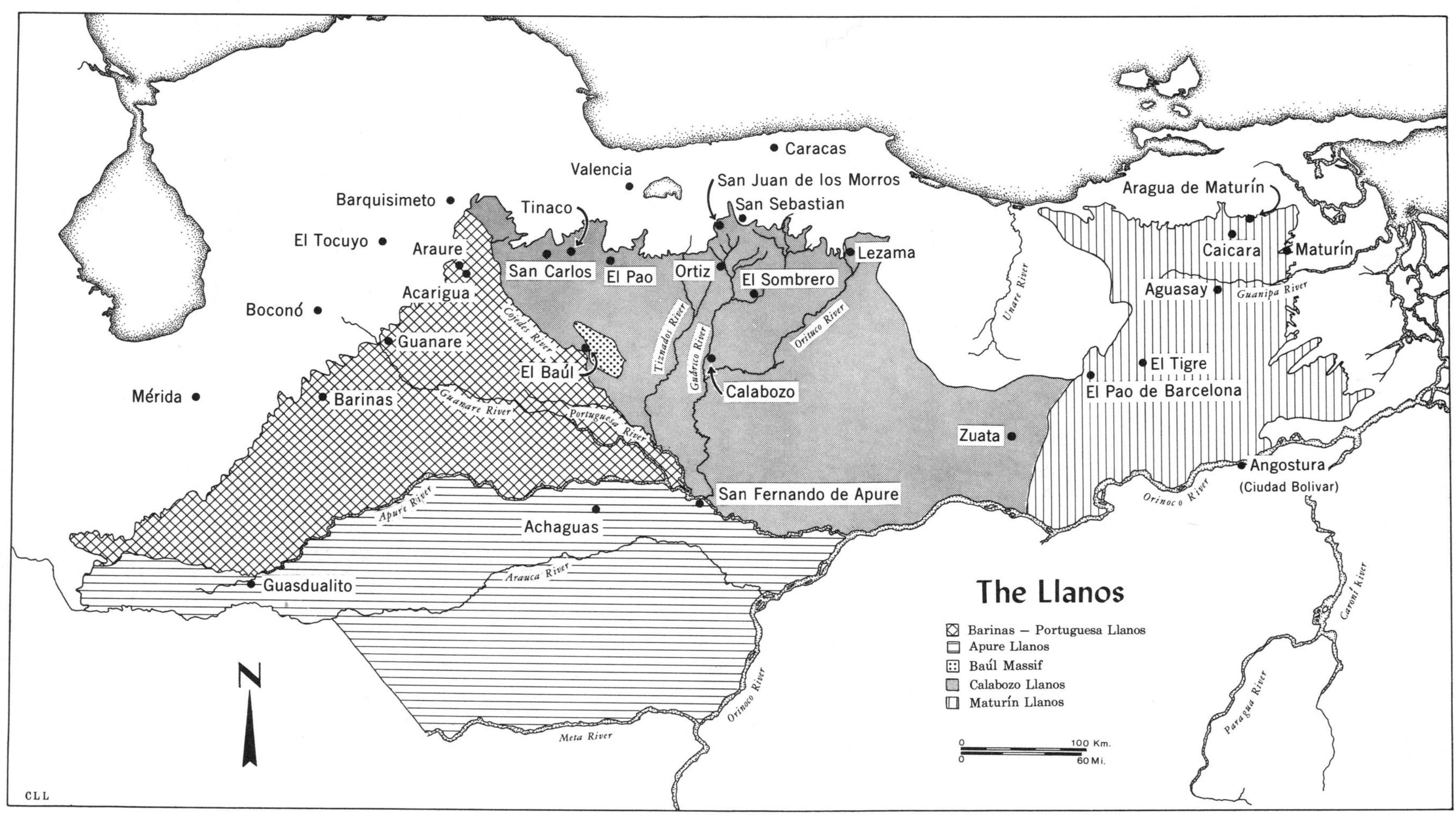
Caracas
Valencia
San Juan de los Morros
San Sebastian
Aragua de Maturín
Barquisimeto
Tinaco
El Tocuyo
Araure
San Carlos
El Pao
Ortiz
El Sombrero
Lezama
Caicara
Maturín
Acarigua
Aguasay
Guanipa River
Boconó
Cojedes River
Tiznados River
Guárico River
Orituco River
Unare River
Guanare
El Baúl
El Tigre
El Pao de Barcelona
Calabozo
Mérida
Barinas
Guanare River
Portuguesa River
Zuata
Angostura
(Ciudad Bolivar)
San Fernando de Apure
Orinoco River
Apure River
Achaguas
Arauca River
Guasdualito
The Llanos
Barinas – Portuguesa Llanos
Apure Llanos
Baúl Massif
Calabozo Llanos
Maturín Llanos
Caroní River
Paragua River
Orinoco River
N
0
100 Km.
0
60 Mi.
Meta River
CLL

Map 1-8

the towns of San Juan de los Morros and Villa de Cura in the eastern foothills and Altos of Platillón, and the town of San Sebastián in the interior valley of the same name which lies just north of the corridor.

To the east of the Fila Maestra the Central Coastal Range gives way to the Unare Depression, but rises again east of Barcelona. This segment has an interior range, the Eastern Interior Mountains, separating the coast of Cumaná from the Eastern Llanos, and a coastal range, the Eastern Littoral Mountains, running along the interior of the Araya and Paria Peninsulas. Of these two formations, only the interior mountains attracted population, to such places as Caripe and San Antonio. In all, these two mountain groups account for 7,700 square kilometers[10] (Map 1-7).

The Llanos

If our traveler moves southward from the Eastern Interior Mountains of the Coastal Range, dropping down to Aragua de Maturín or Caicara, he will find himself entering the Llanos of Maturín. Bordered on the east by the Orinoco Delta, on the south by the Orinoco River, and on the west by the Unare Basin, this subregion has an eastern half of relatively flat grasslands, populated mostly in its northern portion by such towns as Aragua de Maturín, Maturín, Caicara, and Aguasay. Most of the western half of the subregion is dominated by a series of extensive mesas, which break the horizon around such towns as El Tigre and El Pao de Barcelona. From the early years of settlement through to the republican period, this subregion served as one of the major cattle-raising areas of Venezuela (Map 1-8).

As the traveler rides south from El Tigre and swings west around the Unare Basin, he will enter the Llanos of Calabozo a few kilometers before reaching the town of Zuata. This subregion is defined on the south and west by the Orinoco, Apure, Portuguesa, and Cojedes Rivers, and on the north by the Central Coastal Range. A large plain with rolling countryside, meandering streams, and flooded lowlands to the south, the region supported a scattering of towns based on large cattle-raising enterprises. More closely spaced near the foothills of the Coastal Range are towns such as Lezama, Ortiz, El Pao, Tinaco, and San Carlos, while to the south the population becomes sparser, with isolated centers such as Calabozo. Other than the major rivers, the Guárico, the Tiznados, and the Orituco, the only notable geographic feature to break the monotony of these rolling plains with their grass and scrub brush, clumps of trees, and palm forests, are the hills and mesas just east of El Baúl on the Baúl Massif.

As our traveler crosses the Cojedes River at El Baúl, he enters the Llanos of Barinas-Portuguesa. This triangular subregion has its base along the Andean foothills, its southern side following the Apure, and its northern side along the Cojedes-Portuguesa Rivers. In the upper Llanos along the Andean foothills lie most of its towns, such as Barinas, Guanare, and Acarigua-Araure.

South of the Apure our traveler enters the Llanos of Apure, a subregion of flat grassland, subject to frequent flooding by the overflow from the complex system of rivers running east into the Orinoco. The few towns in this subregion, for example Guasdualito, Achaguas, and San Fernando de Apure, are located mostly in a narrow band above the Arauca River. This area, like the rest of the Llanos, is supported principally by stock raising.[11]

Table 1-6. Surface Area of the Llanos

Subregion	Area (Km²)	% of Region
Llanos of Barinas-Portuguesa	51,200	21.6
Llanos of Apure	74,500	31.4
Baúl Massif	680	0.3
Llanos of Calabozo	71,400	30.1
Llanos of Maturín	39,500	16.6
Total	237,280Km²	100.0%

Source: Atlas de Venezuela (Caracas, 1971), pp. 123-124.

Guayana

Having completed his trip through the Llanos, our traveler has only one major region left, Guayana. This largest

Venezuelan region, lying east and south of the Orinoco and perhaps loaded with incalcuable riches, played a very small part in Venezuelan affairs before the nineteenth century. Practically all the principal hamlets and villages of this region, San Félix, Angostura, and Caicara de Orinoco, lie along the rivers of Guayana's western border and exist to serve the Llanos rather than the Guayanés hinterland. For the purposes of this study, Guayana serves only as a backdrop, a potential area of expansion effectively outside the active, Europeanized part of Venezuela. Therefore, we will not ask our traveler to explore the plains, mesas, and mountains which make up the subregions of this area.[12]

Settlement Patterns

During the two and a half centuries following the discovery of the Venezuelan coast by representatives of an expansive and recently consolidated Spain, adventurers, settlers, missionaries, and slaves gradually took possession of these regions we now call Venezuela. That the process took a long time is testimony to the absence of large readily-exploitable mineral deposits within the area and to the resistance of Indian groups unwilling to work for the newcomers and equally unable to resist them. From the sixteenth-century contacts near Coro on the west and Cumaná and her off-shore islands on the east, until the completion of settlement sometime in the second half of the eighteenth century, European expansion into the interior proceeded along systematic and easily understandable lines.[13]

Apart from the earliest contacts by Columbus at the end of the fifteenth century, Europeans became interested in the area when they discovered that the source of pearls traded by the natives lay in the waters around the islands of Margarita, Cubagua, and Coche just north of the Araya Peninsula. From Cubagua, the pearl-fishing center, and later from the new-founded outpost at Coro, came periodic entries of Europeans in search of Indian laborers to enslave and take back either to the Coro deserts, the dangerous pearl fishing grounds off Araya, or the labor-starved Spanish Caribbean islands. The series of entries into Venezuela during the first half of the sixteenth century touched every one of the five major routes into the interior and passed through all the major regions of the country. In the 1530s the Orinoco was charted, and expeditions entered the Llanos through the Unare Basin, striking out overland to the Llanos of Calabozo, or across the Llanos to the foothills of the Andes. From New Granada or Colombia, adventurers came down from the Andes, crossed the Colombian Llanos, and followed the Orinoco to the sea. From a base in the Welser concession in Coro, parties of Europeans traveled through the Segovia Highlands and then entered the Andes. Some reached Colombia, others followed the Andean streams east to the Barinas-Portuguesa Llanos, and still others turned west towards the southern end of the Maracaibo Basin to explore the great lake's shoreline. From Coro, too, came sorties that ranged along the coast eastward to the Yaracuy and then southward into the Llanos, while others surveyed the coast around Maracaibo and braved the hostile Indians and forbidding territory of the Goagira Peninsula, the northernmost part of present-day Colombia.[14]

This generation of explorers in search of gold and Indians left the European survivors of the mid-sixteenth century with a reasonably coherent notion of Venezuelan geography and the realization that no substantial silver or gold mines were to be found. The second generation on the mainland had to make peace with the landscape and adapt its style and activities to the possibilities of the environment. Although most of the interior and coastline had been surveyed, if only in passing, few major towns had appeared. Indeed, by 1550 the only more or less permanent population centers hugged the coast near the pearl fisheries of the east in places like Cumaná on the mainland, and La Asunción or Nueva Cádiz on the island of Cubagua, or they belonged to the western coastal region, like Coro or Maracaibo. The only substantial inland population center, El Tocuyo, owed its existence to its key location in the Segovia Highlands astride the routes into the Andes and out onto the plains.

If that first half century saw the founding of few towns, it did prepare the way for the series of settlements planted throughout that curve of mountains and coastline from the depression of Táchira in the southwest to the Orinoco Delta in the northeast. Ambitious men, radiating outwards from El Tocuyo after 1550 in search of exploitable Indians, suitable soil for agriculture and stockraising, and a healthy climate, established new towns. Some were nearby in the Segovia Highlands, such as Carora (1569) and Barquisimeto (1552), others farther away, such as Trujillo (1557) in the Andes and Valencia (1556) or Caracas (1567) in the Central Coastal Range. A few of these places became in turn principal centers for expansion.

From Caracas came the people who would open the plains of Calabozo with the foundation of San Sebastián (1584) at the edge of the Llanos, or exploit the Barinas-Portuguesa plains from the town of Guanare, founded at the end of the century (1593). Trujillo, too, sponsored an expedition to reestablish Maracaibo (1569). In the east, Cumaná, refounded in the late 1560s, sent men east to Cariaco (1598) and west to Cumanagoto.

From outside the present-day boundaries of Venezuela came adventurers in search of places to stay and grow rich. New Granada provided the people who founded San Cristóbal (1561) and Mérida (1558) in the Andes and who established Santo Tomé at the mouth of the Orinoco. Mérida sent her own to put Gibraltar (1591) on the shores of Lake Maracaibo and to develop the foothills to the east around Barinas (1577) and Pedraza (1591). Of course, some of the towns established during this period failed to survive, either because of a hostile environment or because of the competition from nearby, more prosperous places. Such was the case with Borburata (1549) and Caraballeda (1568) on the coast. Nor did every town remain in the same physical location over time. Cumaná, Trujillo, Barcelona, and Maracaibo were refounded in slightly improved terrain near their original sites.[15]

If the sixteenth century saw the establishment of small population centers located at strategic points along the arc from San Cristóbal through the Coastal Range to the Orinoco Delta, the seventeenth and the first three-quarters of the eighteenth centuries witnessed the slow expansion into the Llanos and the gradual completion of Venezuela's urban network, a structure of hamlets, villages, towns, and a handful of cities destined to remain virtually unchanged in form until the petroleum boom of the mid-twentieth century. During the century and three-quarters required to fill out the network of towns, there were two major impulses toward expansion. Throughout the Andes and parts of the Segovia Highlands and in sections of the western part of the Central Coastal Range, European settlement expanded in response to the insatiable demand for Indian labor to make the Spanish colonists rich or, as more often occurred in Venezuela, to help them survive. Wherever Indians tractable enough to be put to work existed near viable agricultural land, Spaniards established <u>encomiendas</u>, and, to extract the most from each area of encomiendas, they frequently founded hamlets to serve as bases for the <u>encomenderos</u> and their followers. With Indian labor available, colonists also felt free to acquire title to whatever land lay unclaimed or undefended about them. Throughout the Segovia Highlands, encomiendas occurred with considerably less frequency, in part because the terrain offered little encouragement for agricultural enterprise. Here the second colonizing impulse began to play its role. The missionaries found themselves with the task of continuing pacification and conversion in those areas and among those Indians least suitable for the encomienda. The same mixture of encomienda and mission observable in the Segovia Highlands also appeared in the mountains and valleys of the Coastal Range, both in the central branch around Caracas and in the eastern branch behind Cumaná, although the encomiendas in the east were much less significant than those in the center.

As Spanish settlement moved south from the coast or east from the Andes, the seminomadic and frequently dangerous Indians, aided by the inhospitable plains, discouraged the prospective encomendero who found it impossible to collect enough Indians in one place to make an acceptable profit. The missionaries, whose calculus of profit and loss involved different variables, accepted the challenge of taming this wilderness. From the east, various orders of Franciscans planted missions throughout the lower Orinoco and the plains of Maturín. They moved into the Unare Basin, struggling to organize coherent religious communities, and they struck out from posts along the Orinoco

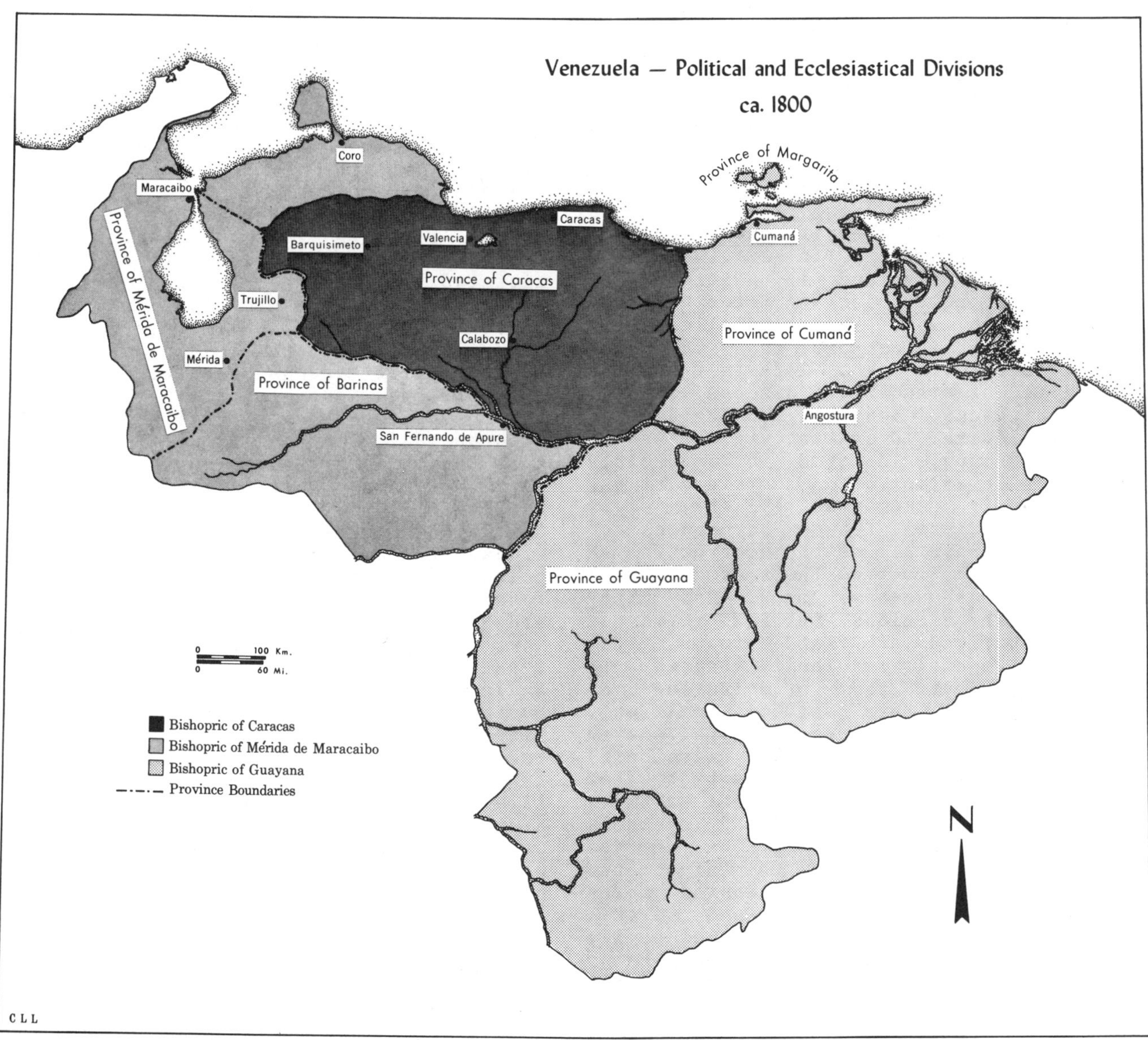
Venezuela — Political and Ecclesiastical Divisions
ca. 1800
Coro
Maracaibo
Province of Margarita
Caracas
Cumaná
Barquisimeto
Valencia
Province of Caracas
Trujillo
Province of Mérida de Maracaibo
Calabozo
Province of Cumaná
Mérida
Province of Barinas
Angostura
San Fernando de Apure
Province of Guayana
0 100 Km.
0 60 Mi.
Bishopric of Caracas
Bishopric of Mérida de Maracaibo
Bishopric of Guayana
Province Boundaries
N
CLL

Map 1-9

into the interior of Guayana. From the mountains and valleys around Caracas, they moved slowly south into the Llanos of Calabozo, scattering mission towns throughout the plains and along the rivers.

Based deep in the Colombian Andes, small parties of Jesuits followed the east-west course of the Apure and Meta, founding towns and establishing missions in an irregular band. They reached the Orinoco and turned southward continuing their work in the territory below the Arauca.

In telling the tale of this missionary expansion which gave Venezuela its territorial integrity and functional framework, it is easy to imagine these missionaries involved in a heroic epic filled with multitudes and triumphs. Few missionaries would have recalled their efforts in that fashion. For the most part, a missionary's life in the wilds consisted of discomfort, disease, danger, disappointment, and all too frequently, an early death. Operating singly or in small groups, isolated in impassible countryside amidst often hostile natives, and rarely supported by what civil authority existed, these harbingers of Spanish culture and of the destruction of native society counted their successes in tens, not thousands, of souls. They founded many missions, but if a third of these survived as viable towns, that merited rejoicing. Their progress in sketching out the organization of Venezuela must have seemed agonizingly slow, taking perhaps four generations to complete. Still, after the missionary tide began to recede from its high water mark in the early 1770s, it left behind a line of hamlets that defined Venezuela and determined the directions of her development far into the nineteenth century. Although many mission towns disappeared from the map and several magnificent mission churches lay abandoned to the ravages of wind, rain, and time, the remaining places carried European domination forward. The untamed regions of the country stayed that way precisely because the missionaries had failed to reach them.[16]

By the 1770s the urban system of Venezuela had reached a point of stability and had acquired sufficient complexity to allow it to carry the developing region through the subsequent century. And it is this stabilized network of hamlets, villages, towns, and cities of the late eighteenth and early nineteenth centuries that provides the focus of this book.

Organization and Jurisdictions

The years of slow expansion into the interior saw Venezuela pass through a long series of political organizations and reorganizations (Map 1-9). Coro served as the capital for most of the area during the early years of the sixteenth century, but with the establishment of other viable settlements, first in El Tocuyo and finally in Caracas, civil and ecclesiastical leaders migrated to those favored towns, and sooner or later the official designations followed. Although some of the confusion in jurisdictions and locations disappeared after Caracas began to develop as the principal administrative center in the seventeenth century, Venezuela's geographical location and settlement pattern that had given the country a three-way external orientation--Colombian, Caribbean, and Atlantic--continued to divide the country until the late-eighteenth century. For much of the colonial period, the provinces of Venezuela, that is Margarita, Caracas, and Nueva Andalucía or Cumaná (created in the sixteenth century), reported separately to the Royal Court or Audiencia in Santo Domingo. But the southernmost portion of the Andes below a line almost half way between Trujillo and Mérida and most of the Maracaibo Basin reported to the Audiencia in Bogotá. In like fashion, ecclesiastical jurisdictions divided the land. The Bishopric of Caracas administered the central portion of Venezuela from the Unare Basin on the east to the Maracaibo Basin on the west, and from the northern coast south to the Apure river. The southern border of the Bishopric ran along a line half way between Trujillo and Mérida, south of which lay the Bishopric of Santa Fé (de Bogotá). From the Unare east reigned the Bishop of Puerto Rico. Until the 1770s the area south of Trujillo belonged to the Bishopric of Santa Fé, but with the creation of the Bishopric of Mérida, this Andean region, plus the western and southern parts of the Maracaibo Basin were governed from the See of Mérida.[17]

The following discussion of

characteristics of towns and people in late colonial Venezuela is confined to the Bishopric of Caracas as it was between approximately 1780 and 1830. This region, while commanding only about twenty percent of the national territory, probably contained some sixty percent of the Europeanized or European controlled population, and perhaps half of the hamlets, villages, towns, and cities.

Parish Church, El Tocuyo

TWO

Counting and Classifying

Like most Latin American countries, Venezuela has a wealth of materials on the size, composition, and characteristics of her colonial population. Much information comes in continuous series that stretch back for some places into the late sixteenth and early seventeenth centuries, but most of the data are in the form of isolated compilations or surveys focused on restricted portions of the region.

For the purposes of the following discussion, I have divided the available information into seven major groups. First are the parish vital statistics that provided data on baptisms, burials, and marriages. Then are those missionary reports that included population estimates. Third are the accounts of travelers to the area, whose observations on population size and composition have proved especially valuable. The fourth group, government surveys, is rich in data on all aspects of the Latin American environment, including information on economics, politics, geography, and social customs, as well as on population. Episcopal visitas often contain demographic observations of remarkable completeness and accuracy. But few sources of population data can equal the information contained in the sixth and seventh groups: the parish household lists collected through much of the eighteenth century, and the annual parish censuses begun in the last quarter of the eighteenth century.

By combining the data contained in these sources, it should be possible to arrive at a rather complete and detailed knowledge of Venezuelan population history through the end of the colonial period. To be sure, some of these sources duplicate the information contained in others, and in some cases the population reports are little better than educated guesses. Nevertheless, a systematic comparison of the data and a careful evaluation of contemporary conditions can lead us to a reasonable approximation of Venezuela's population geography throughout the period.

Before beginning this analysis, however, it is essential to have a notion of the possibilities and problems offered by the sources in each of these seven data groups. To that end, this chapter will place the sources within their proper context and explore some of the ways the data they contain can best be used.[1]

Parish Vital Statistics

Practically every Latin American parish has a set of books that record in greater or lesser detail the occurrence of baptisms, burials, and marriages. Venezuela is no exception to this rule, although little has yet been done to exploit this material for its demographic yield. The neglect stems from the fact that parish records in Venezuela, as in the rest of Spanish America, lie dispersed throughout the country in local archives. Frequently parish priests resist the attempts of scholars to use the archives, and the documents often prove to be in poor condition or partially destroyed. For Venezuelanists, these liabilities are further compounded by the rudimentary state of research on major aspects of Venezuela's colonial past. When few adequate studies of the period exist, most students feel obliged to concentrate on the analysis and description of the major structural elements of government, economics, and society before narrowing their focus to concentrate on micro-history. Moreover, until recently, micro-history at the parish level has been the almost exclusive preserve of the antiquarian, geneologist, or costumbrista.

Added to these impediments is the nature of the methodology required to fully develop these sources. By and large, few students have been inclined to employ family reconstitution techniques to study Venezuela's parish records. Such techniques, while capable of producing excellent results from materials of this kind, require an investment of time and resources out of proportion to the significance of the results obtainable. However unwarranted in theory, this conclusion gains strength when we realize that none of the province- or country-wide data have been fully studied. Indeed, the results of family reconstitution will be difficult to interpret without the analysis from larger scale but necessarily less detailed studies.

Although no comprehensive guide to the parish archives of Venezuela exists, historians interested in local micro-history should begin with Lino Gómez Canedo's _Los archivos históricos de Venezuela_. Although it concentrates primarily on the major national archives, it nevertheless has an excellent section on provincial and regional resources. The next best source of information comes from the elaborate descriptions of parish archives in the books of Bishop Mariano Martí, whose visita of the Bishopric of Caracas at the end of the eighteenth century provides one of the best surveys of the central portion of Venezuela extant. Martí reported on the condition and contents of each parish archive, noting the dates of the earliest surviving parish book. The Martí information current in the late eighteenth century, if used with due regard to the vagaries of climate, civil war, and neglect, still gives the best starting point for any study of Venezuela's colonial population records at the parish level.[2]

Missionary Reports

Throughout Spanish America during the colonial period, the regular clergy provided their superiors with detailed, comprehensive reports on the numbers, dispersion, and characteristics of the native populations exposed to their missionary efforts. In Venezuela these reports constitute one of the few sources of population information outside of the regular government and ecclesiastical accounting system. Unfortunately, most of the accounts published leave much to be desired. Frequently the missionaries speak in terms so vague as to be practically useless. But in spite of this disadvantage, the letters and reports from remote missions are often the only sources of information about the location of obscure towns and settlements. This is especially true for mission towns active and prosperous in the eighteenth century that have subsequently disappeared. The reports also discuss the economic base of regions, describing existing trade patterns and assessing the public health history of the area.

Most of the useable missionary accounts come from the eighteenth century and focus on the Orinoco, Apure, and Llanos of Maturín regions, although there are scattered reports from other areas. These sources must be used with extreme care insofar as they make population estimates, but anyone interested in the development of Venezuela's population, and especially her indigenous population, will find valuable information in the records.[3]

Travelers' Accounts

Of all the sources of population data for Venezuela, none has been used as extensively or received as wide notice as the reports of visitors. While this kind of population reporting suffers from a host of difficulties and a variety of errors, it has at the same time the advantage of accessibility and intelligibility. Indeed, most historians of Venezuela's colonial past use these accounts as the principal source for data on population, partly because of the excellence of the two most important late eighteenth- and early nineteenth-century travelers' accounts by Alexander von Humboldt and François de Pons.

Of the two, Humboldt's has had the greatest impact, and his account represents the most extensive analysis of Venezuela's resources and possibilities available until well into the nineteenth century. A prime example of the Enlightenment polymath, Humboldt took an interest in practically everything. He made every effort to discover the size and composition of the population and to relate its growth to the prevailing economic and social conditions. De Pons, although perhaps more concerned with military affairs, also made a serious but less extensive effort to estimate population size.

Both de Pons and Humboldt traveled widely throughout the country gathering information and observing daily life. But in spite of this intimate acquaintance with Venezuelan conditions, the travelers could hardly have been expected to conduct their own population counts. Instead, they relied on the colonial elite for most of their quantitative information on the country, information which carried with it certain types of inaccuracy and bias.

In the case of population data, Humboldt and de Pons accepted the information provided them by the ecclesiastical authorities, population statistics compiled from the annual parish censuses available in Caracas since at least the mid-1770s. Although neither Humboldt nor de Pons took the figures at face value, both used them as the basis for their own estimates. As a result, neither traveler's information qualifies as an independent check on church-generated population statistics.

Of course the major contributions of these two famous visitors lie not with their population estimates but with their descriptions of the geographic situation, political organization, economic activities, and social structure of Venezuela. Since most of their remarks on these subjects are the result of personal observation and measurement, their value is high indeed. For example, in the effort to locate population centers existing in Venezuela at the end of the century, de Pons and especially Humboldt are indispensable guides.[4]

Special Government Surveys

Under this category come the series of _relaciones geográficas_ compiled in the eighteenth century. By and large this type of document has been thoroughly exploited, described, and analyzed by historians of the Spanish American empire. Nevertheless, it may be useful to give an indication of the utility of these reports for Venezuelan demographic history.

In general, the relaciones geográficas available for Venezuela follow the standard format characteristic of similar reports on other Spanish American areas, that is they contain descriptions of principal geographic features, economic conditions, agricultural conditions, military advantages, and population resources of a given locality. In Venezuela, the reports as a rule focus on the urban centers of each area and then interpret the center in terms of its hinterland. As a source of economic data and agricultural profiles, the relaciones geograficas are excellent, but for population purposes they show very little sophistication. Most of them barely have an estimate of the gross population in the area. Others make a perfunctory effort to separate out subgroups within the population, such as Negro slaves, Indians, or foreigners. On occasion a report will have an estimate of the military potential of an area in terms of the number of able-bodied men of military age in the region.[5]

Also included in this category are special surveys carried out by government officials for various purposes. For example, towns interested in changing their status from _sitio_ to _pueblo_ or from _pueblo_ to _villa_ had to submit extensive files on the state of their population and other characteristics. Likewise, when the Church wanted to create new parishes and requested aid from civil authorities, elaborate files appeared with considerable quantities of population data, sometimes age specific. But if these special surveys appear to be a promising source of population data, they must be used with care. One suspects that a file compiled to prove the populousness and prosperity of a town might be biased, especially if the reward for exaggeration were substantial. The utility of this kind of special report seems even less impressive when we realize that all the population figures come ultimately from the parochial census materials discussed below. Thus, it becomes difficult to use this kind of special survey as an independent check on the accuracy and completeness of the parochial data.

Finally, there is evidence of a considerable body of data collected in the 1770s in a government effort to assess the military strength of the empire. We have the schedule of questions sent out to the civil authorities in each town and the acknowledgements of their receipt. Unfortunately, the returns seem to have passed through the hands of the Caracas authorities on the way to Spain without leaving much of a trace in Venezuela's archives, although they may have been misfiled by the colonial authorities or may appear in some section of the archives not yet consulted. The most likely resting place for these documents, however, is in the Spanish archives. The survey questionnaire and instructions indicate a sophisticated attempt to acquire reliable population information, but we can guess that the extraordinary nature of the survey and its obvious military conscription implications may have seriously compromised its usefulness. Here too, the principal agents of the survey were the parish priests who also supervised the annual parish censuses.

Until a systematic search of the Spanish archives is made, we will of course be unable to determine the importance of the materials held there, but from the available indications, the quantity of that material is quite substantial. However, given the dependence of colonial administrators on the data collection abilities of parish priests, it is likely that the information collected in Spanish archives differs very little from that available from the annual parish censuses.[6]

Episcopal visitas

One of the duties of each new bishop was to conduct a detailed visita of each one of the parishes within his jurisdiction. Although bishops throughout the Spanish American empire honored this requirement in a mostly perfunctory way, a number of conscientious prelates took their duties very seriously and carried out thorough reviews of their sees.

In Venezuela one bishop stands out among all the rest in terms of the comprehensiveness and detail of his episcopal visita. Mariano Martí, Bishop of the See of Caracas, spent the years 1775 to 1783 traveling all over Venezuela visiting his parishes and recording in exceptional detail information on the spiritual and material condition of each parish within his jurisdiction. His records, recently published, constitute a complete description of the Bishopric of Caracas in the last third of the eighteenth century. Not only do the books of the visita include information on the location, boundaries, and physical-geographical features of each parish, but they also contain a wealth of population information.

All of Martí's figures come from the same parochial censuses discussed below and thus duplicate data available from other sources. Furthermore, Martí's visita chronologically spans two different methods of population accounting, and his data are not always comparable between different parishes. Having noted these liabilities, however, we must also acknowledge that Martí's data have certain advantages not present in any other source. Since Martí took a great personal interest in the information his subordinates compiled for him in each town they visited, he often noted inconsistencies in the population data supplied, and on occasion commented on the thoroughness of the parish priests' bookkeeping. This supervisory role exercised by Martí has given a certain consistency to the population reports of his visita. Moreover, in almost every case, Martí's information records population living in towns separately from population living outside and distinguishes people attached to sitios subordinated to towns from population within the town proper. This detailed geographic and locational breakdown is often unavailable in other materials on colonial Venezuelan population.

Martí also took considerable care to document the history of each parish. From his reports, we can usually discover when the parish was founded, which parish it belonged to before being elevated to an independent curacy, and what other places were attached to it for ecclesiastical and administrative purposes. Martí also made every effort to establish the earliest date in the parish registers and frequently commented on their condition. He made recommendations for the creation of new parishes by splitting up excessively large units or rearranging the boundaries of existing units to create parishes of nearly the same geographic and population size.

Although not precisely within the scope of this essay, it is impossible to pass over some of the other features of this remarkable survey. Marti catalogued the physical possessions of each curacy while at the same time describing the shape, construction, and condition of ecclesiastical buildings. He provided thumbnail biographies of the parish priests and assessed their abilities. And he recorded in considerable detail the gossip brought to him about the lives and activities of citizens in each town.[7]

Parish Household Lists: The "Matrículas"

From the mid-eighteenth to almost the beginning of the nineteenth century, parish priests sent in yearly registers or lists of their parishioners. These documents, which reside in the ecclesiastical archive in Caracas, provide an exceptional fund of demographic information. The household lists appear to have been compiled to fulfill the obligation of each parish priest to provide the bishop with a full account of his parishioners, indicating race, sex, marital status, and religious condition. Although the precise instructions received by the priests have yet to appear, it does not stretch the imagination to reconstruct the requirements set out for this annual census. For one thing, the returns for all the parishes in the Bishopric of Caracas show a remarkable uniformity of style and organization. For another, the returns are consistent in content and structure throughout the half-century of their existence.

The matrículas, which constitute the first systematic and regular censuses in Venezuela, were organized around the household as the fundamental census unit. Every individual covered by the census had to be located within a household and bear some relationship to the household head. This notion corresponds directly to the Spaniard's often noted obsession with the location of each individual in physical as well as social space. Indeed, nothing aggravated Spanish bureaucrats more than the unattached, unlocated individual.

But because location of an individual within a household failed to identify his status clearly enough, the household in turn was structured in such a way as to permit the placement of every individual with respect to the household head. Each household was broken down into its component families, and then the families were broken down into their component parts. Where households held multiple families, the individual families would be listed in descending order according to their status within the household. Frequently persons outside the family structure, such as unmarried adults, servants without families of their own, or individual single slaves living within the household, would appear in a separate category within the listing, but still in descending order by social rank. The households themselves were arranged according to the physical location of the building within the city. With this information, it is theoretically possible to reconstruct the organization and distribution of households throughout the parish and recreate patterns of urban residence.

Unfortunately, we do not always have the street plan of Venezuelan parishes, nor do we have a clear indication of the route followed by each census taker. Although in most cases it appears that priests followed the same routes as their predecesors, it is often difficult to verify the consistency of this practice. But because the matrículas are, at the very lowest level, lists of individuals by name, it is usually possible to follow the development of households over time. Sometimes the priests prove rather careless in assigning last names to individuals within the household, and servants, slaves, and women of all ranks usually appear without patronymics.

In addition to physical location within the town and social location within the household, it is possible to collect data on other characteristics of the individuals listed in the matrículas. Sex can be derived from the given names of practically everyone, and marital status is usually evident from the circumstances of the listing or from some specific indication in the entry. Racial designations appear somewhat less often, but still can be determined for the vast majority of individuals. In all but a few isolated cases, no age data are included in the matrículas, but because religious distinctions were in part age dependent, children under seven can be separated out from the adult population. Practically all the entries in the matrícula indicate whether the individual

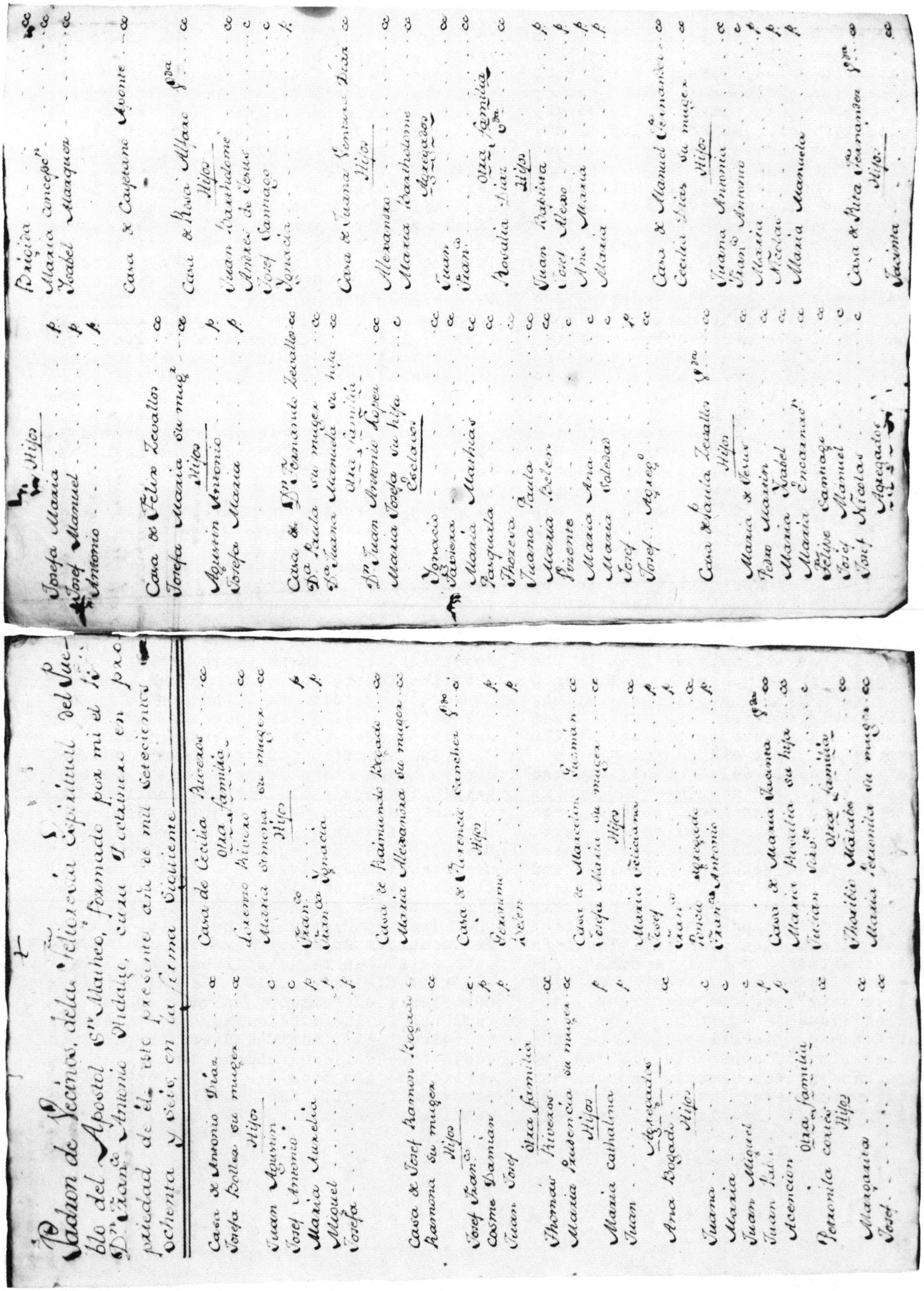

Padron de Vecinos, dela Feligresía Espiritual del Pueblo del Apostol Sr. Matheo, formado por mi el Br. D. Fran.co Antonio Hidalgo, cura y colector en propiedad de él, este presente año de mil setecientos ochenta y seis, en la forma siguiente

Casa de Antonio Díaz c
Josefa Robles su muger c
Hijos
Juan Agustín c
Josef Antonio c
María Aurelia p
Miguel p
Josefa p

Casa de Josef Ramon Rogado c
Ramona su muger c
Hijos
Josef Fran.co c
Cosme Damian p
Juan Josef p
Otra familia
Thomas Riveros c
María Prudencia su muger c
Hijos
María Catharina p
Juan p
Agregados
Ana Bogado c
Hijos
Juana c
María c
Juan Miguel p
Juan Ped.o p
Acencion c
Otra familia
Petronila Concep.on c
Hijos
Margarita c
Josef c

Casa de Cecilia Riveros c
Otra familia
Lorenzo Rivero c
María Simona su muger c
Hijos
Fran.co p
Juan Ignacio p

Casa de Raymundo Rogado c
María Alexandra su muger c

Casa de Florencio Sanchez c
Hijos
Geronimo p
Belen p

Casa de Marcelino Guzman c
Josefa María su muger c
Hijos
María Feliciana c
Josef p
Fran.co p
Poncia agregada c
Juan Antonio p

Casa de María Juana c
María Bonifacia su hija c
Julian Vic.te c
Otra familia
Theodoro Matheo c
María Petronila su muger c

Hijos
Josefa María p
Josef Manuel p
Antonio p

Casa de Felix Zevallos c
Josefa María su muger c
Hijos
Agustín Antonio p
Josefa María p

Casa de D.n Fernando Zevallos c
D.a Paula su muger c
D.a Juana Manuela su hija c
Otra familia
D.n Juan Antonio Lopez c
María Josefa su hija c
Esclavos
Ygnacio c
Xaviera c
María c
Pasquala c
Theresa c
Juana Paula c
María Belen c
Vizente c
María Ana c
María Soledad c
Josef p
Josef Agreg.o c

Casa de Paula Zevallos c
Hijos
María de Jesus c
Pedro Martin c
María Ysabel c
María Encarnacion c
Felipe Santiago c
Josef Manuel c
Josef Nicolas c
Agregados

Brigida c
María Concep.on c
Ysabel Marquez c

Casa de Cayetano Avente c

Casa de Rosa Alfaro c
Hijos
Juan Bartholome c
Andres de Jesus c
Josef Santiago c
Ygnacia p

Casa de Juana Ventura Diaz c
Hijos
Alexandro c
María Bartholome c
Agregados
Juan c
Fran.co c
Otra familia
Rosalia Diaz c
Hijos
Juan Baptista p
Josef Alexo p
Ana María p
María p

Casa de Manuel Fernandez c
Cecilia Diaz su muger c
Hijos
Juana Antonia c
Fran.co Antonio c
María p
Nicolas p
María Manuela p

Casa de Rita Fernandez c
Hijos
Jacinta c

Matricula Page for San Mateo in 1786

Figure 2-1

has taken communion, communion and confession, or is a párvulo--that is, a child under seven not yet required to observe the sacraments.

Without the results of a statistical analysis of these returns over time and space, and without the benefit of a comparison of their data with other sources, it is difficult to assess the value and reliability of the matrículas. In spite of these problems, however, we can make some preliminary observations which may help guide further evaluations. The high degree of standardization of these reports both over time and space indicates a carefully conceived census operation carried out with conscientious regard for the instructions. This conclusion is further buttressed by the physical appearance of the manuscripts themselves. With few exceptions, they are written out with great attention to detail, the formats are internally consistent, and in the cases checked so far, the information changes from year to year. Although it is probable that some parish priests copied the same return year after year, the present state of research on these matrículas does not show that to have been the norm (Figure 2-1).

Since we have not yet encountered the instructions to each parish priest on the methods to be used in taking the census, we cannot be sure about the procedures employed. But from a variety of other sources, some conclusions seem reasonable. With the exception of the major city parishes of the province, practically all of the Venezuelan parishes number between one and four thousand persons. This means that each priest would have had to compile data on a maximum number of households in the range of four to six hundred, a task well within the resources of most parish priests. To be sure, many parishes had no priest at all and their martículas had to be compiled by the curate of a neighboring town. But this situation usually occurred in the less populous parishes, where the number of households concerned may have been half or less of the maximum indicated above.

Having established in theory at least that these matrículas could have been compiled without undue stress by the individual parish priests, it remains to be shown how they did it. Here again we have very little direct evidence. But the organization and physical appearance of the documents themselves would seem to indicate that at least the first matrícula was compiled through a house-to-house survey. Such a procedure had been used before, and since Spanish practice was to use existing procedures and structures as much as possible, one would expect that the same process prevailed in the regular census operation. If the parish priests did indeed compile their original matrícula by a house-to-house survey, their method of updating that survey every year remains to be established.

Several possibilities exist. The curate may have resurveyed the parish every year, although a cursory knowledge of human nature and a basic familiarity with Spanish bureaucracy makes this possibility unlikely. At the other extreme, the priest may have sent in the same return every year, changing only the date. This probably holds true for some parishes over short periods of time, but it is unlikely that any parish would have the same return for the whole period under consideration. For one thing, even the slow moving ecclesiastical bureaucracy might notice this lack of change. For another, few parish priests remained at the same post continuously for thirty years or more. Each new priest would probably want to start off his period with energy and verve calculated to impress his superiors, and the preparation of a new census was one method of doing so. There are some indications in other census materials to support such an interpretation. Finally, we do know that in the cases examined so far the returns have been updated in some fashion.

As is the case in most problems of this kind, the reality can most likely be found somewhere in between the extremes. Until the analysis of these matrículas is completed, however, the following can serve as a possible reconstruction of population accounting administration in the Bishopric of Caracas.

Parish priests in eighteenth-century Venezuela rarely had to care for parishes in excess of four thousand souls. As a result, these men must have had a fairly comprehensive knowledge of who lived where and with whom. Moreover, because of the exaggerated Spanish American concern with social status, it seems reasonable to assume that the parish priest, like everyone else in town, knew everybody, where they lived, and how they ranked on the social scale. Given this intimate knowledge of the town, plus the priest's strategic position as the keeper of vital statistics, records of baptisms, marriages, and burials, it is not difficult to imagine a priest with the requisite knowledge to carry out a thorough yearly updating of his town's matrícula. Every year, sometime after Easter, each parish priest probably sat down with last year's matrícula, his aide, and the parish books, and then proceeded to go through the matrícula household by household. Surely he would know of the deaths, marriages, and births occurring in all but the most remote households. Surely he would know, for example, that a new family in town had rented rooms in a large household in a particular neighborhood. By bringing together his own knowledge of conditions in the parish with the data recorded in the parish books, the priest could thus have made a reliable updating of the previous year's census.

If we can accept this hypothetical sequence of events, it tells us a good deal about the kinds of errors to expect in the matrículas. For example, there is little doubt that the matrículas underenumerated servants, slaves, lower status people, and the children of such individuals. Because the count was based on the household, anyone not belonging to a household was liable to be missed in the census. In like fashion, people living outside the town on haciendas or *hatos* may have been underrepresented in some matrículas, especially if the parish jurisdiction was large geographically and the territory sparsely inhabited. It may also be wise to even out annual fluctuations through the use of moving averages, because it is quite possible that the priest only updated the whole town by a piecemeal process over a period of years.

These initial reflections also have implications for the research design most adequate for the exploitation of these archives. For example, it would be difficult to use these matrículas for the production of global statistics on the size of Venezuela's population near the end of the eighteenth century because of their focus on the urbanized part of a parish's population. Better use of these data would be for the analysis of family patterns and household structure and for the isolation of differential regional patterns, should these exist. Since we have no reliable way of filling out the universe covered in part by the matrículas, this latter type of analysis would seem to offer the most profitable avenue of research at present. Once the data contained in these matrículas have been rendered machine-readable and analyzed, other possibilities for research will undoubtedly appear.[8]

Annual Censuses

Another series of population data for Venezuela, closely related to the matriculas discussed above, comes from annual numerical census returns from the parishes of the Bishopric of Caracas. Covering the same universe as the matrículas and overlapping in chronological period, these returns appear in a variety of formats. All of them, however, have some similar characteristics. They invariably appear on hand-ruled sheets in the form of a rectangular table. Along the stub and the head are arranged the categories within which the data were collected. In addition to the population data, the table contains the name of the parish, the date of the census, the name of the priest responsible, and an occasional note commenting on special circumstances affecting the statistics. There is usually some reference to the ecclesiastical document authorizing the census. Practically all the format types include information on male-female and ecclesiastical categories, but once these minimum requirements have been met, the formats differ quite substantially.

From 1776 until the wars for independence in the Bishopric of Caracas, most of the parishes turned in annual returns according to a standard format labeled here Type III. Evidently a directive requiring a special reporting format was issued for the year 1807 and again for the year 1813. The 1807 version is labeled Type II, and the 1813 version, Type I (Figures 2-2, 2-3, and 2-4).

Direct evidence about the intentions and purposes of the special population accounting methods is extremely difficult to find, at least within Venezuela, but some general conclusions can be drawn from the kinds of questions the data answer. For example, both Type II and

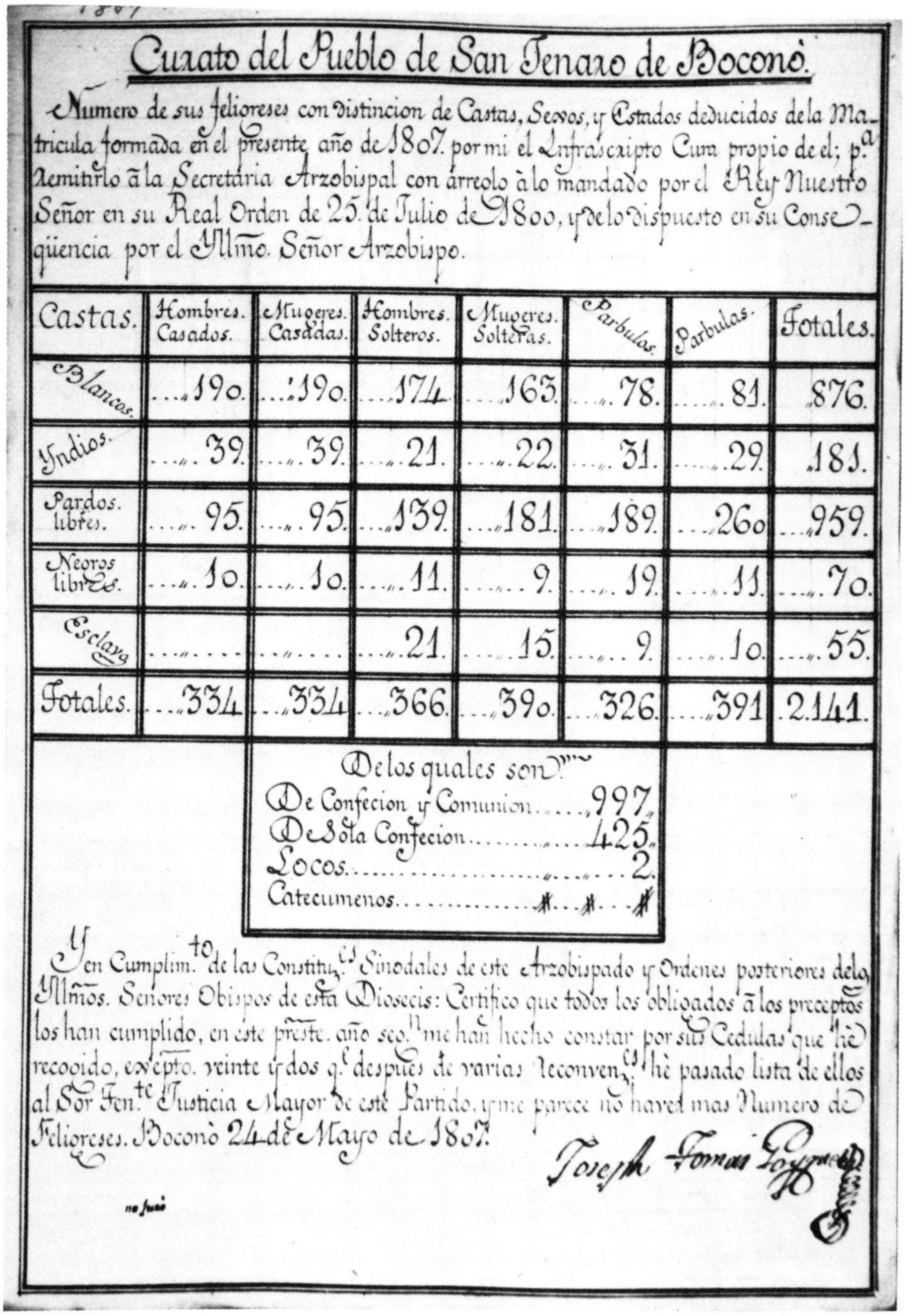

Curato del Pueblo de San Jenaro de Boconó.

Numero de sus feligreses con distincion de Castas, Sexos, y Estados deducidos de la Matricula formada en el presente año de 1807. por mi el Infrascripto Cura propio de el; p.a remitirlo á la Secretaria Arzobispal con arreglo á lo mandado por el Rey Nuestro Señor en su Real Orden de 25. de Julio de 1800, y de lo dispuesto en su consequencia por el Illmo. Señor Arzobispo.

Castas.	Hombres. Casados.	Mugeres. Casadas.	Hombres. Solteros.	Mugeres. Solteras.	Parbulos.	Parbulas.	Totales.
Blancos.	190.	190.	174.	163.	78.	81.	876.
Indios.	39.	39.	21.	22.	31.	29.	181.
Pardos. libres.	95.	95.	139.	181.	189.	260	959.
Negros libres.	10.	10.	11.	9.	19.	11.	70.
Esclavos	...	...	21.	15.	9.	10.	55.
Totales.	334.	334.	366.	390.	326.	391.	2.141.

De los quales son

De Confecion y Comunion .... 997.

De Sola Confecion .... 425.

Locos .... 2.

Catecumenos .... *

Y en Cumplim.to de las Constituc.s Sinodales de este Arzobispado y Ordenes posteriores de los Illmos. Señores Obispos de esta Diocesis: Certifico que todos los obligados á los preceptos los han cumplido, en este pres.te año seg.n me han hecho constar por sus Cedulas que he recogido, excepto. veinte y dos q.e despues de varias reconven.s he pasado lista de ellos al S.or Ten.te Justicia Mayor de este Partido, y me parece no haver mas Numero de Feligreses. Boconó 24 de Mayo de 1807.

Joseph Tomas [illegible]

Type III Census Format for Boconó in 1807

Figure 2-2

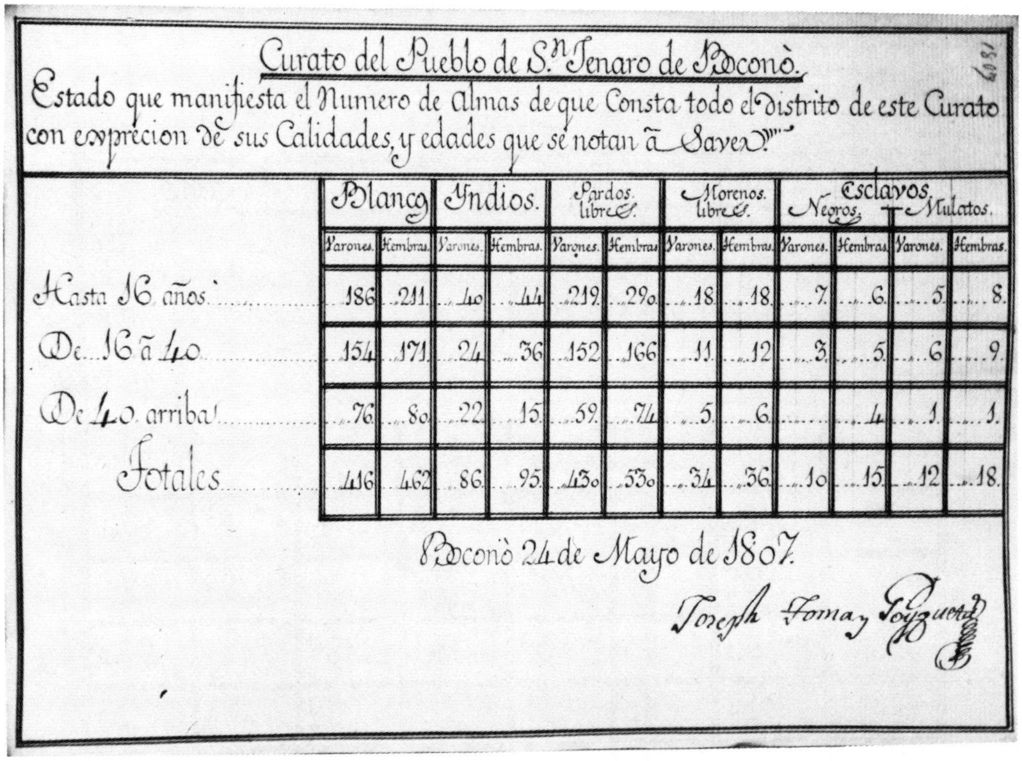

Curato del Pueblo de S.n Jenaro de Boconò.

Estado que manifiesta el Numero de almas de que Consta todo el distrito de este Curato con exprecion de sus Calidades, y edades que se notan á Saver.

1807

	Blancos		Indios.		Pardos libres.		Morenos libres.		Esclavos Negros.		Esclavos Mulatos.	
	Varones.	Hembras.	Varones.	Hembras.	Varones.	Hembras.	Varones.	Hembras.	Varones.	Hembras.	Varones.	Hembras.
Hasta 16 años	186	211	40	44	219	290	18	18	7	6	5	8
De 16 á 40	154	171	24	36	152	166	11	12	3	5	6	9
De 40 arriba	76	80	22	15	59	74	5	6		4	1	1
Totales	416	462	86	95	430	530	34	36	10	15	12	18

Boconò 24 de Mayo de 1807.

Joseph Toma y Goyzueta

Type II Census Format for Boconó in 1807

Figure 2-3

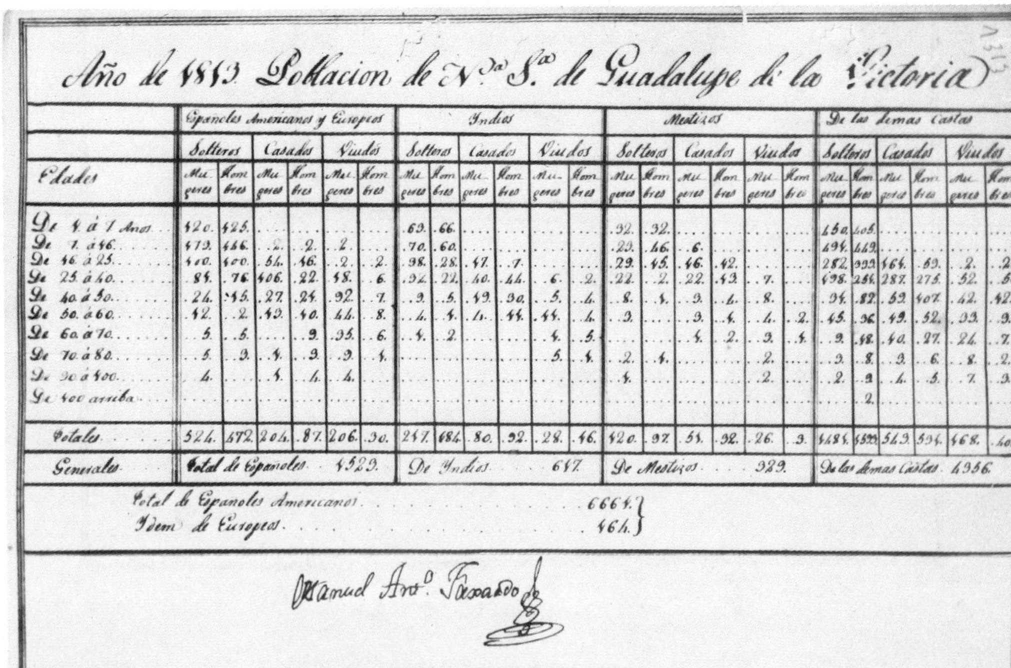

Año de 1813 Poblacion de N.tra S.ra de Guadalupe de la Victoria

Edades	Españoles Americanos y Europeos						Indios						Mestizos						De las demas Castas					
	Solteros		Casados		Viudos		Solteros		Casados		Viudos		Solteros		Casados		Viudos		Solteros		Casados		Viudos	
	Mugeres	Hombres	Mugeres	Hombres	Mugeres	Hombres	Mugeres	Hombres	Mugeres	Hombres	Mugeres	Hombres	Mugeres	Hombres	Mugeres	Hombres	Mugeres	Hombres	Mugeres	Hombres	Mugeres	Hombres	Mugeres	Hombres
De 1 á 7 Años	120	125					63	66					32	32					450	405				
De 7 á 16	179	166	2	2	2		70	60					29	46	6				491	449				
De 16 á 25	110	100	54	16	2	2	98	28	17	7			29	15	16	12			282	333	161	69	2	2
De 25 á 40	81	76	106	22	18	6	92	22	40	44	6	2	22	2	22	13	7		198	251	287	275	52	5
De 40 á 50	24	15	27	21	92	7	9	5	19	30	5	4	8	1	9	4	8		91	82	59	107	42	12
De 50 á 60	12	2	13	10	44	8	4	1	4	11	11	4	9		9	1	4	2	45	36	49	52	33	9
De 60 á 70	5	5		9	35	6	1	2			1	5			1	2	9	1	9	18	40	27	24	7
De 70 á 80	5	9	1	9	9	1					5	1	2	1			2		9	8	9	6	8	2
De 90 á 100	4		1	4	4								1				2		2	9	4	5	7	9
De 100 arriba																				2				
Totales	524	472	204	87	206	30	217	684	80	92	28	16	120	97	51	92	26	9	1481	1533	543	591	168	40
Generales	Total de Españoles 1529						De Indios 617						De Mestizos 329						De las demas Castas 4956					

Total de Españoles Americanos 6661
Idem de Europeos 164

Manuel Ant.o Faxardo

Type I Census Format for La Victoria in 1813

Figure 2-4

Type I formats ask for age data, with the Type I format specifying narrower age ranges than Type II. This demonstrates perhaps a greater interest in true demographic indicators, but it also suggests that the age data may have been requested to answer military manpower questions. The latter supposition seems particularly reasonable when we note that the Type II age categories are 0-16, 16-40, and 40 and above. Of course, the 16-40 age group is the one most liable for military service. It should also be noted that the years 1807 and 1813 are within the critical decades when the Spanish imperial system suffered constant attacks both from within and without. Finally in support of this hypothesis, these two census formats are one-time affairs, special purpose surveys probably not designed for general population accounting, and it is clear that the Type I and Type II censuses form a different category of data from Type III information.[9]

Type III Censuses

From the evidence available at present, there is little doubt that royal bureaucrats designed the Type III census format to provide a steady, uniform, and reliable source of demographic information. Moreover, from the phrasing of the only royal communication on this subject that I have been able to find, this procedure was designed to be used for all of America. (Figure 2-4)

The Type III census returns, on which the preliminary population analysis in this book is based, provide information on the race, sex, marital status, and religious condition of the population of the Bishopric of Caracas at the parish level. The data are presented in tabular form, following a standardized series of conventions. Apparently the reports can be characterized as a *de facto* census. Individuals absent from the parish were evidently excluded from the count, while temporary visitors to the parish were probably included. As a result, persons involved in extended travel have probably been undercounted. Although this would involve a few merchants, some government officials, and perhaps individuals involved in the transportation industry, the number of people actually caught in this circumstance, based on the internal evidence contained in the census returns, seems to have been quite small. Whenever a married man or woman did not appear in the census returns and his or her spouse did appear, the parish priest would note the absence of the spouse and often indicate a reason for the absence.

Even though the census has a fixed date for which it is supposed to be accurate, the small number of individuals considered as absent from the parish would indicate that the census compilers took little pains to determine whether or not a given individual happened to be in town on the particular day of the count. Rather, they most likely considered as absent only those persons habitually away from their homes. Because the census recorded the religious activity of all parishioners, those people absent from town during the Easter period probably ran a greater risk of exclusion from the census than those absent at other times of the year. This chain of explanation cannot, of course, be tested. But it has the virtue of corresponding to the available evidence and at the same time conforming to a commonsense understanding of the operation of Spanish ecclesiastical bureaucracy.

In attempting to assess the coverage of Type III censuses, or for that matter most of the rest of Venezuela's population accounts, it helps considerably to have a notion of the Spanish concept of residence. Within the empire, every citizen, vassal, or slave was expected to have a physical place to which he was attached. Unless he were involved in the process of transferring his residence from one place to another, anyone without a residential location did not legally exist within the system. Vagabonds, runaways, pirates, and smugglers lived in this limbo. Clearly, such people were beyond the limits of civilized society, and as such, could not be considered part of a functioning community.

Since all citizens in good standing had fixed residences, the notion that a census could be taken with reference to those residences and be expected to include all of the King's subjects was perfectly reasonable. As a result, Type III censuses were based on populations whose residential affiliation lay within a parish and who habitually resided there.

A further consideration about the coverage of Type III census data needs to be explained. A town's return covered not only the urbanized part of the parish but also the rural areas subject to the curate's ecclesiastical jurisdiction. In a few large cities this distinction made little difference, since the boundaries of the ecclesiastical jurisdictions coincided with the physical boundaries of the place. But for most of Venezuela, parishes included wide expanses of savanna and vast mountain reaches completely outside the town proper. Indeed, some of the pre-1776 summaries, particularly in the Martí visita, make a careful effort to distinguish between those individuals living inside the town and those living outside. The Type III returns, for the most part, do not separate out the town residents from the rural residents.

This situation leads to some serious complications for the interpretation of the aggregate figures for each parish. One solution to this inside-outside dilemma is to consider the data as representing a population evenly distributed within the parish jurisdiction. Of course, such is not the case, since we know that many characteristics of the population were different for town residents than for rural residents. Another alternative would be to consider the population of the parish to be concentrated at a point source, the location of the parish seat. While this is also an artificial construct, it does have some features to recommend it. In Spanish America, people generally located their place of legal residence within an urban nexus, whether rural village or metropolitan primate city. By considering the population of a parish as concentrated at the point of the parish church, we are able to avoid one of the most difficult problems plaguing an analysis of the kind attempted here, that is, the determination of parish boundaries.

The best single source for information on the size and boundaries of Venezuela's parishes is the report of Bishop Mariano Martí's visita. Even there, however, the geographical descriptions and toponymical terminology are so vague and imprecise that accurate boundary descriptions are almost impossible to derive. In fact, the mere process of locating parish centers is in many cases a job of major proportions. Because of the concentration of Venezuelan population inside towns and the practical difficulties of establishing parish boundaries, I have assumed that the population characteristics analyzed here refer to population aggregates concentrated at the point source defined by the parish church. In like fashion, the regionalizations developed in the course of this study are based on data conceived of in these terms. This procedure has been used with a full understanding of the distortions introduced, and the results of the analysis must be taken within this context.[10]

<u>Temporal and Geographic Coverage (Type III)</u>

Within this framework, the Type III data fall into a two-dimensional matrix whose boundaries help clarify the nature of the data. Along a temporal axis, the census returns are distributed as in Part II, Table 7. Beginning in the 1770s, the number of returns peaks around the turn of the century and tapers off thereafter, although scattered returns exist as late as 1838. Over half of all returns in this group fall in the 1800-1809 decade. Along a geographical axis, we can see that the Type III returns cover mainly that portion of modern Venezuela shaded in Map 3-1 and identified in Map 1-9. This area corresponds roughly to the Bishopric of Caracas after 1800. During the period 1776-1800, the Bishopric had been reduced by the separation of the Coro and Trujillo jurisdictions and their aggregation to the newly created Bishopric of Mérida de Maracaibo. Although the area covered by the Type III censuses represents about twenty percent of Venezuela's surface area, it includes more than sixty percent of Venezuela's population in that period and covers the central coast and valleys, the most important regions of the country from both a socioeconomic and political perspective. The completeness of coverage varies from year to year, with the critical 1800-1809 period showing the highest response.

In an effort to smooth out short-term fluctuations in the data, I have divided the series into four chronological groups. Those returns for parishes reporting before 1800 form the first group, representing about twenty percent of the total number of returns. Those returns for the years 1800 through 1809 make up the second group of about thirty-five percent. The third group of returns covers the years 1810 to 1819 inclusive, about a third of the total. The last group includes the years after 1819, some fifteen percent of the returns.

Because the collection of census returns is rarely complete for all the parishes for every year, some means of estimating the missing data had to be devised. The method adopted here has little to recommend it in terms of statistical elegance but much in terms of practicality. What I have done is to construct a ten year average for each parish. This method, for almost all of the parishes, gives a population value for the mid-point of the two ten year periods 1800-1809 and 1810-1819, in addition to a less reliable mid-point value for the decades preceding 1800 and the decades following 1819.

Such a procedure gives a reasonably accurate representation of Venezuela's population before the dislocations of the independence movement and a comparable picture of her population during the independence era. In the few cases where only one return exists for a given parish within the time period, I have taken that value, whether it occurs at the beginning or the end of the time period, as the best estimator of the mid-point value. To be sure, during the independence era Venezuela's population suffered severe dislocations in selected areas, but the nature of these dislocations has not yet been discovered, nor are there any guides to the magnitude of the changes. Perhaps after the conclusions of this preliminary analysis have been thoroughly evaluated, a more sophisticated estimating formula may be employed, but for the present, the procedure outlined above will probably involve the least risk of serious error.

These manipulations result in two files of population data for late colonial Venezuela possessing a comprehensiveness and consistency rare indeed for Latin America. The first file, composed of the averages for each parish reporting in the period 1800-1809, forms the base for most of this book. The second file, the complete collection of Type III returns, is tabulated and cross-classified in the statistical series that accompanies the analysis.

Census Categories and Definitions (Type III)

In addition to the aggregate population data on the size of parishes within the Bishopric of Caracas, the Type III censuses also divide the population into three categories that need to be defined in terms of the Spanish information system. There appears to be no difficulty with the male-female distinction recorded in the returns. Priests, however, and nuns living in convents, frequently were not included in the tabulations since they were considered outside the traditional civil jurisdictions. They appeared rather in a separate category within the census, without the specificity required in the reporting of the civil population. Although this lack of consistency is regrettable, its effect on the total returns is quite small, as the number of ecclesiastics in any parish was few indeed.

The returns also divided the inhabitants according to what we might call their religious condition, although in modern terms this distinction is more closely allied with civil status. Individuals were first divided into two groups, those over the age of religious responsibility, from seven on up, and those below that age, called párvulos. Adults, in this case people seven years old or older, and children were also separated into male-female groups and differentiated by race. Adults were further divided by civil status, that is married or unmarried. Widows were almost certainly included in the unmarried category, for parish priests frequently noted that the number of married males and females was unequal because of some unusual circumstance. The assumption here, of course, is that all married females had a living male partner and vice versa. Since death broke the marriage bond, it made good sense to include the widows or widowers among the unmarried. It must be emphasized that these civil status distinctions are in fact religious distinctions based on the ecclesiastically defined condition of the individuals involved. As a result, when interpreting the statistics derived from the file, this special character of the definition of single, married, and child must be kept in mind.[11]

But if the religious and sex distinctions are relatively straightforward once the definitions are understood, the same cannot be said of the racial distinctions. Every individual included in the census was cross-classified by racial category. In the Type III censuses in Venezuela, five racial categories were used: white, Indian, _pardo_, Negro, and slave. Although in other parts of America more complex racial designations enjoyed considerable popularity, these five worked so well in Venezuela that most commentators found it difficult to extend the nomenclature. In fact, there is some indication that the term _Negro_ was gradually falling out of use by the end of the eighteenth century. For the purposes of this analysis of the Type III censuses, these terms can be defined in the following way.[12]

Whites were those individuals reputed to be of pure Spanish ancestry without any known trace of African or Indian ancestry. In practice in America, this rigid definition became considerably weakened over time, until by the end of the eighteenth century the term _white_ meant little more than a person with a reasonably close approximation to a Spanish, white stereotype, plus a reasonably prosperous economic condition. In many instances the status of white could be acquired in recompense for distinguished service or substantial financial contribution. As a result, knowing that an individual bore the classification white, we are unable to state with any certainty the nature of his genetic heritage. We can, however, make a series of conditional assumptions about the individual. We can guess that he was either racially white (that is of undiluted white Spanish descent for the last four generations at least) or that he may have deviated somewhat from such genetic purity but have been of sufficient merit and wealth to convince his peers and his sovereign to regard him as white. One suspects that the amount of money and merit required to justify being considered white must have increased substantially with the degree of deviation from the pure white Spanish norm. Because inclusion within this racial group implied access to a variety of privileges, powers, and immunities, admission was jealously controlled by whites and supervised by royal officials. At least in Venezuela, there is considerable evidence that the white elite's control of their group suffered serious erosion during the last decades of imperial rule. In an effort to reduce social tensions and with a commendable interest in feathering the royal nest, the Spanish bureaucracy followed a reasonably consistent policy of expanding the elite by conferring white status on racially nonwhites whose merits were visibly attested to by their generous contributions to the Crown. In spite of the cheapening of white status near the end of the century, this racial category remained one of the best defined and most consistently reported in the census returns. As a legally defined status, jealously guarded, little room remained for the census taker to err in classifying these individuals.

This relative lack of ambiguity in racial classification also occurs with the slave category. With all slaves legally defined as such in a host of official documents, it would appear unlikely that many slaves would have been misclassified. Even though the classification of slaves was relatively clear-cut because of the legal definition, that group contained a wide variety of human types: domestics, artisans, field hands, runaways, newly landed Africans, third generation Venezuelan blacks, and light-colored mulattos.

If the white and slave classifications are straightforward in terms of interpretation, such is not the case with the remaining three categories of Indian, pardo, and Negro. The Indian category, while explicitly racial in theory, in practice involved a combination of cultural and racial criteria. For an individual to be considered an Indian, he had not only to correspond to an Amerindian stereotype, but also to have a cultural level distinguishable from the Spanish norm. In Venezuela, Indians as an identifiable group included those residents of mostly rural parishes who, while not completely assimilated, nevertheless participated in the Spanish labor and market system. Excluded from consideration entirely were those Amerindians who did not form part of the Spanish system, the so-called wild or untamed Indians. But for the Bishopric of Caracas this exclusion poses no serious problem because the areas of significant unassimilated Indian population fall outside the limits of the Bishopric.

It is difficult to know how to regard the Indian category or to imagine how a parish priest might have gone about classifying his parishioners within that category. Until more specific information becomes available, the following explanation will have to suffice. Parish priests undoubtedly employed a pragmatic and what might be called a consensus method for establishing an individual's race for census purposes. If the person in question had obvious Amerindian features and lived in a way stereotyped as Indian, there could have been little difficulty in classifying him. But if the individual had achieved complete acculturation in the sense of speaking colloquial Spanish and living in the Spanish style, the determination of his category might have been considerably more difficult. In such a case the category might have turned on the individual's reputation within the community, on whether his baptismal certificate stipulated that he was an Indian, on his wealth, and on the claims he made for himself. This determination must have been complicated by the extensive miscegenation characteristic of Spanish America. Pure Indian types were probably fairly rare in the more populous areas, and in any event, such individuals were most likely included in the Indian category without problem. But the white-Indian or the Negro-Indian mixture must certainly have produced classification dilemmas. In such a situation, the individuals became part of that category whose stereotype most closely approximated the individual's personal characteristics. Quite obviously such a system leaves much to be desired as a classificatory scheme for census purposes. Equally apparent is the room for wide variation in the interpretations of the standards employed in different spots throughout the country. The Indian-Negro mixtures frequently must have ended up in the pardo category, and some of the more prosperous Indian-white mixtures may have passed as whites.

Although the Indian category poses considerable problems of interpretation, these are small when compared to the difficulties presented by the pardo category. In theory, pardos were people with a mixed African-European ancestry, but in practice this simplicity quickly disappeared. Pardos who lived in legal bondage fell under the category of slave, regardless of their phenotype. Light colored individuals of means or merit who managed to acquire a certificate of whiteness ended up included among the whites. Runaway slaves who escaped detection were often identified as pardos in their place of residence. Products of Indian-Negro liaisons living in areas with small Indian populations must also have been more readily classified as pardos than as Indians. Third or fourth generation free Venezuelans of pure African ancestry were also included within the pardo group. As a result, the range of individual included in the pardo category was wide indeed, and worse yet, the criteria for the category undoubtedly varied from time to time and place to place. Nevertheless, there are some consistencies underlying the use of this catchall term.

Perhaps the best way to comprehend the meaning of the term pardo is to explore the terrain covered by the name. Although at the beginning there was apparently some effort made to define the pardos carefully, by the eighteenth century the classification system which had seemed adequate in the sixteenth century had become completely changed in practice and complicated in theory. Originally these categories of white, Indian, pardo, Negro, and slave had seemed fairly easy to apply, but as a variety of crossbreeds emerged and as more of them achieved an eminence surpassing their supposed racial limitations, the system gradually became modified to accommodate exceptions to the rules. Over time, there was an apparent inflation in the coin of social discrimination in Venezuela. Whites as a group became less and less racially pure and began to include new-made men whose accomplishments allowed them to buy into the white category. At the same time, the bottom-line category of free men, Negro, became used less and less. Negroes were supposed to be individuals of purer African descent than those included in the pardo category. Negroes should have been blacker and closer to an African stereotype than pardos. In fact, by the late eighteenth century few people were included in the Negro classification. Until more evidence on the composition of this group becomes available, I have hypothesized that in the later part of the 1700s those labelled Negroes were actually recently freed slaves whose origin remained fresh in the community's memory. This explanation helps make some sense out of the small number of individuals included in the category. Of course, it is also possible to assume that by the late eighteenth century few Venezuelan blacks had maintained their racial purity, and that therefore few would qualify for inclusion in the Negro category. This explanation, while plausible, lacks a certain feeling of verisimilitude, in part because it only partially explains the low figures, and in part because contemporaries discussing the racial situation tended to lump Negroes and pardos together and to use the terms in such a way as to imply that pardo could refer to nonwhite, non-Indian, and nonslave, but that Negro only referred to black people with a social status somewhat beneath that of pardos. Equally convincing is the lack of concern with racial somatic characteristics in the literature, which implies that the distinction between Negro and pardo may have been based more on relative distance from slavery than on any racial stereotyping.

From the foregoing discussion of this point, the difficulty of interpreting the racial distinctions can readily be appreciated. Before commenting on the utility of these distinctions, a word on the terminology used here is in order. Many designations have been proposed to refer to the Spanish notion of stratifying individuals according to quasi-racial, quasi-social, and quasi-legal criteria. Some have proposed the term social-race to identify these categories. This emphasizes the social nature of the distinctions, while at the same time recognizing their racial basis. Others, wishing to highlight the class or economic basis for these distinctions, have proposed the term racial-class, which has some features to recommend it. But after giving some thought to this problem, I have chosen a thoroughly conservative approach, preferring the notoriously vague concept of race to the semiscientific terms social-race or racial-class. Although the notion of race has taken on an almost vicious derogatory connotation when used outside strictly scientific, genetic contexts, it has much to recommend it as a term for these Spanish American classifications.

Race is the term and concept most Spaniards used when referring to whites, pardos, Indians, Negroes, and slaves. Moreover, although it may have been possible to change racial category by substantial achievements or payments, no one believed that the elevated person had thereby actually changed his race. He may have been able to pass the newfound condition on to his descendents, but unless the phenotype corresponded to the stereotypical norm expected, passage into the new racial category could never be complete. Because most Spaniards saw these ethnic distinctions as inheritable characteristics, I find their notion of race the most approriate term for their classification system.

As for the names for each of the categories within the racial system, I have chosen to translate _blancos_ as whites, _indios_ as Indians, _negros_ as Negroes, and _esclavos_ as slaves, because these English counterparts carry much the same meaning in common speech as their Spanish originals. I have, however, kept the Spanish term _pardo_ rather than translate it as mulatto or something similar. The reason for this is that mulatto in English does not convey the same breadth of meaning as the Spanish term _pardo_. By keeping pardo, I hope to emphasize the special way in which the term was applied, as discussed above. The closest equivalent might well be the present use of black in reference to Afro-Americans in the United States, but the use of that term today is somewhat more inclusive and has political and social overtones not present in the Spanish usage of pardo in eighteenth-century Venezuela. As a result of these considerations, I have stayed with the racial categories of white, Indian, pardo, Negro, and slave. The order of these categories in the discussion and in the data refers, of course, to the order in which these groups always appear in contemporary documents and reflects their theoretical position in the Spanish American social hierarchy.

Even though I have spent a considerable amount of time explaining the problems inherent in the racial classifications employed by late eighteenth- and early nineteenth-century census takers, it must not be assumed that the conceptual and theoretical fuzziness of the terms used renders the categories themselves useless for social analysis. For all the difficulty we may have in understanding the racial distinctions, contemporary Venezuelans had very little trouble attaching categories to specific individuals. And although the meaning and social values attached to the names may have changed gradually over time, it does not follow that contemporaries believed the categorization nothing more than a census taker's exercise. Not only did the various categories have widespread acceptance, but they had a practical impact on the lives of individuals so classified.

With this brief survey of the census-taking methods and classification schemes of Venezuela's eighteenth-century population accounts completed, it is now possible to proceed with the description and analysis of Venezuela's population in the last generation of the colonial period.

Parish Church, Arenales

THREE

Hamlets, Villages, Towns, and Cities

The Urban Nexus and Its Records

Eighteenth-century Venezuelans, like most Spanish Americans, came into the world, grew up, married, raised children, and died within a social matrix arranged around urban or urbanized centers. In that environment, of course, an urban center can range from a few primitive houses clustered around a bit more substantial church, to the major cities composed of a multiplicity of large buildings, spacious plazas, and imposing churches. Nevertheless, whatever the distance separating the smallest parish hamlet in the Llanos from the grandest conglomerate of city parishes in Caracas, these urban centers served their parishioners in much the same way, varying only in complexity and degree. While there are many ways of demonstrating this truism, perhaps the most convincing is to notice how the inhabitants of these regions described themselves and their geography.

When they arrived in the new world and set foot on Tierra Firme, the Spanish adventurers of the sixteenth century began their entries into the continent with the goal of finding either enough Indians or enough gold to justify the establishment of an urban center. And it occurred to almost no one to imagine the exploitation of America's rich resources through some other mechanism than the Iberian town, an urban form transplanted to the Indies and endowed with new functions. Conquistadores, adelantados, governors, merchants, and clerics all looked to the town for direction and control. Even the rebels organized their challenge to royal authority by way of cities. In the sixteenth century, for example, Lope de Aguirre chose to move from town to town in Venezuela in his ill-fated journey towards the overlordship of a part of America.[1]

If it were possible to map the lines of thought, loyalty, interest, and emotion that linked individuals of the Spanish American enterprise to each other and to their sovereign, the lines would reach directly from individuals to the nearest town, from there to the other major towns in the region, and ultimately to the sovereign. Even though the data for such a map are hard to find, we can glimpse the orientation of this mind set through the descriptions contemporaries gave of their time and their places. As we read through the *Recopilación historial de Venezuela* of Fray Pedro Aguado, and follow the efforts of the first explorers, we begin to see how the chronicler envisioned the process of conquest and settlement. He disapproved of the early, Welser period because the Welser's agents failed to get on with the primary business of conquest, the founding of permanent, organized towns. His history proceeds chronologically, but always within a vision of Tierra Firme as a ribbon of coastline connecting an irregular net whose nodes were towns and whose lines were communications routes. His characters move along the lines, they cross mountains and discover great rivers, but their motion, their decisions, and their goals seem regulated more by the presence or absence of Indian towns, the distance to previously established Spanish towns, or the possibility of supporting a new Spanish center, than by the existence of geographic obstacles.

Nor is Aguado alone in this urban conception of the Venezuelan landscape. In 1764, Cisnero's Descripción exacta de la provincia de Benezuela appeared. Cisneros, a merchant for the Caracas Company, wanted to explain the major characteristics of his native land. After a brief summary of Venezuela's geographical features, he confirmed the urban network originally described by Aguado. Cisnero's net, of course, was made of a finer mesh than Aguado's, but the basic structure was virtually identical.

While there is no need to insist on the obvious urban orientation of Venezuela's colonial organization, some of the functional advantages of this organization need emphasizing. The towns and villages that defined the country from the sixteenth century forward provided all the services required in the course of settlement and exploitation. Whatever the strategic resource encountered, whether minerals, Indians, or later, land, the town provided the locus for the distribution of rights and the validation of competing claims. Each competitor for some of America's riches believed his best hope for the maintenance and enforcement of his claim lay in the preservation of town authority. He might try to overthrow town leaders or supplant them, but he never offered to destroy the town's authority. If thwarted by his nearest town, he could appeal upward through increasingly higher authorities in higher-ranking towns, until reaching the final authority of the King and his Councils. In like fashion, the King and his Councils directed the development of the American enterprise by sending their orders throughout the net to be enforced and carried out at the lowest town level.

Given the utility of the net as a governing structure, it is no wonder that the Spanish monarchs reinforced the urban spirit of their people through a variety of legal and administrative measures. Throughout the Spanish empire, nothing lasting and important could be done without the intervention of the urban center. And the more magnificent and permanent the endeavor, the greater the city required to validate it. The simple, yet absolutely fundamental, effort to establish a family line, to create a dynasty in the New World, required as a minimum the intervention of the parish priest in baptism, marriage, and burial. The collection and maintenance of wealth, whether in land, Indians, slaves, or merchandise, demanded the cooperation and services of notaries, lawyers, judges, and public registries, all located and administered in towns. Social status and personal prestige required a substantial urban presence in guilds or Church, in the cabildo or military companies, in large urban houses and substantial retinues. Through these devices, the Spanish American system of gain and loss came to depend more and more on the operation of the urban net. Some people lived outside the net as vagabonds, wanderers, smugglers, thieves, or runaway slaves, but the price they paid was often high. As marginal men, they frequently had to live seminomadic lives, drifting from one distasteful employment to another. For all but the runaway slave, the only hope for an improved life style lay in reentering the network and becoming established in the eyes of a town.

The lowest level of this network, the smallest recognized node, was the parish. Settlements without a parish church always belonged to a nearby parish, and rarely achieved separate recognition by any agency of society. Once such a place grew to a respectable size or became important for some other reason, it would be granted the status of parish, and from that time would begin to function as a recognized part of the net.[2]

During the last quarter of the eighteenth century and continuing well into the first third of the nineteenth, the imperial bureaucracy activated the urban network to provide it with the statistical series on population composition believed necessary for adequate planning. Population accounting at the parish level began of course long before the late 1700s. According to Church regulations, parish priests were obliged to keep careful account of their parishioners, especially to record each parishioner's fulfillment of his religious duties of an annual communion and confession. Each individual in the Spanish empire became a recognized member of the urban network by having his baptism, marriage, and ultimately his burial registered with the parish priest. Throughout his life, he found himself checked off, registered, or in some other way accounted for within the locus of his parish. Whenever his children married, he found himself recorded in the parish book, and each time he participated in a baptism, either as a parent or a godparent, his name and status entered the parochial register. Obviously, this system of personal record keeping worked better in some places than in others, and many recordable events never became part of the official accounts. A hypothesis that expected an underrecording of the activities of some of the less prosperous members of society--free blacks, poor whites, vagabonds, and fugitives--would certainly be justified.

Even considering the opportunities for omissions and incompetence in these parochial accounts, the completeness of the records available to us is remarkable. Life histories can be reconstructed for whole families, especially for the more fortunate members of society, and demographic histories for complete towns. Unfortunately, the combination of information from the variety of sources maintained by colonial ecclesiastics has proved very tedious to use, and only successful to date for small groups. This difficulty in reconstructing whole societies from the parish records derives from the fact that the record-keeping system was designed to permit individuals to recall the particulars of their past when required by the demands of business, family, or law, and to permit the priests to follow the status of each member of their flocks. It is the record keeping system's emphasis on the individual's life history that makes analysis of the parish as a population unit difficult.

In spite of the disaggregated nature of the statistical system for population accounting, a careful examination of this system permits a valuable perspective on the Spanish empire's mechanisms of social organization and control. For both the individual and the monarchy, the key to evaluation of all activity in the empire, and especially to the allocation of reward or punishment, was information. But in the determination of contested issues, the only information normally acceptable came in written and witnessed form. Because of this, every individual with any interest in rewards or punishments kept his activities as carefully documented as possible, or, fearing punishment, tried to suppress the preparation of adverse information. But not just any written document served the purpose. Spanish colonials appeared to believe that information became more reliable as the document became more official, the witnesses more august, and the circumstances more solemn. In matters touching on family, inheritances, status, or personal privileges, parties to the petitions always required written and notarized proofs of birth, parentage, marriage, and _compadrazgo_, information kept and certified by the parish priest at the lowest level of the urban network.

By requiring that all contested matters pass through one of the urban nodes of the network before decisions could be made, the Spanish imperial system acquired a form of built-in stability, a species of moderating influence exercised by established authorities located in the towns and cities of the empire. At the same time, individuals in the system preserved their identification with the empire through their right to appeal directly to the Crown. Thus the Spanish information system linked this extraordinary imperial structure together even more than did the legal systems or administrative apparatus. While government organization might change and legal dispositions might vary from time to time and place to place, the one immutable factor in any important Spanish American situation was the demand for certified, registered, and verified information, most importantly about individuals and their activities. Governors and judges might change, commercial regulations could be varied, bureaucratic terms and formulas shifted, but whatever happened, Spanish Americans knew they would need to produce information recorded, stored, and maintained at the lowest level of parish record keeping. This helps explain why the parish records are so complete, why they maintain their consistency so well over time, and why the eighteenth-century colonial administrators fixed on these records as the principal source for a new kind of population accounting.

In the Bourbon Monarchy's plans to improve the efficiency of Spanish imperial administration, information collection and retrieval assumed a paramount place. With enlightened enthusiasm, they ordered a variety of special censuses, called for new summaries of the American situation, and revised standard ecclesiastical record keeping. In this last effort, they wisely refrained from meddling with the baptismal, marriage, and burial records, the touchstone of imperial continuity. But the Bourbon ministers wanted information in condensed form, with enough detail to permit adequate planning, but not as much as to complicate the establishment of general patterns. So from the lowest level of aggregation in the continuously maintained vital registers, population accounting methods achieved two higher levels of elaboration. The first was the annually-compiled household lists, the matrículas, that appeared in Venezuela at the end of the first half of the eighteenth century. But because of the extreme detail of these records, they could hardly have served the purposes of imperial planners. The second level of aggregation began in the last quarter of the eighteenth century, with summary tables of population compiled at the parish level.

Although the population tables appeared in a variety of forms and styles, a standard form containing information about sex, race, civil status, and an adult-child distinction became the rule in Venezuela in 1776. It is this subset of Venezuelan population records that has provided the basis for this work and for the material collected at the end of the volume.[3]

Individuals within the empire defined themselves at the most basic level in terms of their residential location or affiliation with a parish in a specific location and with a variety of characteristics, so we may better understand the context of eighteenth-century Venezuela by examining what kinds of parishes existed in the Bishopric of Caracas, and how the various parish types were distributed through the region.

Parish Types

This discussion assumes that a knowledge of the parishes of Venezuela may be of considerable help in the effort to understand Spanish American social reality and may provide insights into some of the political, economic, and social transformations occurring during that century of transition, 1750-1850. We are interested in the types, varieties, and characteristics of parishes, that is, the discussion focuses on that residential group organized in an urban center of sufficient importance in the Spanish empire to merit a set of records of its own.

In the abstract, parishes may appear reasonably coherent units amenable to meaningful comparison, but unfortunately the reality of Venezuela failed to conform to this abstraction. In some places parish signified a relatively simple phenomenon, a hamlet, village, town, or city with one principal church, clearly defined boundaries, and no small subsettlements. This idealized parish would have an urban center defined by a gridiron pattern of streets enclosing houses, stores, and at least one plaza. The town proper would be surrounded by agricultural or stock-raising land out to the established borders of the parish. Within this standard parish, most of the population would live in the town proper, but a few individuals, principally slaves, Indians, laborers, and their supervisors, might reside in scattered locations outside the town's gridiron. For the sake of this discussion, I have called this a standard parish (Figure 3-1).

Although the variety of parish types is infinite, two other main patterns can be generalized in eighteenth-century Venezuela, extensions in opposite directions of the standard pattern. What I have called an extended parish looks much like a standard parish. It has the gridiron town proper, the boundaries enclosing agricultural or stock-raising land, and the isolated residences, but in addition, some of these isolated residences have accumulated enough population to form small communities. These sitios often centered on a small chapel or shrine. In spite of their embryonic urban status, these places belonged to the main parish and their residents registered their vital events with the priest in the town proper. Many cases of the formation of new parishes during the eighteenth century arise from sitios whose growth and importance justified their separation from the extended parish. Thus, an extended parish could break into two standard parishes over the course of time. It is difficult at this stage of research to establish exactly what constituted sitio status in Venezuelan practice, and it is unclear how many places can be classified as ex-

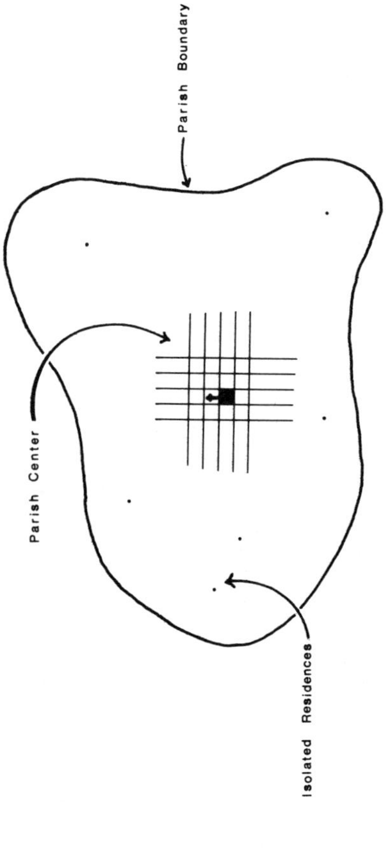

Parish Center
Parish Boundary
Isolated Residences

Standard Parish
Figure 3-1

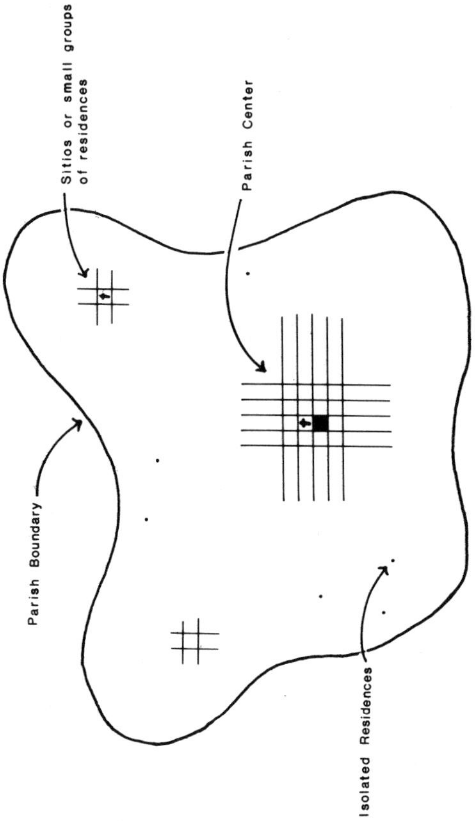

Sitios or small groups of residences
Parish Center
Parish Boundary
Isolated Residences

Extended Parish
Figure 3-2

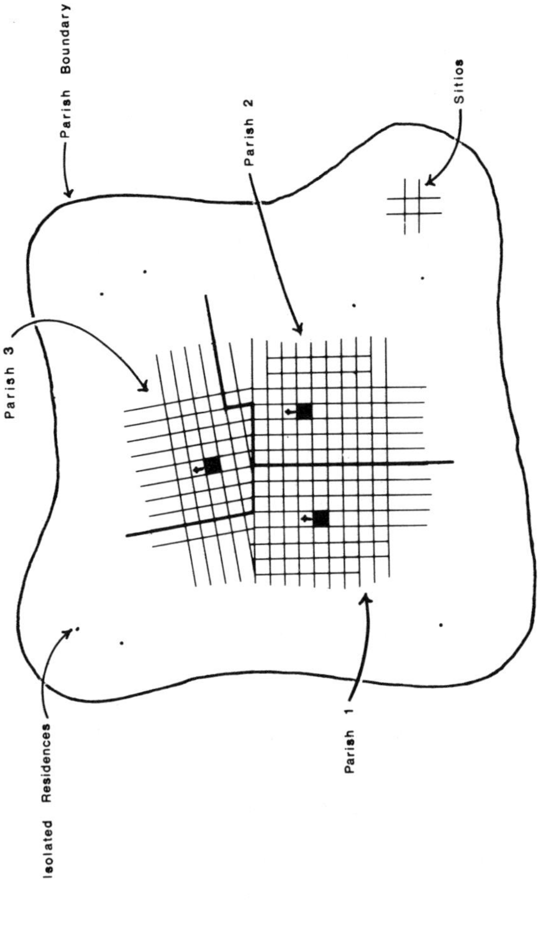

Parish Boundary
Parish 2
Sitios
Parish 3
Isolated Residences
Parish 1

Contracted Parish
Figure 3-3

CLL

tended parishes, but an impressionistic survey of Martí's visita records shows that this extended parish may have been the most prevalent parish type (Figure 3-2).

In a few cases, extremely important ones nonetheless, the parish existed without any nonurban territory, or with only a fragment of territory with isolated residences. This situation only occurred in urban centers large enough to have more than one parish. In the records collected here, two cities, Barquisimeto and San Felipe, had two parishes, and one city, Caracas, had six. I have called this form a <u>contracted parish</u>. Its jurisdiction is contracted, it is bordered on at least one side by another town proper, and the identification of residents to their parish was probably weaker than the identification characteristic of the standard or extended parish. For the purposes of population accounting, the division into multiple parishes within a single town served to keep the record keeping within reasonable bounds[4] (Figure 3-3).

The boundaries of these parishes are in many cases difficult to locate, in part because the geographical nomenclature of the eighteenth century is vague, and in part because some parishes appear never to have defined their borders. In discussing the characteristics of the parishes of the Bishopric of Caracas, another serious analytical problem arises. In spite of an extensive effort to define clearly the limits of the universe of parishes contained within the Bishopric, it has proved impossible at this time to fix the number of parishes subject to ecclesiastical census procedures. As a result, I cannot set a precise measure of the completeness of coverage of this data. While absolute precision may elude me, I can give an educated estimate of completeness, based on the list of parishes and curacies subject to the Bishopric in Mariano Martí's visita in the late 1770s and early 1780s and on the list of parishes from the late 1830s supplied in Agustín Codazzi's <u>Geografía</u>. Neither of these sources can provide the definitive list required, because Martí's visita created some new parishes and missed others, while Codazzi's list is based on civil definitions of <u>parroquia</u> which are not exactly the same as the ecclesiastical census parish units, and his list from 1838 includes places only recently elevated to parish status.

Even with these problems, the disparities between the Martí list, my list from the ecclesiastical census records, and Codazzi's list are not very large. In the period with the highest number of parishes, 1800-1809, the ecclesiastical censuses show data on 194 parishes. Martí has just over 200, as does Codazzi in much the same area. In future studies along these lines it should be possible, by focusing attention exclusively on one region or subregion, to locate and chart the histories of every parish, sitio, or country chapel mentioned in the records. However, such a task is outside the scope of this introduction to the parishes of Venezuela.[5]

As mentioned in Chapter 2, the analysis in Chapters 3 and 4 is based on the 1800-1809 file. The choice of this period as the focus of this population profile was determined by two main considerations. First, the data for 1800-1809 are the most consistent and most comprehensive in the file. Second, the 1809 cutoff permits a concentration on Venezuela's late colonial population characteristics before they were disturbed by the cataclysmic events of the 1810-1824 independence period (Map 3-1).

<u>Urban Categories</u>

Parishes in Venezuela came in a variety of sizes and configurations. Whether standard, contracted, or extended, parishes can also be classified by total population. As is true of practically every classification scheme involving size of urban centers, my divisions are somewhat arbitrary. In deciding where to put the limits of urban categories, I have tried to design limits which make sense in Venezuelan terms, divisions scaled to the orders of magnitude reasonable at the time. As a result, these divisions may not lend themselves to comparative discussion with similar data from the more complex and larger urban networks of viceroyalties, such as Mexico or Peru.

Within the confines of the Bishopric of Caracas, small parishes with populations of up to about 500 accounted for just over ten percent of all parishes. These <u>hamlets</u> existed principally along the Coast, with a few in the Llanos and the Coastal Range. In general, places as

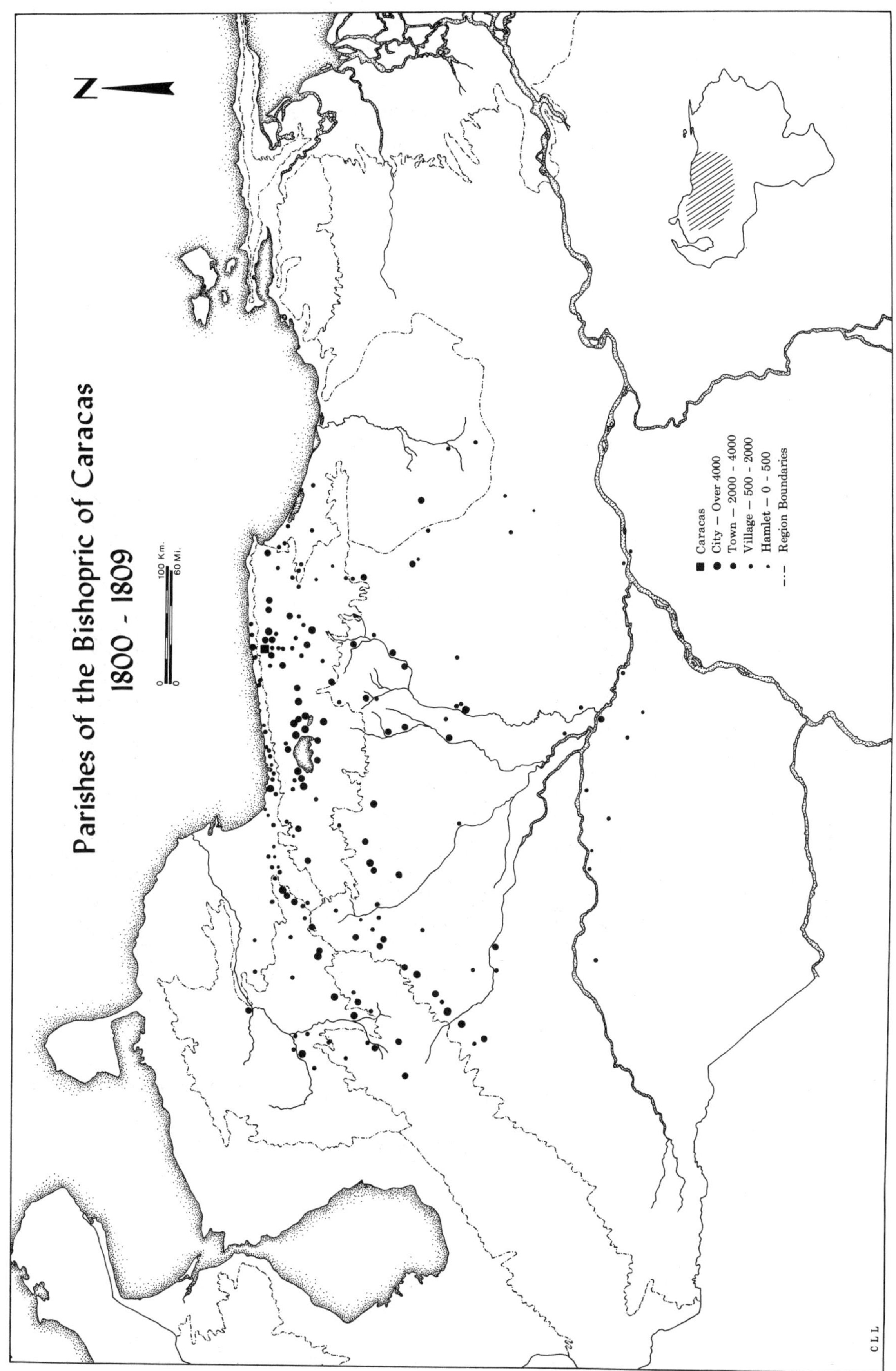
Parishes of the Bishopric of Caracas
1800 - 1809
0
100 Km.
60 Mi.
Caracas
City — Over 4000
Town — 2000 - 4000
Village — 500 - 2000
Hamlet — 0 - 500
Region Boundaries
CLL

Map 3-1

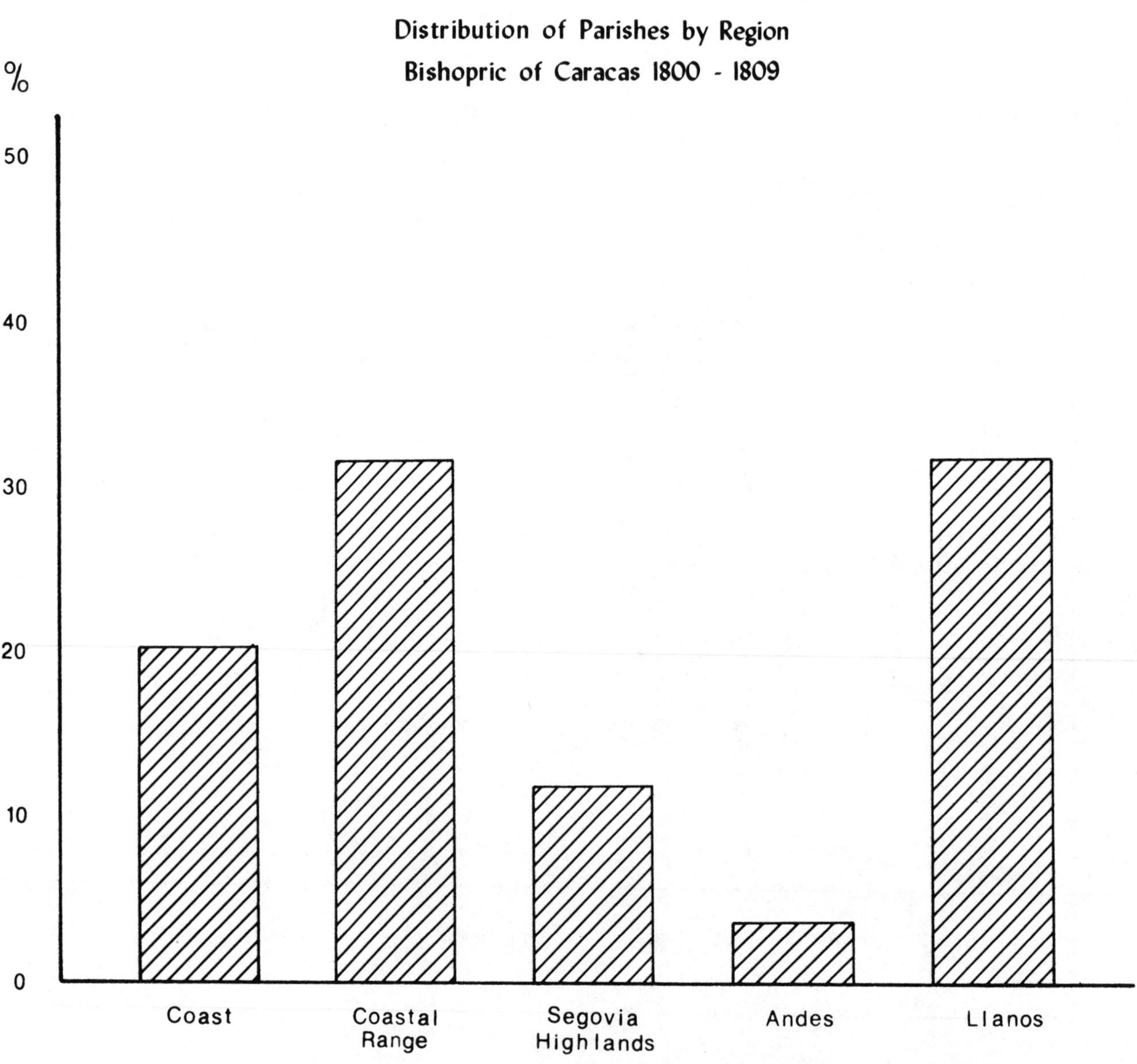
Distribution of Parishes by Region
Bishopric of Caracas 1800 - 1809
%
50
40
30
20
10
0
Coast
Coastal Range
Segovia Highlands
Andes
Llanos
CLL
Source: Appendix A, Table A-3

Figure 3-4

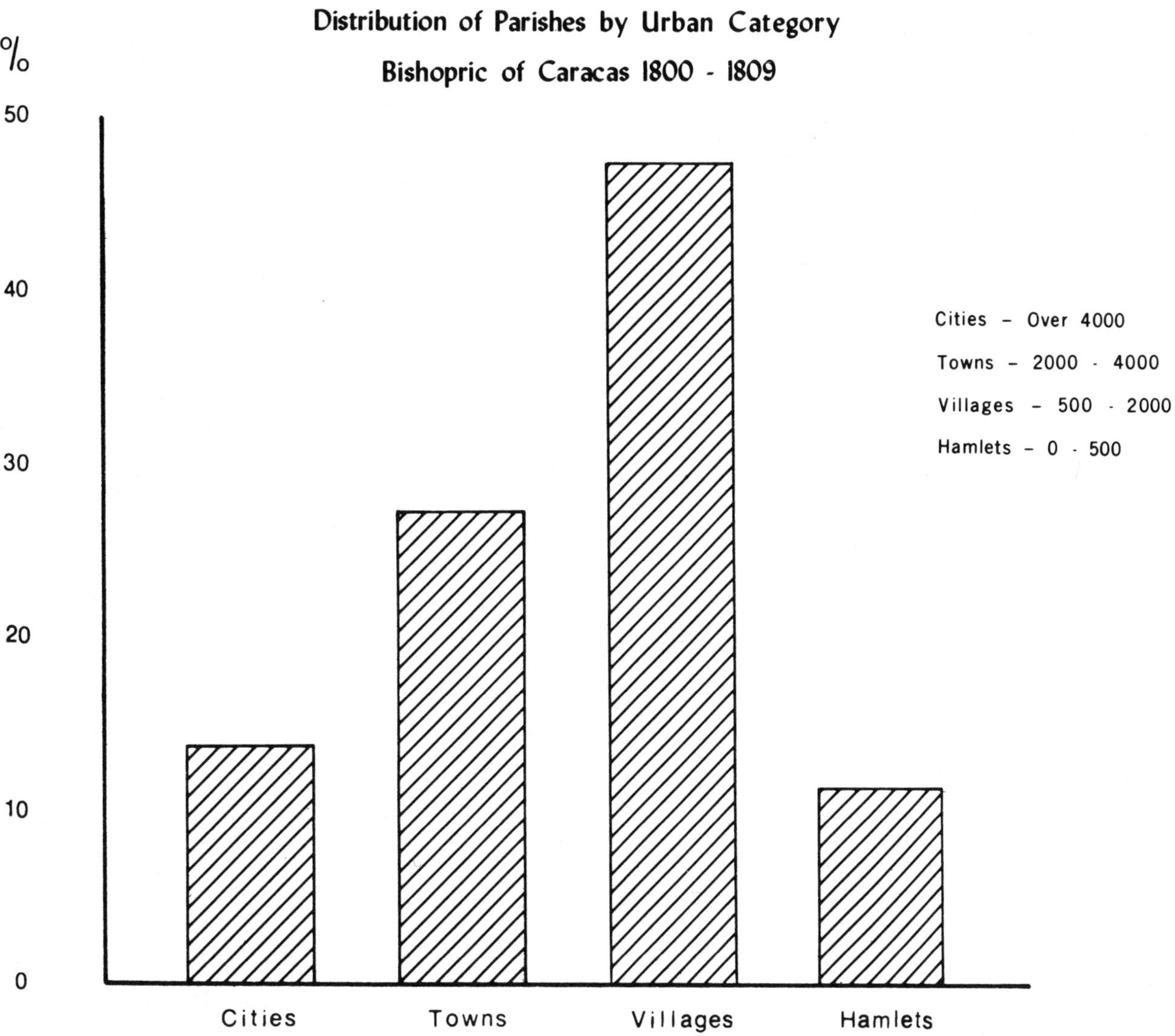
Distribution of Parishes by Urban Category
Bishopric of Caracas 1800 - 1809
%
50
40
30
20
10
0
Cities
Towns
Villages
Hamlets
Cities – Over 4000
Towns – 2000 - 4000
Villages – 500 - 2000
Hamlets – 0 - 500
CLL
Source: Appendix A, Table A-2

Figure 3-5

small as hamlets tended to be subordinate sitios, part of a larger extended parish. But on occasion, missions in the Llanos or strategically located settlements along the Coast achieved parochial status and therefore a separate census return. Other hamlets may well have been prosperous and populated in the past, but by the eighteenth century were reduced in size by epidemics, pirates, or the superior attractions of nearby centers. Over time, the percent of parishes in this category changes only a little, although there is a tendency for there to be more small parishes, more hamlets, in the earlier years than in the later. On further investigation, if this apparent trend is real and not the result of defects in the data, it may well be that the trend is the result of a steady population growth not matched by the creation of new parishes.

Villages of 500 to 2000 individuals account for about half of the parishes during the years 1800-1809. These were places of some substance. Located primarily in the Coast, the Coastal Range, and the Llanos regions, the villages were the most prevalent type of parish. A few villages also existed in the Segovia Highlands and the Andes.

Towns of 2000 to 4000 and cities above 4000 made up the rest of the parishes. Almost a third of all parishes were towns. A few of these towns were actually contracted parishes, located and functioning within a substantial, multiple parish urban center. The same was true for the one-eighth of the parishes qualifying as cities. Over a third of the towns were distributed in the Coastal Range and another third in the Llanos, with the rest scattered about in the Segovia Highlands, the Andes, and along the Coast. But half the cities existed in the Coastal Range, with the rest mostly in the Llanos and the Segovia Highlands[6] (Figures 3-4 and 3-5).

Urban Centers and Their Inhabitants

The distribution of urban centers within the Bishopric by region can provide an indication of the population landscape of late colonial Venezuela, but a greater appreciation of where and how these Spanish colonials lived out their lives can be achieved through a look at the numbers of individuals residing in these places and through an appraisal of whom they lived with. According to the censuses, between 1800 and 1810 some 427,000 people lived in the 194 parishes reporting to the Bishopric. What percentage of Venezuela's total population this represents is difficult to estimate. The only complete estimates for the end of the colonial period are impressionistic, based on the extensive accounts written by Humboldt and de Pons. For the Bishopric of Caracas, these visitors relied on ecclesiastical censuses similar to, or identical with, those presented here. For the rest of the country, they collected informed opinion and what fragmentary information existed in the government archives accessible to them. Both travelers give something on the order of 800,000 individuals as a reasonable estimate of total population. Miguel Izard has brought together a collection of population figures extracted from a variety of official and semiofficial compilations for the 1772-1840 period. If we accept these figures, Venezuela's total population oscillated between about 700,000 and one million during the first decades of the 1800s. Such a total, which is in rough agreement with Humboldt, implies that the Bishopric of Caracas held about one-half of the country's population. Because the Bishopric seems to have included the major areas of high population density, especially the valleys of the Central Coastal Range, our commonsense hypothesis would not have predicted half of Venezuela's population living outside the Bishopric. Either the hypothesis is incorrect or one or both of our sources of data are faulty.

The data available after independence are extremely difficult to compare with the parish-level information because of the problems of establishing equivalences between the population units, usually cantons, of the republican regimes, and the parish units of the colonial period, but a rough estimate gives something on the order of sixty to seventy percent of Venezuela's population to the Bishopric when based on republican data, and fifty percent when based on ecclesiastical data. This maximum difference of maybe twenty percentage points most certainly can be reduced by correcting for those parishes known to exist in 1800-1809 not represented among the 194 of our data file. Because some of the republican censuses helped determine representation in congresses, we might

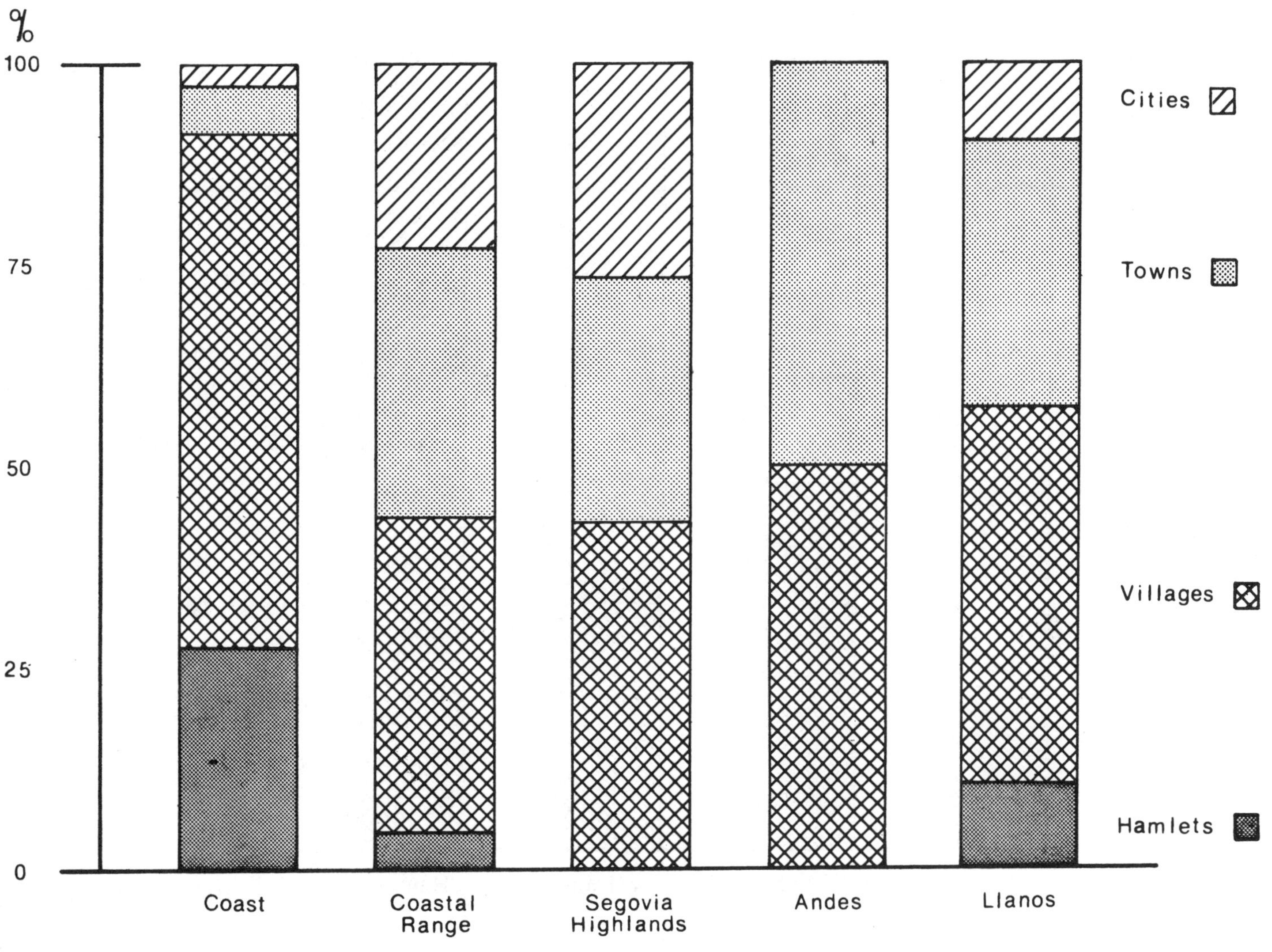
Distribution of Parishes within Regions by Urban Category
Bishopric of Caracas 1800 - 1809
%
100
75
50
25
0
Cities
Towns
Villages
Hamlets
Coast
Coastal Range
Segovia Highlands
Andes
Llanos
CLL
Source: Appendix A, Table A-3 and Part II

Figure 3-6

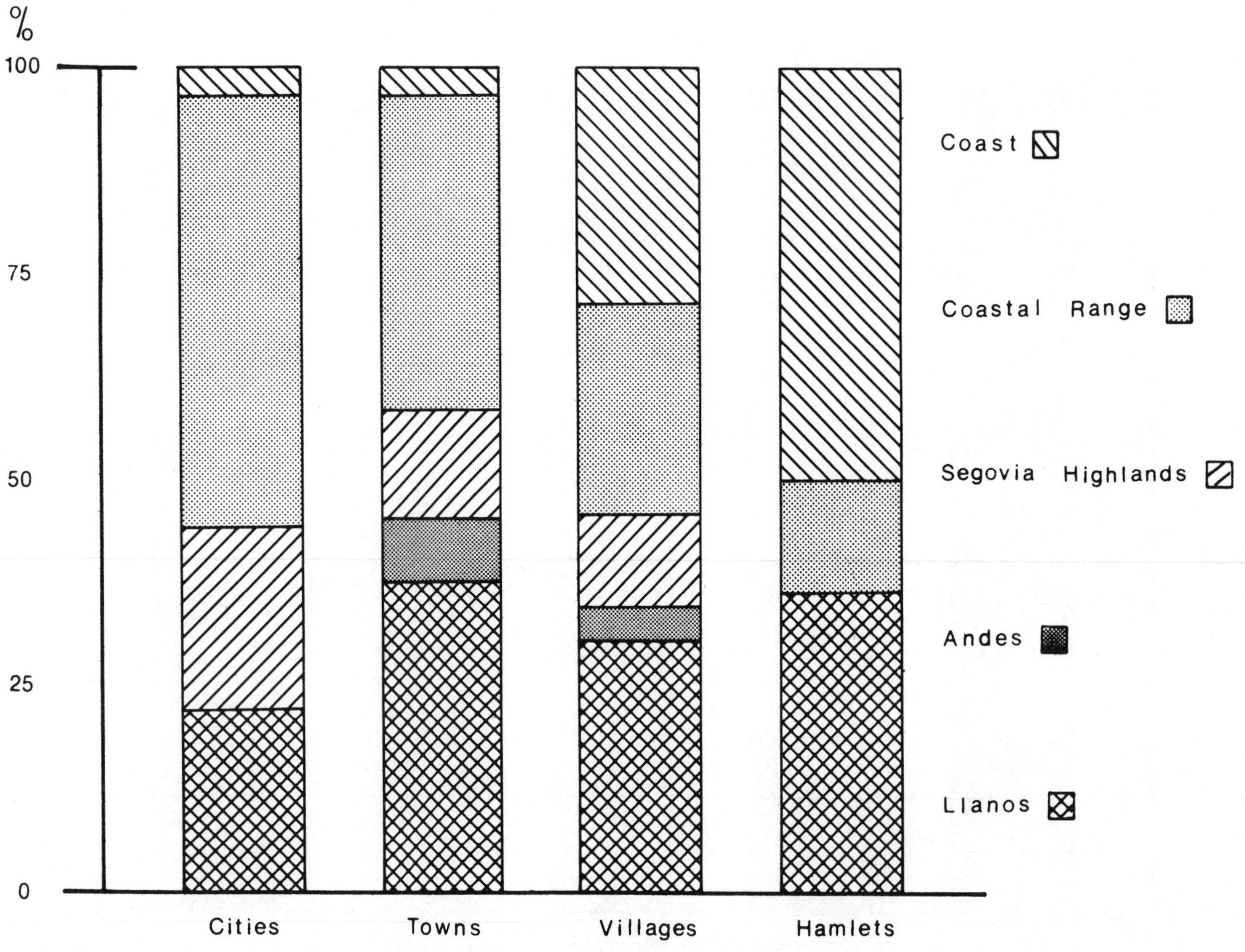
Distribution of Parishes among Regions by Urban Category
Bishopric of Caracas 1800 - 1809
%
100
75
50
25
0
Cities
Towns
Villages
Hamlets
Coast
Coastal Range
Segovia Highlands
Andes
Llanos
CLL
Source: Part II, Tables

Figure 3-7

also anticipate that they may have exaggerated the counts to maximize the allocation due each state. And we know the ecclesiastical censuses almost certainly undercounted the poor, the landless, the vagabond, and the unreduced or "wild" Indians. Republican census takers too had difficulty accounting for the Indians and could never give consistent estimates for the Indian population of Guayana. That state's population varied between 15,000 and 56,000 between 1838 and 1847, the difference probably based on the figure allocated for the unknown and unknowable Indian residents of the vast Guayana region. Similar problems of estimation must have plagued the officials charged with preparing returns for Apure, which can range from 15,000 to 35,000 depending on the source.

How then to resolve these contradictions? Clearly at this stage of the investigation into Venezuela's pre-twentieth-century population, I am in no position to propose estimating formulas that could be counted on to deflate republican figures and inflate colonial data in a reasonably reliable fashion. At the same time, a consideration of the various censuses indicates that I would probably not err greatly by making the following series of assumptions. Of the urbanized, hispanicized population in Venezuela at the end of the colonial period, probably sixty to seventy percent lived within the confines of the Bishopric. This accepts as reasonable a population estimate of 800,000 for all of Venezuela and deducts the estimate of 50,000 that most observers used for uncontrolled Indians. Within the Bishopric, most of the recorded population is probably covered by the censuses collected here. The surviving documents may undercount the recorded population by a maximum figure of two or three percent, or translated into real figures, by about 10,000 people at the very most. This assumes no more than twenty parishes unreported, and it also assumes that these missing parishes were probably hamlets at best, with populations generously put in the 500 person category. Thus out of a total recorded Bishopric population of maybe 437,000, we can work with a selection of parishes totaling 427,000. As for the unrecorded population, I have no means of even attempting a rough guess. Until we have some monographs to guide us, any such attempt will surely lead to fantasy.

In generalizing about the people in the Bishopric of Caracas, I have focused attention on a special subset of the universe made up of all the individuals living in that geographic area. The subset contains a number of biases; it favors the prosperous, the white, the adult, the residentially stable, those living in major population centers, and those living in town. For some purposes, these biases may render the uncorrected data file useless, but for the description of the human landscape and the analysis of its major dimensions, the data can serve as a useful guide. It is imperative, however, that anyone using the data or interpreting these comments keep the limitations of the data and the direction of their biases firmly in mind.

With these caveats made, we can look at the ways that the four hundred thousand plus individuals distributed themselves in space (Figure 3-6). Even though small settlements of no more than 500 inhabitants account for almost ten percent of all parishes, few people chose to locate in such places. Not quite two percent of the population, that is about 7,000 people in all, could be found in the 21 hamlets, an average of 345 people in each parish.

Considerably more people lived in villages of between 500 and 2000 inhabitants, some 110,000 of them in ninety-two parishes. But although half of the parishes in the Bishopric qualify as villages (the largest number of parishes are villages), only twenty-six percent of the Bishopric's people chose to reside in them. Indeed, between them, hamlets and villages contain under one-third of the population.

The rest of the Bishopric's people lived in towns and cities; over seventy percent of the total population lived in this forty percent of the parishes. In absolute numbers, 140,000 people lived in 53 towns, and 170,000 in 27 cities. This would give an average town size of under 3,000 and an average city size of about double this, or 6,000. But before leaving this part of the discussion, we need to look more closely at the parishes qualifying as towns and cities.

Some parishes of the contracted form can and should be aggregated to be considered as the major urban centers they were. Of all the parishes, ten qualify as contracted forms composing three major

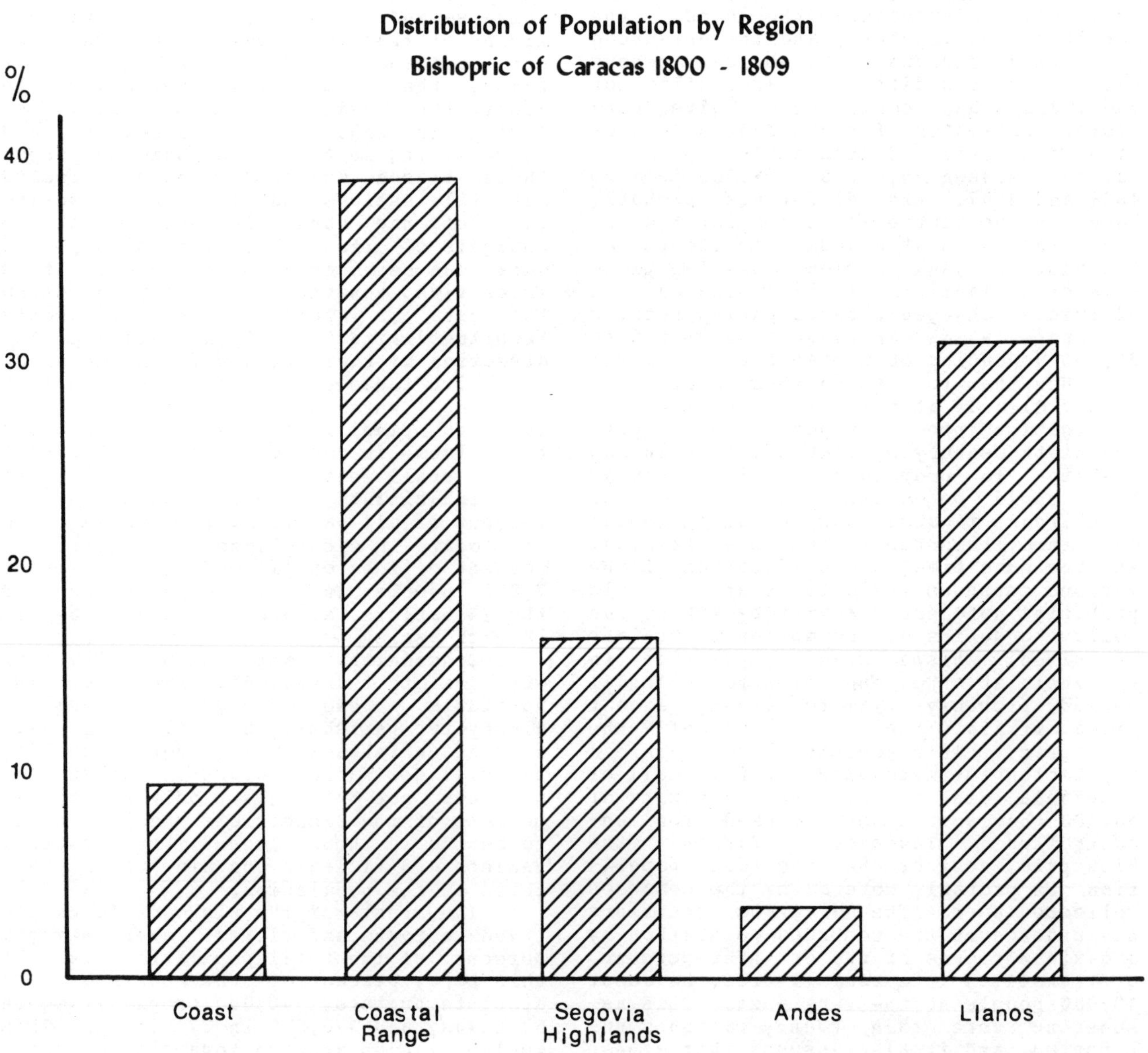
Distribution of Population by Region
Bishopric of Caracas 1800 - 1809
%
40
30
20
10
0
Coast
Coastal Range
Segovia Highlands
Andes
Llanos
CLL
Source: Appendix A, Table A-3

Figure 3-8

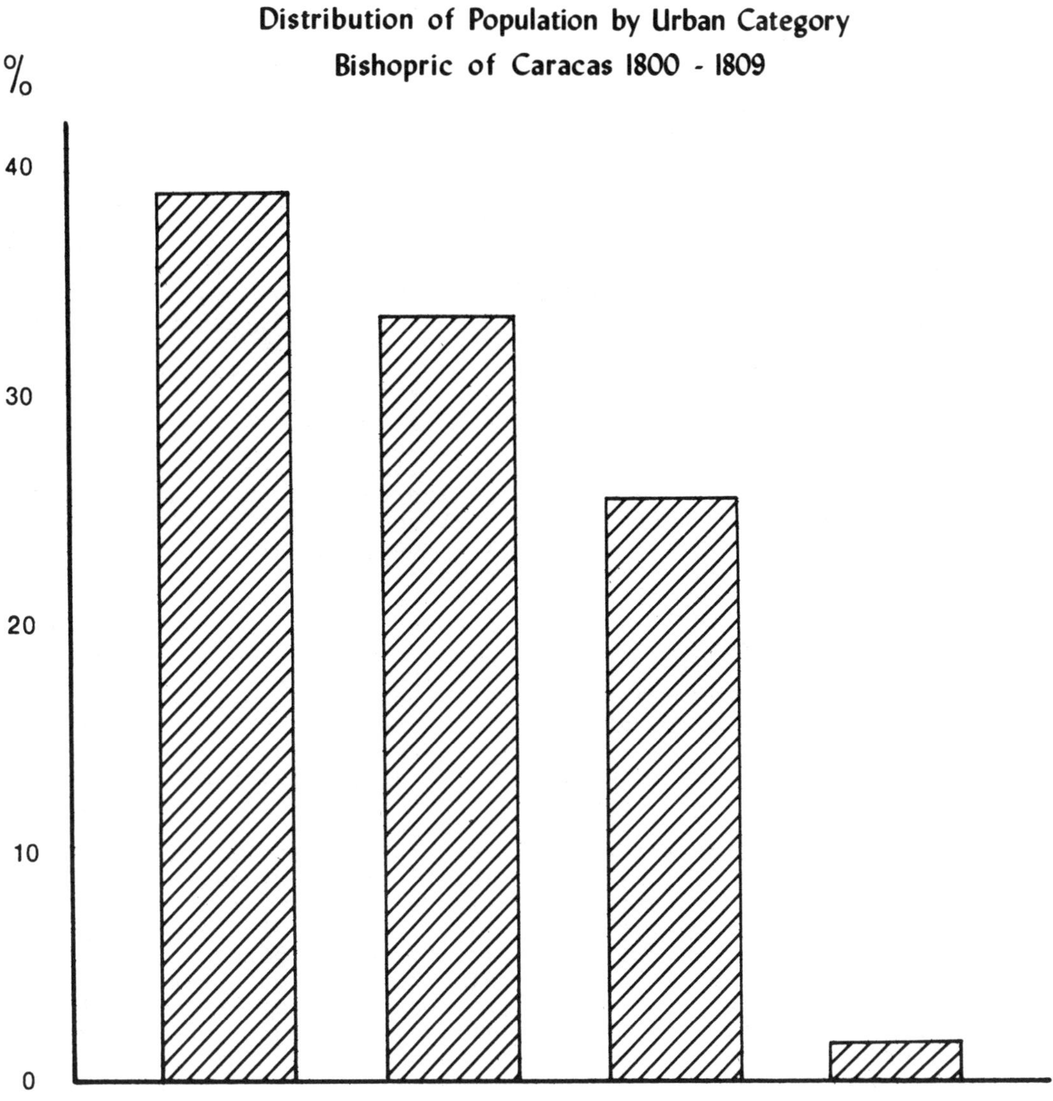
Distribution of Population by Urban Category
Bishopric of Caracas 1800 - 1809
%
40
30
20
10
0
Cities
Towns
Villages
Hamlets
CLL
Source: Appendix A, Table A-2

Figure 3-9

urban centers: Barquisimeto and San Felipe with two parishes each and Caracas with six. San Felipe's two parishes individually qualify for town status, with under 3,000 persons each. Together they place San Felipe in the mid-range of cities in the Bishopric. Barquisimeto's parishes each qualify as cities, and together they make Barquisimeto one of the three largest cities, tied with Guanare, each city having over 11,000 people.

Caracas, as in every other measurable aspect, is the exception to most generalizations about the Bishopric bearing its name. As Venezuela's primate city and only metropolitan center, Caracas attracted about twice the population of any other center in the Bishopric. The metropolis had six parishes, and then later in the nineteenth century, seven: Catedral Oriente and Poniente were two parishes without hinterlands and provided the nucleus of the city, to the north lay Altagracia, to the east Candelaria, and to the south San Pablo and Santa Rosalía. Imbedded in the city was the military parish for the troops stationed in the capital. Together these parishes contained about 24,000 people. This total put the city well outside the limits of the other urban centers and is one of the measures of its primacy.

On first inspection, the total of about 24,000 persons for Caracas appears to be in conflict with all other estimates, which put the city somewhere around 40,000. However, on investigation, those who speak of Caracas as having 40,000 people most often included in this estimate the parishes in the valley of Caracas that are near the city, but not actually a part of the metropolis. Martí's account, which lacks a separate section on Caracas, gives the city 19,000 inhabitants in 1772. Cisneros gave the city 26,000 souls in 1764, but included over twenty other parishes outside the city proper. Martí's figure agrees in the main with the 17,000 total recorded in 1767 in a document published by Arellano Moreno. In light of these figures and the data published here, Codazzi's figure of 40 to 50,000 in 1810-1812 is unacceptable, as is his estimate of 12,000 deaths from the 1812 earthquake. In any case, the estimate of 24,000 for Caracas in the period 1800-1809 would seem at present as close to reality as possible, until we have some micro-history to guide us.

Thus while Caracas, Barquisimeto, and Guanare, along with such major centers as Trujillo, Valencia, San Carlos, and La Victoria, formed the principal poles of urban development, none could compete with Caracas, whose drawing power measured by population totals was at least twice as great as any other center.[7]

From the discussion above, it should be clear that the Bishopric's population distributed itself rather unevenly about the landscape. People tended to live in the larger towns and cities, although the minority in smaller places lived in more parishes. This pattern of unequal distribution also prevails when the population totals are viewed from a purely geographic perspective. Over half the surface area of the Bishopric lay in the Llanos, those gradually descending plains running south and west from the southern foothills of the Coastal Range. The Coast region accounted for under twenty percent, with the Coastal Range and the Segovia Highlands around ten percent each. That part of the Venezuelan Andes that lay within the Bishopric accounted for less than five percent of the surface area covered by the census returns collected here (Figures 3-7, 3-8, 3-9, and 3-10).

In the vast reaches of the Llanos a third of the total population of the Bishopric made their homes. Occupying hamlets, villages, and towns scattered about in a wide gauge pattern along the rivers and trade routes of the Llanos, they lived at a population density of about one person for every square kilometer. Population density, however, is not much of an indication of how individuals might have viewed their environment. The isolated population centers characterizing the Llanos provided stopping places and links in the Spanish imperial network. They focused the population, much of whom lived seminomadic lives in pursuit of cattle, horses, and mules. Moreover, the Llanos by no means appeared as a uniform geographical milieu to those inhabiting its plains and traveling across its meandering streams. By drawing a line through the towns of Guanare in the southwestern edge of the Llanos, along the foothills of the Andes and the Segovia Highlands, through San Carlos and

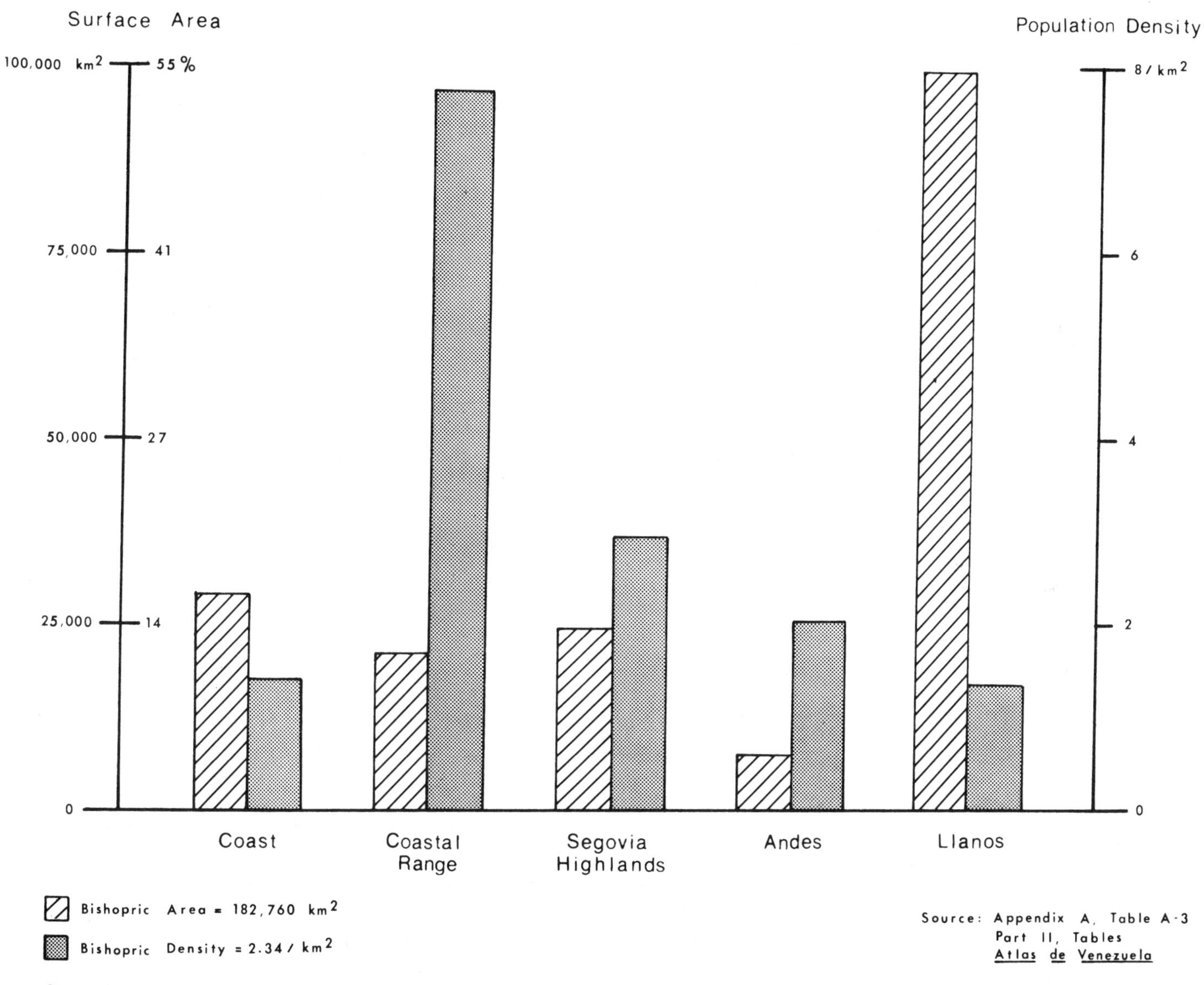
Surface Area and Population Density
Bishopric of Caracas 1800 - 1809
Surface Area
Population Density
100,000 km2
55 %
75,000
41
50,000
27
25,000
14
0
8 / km2
6
4
2
0
Coast
Coastal Range
Segovia Highlands
Andes
Llanos
Bishopric Area = 182,760 km2
Bishopric Density = 2.34 / km2
CLL
Source: Appendix A, Table A-3
Part II, Tables
Atlas de Venezuela

Figure 3-10

El Sombrero, and then sweeping southeastward through Valle de la Pascua to Santa María de Ipire at the edge of the Unare basin, we have defined the area of greatest population and most prosperous settlements in the Llanos. Here ranged the herds of the cattle barons, and throughout this band most of the important llanero towns existed. The other major route through the Llanos extended south from San Sebastián at the boundary between the Central Interior Mountains and the Llanos, through San Juan de los Morros and El Sombrero to Calabozo, and then paralleled the Guárico River south to San Fernando de Apure on the Apure River. San Fernando, a river settlement, served as a transfer point to the trans-Apure Llanos and as the link with the river traffic down the Orinoco to Angostura and the Delta. Because of the structure of the river systems feeding the Apure, and because the Llanos were hemmed in by the Andes and the Coastal Range, the region had a cohesiveness and identity built up over the years by merchants, cowboys, missionaries, and clerics who traveled through the region along the same river routes or followed the same trails leading from town to town across the almost trackless plain. People living here tended to look to the foothill towns of Guanare or Araure-Acarigua, and San Carlos or San Sebastián, as their major connections to the politically dominant, economically important, and more populated regions centered on places such as Barquisimeto, San Felipe, Valencia, or Caracas. In villages and hamlets along the Apure, where the distances weakened the ties to Caracas and the Central Coastal Range, people also thought in terms of commerce and trade through the river system to the Orinoco and then to Angostura en route to the Atlantic. In fact, travelers and Spanish officials who had some experience with the magnificent complex of rivers feeding into the Orinoco predicted that Venezuela's future prosperity depended on the development of these routes connecting the hinterland with the Atlantic and the Colombian Andes. But pirates, hostile Indians, and the general poverty of the Llanos regions prevented the realization of that vision until twentieth-century technology made the minerals of Guayana worth the expense of developing the Orinoco river system.

The northern tip of the Andes that intrudes into the Bishopric was an area without a major city. With a population density just slightly above two persons per square kilometer, the Andean portion of the Bishopric traded with the llanero towns along its eastern foothills and through them to the Central Coastal Range. The inhabitants of the mountains looked to the south to Trujillo and Mérida, and from there to San Cristóbal and into the Nuevo Reino de Granada. Closer to home lay the Maracaibo Basin, a natural trade route restricted by frequent pirate raids. In spite of such inhibitions, trujillanos traveled down to the villages and hamlets along the eastern edge of the lake to send goods and to trade with merchants from Maracaibo and from there into the Caribbean. Finally, the mountain roads north from Trujillo led to the major towns of the Segovia Highlands, El Tocuyo and Barquisimeto, where commerce and trade with the coast of Puerto Cabello and La Guaira or with the valleys of Caracas or Valencia could be carried out. This small portion of the Venezuelan Andes contained only just over three and one-half percent of the Bishopric's population in under five percent of its surface area.

Within the thirteen percent of the Bishopric's area occupied by the Segovia Highlands lay a variety of population centers. El Tocuyo, a major source of men and supplies for the push into the Llanos and the Central Coastal Range in the period of exploration and settlement, and Barquisimeto, a town laying astride the route to the Llanos, the valleys of Valencia and Caracas, and the coast of Puerto Cabello, formed the urban axis of the region supported by places such as Carora or Yaritagua. The people of the Segovia Highlands accounted for about sixteen percent of the total population of the Bishopric, but as the intermediaries between the Coast of Coro, the Maracaibo Basin, the Llanos, and the Central Coastal Range, they prospered throughout the eighteenth century.

The Central Coastal Range proved to be the only region of the Bishopric capable of drawing more people than the Llanos, capturing almost forty percent of the jurisdiction's population. With only just under twelve percent of the Bishopric's surface area, people in the Coastal Range lived about eight to the square kilometer, a population density much higher than that found in any other region. In the intermontane valleys strung out in an east-west line from Valencia through Maracay and Cagua, to the main valley of Caracas, this population concentrated in a variety of towns and cities separated by constellations of villages and hamlets, all living on the rich cacao plantations, the haciendas growing _frutos menores_, and the hatos raising cattle for meat and hides. People came to the Coastal Range from everywhere in the country to participate in the prosperity of the capital city of Caracas, seat of the Captain General, the Bishop and then Archbishop, the offices of the Caracas Company, the major religious establishments, the seat of the Audiencia and the Consulado, and the home of the richest and best-born hidalgos of all Venezuela. From this primate city, protected from pirates by the northern range of mountains along the coast, came the central direction for the Bishopric. Orders from civil and ecclesiastical authorities issued from there, and officials in other places worked to merit appointment to positions in the capital city. The elite, owning cattle ranches in the Llanos, plantations in the valleys of Aragua or Valencia or along the Coast, lived in elaborate style--in Venezuelan terms--in substantial houses located around the central plaza and along its surrounding streets. For most travelers to Venezuela in the eighteenth century, this city and its immediate hinterland in the Central Coastal Range symbolized Venezuela. Given all these advantages, the concentration of population and resources in the area comes as no surprise. And when the density of population in this region is compared with that prevailing in other regions, Caracas's ability to centralize control in her hands after the end of the wars for independence is easier to explain. No other urban center could come close to Caracas, and no other region could hope to compete with the Central Coastal Range.

The remaining ten percent of the Bishopric's population could be found living in the towns, villages, and hamlets dotting the Coast from Rio Chico and Higuerote on the east, through La Guaira and Puerto Cabello in the center, and around past Coro to Maracaibo on the west. Besieged by pirates and exposed to storms and the ravages of Spain's enemies in time of war, these communities thrived on the agriculture of the coastal valleys running into the Coastal Range where cacao grew in abundance, on the trade and commerce fed into the interior through Puerto Cabello and especially the port for Caracas, La Guaira, and on the contraband trade with the Dutch and English carried out through the rivers cutting through the mountains to the sea all along the coast. Coro and Maracaibo, centers of interest and expansion in the earlier years of colonial domination, but no longer part of the Bishopric of Caracas during 1800-1809, maintained their importance as minor trade centers and as strategic outposts defining Venezuela's periphery and maintaining fortresses for the defense of the empire.

This, then, completes a panoramic view of the major characteristics of the parishes and regions of the Bishopric of Caracas. It remains to discuss the composition of the population of the Bishopric: its racial characteristics, its marriage patterns, and its children.

Hacienda, Turmero

FOUR

Race, Sex, Marriage, and Children

Of all the characteristics of Venezuela's population, racial composition shows the most interesting variations and offers the most promising area to begin a social analysis of the Bishopric of Caracas at the close of the colonial period. As explained earlier, the concept of race used in this essay and throughout the book remains necessarily vague. Quasi-genetic and quasi-social in derivation, the classification scheme most commonly used in Venezuela must be understood in terms of late colonial usage and custom. Reviewing briefly the categories and their names, we have a five-part system capable of classifying each person according to his position in the socio-racial hierarchy. Whites, at the top of the social ladder, boasted the closest apparent approximation to a Spanish, non-Moorish stereotype, although the range of genetic heritage within this group must have been wide indeed. Encompassing the descendants of Spanish conquistadores from all over the peninsula, the white category also included Canary Island migrants, Basque merchants, Portuguese residents of the cities, and light-colored, prosperous individuals of African heritage. While the range of racial stock from which these whites came may appear large, whites as a group shared certain privileges and possibilities denied members of other racial categories. Their access to the places of power, wealth, and prominence in the community put them in the best position for advancement. Because of their location on the social scale, we could expect their population characteristics to differ from those of other racial groups.

Indians included the descendants of Venezuela's native population, much reduced by the late colonial period. We could expect these Indians to be of the "tamed" variety, to use the picturesque Spanish exp ression. The degree of acculturation this tamed population might have possessed is difficult to determine, but in the area of the Bishopric of Caracas, most of the Indian villages and hamlets had been under Spanish control for at least a generation, if not two or three. As will be seen later on in this discussion, Indians shared characteristics different from those of other racial groups.

As the largest racial category in the Bishopric of Caracas, pardos probably represented the widest range of racial variation. The one common element linking all the members of the pardo group was derivation from an African ancestor, however remote. Moreover, pardos must have demonstrated, for the most part, a clearly identifiable resemblance to a West African stereotype, for had they looked white, they might well have passed into the elite category. If some did leave the group at the white end of the spectrum, others entered from the darker end, passing from the Negro category upwards to the pardo.

Negroes, perhaps darker in color and closer to the African image, formed a group difficult to define. I have assumed that the one distinguishing mark of Negroes, who were apparently in decline as a group, may have been their closeness

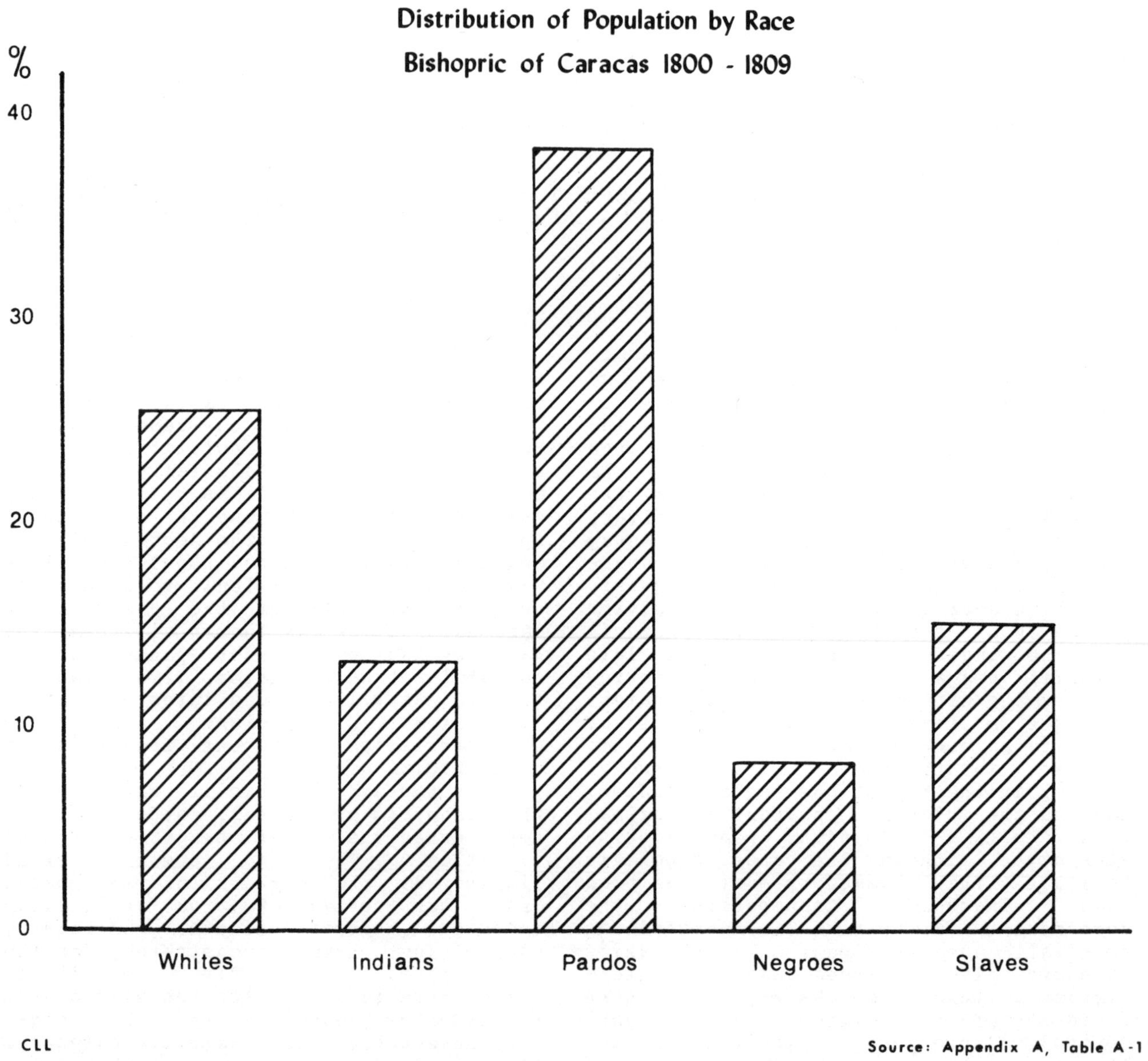

Distribution of Population by Race
Bishopric of Caracas 1800 - 1809

%
40
30
20
10
0

Whites Indians Pardos Negroes Slaves

CLL

Source: Appendix A, Table A-1

Figure 4-1

to the slave condition. Recently freed slaves, their children, or the free children of slaves probably accounted for the bulk of individuals included here.

The slaves themselves, of course, belonged to their group by virtue of legal arrangements, not social or racial distinctions. Slaves could be, and were, of all shades of black, some tending towards the white stereotype, others towards the African. Still, on the average we can assume that slaves presented a more "African" presence to society at large than did their pardo counterparts. While master-slave miscegenation must have occurred frequently, thereby producing some mulatto offspring, the tendency of manumission to free mulattos more readily than blacks may have kept the slave population blacker. Also, the slave group received periodic infusions of pure African blood from the slave trade throughout the colonial period and especially in the last three quarters of the eighteenth century. In any event, slaves demonstrated population patterns different from those of their counterparts in other racial groups.[1]

Because one of the important aspects of this racial system has to do with the elite's perception of the rest of the population, I have introduced a sixth category into this analysis, that of the blacks. Throughout the independence movement and into the republican period, Venezuela's governing elites constantly worried about the disruptive potential of the nonwhite, non-Indian population. They demonstrated a tendency to lump all the Afro-Venezuelans into one group referenced through the use of the code word pardo. But because that designation has a less inclusive meaning in this data and in the colonial period, I have substituted black to refer to the composite group of all identifiable Afro-Venezuelans, a group formed by combining pardos, Negroes, and slaves.[2]

Racial Distribution

The population characteristics of these racial groups can be viewed from a number of perspectives, but the best starting point is to see where they lived in the Bishopric of Caracas.

Taking the entire Bishopric, an area made up of about two hundred parishes and a little less than half a million people, the racial composition breaks down as in Figure 4-1. The largest group were the pardos, followed by the whites, slaves, Indians, and Negroes. If we consolidate the blacks, this division becomes even more striking, with the whites forming only about a quarter of the Bishopric's population. It requires no special insight to understand why a white elite might have been concerned about the motives and behavior of the over sixty percent of the population made up of blacks. This is especially so when we realize that the wars for independence firmly convinced significant sections of Venezuela's elite that the black population harbored intense hatred for whites, and, worse yet, coveted their goods and position in society.

This breakdown of races within the Bishopric hides some important regional differences. Not every part of the country had a majority of blacks, while some places had an even higher black concentration than the Bishopric as a whole. If we reorder our data as in Figure 4-2, some interesting patterns emerge. At the broadest level, it becomes clear that in the Llanos and especially in the Andes, blacks did not predominate to the extent they did in the Coast, the Coastal Range, and the Segovia Highlands. Indeed, it is only in the Andes, of all the Bishopric, that blacks sank to a minority position.

When we look at the regions more closely, the dominance of the pardo element is everywhere apparent, except of course in the Andes, and ranges from a low of thirty-four percent to a high of fifty-seven percent. More striking than these differences, however, are those displayed by the slave group. These captives made up only three percent of the Andean population, but comprised twenty-six percent of the population along the Coast. In every region, Negroes represented only a small fraction of the inhabitants, reaching a peak of thirteen percent in the Segovia Highlands.

This racial distribution of the regional population gives a rather close fit to our understanding of Venezuela's human landscape. That over three-quarters of the Coastal region's population should have been black and that that region should have been one-quarter slave appears reasonable when we consider that the Coast region consisted of ports and agricultural valleys, traditionally

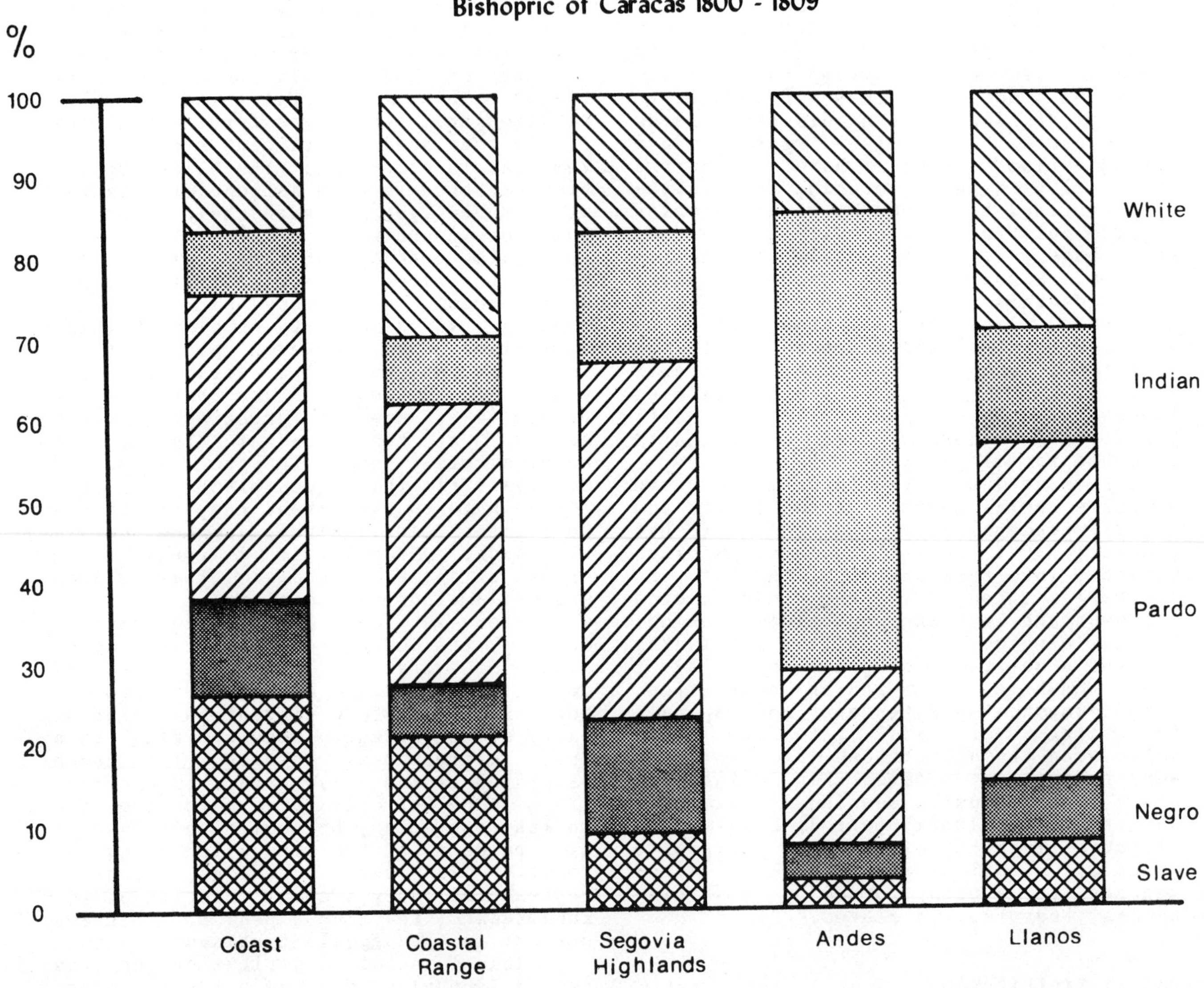
Distribution of Races within Regions
Bishopric of Caracas 1800 - 1809
%
100
90
80
70
60
50
40
30
20
10
0
White
Indian
Pardo
Negro
Slave
Coast
Coastal Range
Segovia Highlands
Andes
Llanos
CLL
Source: Appendix A, Table A-3

Figure 4-2

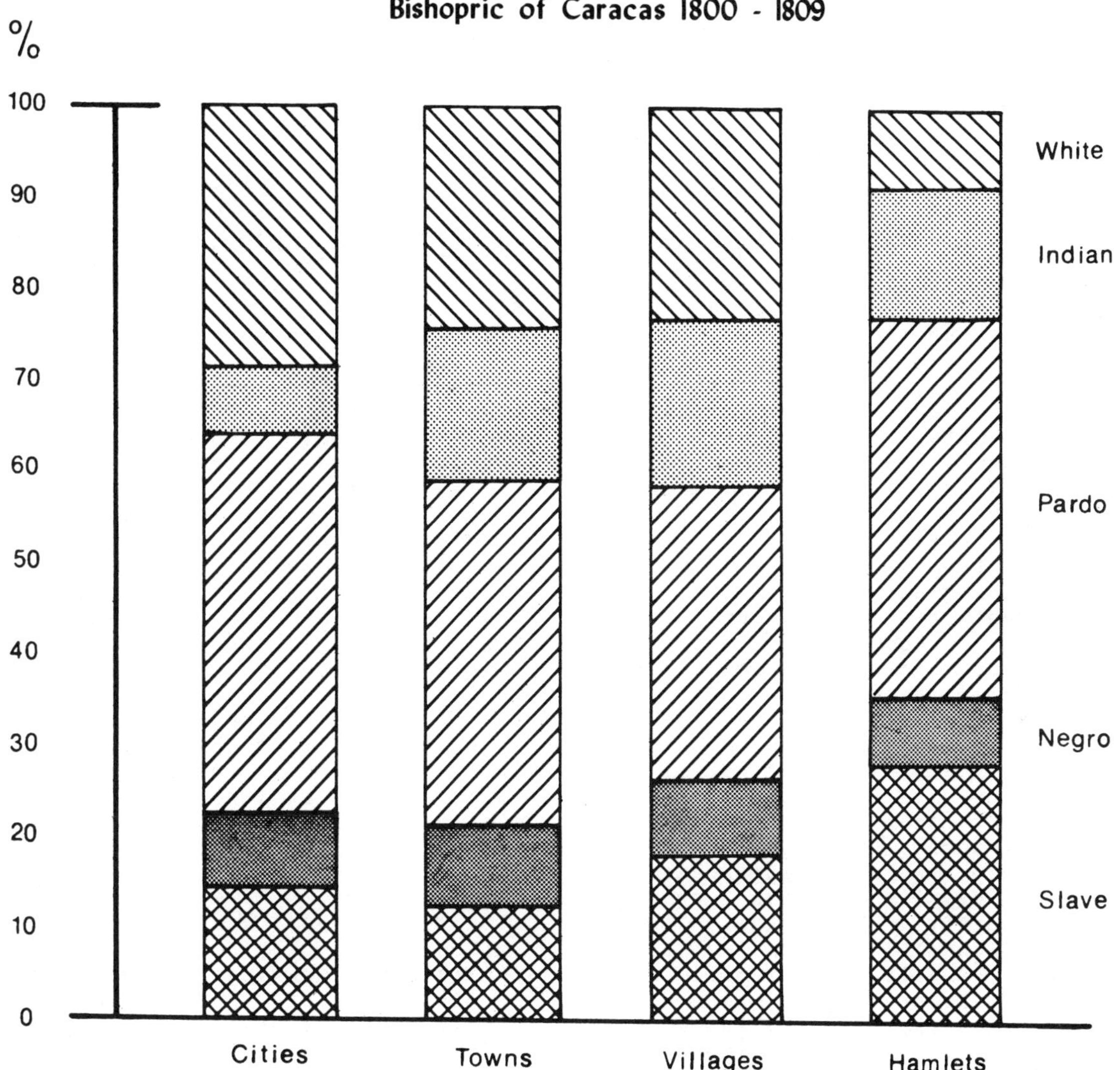
Distribution of Races within Urban Categories
Bishopric of Caracas 1800 - 1809
%
100
90
80
70
60
50
40
30
20
10
0
White
Indian
Pardo
Negro
Slave
Cities
Towns
Villages
Hamlets
CLL
Source: Appendix A, Table A-2

Figure 4-3

cultivated by slaves supervised by pardos and some whites. Furthermore, the unhealthy nature of the region and its hot humid climate drove most of the whites up into the higher elevations, leaving only those members of the colonial elite required to administer the port cities.

The Coastal Range and the Segovia Highlands show similar patterns of racial concentration corresponding to their similarity of geographic features. Still, it is important to note that the Coastal Range had a higher percentage of whites than the Segovia Highlands. This almost certainly reflected the importance of Caracas as an administrative center for the Captaincy General and the concentration of whites in that city. Likewise, the greater probable wealth of the inhabitants of the Coastal Range, along with the highly developed and prosperous plantations in the valleys of this region, may help account for its relatively higher concentration of slaves. Finally, it is useful to note the almost double concentration of Indians in the Segovia Highlands compared to the Coastal Range, reflecting the geographic proximity of the Segovia Highlands region to the Andes, an area dominated by Indians.

We might be able to put forward a hypothetical reconstruction of the allocation of human resources about the Bishopric based on this data. The people available to carry out the tasks of developing Venezuela's resources did not all have the same degree of mobility, or respond to the same pressures for location or relocation. In any given locality, the tendency of the controlling Spanish elite would certainly have been to exploit existing human resources before importing new ones. In the Segovia Highlands, and more so in the Andes, the sizeable and tractable native populations were eventually turned into servants of the Venezuelan economic system. But in an expanding economy always in search of more cheap labor, many tasks could not be carried out by resident Indians, and therefore the more mobile classes of slaves and pardos were brought in to fill the remaining posts.[3]

Along the Coast, a slightly different set of pressures probably helped determine the allocation of human resources. Without a large and docile native population, the white elite had to look elsewhere to find the manpower required to exploit the rich coastal valleys, but because free men must have been disinclined to locate in the insalubrious coastal area, slaves, whose preferences could be ignored, became a major component of the work force. Of course, Venezuelan slave owners never had the resources to staff their coastal enterprises entirely or even mostly with slaves, and here, too, that large class of pardos filled in the places required for the system to function.

In the process of allocating these human resources, the Coastal Range occupied a special place. With its healthy climate and highly prosperous agricultural establishments, and as the center of civil, ecclesiastical, and financial activity, the Coastal Range drew on all classes of people, except Indians. Pardos probably congregated there because of the work and opportunities, whites came in search of wealth and access to central authorities, and slaves were brought to staff elaborate households and to develop the profitable haciendas of the region.

The Llanos, in contrast, provided a special case of an area with a sizeable population composed primarily of nomads, who cared for the cattle herds and horse and mule strings that allowed many Venezuelans to prosper, and who settled, if at all, in hamlets. It is difficult to hypothesize about the motivations and tendencies of the people involved, but we might propose that the Llanos collected the spillover from the surrounding regions, drawing Indians from the Andes and the Llanos themselves, pardos and whites from the Coastal Range, and slaves sent south to help care for the wide-ranging herds.

This scenario should not be construed as anything more than a preliminary working hypothesis. The development of parish-based studies within each region promises to give considerable new information, permitting a modification or revision of this initial hypothesis.

The racial distribution within the urban dimension also shows some interesting variations. From the information in Figure 4-3, we see that those parishes classifed as hamlets, that is places with 0-500 inhabitants, were dominated by blacks. Almost eighty percent of the people in those localities within the

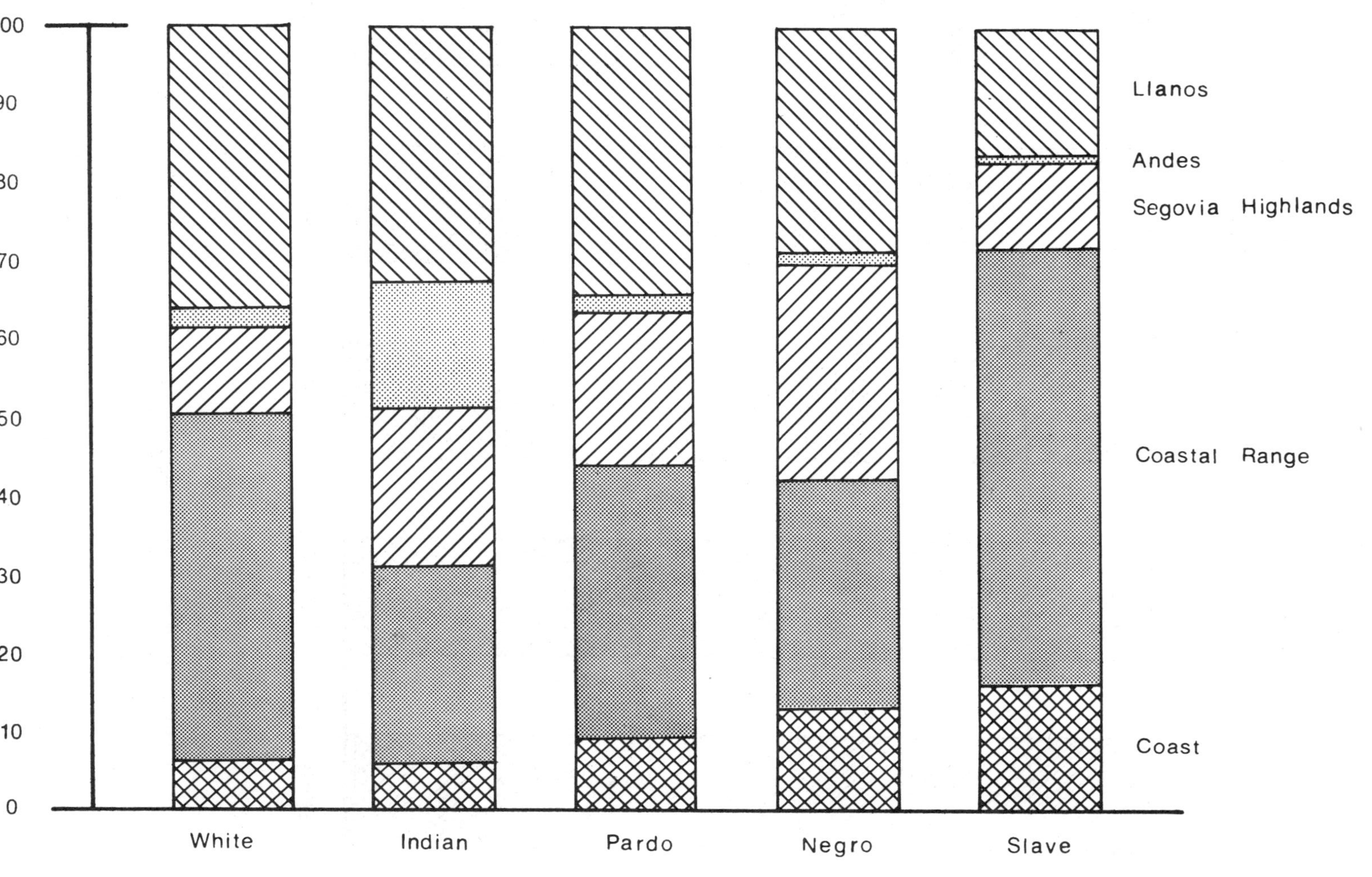
Distribution of Races among Regions
Bishopric of Caracas 1800 - 1809
%
100
90
80
70
60
50
40
30
20
10
0
Llanos
Andes
Segovia Highlands
Coastal Range
Coast
White
Indian
Pardo
Negro
Slave
CLL
Source: Appendix A, Table A-3

Figure 4-4

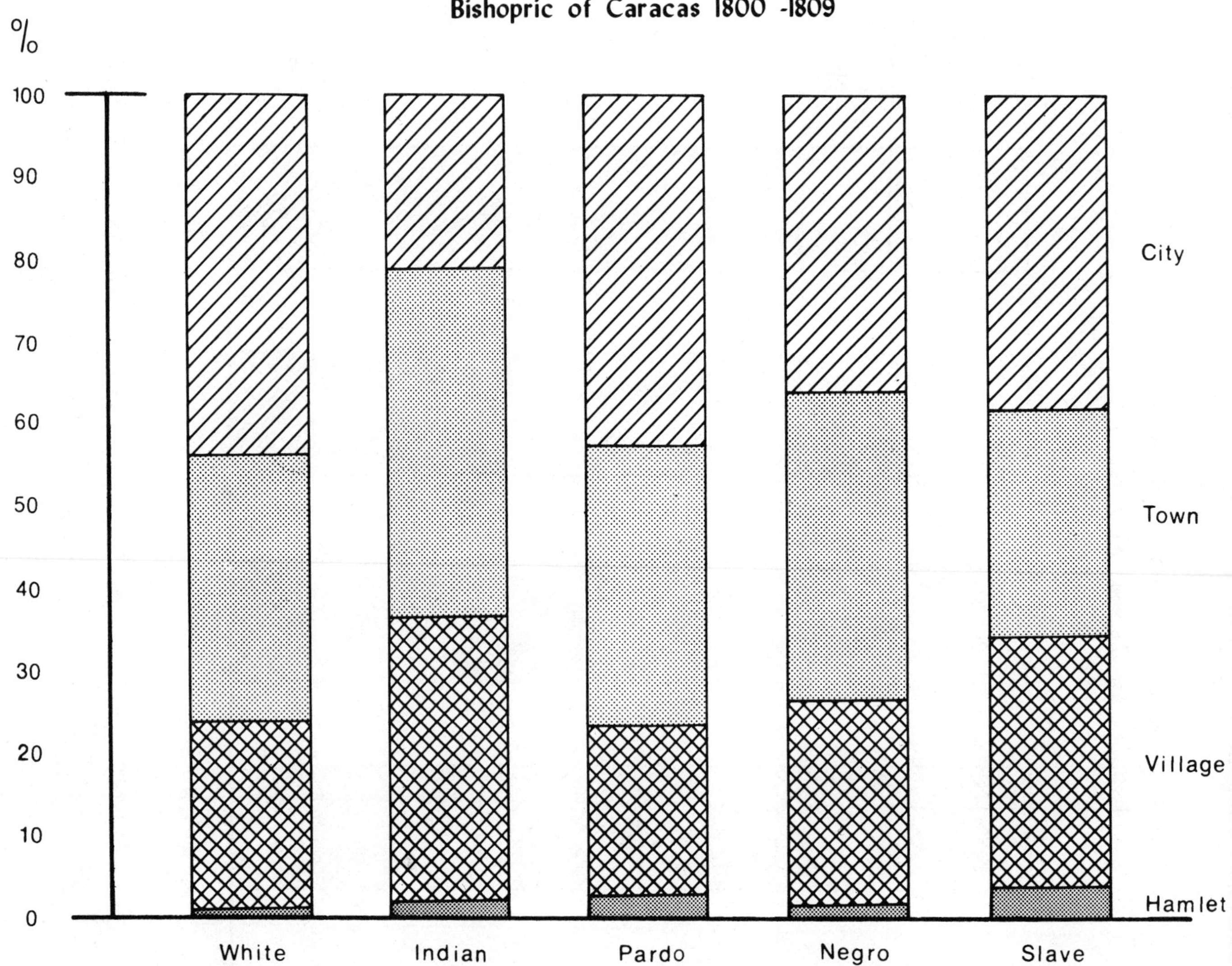
Distribution of Races among Urban Categories
Bishopric of Caracas 1800 -1809
%
100
90
80
70
60
50
40
30
20
10
0
City
Town
Village
Hamlet
White
Indian
Pardo
Negro
Slave
CLL
Source: Appendix A, Table A-2

Figure 4-5

Bishopric belonged in that category. In contrast, villages and towns, demonstrating almost identical patterns of racial concentration, had close to sixty percent blacks. The large places in the Bishopric, those over 4,000 population, showed a higher concentration of blacks than the villages or towns, but a lower concentration than the hamlets.

Another way of looking at this same phenomenon is to consider the percent of the total population that could be found in communities with at least half of their population black. In the Bishopric of 1800-1809, the chances were three out of four that any individual would find himself in one of those communities dominated by blacks. Over seventy percent of the parishes had half or more black residents.

If we can take the distribution of racial groups by urban category as a crude measure of preference patterns, some suggestive comparisons can be made (Figure 4-4). For example, it is striking that the percentages of pardos and whites to be found in cities, towns, villages, and hamlets, appear very close indeed. Pardos and whites, for a variety of reasons, tended to concentrate in the cities and towns and showed a declining preference for places of smaller size. Indians favored villages and towns, while Negroes and slaves were more or less evenly distributed among towns, cities, and villages. Only a very small fraction of any racial group ended up in the Bishopric's hamlets.

Out of this array of tables, charts, diagrams, and figures, some general conclusions about Venezuela's racial landscape can be made. The Bishopric of Caracas, a region over sixty percent black, showed a consistent regional pattern of racial distribution. Blacks concentrated in the Coast and Coastal Range, and were well represented in the Llanos and the Segovia Highlands. Indians could be found in highest concentrations in the Andes, and smaller concentrations appeared in other areas. The whites represented just under a third of the populations of the Llanos and the Coastal Range. Of all the regions, only the Andes had less than half its population from the black category (Figures 4-2 and 4-5).

Blacks represented a strong majority in parishes of all sizes, and three-quarters of the Bishopric's population could have been found in places with at least fifty percent of their populations from the black group.

Having explored these patterns of racial distribution around the Bishopric, we can begin to look at some other measures of population behavior: sex, marriage, and children.

Men and Women

In the Bishopric of Caracas, men and women also distributed themselves among the parishes in characteristic patterns by race, region, and urban category. The male/female ratios derived to illustrate these patterns are population measures with a high degree of predictability. From experience and theory, we can expect the number of males and the number of females in a geographic area to be just about equal. Moreover, we can also expect to find more men than women in the very young ages, and more women than men among the adults. If the number of women and the number of men are exactly equal, the male/female ratios will be 1.0, which when multiplied by 100 for convenience gives 100. With more women than men in the population, the ratio drops below 100, and of course an excess of men will raise the ratio above 100.

Unusual male/female ratios always require careful investigation to determine the causes of deviations from the expected. For example, large male/female differences can result from sex-specific causes of death, such as wars that deplete the male population without seriously affecting the female. Large scale migrations can also tilt the male/female ratios in one direction or the other. Unfortunately, not all disparities in male/female ratios come from significant demographic events. Imbalances in this indicator are frequently the result of an incomplete enumeration that fails to include members of one sex with the completeness it includes members of the other. Because of this, and barring evidence of other reasons for a serious male/female imbalance, the ratios for adults and children can often serve as a check on the consistency and completeness of an enumeration.

In Venezuela, within the Bishopric of Caracas, men and women appeared in the censuses in the ratios displayed in Figure 4-6. The overall ratio of 91.4 is somewhat below the ratio we might have expected for a population of Venezuela's type and experience. Moreover, at the present time no evidence suggests a natural cause for this discrepancy. There were no major wars, no outbreaks of disease that would have affected men more than women, and no major migrations. There is a slight possibility that the Bishopric, by virtue of housing Venezuela's primate city, Caracas, and the country's most prosperous agricultural areas, may have drawn in substantial numbers of females from outside the Bishopric, from the Andes, the Eastern Llanos and Coastal Range, or from the Maracaibo area. However, because we have little evidence to support such a theory, we will have to search elsewhere for an explanation.

To determine what might serve as the norm for Venezuela's population in this matter of male/female ratios and in relation to other indices to be discussed later, I have chosen the model "South" life table in Coale and Demeny's compilation, with a life expectancy at birth of twenty-five years. From the evidence and arguments in Eduardo Arriaga's excellent work on mortality decline in Latin America, I feel confident in assuming that the mortality trends he was able to calculate for 1860 in Latin America can probably be applied to the 1800-1809 period as well, without doing violence to the data.[4] Having accepted the model life table as a close approximation of Venezuela's population age structure, it is a simple matter to compare the male/female ratio of the model with that observed in the Bishopric of Caracas. Figure 4-6 shows the overall sex ratio of the observed data compared with that of the hypothetical model population. Clearly the observed ratio would have to be increased about seven or eight percent to bring it up to the expected level. Before considering any adjustments to the data, however, we should also look closely at the male/female ratios for the children of the Bishopric, again compared with the expected ratios from the model life table. From Figure 4-6, we can see that the two figures for the 0-6 age group differ by only about one percent. We might be safe in supposing that the reporting of children between 0-6 is at least sex consistent; that is, if children are underenumerated, it is probably in about the same amount for boys as for girls. Such a situation could encourage us to readjust our figures for adults upwards to account for the apparent underenumeration of adult males in the census returns. Unfortunately, such a simple procedure improves the utility of the original data little, since much of the variation in male/female ratios between the races must come from a variation in the completeness of reporting each racial group. For the purposes of comparing differences within the Bishopric of Caracas, no useful advantage would be gained at this stage of the investigation by applying correction factors to this data, and such a procedure might introduce new errors.

Looking at these male/female ratios by race for all of the Bishopric, some slight differences among races emerge (Figure 4-7). Among the children, the variation from the overall male/female ratios among the races is no more than plus or minus three percent or so, hardly enough of a spread on which to base any elaborate theories, especially since there seems to be no particular pattern to the variation. Much the same can be said of the overall male/female ratios, which show a similar three to four percent variation around the total ratio. But here a pattern emerges for the first time, rather weak to be sure, but a pattern nevertheless, and one that we will see repeated throughout the data on male/female ratios. Whites and slaves have the highest ratios and the ones closest to the norm of the model life table. Such a phenomenon may suggest that whites and slaves share a characteristic or characteristics that make their men more completely counted than the men of other racial groups. We might suppose that the men of both groups appeared more valuable to society than the men of other groups, and probably had more consistently maintained places of residence, thus being more easily included in the annual parish counts. Slave males, of course, served as an important commercial commodity, whose transfer and sale required the intervention of notaries and other civil officials. As a result of the value of these individuals in a commercial sense, we can safely assume that the location and number of such important commodities would be known and the information available to the parish census takers. Slaves, of course, were not generally liable for tribute payments, nor before the wars of independence did

Male/Female Ratios

Bishopric of Caracas 1800 - 1809 vs. Life Table Ratios

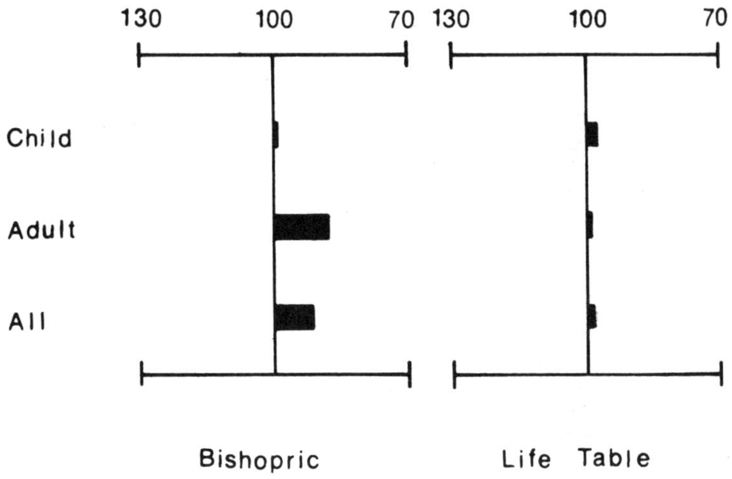

Ratio = (Males/ Females) x (100)
Child = 0-7
Adult = 7 and above

Source: Appendix A, Table A - 4

CLL

Figure 4-6

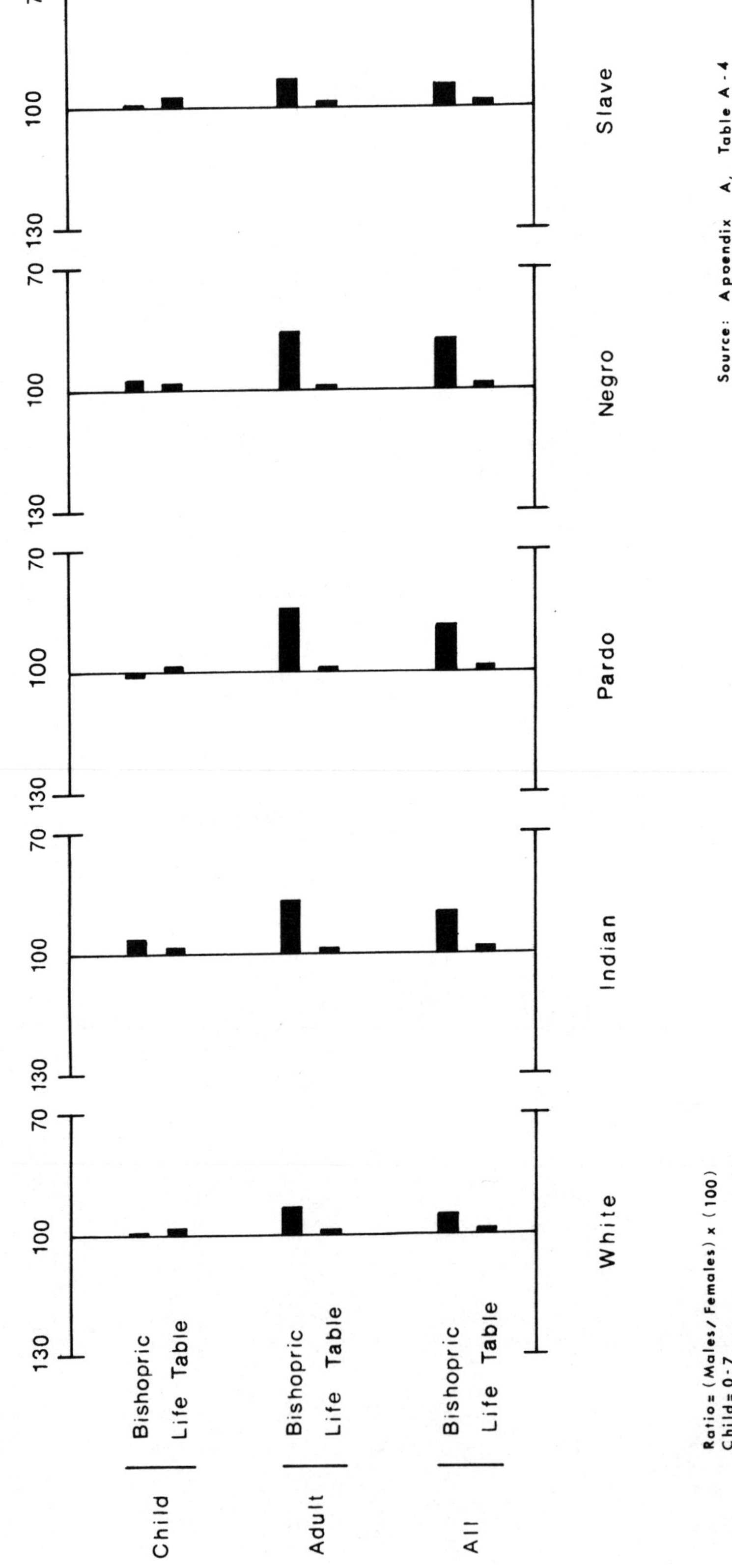
Male/Female Ratios by Race
Bishopric of Caracas 1800 - 1809
130
100
70
White
Indian
Pardo
Negro
Slave
Child
Adult
All
Bishopric
Life Table
Ratio= (Males/Females) x (100)
Child= 0-7
Adult= 7 and above
Source: Appendix A, Table A-4
CLL

Figure 4-7

any military company try to draft them into service. While masters might have had some inclination to understate their slave holdings in hopes of avoiding some kind of tax, they also needed to have all their slaves properly registered and recorded, so that in case of disputes over ownership or sale, the slave's papers would be in order.

From within the white category came the upper strata of Venezuelan society, and though not all whites could be considered members of the elite, their chances of having stable residences, commercial ties, and linkages with better families, were considerably greater than those of pardos, Indians, or Negroes. The mere fact of being fully integrated into the Spanish bureaucratic and commercial system, and of having to maintain linkages with the ecclesiastical and civil bureaucracies, would improve the chances of white males to be included in the censuses. Whites were not liable to tribute payments, and one suspects that the threat of military service did not impress whites as much as it did blacks, thus removing or lessening one reason to avoid population counts.

Although the variation of male/female ratios by race is not particularly impressive over the whole Bishopric, some wide swings in this indicator appear when the data are broken down by region, as in Figure 4-8. One disadvantage of the male/female ratio is that it exaggerates the imbalance between the sexes, implying a more significant deviation from the norm than really exists. Still, the measure does draw our attention to imbalances that need to be explained. For example, the disparity in the number of males and females in the Coast and the Segovia Highland regions is dramatic. On the Coast, this imbalance amounts to about 670 more men than women out of a total regional population of some 6000 individuals. We may suppose this to be the result of the reluctance of married men to bring their wives and families to the unhealthy Coast, to the probable predominance of men in the merchant marine, and to the excess men in the garrison at Puerto Cabello. Such a reasonable explanation does not emerge as readily to explain the excess of women over men in the Segovia Highlands. There are almost 1500 more women than men recorded in this region, out of a total population of twelve thousand souls. This may be partly due to especially poor enumeration of males in the region. We might also hypothesize, albeit on quite meager evidence, that the Segovia Highlands was a region of male outmigrants. We could imagine the males in the area leaving for the Llanos or the Coastal Range in search of work and economic opportunity not available in the less prosperous Segovia Highlands.

In the slave category, the excess of male slaves in the Coast and Llanos regions fits our understanding of these two areas as places where masters would find the employment of male slaves more advantageous than the work of females. Along the hot humid coast, male slaves labored in plantations, where the need for the female slaves' specialties of domestic service would have been less than in other regions of the country. The nomadic life style of the llanero slave would have been less suited to his female counterpart. Because the use of female domestics must have been a primarily urban phenomenon, their absence in the essentially rural areas along the Coast and in the Llanos comes as no surprise. The extraordinary imbalance in the sexes in the Andes is impossible to explain at this time because of the small number of individuals involved. Of the almost 500 slaves in the Andean region of the Bishopric, there were almost 70 more men than women, a situation that could well be the result of idiosyncratic factors. However, the excess of about 700 women out of a population of almost 7000 slaves in the Segovia Highlands does not yield to such an explanation. Here, as with the excess of white women, we might suppose that the male slaves had been exported out of the region to more profitable employment in other parts of the Bishopric, perhaps the Llanos, the Coast, or the Coastal Range. Such a hypothesis has the virtue of corresponding to the similar hypothesis about the white subgroup, although neither hypothesis inspires overwhelming confidence given the rudimentary state of research on Venezuelan social history in the colonial period.

For the rest of the racial categories, the deviations from the normal, that is from the overall ratios for the Bishopric, are hardly large enough to warrant elaborate hypotheses. In general, the greatest departures from the norm occur in the Llanos, the Segovia

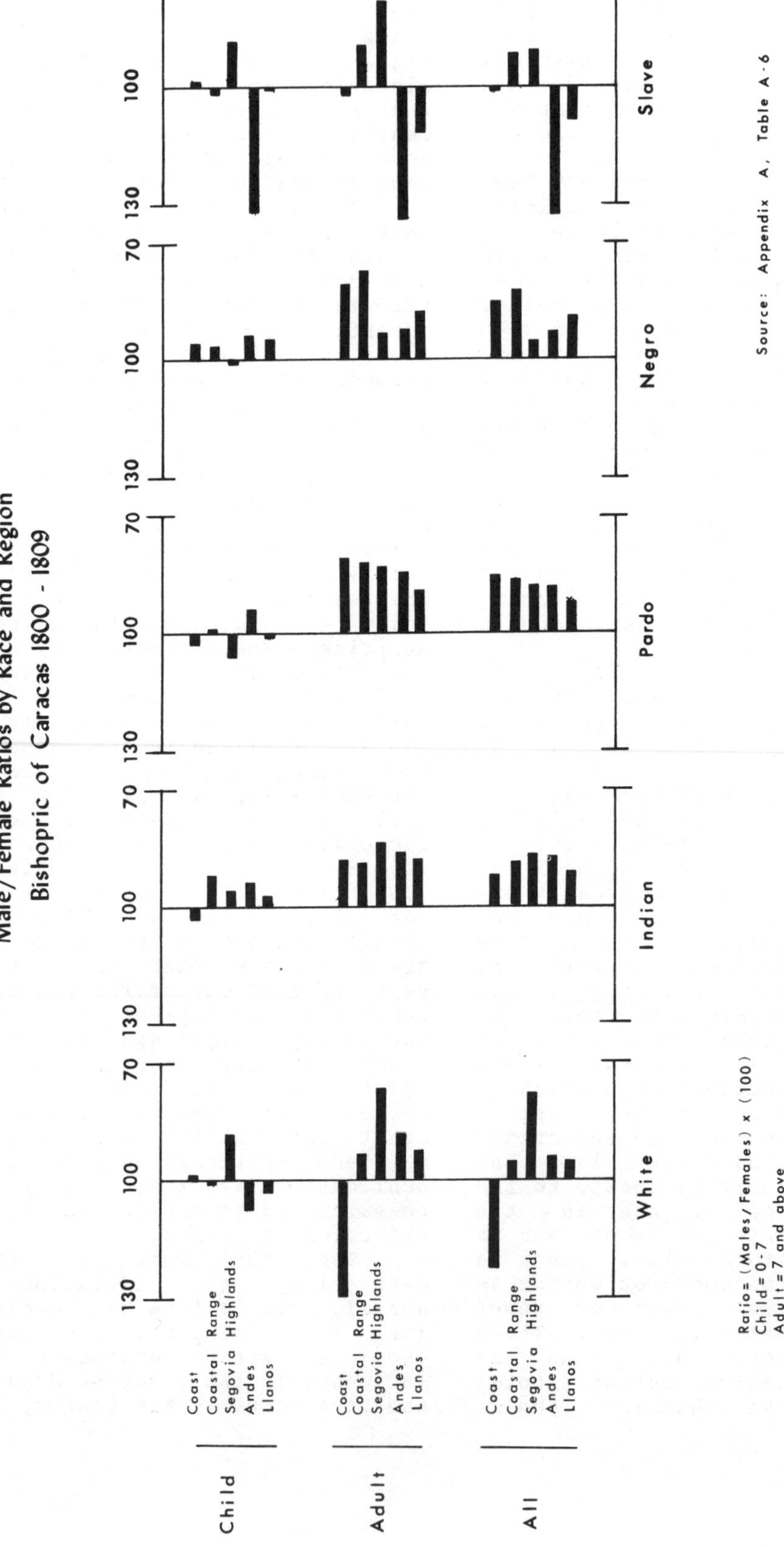
Male/Female Ratios by Race and Region
Bishopric of Caracas 1800 - 1809
Child
Adult
All
Coast
Coastal Range
Segovia Highlands
Andes
Llanos
130
100
70
White
Indian
Pardo
Negro
Slave
Ratio = (Males/Females) x (100)
Child = 0-7
Adult = 7 and above
Source: Appendix A, Table A-6
CLL

Figure 4-8

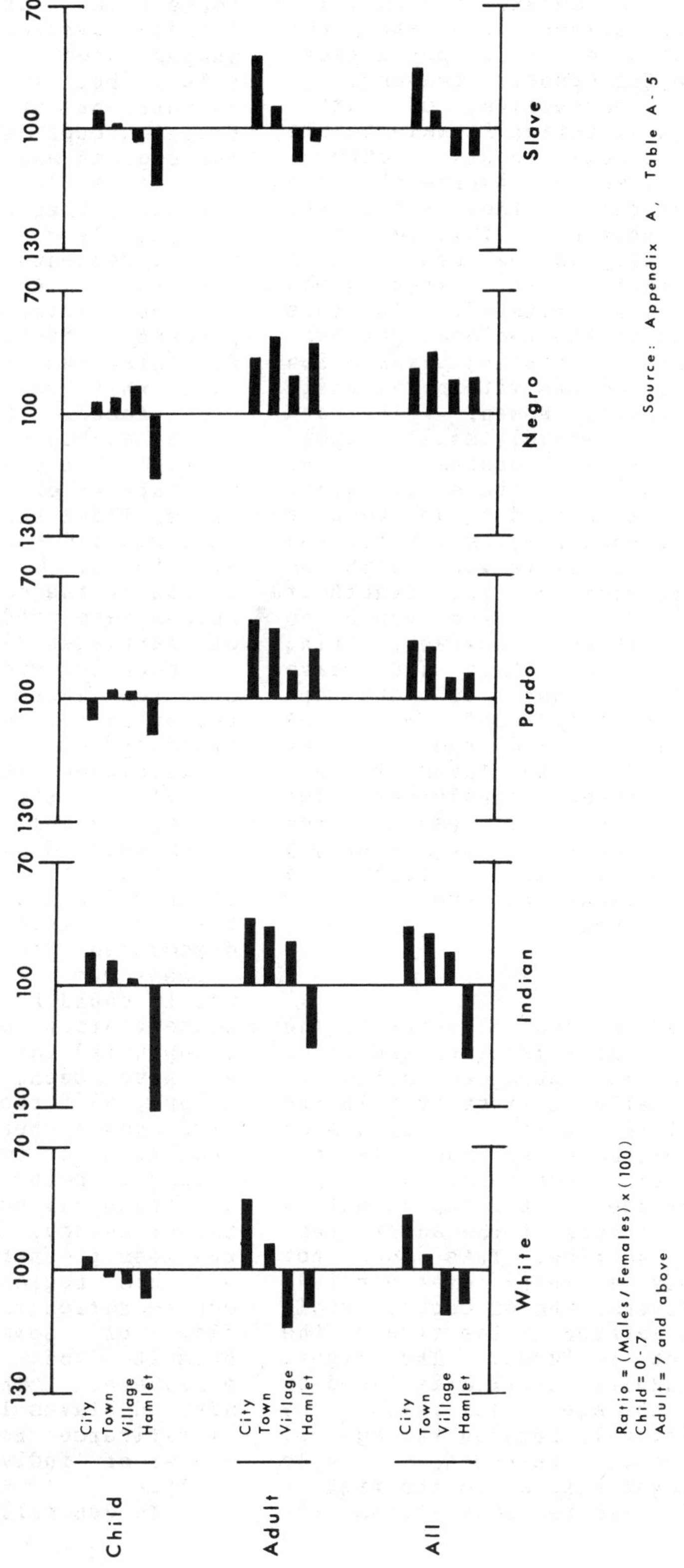
Male/Female Ratios by Race and Urban Category
Bishopric of Caracas 1800 - 1809
130
100
70
White
Indian
Pardo
Negro
Slave
Child
Adult
All
City
Town
Village
Hamlet
Ratio = (Males / Females) x (100)
Child = 0-7
Adult = 7 and above
Source: Appendix A, Table A-5
CLL

Figure 4-9

Highlands, and the Coast, and they involve whites and slaves, the two most mobile elements of the population, although mobile for opposite reasons.

From the perspective of urban categories, the variation in male/female ratios shows a fairly regular pattern. From Figure 4-9, we can observe that the larger the urban center, the larger the excess of women over men. This result is rather unremarkable, as the phenomenon of women concentrating in large urban centers is well-established. In this view, as well as in the regional perspective, the most interesting variation among urban types occurs within the white and slave categories. Women, white and slave, make up a relatively small proportion of their racial groups in the villages and hamlets, where the white women might be disinclined to go because of a lack of opportunity, security, and amenities, and where slave women might be needed less because of the dearth of domestic jobs and of white women to serve. The cities, however, bring together an excess of white and slave women, probably because of the opportunities, security, and amenities available to whites and the need for services performed by the slaves. The extraordinarily high male/female ratio for Indians living in hamlets results from about 90 extra males living there, a number too small to warrant a hypothetical explanation, even in this speculative environment.

Marriage

Inevitably, the men and women of the Bishopric of Caracas married, and in or out of marriage they produced children. Being theoretically a first step in the process, we will begin with a discussion of marriage patterns by race in the regional and urban dimensions.

Throughout the Bishopric, about a third or a bit more of the adults were married at any one time. This does not mean that only a third ever married. Widows and widowers, who of course would not have been married at the time of the census, were not included. The figure for percent adults married is based on "adults" above the age of six years. By including individuals between the ages of seven and about thirteen, people presumably not yet exposed to the risk of marriage, this figure understates the percentage of marriageable adults actually married. The usefulness of this number does not lie in its absolute value, but in its ability to permit comparisons of marital levels between racial groups and the sexes, and among the regions and urban categories.

If we look at Figure 4-10, two important patterns emerge. First, and unsuprisingly given the sex distribution, a higher percentage of men were married than women. Reflecting the probable better enumeration of whites and slaves, the percent difference between men and women for these two groups is considerably less than that between men and women of the other races. The second obvious pattern shows a higher percentage of Indians married than other groups, and a lower percentage of slaves. Indians, by and large, lived under closer supervision by clerics, and many were brought up in mission towns. The recognized role of the Church in the care of Indian souls should indeed have produced a higher incidence of marriages among Indians than among other racial groups. Slaves, objects in commerce whose mobility constituted a factor in every slaveholder's calculations, probably received little incentive to marry, and this, as well as the active denial of the right to marry in some cases, may help account for the slaves' lower married population.

From the regional perspective, the interregional differences are not large, but some interesting patterns can be discovered. The Andes have the highest percentages of married adults. Such a result could be expected from the high concentration of Indians in the area, a group noted for high marriage levels as we have seen. But the other racial groups, with the exception of the slaves, also show higher percentages in the Andes than in other regions. The traditionally stronger role of the Catholic Church in the Andes may be responsible for part of this tendency. We might also expect that the less prosperous and less dynamic role of this region during the period under consideration may have encouraged an outflow of some single individuals in pursuit of better opportunities elsewhere. The lower percentage of married slaves in the Andes is without significance here because of the small number of individuals involved (Figure 4-11).

In general, however, the male-female

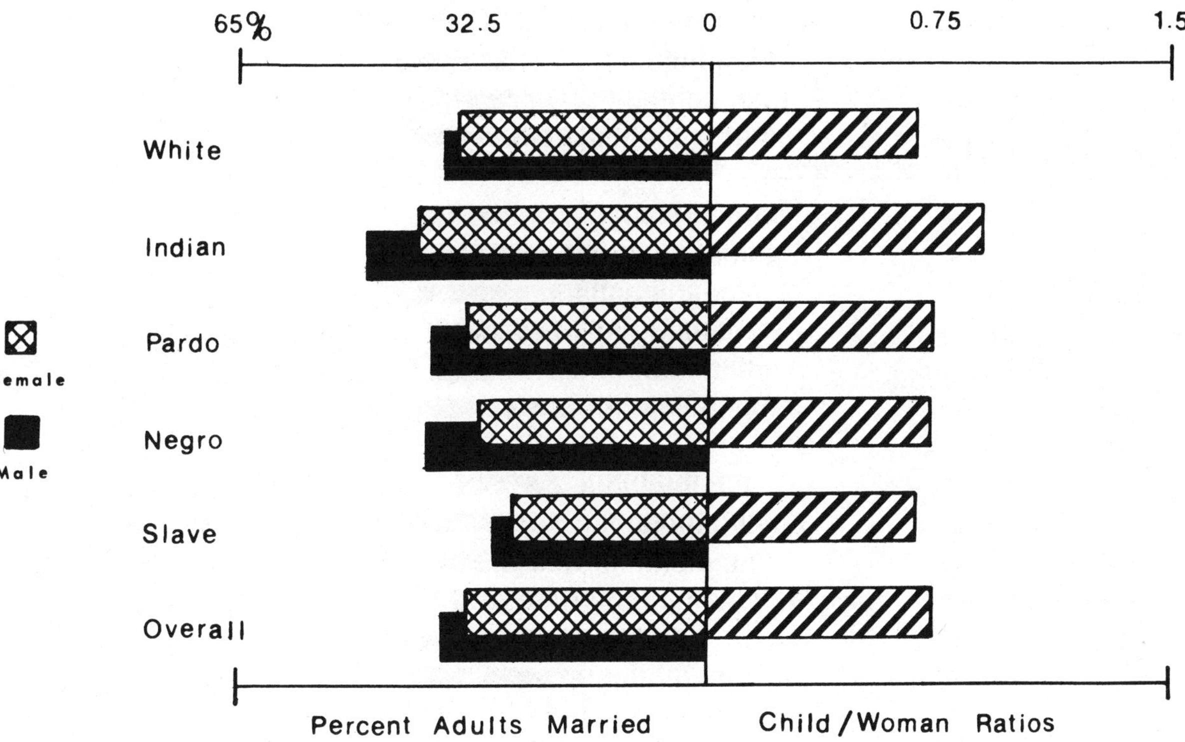
Percent Adults Married and Child/Woman Ratios
Bishopric of Caracas 1800 - 1809
65%
32.5
0
0.75
1.5
White
Indian
Pardo
Negro
Slave
Overall
Female
Male
Percent Adults Married
Child/Woman Ratios
Life Table Ratio = 0.58
Child = 0-7
Adult = 7 and above
Source: Appendix A, Tables A-7 and A-10
CLL

Figure 4-10

Percent Women Married and Child/Woman Ratios by Region
Bishopric of Caracas 1800 - 1809

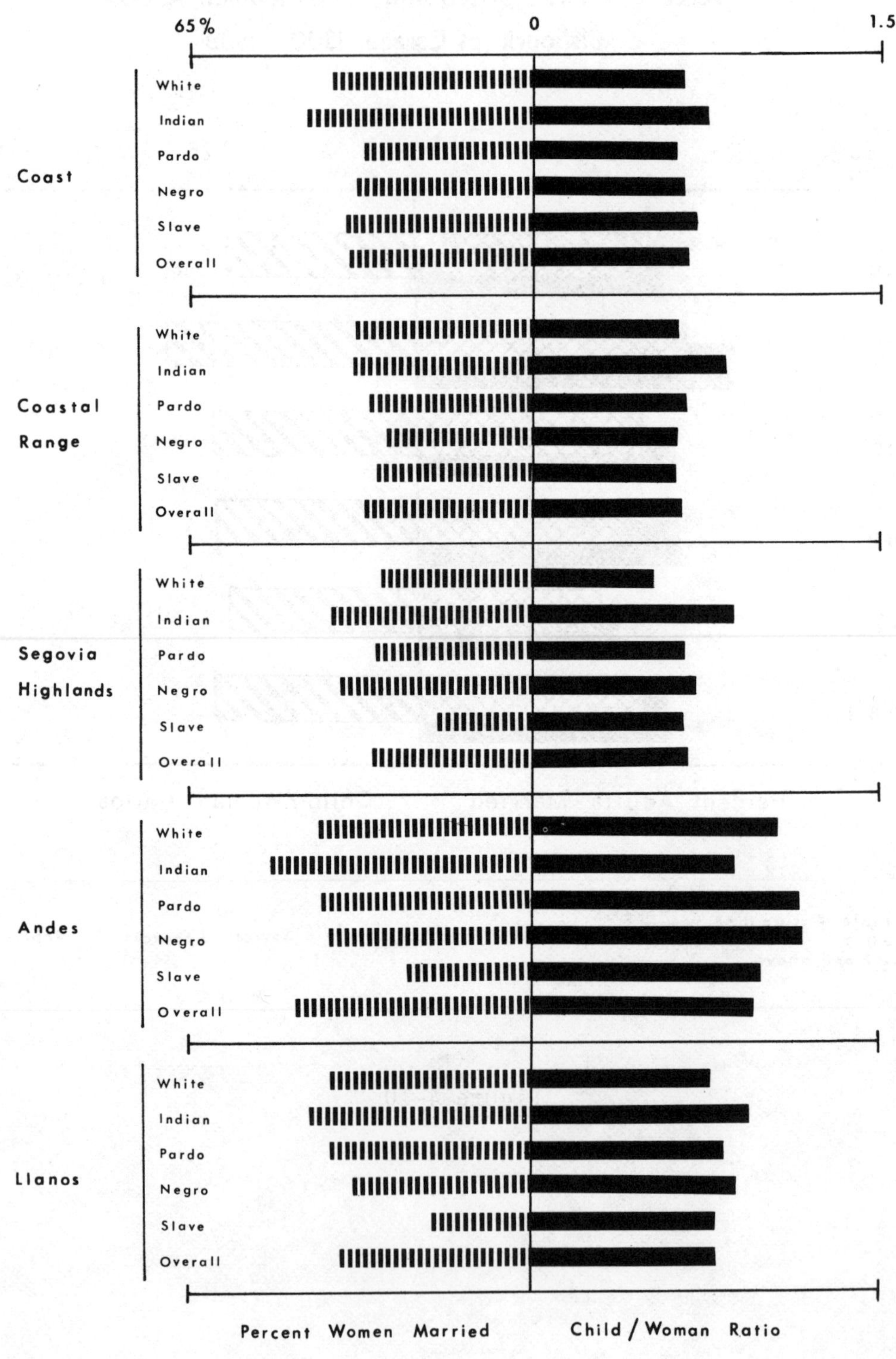

Child = 0 - 7
Adult = 7 and above

Source: Appendix A, Tables A-9 and A-12
CLL

Figure 4-11

Percent Women Married and Child/Woman Ratios by Urban Category
Bishopric of Caracas 1800 - 1809

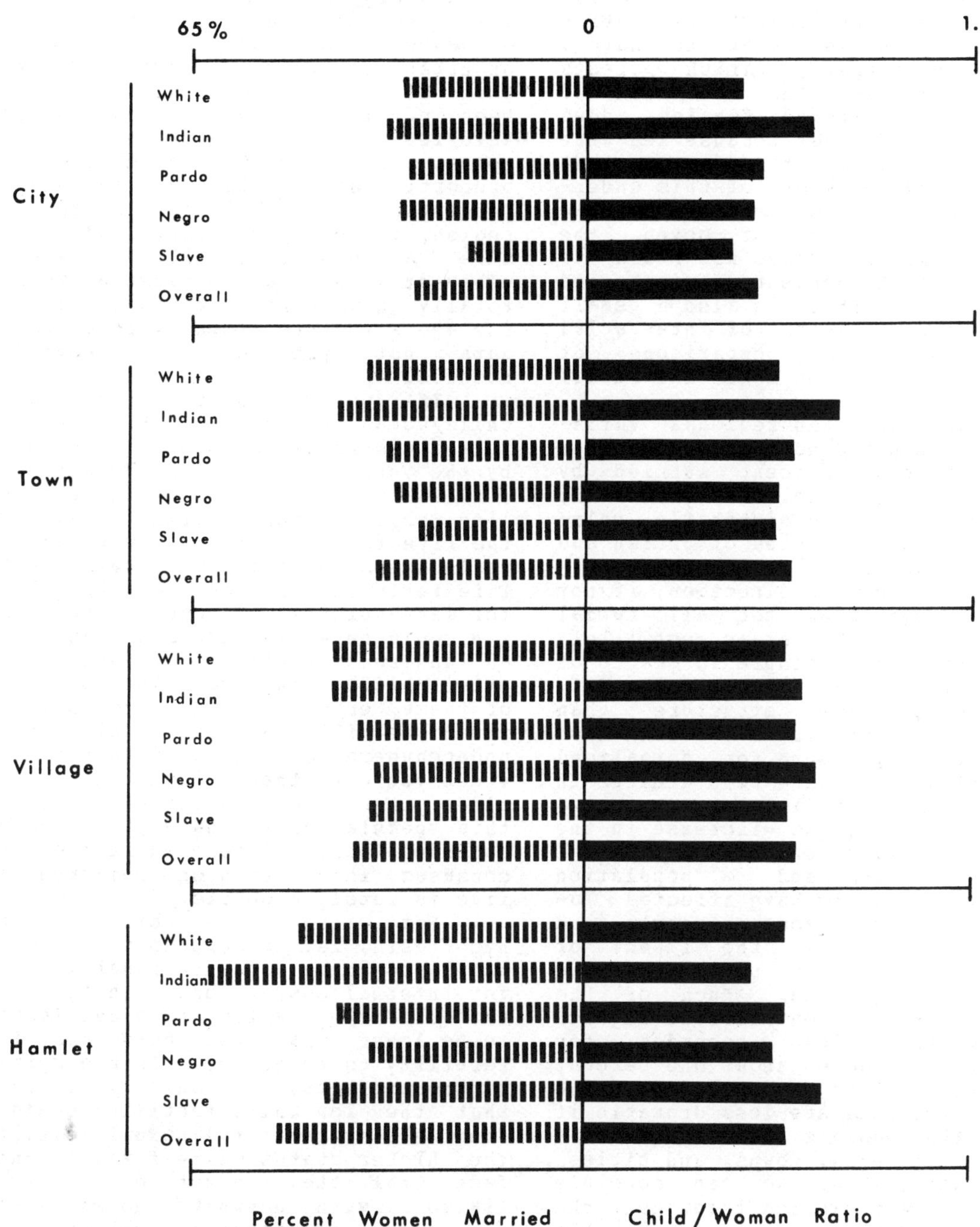

Child = 0 - 7
Adult = 7 and above

Source: Appendix A, Tables A-8 and A-11

CLL

Figure 4-12

percent differences with reference to marriage require little explanation. Much of the difference between male and female percentages throughout these tables can be traced to a bias in the census procedure in favor of married individuals. Since by Church regulation every married female ought to have a living male counterpart, parish priests worked hard to see that the totals of married males and married females added up as they should. But because men were undercounted to a greater degree than women, and because most of this undercounting apparently occurred among single males over the age of seven, the percentage of married males was bound to be higher than the percentage of married females recorded. There is also a small but undetermined number of interracial marriages that makes comparisons of percent married between sexes and racial groups risky.

More important than regional variations are the patterns that emerge from the distribution of percent married by urban category and race. In Figure 4-12, we have a clear and unmistakable relationship between the size of parish and the percent married. And the relationship is in the same direction, if not of the same magnitude, for all racial groups. The large urban areas most likely attracted more single people in search of fame and fortune, and probably had a different, younger, age structure than smaller urban centers. We could also suppose that the pressure for formalized marriage might well have been greater in smaller places than in larger ones, producing a consequent increase in the number of informal unions in the larger parishes. Increased population concentration seems to have affected Indians and slaves most strongly and Negroes least. Even so, the impact of large parishes on the percent married must not be exaggerated. Much of the variation in the percent-married figures comes from the values recorded for hamlets, which housed about one percent of the Bishopric's population. The percent differences are less dramatic if we exclude the hamlets and concentrate instead on villages, towns, and cities.

In summary, then, we can conclude that the percent married throughout the Bishopric of Caracas shows remarkable similarity among the subdivisions of race, urban category, and region.

Children

Children represent the future and much can be learned about the behavior of populations and the family from the analysis of data on children. Unfortunately, Figures 4-10, 4-11, and 4-12 fail to provide us with convincing evidence of important regional, racial, or urban differences. Most of the variations displayed here could easily have been predicted from a knowledge of the male/female ratios and the marriage patterns. Although the evidence of a high proportion of adults married and high percentages of children in the Andes region, for example, might lead us to assume a higher fertility there than elsewhere, such a conclusion would be totally unwarranted without evidence on the age structure of the various regions, data not yet developed from parish records.

If we compare the overall child/woman ratio of the Bishopric--that is the number of children (0-6) divided by the number of women (7 and above)--with what we might get using the model life table mentioned earlier, we see that the life table index is lower than our real-life counterpart. Assuming that the life table is a reasonable approximation for late-colonial Venezuela, the disparity could be explained as a function of an underenumeration of women before and after childbearing age. The presumption of these errors would be to inflate apparent fertility, unless children were underenumerated even more than the adult women younger than about thirteen and older than about thirty-nine. However, this speculation is hardly worth major consideration, since even in the best of censuses, information on children under five is rarely accurate.

For the sake of a working hypothesis, let us suppose that the data displayed here are reasonably accurate for internal comparisons. In that case, we could expect white and slave fertility to be lower than the norm and Indian fertility to be higher. In the spirit of might-have-been, we could also imagine that the low white fertility could stem from less extramarital sexual activity by the higher status white females, and the fact that the product of white male liaisons with nonwhite women would be classified as nonwhite children. We could propose that slave females had at least as high fertility as the average, but that poor sanitation and diet took a heavier toll of slave children, thereby lowering apparent slave fertility. Indians, a high percentage of whom married, demonstrated high fertility because marital fertility might have been higher than illegitimate fertility and because the Church, relatively strong in Indian areas, encouraged large families.

La Blanquera, San Carlos de Austria

FIVE

A City in the Midst of War: San Carlos de Austria

In the preceding chapters, we have seen the Bishopric of Caracas in a variety of dimensions, but from a static viewpoint. Although the data set is not yet good enough to permit an extensive analysis of change over time, we can look more closely at an individual city, town, village, or hamlet, to see how a representative place changed. In selecting the urban center for this analysis, I followed a series of rather ad hoc criteria. In general, I avoided those places that have already been the subject of extensive local history, as mentioned in the notes to Chapter 1. For example, Tucupido, an important urban center on the eastern edge of the Llanos within the Bishopric of Caracas, has been discussed in considerable detail elsewhere. Likewise, I have avoided Caracas, in part because it has been the subject of a host of studies and in part because it is representative of nothing but itself. In order to be able to say something about the movement of a city's or a town's population and to chart the changes that may have occurred in its composition, I needed to choose a place with a reasonably complete series of information and, in addition, a place whose boundaries did not experience drastic changes during the period under study. Finally, I wanted to find an urban center located in a major geographic region of Venezuela. As a result of applying these criteria, I selected the city of San Carlos de Austria. The description offered here must be taken as a first approximation, a summary guide to the further study of the local history of the city and similar places in late colonial and early republican Venezuela. While the urban center selected for examination cannot in any statistical sense be presented as a sample from the universe of places in the Bishopric, nor as typical in any rigorous sense, it is representative of similar places experiencing similar historical conditions. In continuing the study begun here, it should be possible to develop model or typical histories for the various kinds of urban places to be found in Venezuela.

A Llanero City: San Carlos de Austria

Standing on the boundary between the Llanos of Cojedes and the Llanos of Carabobo, San Carlos de Austria qualified as a city according to my criteria, having an average population of 9,545 between the years 1800-1809. This puts it near the top of city parishes in the Bishopric at the end of the colonial period and testifies to San Carlos' prominence as a major distribution point for its region. Here, merchants and stock raisers congregated to take advantage of the fortuitous position of the city astride the trade routes from the cattle hinterland of the Llanos to the Caracas valleys, from the Segovia Highland communities around Barquisimeto, and to Puerto Cabello and the contraband trade areas of the coastline from Puerto Cabello west to Tucacas.

Unlike many other important late-colonial cities, San Carlos originated late in the conquest and colonization of Venezuela. Where major cities such as Barquisimeto came into being during the sixteenth century expansionist wave, San Carlos started out as a missionary outpost in the late seventeenth century. Founded officially by the Capuchins in 1678, San Carlos was designed to provide a Spanish settlement to anchor the growing network of Capuchin missions extending out into the trackless plains.

Under the guidance of the missionaries, the settlement grew rapidly on the trade generated by the development of the Llanos' great cattle herds. By the end of the seventeenth century and the first years of the eighteenth, the town had grown so self-sufficient and so well-established as a Spanish settlement that some Capuchins were prepared to turn the religious administration of the place over to the seculars and withdraw to less well-established missions in other parts of the Llanos. Although some in the Order resisted the effort to secularize the church in San Carlos, the King finally ordered that the transfer of control be made, and in 1720, after almost two decades of dispute, San Carlos became a regular part of the Spanish colonial urban system, administered by civil and secular authorities.[1]

By 1720, then, San Carlos de Austria had emerged as one of the principal places in Venezuela. Travelers commented on its prosperity, and reports on the city from this date through the independence epoch and into the republican period agree that San Carlos was prosperous, populated, and in many ways delightful.

The reasons for this apparent success can be traced to a series of circumstances. Clearly, as mentioned above, the location of the city contributed substantially to its rapid growth. As Spaniards from the plains of Barinas and the Llanos south and west of San Carlos expanded their activities, the city expanded in close step. Not only did San Carlos handle most of the sale and transfer of products destined for internal consumption in the Segovia Highlands and into the valleys of Caracas and even Valencia, but it provided the conduit for products shipped out of the country in legal or illegal trade with Spain and Holland. The enterprising residents of the city grew rich on the sale of hides, tallow, cheese, and cattle on the hoof. They sold large quantities of mules as well, to serve in the extensive transportation industry moving goods between the major cities of the provinces of Venezuela. Of the estimated 3,000 head of cattle sold every year, most went to the Barquisimeto region for beef, while a considerable portion went to the coast, where Dutch contrabandists bought the beef and hides. Although these cattle products and the sale of mules brought the largest part of San Carlos' prosperity, the town accounted for the shipment of a substantial amount of tobacco to the coast as well.

Unfortunately, I have no hard data on the occupations of the residents of this urban center, but the prosperous individuals of the city could clearly be divided into two major groups. First were the merchants whose activities marketing hides, cattle, and mules gave them the income to import a large variety of manufactured products legally through Puerto Cabello and La Guaira-Caracas, or illegally from smugglers along the wide-open coast. The owners of large hatos or stock-raising establishments located throughout the Llanos to the Apure made up the second group. These individuals no doubt lived in San Carlos and established their families there because it was the largest and most substantial urban center with reasonably direct access to their properties. By setting up his principal residence in a city like San Carlos, an enterprising hacendado could maintain his family in the style required by his station in life and in accord with his income. Moreover, I suspect that this pattern of the concentration of the owners of major hatos in the principal llanero centers can be substantiated throughout the region.

Who the people of San Carlos were and where they came from is difficult to determine from the data available in printed sources and the census information, but San Carlos had the reputation of being a center for Isleños, Spaniards from the Canary Islands, a group known for industry, thrift, and entreprenurial talent. If this stereotypical notion is accurate, the Isleños certainly made San Carlos a place to be proud of. In 1780, in recognition of the city's prominent place in the Venezuelan urban network, the King conferred the title of *villa* on the city.[2]

There are, of course, a number of ways of assessing a city's importance in any given context. With the Venezuelan urban network, the easiest is population size. But frequently the bare number of people involved in a city's life fails to convey a sense of the complexity and prosperity of a place. For example, San Carlos served not only as an important commercial center, but also as the head of a civil jurisdiction and the head of an ecclesiastical jurisdiction. As a result, those ecclesiastics serving the parish counted on a substantial income. The curate, according to Mariano Martí, received an income from all sources in 1781 of more than 1600 pesos, while the *sacristán mayor* disposed of more than 600 pesos.

If the priest's income helps give a dimension to the town's prosperity, the healthy state of San Carlos' religious institutions provides an even more impressive indicator. Two religious orders maintained a presence in San Carlos during the last decades of the eighteenth century. The Dominicans kept a Hospice administered by two members of the order. This establishment could afford a well-built chapel on their capital of some 27,588 pesos, a capital that must have produced something on the order of 1200 or 1300 pesos a year. When the Mercederians wanted to establish a convent for their order in 1781, they produced pledges of 28,500 pesos of capital, plus the donation of land for the convent in support of their bid.

Religious charity in San Carlos also extended to the founding of *cofradías*, or brotherhoods, *obras pías*, and special chapels. The obra pía of the Benditas Animas del Purgatorio, established in San Carlos in 1709, maintained a capital of 5,531 pesos that provided an income of over 260 pesos a year, almost five percent. The other obra pía in town, dedicated to the Imaculada Concepción de Nuestra Señora, received a capital clear and free of 1,820 pesos and had litigation in process for another 550 pesos. The cofradía of the Santísimo Sacramento, founded early in the town's history, in 1697, was reconfirmed in 1769 and certified by a royal order in 1771. The cofradía administered a capital of 3,850 pesos. Finally, the town also supported a chapel in one of the neighborhoods west of town, dedicated to San Juan Bautista. This small church had a brick floor, always a sign of prosperity, and an endowment of 1500 pesos.

Of course the monument to San Carlos' prosperity and civic pride, the city church, stood in mute testimony to the city's wealth and prominence. In 1781 Marti found the church remarkably well-built, well-maintained, and pleasing to the eye. The church itself must have been an imposing building, extending over 160 feet in length, with a main nave about thirty-three feet wide. The walls were sturdy and built over a yard thick. The church boasted three altars, three large doors, and an excellent roof of tiles. The floor, paved in brick, and the walls, recently whitewashed, all testified to the careful attention San Carlos paid its main church.

Lest this city appear an urban paradise inhabited by prosperous happy people busy with commercial and stock-raising activities and supporting their favorite religious institutions without a hint of unhappiness or strife, some notion of the town's vices might be in order here. Clearly a substantial number of individuals within San Carlos made their living in direct violation of Spanish laws, trading with the Dutch and probably other foreigners frequenting the coasts. While contraband probably caused few San Carlos merchants much remorse, it was an activity contrary to the law and against the prevailing economic and political wisdom of the empire.

We also know from Mariano Martí's account of his visita that the residents of the city were no more immune from the ordinary kinds of sexual misconduct than the rest of the Bishopric's faithful. In the visita, we can read case after case of moral dereliction: married men taking up with unmarried women, fathers cohabiting with daughters, employers taking unfair advantage of employees. In many cases, these crimes against God's laws were complicated by considerations of social propriety. Bad enough that a married man should be keeping someone else's wife as a concubine, but worse yet that he should be white and she black. These unequal liaisons are always

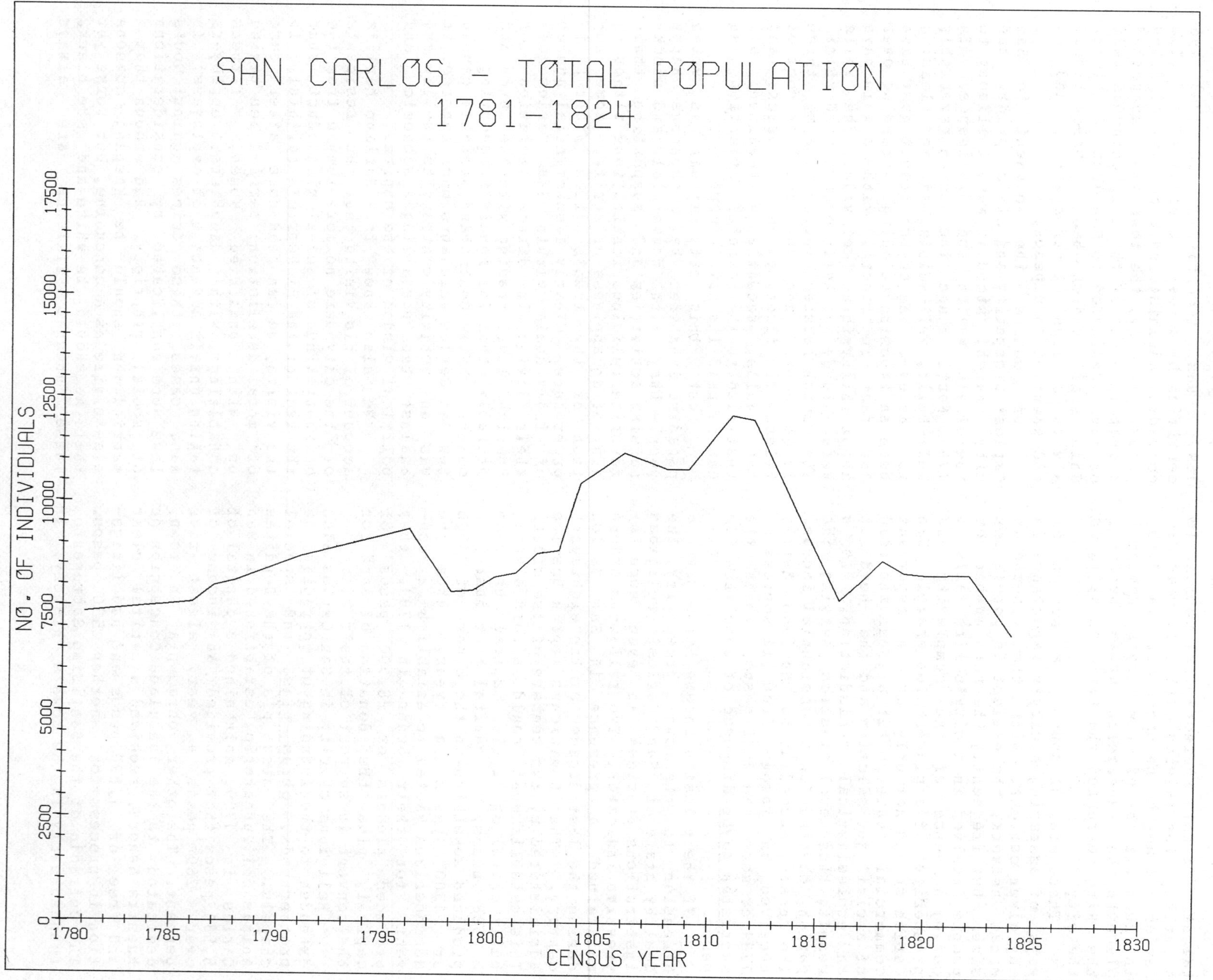
SAN CARLØS - TØTAL PØPULATIØN
1781-1824
NØ. ØF INDIVIDUALS
0
2500
5000
7500
10000
12500
15000
17500
1780
1785
1790
1795
1800
1805
1810
1815
1820
1825
1830
CENSUS YEAR

Figure 5-1

specified in such a way as to indicate that the sin of illicit cohabitation became compounded in evil with the addition of interracial mixture.

To be sure, the reflection of misconduct found in Martí's visita shows only those sins brought to the Bishop's attention during his time in the city. Rarely do we hear of any misconduct not related to sex or failures of the marriage contract. No doubt individuals cheated on prices, lied, stole, and fought. But these must have been regarded as civil transgressions of little interest to the Bishop. Marriage and the sexual relations associated with marriage, however, were always regarded as within the province of Church regulation. Sometimes the Bishop would have to require a man to bring his wife to town from some other city to prevent him from living in sin with other women. In other instances, the Bishop would be asked to coerce a reluctant groom into fulfilling his promises to an all too trusting young woman. Much of the information recorded in the Bishop's books on these themes comes, of course, as the result of gossip. Sometimes, however, the frequency with which a tidbit of malicious gossip turned up in the transcript of the visita indicates that some prominent individual's misconduct was so flagrant and such an affront to the community's standards that a consensus had emerged about his moral culpability. In many of these cases, the Bishop made a determined effort to dissolve the scandalous liaisons. In his efforts to reestablish harmony and tranquility, and eliminate the cause of these scandals, he frequently called on local priests and even the city's civil authorities to guarantee the permanence of the solutions worked out. For all their partiality, the discussion of moral dereliction in the Bishop's books provides a fascinating glimpse into the real lives of real people throughout the Bishopric, and demonstrates unsurprisingly that the residents of San Carlos experienced the same range of human failings as the rest of the inhabitants of the Bishopric.[3]

San Carlos and Independence

The population history of San Carlos during the years 1781-1824 illustrates many of the forces operating on all of Venezuela's parishes throughout these decades. Subjected to the influence of events in Europe and the Caribbean on the price and prospects of her products, Venezuela brought on herself in addition all the dislocations, destruction, and disorganization of the violent and prolonged wars of independence. Because Venezuela began the independence fight as early as any Spanish American colony, and because Venezuelans pursuing Bolivar's dream of a united, independent, and free America felt obligated to liberate all of Spanish South America, that fledgling republic paid a higher price than most of her sister republics for the privilege of managing her own affairs. From 1810 until the final battle at Carabobo in 1823, Venezuela provided men and supplies, and her territory served as a principal battlefield for Bolívar's hemispheric crusade. Below the surface gleam of shining promises, glorious proclamations, and free republics, Venezuela's land displayed the physical scars earned in the cause of Spanish America's independence. Plantations withered or disappeared, and cattle, mules, and horses were swept up and used by the contending armies. Commerce stagnated, civil order weakened and in places disappeared, and people moved from place to place in search of what security and tranquility could be found in those troubled times. Men and women followed the armies from battlefield to battlefield, some as participants, some as supporters, and others in hopes of gaining protection. And the rapid movement of guerrilla bands, highly mobile armies, and expeditionary forces across the land changed the face of many a Venezuelan hamlet, village, town, and city.

San Carlos de Austria was one of those cities. The same conditions that made San Carlos a prosperous place in the late eighteenth century put the city in the center of the independence movement. In the early years of the war, during the unhappy days of Venezuela's First Republic, San Carlos seemed to hold the key to the success or failure of royalist and patriot plans. Fixed at the exchange point between the royalist strongholds of Coro and Maracaibo and the patriot-controlled central mountains and valleys, and, moreover, providing a major gateway to the Llanos, San Carlos felt the brunt of war as strongly as any other place of comparable size during the First Republic. Of course this is not to say that San Carlos provides a typical case

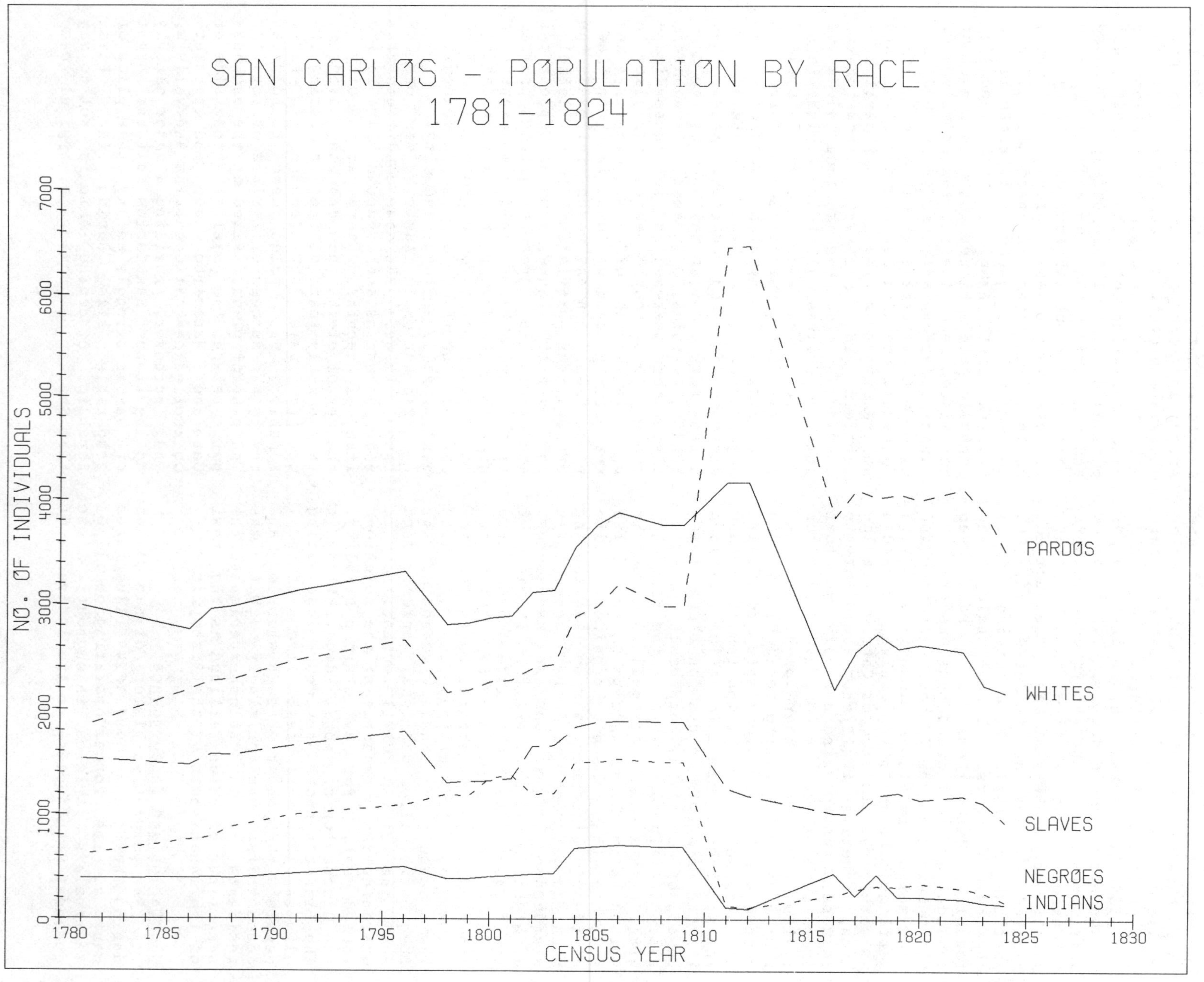
SAN CARLØS - PØPULATIØN BY RACE
1781-1824
NØ. ØF INDIVIDUALS
0
1000
2000
3000
4000
5000
6000
7000
PARDØS
WHITES
SLAVES
NEGRØES
INDIANS
1780
1785
1790
1795
1800
1805
1810
1815
1820
1825
1830
CENSUS YEAR

Figure 5-2

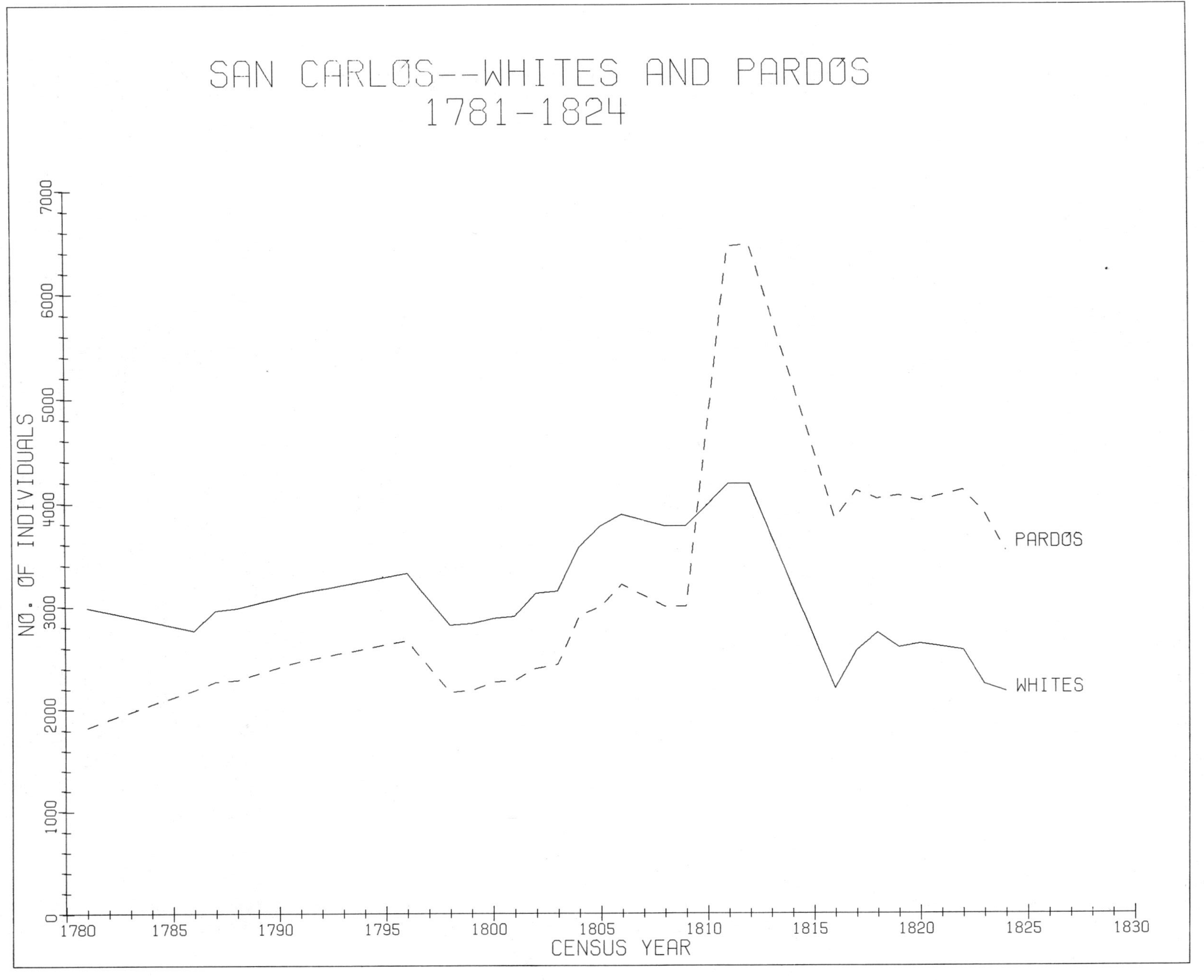
SAN CARLØS--WHITES AND PARDØS
1781-1824
PARDØS
WHITES
NØ. ØF INDIVIDUALS
0
1000
2000
3000
4000
5000
6000
7000
1780
1785
1790
1795
1800
1805
1810
1815
1820
1825
1830
CENSUS YEAR

Figure 5-3

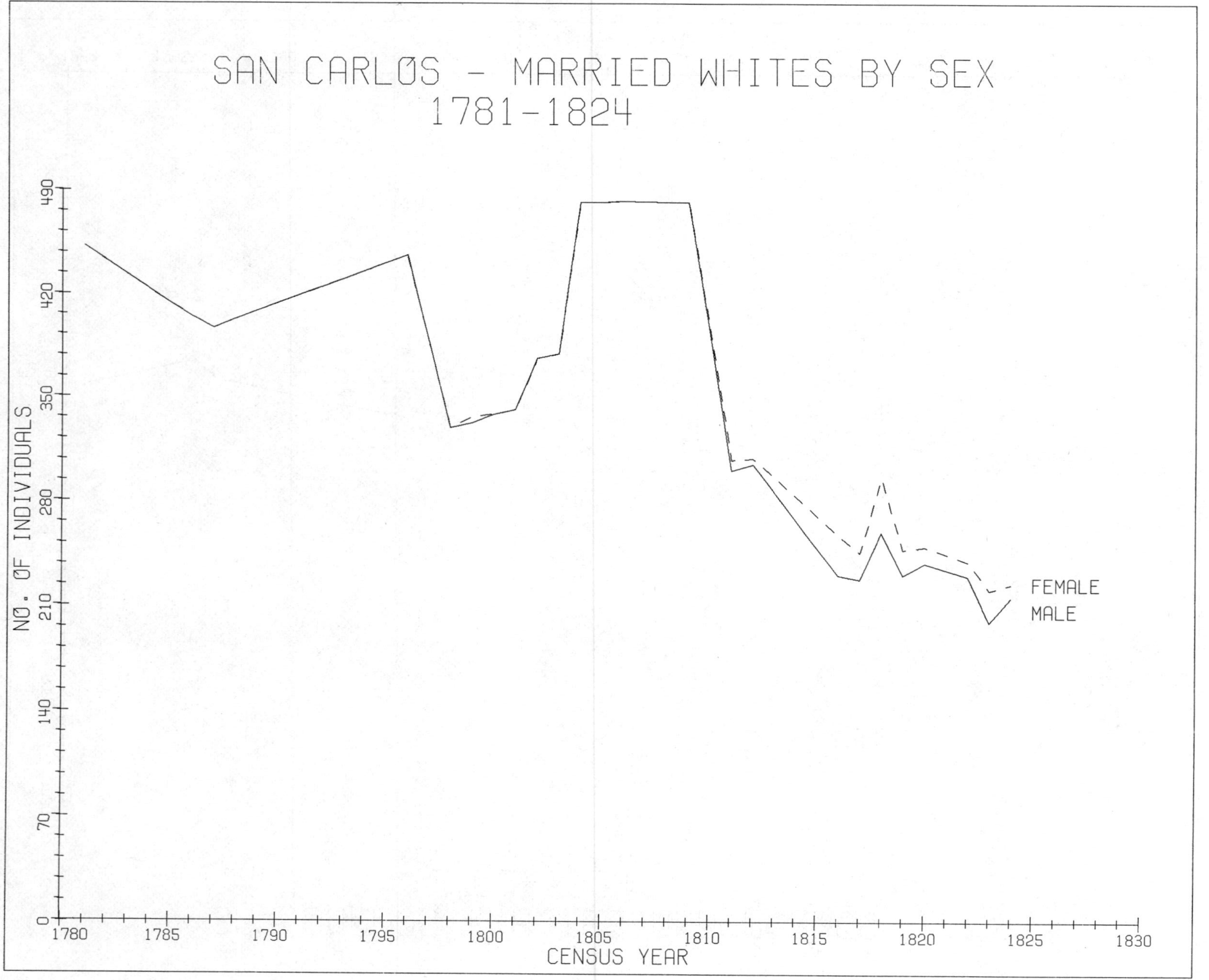
SAN CARLØS - MARRIED WHITES BY SEX
1781-1824
FEMALE
MALE
NØ. ØF INDIVIDUALS
0
70
140
210
280
350
420
490
CENSUS YEAR
1780
1785
1790
1795
1800
1805
1810
1815
1820
1825
1830

Figure 5-4

history in any statistically meaningful sense. Rather, San Carlos' experience provides a useful example of the kind of impact the war experience had on Venezuelan parishes.

In the years preceding the tumult of revolution, San Carlos' population experienced a series of changes of no great magnitude, responding, we may expect, to improvements in economic conditions or difficulties with trade to Europe and the Caribbean. The trend in the population data for this period before 1810 is clearly upward for all racial groups in the city. There also appears to have been relatively little change in the racial composition of the place, with whites, Indians, pardos, Negroes, and slaves all maintaining their shares of total population. This reasonably tranquil state of affairs could not withstand the catastrophic shock of the independence movement and its accompanying warfare (Figures 5-1 and 5-2).

When the war reached San Carlos in the years 1810-1815, the people in the city and the surrounding areas reacted in a way that transformed the population structure for at least a decade. Two important movements dominated the complex trends occurring in San Carlos at the time. The first was the decline in the population of all racial groups except the pardos after 1810. The second was the dramatic increase in the number of pardos between 1811 and 1812 and the decline to levels slightly above the prewar figures after 1812.

Because of the importance of San Carlos as a center of operations in the defense of Caracas and the central valleys against a royalist reconquest, large numbers of troops, mostly pardo, and their officers, mostly white, gathered in the city to prepare the defense and carry out other military maneuvers against the enemy. Unfortunately for the patriot cause, the First Republic was not destined to persevere, and when the royalist troops took San Carlos in the spring of 1812, the republican cause was lost. In spite of the setback, the patriots returned again, this time in the much-praised Campaña Admirable that swept down from the Colombian and Venezuelan Andes, through the San Carlos gateway, and into Caracas. With Caracas once again in patriot hands in the summer of 1813, the republicans attempted to consolidate their gains.

But, as during the First Republic, the patriots underestimated the strength of their opponents. Exploiting the resentments of the black masses, capable Spanish captains began retaking control of towns and villages along the patriot perimeter. Because the war had become less a movement for political independence than an embryonic social revolution, the fury of a war without quarter and without noncombatants drove people from their homes in search of safe havens in the larger towns and the cities. As the royalist armies closed in on the central portion of Venezuela, San Carlos fell in March of 1814, and fugitives and the retiring patriot armies fell back on Caracas and her immediate environs until the end came in July of the same year. With the fall of Caracas imminent, patriots, refugees, soldiers, and frightened citizens fled the city. Some went the easy way, by sea to the eastern part of Venezuela or the Caribbean islands, some trekked overland to the patriot stronghold in Barcelona, and others undoubtedly drifted out from Caracas to lose themselves in the countryside or find their way back to their homes.

In subsequent years, as the patriots rebuilt their armies and began the reconquest of Venezuela from a base in the Eastern Llanos, the population of San Carlos, like that of other cities, fluctuated in response to the fortunes of war and the state of public order in the region. The city recovered some of its 1810-1815 losses during those years, but by the end of the war the city had not regained its pre-independence strength and indeed seemed fixed on a downward trend.[5]

As a consequence of the wars for independence, San Carlos became an urban center overwhelmingly dominated by pardos, Negroes, and slaves. The wave of pardos arriving with the war left behind a substantial residue, while the outflow of whites failed to substantially reverse itself (Figure 5-3).

If these changes appear easy to comprehend as consequences of the independence movement, some of their component parts require somewhat more complex explanations. While definitive statements about the causes and effects of the population changes reflected in

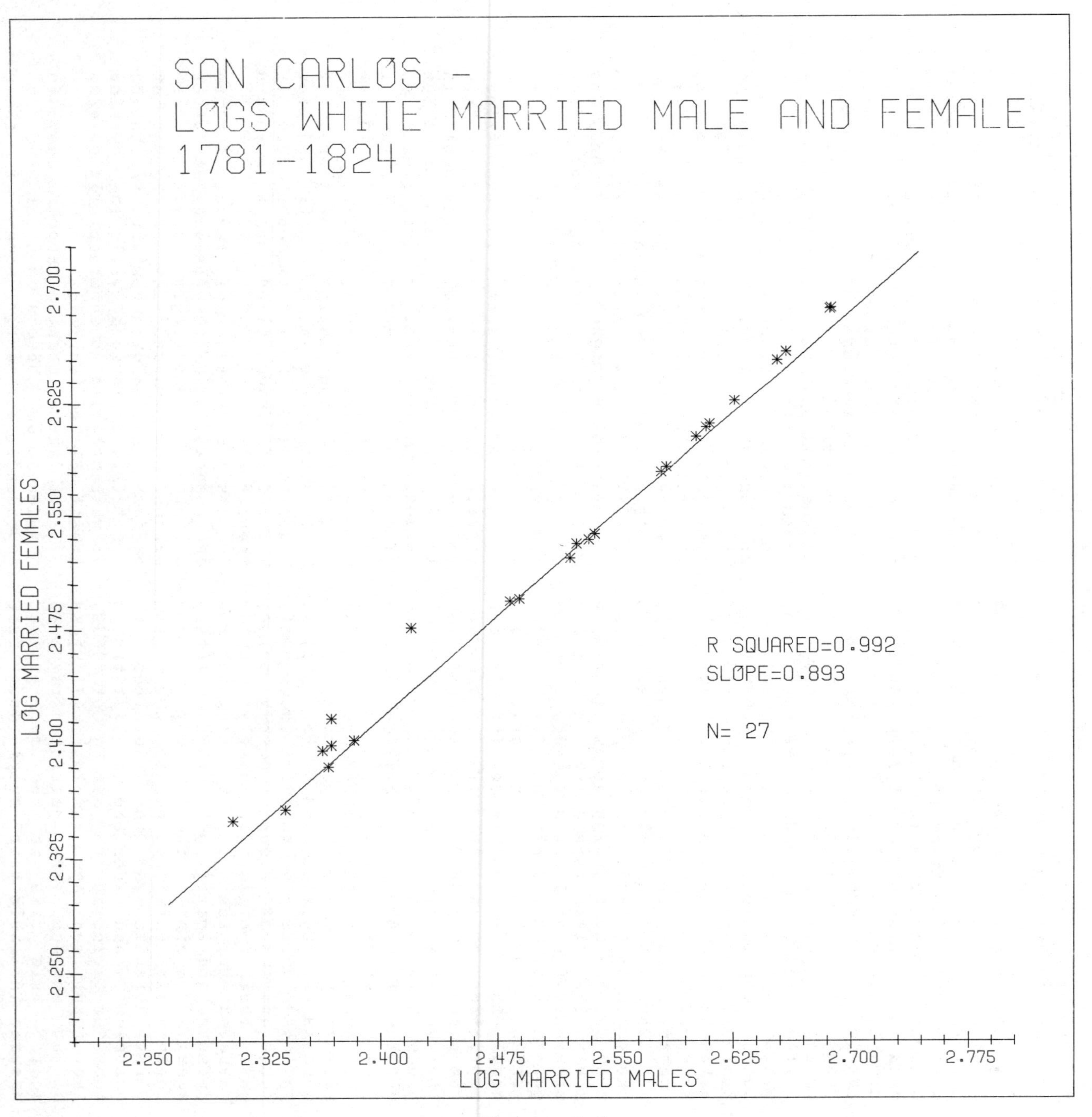
SAN CARLØS -
LØGS WHITE MARRIED MALE AND FEMALE
1781-1824
R SQUARED=0.992
SLØPE=0.893
N= 27
LØG MARRIED FEMALES
2.250
2.325
2.400
2.475
2.550
2.625
2.700
LØG MARRIED MALES
2.250
2.325
2.400
2.475
2.550
2.625
2.700
2.775

Figure 5-5

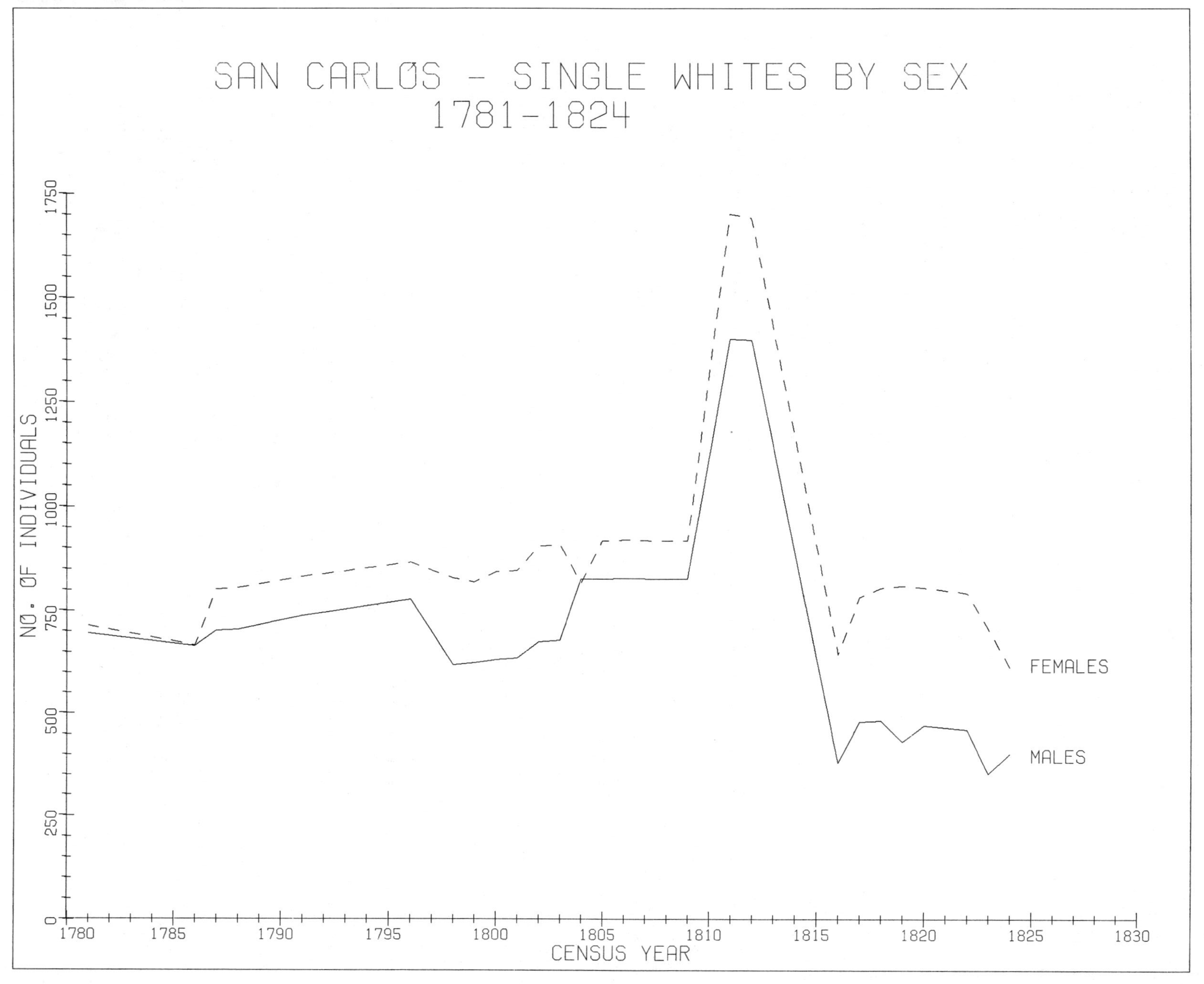
SAN CARLØS - SINGLE WHITES BY SEX
1781-1824
NØ. ØF INDIVIDUALS
0
250
500
750
1000
1250
1500
1750
1780
1785
1790
1795
1800
1805
1810
1815
1820
1825
1830
CENSUS YEAR
FEMALES
MALES

Figure 5-6

the data may elude us, some hypotheses should prove helpful for further investigation.

The striking increase in San Carlos' black population becomes even more impressive when we recognize that practically all the increase came from the pardos, and that Negroes and slaves actually decreased in number at the same time. We can imagine that with the growing intensity of the war and the rumors of the royalists' willingness to recruit slaves, San Carlos' slave owners may have recalled their valuable property from the cattle hinterland and, with their domestics, moved to a safer spot less exposed to confiscation. We can also imagine slaves running off to join guerrilla bands, enlisting in armies, or escaping into the hills or plains. Such explanations gain some support when we note that the loss of slave population between 1809 and 1815 came primarily from the category of single male slaves and secondarily from single female slaves. Before giving too much emphasis to these phenomena, however, we must consider that single male slaves probably were moved about readily by their masters to take advantage of conditions in other places or to work on estates located in other parishes. For example, there was a similar, though not quite so severe, drop in the unmarried male slave population in the late 1790s as well. The unmarried female slaves, while more mobile than their married counterparts, declined less than their unmarried male brethren, most likely because many women in this group worked as domestics and were not as easily moved about.

Married slaves showed somewhat less movement, although the small number of them in San Carlos makes generalizations risky. Still, we might expect married slaves, people with more settled lives and less propensity to wander, to move less than their single counterparts. But before committing ourselves to any theory on slave mobility, it must be emphasized that the data from San Carlos and other cities show an extraordinary amount of population movement in all categories. Only when we realize that the decline in single male slaves amounted to a reduction of three-quarters can we talk about a married male population decline of two-thirds as being less dramatic because it took place less rapidly than the single male decline.

The reduction in Negro population presents some difficult interpretive problems. From our understanding of Venezuela's racial system, no obvious reason for the precipitous decline in Negro population in all categories after 1810 appears. This problem may be more related to the census taker's perceptions of reality than to actual changes in the Negro population. Because the term Negro may have been on the way out as a valid racial label, it is not hard to envision Negroes enlisting or being drafted into the army and being reclassified in the process as pardos, presumably a promotion in the racial scale. Since racial terminology probably extended to the enlistees' families as well, such an explanation helps clarify the trends in the data. Many Negroes may also have fled to other parishes or into the hills and plains to escape participation in the war. Whatever the reasons, Negroes as an identifiable racial group all but disappeared, falling to less than two percent of the population.

Had we any doubts about the total involvement of Venezuela's population in the wars for independence, a survey of the data should eliminate them. In practically every case examined in detail, men and women, married and single, and children of both sexes, were affected by the wars. When large numbers of single pardo men arrived in town, so did large numbers of single women. When married men left, so did the married women. The armies of independence must have moved with large entourages of women and children. Unfortunately, evidence about the functions and composition of these camp followers is hard to find, but it would not be unusual to discover that the women accompanied their husbands or consorts, serving all the functions of a quartermaster corp and medical service.

If the women did indeed move with their men, they evidenced differing degrees of independence in accordance with their race and civil status, as an inspection of the pattern of population movement in San Carlos by sex and civil status indicates. We can measure the degree to which an increase or decrease in population in the white married males, for example, was accompanied by a corresponding change in the equivalent females. In the case of San Carlos, white married adults appear to have migrated at the same rate for both sexes.

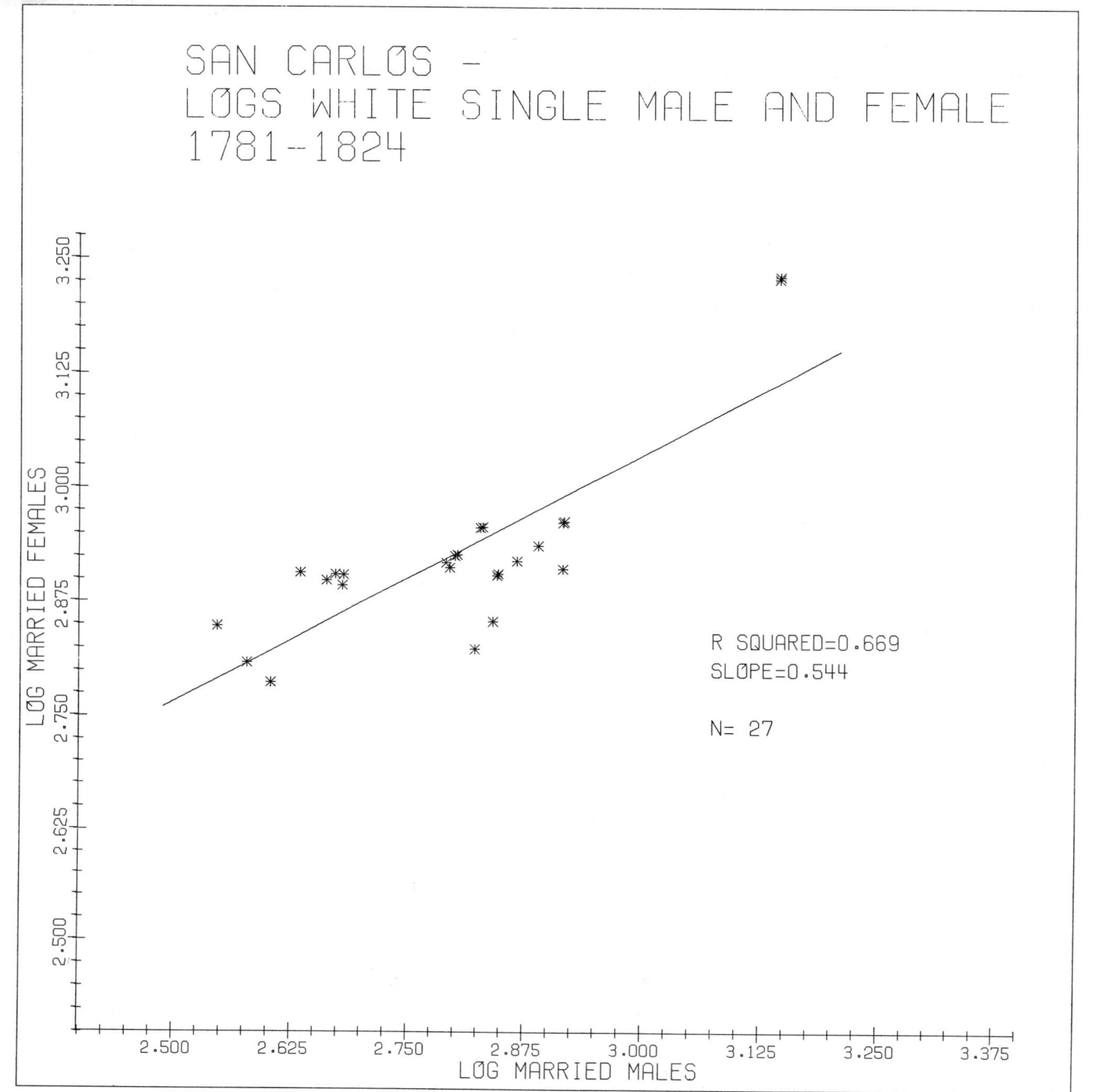

SAN CARLØS -
LØGS WHITE SINGLE MALE AND FEMALE
1781--1824
3.250
3.125
3.000
2.875
2.750
2.625
2.500
LØG MARRIED FEMALES
R SQUARED=0.669
SLØPE=0.544
N= 27
2.500
2.625
2.750
2.875
3.000
3.125
3.250
3.375
LØG MARRIED MALES

Figure 5-7

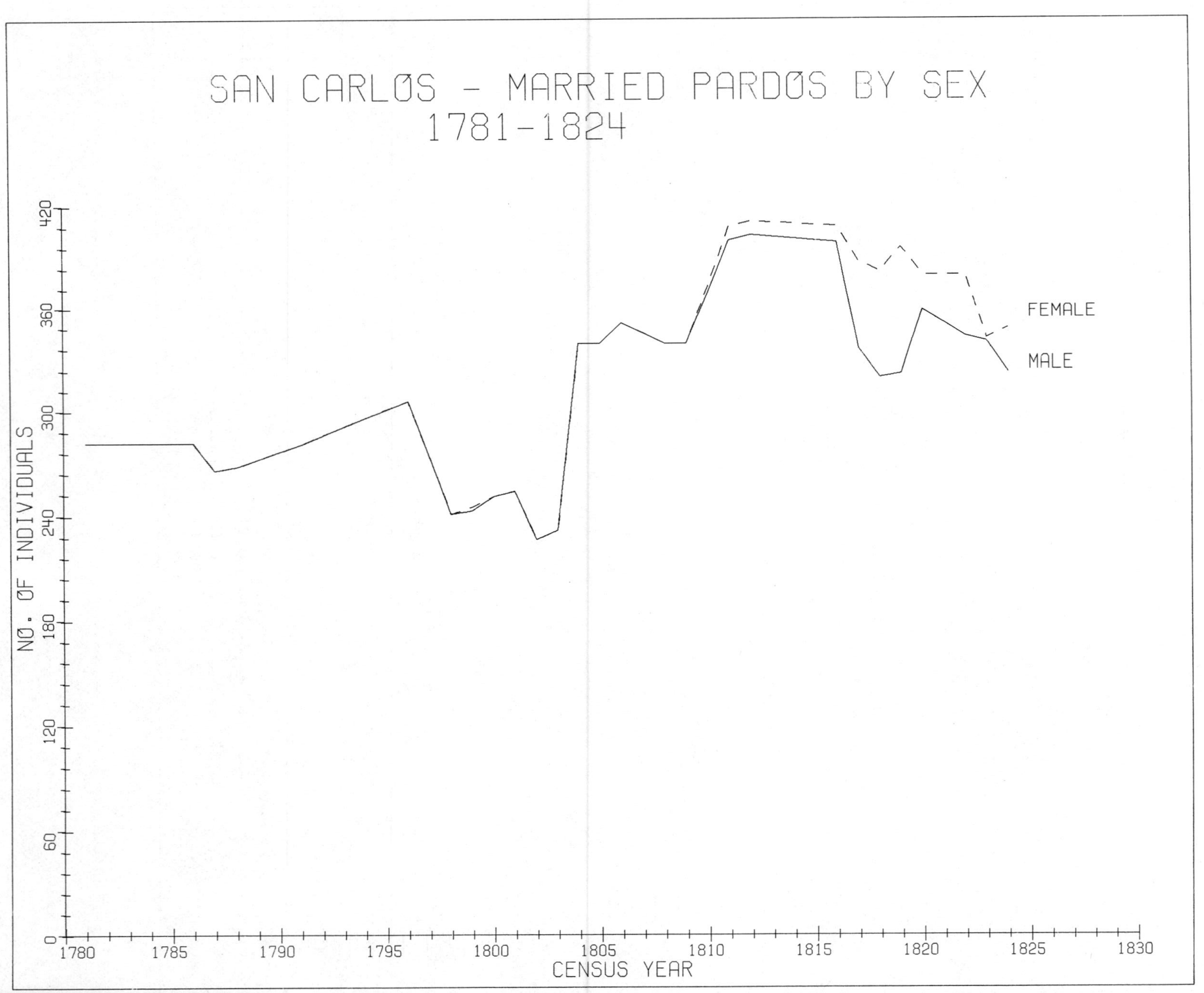
SAN CARLOS - MARRIED PARDOS BY SEX
1781-1824
FEMALE
MALE
NO. OF INDIVIDUALS
0
60
120
180
240
300
360
420
CENSUS YEAR
1780
1785
1790
1795
1800
1805
1810
1815
1820
1825
1830

Not only can we explain almost all of the change in the number of married women by knowing the number of married men, but we can also show that the increase or decrease of say ten men will be accompanied by an almost equal increase or decrease in the number of women[6] (Figures 5-4 and 5-5).

Several conditions may have combined to make this relatively elegant result appear. By and large, whites in the Bishopric of Caracas tended to marry whites, and thus the relationships we are exploring here are not complicated by the possibility of large numbers of white married males not married to white females. Furthermore, we could assume that substantially more whites than members of other racial categories had the economic resources and personal connections to arrange for their wives to move to other areas when they had to leave town for extended campaigns or when conditions in San Carlos looked hazardous. Even taking these things into account, the symmetry of this relationship is remarkable.

A similar relationship prevails among the single white men and women, although to a markedly lesser degree. By knowing the change in the number of white single men in San Carlos, we would only be able to explain two-thirds of the change in the number of white single women. This result should come as no surprise, since we would not expect single women to be attached to single men to the degree married women were attached to their husbands. Moreover, there are quite a few more single women than single men in San Carlos, further reducing, we might suppose, the influence of the men's action on the women. Even though this discussion focuses on single adults, it is important to keep in mind that these adults include people from seven years of age. Individuals between the ages of seven and fifteen might be expected to move with their parents, and their behavior would respond more to the pressures on the married whites than to those on the unmarried (Figures 5-6 and 5-7).

Before considering the performance of the pardo group in this context, some caveats are in order about the assumptions of this discussion. Although in talking about the movement of white adults, I have considered men the independent variable and women the dependent variable, this is not to imply that the causal connection here is absolutely clear. Quite the contrary may have been the case. The purpose of this exploration of the relationship between the changes in the size of San Carlos' male and female populations is to determine if, and to what degree, men and women moved in or out of San Carlos together. The conclusion that they did move together, that is that when men moved out, women moved out too and in about the same number, does not necessarily imply that the men took the women with them, although that may well have occurred, especially in the case of married women and adults between the ages of seven and fifteen. More probable is the assumption that in many cases both men and women responded to the same circumstances, but independently. This situation would have been most likely with single males and females, least likely with married individuals. If we had some way of measuring those forces and then comparing changes in the male or female population, it might be possible to devise a more elegant theory to explain population movement during the wars for independence. Until such information emerges from researches into the social history of those years, we are restricted to the construction of hypotheses based on the trends evident in the data and in the monographs presently available.

Returning to the consideration of the way women and men migrated together during the independence turmoil, it is helpful to compare the performance of the pardos with that of the whites. To a degree almost equal that of the whites, married pardos, male and female, moved together in and out of San Carlos. For every addition or subtraction of a pardo married woman from the city's population, we can find a corresponding change among the pardo men. It is important to observe that most of the movement of married whites was out of the city, while much of the movement of married pardos was in the opposite direction. Likewise, before placing too much emphasis on the similarities between the movement of whites and pardos, it is necessary to evaluate the timing of these movements. In any case, the one sure conclusion that can be offered at this stage is that married pardo men and women showed no less a likelihood to migrate together than did their white counterparts (Figures 5-8 and 5-9).

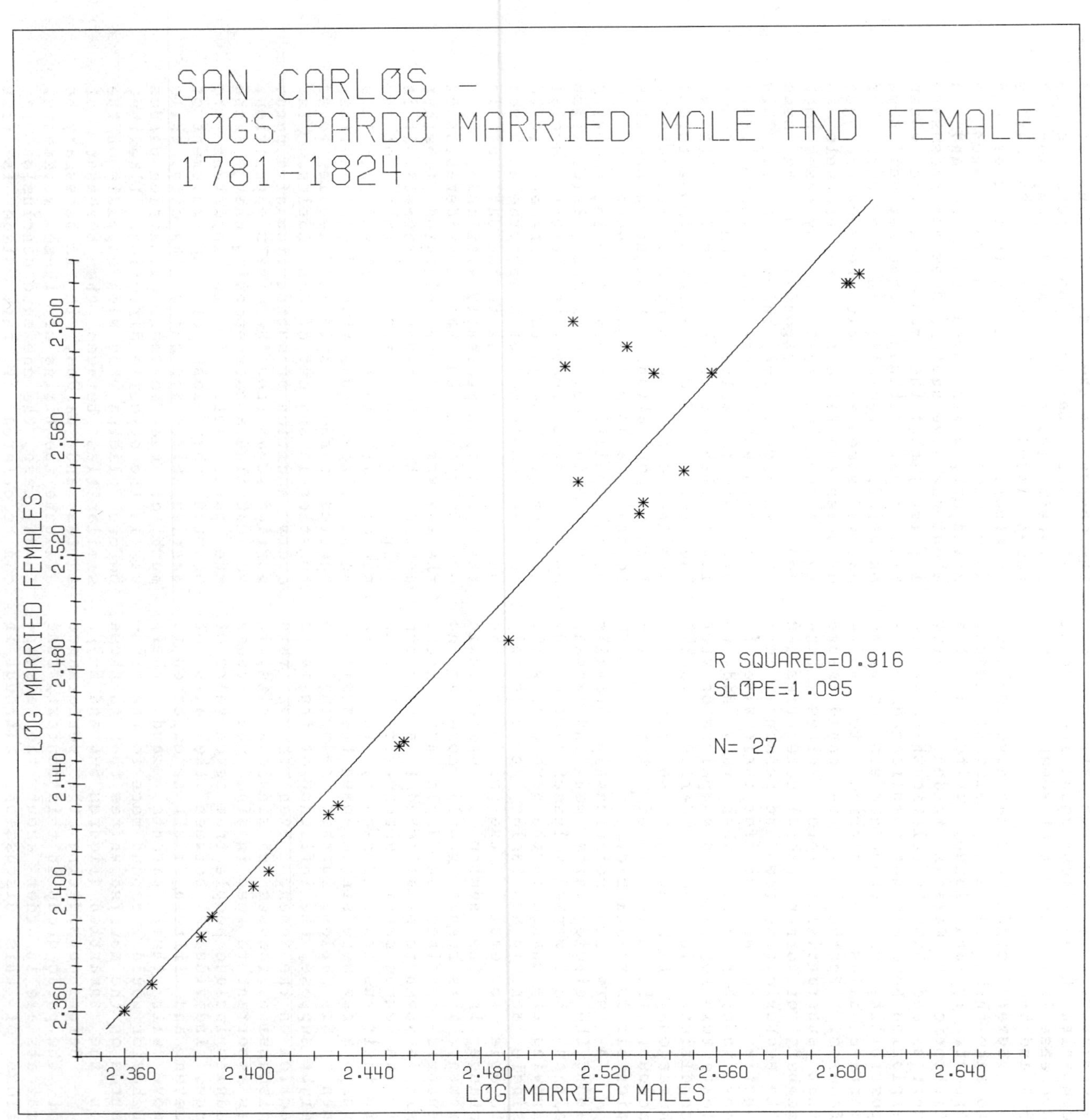

SAN CARLØS -
LØGS PARDØ MARRIED MALE AND FEMALE
1781-1824
R SQUARED=0.916
SLØPE=1.095
N= 27
LØG MARRIED FEMALES
2.360
2.400
2.440
2.480
2.520
2.560
2.600
LØG MARRIED MALES
2.360
2.400
2.440
2.480
2.520
2.560
2.600
2.640

Figure 5-9

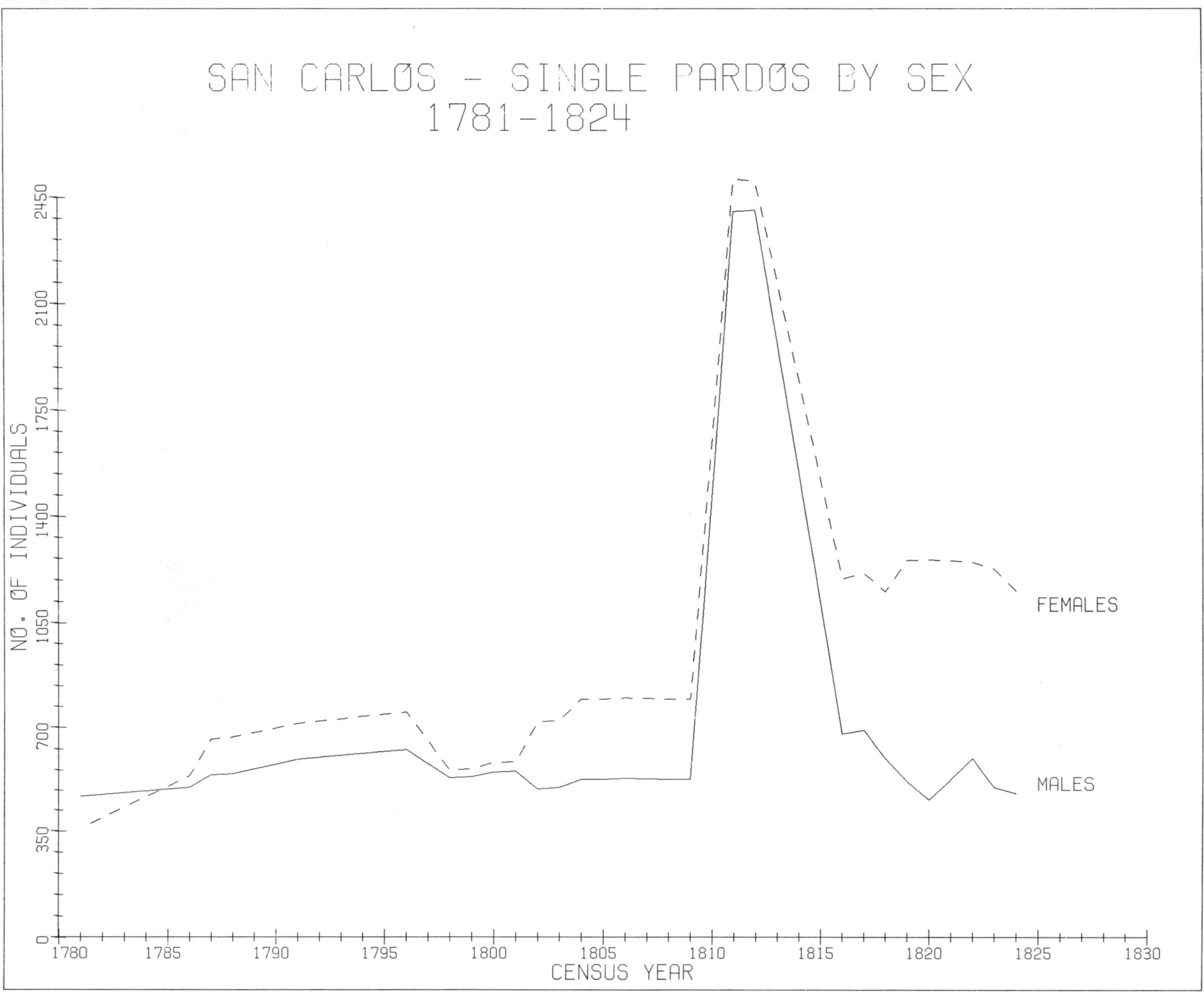
SAN CARLØS - SINGLE PARDØS BY SEX
1781-1824
NØ. ØF INDIVIDUALS
0
350
700
1050
1400
1750
2100
2450
FEMALES
MALES
1780
1785
1790
1795
1800
1805
1810
1815
1820
1825
1830
CENSUS YEAR

Figure 5-10

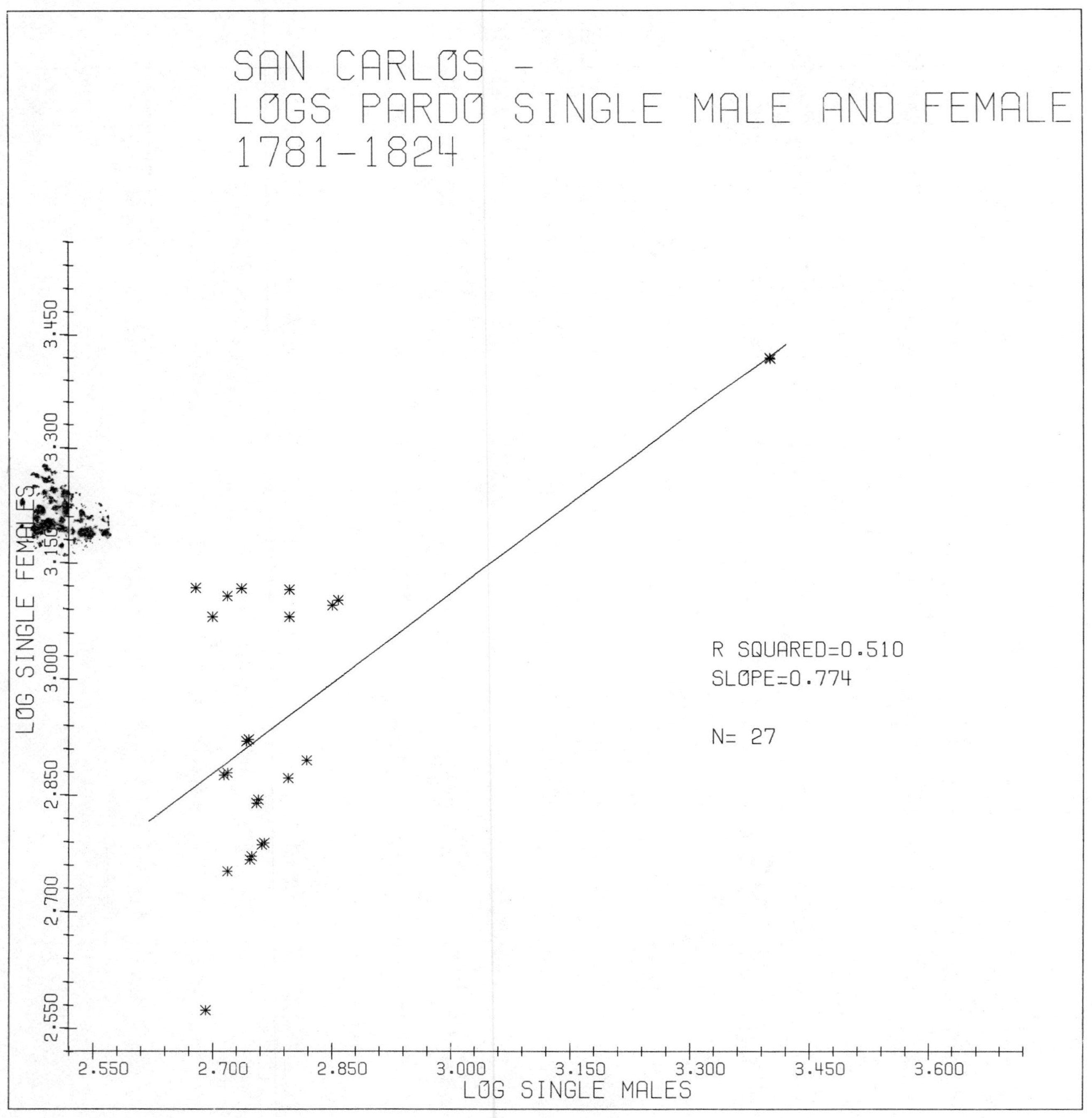
SAN CARLØS -
LØGS PARDØ SINGLE MALE AND FEMALE
1781-1824
R SQUARED=0.510
SLØPE=0.774
N= 27
LØG SINGLE FEMALES
2.550
2.700
2.850
3.000
3.150
3.300
3.450
LØG SINGLE MALES
2.550
2.700
2.850
3.000
3.150
3.300
3.450
3.600

Figure 5-11

When we turn to the single pardos, the situation changes, and the men and women appear to have reacted somewhat differently to the changing circumstances in the San Carlos area. Both men and women came into San Carlos in large numbers in 1810-1812. And both men and women left the city in large numbers before mid-1815. But a significant number of single pardo women stayed on when their male counterparts moved out (Figures 5-10 and 5-11).

Any reasonably imaginative historian can devise a series of hypothetical explanations or alternative stories that fit the data and help clarify the history of Venezuelan independence. One of these stories for San Carlos might go something like this.

Imagine San Carlos de Austria, a prosperous place living on the returns from commerce and a trade based on cattle, hides, beef, mules, and horses, a city of nine to twelve thousand souls serving as the exchange point between the urban centers of the Segovia Highlands and those of the central mountains and valleys, as well as for the less populated plains hinterland. With the coming of independence talk in 1810 and the declaration of independence in 1811, San Carlos, like so many other Venezuelan cities, became caught up in the drama of a political movement whose cost and consequences few people imagined. The city had a representative in Caracas participating in the deliberations of the First Republic, and although San Carlos could certainly be considered a patriot town, its representative demonstrated a reluctance to acquiese in the caraqueño assumption of leadership, a position relatively common among the representatives of Venezuela's major towns and cities.

San Carlos' strategic location quickly made the city a prime concentration point for the patriot forces operating outward from Caracas in the effort to contain the royalist opposition to independence prevalent in the towns of the Segovia Highlands, and especially in Coro and Maracaibo. Large numbers of troops poured into the city, bringing with them a train of women and children, camp followers who took up residence in the parish of San Carlos for a number of years. This army, recruited and dragooned from among the pardos and Negroes of the central valleys and mountains and the plains around San Carlos, followed its white officers partly out of fear of punishment for insubordination and partly in hopes of acquiring some of the spoils of war. The arrival of this horde of newcomers drastically shifted the balance of San Carlos' racial mixture, for while more whites now lived in the parish, they had been buried in an avalanche of pardos. Because pro-independence and royalist propaganda disturbed the countryside, and because the war disrupted normal activity in the ranches and farms in the surrounding area, many people from smaller towns around San Carlos and from isolated haciendas or hatos in the Llanos came into the city in search of some stability. This refugee group grew rapidly larger as guerrilla bands began raiding from strongholds in the rural areas, threatening life and property in the name of King or country. Official depredations also increased as the patriot armies foraged for the food and supplies necessary to maintain their faltering cause.

After the fall of the First Republic, the ebb and flow of soldiers, hangers-on, and refugees continued through the next years. San Carlos witnessed the famous Campaña Admirable when Bolívar swept through on his way to Caracas, and the city suffered all the ravages of war as the royalists pushed in on Caracas from east, west, and south. As a major entryway into the central region, San Carlos collected her share of refugees, people fleeing the increasingly violent and destructive contending armies. As the patriots drew back towards the center, their armies collected sizeable groups of fugitives, and as each city fell to the royalists, the retreating army carried with it new accretions of the homeless and frightened.

With the collapse of the patriots' second attempt to hold the country, San Carlos, like other Venezuelan cities, remained embattled and damaged, although hardly destroyed. Gone were the soldiers and their officers, gone were substantial portions of the colonial white elite, but in their place remained a considerable number of pardos, especially single women, who chose to remain in the city rather than follow the exodus to Caracas in 1814. As the main theater of the war moved to other parts of Venezuela and the continent, until Bolívar stayed in the city en route to the major triumph at Carabobo in 1821, San Carlos, now a city with its pardo population much increased and its white elite much reduced, began the process of restabilization, although her population still showed a tendency to decline.

Such, then, is one story for the history of San Carlos. It is not, of course, the only one possible, but it does reflect what we know about the wars for independence and the population history of San Carlos. Further research may change details, fill in the gaps, or require us to develop alternative hypotheses, but this version gives us a place to start.

Conclusion

During the last half-century before independence, Venezuela experienced a series of dramatic changes in her political organization, her economic base, and her population structure. These transformations, symbolized by the emergence of Caracas as a primate or central city and the creation of the Captaincy-General of Venezuela, brought the colony into what would prove to be a short-lived colonial maturity. By virtue of circumstance and accident, this region of Spanish America found itself the major participant in a continental struggle for independence. Furnishing men, materials, and leadership for a war lasting over a decade, Venezuela emerged at the end with her resources depleted, her population patterns disrupted, and her elite reduced. From a dynamic, prosperous segment of Spain's colonial empire, Venezuela became an impoverished, peripheral member of a North Atlantic commercial empire. Not until the time of Antonio Guzmán Blanco in the late nineteenth century, or even until the emergence of Venezuela as a major supplier cf petroleum in the 1930s, did the country regain its relative position within the Spanish American context.

The preceding chapters have given us a picture of Venezuela's population before the wars. The population base line displayed here represents the Bishopric of Caracas at the peak of its colonial development. And of course it is this fortuitous location in time that gives the analysis its special utility for the study of Venezuela's transitional century.

Although the preliminary nature of this book makes the projection of trends and the elaboration of conclusions difficult, some characteristics of Venezuela's pre-independence population appear relatively well established. For example, the analysis shows the value of structuring the study of Venezuela's population in terms of a regional geographic classification. Although at its present stage of development the population file will not support analyses at the level of subregions, or sub-subregions, the main divisions of the country--the Coast, the Segovia Highlands, the Coastal Range, the Llanos, and the Andes--have proved their usefulness as analytical categories. It must be stressed that the emphasis placed on a relatively detailed geographic framework for this study does not imply any geographically deterministic view of history. Rather, it emphasizes the conviction that if the geographic variable is not the determining one in the historical equation, it is certainly one of the most heavily weighted variables in an analysis of population history.

From the perspective of this book, and within the confines of the Bishopric of Caracas, two monuments to the maturity of Spain's Venezuelan colony and to the dynamism of that colony's last decade stand out. In the first instance, the complex population record system maintained by the Bishopric, from which the material for this book comes, symbolizes the highly developed self-consciousness attained by the colony and the sophistication and spirit of its ecclesiastical bureaucracy. It is certainly no accident that the aggregate standardized censuses began in 1777 and that the best period of collection occurred in the decade 1800-1809. Of course the initiative to prepare the data came from Spain, but the ability of the Bishopric to respond so quickly, so thoroughly, and so well to the directive indicates the recently achieved maturity of the area's institutions. In the traditional centers of colonial power and wealth, the bureaucracies had little of Venezuela's vigor and efficiency. Their size, scale, and age prevented the viceroyalties of Mexico and Peru from generating the kind of complete, standardized, and continuous series available for Venezuela.

In the second instance, the stabilized and fully-developed urban network of the Bishopric of Caracas demonstrates in a concrete, tangible way the proposition that the period 1800-1809 marks a major juncture in Venezuelan history. The hamlets, villages, towns, and cities identified, located, and described in this book constitute an interconnecting urban system so satisfactory that the basic form and organization of that system survived virtually unchanged until the petroleum boom of the 1930s. It is particularly important to emphasize that this urban network acquired its stable, fully-developed form only during the last quarter of the eighteenth century, and that the definitive orientation of the urban system towards the central city of Caracas came as a result of the economic, political, social, and ecclesiastical consolidation of authority in that city at the end of the colonial period.

In following the patterns discovered by the study of race, sex, marriage, and children within the Bishopric of Caracas, the value of an urban-regional framework has been made apparent. The behavior of Venezuela's people as reflected in the data on population characteristics shows a range of variations by region and urban category. And although these two major dimensions of the study hardly exhaust the variables that need to be examined, they do provide a solid base for further analysis.

If the emphasis of this book has been upon the verification and analysis of the urban-regional matrix, that has not been to minimize the rapidly changing characteristics of many component parts of the matrix. The micro-study of San Carlos de Austria illustrates in a dramatic way the frequent and large-scale movement of people in and out of the urban centers. This phenomenon of high population mobility was of course greatly exaggerated by the turmoil of the wars for independence. Even during times of relative peace and prosperity, however, large numbers of Venezuelans appeared ready to move from one parish to another and as a result of these movements the parishes must have experienced the rapid turnover of a significant proportion of their populations.

By identifying and analyzing some of the key characteristics of Venezuela's colonial population, this book has raised more questions than it has answered. And that is all to the good. In subsequent volumes, many of the topics outlined in this one will be explored in depth with the added information provided by the rest of the aggregated census returns from the Bishopric of Caracas. In this continuing inquiry, the next area of interest will be an exploration of the magnitude, direction, timing, composition, and causes of the constant movement of people throughout the Venezuelan urban network.

NOTES

Notes to Introduction

1. Perhaps the best way to survey this rich and extensive literature is through the exceptionally useful bibliographical essay in Charles GIBSON's outstanding survey Spain in America (New York: Harper and Row, 1966). The best guide to the field is, of course, Charles C. GRIFFIN's Latin America: A Guide to the Historical Literature (Austin: University of Texas Press, 1971).

2. Examples of these distinctions are numerous. On the rules governing empires see, for example, Clarence H. HARING, The Spanish Empire in America (New York: Oxford University Press, 1947) or Ernst SCHAEFER, El consejo real y supremo de las Indias; su historia, organización y labor administrativo hasta la terminación de la casa de Austria, 2 vols. (Seville: Imprenta M. Carmona, 1935-47). For an example of the micro approach to families, see Stephanie B. BLANK, "Patrons, Clients, and Kin in Seventeenth-Century Caracas: A Methodological Essay in Colonial Spanish American Social History," Hispanic American Historical Review 54 (1974), 260-283. On the organization of imperial commerce, see, for example, Huguette and Pierre CHAUNU, Seville et l'Atlantique, 1504-1650, 8 vols. in 9 (Paris: A. Colin, 1955-59) and for a micro-level study, see William B. TAYLOR, Landlord and Peasant in Colonial Oaxaca (Stanford: Stanford University Press, 1972). An excellent perspective on this progression of research can be seen in Charles Gibson, "Writings on Colonial Mexico," Hispanic American Historical Review 55 (1975), 287-323. For a survey of some methodological trends in Latin American history, see the essays in Richard GRAHAM and Peter H. SMITH, eds., New Approaches to Latin American History (Austin: University of Texas Press, 1974).

3. One of the major contributions to the history of material culture is, of course, the extraordinarily influential work by Fernand BRAUDEL published in English as Capitalism and Material Life, 1400-1800, trans. Mirian Kochan (New York: Harper and Row, 1973). For a more elaborate statement of Venezuela's position within the North Atlantic hegemony, see John V. LOMBARDI, "Patterns of Venezuela's Past" in John D. MARTZ and David J. MYERS, Venezuela: Is Democracy Institutionalized? (forthcoming). The notion of dependency used here is derived from the excellent discussion in Immanuel WALLERSTEIN, "The Rise and Future Demise of the World Capitalist System. Concepts for Comparative Analysis," Comparative Studies in Society and History 16 (1974), 387-415, and from the provocative study by Stanley J. STEIN and Barbara H. STEIN, The Colonial Heritage of Latin America: Essays on Economic Dependence in Perspective (New York: Oxford University Press, 1970). A survey of the materials available on Venezuela's century of transition is included in the notes to the following chapters. See also John V. LOMBARDI et. al., A Comprehensive Working Bibliography of Venezuelan History (New York: G.K. Hall, forthcoming) for a listing of the major items of interest on Venezuelan history since discovery.

Notes to Chapter 1.

1. The literature on Venezuelan geography is extensive. In these notes, it will only be possible to include some of the important items and more representative pieces from the literature. However, with few exceptions, the books and articles fall into three major categories. First are the contemporary colonial accounts and descriptions that emphasize geographical features. For the most part, these refer to specific regions and will be cited in the sections referring to those regions. The second group includes the works of modern historians and geographers who have approached Venezuela's landscape with a historical perspective. Frequently these works can be classified as ephemeral publications, exegeses on colonial observers, or ceremonial publications honoring the anniversary of town foundations. Even though the value of many of these works can only be described as relative, it is dangerous to ignore them, because buried among the glass and glitter lie a few true jewels of scholarship. Unfortunately, many publications in this category prove extremely difficult to locate, since they are issued by municipal councils and distributed within a small circle. The majority of such items refer to town foundings, a topic of inexhaustible interest. In the course of this chapter, I will have occasion to refer to some of the best and also some of the typical pieces of this genre. Finally, in the third group are those elegant and technically sophisticated geographical works relating to modern petroleum Venezuela. Although some of these have a rather short historical perspective, they have been invaluable aids in the development of the geographic view shown here. The most useful items will appear later on in the notes. Although a few works on Venezuela in time and space may not fit easily into any of these categories, the extraordinary and unusual will be mentioned.

2. Before deciding to adopt the boundaries of these regions, I had the benefit of a long series of studies of Venezuelan regional development. The following items were of particular importance for the regional divisions eventually chosen, and also of considerable assistance in the development of the individual regional descriptions. Pablo VILA, _Geografía de Venezuela_, 2 vols. (Caracas: Ministerio de Educación, Dirección de Cultura y Bellas Artes, 1960-1965), Vol. 1: _El territorio nacional y su ambiente físico_, serves as the starting point for any inquiry into Venezuela's historical geography. Marco Aurelio VILA and Juan J. PERICCHI L., _Zonificación geoeconómica de Venezuela_, 4 vols. (Caracas: Corporación Venezolana de Fomento, 1968) is one of those exceptional works of modern economic geography thoroughly imbued with a historical perspective. Its maps are excellent. Also helpful are Pablo PERALES FRIGOLS, _Manual de geografía económica de Venezuela_, 2d ed. (Caracas: Ediciones EDIME, 1960); Luis Fernando CHAVES, _Geografía agraria de Venezuela_ (Caracas: Universidad Central de Venezuela, Ediciones de la Biblioteca, 1963); and Preston E. JAMES, _Latin America_, 3d ed. (New York: Odessy Press, 1959). One of the most helpful contemporary descriptions of Venezuela's geography is in Joseph Luis de CISNEROS, _Descripción exacta de la provincia de Benezuela, Reproducción de las ediciones de Valencia (1764) y Madrid (1912) con introducción de Enrique Bernardo Núñez_, Biblioteca de Geografía y Historia, Serie Alejandro de Humboldt (Caracas: Editorial Avila Gráfica, 1950). No listing of works on Venezuelan geography would be complete without mention of the extraordinary state by state geographic surveys carried out by Marco Aurelio VILA. Although focused on the economic and human geography of the period since 1930, these volumes help clarify many points of historical interest. Published by the Corporación Venezolana de Fomento in Caracas between 1952 and 1967, in their series Monografías económicas estatales, the following volumes were consulted for this book: _Aspectos geográficos del estado..._ _Anzoátegui_ (1953), _Portuguesa_ (1954), _Sucre_ (1965), _Guárico_ (1965), _Aragua_ (1966), _Carabobo_ (1966), _Yaracuy_ (1966), _Trujillo_ (1966), _Miranda_ (1967), and _Mérida_ (1967); and _Aspectos geográficos... del Zulia_ (1952), _del Táchira_ (1957), _del Distrito Federal_ (1967). In the end, I decided to follow the regional divisions described in the _Atlas de Venezuela_, published by the Ministerio de Obras Públicas, Dirección de Cartografía Nacional, of the

Venezuelan Government (Caracas, 1971), pp. 123-124.

3. The fascination that the Orinoco river system held for all the travelers, missionaries, and explorers of the colonial period is well documented in missionary accounts and naturalists' reports. Most of these can be seen in the items cited below for Guayana, but for a survey of the early efforts to enter the Delta and open up the interior, see José Antonio DE ARMAS CHITTY, _Caracas: Origen y trayectoria de una ciudad_, 2 vols. (Caracas: Fundación Creole, 1967), pp. 21-22. For a contemporary explanation of the difficulties presented by the Delta as an entry point to the mainland, see the relación geográfica of Martín LOPEZ, "Memoria y relación de las tierras que he andado por la Costa Arriba desde la Isla de Margarita hasta el Río Curetin, que es cerca del Marañón, desde el año de 1550,...," in Antonio ARELLANO MORENO, comp., _Relaciones geográficas de Venezuela_, Biblioteca de la Academia Nacional de la Historia, no. 70 (Caracas, 1964), pp. 45-49. At the other end of the period, the Baron von Humboldt eloquently described this magnificent delta and its magical river, the Orinoco, in Alexander von HUMBOLDT, _Viaje a las regiones equinocciales del nuevo continente hecho en 1799, 1800, 1801, 1802, 1803 y 1804_, trans. Lisandro Alvarado, Biblioteca Venezolana de Cultura, Colección "Viajes y naturaleza," 2d ed., 5 vols. (Caracas: Ediciones del Ministerio de Educación, Dirección de Cultura y Bellas Artes, 1956).

4. In addition to the geographic studies cited in the notes above, the sources for the physical descriptions in this book were reinforced by visits to all the regions of the Bishopric of Caracas. Considerable descriptive information is also available on the area around Cumana and Barcelona. For a survey of the settlement and development of the pearl fisheries, the industry that provided the economic motive for the population of this region in the early years, see Jerónimo MARTINEZ MENDOZA, _Venezuela colonial. Investigaciones y noticias para el conocimiento de su historia_ (Caracas: Editorial Arte, 1965). For contemporary accounts from the sixteenth century through the end of the eighteenth, the relaciones geograficas give a number of helpful reports. See for example the following selections from ARELLANO MORENO, _Relaciones geográficas_. Juan de SALAS, "Relación que yo,..., hice y descubrí en la Isla Margarita... (1560s)," pp. 53-56; Rodrigo de NAVARRETE and Antonio BARBUDO, "Relación de las provincias y naciones de los indios llamados aruacas y memoria de Antonio Barbudo sobre los territorios costaneros (1570-1575)," pp. 83-94; and Lope de las VARILLAS, "Relación que hizo..., de la conquista y población de Nueva Córdoba, año 1569," pp. 65-80. For the early seventeenth century we have the relación of Diego SUAREZ DE AMAYA, "Carta de don... al Rey, sobre la pesca de perlas; vela de la salina; mudanza de la ciudad de Cumaná y vacante del obispado de Venezuela (1604)," pp. 277-284. The final two relaciones geográficas present an early and a late eighteenth-century perspective on this part of the coast. Jorge de VILLALONGA, "Descripción de la provincia de Cumaná que hizo en 20 de noviembre de 1720 el Virrey de Santafé ... mediante informe de un práctico que la tenía vista y trajinada," pp. 363-367, and "Informe sobre la Nueva Barcelona, año de 1796," pp. 477-493. Although Trinidad maintained a close relationship with Venezuela throughout most of the colonial period, the island does not fall within the scope of this study. For a good account of Spanish Trinidad and its relationships with the imperial Spanish structure and the colony of Venezuela, see Jesse A. NOEL, _Trinidad, Provincia de Venezuela. Historia de la administración española de Trinidad_, Biblioteca de la Academia Nacional de la Historia, no. 109 (Caracas, 1972).

5. The literature on the Venezuelan missions is extensive, but most of the major items will be cited below. For exceptionally perceptive studies of Tucupido and Zaraza, see the two works by José Antonio DE ARMAS CHITTY, _Tucupido. Formación de un pueblo del llano_ (Caracas: Instituto de Antropología e Historia, Facultad de Humanidades y Educación, Universidad Central de Venezuela, 1961), and _Zaraza. Biografía de un pueblo_ (Caracas: Editorial Avila Gráfica, 1949).

6. Naturally, the early settlers worried much about the possibilities for a major

port along the sweep of coast between Coro and the Unare Basin. But the combination of harsh topography and hostile Indians delayed the establishment of the region's port structure for at least a generation. The following items from ARELLANO MORENO'S _Relaciones geográficas_ proved helpful for the sixteenth century. "Relación de Venezuela (1530 or 1555)," pp. 59-62; Miguel Jerónimo BALLESTEROS, "Carta del obispo de Coro Don... al Rey de España, dándole cuenta de haber tomado posesión de su Mitra, y de como encontró su obispado en 20 octubre de 1550," pp. 15-41; NAVARRETE and BARBUDO, "Relación... (1570-1575)," pp. 83-94; Juan LOPEZ DE VELAZCO, "Corografía de la Gobernación de Venezuela y (de la) Nueva Andalucía, (años de) 1571-1574, por...," pp. 97-109; Diego RUIZ DE VALLEJO, "Carta de... sobre navíos, muerte del Opispo Agreda, frailes doctrineros, puertos, penas de cámara, minas y otros asuntos, 1580," pp. 215-219; Juan Manuel MARTINEZ DE MANZANILLO, "Relación de la Provincia de Venezuela, que envía el Obispo de Coro, año de 1581," pp. 223-231; Diego GIBAJA, "Relación geográfica firmada por...," pp. 287-301. These can be supplemented by two contemporary histories, Pedro de AGUADO, _Recopilación historial de Venezuela_, Biblioteca de la Academia Nacional de la Historia, nos. 62-63, 2 vols. (Caracas, 1963) and José de OVIEDO Y BANOS, _Historia de la conquista y población de la Provincia de Venezuela. Reproducción facsimilar de la edición hecha por Domingo Navas Spínola, en Caracas, 1824_ (Caracas, 1967). An excellent modern account of the coastal settlements can be found in Pablo VILA, _Geografía de Venezuela_, Vol. 1. For a fascinating case study of Puerto Cabello, see the collection of documents from 1729 to 1818 in Manuel PINTO C. and José Guillermo CARILLO, eds., _Proceso de la formación de Puerto Cabello (Documentos)_ (Caracas: Banco del Caribe, 1973).

7. The Maracaibo Basin at the western edge of Venezuela attracted as much interest and inspired similar visions of prosperity and wealth as the Orinoco and Delta on the eastern edge of the territory. Because Lake Maracaibo provided both an entry for pirates and an exit for contraband, colonial administrators often had to explain the geography of the basin to their superiors. A series of reports from the middle of the sixteenth century through the end of the eighteenth can be found in the _Relaciones geográficas_ of ARELLANO MORENO. See Martín LOPEZ, "Memoria y relación... (1550)," pp. 45-49; Rodrigo de ARGUELLES and Gaspar de PARRAGA, "Descripción de la ciudad de Nueva Zamora, su término y Laguna de Maracaybo... (1579)," pp. 203-212; Gonzalo de PIÑA LUDUENA, "Descripción de la Laguna de Maracaibo... (1596)," pp. 241-244; GIBAJA, "Relación... (1607)," pp. 287-301; Juan PACHECO MALDONADO, "Información del estado en que estaba la ciudad de la Nueva Zamora de Maracaibo al tiempo que el capitán... en ella, año de 1607," pp. 305-314; "Noticias de las provincias de Maracaibo y Barinas de la pacificación, y civilidad política moral de indios en ellas... (1787)," pp. 413-433; and José Domingo RUS, "Sobre la Provincia de Maracaibo,..., del 17 de mayo de 1794," pp. 461-473. For a discussion of the dispute over the date for the foundation of the city of Maracaibo, see the notes to AGUADO, _Recopilación historial_, Vol. 1, pp. 1-110.

8. Like other regions of Venezuela, the Segovia Highlands appear frequently in the relaciones geográficas. See, for example, the following items in ARELLANO MORENO, _Relaciones geográficas_: LOPEZ DE VELAZCO, "Corografía... (1571-1574)," pp. 97-109; NAVARRETE and BARBUDO, "Relación de las provincias... (1570-1575)," pp. 83-94; "Descripción de la ciudad del Tocuyo, año de 1578," pp. 143-160; "Relación geográfica de la Nueva Segovia de Barquisimeto, año de 1579," pp. 173-199; MARTINEZ DE MANZANILLO, "Relación... (1581)," pp. 223-231; GIBAJA, "Relación geográfica... (1607)," pp. 287-301; and "Cuidad de Barquisimeto, año de 1745," pp. 371-383. Both AGUADO, _Recopilación historial_, and OVIEDO Y BAÑOS, _Historia_, talk extensively about the Segovia Highlands, and Pablo VILA also reviews the geography and settlement patterns of the region in _Geografía de Venezuela_, Vol. 1.

9. The bulk of the Andes falls outside the area of the Bishopric of Caracas. Still, the comments of colonial observers preserved in the relaciones geográficas and elsewhere shed much light on the lines of trade and commerce linking the

Andes with the rest of Venezuela. In ARELLANO MORENO, Relaciones geográficas, see the following: "Relación geográfica y descripción de la ciudad de Trujillo, año de 1579," pp. 163-171; LOPEZ DE VELAZCO, "Corografía... (1571-1574)," pp. 97-109; MARTINEZ DE MANZANILLO, "Relación... (1581)," pp. 223-301; and RUS, "Sobre la provincia de Maracaibo... (1794)," pp. 462-473. See also Miguel de SANTIESTEBAN, "Viaje muy puntual y curioso que hace por tierra don... desde Lima hasta Caracas en 1740 y 1741," in Antonio ARELLANO MORENO, comp., Documentos para la historia económica de la época colonial. Viajes e informes, Biblioteca de la Academia Nacional de la Historia, no. 93 (Caracas, 1970), pp. 47-176; and AGUADO, Recopilación historial, Vol. 1, especially the notes by Nectario María. Also helpful is the work by Tulio FEBRES CORDERO, Obras completas, 6 vols. in 7 (Bogotá: Editorial Antares, 1960), Vol. 3, pp. 235-237.

10. Practically every account of Venezuela contains more or less elaborate descriptions of the Coastal Range, especially the Central Coastal Range. For examples of the kind of material available, see the items cited in the previous series of notes to this chapter. The sub-divisions used here come, of course, from those developed in the Atlas de Venezuela, pp. 123-124.

11. The historian par excellence of the Venezuelan Llanos is José Antonio DE ARMAS CHITTY. In addition to his works on Tucupido and Zaraza cited earlier, see his Carabobo (Caracas, 1972) and Historia de la tierra de Monagas, Ediciones Cultura del Estado Monagas, no. 3 (Maturín: Ejecutivo del Estado Monagas, 1956). Also very helpful are the missionary accounts and the histories of missions. See, for example, Father BUENAVENTURA DE CARROCERA, Misión de los Capuchinos en los Llanos de Caracas, Biblioteca de la Academia Nacional de la Historia, nos. 111-113, 3 vols. (Caracas, 1972); Father BUENAVENTURA DE CARROCERA, Los primeros historiadores de las misiones capuchinas en Venezuela, Biblioteca de la Academia Nacional de la Historia, no. 69 (Caracas, 1964); José CASSANI, Historia de la provincia de la compañía de Jesús del Nuevo Reino de Granada en la América, Biblioteca de la Academia Nacional de la Historia, no. 85 (Caracas, 1967), especially the excellent notes and introduction by José del Rey; Lino GOMEZ CANEDO, ed., Las misiones de Píritu. Documentos para su historia, Biblioteca de la Academia Nacional de la Historia, nos. 83-84, 2 vols. (Caracas, 1967); Antonio CAULIN, Historia de la Nueva Andalucía, Biblioteca de la Academia Nacional de la Historia, nos. 81-82, 2 vols. (Caracas, 1966), especially the fine introduction by Pablo Ojer; and Matías RUIZ BLANCO, Conversión de Píritu, Biblioteca de la Academia Nacional de la Historia, no. 78 (Caracas, 1965). All historians of Venezuela's colonial past owe a tremendous debt to the Venezuelan Academia Nacional de la Historia for their extensive collection of colonial documents published during the last decade or so. My own reliance on these works will be readily apparent from these notes. Like the rest of Venezuela's regions, the Llanos received attention from the authors of relaciones geograficas and similar reports. From ARELLANO MORENO's Relaciones geográficas, the following proved useful for the region. GIBAJA, "Relación geográfica... (1607)," pp. 287-301; "Relación geográfica de la ciudad del Espíritu Santo de Guanaguanare en que se describe su situación, producciones, frutos, ganado, encomiendas y encomenderos, etc. (1608)," pp. 317-320; and "Informe sobre la Nueva Barcelona, año de 1796," pp. 477-493.

12. Most of the literature on the Guayana region refers to the missions along the Orinoco and its related river systems. Some of the more interesting items are José GUMILLA, El Orinoco Ilustrado y Defendido, Biblioteca de la Academia Nacional de la Historia, no. 68 (Caracas, 1963), especially the introduction by Demetrio Ramos; José GUMILLA, Escritos varios, Biblioteca de la Academia Nacional de la Historia, no. 94 (Caracas, 1970) and the fine introduction by José del Rey; José del REY, ed., Documentos jesuíticos relativos a la historia de la Compañía de Jesús en Venezuela, Biblioteca de la Academia Nacional de la Historia, no. 79 (Caracas, 1966); Felipe Salvador GILII, Ensayo de Historia americana, trans. Antonio Tovar, Biblioteca de la Academia Nacional de la Historia, nos. 71-73, 3 vols. (Caracas, 1965); and Manuel AGUIRRE ELORRIAGA, La Compañía de Jesús en Venezuela (Caracas:

Editorial Condor, 1941). See also the following accounts in ARELLANO MORENO's Relaciones geográficas: Domingo IBARGUEN Y VERA, "Relación sobre El Dorado y sobre la expedición de Antonio Berrio, año (de) 1597," pp. 247-257; Diego RUIZ MALDONADO, "Viaje por los ríos Casanare, Meta y Orinoco, de Santa Fé de Bogotá a Guayana y Trinidad, Realizado en los años 1638-39," pp. 332-360; Fermín SANSINENEA, "Descripción de la Provincia de Guayana y del Río Orinoco (1770)," pp. 401-410; Francisco FERNANDEZ DE BOVADILLA, "Viaje que hizo don... desde La Guayana al Alto Orinoco, año de 1765," pp. 387-398; and "Descripción corográfico-mixta de la provincia Guayana,... 1788," pp. 437-457.

13. From the legion of books and articles on the process of conquest and settlement of Venezuela, I will only include some of the useful items here. Many of the pieces cited in the notes above refer in all or in part to the long drawn-out process of conquest and settlement. The best overall survey of this complex operation is in Pablo VILA, Geografía de Venezuela, Vol. 2.

14. Accounts of this period exist in various versions. See, for example, Demetrio RAMOS PEREZ, El mito del Dorado. Su génesis y proceso con el discovery de Walter Raleigh y otros papeles doradistas, Biblioteca de la Academia Nacional de la Historia, no. 116 (Caracas, 1973), which gives a convincing explanation of the El Dorado myth as a motive for the tremendous drive of the Spanish explorers of the first generation. Both AGUADO, Recopilación historial, and OVIEDO Y BAÑOS, Historia, discuss in detail the settlement, and Pedro SIMÓN, Noticias historiales de Venezuela, Biblioteca de la Academia Nacional de la Historia, nos. 66-67, 2 vols. (Caracas, 1963) has a blow-by-blow account. For the Welser experiment in Coro, see Juan FRIEDE, Los Welser en la conquista de Venezuela, Grandes Libros Venezolanos (Caracas: Ediciones EDIME, 1961). See, too, José Antonio DE ARMAS CHITTY, Influencia de algunas capitulaciones en la geografía de Venezuela (Caracas: Instituto de Antropología e Historia, Universidad Central de Venezuela, 1967). For a vision of the Spanish activities in the eastern region and the problem of the pearl fisheries, see Enrique OTTE, comp., Cedularios de la monarquía española de Margarita, Nueva Andalucía y Caracas, 1533-1604 (Caracas: Fundación John Boulton, Fundación Eugenio Mendoza y Fundación Shell, 1967). Some especially important essays on the Margarita-Cubagua pearl fisheries can be found in Pablo VILA, Visiones geohistóricas de Venezuela (Caracas: Ediciones del Ministerio de Educación, 1969). See in particular the studies entitled "Las perlas y el agua en los comienzos del poblamiento colonial en Tierra Firme y sus islas," pp. 83-94, and the seven essays in Part 5, "De Margarita la de las perlas," pp. 185-276.

15. Because of El Tocuyo's prominence in the early exploration and settlement, practically all of the accounts cited in previous notes mention the town and discuss its role in the expansion of Spanish control over Venezuela. The nature of the literature on individual towns, and of the elaborate polemics over dates of foundation and principal founders can be seen in some of the following. "Documentos relativos a la fundación de la ciudad de Nirgua," Boletín de la Academia Nacional de la Historia (Caracas) (Boletín ANH.C.) 39 (1956), 99; Mario BRICEÑO PEROZO, Araure en la historia (Caracas: Italgráfica, 1969); and Mario BRICEÑO PEROZO, Documentos para la historia de la fundación de Caracas existentes en el Archivo General de la Nación, Biblioteca Venezolana de Historia, no.7 (Caracas: Archivo General de la Nación, 1969); DE ARMAS CHITTY, Caracas, origen y trayectoria; Brother NECTARIO MARIA, Historia de la conquista y fundación de Caracas (Caracas: Comisión Nacional del Cuatricentenario de la Fundación de Caracas, Comité de Obras Culturales, 1966); Brother NECTARIO MARIA, Los orígenes de Maracaibo, Publicaciones de la Junta Cultural de la Universidad del Zulia, no. 2 (Maracaibo, 1959); Brother NECTARIO MARIA, Historia de la fundación de la Nueva Segovia de Barquisimeto a la luz de los documentos de los archivos de España y de Venezuela, 2d ed. (Madrid: Juan Bravo, 1967); Jerónimo MARTINEZ MENDOZA, "Los orígenes de Barcelona," Boletín ANH.C. 54 (1971), 67-71; Manuel PINTO C., Los primeros vecinos de Caracas, recopilación documental (Caracas: Comisión Nacional del Cuatricentenario de la Fundación de Caracas, Comité de Obras Culturales,

1966); and Demetrio RAMOS PEREZ, La fundación de Caracas y el desarrollo de una fecunda polémica. Cauces jurídico-consuetudinarios de la erección de las ciudades americanas (Caracas: Italgráfica, 1967). And these items only touch the surface of the mountain of material on towns and town-founding in the colonial period. I have reserved items on the mission towns for later on in these notes. For a partial survey of early towns, see Ambrosio PERERA, Historia de la organización de pueblos antiguos de Venezuela: génesis, desarrollo y consolidación de pueblos coloniales de Barquisimeto, El Tocuyo, Carora, San Felipe y Nirgua, 3 vols. in 1 (Madrid, 1964).

16. Venezuela's missionary history is amply documented through the diligent efforts of historians and the ambitious publication program of the Academia Nacional de la Historia. Of course the classic work on the encomienda in Venezuela is Eduardo ARCILA FARIAS, El régimen de la encomienda en Venezuela, 2d ed. (Caracas: Instituto de Investigaciones, Facultad de Economía, Universidad Central de Venezuela, 1966). On the Jesuits, see AGUIRRE ELORRIAGA, La Compañía de Jesús en Venezuela; CASSANI, Historia de la Compañía de Jesús; CAULIN, Historia de la Nueva Andalucía; GUMILLA, El Orinoco Ilustrado; GUMILLA, Escritos varios; and REY, Documentos jesuíticos. For the Capuchin missions, see Father BUENAVENTURA DE CARROCERA, Misión de los Capuchinos en Cumaná, Biblioteca de la Academia Nacional de la Historia, nos. 88-90, 3 vols. (Caracas, 1968); BUENAVENTURA DE CARROCERA, Primeros historiadores; BUENAVENTURA DE CARROCERA, Misión de los capuchinos; Cayetano de CARROCERA, "Lista completa de las poblaciones fundadas por los misioneros capuchinos en el Oriente venezolano (1657-1810)," Boletín ANH.C. 54(1971), 120-123; and Froilán de RIONEGRO, ed., Relaciones de las misiones de los pp. Capuchinos en las antiguas provincias españolas, hoy república de Venezuela, 1650-1817 (Seville: Tipografía Zarzuela, 1918). And for the Franciscans, see Cayetano de CARROCERA, "Memoria sobre la orden franciscana en Venezuela," Boletín Histórico (Caracas) 28(1972), 55-80; and GOMEZ CANEDO, Misiones de Píritu. On the Augustinians, see Fernando CAMPO DEL POZO, Historia documentada de los agustinos en Venezuela durante la época colonial, Biblioteca de la Academia Nacional, no. 91 (Caracas, 1968). Venezuela's network of towns can be seen in the maps accompanying this book, at least for the Bishopric of Caracas. Pablo VILA, Geografía de Venezuela, Vol. 2, has many maps showing missions and towns during the colonial period. See also the few old maps reproduced in the Atlas de Venezuela. For a guide to Venezuelan cartography, see Ivan DRENIKOFF, Mapas antiguos de Venezuela. Grabados e impresos antes de 1800 con la reproducción del primer mapa impreso en Venezuela y de mapas antiguos (Caracas: Ediciones del Congreso de la República, 1971).

17. The boundaries discussed here come from the descriptions available in a variety of sources, most of which are listed in these notes. For notes on the bishops involved in the transfer of the episcopal center from Coro to Caracas, see Nicolás E. NAVARRO, Anales eclesiásticos venezolanos, 2d ed. (Caracas: Tipografía Americana, 1951). For a general summary of the evolution of Venezuela as a territorial unit and a discussion of its gradual concentration around Caracas, see José L. SUCRE REYES, La Capitanía General de Venezuela (Barcelona: Editorial R. M., 1969). For a series of documents relating to the separation of Maracaibo from the jurisdiction of Caracas, both in civil and ecclesiastical terms, see Documentos para la historia colonial de los Andes Venezolanos (siglos XVI al XVIII), Fuentes Históricas, no. 1 (Caracas: Universidad Central de Venezuela, 1957). For a general survey of Spanish colonial government in Venezuela, see Carraciolo PARRA PEREZ, El régimen español en Venezuela. Estudio Histórico, 2d ed. (Madrid: Ediciones Cultura Hispánica, 1964); MARTINEZ MENDOZA, Venezuela colonial; and Federico BRITO FIGUEROA, Historia económica y social de Venezuela. Una estructura para su estudio, 2 vols. (Caracas: Dirección de Cultura, Universidad Central de Venezuela, 1966). A quick introduction to the Church during this period is in Mary WATTERS, A History of the Church in Venezuela, 1810-1830 (Chapel Hill: University of North Carolina Press, 1933). Also useful is Guillermo FIGUERA, ed., Documentos para la historia de la iglesia colonial en

Venezuela, Biblioteca de la Academia Nacional de la Historia, nos. 74-75, 2 vols. (Caracas, 1965). See also Luis Alberto SUCRE, Gobernadores y capitanes generales de Venezuela (Caracas: Litografía y Tipografía del Comercio, 1928).

Notes to Chapter 2.

1. In the preparation of this chapter and, indeed, throughout the entire project, I have been aided, nourished, and encouraged by the wealth of information, the sensible methods, and the breadth of interest displayed in the works of Borah and Cook, especially the two volumes by Woodrow W. BORAH and Sherburne F. COOK, Essays in Population History: Mexico and the Caribbean, 2 vols. (Berkeley: University of California Press, 1971-1974). For a panoramic view of Latin American population history, see Nicolás SANCHEZ ALBORNOZ, The Population of Latin America. A History, trans. W.A.R. Richardson (Berkeley: University of California Press, 1974). Students interested in the wide-ranging literature on Latin American population history would do well to consult the excellent notes and comprehensive bibliographies in BORAH and COOK and SANCHEZ ALBORNOZ, plus the essays in Paul DEPREZ, ed., Population and Economics. Proceedings of Section V (Historical Demography) of the Fourth Congress of the International Economic History Association, Indiana University, Bloomington, Indiana, September 9-14, 1968 (Winnipeg: University of Manitoba Press, 1970), especially BORAH's piece on "The Historical Demography of Latin America. Sources, Techniques, Controversies, Yields," pp. 173-205. Because of the easy availability of these excellent works, no attempt will be made here to include everything pertaining to Latin America's colonial demography. See, too, Enrique FLORESCANO, comp., "Bibliografía de historia demográfica de México (época prehispánica-1910)," Historia mexicana 21(1972), 525-537.

2. Perhaps the most intensive use of Venezuelan parish records, although not strictly for demographic purposes, can be found in two studies by Stephanie B. BLANK: "Social Integration and Social Stability in a Colonial Spanish American City, Caracas (1595-1627)," in Indiana University, Latin American Studies Occasional Papers (Bloomington, 1972), and "Patrons, Clients, and Kin in Seventeenth-Century Caracas. A Methodological Essay in Colonial Spanish American Social History," Hispanic American Historical Review 54(1974), 260-283. Parish records in Venezuela come to

us as a result of the order contained in Diego de BAÑOS Y SOTOMAYOR, Constituciones sinodales del obispado de Venezuela y Santiago de León de Caracas. Hechas en la santa iglesia cathedral de dicha ciudad de Caracas, en el año del Señor de 1687 (Madrid: Joseph Rico, 1761), p. 116. For an example of the kind of material available in the smaller parish archives in Venezuela, see Milagros CONTRERAS DAVILA, "El Archivo parroquial de San Miguel de Cubiro," Boletín histórico (Caracas) 28(1972), 146-164. Lino GOMEZ CANEDO's Los Archivos históricos de Venezuela, Monografías y Ensayos, no. 5 (Maracaibo: Universidad del Zulia, Facultad de Humanidades y Educación, 1966) is of course the fundamental guide to Venezuelan archival sources. For the classic explanation of family reconstitution, see Louis HENRY, Manuel de demographie historique (Geneva: Librairie Droz, 1967). For an excellent discussion of the origins of parish records and a country by country survey, see Elio LODOLINI, "Los libros parroquiales y de estado civil en América Latina," Archivum (Revue Internacionale des Archives) (Paris) 8(1958), 95-113. Also see Claude MORIN, "Los libros parroquiales como fuente para la historia demográfica y social novohispana," Historia mexicana 21(1972), 389-418. For Martí's remarks about the state of parochial archives, see Mariano MARTI, Documentos relativos a su visita pastoral de la Diócesis de Caracas, 1771-1784, Biblioteca de la Academia Nacional de la Historia, nos. 95-101, 7 vols. (Caracas, 1969). One of the better examples of local geneological history is Pedro M. ARCAYA U., Población de origen europeo de Coro en la época colonial, Biblioteca de la Academia Nacional de la Historia, no. 114 (Caracas, 1972).

3. For a wide selection of missionary accounts, see the notes to the previous chapter where the major pieces in this category are mentioned.

4. Most travelers' accounts cluster around the turn of the century and the end of the colonial period, but if we consider many of the Spanish reports by explorers and itinerant officials as part of this category, the chronological spread becomes much wider. The best beginning for any survey of travel literature is María Luisa GANZEMULLER DE BLAY, Contribución a la bibliografía de viajes y exploraciones de Venezuela, Colección de 467 fichas (Caracas: Escuela de Biblioteconomía y Archivos, Facultad de Humanidades y Educación, Universidad Central de Venezuela, 1964). The best known are Alexander von HUMBOLDT, Viaje a las regiones equinocciales del nuevo continente hecho en 1799, 1800, 1801, 1802, 1803, y 1804, trans. Lisandro Alvarado, Biblioteca Venezolana de Cultura, Colección "Viajes y naturaleza," 2d ed., 5 vols. (Caracas: Ediciones del Ministerio de Educación, Dirección de Cultura y Bellas Artes, 1956); and François de PONS, Viaje a la parte oriental de Tierra Firma en la América Meridional, trans. Enrique Planchart, Colección Histórico-Económica Venezolana, vols. 4-5, 2 vols. (Caracas: Banco Central de Venezuela, 1960). All of us who use these classic accounts in translation must be wary of translator's slips, as Germán CARRERA DAMAS has reminded us in "La supuesta empresa antiesclavista del conde de Tovar y la formación del peonaje. Estudio crítico del testimonio de Humboldt," Anuario del Instituto de Antropología e Historia (Caracas: Universidad Central de Venezuela) 2(1965), 67-84.

5. Because the relaciones geográficas have been available to scholars for a good many years, they are a relatively well-known and well-consulted source. For Venezuela, see Angel de ALTOLAQUIRRE Y DUVALE, ed., Relaciones geográficas de la gobernación de Venezuela (1767-68) (Madrid: Patronato de Huérfanos de Administración Militar, 1908) and Antonio ARELLANO MORENO, comp. Relaciones geográficas de Venezuela, Biblioteca de la Academia Nacional de la Historia, no. 70 (Caracas, 1964). Also see Antonio ARELLANO MORENO, "Relación geográfica del valle del Tuy, 1768," Boletín ANH.C. 56(1973), 523-529. For examples of relaciones for other parts of America and an extended discussion of the origins of the reports, see Marcos JIMENEZ DE LA ESPADA, ed., Relaciones geográficas de Indias, 4 vols. (Madrid: Ministerio de Fomento, 1881-1897). The text of the King's order for the relaciones geográficas for Venezuela is in the "Descripción de la ciudad del Tocuyo, año de 1578," in ARELLANO MORENO, Relaciones geográficas, pp. 143-160. Like most other Spanish colonial population data

for Venezuela, the relaciones geográficas cluster in the late sixteenth and late eighteenth centuries. See also Charles GIBSON, comp., _The Spanish Tradition in America_ (New York: Harper and Row, 1968), pp. 136-149, for a translated text of the relaciones instructions.

6. The classification of special government surveys outside the relaciones geográficas covers a heterogeneous but extremely rich group of data. Following are some examples of this kind of information. Data on population can be found in Church documents not related to parish administration, as can be seen in Eduardo ARCILA FARIAS et al., _La obra pía de Chuao 1568-1825_, Comisión de Historia de la Propiedad Territorial Agraria en Venezuela, no. 1 (Caracas: Universidad Central de Venezuela, Consejo de Desarrollo Científico y Humanístico, 1968). Miscellaneous reports from towns or regions are also helpful; see Antonio ARELLANO MORENO, "La población de Caracas, Valencia y Puerto Cabello en 1767," _Boletín ANH.C._ 54(1971), 527-531, and his "El primer informe sobre Santiago León de Caracas," _Boletín ANH.C._ 52(1969), 347-352. For similar reports from government officials, see José María AURRECOECHEA, "Memoria geográfico-económico-política del departamento de Venezuela... (1814)," in ARELLANO MORENO, _Relaciones geográficas_, pp. 533-558; and Luis de CHAVEZ Y MENDOZA, "Mensura y descripción de los pueblos de indios situados en las provincias de Nueva Andalucía y Nueva Barcelona... (1782-84)," in César PEREZ RAMIREZ, comp., _Documentos para la historia colonial de Venezuela_ (Caracas: Editorial Crisol, 1946). For a look at some of the materials generated by the military requirement to know the size of a potential army or by the government's requirements for tribute administration, see "New matrículas ordered to assess tribute and taxes 1794," vol. 5, folios 254-256, Reales Cédulas, Archivo General de la Nación, Caracas; and especially the design for a military-oriented census sent out in 1777, "Procedures for taking a military census, 1777," vol. 19, folio 241, Gobernación y Capitanía General, Archivo General de la Nación, Caracas. Included within this category, although slightly outside the chronological framework of this book, is the exceptional survey of Venezuela conducted by Giovanni Battista Agostino CODAZZI in the mid- to late-1830s and published in _Obras escogidas_, Biblioteca Venezolana de Cultura, 2 vols. (Caracas: Dirección de Cultura y Bellas Artes, Departamento de Publicaciones, 1961) and the earlier survey of the province of Caracas by the Sociedad Económica de Amigos del País, published in their _Memorias y estudios 1829-1839_, Colección Histórico-Económica Venezolana, vols. 1-2, 2 vols. (Caracas: Banco Central de Venezuela, 1958).

7. In addition to Martí's extraordinary visita, other prelates visited Venezuela in the eighteenth century. In his introduction to the edition of Martí's visita records published by the Academia Nacional de la Historia, Lino Gómez Canedo refers to three: Martínez de Oneca, Fray Iñigo Abbad y Lasierra, and Manuel Jiménez Pérez (MARTI, _Documentos_, Vol. 1, xxxix-xl). The account of Fray Iñigo Abbad, _Viage a la América_, has been published in facsimile in Caracas, 1974, by the Banco Nacional de Ahorro y Préstamo. Covering the eastern part of Venezuela, plus Puerto Rico and Trinidad, Fray Iñigo evidently arrived in Cumaná with Bishop Manuel Jiménez Pérez of Puerto Rico in 1773. The _Viage_ contains information similar to that found in Martí, but in less detail. Still, it remains one of the best sources for the population of eastern Venezuela at the end of the eighteenth century. There is no way to encapsulate Martí's accomplishment in the space of a footnote; it will be quite a while before we will have mined the Martí documents for all their treasures. It should be mentioned that the seven volumes of the visita fall into four categories. The first two volumes of this edition include Martí's "Libro personal" with his private comments about a wide variety of subjects related to the parishes visited, including a good collection of gossip. The two volumes of "Inventarios" include only a representative selection and abridgement of the original because of the quantity of material involved. These will be indispensable for the historian of material culture. The "Libro de providencias" records the official measures taken by the Bishop during his visita. And the two volumes of the "Compendio" contain the population data. Although this monumental edition has been prepared with the greatest care, the documents must be used

with some caution because an occasional missing page or broken line is not clearly marked and can lead to erroneous identification of parishes. There is an incomplete, earlier edition of the compendio, Mariano MARTI, Relación y testimonio íntegro de la visita general de este obispado de Caracas y Venezuela hecha por el illmo. Senor d.d.... 1771-1784... que la concluyó en el pueblo de Guarenas..., 3 vols. (Caracas: Editorial Sur-América, 1928-1929). For a catalogue of the archive where Martí's originals are preserved, see Jaime SURIA, Catálogo del Archivo Arquidiocesano de Caracas (Madrid: Escuelas Profesionales "Sagrado Corazón de Jesús," 1964).

8. This discussion of the matrículas is based on an examination of the collection of documents of this type preserved in the Sección Parroquias of the Archivo Arquidiocesano, Caracas, and on an intensive study of the matrículas for the parishes of Caracas carried out during the summer of 1973 under the auspices of the Foreign Area Fellowship Program's Collaborative Research Training Project II on The Historical Demography of Venezuela. The participants in that project carefully worked through the matrículas for four Caracas parishes for the year 1788. Although the results of the study are still in draft form, the experience we acquired in the course of the project has permitted me to develop the discussion in this section. The Project, under the joint direction of Professor Germán Carrera Damas (Universidad Central de Venezuela) and myself (Indiana University) included the following individuals to whom I am grateful for the insights that made these remarks possible. G. Reid Andrews (University of Wisconsin--Madison), Anthony Ginsberg (New York University), and Kathy Waldron and Mary B. Floyd (Indiana University) for the United States, and Víctor Gruber, Antonieta Camacho, Carmen Gómez, José Rafael Lovera, and Lourdes Fierro de Suels (all of the Universidad Central de Venezuela). These matrículas have also been studied by the Joint Oxford-Syracuse Population Project, which proposes to analyze all of the eighteenth-century parish level data available in major Spanish American centers. They have published a preliminary study that in the main confirms the conclusions of the FAFP seminar, and contains a very interesting discussion of census-taking procedures in Caracas. See David J. ROBINSON, The Analysis of Eighteenth Century Spanish American Cities: Some Problems and Alternative Solutions, Discussion Paper Series, Department of Geography (Syracuse: Syracuse University, 1975). For the printed version of a fragmentary matrícula of this type, see Francisco TRIAS, "Padrón de varias casas formado en Caracas en 1806," Boletín ANH.C. 12(1929), 218-222 and 299-309. A more elaborate version of this format, giving ages and occupations along with other information, can be seen in the reproduction of a matrícula taken for Los Angeles in J. Gregg LAYNE, "The First Census of the Los Angeles District. Padrón de la Ciudad de Los Angeles y su Jurisdicción. Año 1836," Southern California Quarterly 18(1936), 81-99 and facsimile pages. For an example of a similar population account system modeled on the matrículas used in Venezuela, see the form cited in Note 6 above in vol. 19, folio 241, Gobernación y Capitanía General, Archivo General de la Nación, Caracas.

9. In understanding the annual censuses available for Venezuela, it is helpful to refer to the comparable data from other Latin American countries and Spain for much the same period. See, for example, Marcello CARMAGNANI and Herbert S. KLEIN, "Demografía histórica. La población del obispado de Santiago 1777-1778," Boletín de la Academia Chilena de la Historia 72(1965), 57-74; Luis LIRA MONTT, "Padrones del Reino de Chile existentes en el Archivo de Indias," Revista de Estudios Históricos (Santiago de Chile) 13(1965), 85-88; Alicia V. TJARKS, "Comparative Demographic Analysis of Texas, 1777-1793," Southwestern Historical Quarterly 77:3(1973-74), 291-338; and Antonio DOMINGUEZ ORTIZ, La sociedad española en el siglo XVIII, Monografías Histórico-sociales, vol. 1 (Madrid: Instituto Balmes de Sociología, Departamento de Historia Social, Consejo Superior de Investigaciones Científicas, 1955). In the sequel to this study, the 1813 and 1807, plus other non-standard formats, will be explored in detail. The most extensive publication of late colonial population data has been produced for the Río de la Plata area. This incredibly rich collection of matrículas, padrones, and other popula-

tion lists and summaries can be seen in "Padrones de la ciudad y campaña de Buenos Aires (1726-1810)," "Padrón de la Cuidad de Buenos Aires (1778)," "Padrón de la campaña de Buenos Aires (1778)," "Padrones complementarios de la ciudad de Buenos Aires (1806, 1807, 1809, y 1810)," and "Censo de la ciudad y campaña de Montevideo (1780)," in Volumes 10, 11 and 12 of Emilio RAVIGNANI, ed., Documentos para la historia argentina, 35 vols. (Buenos Aires: Universidad Nacional de Buenos Aires, Instituto de Investigaciones Históricas, 1913-1974).

10. Most of the information for this discussion comes from the annual, Type III, census returns. The population data from these are categorized and summarized in the tables in Part II of this book. The comments appended to each return have not been coded, mostly because the demographic yield of the remarks proved extremely low. But a study of the notes each parish priest appended to his returns sometimes provides an indirect view of the process of census-taking. The innovative features of the Type III census format are made clear by Martí, who received the royal order in the middle of his visita, and promptly changed his method of recording population totals. See MARTI, Relación y testimonio, Vol. 1, p. 6. The short order that put this admirable census-taking procedure into operation runs as follows: "El Rey quiere saver con puntualidad, y certeza el número de vasallos, y havitantes que tiene entodos sus vastos Dominios de América y Filipinas, acuio fin ha resuelto, que todos los Virreyes, y Gobernadores de Indias, y de dhas Islas, hagan exactos Padrones con la devida distinción de clases, estados, y castas detodas las personas de ambos sexos sin excluir los Párbulos. De orden de S. M. lo participo a V. S. para que expida las correspondientes, afin de que todos los Gobernadores, y personas, aquien corresponda desu jurisdición, y distrito, formen desde luego los mencionados Padrones, y repitan todos los años esta operación, remitiéndolos al fin de cada uno por mano de V. S. con la prevención de que han de anotar en cada estado annual, el aumento o diminución, que resultare respecto del anterior. Y para su puntual complimto manda S. M. que cuide de que no haya en ello la menor omisión: que remita asu tpo por esta vía reservada de Indias, los referidos Padrones: y que me de aviso de quedan en esta inteligencia. Dios gue a V. S. ms. as. Sn Lorenzo 10 de novre de 1776. Jph de Gálvez (firmado)," vol. 5, folio 264, Reales Ordenes, Archivo General de la Nación, Caracas. For a discussion of similar royal projects, see DOMINQUEZ ORTIZ, Sociedad española XVIII, pp. 44, 58, and 60; and Jorge NADAL OLLER, La población española, siglos XVI a XX (Barcelona: Ediciones Ariel, 1966), pp. 24-26, 70. For the Mexican counterparts to the Venezuela censuses, see BORAH and COOK, Essays, Vol. 1, especially pages 40 and 50, and TJARKS, "Texas, 1777-1793." See also Trent M. BRADY and John V. LOMBARDI, "The Application of Computers to the Analysis of Census Data: The Bishopric of Caracas, 1780-1820," in DEPREZ, ed., Population and Economics, pp. 271-278.

11. Even though the definition of párvulo is open to some question, since the age of responsibility seems to have varied in practice from time to time and place to place within the Spanish empire, the seven-year level used here seems to fit the data and have the weight of informed opinion behind it. The seven-year level is specified, for example, in a variety of other census documents of the period in Venezuela, and the fifteen-year level, another common break point, appears to have been used more for military purposes than for ecclesiastical population accounting. For a discussion of this point with reference to Mexican data, see BORAH and COOK, Essays, Vols. 1 and 2, and for Spanish practice, see DOMINGUEZ ORTIZ, Sociedad española XVIII, p. 68.

12. To be sure, Venezuelan clerics and others employed the terms mestizo, moreno, and zambo, as well as some of the other less common racial names. But these usages occur so infrequently as to be indications, perhaps, of individuals more accustomed to Mexican than Venezuelan practice. Occasionally, a document may also distinguish between American-born whites and Spanish-born whites, especially in the 1813 census, a one-time exercise. The literature on race mixture and classification in Latin America is extensive. Rather than overburden this account, the reader is

referred to some of the authorities in the field, for example, Magnus MORNER, _Race Mixture in the History of Latin America_ (Boston: Little, Brown and Co., 1967); David W. COHEN and Jack P. GREEN, eds., _Neither Slave nor Free. The Freedmen of African Descent in the Slave Societies of the New World_, The Johns Hopkins Symposia in Comparative History (Baltimore, 1972); and John V. LOMBARDI, "Comparative Slave Systems in the Americas: A Critical Review," in Richard GRAHAM and Peter H. SMITH, eds., _New Approaches to Latin American History_ (Austin: University of Texas Press, 1974), and the notes accompanying these items. For Venezuela, the following proved particularly helpful: Miguel ACOSTA SAIGNES, _Vida de los esclavos negros en Venezuela_ (Caracas: Ediciones Hespérides, 1967); Ermila TROCONIS DE VERACOECHEA, comp., _Documentos para el estudio de los esclavos negros en Venezuela_, Biblioteca de la Academia Nacional de la Historia, no. 103 (Caracas, 1969); and James F. KING, "A Royalist View of the Colored Castes in the Venezuelan War of Independence," _Hispanic American Historical Review_ 33(1953), 526-537. Also very helpful in comprehending the social context of Venezuela's racial terminology are the documents relative to the participation of blacks in the wars for independence. Fear of a race war brought out clearly the tensions involved and displayed the dynamics of the system. See John V. LOMBARDI, _The Decline and Abolition of Negro Slavery in Venezuela, 1820-1854_ (Westport, Conn.: Greenwood, 1971), especially Chapters 2 and 6 and their notes. Also important are the documents in the valuable collection focused on the royalists in Vols. 4-6(1967-69) of the _Anuario de la Instituto de Antropología e Historia_ (Caracas, Universidad Central de Venezuela). On the question of classifying Indians, see Eduardo ARCILA FARIAS, _El régimen de la encomienda en Venezuela_, 2d ed. (Caracas: Instituto de Investigaciones, Facultad de Economía, Universidad Central de Venezuela, 1966). The Indian problem is complicated by the ending of the encomienda in the early eighteenth century, but the continuation of tribute payments until 1811. For the role of blacks in another colony, Frederick P. BOWSER's account gives a valuable perspective, helpful for understanding Venezuela's situation, in _The African Slave in Colonial Peru, 1524-1650_ (Stanford: Stanford University Press, 1974). BORAH and COOK, _Essays_, Vols. 1 and 2, also have a considerable amount of helpful information and commentary on this subject, as on most other matters related to Spanish colonial population accounting.

Notes to Chapter 3.

1. This urban-oriented conquest and settlement pattern is so obvious from the accounts and chronicles of the period, and from the subsequent studies of conquest and colonization, that an elaborate citation of authorities would serve little purpose. Those interested in reviewing the sweep of conquest and colonization in closer detail are referred to the items cited in the notes to Chapter 1. Urban history as a special field within Latin American history has attracted an able core of scholars, whose work is reviewed and discussed in Richard M. MORSE, "Trends and Issues in Latin American Urban Research, 1965-1970," Latin American Research Review 6:1(1971), 3-52 and 6:2(1971), 19-75. For Venezuela, urban studies have for the most part focused on individual towns, especially Caracas, or on twentieth-century urbanization resulting from the post-war oil boom. Without a comprehensive analysis of the colonial Venezuelan urban network, the best source of information and the best view of the Spanish American mind set can be acquired through the better town histories, particularly those that focus on the founding generation. Two of Brother NECTARIO MARIA's books are excellent examples of this type. See Historia de la fundación de la ciudad de Nueva Segovia de Barquisimeto a la luz de los documentos de los archivos de España y de Venezuela, 2d ed. (Madrid: Juan Bravo, 1967); and Los orígenes de Boconó (Madrid: Juan Bravo, 1962). Also important are the works of DE ARMAS CHITTY cited in the previous chapters. For an interesting although not wholly satisfactory procedure for the ordering of colonial urban centers by function and by size, see Jorge E. HARDOY and Carmen ARANOVICH, "Urban Scales and Functions in Spanish America toward the Year 1600: First Conclusions," Latin American Research Review 5:3(1970), 57-110. If we are ever to comprehend the significance and dynamic relationships of the urban net, we will need to develop regional and local studies. An example of what can be done along these lines can be seen in David J. ROBINSON and Teresa THOMAS, "New Towns in Eighteenth Century Northwest Argentina," Journal of Latin American Studies 6:1(1974), 1-33. For a grand view of the formation and structure of colonial Latin American cities, one focusing mostly on the great capitals and infused with a strong eurocentric bias, see George A. KUBLER, "Cities and Cultures in the Colonial Period in Latin America," Diogenes 47(1964), 53-62.

2. In any account of the conquest, settlement, and administration of Spanish America, the student will find myriad examples of the role of towns and town-oriented functions in the establishment and maintenance of the Spanish imperial structure. For the early period, James M. LOCKHART, Spanish Peru, 1532-1560: A Colonial Society (Madison: University of Wisconsin Press, 1968) shows rather elegantly the importance of the urban nucleus in the creation of careers and organization of society. Within a somewhat larger institutional framework, John L. PHELAN's excellent The Kingdom of Quito in the Seventeenth Century: Bureaucratic Politics in the Spanish Empire (Madison: University of Wisconsin Press, 1967) relates the individual's local presence to the demands of the imperial bureaucracy. Unfortunately, we still lack such masterworks for Venezuela. Federico BRITO FIGUEROA's suggestive and imaginative synthesis, La estructura económica de Venezuela colonial (Caracas: Instituto de Investigaciones, Facultad de Economía, Universidad Central de Venezuela, 1963) has some useful insights, as do the classic works on the colonial period by Eduardo ARCILA FARIAS, Economía colonial de Venezuela, Colección Tierra Firme, no. 24 (Mexico: Fondo de Cultura Económica, 1946) and Comercio entre México y Venezuela en los siglos XVII y XVIII (Mexico: El Colegio de México, 1950), along with his Encomienda cited earlier. But because none of these works focus on the local level, with the possible exception of ARCILA FARIAS, Encomienda, they fail to convey a clear notion of the importance of urban nuclei in the colonial Venezuelan frame of reference. A better feel for the situation comes from histories of individual places, the records of cabildos, abstracts of town registers, and similar documents. For some representative samples of this kind of data, see the following items. Nueva Valencia del Rey, Venezuela, Cabildo, Actas del Cabildo de la Nueva Valencia del Rey, 2 vols. (Valencia: Publicaciones del Concejo Municipal del Distrito

Valencia, 1970-71); Petare, Venezuela (Canton), Cabildo, Actas del Cabildo de Petare, 2 vols. (Petare: Concejo Municipal del Distrito Sucre, del Estado Miranda, 1970-); Pedro Manuel ARCAYA U., El Cabildo de Caracas (Caracas: Ediciones del Cuatricentenario de Caracas, 1965); Stephanie B. BLANK, "Social Integration and Social Stability in a Colonial Spanish American City. Caracas (1595-1627)" (Ph.D. diss., University of Wisconsin, Madison, 1971); Erdmann GORMSEN, Barquisimeto. Una ciudad mercantil en Venezuela. Edición venezolana de Barquisimeto, eine Handelsstadt in Venezuela, Heidelberg, 1963, revisada y ampliada, trans. Hannelore Martens de Gormsen (Caracas: Instituto Otto y Magdalena Blohm, 1965); Agustín MILLARES CARLO, Archivo del Registro Principal de Maracaibo. Protocolos de los antiguos escribanos (1790-1836). Indice y extractos (Maracaibo: Centro Histórico del Zulia, 1964); Agustín MILLARES CARLO, Archivo del Concejo de Maracaibo. Expedientes Anexos, 2 vols. (Maracaibo: Centro de Historia del Estado Zulia, 1969); Agustín MILLARES CARLO, Protocolos del siglo XVI. Archivos de los registros principales de Mérida y Caracas, Biblioteca de la Academia Nacional de la Historia, no. 80 (Caracas, 1966); Agustín MILLARES CARLO, Los Archivos municipales de Latinoamérica. Libros de actas y colecciones documentales. Apuntes bibliográficos (Maracaibo: Universidad del Zulia, 1961); Caracas, Cabildo, Actas del cabildo de Caracas, 1573-1629, 6 vols. (Caracas: Editorial Elite, 1943-1951); Manuel PINTO C., Los ejidos de Caracas (Caracas: Ediciones del Consejo Municipal del Distrito Federal, 1968); and Manuel PINTO C., Los primeros vecinos de Caracas. Recopilación documental (Caracas: Comisión Nacional del Cuatricentenario de la Fundación de Caracas, Comité de Obras Culturales, 1966). One way to view the Spanish concern with town living or town-sanctioned residence in Venezuela is through the eyes of Mariano Martí, who during his visita had occasion to comment on the living patterns of his flock. Perhaps most revealing is his comment about a group of individuals living together outside the town proper and evidently carrying on an unauthorized semi-organized existence. Martí ordered them back into the town proper and suggested their houses and agricultural plots be destroyed so there would be no incentive for them to return. See MARTI, Documentos relativos a su visita pastoral de la Diócesis de Caracas, 1771-1784, Biblioteca de la Academia Nacional de la Historia, nos. 95-101, 7 vols. (Caracas, 1969), Vol. 1, pp. 569-570. In the matter of raising sitios to parish status, examples can be seen throughout MARTI, Documentos; one such example is in Vol. 7, p. 312 (a new curato established in sitio of Tapipa, removed from parish of Caucagua, 1784).

3. For a detailed discussion of records for the population history of colonial Venezuela, see Chapter 2 and its accompanying notes.

4. This discussion is based on a close reading of Martí's "Compendio" and the aggregate parish censuses of the Bishopric available in the Archivo Arquidiocesano de Caracas. Unfortunately for the elegance of these ideal type parishes, reality in colonial Venezuela failed to conform to this typology except in an approximate way. Whether the types developed here are useful tools of analysis will depend on the results of parish-based studies, as yet only begun. From the incomplete evidence in MARTI, Documentos, and from a survey of the census returns distinguishing between those living within and those living without the town proper, it would seem that in some areas of the country and in some sizes of parish, half or more of the parishes' population could be found outside the town proper. Naturally where subordinated sitios existed, subject to the jurisdiction and record keeping of the main parish, these outsiders could certainly account for a substantial portion of the parishes' population. And contracted parishes may have had less hinterland to collect outsiders. In spite of these problems, the parish structures defined as standard, extended, and contracted still seem useful analytical devices, because they draw our attention to the structure of these residential units. The hypothesis underlying that structure would read something like this. In a standard parish, individuals have a stronger orientation or identification with the urban nucleus than comparable residents could be expected to have in extended or contracted parishes. Parishioners in standard

parishes presumably had no other embryonic centers on which to focus, as would be the case in an extended parish, nor a coequal parish within the urban nucleus to dilute the primary identification, as would occur in a contracted parish. Having established this analytical scheme at this point, the testing of the construct must await the development of some consistent measures of these characteristics. In the sequel to this book, when the nonstandard data have been processed, it should be possible to determine if this typology can help provide a greater understanding of the dynamics of Venezuela's urban network. For examples of each type of parish, see the following. Standard Parish: Calabozo, MARTI, Documentos, Vol. 7, pp. 17-22 (of the 428 families in this parish, almost 60 percent lived in the town proper in 1780); Extended Parish: El Tocuyo, ibid., Vol. 6, pp. 206-223 (this city had 49 differently named sitios, although some with as few as one family); Contracted Parish: Caracas, San Felipe, Barquisimeto. Neither San Felipe nor Barquisimeto had been divided into two administratively separate parishes at the time of the Martí visita. Caracas, of course, already had several parishes, but for some reason the detailed accounting for Caracas was not included in Martí's visita records. For the special status of these three places, see their records reproduced in Part II of this book. It should be noted that even though San Felipe, for example, counts as a contracted parish, its component fractions may have had sitios attached to them. There is also the complication, in any discussion of parish types, posed by wandering parish sites. Although much more common in the early years of conquest and settlement, the phenomenon is well worth careful consideraion. See Pablo VILA, "Consideraciones sobre poblaciones errantes en el período colonial," Visiones geohistóricas de Venezuela (Caracas: Ediciones del Ministerio de Educación, 1969), pp. 112-120.

5. MARTI, Documentos, Vols. 6-7, and Giovanni Battista Agostino CODAZZI, Obras escogidas, 2 vols. (Caracas: Dirección de Cultura y Bellas Artes, Departamento de Publicaciones, 1961), Vol. 1. See also the list compiled by Eduardo ARCILA FARIAS, El régimen de la encomienda en Venezuela, 2d ed. (Caracas: Instituto de Investigaciones, Facultad de Economía, Universidad Central de Venezuela, 1966), pp. 66-70, from a summary document evidently based on Bishopric sources.

6. Since no one can agree on what it takes to make a town, or tell where urban shades into rural, I have devised these limits for the parishes of the Bishopric of Caracas because they correspond to a reasonable notion of the orders of magnitude involved. In the case of the six parishes of contracted type, their classifications as towns or cities can be misleading, because in every case they are part of urban centers almost twice as large or larger. In subsequent refining of the data introduced here, it may be necessary to reunite these contracted parishes and work with them as the urban units they were in real life.

7. The question of Caracas' primacy within the Venezuelan context and in comparison with other major Latin American urban centers has generated considerable interest. Because at the present time Caracas' primacy is beyond dispute, some tend to project this predominance backward in time. The question, however, is somewhat more complex. Caracas was neither first in time nor predominant in function or population from the early days of Venezuela's settlement, and marking the moment when the city assumed primacy proves a difficult task. A number of authorities have attempted explanations of the primacy of Caracas. For example, Germán CARRERA DAMAS, "Principales momentos del desarrollo histórico de Caracas," in Estudio de Caracas, 6 vols. in 7 (Caracas: Universidad Central de Venezuela, Ediciones de la Biblioteca, 1967-70), Vol. 2, Part 1, pp. 23-102, is particularly helpful in placing the development of the city in perspective. So, too, are the rest of the monographs in the Estudio de Caracas collection. Primacy, of course, is measured as much by function as by size, although population is the easiest variable to measure and has enjoyed considerable popularity among urban analysts. See Surinder K. MEHTA, "Some Demographic and Economic Correlates of Primate Cities: A Case for Revaluation," in Gerald W. BREESE, comp., The City in Newly Developing Countries: Readings in Urbanism and

Urbanization (Englewood Cliffs, N. J.: Prentice-Hall, 1969), pp. 295-308; and Richard M. MORSE, "Trends and Patterns of Latin American Urbanization, 1750-1920," *Comparative Studies in Society and History* 16(1974), 416-447. In any effort to discover the origins of Caracas' primacy, some attention must be paid the concentration of institutions and functions in the city. For Venezuela, see Mercedes M. ALVAREZ F., *El tribunal del Real Consulado de Caracas. Contribución al estudio de nuestras instituciones*, 2 vols. (Caracas: Ediciones del Cuatricentenario de Caracas, 1967); Antonio ARELLANO MORENO, *Caracas: su evolución y su régimen legal* (Caracas: Ediciones del Cuatricentenario de Caracas, 1967); José Antonio DE ARMAS CHITTY, *Caracas: Origen y trayectoria de una ciudad*, 2 vols. (Caracas: Fundación Creole, 1967); Ildefonso LEAL, ed., *Documentos para la historia de la educación en Venezuela. Epoca colonial*, Biblioteca de la Academia Nacional de la Historia, no. 87 (Caracas, 1968). Manuel Nunes DIAS, *El Real Consulado de Caracas (1793-1810)*, trans. Jaime Tello, Biblioteca de la Academia Nacional de la Historia, no. 106 (Caracas, 1971-72); Santiago Gerardo SUAREZ, *Las instituciones militares venezolanas del período hispánico en los archivos*, Biblioteca de la Academia Nacional de la Historia, no. 92 (Caracas, 1969); Ermila TROCONIS DE VERACOECHEA, *Las obras pías en la Iglesia colonial venezolana*, Biblioteca de la Academia Nacional de la Historia, no. 105 (Caracas, 1971). In addition to the institutional aspect of primacy, there is a cultural dimension best seen through material elements such as housing, dress, possessions and the like. See, for example, Enrique MARCO DORTA, ed., *Materiales para la historia de la cultura en Venezuela, 1523-1828. Documentos del Archivo General de Indias de Sevilla* (Caracas: Fundación John Boulton, 1967); Carlos F. DUARTE, ed., *Materiales para la historia de las artes decorativas en Venezuela*, Biblioteca de la Academia Nacional de la Historia, no. 104 (Caracas, 1971); Graziani GASPARINI and Juan Pedro PASANI, *Caracas a través de su arquitectura* (Caracas: Fundación Fina Gómez, 1969). In an effort to clarify some of these problems, Germán Carrera Damas and I have begun a long range project to investigate the "Origins, Structure, and Dynamics of a Primate City: A Case Study of Caracas, 1560-1960," with the cooperation and support of the Mid-West Universities Consortium for International Activities (MUCIA), the Centro de Estudios del Desarrollo (CENDES), Indiana University, and the Universidad Central de Venezuela. Four monographs are underway in this project.

Notes to Chapter 4.

1. On the racial terminology employed here, see the items cited in note 12, Chapter 2.

2. For an extended discussion of the role of slaves and other blacks in the turbulent social atmosphere of post-1810 Venezuela, see John V. LOMBARDI, The Decline and Abolition of Negro Slavery in Venezuela, 1820-1854 (Westport, Conn.: Greenwood, 1971), especially Chapters 2 and 6 and their notes.

3. There is, of course, no way at this stage of research to put this hypothesis to any rigorous test. The causal links suggested here between statistical profiles and human behavior are of necessity made from the most fragile stuff. Nevertheless, this kind of model, for all its simplicity, can help orient our research and focus the discussion on Venezuela's social history. In developing these hypotheses, I have drawn on the range of resources suggested in the notes accompanying this book.

4. For the discussion of male/female ratios and for the choice of a model life table, I have been greatly aided by Eduardo E. ARRIAGA, New Life Tables for Latin American Populations in the Nineteenth and Twentieth Centuries (Berkeley: Institute of International Studies, University of California, 1968) and the same author's Mortality Decline and its Demographic Effects in Latin America (Berkeley: Institute of International Studies, University of California, 1970). As always, Woodrow W. BORAH and Sherburne F. COOK, Essays in Population History, Mexico and the Carribbean, 2 vols. (Berkeley: University of California Press, 1971-1974), Vols. 1 and 2 proved helpful here, although the usefulness of their data as a model for the Venezuelan case is reduced by the relatively high proportion of Indians in the Mexican areas studied by Cook and Borah, a situation rare for the Bishopric of Caracas. The model life table used in this discussion is in the "South" series, presupposing a life expectancy at birth of twenty-five years, from the tables in Ansley J. COALE and Paul DEMENY, Regional Model Life Tables and Stable Populations (Princeton: Princeton University Press, 1966). Although the assumptions underlying the tables do not fit Venezuela's experience exactly, they are close enough to permit some suggestive comparisons between what might have been expected and what the data provide. When current research into the age distributions of these colonial Venezuelan populations progresses further, it will be possible to refine these hypotheses.

5. This discussion is based on the same sources used to develop the analysis in Chapters 1, 2, 3, and 5 of this book.

Notes to Chapter 5.

1. For the foundation date of San Carlos and its role in the Capuchin missionary system, see Father BUENAVENTURA DE CARROCERA, Misión de los Capuchinos en los Llanos de Caracas, Biblioteca de la Academia Nacional de la Historia, nos. 111-113, 3 vols. (Caracas, 1972), especially Vol. 1, pp. 63-68 and 365-466. On the controversy over releasing San Carlos to the secular ecclesiastical administration, see ibid, Vol. 2, pp. 25-26, 32, 40, 49, 50, and 75.

2. For background information, see Mariano MARTI, Documentos relativos a su visita pastoral de la Diócesis de Caracas, 1771-1784, Biblioteca de la Academia Nacional de la Historia, nos. 95-101, 7 vols. (Caracas, 1969), Vol. 2, p. 520, and Vol. 7, pp. 73-83. Also see Guillermo FIGUERA, ed., Documentos para la historia de la iglesia colonial en Venezuela, Biblioteca de la Academia Nacional de la Historia, nos. 74-75, 2 vols. (Caracas, 1965), especially Vol. 2, pp. 102-103; Agustín MARON, "Relación histórico-geográfica de la provincia de Venezuela," in Antonio ARELLANO MORENO, comp., Documentos para la historia económica de la época colonial. Viajes e informes, Biblioteca de la Academia Nacional de la Historia, no. 93 (Caracas, 1970), pp. 411-474; Joseph Luis de CISNEROS, Descripción exacta de la provincia de Benezuela. Reproducción de las ediciones de Valencia (1764) y Madrid (1912), Biblioteca de Geografía y Historia, Serie Alejandro de Humboldt (Caracas: Editorial Avila Gráfica, 1950), pp. 65-66; Pedro José de OLAVARRIAGA, Instrucción general y particular del estado presente de la provincia de Venezuela en los años de 1720 y 1721, Biblioteca de la Academia Nacional de la Historia, no. 76 (Caracas, 1965), p. 262; Giovanni Battista Agostino CODAZZI, Obras escogidas, 2 vols. (Caracas: Dirección de Cultura y Bellas Artes, Departamento de Publicaciones, 1961), Vol. 1, pp. 401-402; François de PONS, Viaje a la parte oriental de Tierra Firme en la América Meridional, trans. Enrique Planchart, Colección Histórico-Económica Venezolana, vols. 4-5, 2 vols. (Caracas: Banco Central de Venezuela, 1960), Vol. 1, pp. 72-75 and Vol. 2, pp. 276-277; and Alexander von HUMBOLDT, Viaje a las regiones equinocciales del nuevo continente hecho en 1799, 1800, 1801, 1802, 1803, y 1804, trans. Lisandro Alvarado, Biblioteca Venezolana de Cultura, Colección "Viajes y naturaleza," 2d ed., 5 vols. (Caracas: Ediciones del Ministerio de Educación, 1956), Vol. 2, p. 240, Vol. 3, pp. 167-168, and Vol. 4, p. 50.

3. All the material on San Carlos' religious institutions and moral character comes from MARTI, Documentos, Vol. 2, pp. 250-268, and Vol. 6, pp. 82-83. A typical item of gossip runs, in free translation, as follows. "Carlos Villasana, white, married to Paula N., is living in sin with Paula Petrona Ximenes, who is married to Silvestre Mesa, a black or free mulatto. Paula Petrona Ximenes is a mestiza or mulata. The sinful couple lives here in this town, while Silvestre Mesa is off in the countryside. The Vicar, and Lieutenant Codessido, in my presence, have resolved that Paula Petrona Ximenes will be sent to her husband, who is located on the other side of the Apure working as a servant on the ranch of don Carlos Moreno" (Vol. 2, p. 251).

4. The literature on the Venezuelan independence movement is most extensive, since no other period of Venezuelan history has so attracted the interest of historians. The best guide to this information is the article by those indefatigable venezolanistas, Pedro GRASES and Manuel PEREZ VILA, "Gran Colombia. Referencias relativas a la bibliografía sobre el período emancipador en los países grancolombianos (desde 1949)," Anuario de Estudios Americanos 21(1964), 733-777. The best survey of the movement can be found in John LYNCH, The Spanish American Revolutions, 1808-1826 (New York: W. W. Norton, 1973), which also has an excellent bibliography. For the student interested in measuring the impact of the wars for independence on Venezuela's economy, the Sociedad Económica de Amigos del País, Memorias y estudios (1829-1839), Colección Histórico-económica Venezolana, vols. 1-2, 2 vols. (Caracas: Banco Central de Venezuela, 1958) sets the pre-war stage, along with Eduardo ARCILA FARIAS' Comercio entre Venezuela y México en los siglos XVII y XVIII (Mexico: El Colegio de México, 1950). And CODAZZI's geography in Obras escogidas gives the status of the postwar economy at the

point of recovery. For a discussion of Venezuelan agriculture and labor problems before and after the war, see Miguel IZARD, "La agricultura venezolana en una época de transición, 1777-1830," Boletín histórico (Caracas) 28(1972), 81-145, and John V. LOMBARDI and James A. HANSON, "The First Venezuelan Coffee Cycle, 1830-1855," Agricultural History 44(1970), 355-367. For a compilation of statistics on Venezuela's economy, see Miguel IZARD, comp., Series estadísticas para la historia de Venezuela (Mérida: Universidad de los Andes, 1970). See also Federico BRITO FIGUEROA, La estructura económica de Venezuela colonial (Caracas: Instituto de Investigaciones, Facultad de Economía, Universidad Central de Venezuela, 1963). Also very helpful is José Rafael REVENGA, La hacienda pública en Venezuela, 1828-1830. Misión de ... como ministro de hacienda (Caracas: Banco Central de Venezuela, 1953).

5. For following the troops in and out of San Carlos, the following works, while hardly exhausting the available literature on the wars, proved most useful either for their specificity about San Carlos, or for their illumination of important themes discussed in this chapter. On the First Republic, see Caracciolo PARRA PEREZ, Historia de la Primera República de Venezuela, Biblioteca de la Academia Nacional de la Historia, nos. 19-20, 2 vols. (Caracas, 1959). Venezuela, Congreso Constituyente 1811-1812, Libro de Actas del Supremo Congreso de Venezuela, 1811-1812, Biblioteca de la Academia Nacional de la Historia, nos. 3-4, 2 vols. (Caracas, 1959) is helpful in understanding the operations of this first Venezuelan government. On the role of Francisco de Miranda in the fall of the First Republic, see Archivo del General Miranda, ed. Vicente Dávila, 24 vols. (Caracas: Editorial Sur-América, 1929-1950), Vol. 24; Francisco de MIRANDA, Textos sobre la independencia, Biblioteca de la Academia Nacional de la Historia, no. 13 (Caracas, 1959); and William Spence ROBERTSON, La vida de Miranda, trans. Julio E. Payro (Caracas: Banco Industrial de Venezuela, 1967). The dominant figure of Venezuelan independence historiography has always been Simón Bolívar. Although there is no room here for an extensive Bolivarian bibliography, some of the more important items are included below. Two useful biographies are Augusto MIJARES, El Libertador, 2d ed. (Caracas: Editorial Arte, 1965) and Gerhard MASUR, Simón Bolívar (Albuquerque: University of New Mexico Press, 1948). The most useful work for this study is by Venezuela's classic bolivarianist, Vicente LECUNA, Crónica razonada de las guerras de Bolívar, 2d ed., 2 vols. (New York: Fundación Vicente Lecuna, 1960). For the definitive edition of Bolívar's writings and letters, see Escritos del Libertador, 10 vols. (Caracas: Sociedad Bolivariana de Venezuela, 1964-). Also helpful is José de AUSTRIA, Bosquejo de la historia militar de Venezuela, Biblioteca de la Academia Nacional de la Historia, nos. 29-30, 2 vols. (Caracas, 1960); Colombia, Laws, statutes, etc., Decretos del Libertador, 3 vols. (Caracas: Publicaciones de la Sociedad Bolivariana de Venezuela, 1961); and Feliciano MONTENEGRO Y COLON, Historia de Venezuela, Biblioteca de la Academia Nacional de la Historia, nos. 26-27, 2 vols. (Caracas, 1960). On the royalist activities in the Venezuelan independence movement, see Stephen K. STOAN, Pablo Morillo and Venezuela, 1815-1820 (Columbus: Ohio State University Press, 1974); "Materiales para el estudio de la ideología realista de la independencia," Anuario del Instituto de Antropología e Historia 4-6(1967-1969); and especially Germán CARRERA DAMAS, Boves. Aspectos socio-económicos de su acción histórica, 2d ed., Colección Vigilia, no. 14 (Caracas: Ministerio de Educación, Dirección Técnica, 1968). The disruptive force of the independence movement in terms of the social and economic structure can be traced through the following items. Charles C. GRIFFIN, Los temas sociales y económicos en la época de la independencia (Caracas: Fundación John Boulton and Fundación Eugenio Mendoza, 1962); Materiales para el estudio de la cuestión agraria en Venezuela (1800-1830) (Caracas: Universidad Central de Venezuela, Consejo de Desarrollo Científico y Humanístico, 1964); John V. LOMBARDI, The Decline and Abolition of Negro Slavery in Venezuela, 1820-1854 (Westport, Conn.: Greenwood, 1971); and James F. KING, "A Royalist View of the Colored Castes in the Venezuelan War of Independence," Hispanic American Historical Review 33(1953), 526-5[illegible]

APPENDIX A

Tables for Part I

Introduction

These tables are computed from the data in Part II of this book, which in turn comes from the Sección Parroquias, Archivo Arquidiocesano de Caracas. The tables in the appendix are derived from the 1800-1809 file. Each parish with one or more returns in those years has one record in the 1800-1809 file. If the parish has more than one return, the values are averages. If the parish has only one return that value is taken as the best estimator of the mid-interval population. Because of its construction, the 1800-1809 file has a few peculiarities that must be taken into consideration. Three urban centers--Caracas, Barquisimeto, and San Felipe--have multiple parishes. Each of these parishes is listed separately in the data file. Nevertheless, the variation introduced by leaving these three cities in their disaggregated form is quite small. In a parallel run of the data with the parishes for Caracas, Barquisimeto, and San Felipe aggregated, the differences in the resulting statistics amounted to one percent or less. Because this preliminary inquiry into the size and composition of Venezuela's colonial population focuses on parishes rather than metropolitan areas, I have stayed with the parish-based file, leaving the preparation of an urban-regional analysis for another time.

A few conventions used in the tables need explanation. Throughout, the percentages and other totals may not add up exactly because of rounding. The terms white, pardo, Indian, Negro, and slave are used here as they have been defined in the preceding chapters. Children are defined as being between the ages of zero and six inclusive, adults as people seven years of age or older. Married individuals exclude widows and widowers. The regions used here are those described in Chapter 1 and the urban categories are those defined in Chapter 3. The life table values are included on some tables mostly as a point of reference. They come from the work by Ansley J. Coale and Paul Demeny, Regional Model Life Tables and Stable Populations (Princeton: Princeton University Press, 1966), p. 658 (Model South, Level 3).

For the technically inclined, the tables in Appendix A were generated in a four-step process. First the data represented in Part II was condensed into the 1800-1809 file through a Fortran program. This file was then processed by SPSS to produce an aggregated data file on the variables. The aggregated file was then processed by a Fortran program that generated the statistics, formatted the output, and produced the tables. I wrote all Fortran programs, which were run at Indiana University's Wrubel Computing Center, Bloomington, Indiana.

TABLE A-1. POPULATION BY RACE (1800-1809)

RACE	PERCENT	POPULATION
WHITE	25.50	108920.30
INDIAN	13.13	56083.30
PARDO	38.22	163275.80
NEGRO	8.07	34463.90
SLAVE	15.09	64462.10
TOTAL	100.00	427205.40

NOTE. TOTAL PERCENT MAY NOT ADD UP TO 100 BECAUSE OF ROUNDING. POPULATION TOTALS EXPRESSED AS FRACTIONS BECAUSE OF AVERAGING DATA IN 1800-1809.

TABLE A-2. POPULATION BY RACE AND URBAN CATEGORY (1800-1809)

--HAMLETS--

RACE	PERCENT POP	PERCENT BISHOPRIC	PERCENT RACE	POP TOTALS
WHITE	8.78	.16	.61	667.30
INDIAN	14.08	.25	1.91	1070.00
PARDO	41.89	.75	1.95	3184.30
NEGRO	7.23	.13	1.59	549.60
SLAVE	28.03	.50	3.31	2130.90
TOTAL	100.00	1.78		7602.10

NUMBER OF PARISHES. 22.00
PARISHES AS PERCENT ALL PARISHES. 11.34

--VILLAGES--

RACE	PERCENT POP	PERCENT BISHOPRIC	PERCENT RACE	POP TOTALS
WHITE	23.37	5.97	23.40	25484.20
INDIAN	17.77	4.54	34.56	19381.10
PARDO	32.63	8.33	21.80	35592.80
NEGRO	7.90	2.02	25.00	8616.20
SLAVE	18.33	4.68	31.02	19995.50
TOTAL	100.00	25.53		109069.80

NUMBER OF PARISHES. 92.00
PARISHES AS PERCENT ALL PARISHES. 47.42

--TOWNS--

RACE	PERCENT POP	PERCENT BISHOPRIC	PERCENT RACE	POP TOTALS
WHITE	24.42	8.24	32.33	35214.30
INDIAN	16.55	5.59	42.57	23872.90
PARDO	37.77	12.75	33.36	54463.80
NEGRO	8.96	3.02	37.47	12914.10
SLAVE	12.30	4.15	27.52	17741.60
TOTAL	100.00	33.76		144206.70

NUMBER OF PARISHES. 53.00
PARISHES AS PERCENT ALL PARISHES. 27.32

--CITIES--

RACE	PERCENT POP	PERCENT BISHOPRIC	PERCENT RACE	POP TOTALS
WHITE	28.59	11.13	43.66	47554.50
INDIAN	7.07	2.75	20.97	11759.30
PARDO	42.11	16.39	42.89	70034.90
NEGRO	7.45	2.90	35.93	12384.00
SLAVE	14.79	5.76	38.15	24594.10
TOTAL	100.00	38.93		166326.80

NUMBER OF PARISHES. 27.00
PARISHES AS PERCENT ALL PARISHES. 13.92

TABLE A-3. POPULATION BY RACE AND REGION (1800-1809)

--COAST REGION--

RACE	PERCENT POP	PERCENT BISHOPRIC	PERCENT RACE	POP TOTALS
WHITE	15.20	1.44	5.66	6164.20
INDIAN	8.09	.77	5.85	3279.60
PARDO	38.84	3.69	9.65	15753.20
NEGRO	11.58	1.10	13.63	4696.70
SLAVE	26.29	2.50	16.54	10660.60
TOTAL	100.00	9.49		40554.30

NUMBER OF PARISHES. 40.00
PARISHES AS PERCENT ALL PARISHES. 20.62

--COASTAL RANGE--

RACE	PERCENT POP	PERCENT BISHOPRIC	PERCENT RACE	POP TOTALS
WHITE	29.36	11.40	44.73	48717.90
INDIAN	8.77	3.41	25.94	14549.80
PARDO	34.32	13.33	34.87	56939.00
NEGRO	5.99	2.33	28.82	9933.30
SLAVE	21.57	8.38	55.52	35789.30
------	------	------		---------
TOTAL	100.00	38.84		165929.30

NUMBER OF PARISHES. 60.00
PARISHES AS PERCENT ALL PARISHES. 30.93

--LLANOS--

RACE	PERCENT POP	PERCENT BISHOPRIC	PERCENT RACE	POP TOTALS
WHITE	29.54	9.28	36.39	39639.30
INDIAN	13.60	4.27	32.55	18253.80
PARDO	41.67	13.09	34.25	55916.80
NEGRO	7.23	2.27	28.17	9707.40
SLAVE	7.94	2.49	16.53	10657.10
------	------	------		---------
TOTAL	100.00	31.41		134174.40

NUMBER OF PARISHES. 62.00
PARISHES AS PERCENT ALL PARISHES. 31.96

--SEGOVIA HIGHLANDS--

RACE	PERCENT POP	PERCENT BISHOPRIC	PERCENT RACE	POP TOTALS
WHITE	17.02	2.82	11.07	12052.80
INDIAN	15.89	2.63	20.07	11255.00
PARDO	44.08	7.31	19.12	31223.20
NEGRO	13.36	2.22	27.46	9464.70
SLAVE	9.65	1.60	10.60	6836.10
------	------	------		---------
TOTAL	100.00	16.58		70831.80

NUMBER OF PARISHES. 23.00
PARISHES AS PERCENT ALL PARISHES. 11.86

--GUAYANA--

RACE	PERCENT POP	PERCENT BISHOPRIC	PERCENT RACE	POP TOTALS
WHITE	26.00	.02	.06	65.00
INDIAN	14.00	.01	.06	35.00
PARDO	50.40	.03	.08	126.00
NEGRO	0.00	0.00	0.00	0.00
SLAVE	9.60	.01	.04	24.00
------	------	------		---------
TOTAL	100.00	.06		250.00

NUMBER OF PARISHES. 1.00
PARISHES AS PERCENT ALL PARISHES. .52

--ANDES--

RACE	PERCENT POP	PERCENT BISHOPRIC	PERCENT RACE	POP TOTALS
WHITE	14.75	.53	2.09	2281.10
INDIAN	56.32	2.04	15.53	8710.10
PARDO	21.45	.78	2.03	3317.60
NEGRO	4.28	.15	1.92	661.80
SLAVE	3.20	.12	.77	495.00
------	------	------		---------
TOTAL	100.00	3.62		15465.60

NUMBER OF PARISHES. 8.00
PARISHES AS PERCENT ALL PARISHES. 4.12

TABLE A-4. MALE/FEMALE RATIOS BY RACE (1800-1809) (M/F)(100)

RACE	OVERALL	ADULT	CHILD
WHITE	94.74	92.97	99.98
INDIAN	89.73	87.04	95.66
PARDO	88.87	84.35	101.17
NEGRO	88.63	85.51	97.04
SLAVE	95.27	93.75	99.72
------	------	------	------
ALL	91.38	88.40	99.50
LIFE TABLE	98.60	98.70	98.10

TABLE A-5. MALE/FEMALE RATIOS BY RACE AND URBAN CATEGORY (1800-1809) (M/F)(100)

--HAMLETS--

RACE	OVERALL	ADULT	CHILD
WHITE	108.99	109.58	107.40
INDIAN	118.10	114.67	130.33
PARDO	93.53	87.76	109.20
NEGRO	91.36	83.06	116.04
SLAVE	106.50	103.15	114.30
------	------	------	------
ALL	101.41	97.01	113.32
LIFE TABLE	98.60	98.70	98.10

--VILLAGES--

RACE	OVERALL	ADULT	CHILD
WHITE	110.52	114.01	101.33
INDIAN	92.55	89.76	99.16
PARDO	95.53	94.13	98.97
NEGRO	92.27	91.36	94.26
SLAVE	106.63	108.35	102.19
------	------	------	------
ALL	100.01	100.16	99.64
LIFE TABLE	98.60	98.70	98.10

--TOWNS--

RACE	OVERALL	ADULT	CHILD
WHITE	96.10	94.35	100.95
INDIAN	88.19	85.29	94.14
PARDO	87.64	83.12	98.90
NEGRO	85.02	80.35	97.51
SLAVE	96.09	94.96	99.24
------	------	------	------
ALL	90.51	87.39	98.35
LIFE TABLE	98.60	98.70	98.10

--CITIES--

RACE	OVERALL	ADULT	CHILD
WHITE	86.13	82.42	98.33
INDIAN	86.12	83.64	91.65
PARDO	86.39	80.65	104.09
NEGRO	89.88	87.28	98.10
SLAVE	85.53	82.41	96.34
------	------	------	------
ALL	86.42	82.11	99.89
LIFE TABLE	98.60	98.70	98.10

TABLE A-6. MALE/FEMALE RATIOS BY RACE AND REGION (1800-1809) (M/F)(100)

--COAST--

RACE	OVERALL	ADULT	CHILD
WHITE	123.20	132.09	96.54
INDIAN	92.35	88.09	103.75
PARDO	85.60	80.43	102.85
NEGRO	85.54	81.66	97.39
SLAVE	101.12	101.99	98.76
------	------	------	------
ALL	95.10	93.38	100.30
LIFE TABLE	98.60	98.70	98.10

--COASTAL RANGE--

RACE	OVERALL	ADULT	CHILD
WHITE	95.45	93.92	100.30
INDIAN	89.88	88.81	92.34
PARDO	86.32	81.93	98.97
NEGRO	82.08	77.55	96.25
SLAVE	92.45	89.49	101.89
------	------	------	------
ALL	90.28	87.34	99.06
LIFE TABLE	98.60	98.70	98.10

--SEGOVIA HIGHLANDS--

RACE	OVERALL	ADULT	CHILD
WHITE	77.79	74.77	88.57
INDIAN	87.63	83.79	96.17
PARDO	88.28	82.69	105.31
NEGRO	95.87	94.05	100.98
SLAVE	80.89	78.25	88.30
------	------	------	------
ALL	86.53	82.37	98.69
LIFE TABLE	98.60	98.70	98.10

--ANDES--

RACE	OVERALL	ADULT	CHILD
WHITE	94.85	88.45	107.42
INDIAN	87.87	85.43	93.21
PARDO	88.30	84.91	93.89
NEGRO	93.45	93.40	93.53
SLAVE	133.93	134.87	131.78
------	------	------	------
ALL	90.40	87.41	96.38
LIFE TABLE	98.60	98.70	98.10

--LLANOS--

RACE	OVERALL	ADULT	CHILD
WHITE	95.61	92.93	102.63
INDIAN	91.30	88.20	97.73
PARDO	92.83	89.23	101.33
NEGRO	89.99	87.82	94.74
SLAVE	108.27	111.33	100.43
------	------	------	------
ALL	94.37	91.78	100.56
LIFE TABLE	98.60	98.70	98.10

--GUAYANA--

RACE	OVERALL	ADULT	CHILD
WHITE	124.14	157.89	60.00
INDIAN	118.75	115.38	133.33
PARDO	117.24	114.29	125.00
NEGRO	0.00	0.00	0.00
SLAVE	200.00	214.29	100.00
------	------	------	------
ALL	125.23	133.33	103.33
LIFE TABLE	98.60	98.70	98.10

TABLE A-7. PERCENT MARRIED BY RACE AND SEX (1800-1809)

RACE	PERCENT ADULTS MARRIED		
	MALES	FEMALES	ALL ADULTS
WHITE	37.43	34.80	36.07
INDIAN	45.78	39.98	42.68
PARDO	37.85	32.86	35.14
NEGRO	38.46	32.17	35.07
SLAVE	28.28	27.04	27.64
------	------	------	------
ALL	37.23	33.31	35.15

NOTE. ADULTS ARE SEVEN YEARS OR OLDER.

TABLE A-8. PERCENT MARRIED BY RACE, SEX, AND URBAN CATEGORY (1800-1809)

--HAMLETS--

RACE	PERCENT ADULTS MARRIED		
	MALES	FEMALES	ALL ADULTS
WHITE	45.71	47.16	46.40
INDIAN	54.20	62.23	57.94
PARDO	46.09	40.71	43.23
NEGRO	45.55	35.64	40.14
SLAVE	40.96	42.68	41.81
------	------	------	------
ALL	45.92	44.37	45.13

NOTE. ADULTS ARE SEVEN YEARS OR OLDER.

--VILLAGES--

RACE	PERCENT ADULTS MARRIED		
	MALES	FEMALES	ALL ADULTS
WHITE	37.11	41.75	39.28
INDIAN	46.94	42.13	44.41
PARDO	40.03	38.11	39.04
NEGRO	39.78	34.51	37.02
SLAVE	32.44	35.75	34.03
------	------	------	------
ALL	38.92	38.95	38.93

NOTE. ADULTS ARE SEVEN YEARS OR OLDER.

--TOWNS--

RACE	PERCENT ADULTS MARRIED		
	MALES	FEMALES	ALL ADULTS
WHITE	38.51	36.16	37.30
INDIAN	47.97	40.71	44.05
PARDO	38.76	33.45	35.86
NEGRO	40.12	31.72	35.46
SLAVE	28.94	27.73	28.32
------	------	------	------
ALL	38.92	34.39	36.50

NOTE. ADULTS ARE SEVEN YEARS OR OLDER.

--CITIES--

RACE	PERCENT ADULTS MARRIED		
	MALES	FEMALES	ALL ADULTS
WHITE	36.67	30.62	33.36
INDIAN	38.38	33.13	35.52
PARDO	35.63	29.71	32.35
NEGRO	35.75	31.04	33.24
SLAVE	22.95	19.59	21.11
------	------	------	------
ALL	34.18	28.75	31.20

NOTE. ADULTS ARE SEVEN YEARS OR OLDER.

TABLE A-9. PERCENT MARRIED BY RACE, SEX, AND REGION (1800-1809)

--COAST--

RACE	PERCENT ADULTS MARRIED		
	MALES	FEMALES	ALL ADULTS
WHITE	32.95	37.71	35.00
INDIAN	47.58	42.34	44.79
PARDO	38.94	31.62	34.88
NEGRO	40.86	32.67	36.35
SLAVE	34.15	35.04	34.59
------	------	------	------
ALL	37.37	34.25	35.76

NOTE. ADULTS ARE SEVEN YEARS OR OLDER.

--COASTAL RANGE--

RACE	PERCENT ADULTS MARRIED		
	MALES	FEMALES	ALL ADULTS
WHITE	34.82	33.22	34.00
INDIAN	37.94	33.79	35.75
PARDO	35.43	29.89	32.38
NEGRO	35.96	27.42	31.15
SLAVE	31.20	28.90	29.99
------	------	------	------
ALL	34.54	30.81	32.55

NOTE. ADULTS ARE SEVEN YEARS OR OLDER.

--SEGOVIA HIGHLANDS--

RACE	PERCENT ADULTS MARRIED		
	MALES	FEMALES	ALL ADULTS
WHITE	37.38	28.33	32.20
INDIAN	43.56	37.12	40.05
PARDO	34.29	29.59	31.72
NEGRO	38.85	35.63	37.19
SLAVE	24.01	17.81	20.53
------	------	------	------
ALL	35.89	30.05	32.69

NOTE. ADULTS ARE SEVEN YEARS OR OLDER.

--ANDES--

RACE	PERCENT ADULTS MARRIED		
	MALES	FEMALES	ALL ADULTS
WHITE	42.47	39.90	41.11
INDIAN	57.71	49.35	53.20
PARDO	46.85	39.86	43.07
NEGRO	45.51	37.75	41.50
SLAVE	19.01	23.20	20.80
------	------	------	------
ALL	51.23	44.91	47.85

NOTE. ADULTS ARE SEVEN YEARS OR OLDER.

--LLANOS--

RACE	PERCENT ADULTS MARRIED		
	MALES	FEMALES	ALL ADULTS
WHITE	41.49	38.45	39.91
INDIAN	47.66	41.87	44.58
PARDO	41.53	38.13	39.74
NEGRO	38.98	33.65	36.14
SLAVE	16.34	18.57	17.40
------	------	------	------
ALL	39.81	36.92	38.30

NOTE. ADULTS ARE SEVEN YEARS OR OLDER.

--GUAYANA--

RACE	PERCENT ADULTS MARRIED		
	MALES	FEMALES	ALL ADULTS
WHITE	43.33	68.42	53.06
INDIAN	40.00	46.15	42.86
PARDO	56.25	64.29	60.00
NEGRO	0.00	0.00	0.00
SLAVE	20.00	42.86	27.27
------	------	------	------
ALL	45.37	60.49	51.85

NOTE. ADULTS ARE SEVEN YEARS OR OLDER.

TABLE A-10. CHILD/WOMAN RATIOS BY RACE (1800-1809)

RACE	CHILD/WOMAN
WHITE	.68
INDIAN	.88
PARDO	.74
NEGRO	.73
SLAVE	.68
------	-----
ALL	.73
LIFE TABLE	.58

CHILDREN AS PERCENT OF POPULATION. 27.96
CHILD IS AGES 0-6 YEARS.
ADULT WOMAN IS AGES 7 YEARS AND OLDER.

TABLE A-11. CHILD/WOMAN RATIOS BY RACE AND URBAN CATEGORY (1800-1809)

--HAMLETS--

RACE	CHILD/WOMAN
WHITE	.77
INDIAN	.65
PARDO	.77
NEGRO	.73
SLAVE	.92
------	-----
ALL	.79
LIFE TABLE	.58

CHILDREN AS PERCENT OF POPULATION. 28.60
CHILD IS AGES 0-6 YEARS.
ADULT WOMAN IS AGES 7 YEARS AND OLDER.

--VILLAGES--

RACE	CHILD/WOMAN
WHITE	.77
INDIAN	.84
PARDO	.81
NEGRO	.89
SLAVE	.78
------	-----
ALL	.81
LIFE TABLE	.58

CHILDREN AS PERCENT OF POPULATION. 28.69
CHILD IS AGES 0-6 YEARS.
ADULT WOMAN IS AGES 7 YEARS AND OLDER.

--TOWNS--

RACE	CHILD/WOMAN
WHITE	.73
INDIAN	.94
PARDO	.80
NEGRO	.74
SLAVE	.72
------	-----
ALL	.79
LIFE TABLE	.58

CHILDREN AS PERCENT OF POPULATION. 29.62
CHILD IS AGES 0-6 YEARS.
ADULT WOMAN IS AGES 7 YEARS AND OLDER.

--CITIES--

RACE	CHILD/WOMAN
WHITE	.60
INDIAN	.86
PARDO	.66
NEGRO	.63
SLAVE	.57
------	-----
ALL	.64
LIFE TABLE	.58

CHILDREN AS PERCENT OF POPULATION. 26.CO
CHILD IS AGES 0-6 YEARS.
ADULT WOMAN IS AGES 7 YEARS AND OLDER.

TABLE A-12. CHILD/WOMAN RATIOS BY RACE AND REGION (1800-1809)

--COAST--

RACE	CHILD/WOMAN
WHITE	.66
INDIAN	.76
PARDO	.61
NEGRO	.65
SLAVE	.73
------	-----
ALL	.66
LIFE TABLE	.58

CHILDREN AS PERCENT OF POPULATION. 25.51
CHILD IS AGES 0-6 YEARS.
ADULT WOMAN IS AGES 7 YEARS AND OLDER.

--COASTAL RANGE--

RACE	CHILD/WOMAN
WHITE	.63
INDIAN	.83
PARDO	.69
NEGRO	.63
SLAVE	.63
------	-----
ALL	.67
LIFE TABLE	.58

CHILDREN AS PERCENT OF POPULATION. 26.29
CHILD IS AGES 0-6 YEARS.
ADULT WOMAN IS AGES 7 YEARS AND OLDER.

--SEGOVIA HIGHLANDS--

RACE	CHILD/WOMAN
WHITE	.53
INDIAN	.88
PARDO	.67
NEGRO	.71
SLAVE	.67
------	-----
ALL	.68
LIFE TABLE	.58

CHILDREN AS PERCENT OF POPULATION. 27.21
CHILD IS AGES 0-6 YEARS.
ADULT WOMAN IS AGES 7 YEARS AND OLDER.

--ANDES--

RACE	CHILD/WOMAN
WHITE	1.06
INDIAN	.88
PARDO	1.17
NEGRO	1.18
SLAVE	1.01
------	-----
ALL	.98
LIFE TABLE	.58

CHILDREN AS PERCENT OF POPULATION. 34.39
CHILD IS AGES 0-6 YEARS.
ADULT WOMAN IS AGES 7 YEARS AND OLDER.

--LLANOS--

RACE	CHILD/WOMAN
WHITE	.77
INDIAN	.95
PARDO	.85
NEGRO	.89
SLAVE	.78
------	-----
ALL	.84
LIFE TABLE	.58

CHILDREN AS PERCENT OF POPULATION. 30.43
CHILD IS AGES 0-6 YEARS.
ADULT WOMAN IS AGES 7 YEARS AND OLDER.

--GUAYANA--

RACE	CHILD/WOMAN
WHITE	.84
INDIAN	.54
PARDO	.86
NEGRO	0.00
SLAVE	.29
------	-----
ALL	.75
LIFE TABLE	.58

CHILDREN AS PERCENT OF POPULATION. 24.40
CHILD IS AGES 0-6 YEARS.
ADULT WOMAN IS AGES 7 YEARS AND OLDER.

APPENDIX B

Parish Name Lists and Location Maps

<u>Introduction</u>

The four lists in Appendix B make up a guide to the parishes and parish names used in Parts I and II of this book. For those looking for a particular parish in the text or in the tables, the "Master Parish Name File" will indicate the parish name identifying each place in the study. If the name sought appears followed by **SEE..., that indicates that the parish is listed under the name following **SEE.... For example, in looking up Santa María de Altagracia, we discover that it is listed in the data file under Caracas-Altagracia. The master name file attempts to list most of the possible and all of the likely variants of any parish name. If a parish does not appear in this list, it is not included in the data and does not form part of this study. All alphabetizing in this book follows the English alphabet with no provision for treating <u>ll</u>, <u>rr</u>, or <u>ch</u> as separate letters. The <u>ñ</u> is treated as an <u>n</u>.

Should a reader want to locate any particular parish on the map or find its regional designation, the list headed "Parish Names with Regions, Modern States, and Number of Returns" will have that information. For Caracas-Altagracia, we see that it is in the Coastal Range, is located in the Distrito Federal, and has fifteen returns included in this data file.

The "Parishes Arranged by Region" is a permutation of the previous list to permit easy location of all the parishes in any region, and the "Parishes Arranged by State" is the same sort of list for locating the places covered in any particular state.

Although in most cases location of the parishes mentioned in the data proved reasonably unambiguous, some confusion still exists for a few tiny hamlets in the Llanos and elsewhere.

The maps included at the end of the name lists are designed to help locate the parishes within regions. Only parishes represented by at least one census return in the tables in Part II of this book are included on the maps. Because these are location maps, we have made no distinction between parishes of differing size. Readers interested in total population for these parishes should turn to Part II, Table 7.

The location of each parish on the maps has been determined by consulting the <u>Atlas de Venezuela</u> (Caracas: Ministerio de Obras Públicas, Dirección de Cartografía Nacional, 1971) and wherever that has proved inconclusive, the sheets of the 1:100,000 map series (Ministerio de Obras Públicas, Dirección de Cartografía Nacional) have been used. In the few cases where a colonial parish has not survived to appear on modern maps, I have placed the parish as best as can be determined from the description in Mariano Martí's <u>Compendio</u>, vols. 6 and 7 of <u>Documentos relativos a su visita pastoral de la Diócesis de Caracas, 1771-1784</u>, Biblioteca de la Academia Nacional de la Historia, nos. 95-101, 7 vols. (Caracas, 1969).

--A--

ACARIGUA
ACHAGUAS
AGUA BLANCA
AGUA CULEBRAS
AGUA DE CULEBRAS
    **SEE AGUA CULEBRAS
AGUACALIENTE
ALPARGATON
ALTAGRACIA
    **SEE ALTAGRACIA DE ORITUCO
ALTAGRACIA DE CARACAS
    **SEE CARACAS-ALTAGRACIA
ALTAGRACIA DE CURARIGUA
    **SEE CURARIGUA
ALTAGRACIA DE CURIEPE
    **SEE CURIEPE
ALTAGRACIA DE IGUANA
    **SEE IGUANA
ALTAGRACIA DE ORITUCO
ALTAGRACIA DE QUIBOR
    **SEE QUIBOR
ALTAMIRA
ALTAR
    **SEE SANTA INES DEL ALTAR
ANTIMANO
ANUNCIACION DE NRA. SRA. DE VALENCIA
    **SEE VALENCIA
APARICION
APARICION DE COROMOTO DE TUCUPIDO
    **SEE TUCUPIDO DE GUANARE
APURITO
ARAGUITA
ARAURE
AREGUE
ARENALES
ARICHUNA
AROA
ASUNCION DEL VALLE DE LA PASCUA
    **SEE VALLE DE LA PASCUA
ATAMAICA
AYAMANES

--B--

BANCO LARGO
BARBACOAS DE LOS LLANOS
BARBACOAS DEL TOCUYO
BARQUISIMETO
BARQUISIMETO, MITAD DE(1)
BARQUISIMETO, MITAD DE(2)
BARUTA
BAUL
BOBARE
BOCA DEL TINACO
    **SEE BAUL
BOCONO
BOCONO DE GUANARE
    **SEE BOCONO
BOCONOITO
    **SEE BOCONO
BORBURATA
BUEN CONSEJO
    **SEE EL CONSEJO
BUEN JESUS DE PETARE
    **SEE PETARE
BURERITO
BURIA

--C--

CABRIA
CABRUTA
CACIGUA
    **SEE CASIGUA
CAGUA
CAICARA DEL ORINOCO
CALABOZO
CALVARIO
    **SEE EL CALVARIO
CAMAGUAN
CAMATAGUA
CANDELARIA
    **SEE CARACAS-CANDELARIA
CANDELARIA DE CARABALLEDA
    **SEE CARABALLEDA
CANDELARIA DE PANAQUIRE
    **SEE PANAQUIRE
CANIZOS
    **SEE LOS CANIZOS
CANOABO
CAPAYA
CARA
    **SEE SAN FRANCISCO DE CARA
CARABALLEDA
CARACAS-ALTAGRACIA
CARACAS-CANDELARIA
CARACAS-CATEDRAL ORIENTE
CARACAS-CATEDRAL PONIENTE
CARACAS-CURATO CASTRENSE
CARACAS-SAN PABLO
CARACAS-SANTA ROSALIA
CARAMACATE
CARAYACA
CARMEN DE BANCO LARGO
    **SEE BANCO LARGO
CARMEN DE BURIA
    **SEE BURIA
CARORA
CARUAO

CASIGUA
CASTILLO DE SAN FELIPE DE PUERTO CABELLO
    **SEE PUERTO CABELLO, CASTILLO
CATA
CATEDRAL NACIENTE
    **SEE CARACAS-CATEDRAL ORIENTE
CATEDRAL ORIENTE
    **SEE CARACAS-CATEDRAL ORIENTE
CATEDRAL PONIENTE
    **SEE CARACAS-CATEDRAL PONIENTE
CAUCAGUA
CEPE
    **SEE CHUAO
CERRITO
CERRITO DE SANTA ROSA
    **SEE CERRITO
CERRO NEGRO
    **SEE SANTA INES DEL ALTAR
CHABASQUEN
CHACAO
CHAGUARAMAL
CHAGUARAMAS
CHARALLAVE
CHAVASQUEN
    **SEE CHABASQUEN
CHIQUINQUIRA
    **SEE AREGUE
CHIVACOA
CHORONI
CHUAO
CHUAO
    **SEE CHUAO
COCOROTE
COCUIZAS
    **SEE SAN ANTONIO DE LAS COCUIZAS
COJEDES
CONC. DE TARIA
    **SEE TARIA
COPACABANA DE LOS GUARENAS
    **SEE GUARENAS
CORTEZA
    **SEE APARICION
CRUZ DE GUARICO
    **SEE GUARICO
CUA
CUARA
    **SEE QUARA
CUBIRO
CUNAVICHE
CUPIRA
CURA
    **SEE VILLA DE CURA
CURARIGUA
CURATO CASTRENSE DE CARACAS
    **SEE CARACAS-CURATO CASTRENSE
CURIEPE
CUYAGUA

--D--

DIVINA PASTORA DE GUANARE VIEJO
    **SEE GUANARE VIEJO
DIVINA PASTORA DEL JOBAL
DUACA

--E--

EL ALTAR
    **SEE SANTA INES DEL ALTAR
EL BAUL
    **SEE BAUL
EL BUEN CONSEJO
    **SEE EL CONSEJO
EL BUEN JESUS DE PETARE
    **SEE PETARE
EL CALVARIO
EL CARMEN DE BANCO LARGO
    **SEE BANCO LARGO
EL CARMEN DE BURIA
    **SEE BURIA
EL CERRITO
    **SEE CERRITO
EL CONSEJO
EL GUAPO
EL HATILLO
EL PAO
EL PILAR
    **SEE ARAURE
EL RASTRO
EL ROSARIO
    **SEE ANTIMANO
EL ROSARIO
    **SEE ALTAMIRA
EL ROSARIO DE BARUTA
    **SEE BARUTA
EL ROSARIO DE CASIGUA
    **SEE CASIGUA
EL ROSARIO DE GUIGUE
    **SEE GUIGUE
EL ROSARIO DE HUMOCARO BAJO
    **SEE HUMOCARO BAJO
EL ROSARIO DE LA VEGA
    **SEE LA VEGA
EL ROSARIO DE MARACA
    **SEE MARACA
EL ROSARIO DE MARIN
    **SEE CUA
EL ROSARIO DE TAGUAI
    **SEE TAGUAI
EL SOMBRERO
EL TINACO
    **SEE TINACO
EL TINAQUILLO
    **SEE TINAQUILLO

EL TOCUYO
EL VALLE
EL VALLE DE CABRIA
**SEE CABRIA
EL VALLE DE CAUCAGUA
**SEE CAUCAGUA
EL VALLE DE CHORONI
**SEE CHORONI
EL VALLE DE CUYAGUA
**SEE CUYAGUA
EL VALLE DE GUATIRE
**SEE GUATIRE
EL VALLE DE LA PURA Y LIMPIA CONCEPCION DE CUYAGUA
**SEE CUYAGUA
EL VALLE DE MORON
**SEE MORON
EL VALLE DE MOROTURO
**SEE MOROTURO
EL VALLE DE TURIAMO
**SEE TURIAMO
EL VALLE DE URAMA
**SEE URAMA
ESPINO

--F--

FARMAS
**SEE TARMAS

--G--

GOAIGOAZA
**SEE GUAIGUAZA
GUACARA
GUADALUPE DE BOBARE
**SEE BOBARE
GUADARRAMA
GUAIGUAZA
GUAIRA
**SEE LA GUAIRA
GUAIRA DE PARACOTOS
**SEE PARACOTOS
GUAMA
GUANARE
GUANARE VIEJO
GUANARITO
GUAPO
**SEE EL GUAPO
GUARDATINAJAS
GUARENAS
GUARICO
GUASGUAS
GUATIRE
GUAYABAL
GUAYGUAZA
**SEE GUAIGUAZA
GUAYOS
**SEE LOS GUAYOS
GUAYRA
**SEE LA GUAIRA
GUAYRA
**SEE LA GUAIRA, CURATO CASTRENSE
GUAYRA DE PARACOTOS
**SEE PARACOTOS
GUIGUE
GUIRIPA

--H--

HORTIZ
**SEE ORTIZ
HOSPINO
**SEE OSPINO
HUMOCARO ALTO
HUMOCARO BAJO

--I--

IGUANA
IMCDA. CONC. DE CUYAGUA
**SEE CUYAGUA
IMCDA. CONC. DE GUAIGUAZA
**SEE GUAIGUAZA
IMCDA. CONC. DE NRA. SRA. DE BARBACOAS
**SEE BARBACOAS DE LOS LLANOS
IMCDA. CONC. DE NRA. SRA. DE CAMATAGUA
**SEE CAMATAGUA
IMCDA. CONC. DE NRA. SRA. DE CUPIRA
**SEE CUPIRA
IMCDA. CONC. DE NRA. SRA. DE MARIARA
**SEE MARIARA
IMCDA. CONC. DE NRA. SRA. DE MONTALBAN
**SEE MONTALBAN
IMCDA. CONC. DE NRA. SRA. DEL SOMBRERO
**SEE EL SOMBRERO
IMCDA. CONC. DE NRA. SRA. DEL TOCUYO
**SEE EL TOCUYO
IPIRE
**SEE SANTA MARIA DE IPIRE

--J--

JESUS DE PETARE
**SEE PETARE
JESUS, MARIA Y JOSE DE TACARIGUA
**SEE TACARIGUA DE MAMPORAL
JOBAL
**SEE DIVINA PASTORA DEL JOBAL
JUJURE
**SEE TUREN

--L--

LA ANUNCIACION DE NRA. SRA. DE VALENCIA
**SEE VALENCIA
LA ANUNCIACION DE NRA. SRA. DEL VALLE DE LA SANTA CRUZ DE CAUCAGUA
**SEE CAUCAGUA
LA ANUNCIACION DEL VALLE DE MOROTURO
**SEE MOROTURO
LA APARICION DE COROMOTO DE TUCUPIDO
**SEE TUCUPIDO DE GUANARE
LA ASUNCION DEL VALLE DE LA PASCUA
**SEE VALLE DE LA PASCUA
LA BORBURATA
**SEE BORBURATA
LA CANDELARIA
**SEE CARACAS-CANDELARIA
LA CONC. DE TARIA
**SEE TARIA
LA CONCEPCION DE CUYAGUA
**SEE CUYAGUA
LA CORTEZA
**SEE APARICION
LA DIVINA PASTORA DE GUANARE VIEJO
**SEE GUANARE VIEJO
LA DIVINA PASTORA DEL JOBAL
**SEE DIVINA PASTORA DEL JOBAL
LA GUAIRA
LA GUAIRA DE PARACOTOS
**SEE PARACOTOS
LA GUAIRA, CURATO CASTRENSE
LA HUMILDAD Y PACIENCIA DE NRO. SR. JESUCRISTO DE CAMAGUAN
**SEE CAMAGUAN
LA IMCDA. CONC. DE CUYAGUA
**SEE CUYAGUA
LA IMCDA. CONC. DE GUAIGUAZA
**SEE GUAIGUAZA
LA IMCDA. CONC. DE NRA. SRA. DE BARQUISIMETO
**SEE BARQUISIMETO
LA IMCDA. CONC. DE NRA. SRA. DE CAMATAGUA
**SEE CAMATAGUA
LA IMCDA. CONC. DE NRA. SRA. DE CUPIRA
**SEE CUPIRA
LA IMCDA. CONC. DE NRA. SRA. DE MARIARA
**SEE MARIARA
LA IMCDA. CONC. DE NRA. SRA. DE MONTALBAN
**SEE MONTALBAN
LA IMCDA. CONC. DE NRA. SRA. DE PAYARA
**SEE PAYARA
LA IMCDA. CONC. DE NRA. SRA. DEL SOMBRERO
**SEE EL SOMBRERO
LA IMCDA. CONC. DE NRA. SRA. DEL TOCUYO
**SEE EL TOCUYO
LA MERCED
**SEE ARENALES
LA MISION
**SEE LOS ANGELES
LA MISION BAJA
**SEE LOS ANGELES
LA MISSION ALTA
**SEE LA SANTISIMA TRINIDAD
LA SABANA DE OCUMARE
**SEE OCUMARE DEL TUY
LA SABANETA DE TUREN
**SEE SABANETA
LA SANTA CRUZ DE GUARICO
**SEE GUARICO
LA SANTISIMA CRUZ DE MACAIRITA
**SEE MACAIRITA
LA SANTISIMA TRINIDAD
LA SANTISIMA TRINIDAD DE MARCHENA
**SEE LA SANTISIMA TRINIDAD
LA VEGA
LA VICTORIA
LA VICTORIA DE NIRGUA
**SEE NIRGUA
LAGUNITAS
**SEE DIVINA PASTORA DEL JOBAL
LAS COCUIZAS
**SEE SAN ANTONIO DE LAS COCUIZAS
LAS GUASGUAS
**SEE GUASGUAS
LAS TINAJAS
**SEE TINAJAS
LESAMA
**SEE LEZAMA
LEZAMA
LOS ACHAGUAS
**SEE ACHAGUAS
LOS ANGELES
LOS ANGELES DE SETENTA
LOS ARENALES
**SEE ARENALES
LOS AYAMANES
**SEE AYAMANES
LOS CANIZOS
LOS GUARENAS
**SEE GUARENAS
LOS GUAYOS
LOS TEQUES

--M--

MACAIRA
MACAIRITA
MACARAO
MACUTO
**SEE CARABALLEDA
MAGDALENA DE MAGDALENO
**SEE MAGDALENO
MAGDALENO
MAIQUETIA

MAMON
**SEE EL CONSEJO
MAMPORAL
MANAPIRE
MAPUEY
**SEE SAN JOSE
MARACA
MARACAY
MARASMA
**SEE CAPAYA
MARCHENA
**SEE LA SANTISIMA TRINIDAD
MARIA
MARIA MAGDALENA DE MAGDALENO
**SEE MAGDALENO
MARIARA
MARIN
**SEE CUA
MAYQUETIA
**SEE MAIQUETIA
MISION BAJA
**SEE LOS ANGELES
MISSION ALTA
**SEE LA SANTISIMA TRINIDAD
MONTALBAN
MONTALVAN
**SEE MONTALBAN
MORON
MORCTURO
MORRONCITO
**SEE GUANARE VIEJO
MORRONES
**SEE GUANARE VIEJO

--N--

NAGUANAGUA
NAIGUATA
NAYGUATA
**SEE NAIGUATA
NIRGUA
NRA. SRA. DE ALTAGRACIA DE CURARIGUA
**SEE CURARIGUA
NRA. SRA. DE ALTAGRACIA DE IGUANA
**SEE IGUANA
NRA. SRA. DE ALTAGRACIA DE ORITUCO
**SEE ALTAGRACIA DE ORITUCO
NRA. SRA. DE ALTAGRACIA DE QUIBOR
**SEE QUIBOR
NRA. SRA. DE ALTAGRACIA Y DEL SENOR SAN JOSE DE CURIEPE
**SEE CURIEPE
NRA. SRA. DE BARBACOAS
**SEE BARBACOAS DE LOS LLANOS
NRA. SRA. DE BARQUISIMETO
**SEE BARQUISIMETO
NRA. SRA. DE BEGONA DE NAGUANAGUA
**SEE NAGUANAGUA
NRA. SRA. DE CAMATAGUA
**SEE CAMATAGUA
NRA. SRA. DE CANDELARIA DE CARABALLEDA
**SEE CARABALLEDA
NRA. SRA. DE CANDELARIA DE PANAQUIRE
**SEE PANAQUIRE
NRA. SRA. DE CANDELARIA DE TARMAS
**SEE TARMAS
NRA. SRA. DE CANDELARIA DE TURMERO
**SEE TURMERO
NRA. SRA. DE CHIQUINQUIRA DE AREGUE
**SEE AREGUE
NRA. SRA. DE CHIQUINQUIRA DEL TINACO
**SEE TINACO
NRA. SRA. DE COPACABANA DE LOS GUARENAS
**SEE GUARENAS
NRA. SRA. DE CUPIRA
**SEE CUPIRA
NRA. SRA. DE GUADALUPE DE BOBARE
**SEE BOBARE
NRA. SRA. DE GUADALUPE DE LA VICTORIA
**SEE LA VICTORIA
NRA. SRA. DE LA APARICION DE COROMOTO DE TUCUPIDO
**SEE TUCUPIDO DE GUANARE
NRA. SRA. DE LA APARICION DE LA CORTEZA
**SEE APARICION
NRA. SRA. DE LA ASUNCION DEL VALLE DE LA PASCUA
**SEE VALLE DE LA PASCUA
NRA. SRA. DE LA ASUNCION DEL VALLE DE LA PASCUA
**SEE EL VALLE
NRA. SRA. DE LA CANDELARIA
**SEE CARACAS-CANDELARIA
NRA. SRA. DE LA CARIDAD DE LAS TINAJAS
**SEE TINAJAS
NRA. SRA. DE LA CONC. DE TARIA
**SEE TARIA
NRA. SRA. DE LA IMCDA. CONC. DE GUAIGUAZA
**SEE GUAIGUAZA
NRA. SRA. DE LA INIESTRA DE MARASMA, VALLE DE CAPAYA
**SEE CAPAYA
NRA. SRA. DE LA MERCED DE LOS ARENALES
**SEE ARENALES
NRA. SRA. DE LA MERCED DE RIO CHICO
**SEE RIO CHICO
NRA. SRA. DE LA PAZ DE GUANARITO
**SEE GUANARITO
NRA. SRA. DE LA VICTORIA DE NIRGUA
**SEE NIRGUA
NRA. SRA. DE LOS ANGELES
**SEE LOS ANGELES
NRA. SRA. DE LOS ANGELES DE SETENTA
**SEE LOS ANGELES DE SETENTA
NRA. SRA. DE LOS DOLORES DE TOCUYITO
**SEE TOCUYITO

NRA. SRA. DE MACARAO
    **SEE MACARAO
NRA. SRA. DE MARIARA
    **SEE MARIARA
NRA. SRA. DE MONTALBAN
    **SEE MONTALBAN
NRA. SRA. DE VALENCIA
    **SEE VALENCIA
NRA. SRA. DEL BUEN CONSEJO DEL MAMON
    **SEE EL CONSEJO
NRA. SRA. DEL CARMEN DE BANCO LARGO
    **SEE BANCO LARGO
NRA. SRA. DEL CARMEN DE BURIA
    **SEE BURIA
NRA. SRA. DEL PILAR DE ARAURE
    **SEE ARAURE
NRA. SRA. DEL ROSARIO DE ALTAMIRA
    **SEE ALTAMIRA
NRA. SRA. DEL ROSARIO DE ANTIMANO
    **SEE ANTIMANO
NRA. SRA. DEL ROSARIO DE BARUTA
    **SEE BARUTA
NRA. SRA. DEL ROSARIO DE CASIGUA
    **SEE CASIGUA
NRA. SRA. DEL ROSARIO DE CHIQUINQUIRA
    **SEE AREGUE
NRA. SRA. DEL ROSARIO DE GUIGUE
    **SEE GUIGUE
NRA. SRA. DEL ROSARIO DE HUMOCARO BAJO
    **SEE HUMOCARO BAJO
NRA. SRA. DEL ROSARIO DE LA VEGA
    **SEE LA VEGA
NRA. SRA. DEL ROSARIO DE MARACA
    **SEE MARACA
NRA. SRA. DEL ROSARIO DE MARIN
    **SEE CUA
NRA. SRA. DEL ROSARIO DE TAGUAI
    **SEE TAGUAI
NRA. SRA. DEL SOCORRO DEL TINAQUILLO
    **SEE TINAQUILLO
NRA. SRA. DEL SOMBRERO
    **SEE EL SOMBRERO
NRA. SRA. DEL TOCUYO
    **SEE EL TOCUYO
NRA. SRA. DEL VALLE DE CAUCAGUA
    **SEE CAUCAGUA
NRA. SRA. DEL VALLE DE LA PASCUA
    **SEE VALLE DE LA PASCUA
NRO. SR. JOSE DE LA SABANA DE CARUAO
    **SEE CARUAO

--O--

OCUMARE
    **SEE OCUMARE DEL TUY
OCUMARE DE LA COSTA
OCUMARE DEL TUY
ONOTO
    **SEE SAN RAFAEL DE ONOTO
ORACHICHE
    **SEE URACHICHE
ORITUCO
    **SEE ALTAGRACIA DE ORITUCO
ORITUCO
    **SEE SAN RAFAEL DE ORITUCO
ORTIZ
OSPINO

--P--

PACAIRIGUA
    **SEE GUATIRE
PANAQUIRE
PAO
    **SEE EL PAO
PARACOTOS
PARAISO DE CHABASQUEN
    **SEE CHABASQUEN
PARAPARA
PASCUA
    **SEE VALLE DE LA PASCUA
PATANEMO
PAYARA
PETARE
PILAR
    **SEE ARAURE
PUERTO CABELLO
PUERTO CABELLO, CASTILLO

--Q--

QUARA
QUIBOR

--R--

RASTRO
    **SEE EL RASTRO
RIO CHICO
RIO DEL TOCUYO
ROSARIO
    **SEE ANTIMANO
ROSARIO
    **SEE ALTAMIRA
ROSARIO DE BARUTA
    **SEE BARUTA
ROSARIO DE CASIGUA
    **SEE CASIGUA
ROSARIO DE GUIGUE
    **SEE GUIGUE
ROSARIO DE HUMOCARO BAJO
    **SEE HUMOCARO BAJO
ROSARIO DE LA VEGA
    **SEE LA VEGA

ROSARIO DE MARACA
**SEE MARACA
ROSARIO DE MARIN
**SEE CUA
ROSARIO DE TAGUAI
**SEE TAGUAI

--S--

SABANA DE CARUAO
**SEE CARUAO
SABANA DE OCUMARE
**SEE OCUMARE DEL TUY
SABANETA
SAN AGUSTIN DE GUACARA
**SEE GUACARA
SAN ANTONIO DE LAS COCUIZAS
SAN ANTONIO DE LOS ALTOS
SAN ANTONIO DE LOS NARANJOS DE HUMOCARO ALTO
**SEE HUMOCARO ALTO
SAN ANTONIO DE PADUA DE HUMOCARO ALTO
**SEE HUMOCARO ALTO
SAN ANTONIO DE PADUA DE JUJURE
**SEE TUREN
SAN ANTONIO DE PADUA DE LAS COCUIZAS
**SEE SAN ANTONIO DE LAS COCUIZAS
SAN ANTONIO DE PADUA DE TUREN
**SEE TUREN
SAN ANTONIO PADUA DE LOS GUAYOS
**SEE LOS GUAYOS
SAN BARTOLOME DE MACUTO
**SEE CARABALLEDA
SAN CARLOS
SAN CARLOS DE AUSTRIA
**SEE SAN CARLOS
SAN DIEGO DE ALCALA
SAN DIEGO DE ALCALA DE LA SABANA DE OCUMARE
**SEE OCUMARE DEL TUY
SAN DIEGO DE LOS ALTOS
SAN FELIPE
SAN FELIPE DE BARBACOAS
**SEE BARBACOAS DEL TOCUYO
SAN FELIPE DE PUERTO CABELLO
**SEE PUERTO CABELLO, CASTILLO
SAN FELIPE DE TUCURAGUA
**SEE TUCURAGUA
SAN FELIPE NERI DE LOS TEQUES
**SEE LOS TEQUES
SAN FELIPE NERI DE LOS VALLES DE CHUAO Y SEPE
**SEE CHUAO
SAN FELIPE NERI DEL GUAPO
**SEE EL GUAPO
SAN FELIPE, MITAD DE (1)
SAN FELIPE, MITAD DE (2)
SAN FERNANDO DE APURE
SAN FERNANDO DE CACHICAMO
SAN FERNANDO DE OSPINO
**SEE OSPINO
SAN FRANCISCO DE ASIS DE COJEDES
**SEE COJEDES
SAN FRANCISCO DE ASIS DE NAIGUATA
**SEE NAIGUATA
SAN FRANCISCO DE CAMATAGUA
**SEE CAMATAGUA
SAN FRANCISCO DE CARA
SAN FRANCISCO DE TIZNADOS
SAN FRANCISCO DE YARE
SAN FRANCISCO DEL VALLE DE CATA
**SEE CATA
SAN FRANCISCO DEL VALLE DE MORON
**SEE MORON
SAN FRANCISCO JAVIER DE AGUA DE CULEBRAS
**SEE AGUA CULEBRAS
SAN FRANCISCO JAVIER DE ARAGUITA
**SEE ARAGUITA
SAN FRANCISCO JAVIER DE LEZAMA
**SEE LEZAMA
SAN GABRIEL DE CHAGUARAMAL
**SEE CHAGUARAMAL
SAN GENARO DE BOCONO
**SEE BOCONO
SAN GERONIMO DE GUAYABAL
**SEE GUAYABAL
SAN HILARIO DE TEMERLA
**SEE TEMERLA
SAN IGNACIO DE LOYOLA DE CABRUTA
**SEE CABRUTA
SAN JAIME
SAN JAVIER
**SEE AGUA CULEBRAS
SAN JAYME
**SEE SAN JAIME
SAN JERONIMO DE BARBACOAS
**SEE BARBACOAS DE LOS LLANOS
SAN JERONIMO DE COCOROTO
**SEE COCOROTE
SAN JOAQUIN DE CARABOBO
**SEE SAN PEDRO
SAN JORGE DE BURERITO
**SEE BURERITO
SAN JOSE
SAN JOSE DE APURE
SAN JOSE DE APURITO
**SEE APURITO
SAN JOSE DE CAGUA
**SEE CAGUA
SAN JOSE DE CANOABO
**SEE CANOABO
SAN JOSE DE CARAYACA
**SEE CARAYACA
SAN JOSE DE CARUAO
**SEE CARUAO

SAN JOSE DE CHACAO
    **SEE CHACAO
SAN JOSE DE CHIVACOA
    **SEE CHIVACOA
SAN JOSE DE CURIEPE
    **SEE CURIEPE
SAN JOSE DE GUAMA
    **SEE GUAMA
SAN JOSE DE LEONISA DE CUNAVICHE
    **SEE CUNAVICHE
SAN JOSE DE MAPUEY
    **SEE SAN JOSE
SAN JOSE DE MARACAY
    **SEE MARACAY
SAN JOSE DE PUERTO CABELLO
    **SEE PUERTO CABELLO
SAN JOSE DE SIQUISIQUE
    **SEE SIQUISIQUE
SAN JOSE DE TACATA
    **SEE TACATA
SAN JOSE DE TIZNADOS
SAN JUAN BAUTISTA DE CARORA
    **SEE CARORA
SAN JUAN BAUTISTA DE DUACA
    **SEE DUACA
SAN JUAN BAUTISTA DE ESPINO
    **SEE ESPINO
SAN JUAN BAUTISTA DE LA BORBURATA
    **SEE BORBURATA
SAN JUAN BAUTISTA DE ORACHICHE
    **SEE URACHICHE
SAN JUAN BAUTISTA DE PATANEMO
    **SEE PATANEMO
SAN JUAN BAUTISTA DE URACHICHE
    **SEE URACHICHE
SAN JUAN BAUTISTA DEL PAO
    **SEE EL PAO
SAN JUAN BAUTISTA DEL VALLE DE URAMA
    **SEE URAMA
SAN JUAN BAUTISTA Y SENOR SAN JOSE DE
  TACATA
    **SEE TACATA
SAN JUAN DE LOS MORROS
SAN JUAN DE PAYARA
    **SEE PAYARA
SAN JUAN EVANGELISTA DE LA GUAIRA DE
  PARACOTOS
    **SEE PARACOTOS
SAN JUAN NEPOMUCENO DE TAPIPA
    **SEE TAPIPA
SAN LORENZO DE CHAGUARAMAS
    **SEE CHAGUARAMAS
SAN LUIS BELTRAN DEL VALLE DE CABRIA
    **SEE CABRIA
SAN LUIS DE CURA
    **SEE VILLA DE CURA
SAN MATEO
SAN MIGUEL DE ACARIGUA
    **SEE ACARIGUA
SAN MIGUEL DE BURIA
    **SEE BURIA
SAN MIGUEL DE CAICARA
    **SEE CAICARA DEL ORINOCO
SAN MIGUEL DE CUBIRO
    **SEE CUBIRO
SAN MIGUEL DE LA BOCA DEL TINACO
    **SEE BAUL
SAN MIGUEL DE LOS AYAMANES
    **SEE AYAMANES
SAN MIGUEL DE TRUJILLO
SAN MIGUEL DE TURIAMO
    **SEE TURIAMO
SAN MIGUEL DEL VALLE DE AROA
    **SEE AROA
SAN MIGUEL DEL VALLE DE TURIAMO
    **SEE TURIAMO
SAN NICOLAS DE BARI DE LOS CANIZOS
    **SEE LOS CANIZOS
SAN NICOLAS DE BARI DE SARARE
    **SEE SARARE
SAN NICOLAS DE BARI DEL RASTRO
    **SEE EL RASTRO
SAN NICOLAS DE TOLENTINO
SAN PABLO
    **SEE CARACAS-SAN PABLO
SAN PEDRO
SAN PEDRO
    **SEE SAN PEDRO
SAN PEDRO ALCANTARA DE MARIA
    **SEE MARIA
SAN PEDRO APOSTOL DE LA GUAIRA
    **SEE LA GUAIRA
SAN PEDRO DEL CALVARIO
    **SEE EL CALVARIO
SAN RAFAEL DE ATAMAICA
    **SEE ATAMAICA
SAN RAFAEL DE LAS GUASGUAS
    **SEE GUASGUAS
SAN RAFAEL DE ONOTO
SAN RAFAEL DE ORITUCO
SAN SEBASTIAN DE LOS REYES
SAN SEBASTIAN DE MAIQUETIA
    **SEE MAIQUETIA
SAN SEBASTIAN DE OCUMARE DE LA COSTA
    **SEE OCUMARE DE LA COSTA
SAN VICENTE FERRER DEL VALLE DE
  ALPARGATON
    **SEE ALPARGATON
SAN XAVIER
    **SEE AGUA CULEBRAS
SANARE
SANTA ANA DE SANARE
    **SEE SANARE
SANTA BARBARA
    **SEE ACHAGUAS

SANTA BARBARA DE AGUA BLANCA
**SEE AGUA BLANCA
SANTA BARBARA DE APURE DE ARICHUNA
**SEE ARICHUNA
SANTA BARBARA DE ARICHUNA
**SEE ARICHUNA
SANTA BARBARA DE GUARDATINAJAS
**SEE GUARDATINAJAS
SANTA BARBARA DE LOS ACHAGUAS
**SEE ACHAGUAS
SANTA CATALINA DE QUARA
**SEE QUARA
SANTA CATALINA DE SENA DE PARAPARA
**SEE PARAPARA
SANTA CLARA DE CARAMACATE
**SEE CARAMACATE
SANTA CLARA DEL VALLE DE CHORONI
**SEE CHORONI
SANTA CRUZ DE ARAGUA
SANTA CRUZ DE GUARICO
**SEE GUARICO
SANTA CRUZ DE MACAIRA
**SEE MACAIRA
SANTA CRUZ DE PACAIRIGUA EN EL VALLE DE GUATIRE
**SEE GUATIRE
SANTA INES DEL ALTAR
SANTA LUCIA
SANTA LUCIA DE APURE
**SEE SAN JOSE DE APURE
SANTA LUCIA DE YARITAGUA
**SEE YARITAGUA
SANTA MARIA DE ALTAGRACIA
**SEE CARACAS-ALTAGRACIA
SANTA MARIA DE IPIRE
SANTA RITA DE MANAPIRE
**SEE MANAPIRE
SANTA ROSA DE LIMA
SANTA ROSA DE LIMA DE CHARALLAVE
**SEE CHARALLAVE
SANTA ROSA DE LIMA DE ORTIZ
**SEE ORTIZ
SANTA ROSA DEL CERRITO
**SEE CERRITO
SANTA ROSALIA
**SEE CARACAS-SANTA ROSALIA
SANTA ROSALIA DEL HATILLO
**SEE EL HATILLO
SANTA TERESA DE JESUS
SANTIAGO DEL RIO DEL TOCUYO
**SEE RIO DEL TOCUYO
SANTISIMA CRUZ DE MACAIRITA
**SEE MACAIRITA
SANTISIMA TRINIDAD DE MARCHENA
**SEE LA SANTISIMA TRINIDAD
SANTO DOMINGO DE MAMPORAL
**SEE MAMPORAL
SANTO TOMAI DE GUACARRAMA
**SEE GUADARRAMA
SANTO TOMAS DE GUACARRAMA
**SEE GUADARRAMA
SANTO TOMAS DE TUCUPIDO
**SEE TUCUPIDO
SARARE
SEPE
**SEE CHUAO
SIQUISIQUE
SOMBRERO
**SEE EL SOMBRERO

--T--

TACARIGUA DE MAMPORAL
TACATA
TAGUAI
TAGUAY
**SEE TAGUAI
TAPIPA
TARIA
TARMAS
TEMERLA
TEQUES
**SEE LOS TEQUES
TIMERLA
**SEE TEMERLA
TINACO
TINAJAS
TINAQUILLO
TISNADOS
**SEE SAN FRANCISCO DE TIZNADOS
TIZNADOS
**SEE SAN FRANCISCO DE TIZNADOS
TIZNADOS
**SEE SAN JOSE DE TIZNADOS
TOCUYITO
TOCUYO
**SEE EL TOCUYO
TODOS LOS SANTOS DE CALABOZO
**SEE CALABOZO
TRINIDAD
**SEE LA SANTISIMA TRINIDAD
TUCUPIDO
TUCUPIDO DE GUANARE
TUCURAGUA
TUPEN
TURIAMO
TURMERO

--U--

URACHICHE
URAMA

--V--

VALENCIA
VALLE DE AGUACALIENTE
**SEE AGUACALIENTE
VALLE DE ALPARGATON
**SEE ALPARGATON
VALLE DE AROA
**SEE AROA
VALLE DE BORBURATA
**SEE BORBURATA
VALLE DE CABRIA
**SEE CABRIA
VALLE DE CAPAYA
**SEE CAPAYA
VALLE DE CAUCAGUA
**SEE CAUCAGUA
VALLE DE CHORONI
**SEE CHORONI
VALLE DE CHUAO
**SEE CHUAO
VALLE DE CHUAO Y SEPE
**SEE CHUAO
VALLE DE CURARIGUA DE LEAL
**SEE CURARIGUA
VALLE DE GUATIRE
**SEE GUATIRE
VALLE DE LA PASCUA
VALLE DE MORON
**SEE MORON
VALLE DE MOROTURO
**SEE MOROTURO
VALLE DE NRA. SRA. DEL ROSARIO DE MARIN O CUA
**SEE CUA
VALLE DE PASCUA
**SEE VALLE DE LA PASCUA
VALLE DE SAN FRANCISCO DE CATA
**SEE CATA
VALLE DE SAN FRANCISCO DE PAULA DE YARE
**SEE SAN FRANCISCO DE YARE
VALLE DE SEPE
**SEE CHUAO
VALLE DE TURIAMO
**SEE TURIAMO
VALLE DE URAMA
**SEE URAMA
VEGA
**SEE LA VEGA
VICTORIA
**SEE LA VICTORIA
VICTORIA DE NIRGUA
**SEE NIRGUA
VILLA DE CURA
VILLA DE SAN LUIS DE CURA
**SEE VILLA DE CURA

--Y--

YARE
**SEE SAN FRANCISCO DE YARE
YARITAGUA
YUJURE
**SEE TUREN

--Z--

ZARAZA
**SEE CHAGUARAMAL

PARISH NAMES WITH REGIONS, MODERN STATES, AND NUMBER OF RETURNS

PARISH NAME	REGION NAME	STATE NAME	NUMBER OF RETURNS
--A--			
ACARIGUA	LLANOS	PORTUGUESA	10
ACHAGUAS	LLANOS	APURE	6
AGUA BLANCA	LLANOS	PORTUGUESA	10
AGUA CULEBRAS	COAST	YARACUY	16
AGUACALIENTE	COASTRANGE	CARABOBO	7
ALPARGATON	COAST	CARABOBO	7
ALTAGRACIA DE ORITUCO	COASTRANGE	GUARICO	9
ALTAMIRA	LLANOS	GUARICO	1
ANTIMANO	COASTRANGE	D.F.	2
APARICION	LLANOS	PORTUGUESA	9
APURITO	LLANOS	APURE	3
ARAGUITA	COASTRANGE	MIRANDA	11
ARAURE	LLANOS	PORTUGUESA	15
AREGUE	SEGOVIA	LARA	6
ARENALES	SEGOVIA	LARA	6
ARICHUNA	LLANOS	APURE	2
AROA	COAST	YARACUY	7
ATAMAICA	LLANOS	APURE	2
AYAMANES	COAST	LARA	7
--B--			
BANCO LARGO	LLANOS	APURE	2
BARBACOAS DE LOS LLANOS	LLANOS	ARAGUA	9
BARBACOAS DEL TOCUYO	ANDES	LARA	16
BARQUISIMETO	SEGOVIA	LARA	2
BARQUISIMETO, MITAD DE(1)	SEGOVIA	LARA	13
BARQUISIMETO, MITAD DE(2)	SEGOVIA	LARA	13
BARUTA	COASTRANGE	MIRANDA	9
BAUL	LLANOS	COJEDES	10
BOBARE	SEGOVIA	LARA	9
BOCONO	LLANOS	PORTUGUESA	14
BORBURATA	COAST	CARABOBO	7
BURERITO	SEGOVIA	LARA	5
BURIA	LLANOS	LARA	12
--C--			
CABRIA	COAST	YARACUY	3
CABRUTA	LLANOS	GUARICO	4
CAGUA	COASTRANGE	ARAGUA	13
CAICARA DEL ORINOCO	GUAYANA	BOLIVAR	1
CALABOZO	LLANOS	GUARICO	12
CAMAGUAN	LLANOS	GUARICO	7
CAMATAGUA	LLANOS	ARAGUA	8
CANOABO	COASTRANGE	CARABOBO	15
CAPAYA	COASTRANGE	MIRANDA	15
CARABALLEDA	COAST	D.F.	2

PARISH NAME	REGION NAME	STATE NAME	NUMBER OF RETURNS
CARACAS-ALTAGRACIA	COASTRANGE	D.F.	15
CARACAS-CANDELARIA	COASTRANGE	D.F.	16
CARACAS-CATEDRAL ORIENTE	COASTRANGE	D.F.	13
CARACAS-CATEDRAL PONIENTE	COASTRANGE	D.F.	13
CARACAS-CURATO CASTRENSE	COASTRANGE	D.F.	7
CARACAS-SAN PABLO	COASTRANGE	D.F.	17
CARACAS-SANTA ROSALIA	COASTRANGE	D.F.	21
CARAMACATE	LLANOS	PORTUGUESA	27
CARAYACA	COAST	D.F.	13
CARORA	SEGOVIA	LARA	5
CARUAO	COAST	D.F.	2
CASIGUA	COAST	FALCON	1
CATA	COAST	ARAGUA	3
CAUCAGUA	COASTRANGE	MIRANDA	16
CERRITO	SEGOVIA	LARA	1
CHABASQUEN	ANDES	PORTUGUESA	15
CHACAO	COASTRANGE	MIRANDA	9
CHAGUARAMAL	COAST	GUARICO	3
CHAGUARAMAS	LLANOS	GUARICO	7
CHARALLAVE	COASTRANGE	MIRANDA	13
CHIVACOA	COAST	YARACUY	16
CHORONI	COAST	ARAGUA	7
CHUAO	COAST	ARAGUA	5
COCOROTE	SEGOVIA	YARACUY	18
COJEDES	LLANOS	COJEDES	29
CUA	COASTRANGE	MIRANDA	10
CUBIRO	ANDES	LARA	15
CUNAVICHE	LLANOS	APURE	1
CUPIRA	COAST	MIRANDA	9
CURARIGUA	SEGOVIA	LARA	14
CURIEPE	COASTRANGE	MIRANDA	14
CUYAGUA	COAST	ARAGUA	7
--D--			
DIVINA PASTORA DEL JOBAL	LLANOS	COJEDES	27
DUACA	SEGOVIA	LARA	13
--E--			
EL CALVARIO	LLANOS	GUARICO	7
EL CONSEJO	COASTRANGE	ARAGUA	15
EL GUAPO	COAST	MIRANDA	11
EL HATILLO	COASTRANGE	MIRANDA	8
EL PAO	LLANOS	COJEDES	31
EL RASTRO	LLANOS	GUARICO	6
EL SOMBRERO	LLANOS	GUARICO	9
EL TOCUYO	SEGOVIA	LARA	16
EL VALLE	COASTRANGE	D.F.	12
ESPINO	LLANOS	GUARICO	2
--G--			
GUACARA	COASTRANGE	CARABOBO	7

PARISH NAME	REGION NAME	STATE NAME	NUMBER OF RETURNS
GUADARRAMA	LLANOS	BARINAS	1
GUAIGUAZA	COAST	CARABOBO	7
GUAMA	SEGOVIA	YARACUY	15
GUANARE	LLANOS	PORTUGUESA	12
GUANARE VIEJO	LLANOS	PORTUGUESA	12
GUANARITO	LLANOS	PORTUGUESA	10
GUARDATINAJAS	LLANOS	GUARICO	10
GUARENAS	COASTRANGE	MIRANDA	9
GUARICO	ANDES	LARA	15
GUASGUAS	LLANOS	PORTUGUESA	9
GUATIRE	COASTRANGE	MIRANDA	10
GUAYABAL	LLANOS	GUARICO	2
GUIGUE	COASTRANGE	CARABOBO	8
GUIRIPA	COASTRANGE	ARAGUA	9
--H--			
HUMOCARO ALTO	ANDES	LARA	15
HUMOCARO BAJO	ANDES	LARA	13
--I--			
IGUANA	LLANOS	GUARICO	8
--L--			
LA GUAIRA	COAST	D.F.	13
LA GUAIRA, CURATO CASTRENSE	COAST	D.F.	6
LA SANTISIMA TRINIDAD	LLANOS	GUARICO	11
LA VEGA	COASTRANGE	D.F.	16
LA VICTORIA	COASTRANGE	ARAGUA	12
LEZAMA	LLANOS	GUARICO	11
LOS ANGELES	LLANOS	GUARICO	12
LOS ANGELES DE SETENTA	LLANOS	APURE	5
LOS CANIZOS	COAST	YARACUY	13
LOS GUAYOS	COASTRANGE	CARABOBO	7
LOS TEQUES	COASTRANGE	MIRANDA	8
--M--			
MACAIRA	COASTRANGE	GUARICO	10
MACAIRITA	COASTRANGE	MIRANDA	1
MACARAO	COASTRANGE	D.F.	18
MAGDALENO	COASTRANGE	ARAGUA	7
MAIQUETIA	COAST	D.F.	10
MAMPORAL	COAST	MIRANDA	13
MANAPIRE	LLANOS	GUARICO	4
MARACA	LLANOS	PORTUGUESA	10
MARACAY	COASTRANGE	ARAGUA	14
MARIA	LLANOS	PORTUGUESA	6
MARIARA	COASTRANGE	CARABOBO	9
MONTALBAN	COASTRANGE	CARABOBO	12
MORON	COAST	CARABOBO	7
MOROTURO	COAST	LARA	7

PARISH NAME	REGION NAME	STATE NAME	NUMBER OF RETURNS
--N--			
NAGUANAGUA	COASTRANGE	CARABOBO	6
NAIGUATA	COAST	D.F.	10
NIRGUA	COASTRANGE	YARACUY	15
--O--			
OCUMARE DE LA COSTA	COAST	ARAGUA	10
OCUMARE DEL TUY	COASTRANGE	MIRANDA	11
ORTIZ	LLANOS	GUARICO	11
OSPINO	LLANOS	PORTUGUESA	11
--P--			
PANAQUIRE	COAST	MIRANDA	11
PARACOTOS	COASTRANGE	MIRANDA	16
PARAPARA	LLANOS	GUARICO	11
PATANEMO	COAST	CARABOBO	7
PAYARA	LLANOS	APURE	7
PETARE	COASTRANGE	MIRANDA	16
PUERTO CABELLO	COAST	CARABOBO	8
PUERTO CABELLO, CASTILLO	COAST	CARABOBO	11
--Q--			
QUARA	SEGOVIA	YARACUY	16
QUIBOR	SEGOVIA	LARA	15
--R--			
RIO CHICO	COAST	MIRANDA	14
RIO DEL TOCUYO	SEGOVIA	LARA	7
--S--			
SABANETA	LLANOS	BARINAS	7
SAN ANTONIO DE LAS COCUIZAS	LLANOS	BARINAS	1
SAN ANTONIO DE LOS ALTOS	COASTRANGE	MIRANDA	16
SAN CARLOS	LLANOS	COJEDES	27
SAN DIEGO DE ALCALA	COASTRANGE	CARABOBO	6
SAN DIEGO DE LOS ALTOS	COASTRANGE	MIRANDA	15
SAN FELIPE	SEGOVIA	YARACUY	10
SAN FELIPE, MITAD DE (1)	SEGOVIA	YARACUY	6
SAN FELIPE, MITAD DE (2)	SEGOVIA	YARACUY	5
SAN FERNANDO DE APURE	LLANOS	APURE	4
SAN FERNANDO DE CACHICAMO	LLANOS	GUARICO	6
SAN FRANCISCO DE CARA	LLANOS	ARAGUA	2
SAN FRANCISCO DE TIZNADOS	LLANOS	GUARICO	10
SAN FRANCISCO DE YARE	COASTRANGE	MIRANDA	13
SAN JAIME	LLANOS	BARINAS	1
SAN JOSE	LLANOS	COJEDES	23
SAN JOSE DE APURE	LLANOS	APURE	6

PARISH NAME	REGION NAME	STATE NAME	NUMBER OF RETURNS
SAN JOSE DE TIZNADOS	LLANOS	GUARICO	11
SAN JUAN DE LOS MORROS	LLANOS	GUARICO	8
SAN MATEO	COASTRANGE	ARAGUA	14
SAN MIGUEL DE TRUJILLO	ANDES	TRUJILLO	1
SAN NICOLAS DE TOLENTINO	COAST	YARACUY	5
SAN PEDRO	COASTRANGE	MIRANDA	4
SAN RAFAEL DE ONOTO	LLANOS	PORTUGUESA	5
SAN RAFAEL DE ORITUCO	LLANOS	GUARICO	10
SAN SEBASTIAN DE LOS REYES	COASTRANGE	ARAGUA	9
SANARE	ANDES	LARA	15
SANTA CRUZ DE ARAGUA	COASTRANGE	ARAGUA	11
SANTA INES DEL ALTAR	LLANOS	LARA	12
SANTA LUCIA	COASTRANGE	MIRANDA	13
SANTA MARIA DE IPIRE	COAST	GUARICO	3
SANTA ROSA DE LIMA	SEGOVIA	LARA	13
SANTA TERESA DE JESUS	COASTRANGE	MIRANDA	14
SARARE	LLANOS	LARA	11
SIQUISIQUE	SEGOVIA	LARA	5
--T--			
TACARIGUA DE MAMPORAL	COAST	MIRANDA	13
TACATA	COASTRANGE	MIRANDA	13
TAGUAI	COASTRANGE	ARAGUA	5
TAPIPA	COASTRANGE	MIRANDA	14
TARIA	COAST	YARACUY	3
TARMAS	COAST	D.F.	14
TEMERLA	COASTRANGE	YARACUY	13
TINACO	LLANOS	COJEDES	41
TINAJAS	SEGOVIA	YARACUY	16
TINAQUILLO	LLANOS	COJEDES	31
TOCUYITO	COASTRANGE	CARABOBO	5
TUCUPIDO	COAST	GUARICO	4
TUCUPIDO DE GUANARE	LLANOS	PORTUGUESA	9
TUCURAGUA	COAST	YARACUY	9
TUREN	LLANOS	PORTUGUESA	8
TURIAMO	COAST	ARAGUA	7
TURMERO	COASTRANGE	ARAGUA	9
--U--			
URACHICHE	SEGOVIA	YARACUY	16
URAMA	COAST	CARABOBO	9
--V--			
VALENCIA	COASTRANGE	CARABOBO	11
VALLE DE LA PASCUA	LLANOS	GUARICO	5
VILLA DE CURA	COASTRANGE	ARAGUA	14
--Y--			
YARITAGUA	SEGOVIA	YARACUY	15

TOTAL PARISHES 206 TOTAL RETURNS 2089

PARISH NAME	STATE NAME
ANDES	
BARBACOAS DEL TOCUYO	LARA
CHABASQUEN	PORTUGUESA
CUBIRO	LARA
GUARICO	LARA
HUMOCARO ALTO	LARA
HUMOCARO BAJO	LARA
SAN MIGUEL DE TRUJILLO	TRUJILLO
SANARE	LARA
COAST	
AGUA CULEBRAS	YARACUY
ALPARGATON	CARABOBO
AROA	YARACUY
AYAMANES	LARA
BORBURATA	CARABOBO
CABRIA	YARACUY
CARABALLEDA	D.F.
CARAYACA	D.F.
CARUAO	D.F.
CASIGUA	FALCON
CATA	ARAGUA
CHAGUARAMAL	GUARICO
CHIVACOA	YARACUY
CHORONI	ARAGUA
CHUAO	ARAGUA
CUPIRA	MIRANDA
CUYAGUA	ARAGUA
EL GUAPO	MIRANDA
GUAIGUAZA	CARABOBO
LA GUAIRA	D.F.
LA GUAIRA, CURATO CASTRENSE	D.F.
LOS CANIZOS	YARACUY
MAIQUETIA	D.F.
MAMPORAL	MIRANDA
MORON	CARABOBO
MOROTURO	LARA
NAIGUATA	D.F.
OCUMARE DE LA COSTA	ARAGUA
PANAQUIRE	MIRANDA
PATANEMO	CARABOBO
PUERTO CABELLO	CARABOBO
PUERTO CABELLO, CASTILLO	CARABOBO
RIO CHICO	MIRANDA
SAN NICOLAS DE TOLENTINO	YARACUY
SANTA MARIA DE IPIRE	GUARICO
TACARIGUA DE MAMPORAL	MIRANDA
TARIA	YARACUY
TARMAS	D.F.
TUCUPIDO	GUARICO
TUCURAGUA	YARACUY
TURIAMO	ARAGUA
URAMA	CARABOBO
COASTRANGE	
AGUACALIENTE	CARABOBO
ALTAGRACIA DE ORITUCO	GUARICO
ANTIMANO	D.F.
ARAGUITA	MIRANDA
BARUTA	MIRANDA
CAGUA	ARAGUA
CANOABO	CARABOBO
CAPAYA	MIRANDA
CARACAS-ALTAGRACIA	D.F.
CARACAS-CANDELARIA	D.F.
CARACAS-CATEDRAL ORIENTE	D.F.
CARACAS-CATEDRAL PONIENTE	D.F.
CARACAS-CURATO CASTRENSE	D.F.
CARACAS-SAN PABLO	D.F.
CARACAS-SANTA ROSALIA	D.F.
CAUCAGUA	MIRANDA
CHACAO	MIRANDA
CHARALLAVE	MIRANDA
CUA	MIRANDA
CURIEPE	MIRANDA
EL CONSEJO	ARAGUA
EL HATILLO	MIRANDA
EL VALLE	D.F.
GUACARA	CARABOBO
GUARENAS	MIRANDA
GUATIRE	MIRANDA
GUIGUE	CARABOBO
GUIRIPA	ARAGUA
LA VEGA	D.F.
LA VICTORIA	ARAGUA
LOS GUAYOS	CARABOBO
LOS TEQUES	MIRANDA
MACAIRA	GUARICO
MACAIRITA	MIRANDA
MACARAO	D.F.
MAGDALENO	ARAGUA
MARACAY	ARAGUA
MARIARA	CARABOBO
MONTALBAN	CARABOBO
NAGUANAGUA	CARABOBO
NIRGUA	YARACUY
OCUMARE DEL TUY	MIRANDA
PARACOTOS	MIRANDA
PETARE	MIRANDA
SAN ANTONIO DE LOS ALTOS	MIRANDA
SAN DIEGO DE ALCALA	CARABOBO
SAN DIEGO DE LOS ALTOS	MIRANDA

PARISH NAME	STATE NAME
SAN FRANCISCO DE YARE	MIRANDA
SAN MATEO	ARAGUA
SAN PEDRO	MIRANDA
SAN SEBASTIAN DE LOS REYES	ARAGUA
SANTA CRUZ DE ARAGUA	ARAGUA
SANTA LUCIA	MIRANDA
SANTA TERESA DE JESUS	MIRANDA
TACATA	MIRANDA
TAGUAI	ARAGUA
TAPIPA	MIRANDA
TEMERLA	YARACUY
TOCUYITO	CARABOBO
TURMERO	ARAGUA
VALENCIA	CARABOBO
VILLA DE CURA	ARAGUA

GUAYANA

PARISH NAME	STATE NAME
CAICARA DEL ORINOCO	BOLIVAR

LLANOS

PARISH NAME	STATE NAME
ACARIGUA	PORTUGUESA
ACHAGUAS	APURE
AGUA BLANCA	PORTUGUESA
ALTAMIRA	GUARICO
APARICION	PORTUGUESA
APURITO	APURE
ARAURE	PORTUGUESA
ARICHUNA	APURE
ATAMAICA	APURE
BANCO LARGO	APURE
BARBACOAS DE LOS LLANOS	ARAGUA
BAUL	COJEDES
BOCONO	PORTUGUESA
BURIA	LARA
CABRUTA	GUARICO
CALABOZO	GUARICO
CAMAGUAN	GUARICO
CAMATAGUA	ARAGUA
CARAMACATE	PORTUGUESA
CHAGUARAMAS	GUARICO
COJEDES	COJEDES
CUNAVICHE	APURE
DIVINA PASTORA DEL JOBAL	COJEDES
EL CALVARIO	GUARICO
EL PAO	COJEDES
EL RASTRO	GUARICO
EL SOMBRERO	GUARICO
ESPINO	GUARICO
GUADARRAMA	BARINAS
GUANARE	PORTUGUESA
GUANARE VIEJO	PORTUGUESA
GUANARITO	PORTUGUESA
GUARDATINAJAS	GUARICO
GUASGUAS	PORTUGUESA
GUAYABAL	GUARICO
IGUANA	GUARICO
LA SANTISIMA TRINIDAD	GUARICO
LEZAMA	GUARICO
LOS ANGELES	GUARICO
LOS ANGELES DE SETENTA	APURE
MANAPIRE	GUARICO
MARACA	PORTUGUESA
MARIA	PORTUGUESA
ORTIZ	GUARICO
OSPINO	PORTUGUESA
PARAPARA	GUARICO
PAYARA	APURE
SABANETA	BARINAS
SAN ANTONIO DE LAS COCUIZAS	BARINAS
SAN CARLOS	COJEDES
SAN FERNANDO DE APURE	APURE
SAN FERNANDO DE CACHICAMO	GUARICO
SAN FRANCISCO DE CARA	ARAGUA
SAN FRANCISCO DE TIZNADOS	GUARICO
SAN JAIME	BARINAS
SAN JOSE	COJEDES
SAN JOSE DE APURE	APURE
SAN JOSE DE TIZNADOS	GUARICO
SAN JUAN DE LOS MORROS	GUARICO
SAN RAFAEL DE ONOTO	PORTUGUESA
SAN RAFAEL DE ORITUCO	GUARICO
SANTA INES DEL ALTAR	LARA
SARARE	LARA
TINACO	COJEDES
TINAQUILLO	COJEDES
TUCUPIDO DE GUANARE	PORTUGUESA
TUREN	PORTUGUESA
VALLE DE LA PASCUA	GUARICO

SEGOVIA

PARISH NAME	STATE NAME
AREGUE	LARA
ARENALES	LARA
BARQUISIMETO	LARA
BARQUISIMETO, MITAD DE(1)	LARA
BARQUISIMETO, MITAD DE(2)	LARA
BOBARE	LARA
BURERITO	LARA
CARORA	LARA
CERRITO	LARA
COCOROTE	YARACUY
CURARIGUA	LARA
DUACA	LARA
EL TOCUYO	LARA
GUAMA	YARACUY
QUARA	YARACUY

PARISH NAME	STATE NAME
QUIBOR	LARA
RIO DEL TOCUYO	LARA
SAN FELIPE	YARACUY
SAN FELIPE, MITAD DE (1)	YARACUY
SAN FELIPE, MITAD DE (2)	YARACUY
SANTA ROSA DE LIMA	LARA
SIQUISIQUE	LARA
TINAJAS	YARACUY
URACHICHE	YARACUY
YARITAGUA	YARACUY

PARISHES ARRANGED BY STATE

APPENDIX B,

PARISH NAME	REGION NAME
APURE	
ACHAGUAS	LLANOS
APURITO	LLANOS
ARICHUNA	LLANOS
ATAMAICA	LLANOS
BANCO LARGO	LLANOS
CUNAVICHE	LLANOS
LOS ANGELES DE SETENTA	LLANOS
PAYARA	LLANOS
SAN FERNANDO DE APURE	LLANOS
SAN JOSE DE APURE	LLANOS
ARAGUA	
BARBACOAS DE LOS LLANOS	LLANOS
CAGUA	COASTRANGE
CAMATAGUA	LLANOS
CATA	COAST
CHORONI	COAST
CHUAO	COAST
CUYAGUA	COAST
EL CONSEJO	COASTRANGE
GUIRIPA	COASTRANGE
LA VICTORIA	COASTRANGE
MAGDALENO	COASTRANGE
MARACAY	COASTRANGE
OCUMARE DE LA COSTA	COAST
SAN FRANCISCO DE CARA	LLANOS
SAN MATEO	COASTRANGE
SAN SEBASTIAN DE LOS REYES	COASTRANGE
SANTA CRUZ DE ARAGUA	COASTRANGE
TAGUAI	COASTRANGE
TURIAMO	COAST
TURMERO	COASTRANGE
VILLA DE CURA	COASTRANGE
BARINAS	
GUADARRAMA	LLANOS
SABANETA	LLANOS
SAN ANTONIO DE LAS COCUIZAS	LLANOS
SAN JAIME	LLANOS
BOLIVAR	
CAICARA DEL ORINOCO	GUAYANA
CARABOBO	
AGUACALIENTE	COASTRANGE
ALPARGATON	COAST
BORBURATA	COAST
CANOABO	COASTRANGE
GUACARA	COASTRANGE
GUAIGUAZA	COAST
GUIGUE	COASTRANGE
LOS GUAYOS	COASTRANGE
MARIARA	COASTRANGE
MONTALBAN	COASTRANGE
MORON	COAST
NAGUANAGUA	COASTRANGE
PATANEMO	COAST
PUERTO CABELLO	COAST
PUERTO CABELLO, CASTILLO	COAST
SAN DIEGO DE ALCALA	COASTRANGE
TOCUYITO	COASTRANGE
URAMA	COAST
VALENCIA	COASTRANGE
COJEDES	
BAUL	LLANOS
COJEDES	LLANOS
DIVINA PASTORA DEL JOBAL	LLANOS
EL PAO	LLANOS
SAN CARLOS	LLANOS
SAN JOSE	LLANOS
TINACO	LLANOS
TINAQUILLO	LLANOS
D.F.	
ANTIMANO	COASTRANGE
CARABALLEDA	COAST
CARACAS-ALTAGRACIA	COASTRANGE
CARACAS-CANDELARIA	COASTRANGE
CARACAS-CATEDRAL ORIENTE	COASTRANGE
CARACAS-CATEDRAL PONIENTE	COASTRANGE
CARACAS-CURATO CASTRENSE	COASTRANGE
CARACAS-SAN PABLO	COASTRANGE
CARACAS-SANTA ROSALIA	COASTRANGE
CARAYACA	COAST
CARUAO	COAST
EL VALLE	COASTRANGE
LA GUAIRA	COAST
LA GUAIRA, CURATO CASTRENSE	COAST
LA VEGA	COASTRANGE
MACARAO	COASTRANGE
MAIQUETIA	COAST
NAIGUATA	COAST

PARISH NAME	REGION NAME
TARMAS	COAST
FALCON	
CASIGUA	COAST
GUARICO	
ALTAGRACIA DE ORITUCO	COASTRANGE
ALTAMIRA	LLANOS
CABRUTA	LLANOS
CALABOZO	LLANOS
CAMAGUAN	LLANOS
CHAGUARAMAL	COAST
CHAGUARAMAS	LLANOS
EL CALVARIO	LLANOS
EL RASTRO	LLANOS
EL SOMBRERO	LLANOS
ESPINO	LLANOS
GUARDATINAJAS	LLANOS
GUAYABAL	LLANOS
IGUANA	LLANOS
LA SANTISIMA TRINIDAD	LLANOS
LEZAMA	LLANOS
LOS ANGELES	LLANOS
MACAIRA	COASTRANGE
MANAPIRE	LLANOS
ORTIZ	LLANOS
PARAPARA	LLANOS
SAN FERNANDO DE CACHICAMO	LLANOS
SAN FRANCISCO DE TIZNADOS	LLANOS
SAN JOSE DE TIZNADOS	LLANOS
SAN JUAN DE LOS MORROS	LLANOS
SAN RAFAEL DE ORITUCO	LLANOS
SANTA MARIA DE IPIRE	COAST
TUCUPIDO	COAST
VALLE DE LA PASCUA	LLANOS
LARA	
AREGUE	SEGOVIA
ARENALES	SEGOVIA
AYAMANES	COAST
BARBACOAS DEL TOCUYO	ANDES
BARQUISIMETO	SEGOVIA
BARQUISIMETO, MITAD DE(1)	SEGOVIA
BARQUISIMETO, MITAD DE(2)	SEGOVIA
BOBARE	SEGOVIA
BURERITO	SEGOVIA
BURIA	LLANOS
CARORA	SEGOVIA
CERRITO	SEGOVIA
CUBIRO	ANDES
CURARIGUA	SEGOVIA

PARISH NAME	REGION NAME
DUACA	SEGOVIA
EL TOCUYO	SEGOVIA
GUARICO	ANDES
HUMOCARO ALTO	ANDES
HUMOCARO BAJO	ANDES
MOROTURO	COAST
QUIBOR	SEGOVIA
RIO DEL TOCUYO	SEGOVIA
SANARE	ANDES
SANTA INES DEL ALTAR	LLANOS
SANTA ROSA DE LIMA	SEGOVIA
SARARE	LLANOS
SIQUISIQUE	SEGOVIA
MIRANDA	
ARAGUITA	COASTRANGE
BARUTA	COASTRANGE
CAPAYA	COASTRANGE
CAUCAGUA	COASTRANGE
CHACAO	COASTRANGE
CHARALLAVE	COASTRANGE
CUA	COASTRANGE
CUPIRA	COAST
CURIEPE	COASTRANGE
EL GUAPO	COAST
EL HATILLO	COASTRANGE
GUARENAS	COASTRANGE
GUATIRE	COASTRANGE
LOS TEQUES	COASTRANGE
MACAIRITA	COASTRANGE
MAMPORAL	COAST
OCUMARE DEL TUY	COASTRANGE
PANAQUIRE	COAST
PARACOTOS	COASTRANGE
PETARE	COASTRANGE
RIO CHICO	COAST
SAN ANTONIO DE LOS ALTOS	COASTRANGE
SAN DIEGO DE LOS ALTOS	COASTRANGE
SAN FRANCISCO DE YARE	COASTRANGE
SAN PEDRO	COASTRANGE
SANTA LUCIA	COASTRANGE
SANTA TERESA DE JESUS	COASTRANGE
TACARIGUA DE MAMPORAL	COAST
TACATA	COASTRANGE
TAPIPA	COASTRANGE
PORTUGUESA	
ACARIGUA	LLANOS
AGUA BLANCA	LLANOS
APARICION	LLANOS
ARAURE	LLANOS
BOCONO	LLANOS

PARISH NAME	REGION NAME
CARAMACATE	LLANOS
CHABASQUEN	ANDES
GUANARE	LLANOS
GUANARE VIEJO	LLANOS
GUANARITO	LLANOS
GUASGUAS	LLANOS
MARACA	LLANOS
MARIA	LLANOS
OSPINO	LLANOS
SAN RAFAEL DE ONOTO	LLANOS
TUCUPIDO DE GUANARE	LLANOS
TUREN	LLANOS
TRUJILLO	
SAN MIGUEL DE TRUJILLO	ANDES
YARACUY	
AGUA CULEBRAS	COAST
AROA	COAST
CABRIA	COAST
CHIVACOA	COAST
COCOROTE	SEGOVIA
GUAMA	SEGOVIA
LOS CANIZOS	COAST
NIRGUA	COASTRANGE
QUARA	SEGOVIA
SAN FELIPE	SEGOVIA
SAN FELIPE, MITAD DE (1)	SEGOVIA
SAN FELIPE, MITAD DE (2)	SEGOVIA
SAN NICOLAS DE TOLENTINO	COAST
TARIA	COAST
TEMERLA	COASTRANGE
TINAJAS	SEGOVIA
TUCURAGUA	COAST
URACHICHE	SEGOVIA
YARITAGUA	SEGOVIA

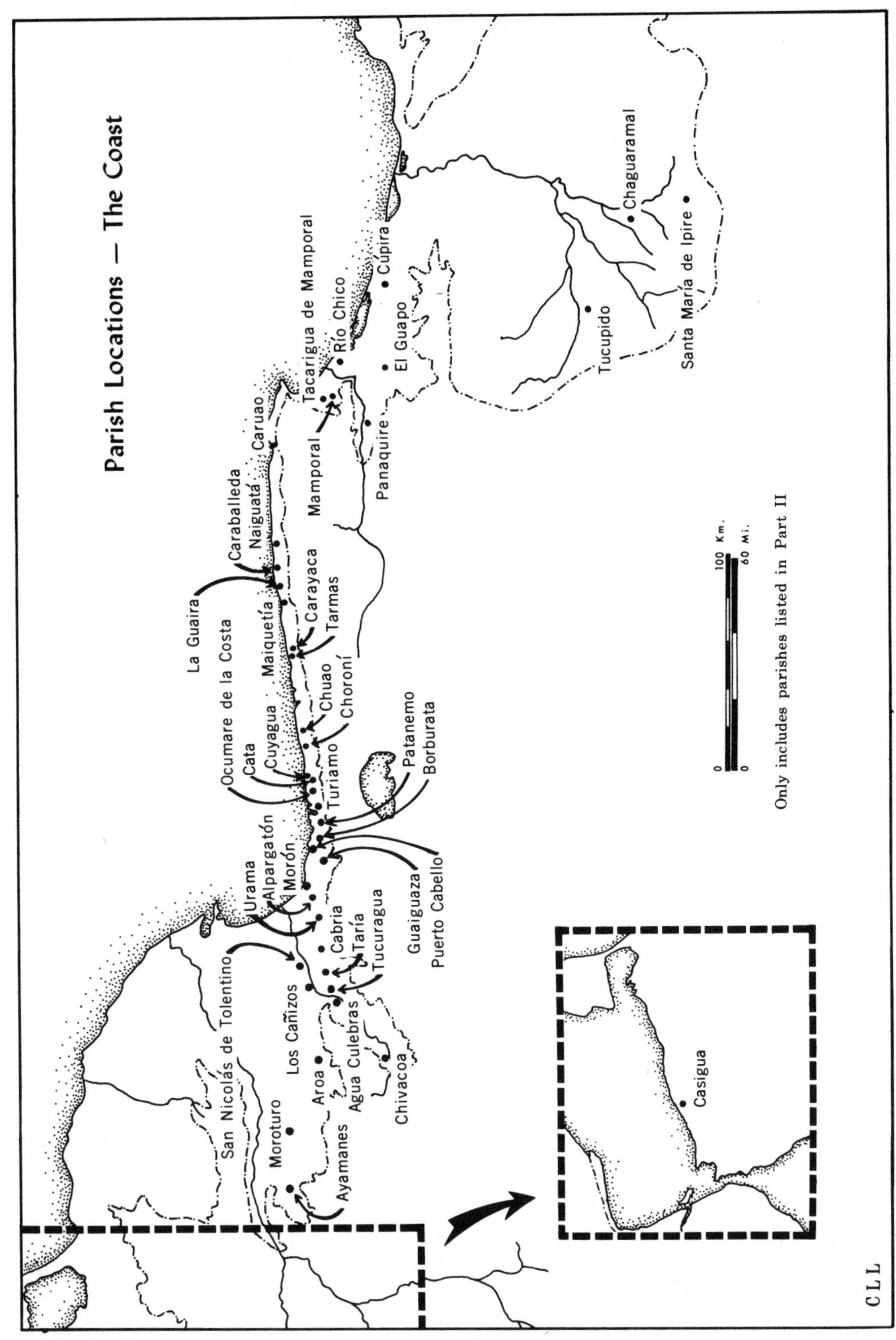

Parish Locations — The Coast
La Guaira
Caraballeda
Naiguatá
Caruao
Maiquetía
Carayaca
Tarmas
Ocumare de la Costa
Cata
Cuyagua
Chuao
Choroní
Turiamo
Patanemo
Borburata
Urama
Alpargatón
Morón
Guaiguaza
Puerto Cabello
San Nicolás de Tolentino
Cabria
Taría
Tucuragua
Los Cañizos
Aroa
Agua Culebras
Chivacoa
Moroturo
Ayamanes
Mamporal
Tacarigua de Mamporal
Río Chico
Panaquire
El Guapo
Cúpira
Tucupido
Chaguaramal
Santa María de Ipire
Casigua
0
100 Km.
0
60 Mi.
Only includes parishes listed in Part II
CLL

MAP B-1

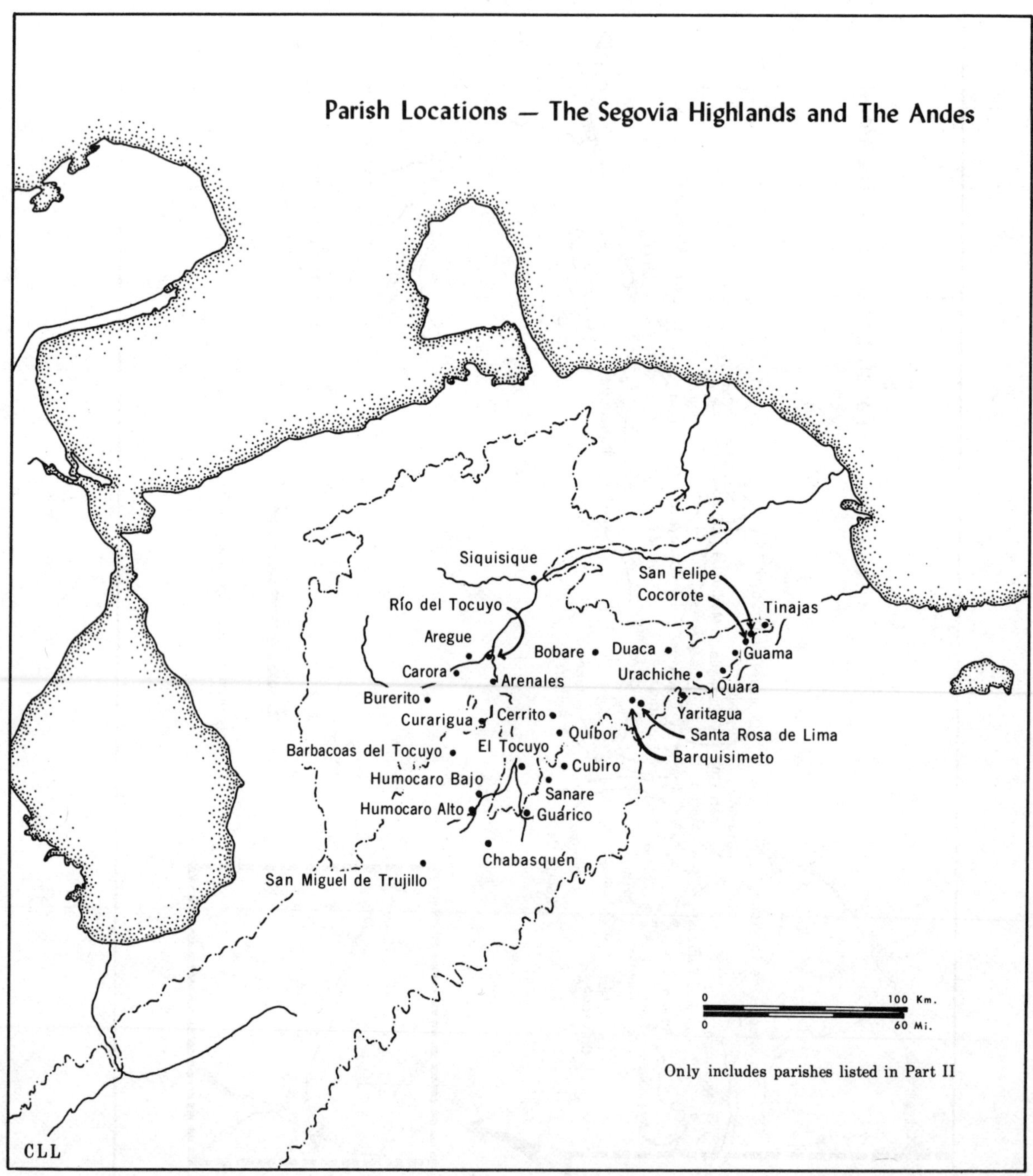
Parish Locations — The Segovia Highlands and The Andes
Siquisique
San Felipe
Cocorote
Tinajas
Río del Tocuyo
Aregue
Bobare
Duaca
Guama
Carora
Arenales
Urachiche
Quara
Burerito
Curarigua
Cerrito
Yaritagua
Santa Rosa de Lima
Quíbor
Barquisimeto
Barbacoas del Tocuyo
El Tocuyo
Cubiro
Humocaro Bajo
Sanare
Humocaro Alto
Guárico
Chabasquén
San Miguel de Trujillo
0
100 Km.
0
60 Mi.
Only includes parishes listed in Part II
CLL

Map B-2

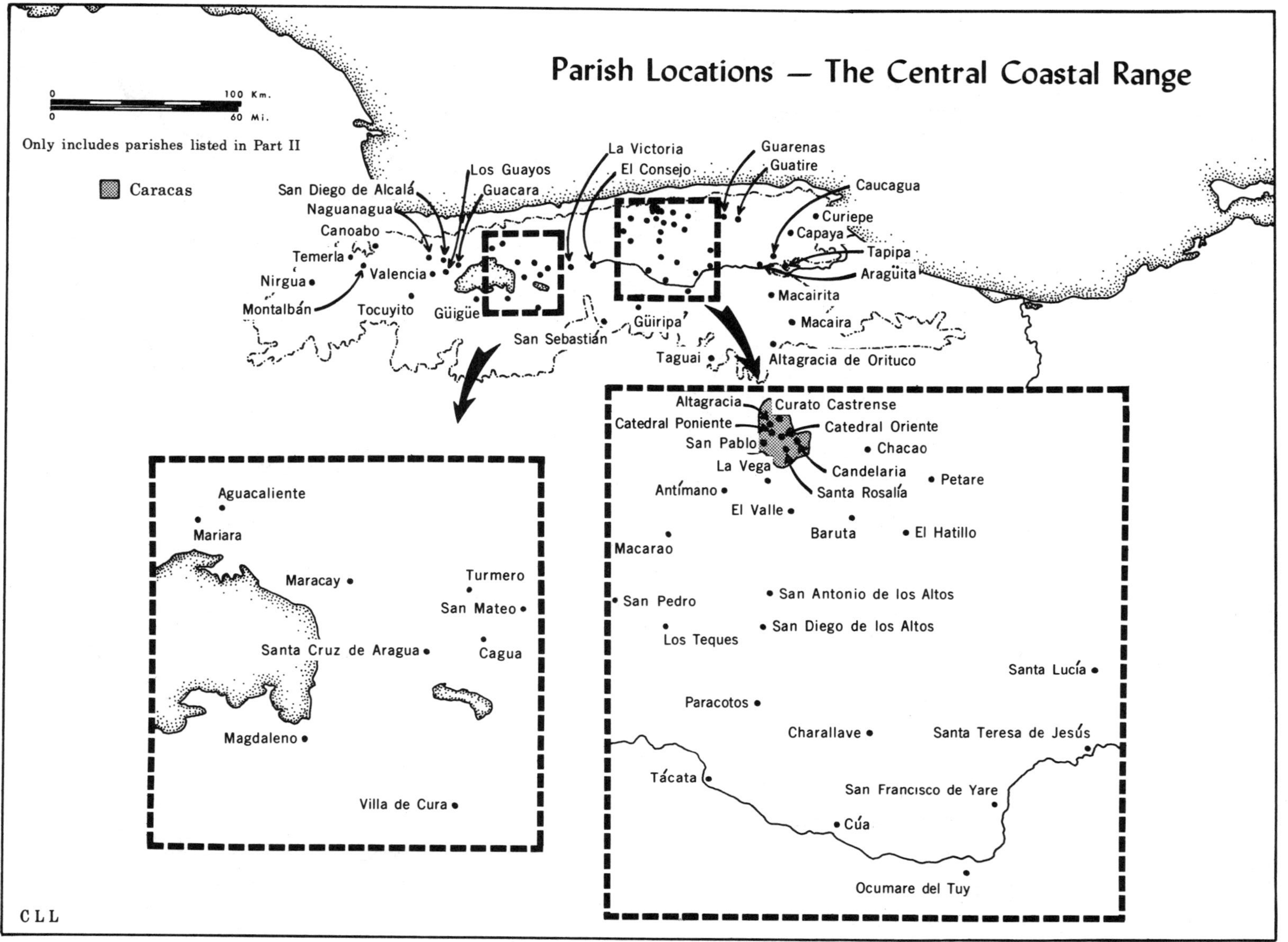
Parish Locations — The Central Coastal Range
Caracas
Only includes parishes listed in Part II
0 100 Km.
0 60 Mi.
Los Guayos
Guacara
San Diego de Alcalá
Naguanagua
Canoabo
Temería
Nirgua
Montalbán
Valencia
Tocuyito
Güigüe
La Victoria
El Consejo
San Sebastián
Güiripa
Taguai
Guarenas
Guatire
Caucagua
Curiepe
Capaya
Tapipa
Aragüita
Macairita
Macaira
Altagracia de Orituco
Altagracia
Catedral Poniente
San Pablo
La Vega
Antímano
Curato Castrense
Catedral Oriente
Chacao
Candelaria
Santa Rosalía
Petare
El Valle
Baruta
El Hatillo
Macarao
San Pedro
San Antonio de los Altos
San Diego de los Altos
Los Teques
Paracotos
Charallave
Santa Lucía
Santa Teresa de Jesús
San Francisco de Yare
Cúa
Tácata
Ocumare del Tuy
Aguacaliente
Mariara
Maracay
Turmero
San Mateo
Cagua
Santa Cruz de Aragua
Villa de Cura
Magdaleno
CLL

Map B-3

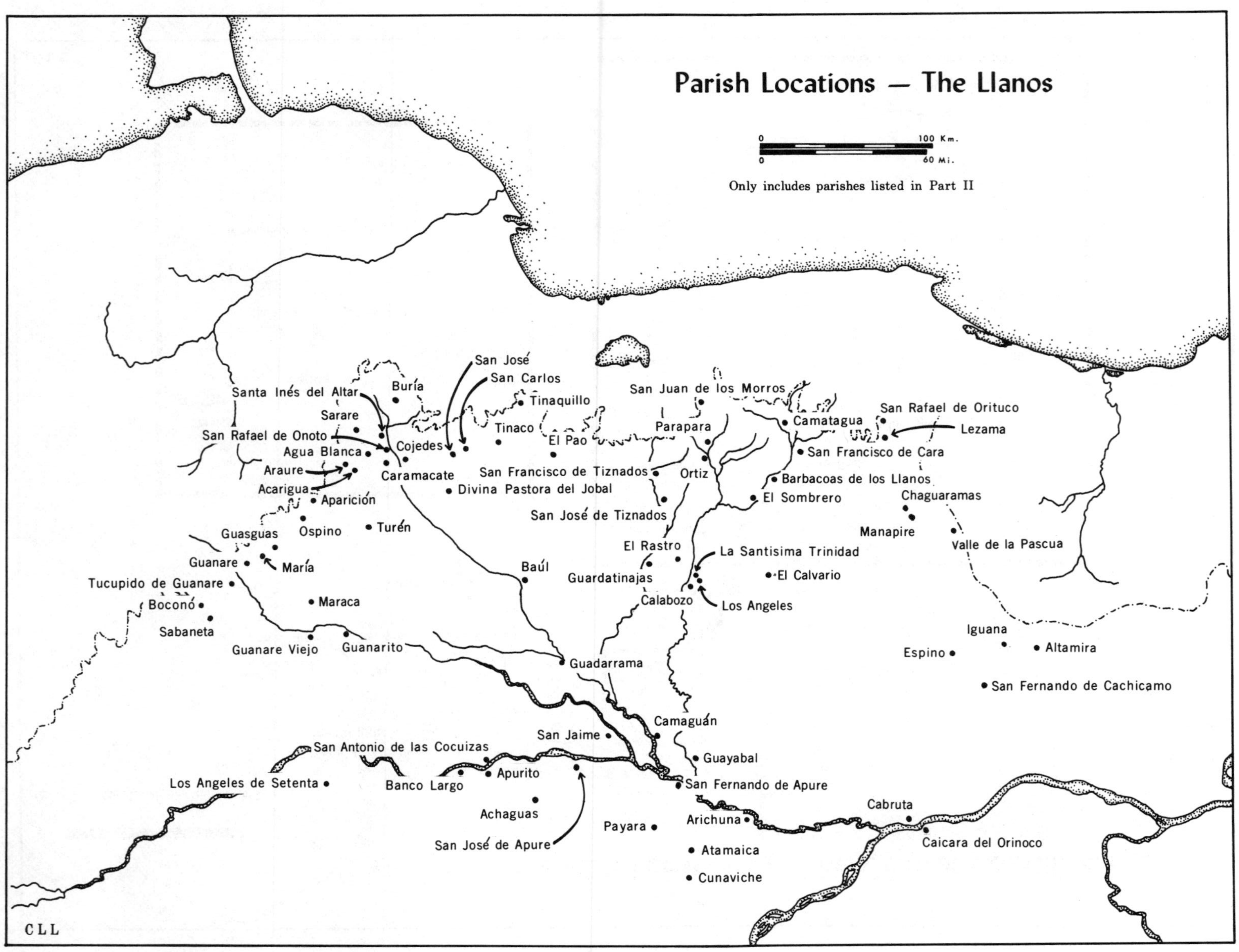
Parish Locations — The Llanos
0 100 Km.
0 60 Mi.
Only includes parishes listed in Part II
San José
San Carlos
Santa Inés del Altar
Buría
Tinaquillo
San Juan de los Morros
Sarare
Tinaco
Parapara
Camatagua
San Rafael de Orituco
Lezama
San Rafael de Onoto
El Pao
Agua Blanca
Cojedes
San Francisco de Cara
Araure
Caramacate
San Francisco de Tiznados
Ortiz
Barbacoas de los Llanos
Acarigua
Divina Pastora del Jobal
El Sombrero
Chaguaramas
Aparición
San José de Tiznados
Guasguas
Ospino
Turén
Manapire
Valle de la Pascua
El Rastro
La Santisima Trinidad
Guanare
María
Baúl
El Calvario
Tucupido de Guanare
Guardatinajas
Boconó
Maraca
Calabozo
Los Angeles
Sabaneta
Iguana
Guanare Viejo
Guanarito
Espino
Altamira
Guadarrama
San Fernando de Cachicamo
Camaguán
San Jaime
San Antonio de las Cocuizas
Guayabal
Apurito
Los Angeles de Setenta
Banco Largo
San Fernando de Apure
Cabruta
Achaguas
Arichuna
Payara
Caicara del Orinoco
San José de Apure
Atamaica
Cunaviche
CLL

Part II

A Workbook in the Historical Demography of Venezuela

The Bishopric of Caracas, 1771-1838

Introduction

The following tables present data originally in Type III census format located in the Sección Parroquias, Archivo Arquidiocesano de Caracas. Some review of the procedures used to produce these tables from the manuscript census returns may help in the evaluation of the data's usefulness and accuracy. In general terms, the process of making this data available to scholars in a systematic and reliable form can be divided into three parts: collection, classification and coding, and verification.

The universe of all population data in the Sección Parroquias includes documents of widely varying types, from the detailed and voluminous matrículas, or household lists, to the standardized summary annual census returns. This current effort focuses on that part of those records already in an aggregated format, and these tables are based on the subset of aggregated data that conforms to, or can be made to conform to, Type III format. In subsequent publications, the rest of the aggregate data formats will be processed and made available, although their consistency and reliability appear somewhat less than what we can expect from the Type III data. All of the aggregated census information from the Sección Parroquias was separated out from the nominal or household list data and microfilmed. The nearly four thousand folios thus collected on microfilm became the main file for this project. A copy of the original file is available at the Fundación John Boulton in Caracas. The next step transferred the microfilm to Xerox sheets for coding purposes.

At the beginning, the coding scheme attempted to preserve some information from the parish priests' notes appended to the end of each yearly return. This proved unworkable because most of the notes appeared ritualized, noting principally that the number of married men and the number of married women in any given racial category failed to coincide because some men were absent from the parish or because some interracial marriages had occurred. In the few cases of idiosyncratic notes, usually in reference to the absence of men in the independence wars or the flight of people into the hills to avoid military service after 1810, the information seemed more appropriate for traditional historical notes than for the quantitative data file presented here.

In the design for coding, every effort was made to preserve the greatest amount of detail from the documents. As a result, for every major census-taking format, a special coding format exists. In practice, this worked out to about five different coding schemes, with Type III representing the vast majority of the useable returns.

If designing the coding schemes caused relatively few problems, their application to the data in hand proved more complex than imagined. The principal difficulty came from ambiguities and inconsistencies in the naming of parishes. In retrospect, and with the lore accumulated from research into

Venezuela's local history, the number of missteps and the amount of time spent in the location and identification of parish sites seems incredible. However, without a comprehensive guide other than Marti's visita, such false starts must have been inevitable. The final name file only holds some two hundred names, but to be sure of all these places and to avoid identifying two parishes with similar names as one, a file of at least three times that many place names had to be developed. In some cases it took two or three passes through the data and extensive external research to identify and locate obscure places or to reconcile multiple names for single parishes. The cross-reference name file contains all the possible variants for the parishes included in this study and in the tables.

Fortunately, most parish priests working with Type III format turned in remarkably consistent returns. But on occasion, returns appeared with slightly nonstandard responses. In these cases, a simple procedure resolved most difficulties. If the return could be reconciled into the Type III format by the combination of categories, that was done and the return entered the Type III file. If not, the return became part of a small file of completely nonstandard returns and will be processed for the next publication based on this data. Most of the reconcilable departures from standard Type III format involved separate listings for Indian-white mixtures, or _mestizos_, (Type III combines mestizos and blancos in the same category), or the listing of widows separate from singles. In a few cases, slaves might be divided into _zambo_ (an Indian-Negro mixture) and Negro categories (Type III only admits of one kind of slave).

As anyone familiar with Latin American colonial documents might suspect, some of the census returns had missing pieces, blots, and worm holes. Wherever the missing cells could be reconstructed through the use of column and row totals in the document, that was done and the return included in the file. Where the illegible or broken portions of the documents made such reconstruction impossible, the return was excluded. In the file of Type III data, then, there are no missing entries. The parish priest's row and column totals were ignored otherwise.

Most of the categories of the coding scheme are self-explanatory, especially after the discussion in Chapters 1 and 2 of this book. But the category of ecclesiastics requires some explanation. The Type III format did not require church men and women to distinguish their sex, race, or religious condition in a consistent and satisfactory way. Sometimes we have some information beyond the number of clerics, but frequently we do not. Moreover, ecclesiastics did not enter the main part of the census return as a rule, but almost invariably were added in at the end in an undifferentiated category. So, too, by the way, were the rare _locos_ recorded in the censuses. With a few notable exceptions, the parishes of Caracas the most extreme, most places had one or no ecclesiastics associated with them, and we can assume that each such individual was the parish priest or a missionary. The utility of the ecclesiastic category is further reduced because priests showed a relatively casual attitude toward identifying the number of clerics in any given place, a fault made even more obvious by their careful attention to detail in preparing the rest of the census return.

After all the parishes in the file had been identified, and their population categories coded, each record received three kinds of identifying information. First was a parish number, that is an arbitrary identifier that originally had the virtue of locating the parish within a _vicariato_, or ecclesiastical subdivision, of the Bishopric, with the first two digits indicating the jurisdiction. But in the process of checking names and verifying parish locations, the system proved unworkable, so that some parishes have only identification numbers without vicariato codes. These IDs form the unique identifier for each parish and remained unchanged throughout the project, even though the parish name and location may have been changed to correspond to new information. Associated with the parish ID is the year, and these two numbers together provide each record, each census return, with a unique identification number.

The second set of numbers associated with each parish is a location code that places the center in a region, a subregion, and a sub-subregion, and locates it within a modern state as well. These come from the _Atlas de Venezuela_. In fact, locating each parish on the map proved very difficult for a number of hamlets and villages, but with the aid of Mariano Marti and other sources, every parish received a region code and a state code. Naturally, given the scale of the map and the insecurity about some place locations, a few errors may exist in these identifications. But if the subsubregions may be open to question, the subregions are much more securely assigned, as are the regions. The state codes exist simply to help locate parishes on Venezuela's modern maps. These are based on the state divisions as of 1960.

The parish name used in these tables is the fourth identifier included on every record. Choosing the short name for each parish proved a less clear-cut decision than I had expected. In general, I have tried to assign each parish the version of its name that satisfies as many of the following criteria as possible. The name must be unique, it must be one of the variants of the parish's full name in common usage in the eighteenth-century or in present-day cartography, and it must be thirty characters or less. Scholars searching for a particular place should consult the main name file, where all the alternative names for the parishes are cross-classified with the name used in the tables. Clearly, in this business of picking names a foreigner works at a severe disadvantage. But I anticipate that any errors will be quickly noted by my Venezuelan colleagues and brought to my attention.

In an operation of this kind, the procedures used to ensure the accuracy of transcription, punching, and recording assume considerable importance. While a machine-readable data file is a joy to work with, it is very tedious to compile. For the file of Type III data, we initially coded up the data on code sheets, had the sheets punched onto cards, and listed the file on the printer. Through inspection of unlikely totals and discontinuous series, keypunching errors, mostly column shifts, were corrected. With a reasonably accurate file prepared, the initial data manipulations for the tables were carried out, programs written to produce statistics, and so forth. After some experience with the file and with a better knowledge of colonial Venezuelan census techniques, we took the machine-readable file and checked every record against the original on Xerox or microfilm. This second pass through the data turned up a few misinterpreted digits and mispunched codes, although most of these involved small errors. This second pass also permitted us to recheck the parish names and identifications against those developed after the first pass. As a result of these procedures, this data file represents the original returns as closely as is humanly possible.

The experience of working with this data has brought home forcefully the importance of observing the maxims laid down in every treatise on quantitative historical methods. Consistency of coding is absolutely essential. Most of the errors turned up in the second pass involved varying interpretations of ambiguous clerical script by different coders. It is indeed true that while the tedium and boredom associated with coding is mind-numbing as well as time-consuming, there is no substitute for careful coding and elaborate cross-checking procedures. The data have enough possibilities for error all their own without those added in transcription and coding.

Some Technical Notes

Although of little significance to the interpretation of these tables or to the use of this book, a brief description of the hardware and software used in producing this book may be of interest to the aficionado. The tables and all the calculations and file management routines were done at Indiana University's Marshal H. Wrubel Computing Center on a Control Data Corporation 6600 computer. The tables in the form presented here come from a series of simple Fortran IV programs that I wrote. I generated the statistics for the discussion in Chapters 2, 3, 4, and 5 through the use of the Statistical Package for the Social Sciences, and I designed the graphs through Indiana University's Plotter Package, working with a Calcomp Plotter and a Versatec 1200 electrostatic plotter. The drafts of this book were circulated to a variety of scholars here and in Venezuela in a version produced by INSTEP, a text-formatting package developed by the WCC staff at Indiana University. A slightly modified version of INSTEP produced the copy for this publication.

When the rest of the aggregate data from the Archivo Arquidiocesano is verified and corrected, the entire data set will be made available to scholars on magnetic tape. The Type III file contains approximately 4,000 records of 115 characters. The remaining census data of less tractable format will about double the size of the final file. While by computer standards the file is quite small, most of us historians will find it a substantial collection of machine-readable population data.

TABLES 1 THROUGH 7

TABLE 1. PARISH POPULATION BY SEX AND RACE

YEAR	TOTAL		WHITE		INDIAN		PARDO		NEGRO		SLAVE	
	M	F	M	F	M	F	M	F	M	F	M	F
ACARIGUA												
1778	425	510	0	0	425	510	0	0	0	0	0	0
1802	1024	1197	193	241	593	683	231	245	4	13	3	15
1803	1252	1297	215	263	784	756	235	249	11	14	7	15
1804	1238	1332	216	267	778	795	235	253	4	7	5	10
1805	1209	1316	216	260	753	801	230	243	5	4	5	8
1808	1188	1375	196	219	765	886	222	259	3	4	2	7
1809	1201	1382	202	214	775	900	220	261	3	3	1	4
1810	1109	1193	196	219	708	729	198	234	4	3	3	8
1812	1113	1213	203	219	707	739	197	235	3	6	3	14
1829	451	536	139	195	18	31	281	285	12	7	1	18
ACHAGUAS												
1780	88	68	8	6	76	58	3	2	0	0	1	2
1801	554	550	62	58	53	53	422	413	9	17	8	9
1804	1247	1266	196	176	64	60	870	902	71	75	46	53
1806	650	588	104	96	169	146	283	302	26	21	68	23
1809	960	962	189	173	150	136	527	547	25	28	69	78
1811	1233	1242	225	226	164	164	697	687	36	44	111	121
AGUA BLANCA												
1779	241	286	12	16	119	147	108	119	0	0	2	4
1801	287	300	46	46	124	98	117	156	0	0	0	0
1802	270	287	39	45	96	111	135	131	0	0	0	0
1803	270	287	39	45	96	111	135	131	0	0	0	0
1804	488	432	94	80	176	160	218	192	0	0	0	0
1805	360	357	74	72	124	116	162	168	0	0	0	1
1808	380	415	21	20	163	194	193	199	1	0	2	2
1812	414	470	30	30	165	184	213	253	6	3	0	0
1815	373	431	80	94	108	119	185	218	0	0	0	0
1830	356	413	97	107	94	128	163	178	0	0	2	0
AGUA CULEBRAS												
1781	887	1019	129	152	99	116	549	640	6	9	104	102
1802	566	647	59	78	75	97	399	445	5	11	28	16
1803	441	622	47	66	57	79	317	459	5	10	15	8
1804	318	428	48	56	40	62	209	285	4	9	17	16
1805	550	659	66	67	41	65	396	489	5	8	42	30
1807	406	475	43	46	48	58	300	350	6	8	9	13
1808	466	528	47	51	54	59	340	394	8	9	17	15
1809	468	539	48	60	54	59	340	394	9	11	17	15
1811	407	448	46	48	45	45	289	336	8	7	19	12
1812	360	428	33	37	45	48	263	318	4	6	15	19
1815	303	358	18	17	30	23	245	307	1	4	9	7
1817	171	237	14	17	33	44	119	171	0	0	5	5
1818	292	342	19	22	37	42	229	271	0	0	7	7

TABLE 1. PARISH POPULATION BY SEX AND RACE (CONTINUED)

YEAR	TOTAL M	TOTAL F	WHITE M	WHITE F	INDIAN M	INDIAN F	PARDO M	PARDO F	NEGRO M	NEGRO F	SLAVE M	SLAVE F
1819	226	342	19	22	18	27	182	286	0	0	7	7
1820	318	433	14	22	0	0	254	329	26	46	24	36
1821	305	427	14	13	26	37	241	321	24	54	0	2
AGUACALIENTE												
1803	261	246	42	34	0	0	209	202	0	0	10	10
1804	242	267	49	31	0	0	181	222	0	0	12	14
1805	250	286	53	62	0	0	157	177	15	16	25	31
1806	234	250	38	34	0	0	159	189	0	0	37	27
1807	273	275	36	26	0	0	196	208	0	0	41	41
1818	160	219	4	2	0	0	131	193	0	0	25	24
1819	163	231	5	2	0	0	139	197	0	0	19	32
ALPARGATON												
1804	107	132	0	0	0	0	79	95	28	37	0	0
1805	117	110	0	0	0	0	89	71	28	39	0	0
1806	83	100	0	0	0	0	60	73	23	27	0	0
1807	116	100	0	0	0	0	70	46	46	54	0	0
1818	79	112	0	0	0	0	79	112	0	0	0	0
1819	73	83	0	0	0	0	73	83	0	0	0	0
1820	162	184	0	0	0	0	126	139	36	45	0	0
ALTAGRACIA DE ORITUCO												
1783	500	468	116	119	193	208	10	7	103	76	78	58
1802	772	843	256	278	261	298	182	194	5	6	68	67
1803	821	831	234	244	295	281	189	203	14	12	89	91
1804	884	901	240	266	257	297	204	217	24	21	159	100
1806	909	894	307	320	272	266	190	175	27	31	113	102
1807	961	904	319	329	284	271	201	156	34	36	123	112
1809	995	943	328	309	303	292	213	183	38	41	113	118
1810	974	931	320	303	291	285	209	183	44	44	110	116
1811	965	935	307	320	306	289	195	177	36	40	121	109
ALTAMIRA												
1783	174	178	0	0	174	178	0	0	0	0	0	0
ANTIMANO												
1811	797	489	40	26	120	92	81	51	55	39	501	281
1819	545	631	139	123	83	100	170	213	11	13	142	182
APARICION												
1802	1138	1235	300	317	311	336	344	374	138	155	45	53
1803	1107	1224	318	311	270	333	346	377	142	159	31	44
1804	1699	1689	506	492	322	337	815	807	0	0	56	53
1805	1511	1587	216	227	290	332	910	921	44	53	51	54

TABLE 1. PARISH POPULATION BY SEX AND RACE (CONTINUED)

YEAR	TOTAL		WHITE		INDIAN		PARDO		NEGRO		SLAVE	
	M	F	M	F	M	F	M	F	M	F	M	F
1808	1584	1713	395	348	351	424	790	876	0	0	48	65
1809	1323	1419	394	422	222	235	654	711	0	0	53	51
1810	1508	1670	375	405	306	381	775	816	0	0	52	68
1811	1445	1546	360	338	295	375	738	773	0	0	52	60
1812	1160	1294	370	349	232	325	531	603	0	0	27	17
APURITO												
1802	237	209	13	14	18	19	137	129	42	33	27	14
1806	200	207	39	46	22	25	126	131	0	0	13	5
1807	256	289	57	65	49	55	131	143	10	13	9	13
ARAGUITA												
1784	440	444	19	13	50	52	71	64	12	10	288	305
1802	310	351	10	10	30	25	9	14	12	12	249	290
1803	270	311	11	12	7	10	1	3	17	11	234	275
1804	278	298	11	10	5	6	7	7	18	16	237	259
1805	239	265	11	7	7	7	5	4	8	1	208	246
1807	321	290	12	6	6	2	44	20	3	13	256	249
1810	235	273	22	18	14	16	52	36	8	23	139	180
1811	230	249	24	14	11	19	61	47	11	16	123	153
1812	180	211	21	16	11	13	40	33	7	14	101	135
1816	197	258	28	30	17	15	24	30	18	20	110	163
1819	208	245	35	33	7	6	25	25	17	15	124	166
ARAURE												
1778	1369	1472	639	659	127	124	342	374	127	147	134	168
1798	3571	3957	1271	1384	637	658	1508	1728	155	187	0	0
1799	3691	4013	1352	1415	658	654	1522	1754	159	190	0	0
1800	3740	4095	1325	1443	687	669	1553	1778	175	205	0	0
1801	1281	1387	261	300	37	43	895	920	88	124	0	0
1802	1531	1754	494	570	76	66	824	953	40	32	97	133
1803	1485	1645	507	528	54	58	807	895	26	33	91	131
1804	1269	1335	461	504	65	66	649	618	14	22	80	125
1805	1251	1625	449	951	72	82	615	490	28	19	87	83
1808	1445	1616	441	481	157	145	731	844	4	11	112	135
1809	1420	1714	466	523	150	177	706	862	4	6	94	146
1810	1437	1730	473	527	150	177	706	872	8	6	100	148
1811	1598	1846	617	636	150	178	711	872	16	12	104	148
1812	1445	1767	479	546	145	181	698	880	19	16	104	144
1829	1874	2355	785	1011	159	145	848	1078	65	82	17	39
AREGUE												
1802	301	403	45	59	140	211	105	122	0	0	11	11
1803	385	467	35	40	235	286	105	132	0	0	10	9
1804	344	409	36	42	215	286	85	72	0	0	8	9
1805	334	364	54	55	176	204	90	92	0	0	14	13
1809	481	499	56	64	318	316	91	105	1	1	15	13

TABLE 1. PARISH POPULATION BY SEX AND RACE (CONTINUED)

YEAR	TOTAL		WHITE		INDIAN		PARDO		NEGRO		SLAVE	
	M	F	M	F	M	F	M	F	M	F	M	F
1815	403	535	71	107	206	257	111	146	0	0	15	25
ARENALES												
1802	441	461	74	74	49	41	191	208	61	67	66	71
1803	440	485	83	102	51	37	190	214	47	61	69	71
1804	453	469	77	88	54	36	204	231	44	45	74	69
1805	443	464	64	78	59	48	179	179	70	96	71	63
1807	442	465	58	68	54	47	213	223	47	56	70	71
1809	455	464	60	40	79	72	196	215	66	75	54	62
ARICHUNA												
1801	296	293	75	66	144	148	55	60	17	13	5	6
1804	408	447	70	82	214	241	67	67	30	34	27	23
AROA												
1802	962	626	61	57	61	64	685	367	69	70	86	68
1805	742	720	101	91	46	38	341	359	202	187	52	45
1807	719	749	100	93	47	51	337	375	200	194	35	36
1808	724	849	39	55	47	64	314	395	194	219	130	116
1809	697	761	65	49	33	40	510	573	38	39	51	60
1817	466	500	60	56	0	0	379	415	11	12	16	17
1818	686	703	107	111	66	53	418	453	95	86	0	0
ATAMAICA												
1780	69	64	2	3	65	60	0	1	2	0	0	0
1802	176	160	59	52	71	70	34	33	1	0	11	5
AYAMANES												
1802	258	266	17	31	241	235	0	0	0	0	0	0
1803	210	252	28	25	180	226	2	1	0	0	0	0
1804	234	249	19	11	201	230	14	8	0	0	0	0
1805	192	233	26	30	160	200	6	3	0	0	0	0
1807	281	340	43	46	216	275	22	19	0	0	0	0
1808	296	338	52	53	219	266	25	19	0	0	0	0
1815	252	381	46	49	168	281	38	50	0	0	0	1
BANCO LARGO												
1805	619	685	175	201	85	95	139	157	107	123	113	109
1809	534	630	88	104	51	68	337	380	17	24	41	54
BARBACOAS DE LOS LLANOS												
1782	659	662	315	256	92	133	72	100	139	127	41	46
1783	850	864	315	256	92	139	172	206	230	217	41	46
1802	1269	1289	474	409	204	253	453	495	49	54	89	78

TABLE 1. PARISH POPULATION BY SEX AND RACE (CONTINUED)

YEAR	TOTAL		WHITE		INDIAN		PARDO		NEGRO		SLAVE	
	M	F	M	F	M	F	M	F	M	F	M	F
1803	1222	1162	500	389	151	177	312	343	206	201	53	52
1804	1354	1362	509	459	142	167	152	161	428	487	123	88
1805	1541	1569	469	458	108	136	379	421	484	471	101	83
1809	1700	1541	548	531	235	231	429	409	405	299	83	71
1810	1591	1465	542	528	208	180	419	394	354	318	68	45
1811	1573	1472	543	526	198	172	419	402	347	315	66	57
	BARBACOAS DEL TOCUYO											
1802	303	303	57	56	119	122	47	41	72	76	8	8
1803	246	291	36	51	115	137	33	40	51	53	11	10
1804	269	331	50	65	110	144	39	46	55	63	15	13
1805	306	325	42	61	144	138	40	52	57	57	23	17
1806	294	336	43	52	117	135	47	55	72	80	15	14
1807	299	343	48	57	118	138	48	58	75	81	10	9
1808	320	353	57	62	122	140	55	65	71	71	15	15
1809	334	364	61	65	127	144	61	67	69	71	16	17
1810	368	380	63	68	138	147	73	74	73	76	21	15
1812	286	318	77	62	88	120	101	118	15	16	5	2
1815	332	370	55	51	113	129	141	174	9	4	14	12
1816	300	334	58	50	109	124	109	139	13	12	11	9
1817	384	382	45	42	151	124	162	192	9	12	17	12
1818	325	324	37	35	112	108	148	162	10	5	18	14
1819	365	410	48	44	125	137	148	190	24	27	20	12
1820	376	399	55	44	124	135	170	195	6	10	21	15
	BARQUISIMETO											
1779	4315	4461	362	452	354	306	2563	2547	637	738	399	418
1815	5490	7106	368	400	641	801	3994	5252	187	299	300	354
	BARQUISIMETO, MITAD DE(1)											
1802	2461	2706	399	460	310	344	1077	1160	515	560	160	182
1803	2466	2723	400	464	314	353	1079	1167	512	558	161	181
1804	2520	3175	405	468	321	359	1087	1167	522	972	185	209
1805	2530	2794	401	470	297	333	1142	1235	525	558	165	198
1807	2947	3045	211	221	313	254	1860	1914	239	261	324	395
1808	2895	3148	222	223	314	323	1781	1924	245	288	333	390
1809	3070	3312	235	242	227	340	1951	2012	287	305	370	413
1810	2948	3045	211	221	313	254	1860	1914	239	261	325	395
1811	3094	3345	251	245	249	355	1961	2019	270	304	363	422
1817	2667	3242	128	156	585	701	1878	2310	3	12	73	63
1818	2064	2480	58	72	540	554	1335	1697	65	98	66	59
1819	1969	2521	62	79	528	544	1251	1726	63	100	65	72
1820	1963	2566	59	104	439	531	1315	1797	77	59	73	75
	BARQUISIMETO, MITAD DE(2)											
1802	2483	2927	323	393	97	125	1677	1936	146	172	240	301
1803	3503	2469	327	989	144	108	1758	618	1020	440	254	314

TABLE 1. PARISH POPULATION BY SEX AND RACE (CONTINUED)

YEAR	TOTAL		WHITE		INDIAN		PARDO		NEGRO		SLAVE	
	M	F	M	F	M	F	M	F	M	F	M	F
1804	3461	2445	330	960	146	116	1686	608	1044	451	255	310
1805	3475	2487	331	965	144	115	1692	624	1044	458	264	325
1807	3460	2470	336	973	147	114	1684	621	1037	451	256	311
1808	3343	2189	310	854	131	99	1603	544	1069	426	230	266
1809	3382	2246	325	876	171	109	1081	552	1565	433	240	276
1810	3382	2246	325	876	171	109	1081	552	1565	433	240	276
1811	3375	3318	373	910	179	153	1100	801	1469	1179	254	275
1817	2992	3941	209	248	118	155	2359	3141	121	161	185	236
1818	2690	4019	232	298	131	168	2004	3114	136	194	187	245
1819	2706	4091	240	315	137	196	2005	3120	133	206	191	254
1820	2738	4086	282	317	144	184	1980	3134	139	203	193	248
	BARUTA											
1802	1013	1033	436	431	354	373	74	68	36	31	113	130
1803	1055	1054	406	405	398	400	86	70	48	48	117	131
1804	1066	1058	422	406	387	388	80	77	52	52	125	135
1805	1044	1022	368	358	412	404	79	84	39	45	146	131
1811	1037	992	414	395	375	330	64	68	36	35	148	164
1816	536	619	192	248	183	211	31	35	42	37	88	88
1817	670	875	278	338	233	314	60	94	14	17	85	112
1819	1208	1451	286	292	220	318	55	64	7	11	640	766
1820	812	898	365	342	231	298	101	124	18	21	97	113
	BAUL											
1781	285	253	104	97	95	73	25	26	58	54	3	3
1802	1039	987	380	362	171	145	300	249	124	177	64	54
1805	852	908	367	360	174	169	264	315	37	54	10	10
1811	1296	1370	500	550	223	233	428	426	0	0	145	161
1812	1028	1195	395	489	184	212	381	407	0	0	68	87
1815	761	799	307	332	90	117	286	263	21	20	57	67
1816	1008	989	430	371	104	117	373	384	28	28	73	89
1817	1094	1179	504	488	103	127	391	443	34	48	62	73
1825	1275	1370	383	404	179	197	690	754	10	4	13	11
1829	807	868	291	299	14	19	354	382	124	138	24	30
	BOBARE											
1779	143	154	0	0	143	154	0	0	0	0	0	0
1802	270	310	0	0	270	310	0	0	0	0	0	0
1803	270	310	0	0	270	310	0	0	0	0	0	0
1804	282	307	0	0	282	307	0	0	0	0	0	0
1805	278	263	0	0	278	263	0	0	0	0	0	0
1806	278	263	0	0	278	263	0	0	0	0	0	0
1808	287	306	0	0	287	306	0	0	0	0	0	0
1811	406	409	0	0	406	409	0	0	0	0	0	0
1820	236	232	0	0	225	216	9	15	0	0	2	1

TABLE 1. PARISH POPULATION BY SEX AND RACE (CONTINUED)

YEAR	TOTAL M	TOTAL F	WHITE M	WHITE F	INDIAN M	INDIAN F	PARDO M	PARDO F	NEGRO M	NEGRO F	SLAVE M	SLAVE F
BOCONO												
1778	977	1084	465	513	107	125	387	426	2	6	16	14
1795	1232	1272	576	580	124	119	470	507	27	18	35	48
1796	1082	1104	525	526	101	86	423	456	12	15	21	21
1798	1376	1329	774	683	112	110	450	491	13	10	27	35
1799	1177	1223	562	573	110	107	460	501	22	10	23	32
1800	1022	1040	492	489	100	90	395	421	13	10	22	30
1802	853	874	258	225	136	139	432	476	19	16	8	18
1803	998	1014	312	270	157	156	494	546	25	20	10	22
1804	932	1024	314	273	86	157	495	545	27	21	10	28
1805	1102	1181	646	696	112	94	303	340	24	29	17	22
1806	896	1022	331	328	92	109	428	540	31	24	14	21
1807	1026	1115	442	434	91	90	423	536	40	30	30	25
1808	854	836	397	393	84	94	300	302	40	28	33	19
1810	687	781	278	331	89	98	307	340	0	0	13	12
BORBURATA												
1803	355	340	15	8	8	5	99	102	126	131	107	94
1804	393	361	19	7	7	4	106	97	149	156	112	97
1805	371	365	20	12	3	2	83	88	153	164	112	99
1806	406	375	26	19	2	3	98	85	180	172	100	96
1807	403	376	16	11	2	3	98	93	184	175	103	94
1818	262	315	7	1	1	2	63	90	109	127	82	95
1819	300	364	9	5	1	4	80	102	122	151	88	102
BURERITO												
1802	548	553	6	0	10	3	334	412	155	122	43	16
1803	560	558	6	0	8	3	104	114	403	424	39	17
1804	499	622	0	0	11	19	353	441	109	137	26	25
1807	496	494	3	4	1	1	274	306	184	166	34	17
1809	530	618	3	2	1	0	287	343	204	241	35	32
BURIA												
1779	224	229	16	11	60	69	135	130	11	16	2	3
1802	382	403	8	9	55	54	278	311	31	26	10	3
1803	351	380	6	7	31	35	278	311	30	26	6	1
1804	380	343	10	10	50	36	304	286	5	7	11	4
1805	390	429	11	8	47	49	321	364	5	5	6	3
1807	393	447	18	13	43	54	315	370	7	6	10	4
1809	346	391	12	10	35	42	291	334	3	4	5	1
1810	452	484	13	11	35	42	395	424	5	7	4	0
1811	495	540	14	12	44	40	427	482	5	5	5	1
1817	327	461	24	22	35	42	251	376	14	21	3	0
1818	324	513	45	76	18	48	257	389	0	0	4	0
1819	403	594	21	30	59	84	171	296	145	180	7	4

TABLE 1. PARISH POPULATION BY SEX AND RACE (CONTINUED)

YEAR	TOTAL M	TOTAL F	WHITE M	WHITE F	INDIAN M	INDIAN F	PARDO M	PARDO F	NEGRO M	NEGRO F	SLAVE M	SLAVE F
CABRIA												
1802	106	94	0	0	0	0	106	93	0	0	0	1
1803	90	122	0	0	0	0	90	122	0	0	0	0
1808	91	86	0	0	0	0	90	83	1	3	0	0
CABRUTA												
1780	128	91	53	45	11	10	32	27	5	5	27	4
1806	114	112	13	13	89	88	12	10	0	0	0	1
1808	218	164	4	7	208	148	5	9	1	0	0	0
1810	237	208	27	18	180	159	30	31	0	0	0	0
CAGUA												
1781	2680	2826	1177	1212	135	161	1238	1323	0	0	130	130
1802	2031	2686	628	1008	64	79	1062	1304	68	79	209	216
1803	2066	2425	618	664	69	64	1167	1453	10	15	202	229
1804	2020	2643	624	779	124	99	961	1454	43	41	268	270
1805	2095	2401	584	708	53	52	1167	1333	41	47	250	261
1806	2114	2554	579	732	61	69	1189	1427	48	57	237	269
1808	1977	2522	541	729	71	72	1133	1453	22	13	210	255
1809	2005	2576	551	741	87	70	1099	1461	22	24	246	280
1811	1934	2362	485	696	69	62	1110	1257	33	46	237	301
1815	1465	2055	481	664	211	224	473	892	18	21	282	254
1816	1634	1802	511	684	249	247	523	538	48	51	303	282
1817	1709	2277	526	699	264	262	538	953	63	66	318	297
1818	1646	2266	508	694	242	262	522	950	56	66	318	294
CAICARA DEL ORINOCO												
1802	139	111	36	29	19	16	68	58	0	0	16	8
CALABOZO												
1780	1888	1560	768	643	68	40	627	566	96	75	329	236
1802	2138	2540	677	812	65	96	927	1091	80	94	389	447
1803	2197	2564	702	818	60	101	942	1075	98	120	395	450
1804	2203	2536	695	807	57	99	945	1061	104	123	402	446
1805	2237	2583	722	827	65	101	950	1057	110	142	390	456
1807	1948	2185	605	680	55	84	870	936	98	111	320	374
1808	1847	2064	526	568	54	67	866	970	111	111	290	348
1810	1803	1962	536	548	27	26	949	977	27	33	264	378
1812	1256	1683	440	505	23	26	619	811	13	25	161	316
1817	749	1236	270	351	0	0	345	659	0	0	134	226
1818	566	988	235	329	0	0	257	467	0	0	74	192
1822	481	946	158	210	0	0	258	610	0	0	65	126

TABLE 1. PARISH POPULATION BY SEX AND RACE (CONTINUED)

YEAR	TOTAL M	TOTAL F	WHITE M	WHITE F	INDIAN M	INDIAN F	PARDO M	PARDO F	NEGRO M	NEGRO F	SLAVE M	SLAVE F
CAMAGUAN												
1780	419	320	36	29	213	214	32	23	13	11	125	43
1801	463	437	93	86	242	231	88	92	19	17	21	11
1802	447	419	101	83	204	203	101	104	19	17	22	12
1803	551	521	98	88	248	241	172	157	12	20	21	15
1804	553	535	107	96	249	251	164	163	7	11	26	14
1812	543	564	102	92	184	219	227	213	8	8	22	32
1817	541	596	125	134	134	148	233	260	26	35	23	19
CAMATAGUA												
1783	1080	1183	280	249	236	263	118	126	368	451	78	94
1802	913	1238	177	233	377	543	112	143	87	130	160	189
1803	897	1231	181	234	361	537	108	141	84	126	163	193
1804	1008	1297	126	150	229	313	243	321	255	320	155	193
1805	894	1217	181	227	361	537	108	141	84	126	160	186
1806	894	1217	181	227	361	537	108	141	84	126	160	186
1808	894	1217	181	227	361	537	108	141	84	126	160	186
1811	870	787	104	103	171	159	495	469	0	0	100	56
CANOABO												
1781	556	566	58	39	0	0	413	408	0	0	85	119
1788	532	560	33	32	0	0	392	396	0	0	107	132
1802	487	594	26	29	0	0	391	466	0	0	70	99
1803	461	580	26	23	0	0	367	467	0	0	68	90
1804	480	583	35	33	0	0	375	461	0	0	70	89
1805	519	615	18	23	0	0	401	485	0	0	100	107
1806	616	604	38	46	0	0	478	438	11	14	89	106
1807	564	586	48	51	0	0	418	418	14	16	84	101
1808	578	616	48	55	0	0	419	414	16	37	95	110
1809	596	618	58	57	0	0	413	423	19	19	106	119
1810	463	574	30	34	4	3	337	422	23	26	69	89
1815	388	451	29	24	0	0	266	324	7	8	86	95
1817	469	527	33	37	4	8	321	344	27	37	84	101
1819	618	669	48	58	10	18	376	402	44	44	140	147
1820	630	680	51	60	10	18	382	408	47	47	140	147
CAPAYA												
1784	603	649	31	14	99	116	65	80	67	66	341	373
1802	574	621	24	4	111	113	106	160	9	11	324	333
1803	731	645	20	7	99	108	60	79	59	59	493	392
1804	698	658	19	3	102	95	77	84	41	49	459	427
1805	653	702	22	2	96	109	77	83	109	131	349	377
1806	769	673	9	1	76	80	94	94	151	148	439	350
1807	800	694	15	7	55	51	214	199	69	57	447	380
1808	760	696	15	7	55	53	214	199	69	57	407	380
1809	522	582	18	3	64	86	42	41	63	73	335	379

TABLE 1. PARISH POPULATION BY SEX AND RACE (CONTINUED)

YEAR	TOTAL		WHITE		INDIAN		PARDO		NEGRO		SLAVE	
	M	F	M	F	M	F	M	F	M	F	M	F
1811	562	611	21	13	71	86	134	153	38	56	298	303
1812	554	581	22	5	140	145	126	151	23	33	243	247
1817	398	505	11	9	34	46	117	172	11	29	225	249
1818	473	540	15	10	46	52	110	164	27	35	275	279
1819	450	591	11	9	49	56	128	194	24	44	238	288
1820	477	583	14	10	48	56	131	184	32	31	252	302
CARABALLEDA												
1802	611	579	93	63	99	116	107	128	0	0	312	272
1804	573	524	81	64	90	107	93	99	0	0	309	254
CARACAS-ALTAGRACIA												
1796	2419	3822	691	1055	0	0	1147	1833	182	256	399	678
1802	2224	3550	776	998	15	27	962	1566	170	367	301	592
1803	2284	3673	843	1197	13	30	906	1444	192	427	330	575
1804	2388	4030	937	1241	19	65	951	1693	174	405	307	626
1805	2483	3968	771	1131	50	103	1088	1577	181	341	393	816
1807	2242	3937	746	1103	33	80	960	1633	144	325	359	796
1808	2293	3958	729	1100	32	65	995	1623	149	331	388	839
1810	2340	4053	736	1098	25	41	972	1682	198	336	409	896
1811	1873	3373	687	998	8	17	763	1525	126	257	289	576
1815	802	1311	272	503	20	36	266	524	155	128	89	120
1816	636	1129	296	478	7	7	257	483	28	74	48	87
1817	699	1384	298	565	2	8	285	567	50	95	64	149
1818	709	1482	338	623	10	24	230	586	26	85	105	164
1819	783	1424	339	614	22	48	259	528	27	70	86	164
1820	721	1234	321	381	28	36	247	567	35	69	90	181
CARACAS-CANDELARIA												
1800	1370	1983	428	554	9	19	625	1002	69	110	239	298
1802	1486	2052	569	739	28	58	560	788	105	177	224	290
1803	1365	1984	527	703	34	81	482	699	113	211	209	290
1804	1475	2098	574	769	23	50	539	792	119	203	220	284
1805	1425	2118	533	702	26	53	504	834	131	246	231	283
1806	1529	2171	557	729	38	67	544	847	131	238	259	290
1808	1577	2350	518	711	24	49	680	1072	124	183	231	335
1809	1638	2402	585	747	31	53	702	1130	88	155	232	317
1811	1222	2117	492	798	15	26	438	837	105	196	172	260
1815	695	1466	246	539	15	49	273	532	90	185	71	161
1816	996	1729	285	480	17	22	466	677	47	69	181	481
1817	984	1686	276	473	24	35	374	745	163	241	147	192
1818	913	1664	283	444	13	14	433	864	63	131	121	211
1819	926	1588	258	445	9	17	428	747	81	156	150	223
1820	895	1552	303	454	2	10	445	851	32	76	113	161
1821	880	1571	263	431	11	15	406	764	67	140	133	221

TABLE 1. PARISH POPULATION BY SEX AND RACE (CONTINUED)

YEAR	TOTAL		WHITE		INDIAN		PARDO		NEGRO		SLAVE	
	M	F	M	F	M	F	M	F	M	F	M	F
CARACAS-CATEDRAL ORIENTE												
1801	1757	2848	654	808	14	46	510	868	76	156	503	970
1802	1815	2877	677	745	24	51	498	853	106	178	510	1050
1803	1782	2706	670	754	20	27	455	796	86	163	551	966
1804	1815	2726	678	646	9	41	540	856	78	146	510	1037
1805	1921	2953	731	815	14	49	548	911	80	169	548	1009
1807	1670	2817	636	788	11	34	428	899	69	167	526	929
1809	1838	2957	714	826	12	42	536	964	75	183	501	942
1811	1837	2761	630	753	12	24	639	915	125	68	431	1001
1815	724	1634	281	497	6	21	240	609	19	49	178	458
1816	1055	1428	250	464	51	65	390	489	99	107	265	303
1817	903	1982	335	640	14	32	257	620	56	120	241	570
1818	974	1782	363	504	29	55	292	578	59	134	231	511
1819	1134	2166	432	661	17	23	338	790	38	79	309	613
CARACAS-CATEDRAL PONIENTE												
1802	1438	2037	535	501	33	56	440	731	54	96	376	653
1803	1635	2196	585	536	29	44	512	798	87	118	422	700
1805	1679	2112	700	543	40	96	470	649	95	151	374	673
1807	1640	2253	598	575	44	87	476	708	122	187	400	696
1808	1652	2229	620	552	38	71	483	747	106	149	405	710
1810	1696	2274	610	561	55	67	522	768	84	165	425	713
1811	1630	2268	604	567	38	64	490	773	87	173	411	691
1815	709	1652	352	554	28	60	198	561	46	91	85	386
1816	1476	1663	478	608	11	23	394	365	268	270	325	397
1817	1125	2032	496	645	18	39	341	751	83	147	187	450
1818	1253	1973	606	666	10	25	267	633	59	114	311	535
1819	1129	2059	564	691	9	33	240	664	63	138	253	533
1822	799	1853	387	627	218	679	10	32	43	106	141	409
CARACAS-CURATO CASTRENSE												
1803	686	275	611	157	0	4	36	23	0	10	39	81
1804	804	288	711	163	0	2	36	21	2	3	55	99
1805	957	302	859	180	2	7	50	21	0	4	46	90
1807	2536	709	1690	398	2	3	763	158	5	15	76	135
1809	1499	534	1118	308	2	7	297	104	4	8	78	107
1810	823	261	774	178	1	7	5	10	2	3	41	63
1811	859	356	696	182	1	5	76	44	22	13	64	112
CARACAS-SAN PABLO												
1799	2251	3573	915	1110	8	33	848	1548	113	177	367	705
1801	2304	3643	874	1093	7	59	915	1545	108	160	400	786
1802	2544	3743	790	1115	42	56	1006	1487	191	247	515	838
1803	2563	3356	1146	1138	33	40	789	1466	49	52	546	660
1804	2391	3337	962	1190	19	47	888	1371	79	82	443	647
1805	3333	3280	1173	1259	28	77	1179	991	559	567	394	386

TABLE 1. PARISH POPULATION BY SEX AND RACE (CONTINUED)

YEAR	TOTAL		WHITE		INDIAN		PARDO		NEGRO		SLAVE	
	M	F	M	F	M	F	M	F	M	F	M	F
1806	3069	3038	1000	1130	34	73	1165	889	486	564	384	382
1807	3103	3317	1000	1130	34	73	1165	1090	520	564	384	460
1808	2960	2883	1100	950	40	30	1250	1114	320	335	250	454
1809	2306	2466	609	709	149	139	450	578	539	508	559	532
1810	2755	3236	560	960	58	75	902	951	580	455	655	795
1811	2497	2833	700	650	89	150	900	1030	385	415	423	588
1815	3751	3110	626	852	126	163	1100	1150	230	290	1669	655
1816	2447	3770	805	1263	9	15	866	1613	230	199	537	680
1817	2772	4097	1008	1403	9	15	988	1713	231	199	536	767
1818	3573	4642	1509	1565	19	25	978	1690	628	729	439	633
1820	2787	4787	1146	1996	28	87	1101	1577	102	269	410	858
CARACAS-SANTA ROSALIA												
1795	1979	2697	834	959	0	0	880	1314	0	0	265	424
1796	2036	3033	796	859	0	0	965	1719	0	0	275	455
1798	1947	2745	815	867	0	0	872	1417	0	0	260	461
1799	1935	2687	738	854	0	0	923	1402	0	0	274	431
1802	2012	3070	752	931	22	55	870	1384	84	170	284	530
1803	2008	3157	705	906	30	63	908	1357	96	171	269	660
1804	2256	2884	715	871	42	50	1066	1250	95	130	338	583
1805	2356	2673	760	956	24	65	1077	947	99	130	396	575
1806	2190	3261	885	1002	27	97	830	1552	115	217	333	393
1807	1962	3426	751	993	36	98	719	1482	95	233	361	620
1808	1966	3474	710	991	32	94	733	1495	101	249	390	645
1809	1939	3528	732	1133	61	154	674	1429	135	269	337	543
1810	2028	3420	727	1038	57	98	827	1481	114	231	303	572
1811	2024	4446	717	1010	38	102	751	2410	112	265	406	659
1815	1195	2145	435	796	10	35	463	855	69	123	218	336
1816	1163	2540	501	844	6	13	413	1045	48	154	195	484
1817	1314	2242	522	813	3	4	483	956	152	165	154	304
1818	1563	2493	548	895	3	14	640	1020	196	259	176	305
1819	1618	2387	704	888	10	17	399	714	308	479	197	289
1820	1737	2352	813	1096	13	17	604	846	136	173	171	220
1822	1723	2572	719	1006	10	16	690	1149	93	126	211	275
CARAMACATE												
1779	93	88	11	8	73	60	9	20	0	0	0	0
1799	197	175	70	55	38	43	77	72	9	1	3	4
1801	218	203	57	44	32	40	115	105	14	13	0	1
1802	295	273	53	39	30	33	208	195	0	0	4	6
1803	318	324	73	71	52	47	187	201	3	0	3	5
1804	236	276	48	40	37	34	150	197	0	0	1	5
1805	269	281	58	44	42	38	168	198	0	0	1	1
1806	253	279	55	44	37	33	158	200	1	1	2	1
1807	247	226	29	29	45	45	164	147	8	5	1	0
1809	315	305	40	41	52	112	217	150	4	2	2	0
1811	265	261	28	26	51	54	186	181	0	0	0	0
1812	238	241	30	28	46	47	162	166	0	0	0	0
1817	132	164	17	21	22	20	113	123	0	0	0	0

TABLE 1. PARISH POPULATION BY SEX AND RACE (CONTINUED)

YEAR	TOTAL		WHITE		INDIAN		PARDO		NEGRO		SLAVE	
	M	F	M	F	M	F	M	F	M	F	M	F
1818	127	165	16	16	27	30	84	119	0	0	0	0
1819	154	173	22	23	30	27	102	123	0	0	0	0
1822	97	155	11	17	15	15	70	123	1	0	0	0
1823	86	123	9	11	12	10	64	102	0	0	1	0
1828	92	129	15	15	12	10	64	102	1	0	0	2
1829	114	158	10	13	23	34	80	111	1	0	0	0
1831	129	160	16	21	30	38	80	100	2	1	1	0
1832	128	159	15	20	30	38	79	99	3	2	1	0
1833	125	154	9	14	29	35	82	98	5	7	0	0
1834	137	165	14	16	30	34	83	101	10	14	0	0
1835	165	190	17	22	39	45	95	105	14	18	0	0
1836	178	202	18	23	46	49	98	110	16	20	0	0
1837	190	215	20	24	50	54	104	115	16	22	0	0
1838	206	233	20	24	62	69	107	116	17	24	0	0
CARAYACA												
1802	424	359	118	92	8	9	76	60	76	60	146	138
1804	366	284	62	44	32	32	72	49	64	44	136	115
1805	361	313	70	58	18	11	106	99	37	36	130	109
1807	361	313	70	58	18	11	106	99	37	36	130	109
1808	361	313	70	58	18	11	106	99	37	36	130	109
1809	361	313	70	58	18	11	106	99	37	36	130	109
1810	361	313	70	58	18	11	106	99	37	36	130	109
1811	368	305	70	61	18	11	81	80	30	26	169	127
1817	470	441	132	114	1	0	171	163	49	55	117	109
1818	533	507	189	195	6	3	183	193	31	19	124	97
1819	450	422	144	143	10	1	148	139	21	20	127	119
1820	479	472	144	169	9	5	147	155	30	24	149	119
1833	677	1015	151	196	29	60	192	293	100	145	205	321
CARORA												
1802	2004	2855	183	253	12	26	1419	2056	140	225	250	295
1803	2226	3092	173	273	17	25	1623	2248	154	235	259	311
1804	2354	3230	191	304	17	32	1745	2395	146	217	255	282
1809	2466	3666	223	332	21	41	1800	2782	186	258	236	253
1815	2402	3193	141	239	4	7	2050	2625	64	56	143	266
CARUAO												
1811	232	311	2	0	0	0	55	52	2	5	173	254
1815	289	273	0	0	1	3	6	4	12	23	270	243
CASIGUA												
1780	1235	1320	357	392	25	24	394	482	185	177	274	245
CATA												
1803	256	262	8	0	0	0	0	0	97	105	151	157

TABLE 1. PARISH POPULATION BY SEX AND RACE (CONTINUED)

YEAR	TOTAL		WHITE		INDIAN		PARDO		NEGRO		SLAVE	
	M	F	M	F	M	F	M	F	M	F	M	F
1804	255	268	6	4	0	0	0	0	101	109	148	155
1805	262	285	8	4	0	0	27	31	74	81	153	169
CAUCAGUA												
1784	1276	1146	71	70	64	70	160	146	79	71	902	789
1802	888	976	38	38	57	78	106	120	92	94	595	646
1803	887	913	39	34	45	65	105	99	91	95	607	620
1804	887	952	39	37	49	66	104	107	92	107	603	635
1805	902	940	39	29	47	63	117	109	95	111	604	628
1806	899	951	38	30	45	64	114	118	95	107	607	632
1807	878	919	43	33	56	63	89	96	102	115	588	612
1808	829	732	41	35	39	59	77	66	61	55	611	517
1809	791	844	35	30	69	81	70	74	53	69	564	590
1811	671	769	51	41	38	48	140	173	14	20	428	487
1812	737	937	73	90	63	87	151	206	40	53	410	501
1816	684	821	53	48	32	50	84	142	36	49	479	532
1817	593	764	33	40	28	51	86	143	17	35	429	495
1818	566	739	32	31	31	79	88	137	8	20	407	472
1819	669	843	48	41	49	75	127	184	22	33	423	510
1820	710	885	51	69	53	78	141	194	25	40	440	504
CERRITO												
1779	1567	1777	423	442	146	175	949	1089	2	3	47	68
CHABASQUEN												
1802	911	1178	62	79	734	959	103	124	3	5	9	11
1803	918	1185	61	78	734	964	108	128	3	3	12	12
1804	926	1205	61	80	736	976	112	133	4	4	13	12
1805	935	1206	67	86	744	977	105	123	5	6	14	14
1806	940	1214	69	90	745	975	108	128	5	7	13	14
1808	932	1182	56	72	755	981	111	120	7	7	3	2
1809	918	1165	8	16	784	1002	114	139	4	5	8	3
1812	664	608	22	26	465	423	164	146	10	7	3	6
1815	655	634	21	26	453	431	167	161	8	8	6	8
1816	681	717	37	44	471	445	148	183	22	32	3	13
1817	688	717	36	39	470	454	157	186	23	30	2	8
1818	688	717	36	39	470	454	157	186	23	30	2	8
1819	335	476	14	25	236	315	74	112	10	14	1	10
1820	564	768	80	109	376	511	101	141	3	1	4	6
1829	800	847	102	99	382	427	237	213	78	106	1	2
CHACAO												
1802	1018	1017	280	312	24	25	180	178	163	175	371	327
1803	1062	1041	294	326	20	26	237	235	132	146	379	308
1804	1096	1059	305	339	19	24	218	226	142	145	412	325
1805	1018	1030	286	313	12	13	229	256	127	142	364	306
1808	1035	979	323	319	3	1	143	133	278	254	288	272

TABLE 1. PARISH POPULATION BY SEX AND RACE (CONTINUED)

YEAR	TOTAL		WHITE		INDIAN		PARDO		NEGRO		SLAVE	
	M	F	M	F	M	F	M	F	M	F	M	F
1811	1023	1068	244	267	11	15	209	227	140	152	419	407
1815	841	1165	241	382	14	13	177	259	124	156	285	355
1818	1070	1168	420	487	1	1	413	443	45	58	191	179
1819	999	1086	377	407	0	0	387	411	54	69	181	199
CHAGUARAMAL												
1783	843	764	248	203	68	59	344	349	34	36	149	117
1804	1005	898	311	259	77	50	555	537	13	12	49	40
1805	933	1052	157	211	38	49	384	449	71	73	283	270
CHAGUARAMAS												
1783	1161	1141	381	399	47	45	216	273	195	181	322	243
1802	1292	1073	295	224	82	57	525	536	40	47	350	209
1803	1317	1102	317	224	57	37	578	587	0	0	365	254
1804	1265	1174	334	237	62	42	588	594	0	0	281	301
1805	1356	1115	236	207	123	113	577	510	75	80	345	205
1808	1483	1335	338	294	76	89	611	653	117	114	341	185
1810	1559	1293	354	285	105	115	672	660	72	45	356	188
CHARALLAVE												
1783	417	401	61	64	239	216	94	102	15	9	8	10
1802	950	903	346	354	417	369	105	100	55	40	27	40
1803	928	886	312	321	398	371	110	92	85	70	23	32
1804	750	704	338	311	226	223	87	75	72	74	27	21
1805	809	816	323	371	256	245	136	118	61	52	33	30
1806	759	723	302	328	247	191	137	133	42	40	31	31
1807	776	762	293	323	273	252	132	114	38	37	40	36
1808	804	826	389	421	195	177	154	153	35	30	31	45
1810	1001	943	434	427	301	286	198	159	28	16	40	55
1811	1032	1111	459	508	270	286	220	224	30	42	53	51
1815	838	1002	366	438	260	307	133	160	46	50	33	47
1816	961	1122	399	500	291	349	212	202	31	26	28	45
1817	975	1095	375	443	312	357	237	213	24	36	27	46
CHIVACOA												
1782	882	1147	35	26	456	600	347	467	37	49	7	5
1802	473	606	14	18	248	313	185	244	12	12	14	19
1803	579	739	21	26	280	358	15	17	249	327	14	11
1804	596	704	31	40	289	316	230	289	25	34	21	25
1805	596	775	27	33	322	413	203	280	26	33	18	16
1807	625	783	31	41	347	399	200	284	27	28	20	31
1808	732	899	34	53	366	412	280	362	31	40	21	32
1809	682	903	37	45	281	395	291	383	50	54	23	26
1810	834	926	32	41	453	452	285	347	47	60	17	26
1811	744	944	33	45	330	411	285	362	78	101	18	25
1812	750	944	33	40	327	404	298	387	74	91	18	22
1815	863	1066	41	45	345	435	420	517	42	49	15	20

TABLE 1. PARISH POPULATION BY SEX AND RACE (CONTINUED)

YEAR	TOTAL		WHITE		INDIAN		PARDO		NEGRO		SLAVE	
	M	F	M	F	M	F	M	F	M	F	M	F
1816	914	1000	46	58	390	404	332	393	132	129	14	16
1817	866	1005	46	50	373	463	398	441	42	38	7	13
1818	807	1057	75	94	303	438	337	428	84	83	8	14
1819	775	1033	69	89	297	427	318	419	82	85	9	13
CHORONI												
1802	733	813	81	83	7	10	465	543	14	21	166	156
1803	727	815	72	71	7	10	463	546	14	22	171	166
1804	713	806	75	71	7	10	494	587	17	24	120	114
1805	694	757	74	74	6	7	450	500	9	11	155	165
1808	726	813	88	81	5	11	465	531	8	17	160	173
1809	766	785	95	81	8	12	478	494	13	23	172	175
1819	330	521	25	38	0	0	246	360	0	0	59	123
CHUAO												
1802	155	170	1	0	0	0	10	5	0	0	144	165
1803	156	173	0	0	0	0	8	3	1	0	147	170
1804	170	178	2	0	0	0	5	3	1	0	162	175
1805	169	187	1	0	0	0	9	11	1	0	158	176
1819	175	209	4	5	0	0	12	7	0	2	159	195
COCOROTE												
1781	926	1186	108	125	425	626	244	251	83	111	66	73
1782	918	1153	108	125	425	626	244	251	83	97	58	54
1788	782	1079	87	109	285	449	233	307	112	145	65	69
1791	729	1052	89	139	249	372	253	351	96	133	42	57
1794	839	1168	118	163	262	402	304	407	108	141	47	55
1802	868	1161	167	227	167	241	473	603	17	28	44	62
1803	934	1198	171	193	217	226	469	685	28	39	49	55
1804	877	1150	107	144	229	320	331	442	162	175	48	69
1805	898	1140	98	109	294	373	337	438	123	147	46	73
1807	926	1192	100	110	252	359	367	476	165	188	42	59
1808	885	1151	102	140	266	352	274	386	199	218	44	55
1809	917	1077	107	121	278	313	308	388	182	207	42	48
1811	884	1128	110	125	132	183	465	598	157	193	20	29
1812	780	958	107	127	222	300	260	304	155	195	36	32
1817	611	1030	43	41	202	329	271	511	91	139	4	10
1818	669	973	119	161	175	316	353	468	0	0	22	28
1820	611	1030	43	41	202	329	271	511	91	139	4	10
1821	800	1092	115	138	225	314	455	633	0	0	5	7
COJEDES												
1779	656	655	131	130	388	398	136	126	0	0	1	1
1799	890	847	307	307	242	234	209	225	26	26	106	55
1801	813	851	320	313	207	259	214	227	26	28	46	24
1802	949	979	256	246	243	265	355	386	7	5	88	77
1803	922	858	271	261	254	240	321	293	1	1	75	63

TABLE 1. PARISH POPULATION BY SEX AND RACE (CONTINUED)

YEAR	TOTAL		WHITE		INDIAN		PARDO		NEGRO		SLAVE	
	M	F	M	F	M	F	M	F	M	F	M	F
1804	915	864	244	254	259	241	333	299	1	1	78	69
1805	961	854	272	260	253	245	345	283	2	3	89	63
1806	985	937	246	259	296	273	359	336	1	1	83	68
1807	978	919	258	246	285	270	344	321	2	2	89	80
1808	1020	875	274	244	290	253	315	309	1	1	140	68
1809	966	958	223	242	300	288	341	352	3	6	99	70
1811	687	784	104	109	283	349	235	251	0	0	65	75
1812	698	814	117	124	270	352	240	259	0	0	71	79
1816	713	833	116	121	273	360	249	270	0	0	75	82
1817	698	831	116	120	269	358	238	273	0	0	75	80
1818	707	848	108	127	280	352	244	285	0	0	75	84
1819	703	810	97	119	271	332	248	258	12	15	75	86
1820	678	788	108	128	218	274	280	301	24	31	48	54
1822	621	668	86	97	194	214	284	302	20	18	37	37
1823	538	598	72	83	161	190	270	289	20	16	15	20
1824	503	591	66	85	147	180	254	289	21	17	15	20
1829	541	633	83	93	137	192	280	304	20	16	21	28
1831	549	629	72	87	170	192	267	305	19	17	21	28
1833	532	612	73	85	163	187	266	312	14	12	16	16
1834	533	598	69	80	167	179	267	312	14	12	16	15
1835	581	632	81	91	180	194	282	311	23	22	15	14
1836	593	647	85	99	181	193	289	319	23	22	15	14
1837	612	648	87	100	183	190	299	318	28	26	15	14
1838	604	647	87	101	184	192	293	314	25	26	15	14
CUA												
1783	789	742	64	37	18	20	98	111	79	66	530	508
1803	1282	1273	127	86	107	93	253	257	127	113	668	724
1805	1087	1186	168	127	72	74	170	218	115	134	562	633
1810	1516	1568	216	160	131	159	326	338	142	139	701	772
1812	1552	1629	251	267	45	61	312	326	61	139	883	836
1815	1234	1445	124	106	62	103	346	430	92	100	610	706
1816	1320	1652	165	164	88	134	400	509	78	119	589	726
1818	1634	1656	266	278	58	63	338	362	68	127	904	826
1820	1290	1717	145	145	190	225	223	290	123	143	609	914
1821	1610	1576	110	138	38	45	440	446	36	37	986	910
CUBIRO												
1802	363	383	8	4	317	352	14	18	5	3	19	6
1803	392	404	5	6	361	377	3	4	3	5	20	12
1804	363	386	4	6	319	349	18	22	2	0	20	9
1805	448	449	2	0	385	405	22	32	18	4	21	8
1806	421	437	3	0	359	386	24	32	11	5	24	14
1807	428	437	2	0	366	387	25	32	11	5	24	13
1808	428	421	3	0	365	370	24	32	12	5	24	14
1809	438	431	3	0	379	380	20	32	12	5	24	14
1810	443	433	3	0	380	382	24	32	12	5	24	14
1815	360	360	3	0	305	311	30	29	13	5	9	15
1816	475	400	3	0	430	357	28	27	3	3	11	13

TABLE 1. PARISH POPULATION BY SEX AND RACE (CONTINUED)

YEAR	TOTAL		WHITE		INDIAN		PARDO		NEGRO		SLAVE	
	M	F	M	F	M	F	M	F	M	F	M	F
1817	481	408	3	0	433	357	28	32	5	7	12	12
1818	396	408	7	3	329	350	50	44	6	5	4	6
1819	391	406	6	3	325	348	50	44	6	5	4	6
1820	378	392	7	5	309	332	50	44	8	5	4	6
CUNAVICHE												
1780	193	200	1	0	191	199	0	1	1	0	0	0
CUPIRA												
1784	448	410	122	99	19	27	131	117	64	76	112	91
1802	287	295	65	65	14	11	82	104	81	81	45	34
1803	292	281	58	61	15	11	93	103	79	70	47	36
1804	275	272	50	57	14	11	103	99	67	70	41	35
1805	252	260	52	47	11	10	57	79	84	90	48	34
1807	245	260	33	35	14	17	68	83	87	87	43	38
1808	234	262	28	36	11	15	91	111	63	61	41	39
1809	239	246	28	30	13	14	88	100	72	61	38	41
1811	277	299	33	45	61	64	71	77	82	73	30	40
CURARIGUA												
1802	468	842	57	46	12	14	67	75	302	275	30	432
1803	463	511	67	80	10	12	103	115	253	291	30	13
1804	425	441	66	70	20	25	131	140	181	194	27	12
1805	523	556	88	97	15	19	82	100	311	323	27	17
1806	442	431	71	68	30	35	88	94	227	222	26	12
1807	436	436	75	78	29	31	92	97	228	223	12	7
1808	454	463	82	92	35	35	100	104	225	226	12	6
1809	455	458	84	92	34	29	94	105	230	224	13	8
1810	577	472	90	91	28	27	109	114	240	235	110	5
1816	633	658	54	68	0	0	539	550	23	20	17	20
1817	612	685	57	54	0	0	475	548	63	61	17	22
1818	491	562	57	67	0	0	372	420	49	56	13	19
1819	596	649	102	81	41	29	362	448	75	84	16	7
1820	599	688	91	91	31	20	391	457	66	107	20	13
CURIEPE												
1784	670	690	34	17	13	3	139	156	254	292	230	222
1803	937	983	48	24	30	22	283	263	266	357	310	317
1804	876	987	38	23	31	22	146	236	314	373	347	333
1805	1030	1010	36	24	23	7	218	233	381	399	372	347
1806	1024	1114	39	18	28	14	294	365	321	376	342	341
1807	1080	1049	34	15	44	25	286	297	363	389	353	323
1808	1093	1079	34	15	45	28	289	306	372	399	353	331
1811	1180	1040	52	23	52	45	314	332	392	340	370	300
1812	1243	1077	57	28	67	50	332	351	415	350	372	298
1816	704	914	26	27	8	3	199	273	195	292	276	319
1817	614	849	24	15	12	14	213	354	166	250	199	216

TABLE 1. PARISH POPULATION BY SEX AND RACE (CONTINUED)

YEAR	TOTAL		WHITE		INDIAN		PARDO		NEGRO		SLAVE	
	M	F	M	F	M	F	M	F	M	F	M	F
1818	707	947	35	31	21	12	265	386	180	267	206	251
1819	770	989	34	30	21	12	291	405	198	282	226	260
1820	832	1063	28	34	29	16	316	417	229	310	230	286
CUYAGUA												
1802	228	243	11	5	15	24	47	63	40	41	115	110
1803	223	233	6	3	5	5	42	45	60	76	110	104
1804	213	239	6	1	3	7	55	53	40	74	109	104
1805	235	258	13	3	3	6	48	55	40	60	131	134
1808	233	220	11	7	5	5	35	36	61	76	121	96
1809	249	248	7	4	4	3	40	42	57	69	141	130
1815	236	225	30	16	4	9	60	56	2	0	140	144
DIVINA PASTORA DEL JOBAL												
1781	1026	1010	172	175	420	379	336	379	36	40	62	37
1798	1401	1475	373	348	211	238	501	565	276	276	40	48
1799	1411	1465	385	346	210	174	497	573	277	319	42	53
1801	1276	1331	275	278	225	238	740	775	7	6	29	34
1802	1208	1494	331	370	209	292	478	569	138	210	52	53
1803	1237	1504	338	371	215	291	488	573	143	215	53	54
1804	1175	1194	331	376	206	186	551	551	45	39	42	42
1805	1300	1286	403	370	143	166	564	497	143	207	47	46
1806	1292	1388	405	450	191	202	654	687	2	2	40	47
1807	1123	1184	384	385	134	140	545	608	5	7	55	44
1808	1163	1307	374	405	143	154	606	700	7	3	33	45
1809	1300	1286	403	370	143	166	564	497	143	207	47	46
1811	1138	1238	350	349	227	250	534	593	0	0	27	46
1815	1169	1251	139	161	324	269	594	680	102	108	10	33
1816	1216	1270	159	163	334	269	600	681	112	122	11	35
1817	1243	1312	144	161	324	259	667	753	98	107	10	32
1818	997	1261	147	214	299	288	423	568	101	154	27	37
1819	2081	1918	322	294	266	279	1467	1271	5	8	21	66
1820	1448	1535	328	347	145	166	957	984	8	14	10	24
1822	1149	1574	237	391	239	339	649	789	4	0	20	55
1824	914	1065	133	132	117	141	646	760	6	3	12	29
1825	961	1148	137	164	116	150	690	802	6	3	12	29
1829	767	993	101	116	43	49	600	781	0	0	23	47
1830	756	979	101	116	43	49	600	791	12	23	0	0
1832	756	979	101	116	43	49	600	791	12	23	0	0
1833	672	940	97	132	43	60	501	686	30	56	1	6
1834	674	946	97	132	43	60	501	686	30	56	3	12
DUACA												
1779	261	290	48	50	147	167	56	57	5	5	5	11
1802	220	268	53	58	100	130	58	72	6	8	3	0
1803	163	266	5	9	75	152	79	102	0	0	4	3
1804	163	266	5	9	75	152	79	102	0	0	4	3
1805	236	319	60	78	95	132	79	107	0	0	2	2

TABLE 1. PARISH POPULATION BY SEX AND RACE (CONTINUED)

YEAR	TOTAL		WHITE		INDIAN		PARDO		NEGRO		SLAVE	
	M	F	M	F	M	F	M	F	M	F	M	F
1807	302	315	73	75	141	148	60	62	24	30	4	0
1808	280	300	60	60	164	176	55	60	1	2	0	2
1809	293	311	51	56	171	170	69	82	2	2	0	1
1810	305	311	63	56	168	170	69	82	2	2	3	1
1811	341	351	52	58	231	243	58	50	0	0	0	0
1815	220	267	9	9	73	106	138	152	0	0	0	0
1816	252	289	9	9	73	106	170	174	0	0	0	0
1818	519	458	136	139	163	131	212	179	8	9	0	0
EL CALVARIO												
1783	383	270	132	90	24	32	31	36	32	26	164	86
1802	671	591	215	202	29	27	151	133	76	88	200	141
1803	678	586	211	209	24	28	158	131	74	80	211	138
1804	700	642	226	231	36	46	145	142	82	81	211	142
1805	737	673	234	234	45	49	151	139	82	92	225	159
1808	774	677	250	245	44	45	152	143	79	79	249	165
1812	916	936	282	291	53	70	209	237	118	144	254	194
EL CONSEJO												
1781	1105	1010	354	249	0	0	291	277	0	0	460	484
1795	1262	1241	175	170	23	16	505	503	28	34	531	518
1796	1208	1179	223	200	5	4	432	431	9	8	539	536
1802	1516	1304	227	219	21	22	485	395	33	31	750	637
1803	1606	1319	232	226	21	22	570	402	33	32	750	637
1804	1603	1382	255	249	30	30	505	412	45	39	768	652
1805	1618	1389	259	242	28	31	509	410	44	44	778	662
1806	1323	1594	234	228	22	29	376	523	44	53	647	761
1807	1560	1348	236	228	30	31	494	404	42	40	758	645
1808	1578	1360	239	231	34	33	498	406	45	43	762	647
1809	1455	1243	215	207	9	10	473	383	21	19	737	624
1811	1488	1252	229	212	8	10	479	380	26	26	746	624
1817	1506	1611	287	268	120	137	542	642	0	0	557	564
1818	1547	1698	307	327	132	147	546	655	0	0	562	569
1833	1308	1295	290	272	123	108	433	451	0	0	462	464
EL GUAPO												
1784	257	225	87	56	31	41	49	39	16	27	74	62
1802	619	613	78	73	41	43	83	88	138	146	279	263
1803	731	707	115	103	59	60	176	162	89	97	292	285
1804	746	718	115	103	59	60	176	162	104	108	292	285
1805	755	776	107	115	56	62	162	169	147	150	283	280
1807	789	806	117	132	62	62	182	174	175	180	253	258
1808	778	799	108	126	62	62	180	173	175	180	253	258
1809	778	799	108	126	62	62	180	173	175	180	253	258
1811	839	815	126	113	57	52	162	170	135	152	359	328
1812	748	797	88	95	58	67	163	172	150	176	289	287
1820	595	730	104	132	66	105	216	254	39	35	170	204

TABLE 1. PARISH POPULATION BY SEX AND RACE (CONTINUED)

YEAR	TOTAL		WHITE		INDIAN		PARDO		NEGRO		SLAVE	
	M	F	M	F	M	F	M	F	M	F	M	F
EL HATILLO												
1802	581	489	321	268	34	23	108	70	35	47	83	81
1803	581	489	321	268	34	23	108	70	35	47	83	81
1804	629	554	324	283	41	29	118	94	44	49	102	99
1805	718	629	358	299	45	37	140	114	58	64	117	115
1806	805	719	403	364	46	32	99	89	89	82	168	152
1808	826	819	403	464	46	32	109	89	98	82	170	152
1815	916	811	395	368	0	0	240	196	0	0	281	247
1818	650	763	250	266	0	0	228	275	0	0	172	222
EL PAO												
1781	1681	1646	238	222	28	26	1158	1222	61	65	196	111
1791	1967	2134	226	253	99	141	1345	1469	192	267	105	54
1792	1862	2144	226	256	191	278	1004	1185	271	375	170	50
1794	2116	2330	249	271	153	185	1097	1232	430	593	187	49
1796	2154	2421	243	284	239	287	1047	1245	425	524	200	81
1798	2422	2472	284	335	239	287	1041	1084	613	701	245	65
1801	2395	2320	351	393	123	98	1551	1485	185	250	185	94
1802	2078	2470	191	258	61	73	1404	1718	199	286	223	135
1803	2530	2575	411	481	68	46	1642	1726	182	237	227	85
1804	2656	2908	395	473	30	36	1889	2078	125	232	217	89
1805	2805	3028	395	473	30	36	2012	2198	145	232	223	89
1808	2776	3110	390	434	35	56	1965	2274	201	256	185	90
1809	3069	2751	321	305	240	224	2222	1945	149	160	137	117
1811	2933	3358	395	449	95	110	1850	2294	312	342	281	163
1812	2461	2967	362	415	89	114	1534	2005	229	323	247	110
1815	2974	3534	500	537	17	32	2341	2884	40	47	76	34
1816	2997	3634	531	569	20	37	2317	2932	54	55	75	41
1817	2865	3432	550	690	16	14	2041	2522	54	85	204	121
1818	2621	3161	425	472	61	108	1874	2347	91	123	170	111
1819	2259	2758	356	368	66	76	1630	2108	68	81	139	125
1821	2375	3296	397	506	24	33	1729	2472	95	146	130	139
1823	3738	3967	453	634	32	28	2967	3025	134	158	152	122
1824	3712	4198	415	645	29	26	2974	3265	113	125	181	137
1825	3004	3164	495	421	29	32	2254	2444	122	201	104	66
1826	3038	3288	513	541	28	35	2273	2436	116	208	108	68
1827	3180	3015	380	462	30	28	1970	2274	482	119	318	132
1829	3727	4140	61	75	33	37	3470	3828	115	142	48	58
1835	4067	4354	169	180	0	0	3761	4006	70	75	67	93
1836	4219	4520	190	207	0	0	3869	4122	87	91	73	100
1837	4440	4765	200	219	0	0	4111	4335	54	110	75	101
1838	4571	4815	214	234	0	0	4218	4404	67	77	72	100
EL RASTRO												
1807	519	510	263	233	10	7	167	168	14	15	65	87
1810	709	686	343	274	24	13	264	277	24	23	54	99
1811	754	709	360	303	25	15	276	257	37	32	56	102

TABLE 1. PARISH POPULATION BY SEX AND RACE (CONTINUED)

YEAR	TOTAL M	TOTAL F	WHITE M	WHITE F	INDIAN M	INDIAN F	PARDO M	PARDO F	NEGRO M	NEGRO F	SLAVE M	SLAVE F
1812	633	613	368	312	5	10	186	167	0	0	74	124
1817	520	584	242	233	10	12	193	217	14	16	61	106
1822	449	567	202	229	50	77	171	195	12	11	14	55
EL SOMBRERO												
1781	1034	1012	325	232	6	1	629	728	5	9	69	42
1783	1120	1059	354	247	13	7	3	0	664	723	86	82
1802	1486	1605	409	393	48	66	744	832	162	189	123	125
1803	1552	1708	411	402	50	58	797	894	165	219	129	135
1804	1687	1815	470	422	60	68	849	954	161	224	147	147
1805	1723	1834	435	452	39	42	896	974	167	197	136	169
1809	2284	2301	572	499	72	74	1228	1247	269	306	143	175
1810	2369	2371	587	514	87	89	1247	1267	279	316	169	185
1811	2369	2371	587	514	87	89	1247	1267	279	316	169	185
EL TOCUYO												
1802	4451	4722	754	854	197	192	2335	2353	435	515	730	808
1803	4538	4878	775	876	187	195	2358	2449	474	529	744	829
1804	4340	5129	609	734	88	115	2297	2764	634	768	712	748
1805	4455	4826	770	853	187	188	2341	2450	445	540	712	795
1806	4414	4812	780	850	205	206	2312	2440	427	476	690	840
1807	4397	5130	629	717	88	109	2340	2813	654	764	686	727
1808	4434	5099	638	713	101	105	2338	2783	657	766	700	732
1809	4450	5187	627	754	101	106	2394	2809	664	761	664	757
1810	4502	5111	657	649	89	103	2398	2830	692	733	666	796
1812	4477	5201	628	758	97	113	2426	2813	668	758	658	759
1815	4082	5342	588	836	50	70	2713	3598	182	219	549	619
1816	4275	5461	634	852	52	78	2799	3612	206	266	584	653
1817	4212	5280	608	928	68	111	2756	3232	183	331	597	678
1818	4250	5081	577	744	89	104	2328	2752	617	750	639	731
1819	4876	6043	779	764	58	58	3394	4599	15	13	630	609
1820	4435	5614	757	909	24	27	3132	4105	41	32	481	541
EL VALLE												
1798	453	563	107	125	140	192	82	97	45	52	79	97
1802	585	647	203	193	105	144	91	105	68	70	118	135
1803	614	683	212	202	115	152	93	111	70	74	124	144
1804	671	745	230	227	123	159	101	120	76	86	141	153
1805	743	785	239	234	136	162	107	122	103	104	158	163
1809	765	817	247	246	142	166	108	125	108	116	160	164
1815	659	956	268	383	84	98	134	201	65	82	108	192
1816	767	1028	306	405	94	99	155	211	83	91	129	222
1817	1009	1194	367	447	153	170	218	242	98	93	173	242
1818	697	939	306	381	75	106	165	231	48	83	103	138
1819	730	921	302	365	62	86	189	233	46	71	131	166
1820	801	1031	309	387	71	106	203	262	72	85	146	191

TABLE 1. PARISH POPULATION BY SEX AND RACE (CONTINUED)

YEAR	TOTAL M	TOTAL F	WHITE M	WHITE F	INDIAN M	INDIAN F	PARDO M	PARDO F	NEGRO M	NEGRO F	SLAVE M	SLAVE F
	ESPINO											
1804	294	294	53	49	6	6	162	178	7	8	66	53
1807	456	563	75	134	54	141	219	216	6	3	102	69
	GUACARA											
1781	1497	1583	432	492	287	282	443	478	18	18	317	313
1802	2222	2366	564	740	477	504	1006	952	9	7	166	163
1803	2430	2585	629	821	516	522	1092	1060	15	11	178	171
1804	2525	2866	700	805	488	503	1124	1331	25	20	188	207
1805	2168	2560	625	776	482	481	832	1089	22	16	207	198
1808	2462	2463	665	710	327	343	1263	1201	22	24	185	185
1816	2286	2773	570	710	356	370	1222	1520	14	15	124	158
	GUACARRAMA											
1820	552	775	151	215	24	34	91	115	279	403	7	8
	GUAIGUAZA											
1803	338	396	14	15	1	0	117	130	84	157	122	94
1804	336	337	20	20	0	0	161	160	47	52	108	105
1805	333	329	20	19	1	1	161	159	47	54	104	96
1806	296	295	20	17	0	0	111	129	50	53	115	96
1807	317	331	20	12	0	0	131	150	46	39	120	130
1818	235	217	12	4	0	0	85	70	0	0	138	143
1819	271	285	13	7	0	0	113	134	0	0	145	144
	GUAMA											
1781	1009	1248	183	183	295	412	375	469	101	102	55	82
1794	1204	1582	136	168	248	532	606	674	127	117	87	91
1803	1440	1800	77	98	310	447	919	1131	36	25	98	99
1804	1673	1919	70	91	411	438	1100	1277	19	20	73	93
1805	1454	1809	94	100	344	440	902	1112	32	44	82	113
1807	1454	1765	116	136	350	431	818	1015	103	112	67	71
1808	1540	1866	144	170	366	425	874	1071	105	126	51	74
1809	1489	1803	126	158	350	432	851	1023	104	120	58	70
1810	1481	1778	80	82	367	446	882	1071	98	115	54	64
1811	1569	1895	99	105	405	486	920	1137	106	119	39	48
1812	1469	1802	85	89	355	436	867	1095	102	119	60	63
1817	1278	1716	142	172	269	367	734	1016	91	98	42	63
1818	1187	1526	109	126	255	360	791	994	6	25	26	21
1819	890	1239	119	123	187	226	452	694	99	136	33	60
1820	1002	1571	103	154	189	324	582	906	97	132	31	55
	GUANARE											
1788	3990	4292	1823	1957	192	206	1504	1595	107	102	364	432

TABLE 1. PARISH POPULATION BY SEX AND RACE (CONTINUED)

YEAR	TOTAL		WHITE		INDIAN		PARDO		NEGRO		SLAVE	
	M	F	M	F	M	F	M	F	M	F	M	F
1791	3538	3995	1203	1305	52	83	1747	2037	105	104	431	466
1792	4031	3978	1856	1599	124	155	1550	1660	105	105	396	459
1802	6711	6699	2443	2390	370	386	3355	3375	88	63	455	485
1803	5456	5584	2107	2191	320	304	2427	2494	96	101	506	494
1804	4893	5187	1947	1910	274	315	2277	2441	61	86	334	435
1807	5099	5704	1906	2039	293	343	2402	2735	121	133	377	454
1808	5387	6067	1970	2106	390	494	2506	2856	101	132	420	479
1809	5266	5759	2086	2235	244	298	2313	2395	62	79	561	752
1810	3752	4048	1359	1671	404	409	1457	1432	126	142	406	394
1811	3909	4848	1343	1686	316	410	1617	1940	179	217	454	595
1817	3105	3685	941	1151	213	190	1632	2044	65	85	254	215
GUANARE VIEJO												
1778	247	218	75	77	77	58	90	78	0	0	5	5
1782	441	486	99	108	150	165	186	206	0	0	6	7
1801	695	657	249	207	290	289	151	152	0	0	5	9
1802	691	648	250	200	289	296	145	145	0	0	7	7
1803	790	793	258	255	225	215	300	313	3	5	4	5
1804	1134	1086	437	420	134	229	557	427	0	0	6	10
1805	789	725	339	260	181	218	264	241	0	0	5	6
1806	864	1112	342	416	133	229	386	463	0	0	3	4
1807	843	866	356	319	172	239	310	303	0	0	5	5
1808	1457	1596	546	561	263	372	641	658	0	0	7	5
1811	738	856	279	285	138	202	317	362	0	0	4	7
1813	749	767	242	253	262	251	238	258	0	0	7	5
GUANARITO												
1778	505	457	112	99	142	126	244	224	0	0	7	8
1801	866	936	182	210	279	309	265	279	91	88	49	50
1802	915	901	357	345	102	100	389	391	32	29	35	36
1803	1598	1666	645	648	98	170	630	626	120	133	105	89
1804	1449	1554	551	558	149	151	675	774	0	0	74	71
1805	1508	1550	523	532	154	148	576	583	164	182	91	105
1807	2635	2524	825	811	240	287	1357	1292	20	9	193	125
1808	2103	2398	902	985	109	153	993	1127	53	80	46	53
1810	2164	2410	924	990	111	154	1038	1142	45	71	46	53
1811	2268	2524	965	1029	127	167	1068	1196	53	74	55	58
GUARDATINAJAS												
1780	269	206	32	35	117	110	47	37	72	23	1	1
1804	1162	1066	296	230	124	153	292	268	349	320	101	95
1805	1172	1067	299	232	111	154	295	269	358	315	109	97
1807	1167	1117	294	211	108	130	248	253	407	420	110	103
1808	1221	1142	299	217	110	147	252	259	437	418	123	101
1809	1240	1104	347	254	109	133	265	267	393	342	126	108
1810	1154	1099	281	244	104	150	620	567	41	35	108	103
1811	1352	1182	304	236	157	163	679	599	60	45	152	139
1812	1333	1268	252	249	164	178	688	630	70	61	159	150

TABLE 1. PARISH POPULATION BY SEX AND RACE (CONTINUED)

YEAR	TOTAL M	TOTAL F	WHITE M	WHITE F	INDIAN M	INDIAN F	PARDO M	PARDO F	NEGRO M	NEGRO F	SLAVE M	SLAVE F
1816	1213	1247	232	237	154	171	675	696	15	23	137	120
GUARENAS												
1784	1114	1219	444	463	286	289	137	136	148	145	99	186
1802	1404	1497	489	494	176	232	110	136	262	293	367	342
1803	1465	1560	503	510	191	243	120	152	280	305	371	350
1804	1403	1596	482	522	170	227	100	126	296	359	355	362
1805	1425	1625	494	529	173	230	101	132	295	368	362	366
1808	897	963	289	292	110	134	89	76	119	151	290	310
1809	1316	1350	478	456	128	151	189	196	172	195	349	352
1811	1613	1599	551	510	156	180	379	371	161	172	366	366
1816	1146	1465	342	435	63	107	406	568	23	12	312	343
GUARICO												
1803	1069	965	132	122	456	462	352	296	79	46	50	39
1804	954	1046	153	161	363	395	316	350	73	96	49	44
1805	892	940	98	112	428	422	299	350	29	28	38	28
1806	915	993	100	138	438	435	309	360	29	30	39	30
1807	882	988	96	112	381	448	332	381	29	13	44	34
1808	872	966	95	105	375	433	332	381	29	13	41	34
1809	932	1021	105	118	396	447	353	393	35	25	43	38
1810	1031	1131	128	111	412	496	367	402	62	63	62	59
1812	1007	1107	126	117	355	430	377	413	75	76	74	71
1815	1090	1135	51	61	428	454	553	553	28	32	30	35
1816	1092	1156	52	64	429	459	553	563	28	32	30	38
1817	1145	1206	82	85	440	473	565	578	28	32	30	38
1818	1141	1197	82	94	434	464	563	573	32	28	30	38
1819	1187	1306	83	99	447	484	593	644	27	32	37	47
1820	1293	1411	88	100	488	525	627	686	47	44	43	56
GUASGUAS												
1802	1689	1906	748	851	311	346	614	679	0	0	16	30
1803	1643	1801	724	738	300	360	602	672	0	0	17	31
1804	1543	1782	685	796	272	327	567	630	0	0	19	29
1805	1618	1901	714	836	300	357	586	680	0	0	18	28
1806	1770	2033	793	904	359	390	600	706	0	0	18	33
1807	1763	2051	798	898	320	390	626	732	0	0	19	31
1808	1792	2086	802	919	344	390	630	750	0	0	16	27
1809	1919	2180	839	894	372	420	690	839	0	0	18	27
1810	1765	2080	802	967	337	406	524	567	85	109	17	31
GUATIRE												
1784	964	978	148	121	16	6	185	231	103	135	512	485
1802	1115	1109	92	106	22	12	242	254	151	190	608	547
1803	1135	1119	140	115	14	10	234	245	167	202	580	547
1805	1022	1155	140	119	15	5	214	254	161	207	492	570
1807	992	1073	90	113	2	2	296	376	28	29	576	553

TABLE 1. PARISH POPULATION BY SEX AND RACE (CONTINUED)

YEAR	TOTAL		WHITE		INDIAN		PARDO		NEGRO		SLAVE	
	M	F	M	F	M	F	M	F	M	F	M	F
1809	992	1073	90	113	2	2	296	376	28	29	576	553
1811	1169	1160	128	121	34	25	288	321	101	116	618	577
1815	1056	1104	126	111	26	24	261	308	92	110	551	551
1816	1195	1148	134	114	33	23	323	370	117	142	588	499
1817	1157	1335	116	101	22	25	428	605	38	37	553	567
	GUAYABAL											
1804	789	703	98	121	48	57	283	316	92	106	268	103
1817	744	778	180	197	39	44	443	448	45	52	37	37
	GUIGUE											
1781	1235	1197	381	374	52	56	356	353	222	204	224	210
1802	1277	1369	299	292	39	54	679	713	55	61	205	249
1803	1278	1363	284	290	52	60	667	717	52	50	223	246
1804	1243	1412	272	303	54	65	672	727	51	54	194	263
1805	1319	1416	272	297	62	68	683	732	45	54	257	265
1808	1424	1551	295	318	53	68	695	735	56	75	325	355
1809	1484	1599	319	329	62	81	704	732	53	84	346	373
1817	1332	1514	100	105	82	112	705	822	135	192	310	283
	GUIRIPA											
1802	519	475	251	246	60	45	160	149	7	0	41	35
1803	490	454	248	252	48	31	148	140	6	0	40	31
1804	510	481	229	211	58	45	175	181	8	1	40	43
1805	530	484	229	204	60	42	193	190	8	1	40	47
1806	459	461	188	198	44	51	170	157	7	6	50	49
1807	509	489	141	136	153	138	160	155	10	8	45	52
1808	520	495	142	126	142	146	177	166	11	6	48	51
1809	531	527	131	128	140	132	203	209	11	10	46	48
1811	511	493	224	216	37	25	199	200	0	0	51	52
	HUMOCARO ALTO											
1802	1242	1357	59	73	1028	1126	123	123	3	5	29	30
1803	1264	1372	60	74	1052	1147	127	127	2	4	23	20
1804	1450	1462	65	69	1224	1229	136	138	3	5	22	21
1805	1354	1404	67	70	1119	1161	140	143	3	5	25	25
1806	1230	1518	58	72	1003	1273	145	143	2	3	22	27
1807	1209	1505	58	72	973	1252	150	154	2	4	26	23
1808	1172	1486	53	71	941	1233	150	155	2	4	26	23
1809	1046	1424	60	78	822	1148	136	170	2	3	26	25
1810	981	1227	58	76	766	964	138	170	6	4	13	13
1815	654	743	37	59	542	591	62	79	3	3	10	11
1816	821	992	68	101	672	683	58	181	6	7	17	20
1817	815	1019	43	100	694	703	54	188	6	7	18	21
1818	763	1031	41	102	640	709	59	193	4	6	19	21
1819	700	912	38	61	574	630	64	191	4	6	20	24
1820	817	991	47	70	657	747	91	146	9	5	13	23

TABLE 1. PARISH POPULATION BY SEX AND RACE (CONTINUED)

YEAR	TOTAL		WHITE		INDIAN		PARDO		NEGRO		SLAVE	
	M	F	M	F	M	F	M	F	M	F	M	F
HUMOCARO BAJO												
1803	776	963	206	274	332	408	114	141	71	87	53	53
1804	776	963	206	274	332	408	114	141	71	87	53	53
1806	687	735	106	135	304	313	217	230	2	4	58	53
1807	679	891	106	142	293	403	213	278	5	4	62	64
1808	833	1113	130	164	375	509	254	340	9	10	65	90
1809	861	1291	129	176	411	570	244	408	11	16	66	121
1810	868	1320	124	172	407	580	252	423	10	18	75	127
1815	547	1160	100	222	268	563	124	274	7	14	48	87
1816	593	1195	107	225	267	546	160	307	7	12	52	105
1817	600	1180	107	221	283	531	152	313	5	13	53	102
1818	614	1115	140	208	275	509	145	294	4	10	50	94
1819	592	888	136	190	287	390	133	248	3	8	33	52
1820	599	914	135	186	286	404	139	268	1	3	38	53
IGUANA												
1783	75	64	2	0	68	60	2	0	3	4	0	0
1801	177	133	0	0	164	124	11	8	2	1	0	0
1802	184	139	0	0	171	130	11	8	2	1	0	0
1803	190	152	2	2	177	140	11	9	0	1	0	0
1804	167	128	0	0	160	121	7	6	0	1	0	0
1805	175	130	0	0	167	124	8	6	0	0	0	0
1806	211	151	0	0	203	145	8	6	0	0	0	0
1807	183	147	0	0	181	147	2	0	0	0	0	0
LA GUAIRA												
1802	1763	2292	586	547	30	36	647	1054	214	337	286	318
1804	1528	1741	485	512	17	17	580	662	252	291	194	259
1805	1489	2037	462	405	3	3	627	1026	184	323	213	280
1807	1336	1862	469	420	8	10	477	822	201	360	181	250
1809	1181	2091	370	354	3	7	538	1220	130	270	140	240
1810	1392	1875	423	399	5	4	524	904	275	355	165	213
1811	1291	2026	384	343	12	13	578	1141	149	263	168	266
1815	663	1156	282	372	26	36	189	429	70	167	96	152
1816	843	1121	330	400	47	66	310	365	62	162	94	128
1817	1032	1682	347	413	42	60	408	827	125	241	110	141
1818	1040	1949	265	357	51	49	445	1136	137	193	142	214
1819	1244	1640	257	312	166	162	331	696	318	301	172	169
1820	1276	1729	279	375	96	184	410	494	284	412	207	264
LA GUAIRA, CURATO CASTRENSE												
1802	263	47	247	33	0	0	3	1	1	2	12	11
1803	257	23	247	13	0	0	1	1	2	1	7	8
1804	410	47	367	23	0	0	37	15	1	1	5	8
1805	599	66	447	37	0	0	140	15	3	2	9	12
1807	707	75	390	38	0	0	305	25	4	1	8	11

TABLE 1. PARISH POPULATION BY SEX AND RACE (CONTINUED)

YEAR	TOTAL		WHITE		INDIAN		PARDO		NEGRO		SLAVE	
	M	F	M	F	M	F	M	F	M	F	M	F
1808	497	44	327	29	0	1	162	2	3	1	5	11
LA SANTISIMA TRINIDAD												
1780	276	291	10	9	163	157	48	56	49	63	6	6
1802	1077	882	80	40	59	59	516	437	332	315	90	31
1803	1043	907	36	33	42	64	561	459	358	340	46	11
1804	864	864	50	70	75	84	351	385	337	298	51	27
1805	869	875	47	42	47	38	363	347	368	384	44	64
1807	581	581	48	45	60	62	176	153	247	288	50	33
1808	623	571	60	74	91	85	403	375	14	12	55	25
1809	597	576	48	62	83	78	382	393	20	17	64	26
1810	527	547	36	36	71	83	376	402	22	18	22	8
1811	614	592	40	44	88	100	386	410	16	15	84	23
1812	469	470	30	25	66	74	336	343	9	11	28	17
LA VEGA												
1802	1119	1075	297	306	192	208	237	248	39	37	354	276
1803	1195	1130	329	311	198	212	247	267	39	37	382	303
1804	1170	1041	247	222	250	252	247	270	83	71	343	226
1805	1189	1096	249	216	253	277	239	265	90	96	358	242
1809	529	587	127	147	120	120	149	170	21	25	112	125
1810	498	554	121	139	110	114	131	164	20	22	116	115
1811	450	510	98	129	91	79	136	180	17	23	108	99
1815	309	489	85	145	28	43	91	154	15	28	90	119
1816	342	503	107	156	23	46	95	168	20	28	97	105
1817	333	404	101	115	40	37	90	155	15	14	87	83
1818	298	441	120	178	27	37	78	128	6	16	67	82
1819	304	427	103	127	50	69	78	135	5	16	68	80
1820	303	408	82	106	48	83	96	137	7	14	70	68
1821	326	394	76	101	56	76	80	124	6	12	108	81
1822	317	357	73	109	49	45	98	117	8	13	89	73
1823	307	346	87	122	28	29	106	120	14	14	72	61
LA VICTORIA												
1780	2415	2895	643	790	387	450	829	1005	192	215	364	435
1802	2832	3388	722	853	331	417	1024	1354	84	87	671	677
1803	3190	3510	780	805	433	533	1072	1312	94	100	811	760
1804	3157	3470	787	807	421	548	1034	1262	91	93	824	760
1805	3236	3653	793	825	442	544	1082	1321	108	121	811	842
1806	3288	3703	803	837	452	553	1093	1332	117	128	823	853
1808	3406	3711	855	942	420	445	1080	1276	109	111	942	937
1809	3377	3795	820	855	470	571	1111	1350	135	146	841	873
1811	3808	4292	729	930	551	522	1369	1510	132	177	1027	1153
1816	2156	2499	429	735	204	317	1289	1075	0	0	234	372
1817	2156	2499	429	735	204	317	1289	1075	0	0	234	372
1818	2156	2499	429	735	204	317	1289	1075	0	0	234	372

TABLE 1. PARISH POPULATION BY SEX AND RACE (CONTINUED)

YEAR	TOTAL M	TOTAL F	WHITE M	WHITE F	INDIAN M	INDIAN F	PARDO M	PARDO F	NEGRO M	NEGRO F	SLAVE M	SLAVE F
LEZAMA												
1783	787	777	241	264	276	259	113	119	93	88	64	47
1802	1134	1254	395	418	264	309	311	349	50	67	114	111
1803	1134	1254	395	418	264	309	311	349	50	67	114	111
1804	1134	1254	395	418	264	309	311	349	50	67	114	111
1805	1134	1254	395	418	264	309	311	349	50	67	114	111
1806	1134	1254	395	418	264	309	311	349	50	67	114	111
1807	1134	1254	395	418	264	309	311	349	50	67	114	111
1808	1134	1254	395	418	264	309	311	349	50	67	114	111
1809	1134	1254	395	418	264	309	311	349	50	67	114	111
1810	1134	1254	395	418	264	309	311	349	50	67	114	111
1811	1134	1254	395	418	264	309	311	349	50	67	114	111
LOS ANGELES												
1780	219	200	1	10	170	145	38	39	9	6	1	0
1803	215	237	8	13	90	105	115	118	0	0	2	1
1804	235	241	9	13	105	111	119	116	0	0	2	1
1805	223	260	15	13	98	121	108	124	0	0	2	2
1807	217	257	14	12	96	115	103	128	0	0	4	2
1808	227	252	13	9	83	112	130	130	0	0	1	1
1809	490	430	122	111	90	93	242	214	0	0	36	12
1810	494	433	117	103	96	106	246	213	0	0	35	11
1811	532	479	132	129	91	111	260	223	0	0	49	16
1812	520	447	112	103	98	110	268	215	0	0	42	19
1816	456	490	88	108	79	91	256	276	0	0	33	15
1817	474	538	116	133	76	100	246	286	0	0	36	19
LOS ANGELES DE SETENTA												
1801	521	593	331	391	40	45	121	127	0	0	29	30
1805	380	398	170	186	52	56	104	124	0	0	54	32
1806	436	443	186	203	76	54	121	146	0	0	53	40
1807	493	603	192	238	120	144	150	187	0	0	31	34
1809	440	541	182	216	88	109	133	162	0	0	37	54
LOS CANIZOS												
1802	430	402	40	29	0	0	215	224	16	14	159	135
1803	382	430	33	32	0	0	212	237	13	11	124	150
1804	410	412	45	37	0	0	216	216	11	7	138	152
1805	371	404	41	33	0	0	165	190	39	40	126	141
1807	384	380	33	28	0	0	186	195	35	25	130	132
1808	406	423	40	34	0	0	224	245	11	9	131	135
1809	409	429	39	34	0	0	228	248	11	9	131	138
1810	420	529	33	27	0	0	232	326	10	10	145	166
1811	402	474	31	25	0	0	242	293	5	6	124	150
1813	253	316	6	4	0	0	163	189	29	45	55	78
1818	181	231	8	4	0	0	109	141	0	0	64	86

TABLE 1. PARISH POPULATION BY SEX AND RACE (CONTINUED)

YEAR	TOTAL		WHITE		INDIAN		PARDO		NEGRO		SLAVE	
	M	F	M	F	M	F	M	F	M	F	M	F
1819	200	252	12	8	0	0	124	159	0	0	64	85
1820	191	251	12	8	0	0	121	158	0	0	58	85
LOS GUAYOS												
1781	629	613	208	177	290	314	130	120	0	0	1	2
1795	1298	1294	371	344	427	430	473	496	0	0	27	24
1802	2050	2040	405	352	667	736	815	848	32	20	131	84
1803	1766	1846	355	297	1012	1131	271	333	15	12	113	73
1804	1619	1698	443	424	367	414	681	773	13	15	115	72
1805	1604	1803	413	429	377	482	712	813	8	13	94	66
1816	1464	1559	366	409	272	301	758	793	14	10	54	46
LOS TEQUES												
1796	1100	1084	668	673	83	87	224	192	21	26	104	106
1799	1156	1153	683	694	83	87	239	211	33	45	118	116
1800	1156	1153	683	694	83	87	239	211	33	45	118	116
1801	1234	1247	704	715	88	95	262	231	50	60	130	146
1805	1475	1298	848	753	129	113	142	68	22	31	334	333
1811	816	1179	243	368	20	29	384	565	58	84	111	133
1816	1133	1222	646	682	100	109	242	258	7	13	138	160
1817	1082	1151	628	662	86	94	238	241	9	13	121	141
MACAIRA												
1784	311	278	4	1	56	47	33	29	8	3	210	198
1802	169	149	1	0	17	11	15	7	3	4	133	127
1803	164	139	1	0	17	8	1	2	9	3	136	126
1804	144	136	1	0	15	12	3	5	7	3	118	116
1806	130	129	1	1	14	14	0	0	8	4	107	110
1807	145	132	0	0	10	8	0	0	6	4	129	120
1808	101	118	0	0	17	16	0	0	12	8	72	94
1809	100	110	1	0	8	8	9	9	5	1	77	92
1811	57	53	0	0	10	10	0	0	1	1	46	42
1817	67	56	0	0	3	1	8	7	1	2	55	46
MACAIRITA												
1805	136	128	0	0	13	10	0	0	6	2	117	116
MACARAO												
1802	517	652	212	248	54	72	91	129	23	36	137	167
1803	552	561	130	197	60	61	158	126	26	38	178	139
1804	625	629	266	266	60	63	134	153	16	27	149	120
1805	568	607	238	259	49	58	116	131	16	22	149	137
1807	586	674	248	286	62	79	94	117	17	20	165	172
1808	587	653	277	306	56	65	110	122	21	25	123	135
1809	560	690	265	300	57	71	65	103	14	26	159	190
1810	718	670	294	298	75	68	125	118	21	27	203	159

TABLE 1. PARISH POPULATION BY SEX AND RACE (CONTINUED)

YEAR	TOTAL		WHITE		INDIAN		PARDO		NEGRO		SLAVE	
	M	F	M	F	M	F	M	F	M	F	M	F
1811	550	622	258	283	64	71	86	101	17	26	125	141
1812	536	604	251	301	28	33	73	79	14	17	170	174
1815	548	669	229	280	49	67	72	100	11	21	187	201
1816	590	701	249	292	50	71	85	110	18	25	188	203
1817	489	609	246	309	40	49	60	89	9	16	134	146
1818	485	609	242	309	40	49	60	89	9	16	134	146
1819	508	623	250	310	43	52	65	93	12	20	138	148
1820	508	623	250	310	43	52	65	93	12	20	138	148
1822	525	660	203	261	84	99	69	91	46	62	123	147
1823	617	747	273	311	95	112	79	104	42	66	128	154
MAGDALENO												
1802	1157	1255	411	432	62	72	602	679	7	9	75	63
1803	1349	1361	367	367	118	172	724	686	87	80	53	56
1804	1277	1314	374	395	18	21	789	833	15	7	81	58
1805	1244	1274	428	456	19	16	676	724	16	4	105	74
1806	1333	1315	438	456	26	23	726	703	39	53	104	80
1809	613	613	127	92	15	21	331	352	44	48	96	100
1816	1370	1428	433	458	27	27	786	801	51	72	73	70
MAIQUETIA												
1796	861	936	185	211	46	36	442	528	0	0	188	161
1802	771	883	204	250	31	24	213	267	140	170	183	172
1804	726	837	193	219	34	37	251	333	70	91	178	157
1805	776	854	193	211	32	43	279	337	86	96	186	167
1807	778	992	196	279	35	38	280	338	90	160	177	177
1811	787	955	188	251	50	47	275	341	111	167	163	149
1815	803	1014	247	248	39	62	201	296	200	271	116	137
1816	526	744	119	182	70	70	117	224	77	115	143	153
1817	454	873	124	231	26	37	137	324	35	85	132	196
1819	803	1014	247	248	39	62	201	296	200	271	116	137
MAMPORAL												
1784	253	268	21	25	17	12	26	32	30	31	159	168
1802	235	253	21	21	10	15	28	30	21	23	155	164
1804	243	244	21	15	17	10	35	46	34	40	136	133
1805	279	278	25	20	28	20	50	56	23	39	153	143
1807	269	272	24	13	16	18	58	66	20	36	151	139
1808	274	284	33	22	20	18	50	43	32	55	139	146
1809	248	273	17	9	20	12	29	46	57	68	125	138
1811	246	266	30	18	19	21	60	73	28	27	109	127
1812	238	273	23	20	31	16	76	63	19	35	89	139
1816	126	148	2	3	4	4	43	42	7	3	70	96
1817	139	135	4	4	16	10	0	0	45	28	74	93
1818	169	149	7	4	1	6	40	42	9	6	112	91
1820	137	158	3	0	4	6	35	47	6	10	89	95

TABLE 1. PARISH POPULATION BY SEX AND RACE (CONTINUED)

YEAR	TOTAL		WHITE		INDIAN		PARDO		NEGRO		SLAVE	
	M	F	M	F	M	F	M	F	M	F	M	F
MANAPIRE												
1804	291	195	75	55	29	24	92	75	5	4	90	37
1807	260	206	65	61	20	15	78	83	8	6	89	41
1808	263	208	65	61	23	17	78	83	8	6	89	41
1810	298	223	78	68	18	14	108	89	5	6	89	46
MARACA												
1778	427	446	118	117	165	168	139	150	4	1	1	10
1803	811	936	50	72	456	533	288	317	7	5	10	9
1804	750	886	270	339	204	232	249	290	17	17	10	8
1805	884	1051	274	366	291	332	297	335	13	14	9	4
1806	785	934	225	305	309	342	229	262	13	19	9	6
1807	822	926	230	296	345	364	202	215	31	37	14	14
1808	671	793	203	259	268	319	156	168	31	34	13	13
1809	714	791	199	233	298	328	171	185	32	30	14	15
1810	659	759	193	227	251	307	163	179	36	33	16	13
1817	300	338	107	140	91	87	89	101	3	2	10	8
MARACAY												
1782	2885	2679	867	750	604	451	1132	1189	40	43	242	246
1796	3888	4045	1689	1627	0	0	1429	1620	225	276	545	522
1802	4414	3796	1223	1094	116	61	1834	1450	188	193	1053	998
1803	4508	3866	1254	1113	121	68	1877	1481	193	197	1063	1007
1804	4795	4171	1302	1233	119	69	2015	1595	204	213	1155	1061
1805	3961	4413	1305	1465	59	58	1785	2093	14	6	798	791
1808	4034	4468	1333	1486	73	72	1797	2101	22	12	809	797
1809	4148	3781	1254	1028	61	68	1577	1481	193	197	1063	1007
1811	3827	3511	1200	970	106	42	1410	1400	165	150	946	949
1816	2948	3479	264	437	253	428	961	999	140	180	1330	1435
1817	2140	3113	566	910	17	25	936	1590	32	46	589	542
1818	2951	3055	850	891	103	85	1157	1227	199	178	642	674
1819	3206	3217	998	940	133	115	1196	1266	214	194	665	702
1820	3215	3327	907	942	143	123	1203	1276	258	229	704	757
MARIA												
1803	394	451	190	208	86	104	79	88	32	43	7	8
1804	635	734	305	334	107	132	203	245	6	6	14	17
1805	683	745	310	323	94	115	253	281	9	7	17	19
1806	699	774	316	335	102	117	253	293	10	8	18	21
1807	719	810	320	362	96	105	280	321	8	6	15	16
1811	694	765	246	270	141	152	261	304	30	22	16	17
MARIARA												
1802	1114	1110	304	238	51	61	503	529	91	110	165	172
1803	1187	1092	313	250	36	32	495	485	137	134	206	191

TABLE 1. PARISH POPULATION BY SEX AND RACE (CONTINUED)

YEAR	TOTAL		WHITE		INDIAN		PARDO		NEGRO		SLAVE	
	M	F	M	F	M	F	M	F	M	F	M	F
1804	1126	1062	299	231	30	27	519	521	125	116	153	167
1805	1310	1239	343	291	32	31	673	682	103	77	159	158
1809	1608	1646	417	400	145	139	640	675	192	197	214	235
1815	1455	1477	359	331	62	57	718	800	129	99	187	190
1816	1575	1695	369	397	26	20	940	1070	67	64	173	144
1817	1733	1753	444	437	46	35	985	988	85	111	173	182
1818	1619	1777	483	506	24	24	887	1017	68	60	157	170
MONTALBAN												
1781	753	772	288	288	26	30	305	294	14	8	120	152
1802	1097	1176	421	408	0	0	439	470	59	91	178	207
1803	1274	1286	492	483	0	0	589	586	55	26	138	191
1804	1307	1317	507	494	0	0	602	602	61	31	137	190
1805	1277	1318	513	505	0	0	603	611	61	35	100	167
1806	1222	1402	482	602	0	0	592	610	54	31	94	159
1808	1210	1455	463	656	0	0	576	604	92	63	79	132
1810	1347	1371	565	511	6	4	601	642	68	105	107	109
1815	1504	1514	461	480	9	7	743	713	82	82	209	232
1817	1692	1680	542	540	13	9	864	817	84	84	189	230
1818	1308	1523	410	486	10	10	710	800	54	67	124	160
1820	1817	1929	668	702	12	15	891	947	121	121	125	144
MORON												
1804	161	136	0	0	0	0	86	77	7	0	68	59
1805	165	137	0	0	0	0	84	72	14	12	67	53
1806	149	153	0	0	0	0	77	74	16	17	56	62
1807	175	162	0	0	0	0	84	82	17	20	74	60
1818	163	184	0	0	0	0	104	135	0	0	59	49
1819	166	168	0	0	0	0	102	113	0	0	64	55
1820	283	304	5	4	0	0	169	177	46	51	63	72
MOROTURO												
1802	165	192	21	29	1	1	35	37	94	99	14	26
1804	246	275	20	18	54	61	69	69	92	111	11	16
1805	252	283	25	42	35	46	70	72	106	108	16	15
1807	178	203	16	12	25	32	112	140	14	12	11	7
1808	234	275	20	18	49	61	64	69	92	111	9	16
1809	208	224	27	27	21	12	146	172	4	4	10	9
1815	238	275	14	18	54	61	69	69	92	111	9	16
NAGUANAGUA												
1802	760	686	340	346	2	3	247	239	1	1	170	97
1803	814	786	371	399	2	3	256	289	1	1	184	94
1804	700	640	293	311	4	4	241	233	1	1	161	91
1805	838	782	296	346	4	4	389	314	2	0	147	118
1809	696	722	310	343	3	5	236	264	3	0	144	110
1816	891	863	305	319	34	39	278	260	26	25	248	220

TABLE 1. PARISH POPULATION BY SEX AND RACE (CONTINUED)

YEAR	TOTAL		WHITE		INDIAN		PARDO		NEGRO		SLAVE	
	M	F	M	F	M	F	M	F	M	F	M	F
NAIGUATA												
1801	400	371	27	13	75	87	13	8	6	3	279	260
1802	401	351	16	10	79	82	8	5	9	6	289	248
1804	413	344	15	13	116	86	1	1	3	3	277	241
1805	348	350	22	18	73	84	7	4	1	2	245	242
1809	366	374	23	17	74	82	2	5	1	2	266	268
1810	394	381	24	14	72	68	4	12	4	9	290	278
1811	390	401	35	20	87	101	12	10	11	6	245	264
1816	256	294	16	20	60	49	13	23	10	12	157	190
1817	310	356	29	25	53	56	19	33	23	22	186	220
1822	221	289	18	9	48	69	23	30	13	12	119	169
NIRGUA												
1781	1566	1738	23	9	0	0	1534	1718	0	0	9	11
1802	1445	1645	16	13	0	0	1412	1607	0	0	17	25
1803	1590	1584	16	19	0	0	1561	1549	0	0	13	16
1804	1597	1585	20	20	0	0	1564	1549	0	0	13	16
1805	1233	1581	31	29	0	0	1151	1500	0	0	51	52
1806	1253	1603	36	32	0	0	1166	1517	0	0	51	54
1807	1234	1582	31	29	0	0	1152	1501	0	0	51	52
1808	2064	2224	57	66	2	8	1614	1636	334	431	57	83
1809	1650	2419	33	49	1	2	1043	1696	548	636	25	36
1810	2251	2417	45	51	13	17	1493	1564	663	730	37	55
1813	1499	1858	32	23	0	0	1448	1809	0	0	19	26
1817	1465	1846	30	23	0	0	1416	1797	0	0	19	26
1819	1353	1905	32	23	0	0	1300	1856	0	0	21	26
1820	1329	1939	28	26	0	0	1270	1883	0	0	31	30
1821	1300	1779	18	13	0	0	1268	1742	0	0	14	24
OCUMARE DE LA COSTA												
1802	1159	1359	45	41	2	2	401	432	52	46	659	838
1803	986	1049	40	45	5	4	378	402	121	139	442	459
1804	678	836	50	47	3	2	144	182	103	130	378	475
1805	1114	1112	45	41	0	1	287	351	17	20	765	699
1809	844	818	54	44	0	0	296	315	29	25	465	434
1815	671	858	37	43	0	0	255	352	20	41	359	422
1816	661	879	26	30	0	0	217	325	31	69	387	455
1817	697	852	28	37	0	0	252	350	24	59	393	406
1819	522	632	36	20	1	2	194	218	20	57	271	335
1820	605	722	54	56	1	2	224	247	54	87	272	330
OCUMARE DEL TUY												
1783	1054	1087	171	182	35	24	215	241	84	130	549	510
1802	2021	2082	287	298	188	206	423	509	109	172	1014	897
1803	1855	2286	666	770	205	235	242	382	210	344	532	555
1804	2335	2418	282	314	189	212	490	561	157	186	1217	1145

TABLE 1. PARISH POPULATION BY SEX AND RACE (CONTINUED)

YEAR	TOTAL		WHITE		INDIAN		PARDO		NEGRO		SLAVE	
	M	F	M	F	M	F	M	F	M	F	M	F
1805	2404	2482	339	364	192	217	493	564	160	189	1220	1148
1810	2299	2392	267	271	176	173	480	573	94	99	1282	1276
1811	1617	1829	247	247	154	144	398	508	100	106	718	824
1815	681	763	88	122	47	58	115	122	34	42	397	419
1820	1815	2214	258	250	71	113	459	670	165	197	862	984
1821	1677	2148	301	359	27	57	373	526	116	188	860	1018
1822	1565	2278	245	302	77	125	312	667	146	214	785	970
ORTIZ												
1780	625	568	412	384	47	48	46	53	55	35	65	48
1802	1003	697	659	478	20	24	52	74	149	67	123	54
1803	742	761	486	539	31	24	94	106	62	50	69	42
1804	790	769	537	541	39	47	106	98	31	27	77	56
1805	786	784	541	559	40	49	104	95	25	27	76	54
1806	976	799	750	577	33	33	90	93	20	35	83	61
1807	928	968	503	534	25	29	260	290	52	50	88	65
1808	958	983	520	538	33	27	266	301	50	56	89	61
1809	970	1015	513	545	34	35	272	293	59	69	92	73
1810	988	1031	524	557	34	40	279	291	56	68	95	75
1813	987	988	670	694	25	32	152	147	42	44	98	71
OSPINO												
1802	2780	3241	842	967	372	507	1378	1537	69	72	119	158
1803	2797	3270	843	962	381	509	1375	1554	67	78	131	167
1804	2982	3393	853	1022	543	528	1381	1579	80	106	125	158
1805	3008	3411	889	1009	574	642	1379	1548	40	46	126	166
1806	3185	3582	953	1072	606	664	1438	1617	52	57	136	172
1807	3238	3624	958	1087	594	657	1480	1633	62	70	144	177
1808	3400	3702	1116	1181	485	727	1572	1488	101	121	126	185
1809	3401	3876	919	999	677	924	1575	1664	107	124	123	165
1810	3375	3876	919	999	675	924	1553	1664	103	124	125	165
1811	2650	3023	937	1038	308	383	1160	1301	122	121	123	180
1817	2583	2923	937	1038	308	383	1093	1201	122	121	123	180
PANAQUIRE												
1784	257	207	21	19	33	19	33	25	1	2	169	142
1802	494	417	43	22	50	36	47	36	3	3	351	320
1803	445	391	45	29	45	29	41	37	0	1	314	295
1804	443	368	36	20	47	29	40	22	1	1	319	296
1805	453	376	36	20	36	34	39	32	9	5	333	285
1807	457	366	32	21	31	18	55	40	4	0	335	287
1808	459	376	31	25	33	19	55	40	3	3	337	289
1809	429	392	36	24	35	30	53	42	6	3	299	293
1811	400	367	25	12	33	19	47	42	8	17	287	277
1812	412	385	23	17	36	33	55	51	10	16	288	268
1816	274	319	16	8	10	10	39	65	11	16	198	220

TABLE 1. PARISH POPULATION BY SEX AND RACE (CONTINUED)

YEAR	TOTAL M	TOTAL F	WHITE M	WHITE F	INDIAN M	INDIAN F	PARDO M	PARDO F	NEGRO M	NEGRO F	SLAVE M	SLAVE F
PARACOTOS												
1783	1014	834	223	173	346	252	231	181	70	70	144	158
1802	1008	881	337	289	229	213	286	254	28	26	128	99
1803	1142	923	346	301	216	218	307	266	38	25	235	113
1804	921	843	371	344	208	186	236	212	28	18	78	83
1805	1014	952	378	351	268	254	244	223	32	22	92	102
1806	1050	1039	477	499	267	257	198	185	18	14	90	84
1807	1038	1092	458	499	272	254	198	185	18	22	92	132
1808	1089	1108	478	519	289	279	208	195	23	27	91	88
1809	769	862	274	295	198	245	113	121	43	44	141	157
1810	858	899	318	340	230	224	123	129	43	44	144	162
1811	940	963	356	367	251	244	136	136	44	51	153	165
1812	963	1039	296	303	229	245	168	197	69	83	201	211
1816	880	931	268	258	138	153	188	234	186	207	100	79
1817	888	953	270	263	132	161	198	234	185	204	103	91
1819	848	955	363	394	294	338	93	112	0	0	98	111
1820	852	960	366	395	294	341	92	112	0	0	100	112
PARAPARA												
1780	1036	972	285	262	46	64	471	423	132	125	102	98
1781	1028	964	282	260	47	63	469	421	130	123	100	97
1782	1053	979	285	200	53	111	479	431	136	129	100	108
1788	1039	939	286	200	53	71	479	431	112	129	109	108
1802	1044	1049	275	257	46	40	328	376	329	323	66	53
1803	1098	1121	292	289	31	34	355	381	350	357	70	60
1805	1102	1129	302	296	18	22	373	405	340	350	69	56
1807	1143	1187	240	248	6	12	685	709	149	159	63	59
1809	1237	1243	269	271	8	15	746	733	150	160	64	64
1810	1282	1303	271	275	9	17	771	766	156	171	75	74
1811	1315	1458	287	322	10	19	795	875	160	178	63	64
PATANEMO												
1802	218	244	6	6	1	1	98	96	19	34	94	107
1803	223	246	7	9	4	4	95	99	20	34	97	100
1804	248	247	7	6	3	1	114	135	21	24	103	81
1805	264	269	7	8	4	2	117	143	21	31	115	85
1808	246	267	5	5	2	0	103	133	25	30	111	99
1818	205	206	4	3	3	1	128	140	5	2	65	60
1819	244	228	5	3	3	3	138	145	15	14	83	63
PAYARA												
1780	450	458	24	15	372	419	14	8	1	0	39	16
1802	537	538	81	90	260	247	147	148	26	30	21	23
1804	621	604	114	114	268	245	172	174	33	37	34	34
1805	726	699	142	144	292	260	206	204	42	46	44	45
1806	729	704	145	146	292	261	206	206	42	46	44	45

TABLE 1. PARISH POPULATION BY SEX AND RACE (CONTINUED)

YEAR	TOTAL		WHITE		INDIAN		PARDO		NEGRO		SLAVE	
	M	F	M	F	M	F	M	F	M	F	M	F
1807	720	775	145	169	282	288	213	235	38	44	42	39
1812	696	729	140	146	270	282	194	216	44	44	48	41
PETARE												
1802	1858	1982	527	598	304	355	350	298	213	239	464	492
1803	1898	1977	537	602	307	351	365	293	216	240	473	491
1804	1936	1963	575	591	299	359	381	355	241	250	440	408
1805	2175	2067	539	524	263	295	499	563	100	118	774	567
1806	2066	2064	501	529	255	274	500	548	84	118	726	595
1807	2314	2243	559	584	262	278	575	606	86	88	832	687
1811	2147	2202	552	594	217	199	393	402	249	254	736	753
1812	2241	2307	554	532	311	318	282	301	209	244	885	912
1815	1703	1741	480	492	172	173	230	246	181	186	640	644
1816	2075	2433	531	679	149	172	289	361	435	590	671	631
1817	2029	2345	445	505	171	216	297	399	436	574	680	651
1818	1557	1843	365	465	166	200	358	511	86	109	582	558
1819	1681	1989	401	507	174	212	415	580	86	109	605	581
1820	1785	2069	424	527	178	214	457	613	90	114	636	601
1821	1840	2122	424	530	184	219	480	631	98	120	654	622
1822	1886	1862	437	447	186	218	490	461	123	117	650	619
PUERTO CABELLO												
1803	2122	2784	444	420	14	44	1093	1580	282	378	289	362
1804	2236	2977	504	527	9	19	1192	1773	242	311	289	347
1805	2147	3084	400	526	9	16	1198	1863	255	303	285	376
1806	2149	3245	511	555	7	25	962	1812	348	458	321	395
1811	2160	3322	433	542	26	40	1044	1464	417	824	240	452
1817	1591	2051	611	661	128	172	402	574	210	254	240	390
1819	1406	1873	561	735	25	30	632	859	117	155	71	94
1820	1052	2060	362	382	23	18	397	1230	140	210	130	220
PUERTO CABELLO, CASTILLO												
1801	389	134	332	98	8	0	16	4	0	0	33	32
1802	251	66	233	37	0	0	0	2	0	0	18	27
1804	334	148	203	50	0	0	90	53	0	0	41	45
1805	534	203	262	78	0	0	206	66	0	0	66	59
1806	862	210	477	104	1	6	311	53	0	0	73	47
1807	830	232	436	106	5	5	322	72	0	0	67	49
1808	927	271	496	131	9	7	348	83	0	0	74	50
1809	855	284	451	123	17	9	303	101	0	0	84	51
1810	1185	256	638	85	17	7	476	119	0	0	54	45
1819	796	56	230	32	51	0	376	0	103	0	36	24
1820	665	45	162	33	50	0	320	0	97	0	36	12
QUARA												
1782	480	577	11	9	453	543	9	12	7	12	0	1
1791	374	431	10	9	349	403	15	18	0	1	0	0

TABLE 1. PARISH POPULATION BY SEX AND RACE (CONTINUED)

YEAR	TOTAL		WHITE		INDIAN		PARDO		NEGRO		SLAVE	
	M	F	M	F	M	F	M	F	M	F	M	F
1802	325	390	11	11	289	351	24	28	0	0	1	0
1803	314	389	13	12	293	359	0	3	7	15	1	0
1804	353	380	5	5	339	363	2	6	7	6	0	0
1805	386	461	11	10	315	402	22	15	38	34	0	0
1807	411	399	15	11	337	336	41	36	17	16	1	0
1808	423	484	19	15	352	424	37	30	15	15	0	0
1809	420	471	18	10	354	404	28	30	20	27	0	0
1810	423	477	8	7	366	423	40	36	9	11	0	0
1811	389	543	15	7	314	474	41	38	19	24	0	0
1815	401	529	15	11	328	438	48	62	10	18	0	0
1816	424	511	17	10	339	414	57	56	11	31	0	0
1817	436	511	15	10	348	419	56	55	17	27	0	0
1818	467	538	13	10	338	375	67	87	39	55	10	11
1819	369	490	13	11	250	332	59	79	34	53	13	15

QUIBOR

YEAR	TOTAL M	TOTAL F	WHITE M	WHITE F	INDIAN M	INDIAN F	PARDO M	PARDO F	NEGRO M	NEGRO F	SLAVE M	SLAVE F
1802	3182	3623	1053	1219	603	725	807	869	441	492	278	318
1803	3102	3576	1053	1217	523	730	807	869	441	442	278	318
1804	3317	3681	1076	1231	615	734	864	901	456	484	306	331
1805	3498	3910	1125	1282	675	790	883	946	496	534	319	358
1806	3497	3909	1124	1281	675	790	883	946	496	534	319	358
1807	3480	3928	1125	1282	675	790	865	964	496	534	319	358
1808	3792	4232	1183	1337	708	818	1013	1123	545	577	343	377
1810	4687	5283	1332	1498	865	1033	2333	2577	30	32	127	143
1812	3900	4546	1113	1315	483	661	1666	1838	281	321	357	411
1815	4115	4791	1178	1395	523	706	1776	1958	281	321	357	411
1816	4072	4634	1136	1315	508	700	1791	1919	272	308	365	392
1817	4631	5373	1326	1507	580	803	2018	2272	301	358	406	433
1818	4202	5578	1061	1559	556	925	1938	2290	283	363	364	441
1819	4076	5200	1223	1547	507	731	1718	2165	233	347	395	410
1820	4495	5666	1355	1720	596	788	1843	2314	276	402	425	442

RIO CHICO

YEAR	TOTAL M	TOTAL F	WHITE M	WHITE F	INDIAN M	INDIAN F	PARDO M	PARDO F	NEGRO M	NEGRO F	SLAVE M	SLAVE F
1802	429	440	40	10	22	17	57	48	66	77	244	288
1803	449	465	43	12	24	23	62	54	68	80	252	296
1804	491	508	31	15	15	12	90	93	72	78	283	310
1805	632	508	55	17	31	34	83	60	60	55	403	342
1806	702	528	60	17	36	38	86	65	61	55	459	353
1807	734	552	60	17	38	40	91	70	68	62	477	363
1808	762	568	60	18	40	43	92	74	72	60	498	373
1809	769	573	63	19	40	43	92	74	72	60	502	377
1810	822	620	83	27	46	49	100	86	81	71	512	387
1811	876	699	89	41	59	59	116	112	86	72	526	415
1812	792	628	68	27	42	45	93	86	72	79	517	391
1816	652	773	61	51	49	76	148	180	35	42	359	424
1817	668	711	68	40	51	49	93	130	56	57	400	435
1819	712	705	59	48	47	46	110	154	52	54	444	403

TABLE 1. PARISH POPULATION BY SEX AND RACE (CONTINUED)

YEAR	TOTAL		WHITE		INDIAN		PARDO		NEGRO		SLAVE	
	M	F	M	F	M	F	M	F	M	F	M	F
RIO DEL TOCUYO												
1802	947	940	190	192	596	582	132	128	0	0	29	38
1803	881	932	173	179	536	551	134	159	0	0	38	43
1804	806	833	104	111	567	585	90	90	0	0	45	47
1805	849	866	110	114	585	605	106	97	0	0	48	50
1808	882	887	107	131	661	623	46	63	0	0	68	70
1809	1053	1341	251	291	509	749	136	125	0	0	157	176
1815	1099	1287	206	229	738	837	121	169	0	0	34	52
SABANETA												
1805	1052	1073	349	380	104	122	550	528	22	22	27	21
1808	1175	1208	227	172	292	345	618	655	14	22	24	14
1809	1649	1351	565	458	215	127	822	742	22	19	25	5
1810	1855	1665	600	505	250	165	900	915	70	68	35	12
1811	2182	1875	742	656	300	220	991	893	85	85	64	21
1812	1162	1223	499	388	220	340	309	340	86	113	48	42
1816	1016	1230	335	397	42	51	639	782	0	0	0	0
SAN ANTONIO DE LAS COCUIZAS												
1780	502	570	46	59	57	58	300	347	83	96	16	10
SAN ANTONIO DE LOS ALTOS												
1796	248	223	209	193	0	0	19	11	3	3	17	16
1802	255	200	206	168	4	2	15	18	0	1	30	11
1803	283	221	227	180	20	16	4	7	1	1	31	17
1804	288	217	231	176	7	3	8	8	0	2	42	28
1805	374	242	247	183	15	9	20	9	0	1	92	40
1808	697	392	310	219	43	9	83	34	6	2	255	128
1809	518	451	272	206	16	6	19	19	0	3	211	217
1810	504	356	247	192	2	9	36	29	2	2	217	124
1811	474	383	253	214	2	4	33	33	1	1	185	131
1812	447	381	227	220	2	1	23	38	3	3	192	119
1815	283	305	129	135	4	6	32	53	2	2	116	109
1816	284	288	139	147	5	9	21	35	1	1	118	96
1817	265	268	138	138	3	1	15	29	2	2	107	98
1818	274	295	147	147	9	9	25	47	1	2	92	90
1819	282	301	153	163	2	4	35	43	3	6	89	85
1820	336	350	167	180	14	19	43	57	10	7	102	87
SAN CARLOS												
1781	3706	3640	1504	1484	207	181	961	868	283	329	751	778
1786	3729	3849	1384	1381	187	207	1051	1137	349	409	758	715
1787	3826	4160	1440	1519	209	189	1060	1213	371	413	746	826
1788	3847	4264	1450	1533	205	186	1069	1218	368	516	755	811
1791	4137	4569	1527	1605	226	211	1163	1309	424	577	797	867

TABLE 1. PARISH POPULATION BY SEX AND RACE (CONTINUED)

YEAR	TOTAL		WHITE		INDIAN		PARDO		NEGRO		SLAVE	
	M	F	M	F	M	F	M	F	M	F	M	F
1796	4452	4921	1619	1701	256	248	1255	1409	465	628	857	935
1798	3619	4234	1280	1531	169	216	1082	1081	556	637	532	769
1799	3623	4265	1293	1533	169	220	1089	1093	533	641	539	778
1800	3835	4386	1316	1563	177	229	1129	1135	671	676	542	783
1801	3878	4433	1326	1570	183	234	1139	1143	682	697	548	794
1802	4146	4659	1468	1656	220	212	1098	1302	526	672	834	817
1803	4188	4696	1478	1665	222	216	1119	1317	529	676	840	822
1804	5133	5343	1803	1754	340	342	1344	1554	695	806	951	887
1805	5274	5571	1865	1901	349	349	1387	1606	695	806	978	909
1806	5457	5768	1910	1971	355	356	1493	1713	710	824	989	904
1808	5276	5570	1865	1901	351	348	1387	1606	695	806	978	909
1809	5274	5571	1865	1901	349	349	1387	1606	695	806	978	909
1811	5747	6381	1906	2265	56	62	3154	3298	61	69	570	687
1812	5724	6311	1913	2258	45	56	3168	3300	54	59	544	638
1816	3368	4358	969	1227	218	224	1655	2183	121	109	405	615
1817	3248	4942	1074	1490	94	133	1612	2491	92	194	376	634
1818	3544	5156	1135	1597	183	251	1616	2410	108	213	502	685
1819	3190	5199	1045	1545	69	148	1472	2587	93	219	511	700
1820	3278	5070	1089	1538	81	137	1442	2565	175	173	491	657
1822	3295	5059	1060	1507	91	106	1554	2555	97	203	493	688
1823	2922	4751	875	1364	78	86	1425	2469	92	166	452	666
1824	2719	4222	932	1237	65	82	1302	2220	66	104	354	579
SAN DIEGO DE ALCALA												
1781	370	424	106	112	91	103	158	189	0	0	15	20
1802	506	787	96	162	82	133	225	318	93	163	10	11
1803	298	432	55	82	77	121	130	185	27	34	9	10
1804	417	508	104	129	74	93	147	172	84	106	8	8
1805	405	432	96	110	93	91	185	208	20	13	11	10
1809	392	409	80	79	104	77	180	231	22	15	6	7
SAN DIEGO DE LOS ALTOS												
1802	418	426	217	210	102	116	45	54	6	5	48	41
1803	444	493	199	213	136	144	32	46	34	42	43	48
1804	450	409	240	209	98	100	45	42	17	19	50	39
1805	479	438	247	220	109	108	47	45	24	26	52	39
1807	519	506	244	243	144	150	51	50	17	22	63	41
1808	538	519	243	240	146	155	57	47	21	24	71	53
1809	618	588	257	257	172	173	73	53	37	44	79	61
1810	587	645	258	270	161	184	66	81	26	23	76	87
1811	610	645	265	286	168	186	58	56	32	26	87	91
1815	595	633	259	293	149	154	50	48	45	51	92	87
1816	553	593	237	258	142	164	52	55	23	31	99	85
1817	532	593	243	286	118	139	47	46	35	43	89	79
1818	524	554	240	247	122	156	46	53	97	75	19	23
1819	557	575	227	228	153	187	53	51	24	22	100	87
1820	587	611	228	240	158	178	68	83	25	27	108	83

TABLE 1. PARISH POPULATION BY SEX AND RACE (CONTINUED)

YEAR	TOTAL		WHITE		INDIAN		PARDO		NEGRO		SLAVE	
	M	F	M	F	M	F	M	F	M	F	M	F
SAN FELIPE												
1782	2441	2579	485	822	157	99	1576	1449	112	120	111	89
1802	2650	3420	700	800	290	350	960	1210	290	350	410	710
1803	2532	3135	670	760	295	318	932	1175	260	307	375	575
1804	1827	2739	350	531	38	71	1138	1648	40	79	261	410
1805	2083	3044	368	543	20	41	1355	1970	55	83	285	407
1817	1367	1700	142	194	11	14	1092	1341	25	25	97	126
1818	1111	2113	233	675	0	0	755	1154	3	6	120	278
1819	1470	1823	168	233	18	21	1142	1384	35	41	107	144
1820	1471	1910	174	242	24	29	1118	1433	43	53	112	153
1821	1193	1563	138	197	18	21	895	1180	35	41	107	124
SAN FELIPE, MITAD DE (1)												
1807	1280	1581	201	297	19	19	835	1030	18	15	207	220
1808	1297	1592	211	297	19	19	841	1040	18	15	208	221
1809	1234	1520	186	291	14	17	796	938	12	16	226	258
1810	1277	1585	209	297	14	18	832	1030	18	21	204	219
1811	1277	1585	209	297	14	18	832	1030	18	21	204	219
1812	1032	993	94	114	5	3	825	745	5	5	103	126
SAN FELIPE, MITAD DE (2)												
1807	1143	1699	203	274	17	28	774	1173	23	25	126	199
1808	1190	1697	203	268	28	53	790	1118	41	57	128	201
1809	1165	1673	191	251	54	83	767	1059	48	75	105	205
1810	1190	1688	185	259	56	82	773	1058	49	80	127	209
1811	1114	1763	173	262	39	45	758	1218	40	58	104	180
SAN FERNANDO DE APURE												
1801	1528	2036	555	773	114	144	766	983	34	46	59	90
1805	734	841	363	391	108	128	246	304	0	0	17	18
1806	1143	1321	493	531	213	283	411	475	0	0	26	32
1816	858	974	323	399	46	69	345	367	75	73	69	66
SAN FERNANDO DE CACHICAMO												
1783	232	188	62	43	5	9	78	61	24	23	63	52
1802	223	201	47	50	20	13	87	92	22	20	47	26
1803	218	197	47	45	21	14	79	90	27	22	44	26
1805	212	227	43	42	14	8	117	138	4	7	34	32
1806	264	249	65	56	19	13	135	141	6	4	39	35
1807	265	238	66	57	19	13	135	141	6	4	39	23
SAN FRANCISCO DE CARA												
1783	574	595	110	126	16	16	415	410	0	0	33	43
1802	721	787	184	186	17	22	390	462	42	30	88	87

TABLE 1. PARISH POPULATION BY SEX AND RACE (CONTINUED)

YEAR	TOTAL M	TOTAL F	WHITE M	WHITE F	INDIAN M	INDIAN F	PARDO M	PARDO F	NEGRO M	NEGRO F	SLAVE M	SLAVE F
SAN FRANCISCO DE TIZNADOS												
1780	1228	1012	166	117	73	63	172	172	607	525	210	135
1801	850	896	103	94	19	22	602	705	0	0	126	75
1802	1010	977	111	100	9	9	505	447	273	359	112	62
1803	1049	1005	145	139	10	11	488	515	262	268	144	72
1805	1108	1073	166	150	11	19	789	820	9	8	133	76
1807	1199	1169	138	172	11	19	854	887	9	11	137	80
1808	1193	1168	173	163	11	19	861	893	9	11	139	82
1809	1225	1198	179	168	14	21	877	913	12	12	143	84
1811	1103	1127	240	236	94	94	482	488	199	220	88	89
1812	1176	1289	235	242	98	118	536	633	184	193	123	103
SAN FRANCISCO DE YARE												
1783	673	626	28	26	68	64	74	52	69	68	434	416
1802	903	863	48	43	114	119	42	36	136	168	563	497
1803	824	916	45	34	113	127	48	44	158	196	460	515
1804	819	914	36	38	107	119	32	31	155	203	489	523
1805	829	896	48	33	102	119	35	30	160	206	484	508
1810	1071	1074	48	40	137	148	229	264	46	53	611	569
1811	1078	1074	48	40	137	148	232	264	50	53	611	569
1815	525	809	29	30	62	76	64	88	20	29	350	586
1817	981	1115	50	40	172	219	157	255	104	54	498	547
1818	761	952	47	31	97	95	179	257	41	64	397	505
1820	849	986	68	54	84	91	120	144	88	131	489	566
1821	955	1051	77	52	125	161	175	213	52	76	526	549
1822	983	975	62	55	92	107	191	215	59	63	579	535
SAN JAIME												
1780	1087	877	416	340	62	45	473	367	58	30	78	95
SAN JOSE												
1781	561	538	92	78	160	177	272	239	11	10	26	34
1788	760	756	40	46	137	143	538	520	25	26	20	21
1790	891	836	186	201	146	170	496	423	37	42	26	0
1791	891	836	186	201	146	170	496	423	37	42	26	0
1792	997	1105	197	296	172	207	599	564	17	16	12	22
1794	997	1045	197	236	172	207	599	564	17	16	12	22
1795	1127	1119	247	235	155	184	318	326	383	346	24	28
1798	1256	1261	277	284	185	216	348	346	415	377	31	38
1799	1256	1261	277	284	185	216	348	346	415	377	31	38
1800	1273	1262	277	284	185	216	368	346	415	377	28	39
1801	1269	1303	263	274	191	220	390	402	417	397	8	10
1803	1243	1300	243	263	188	195	776	805	19	18	17	19
1804	1266	1294	245	271	176	104	805	867	18	19	22	33
1805	952	968	201	200	134	140	586	587	11	17	20	24
1807	768	856	182	225	70	96	498	516	0	0	18	19

TABLE 1. PARISH POPULATION BY SEX AND RACE (CONTINUED)

YEAR	TOTAL		WHITE		INDIAN		PARDO		NEGRO		SLAVE	
	M	F	M	F	M	F	M	F	M	F	M	F
1808	768	857	184	230	68	91	493	517	0	0	23	19
1811	749	848	169	216	78	97	485	514	0	0	17	21
1812	698	867	128	187	37	58	527	608	6	14	0	0
1815	792	947	28	41	84	82	664	805	6	11	10	8
1818	544	1080	150	310	140	237	248	524	4	6	2	3
1819	661	1008	181	200	221	297	250	500	6	6	3	5
1822	700	1292	228	350	187	231	267	658	9	34	9	19
1823	646	1046	211	280	158	187	266	549	3	16	8	14
SAN JOSE DE APURE												
1802	277	282	39	36	104	111	90	92	39	40	5	3
1804	335	384	71	87	102	110	94	108	66	79	2	0
1806	320	336	66	77	102	110	91	80	57	69	4	0
1807	289	326	55	73	101	104	79	81	51	68	3	0
1808	280	313	57	70	95	101	73	80	52	62	3	0
1809	280	313	57	70	95	101	73	80	52	62	3	0
SAN JOSE DE TIZNADOS												
1802	949	916	193	152	39	37	575	619	31	32	111	76
1803	1009	985	195	164	62	58	594	662	51	32	107	69
1804	962	976	196	162	63	78	565	645	54	30	84	61
1805	949	1018	190	183	64	79	580	670	41	25	74	61
1807	1052	1136	205	162	43	68	575	668	157	174	72	64
1808	985	1024	166	133	45	37	624	732	65	76	85	46
1809	1038	1050	202	161	34	29	636	690	97	116	69	54
1810	1074	1187	178	148	59	70	699	768	93	100	45	101
1812	1099	1172	151	135	60	72	721	808	86	98	81	59
1816	923	1181	164	190	57	79	468	632	163	226	71	54
1817	1219	1508	209	245	70	96	677	865	185	235	78	67
SAN JUAN DE LOS MORROS												
1802	588	644	260	281	55	45	117	142	101	128	55	48
1803	587	640	275	296	51	44	122	146	93	103	46	51
1805	656	733	325	338	64	55	153	199	68	82	46	59
1806	665	765	325	332	53	63	109	138	132	174	46	58
1807	713	780	331	343	67	70	148	156	119	151	48	60
1809	758	870	360	391	56	67	158	191	130	155	54	66
1810	753	869	367	387	59	71	158	179	121	169	48	63
1811	734	834	362	393	56	46	158	191	105	136	53	68
SAN MATEO												
1781	1044	1209	272	336	129	178	463	498	0	0	180	197
1802	1102	1174	306	335	82	127	411	437	6	7	297	268
1803	1079	1139	277	329	124	123	367	384	30	34	281	269
1804	1080	1174	265	310	125	152	355	399	24	32	311	281
1805	1095	1191	293	341	126	139	355	407	25	27	296	277
1806	1093	1188	266	347	101	110	407	439	24	31	295	261

TABLE 1. PARISH POPULATION BY SEX AND RACE (CONTINUED)

YEAR	TOTAL		WHITE		INDIAN		PARDO		NEGRO		SLAVE	
	M	F	M	F	M	F	M	F	M	F	M	F
1808	1051	1073	288	326	127	98	326	360	39	42	271	247
1809	1143	1272	330	392	135	146	357	425	34	38	287	271
1811	1190	1318	347	381	123	141	392	480	31	29	297	287
1815	729	1157	242	412	67	93	257	419	24	35	139	198
1816	764	1109	246	385	76	105	284	394	24	34	134	191
1817	789	1126	242	378	89	113	290	414	26	35	142	186
1818	802	1128	249	368	95	116	281	413	30	38	147	193
1821	1010	1418	308	418	112	151	354	553	39	39	197	257
	SAN MIGUEL DE TRUJILLO											
1808	1216	1127	497	441	123	110	484	522	37	41	75	13
	SAN NICOLAS DE TOLENTINO											
1803	282	289	1	0	8	2	158	157	49	60	66	70
1808	310	387	24	27	33	26	131	209	24	38	98	87
1818	134	157	0	0	0	0	134	157	0	0	0	0
1820	191	251	12	8	0	0	121	158	0	0	58	85
1821	186	251	0	0	12	8	116	158	58	85	0	0
	SAN PEDRO											
1810	509	512	265	275	4	3	176	164	0	0	64	70
1811	586	565	285	283	18	20	220	182	0	0	63	80
1816	444	494	242	261	9	11	171	189	0	0	22	33
1817	410	459	226	250	10	9	155	171	0	0	19	29
	SAN RAFAEL DE CNOTO											
1779	305	293	133	122	135	138	26	24	6	7	5	2
1810	651	679	210	219	162	170	264	285	2	0	13	5
1811	628	645	169	174	168	161	274	307	2	0	15	3
1828	387	460	73	83	142	173	159	188	12	16	1	0
1829	393	434	72	76	131	157	173	183	13	17	4	1
	SAN RAFAEL DE ORITUCO											
1783	803	784	301	277	20	21	203	187	122	142	157	157
1802	473	498	109	82	0	0	273	312	0	0	91	104
1803	469	503	106	94	0	0	275	312	0	0	88	97
1804	511	549	131	124	0	0	305	334	0	0	75	91
1805	498	570	142	119	0	0	284	353	0	0	72	98
1806	567	619	143	132	0	0	343	394	0	0	81	93
1808	571	643	158	162	0	0	331	373	0	0	82	108
1809	514	570	153	169	19	29	264	289	18	13	60	70
1810	677	806	199	238	20	16	410	494	16	23	32	35
1811	625	939	199	238	20	16	316	410	44	213	46	62

TABLE 1. PARISH POPULATION BY SEX AND RACE (CONTINUED)

YEAR	TOTAL		WHITE		INDIAN		PARDO		NEGRO		SLAVE	
	M	F	M	F	M	F	M	F	M	F	M	F
SAN SEBASTIAN DE LOS REYES												
1783	1356	1551	325	397	307	315	607	663	28	29	89	147
1802	1460	1752	453	532	98	108	762	940	28	29	119	143
1803	1487	1823	469	535	99	172	770	947	31	28	118	141
1804	1512	1872	481	555	97	179	783	963	32	32	119	143
1805	1526	1861	477	550	92	183	802	961	37	32	118	135
1806	1513	1820	493	547	81	161	794	960	47	45	98	107
1809	1450	1638	445	530	104	98	742	839	49	48	110	123
1810	1484	1728	478	527	101	118	751	895	50	69	104	119
1811	1484	1761	477	537	100	118	748	906	52	71	107	129
SANARE												
1803	1528	1753	193	213	889	1053	264	295	159	171	23	21
1804	1550	1765	195	217	897	1054	268	301	164	172	26	21
1805	1528	1753	193	213	889	1053	264	295	159	171	23	21
1806	1573	1534	185	202	1009	909	226	244	116	138	37	41
1807	1560	1540	179	203	1005	899	215	256	116	138	45	44
1808	1550	1542	182	205	1012	915	209	254	102	124	45	44
1809	1555	1549	183	196	1012	915	229	275	92	124	39	39
1810	1560	1558	188	199	996	912	240	279	86	129	50	39
1812	1249	1302	173	198	777	787	222	238	56	57	21	22
1815	1069	1179	146	167	650	709	216	235	37	45	20	23
1816	1284	1380	169	195	836	867	228	251	39	55	12	12
1817	1341	1440	169	198	836	867	228	251	76	91	32	33
1818	1284	1380	169	195	836	867	228	251	39	55	12	12
1819	1062	1170	146	167	650	709	216	235	37	45	13	14
1820	1341	1437	169	195	836	867	228	251	76	91	32	33
SANTA CRUZ DE ARAGUA												
1802	2929	3135	1634	1757	38	26	1180	1270	33	34	44	48
1803	2615	3052	1277	1771	55	49	1218	1168	18	33	47	31
1804	3097	3041	1667	1700	47	30	1345	1269	7	10	31	32
1805	2717	2994	1482	1720	26	39	1177	1206	1	2	31	27
1808	2693	3024	1560	1751	33	28	1053	1167	10	30	37	48
1811	2265	1773	1409	898	17	22	570	815	231	19	38	19
1815	1884	2432	940	1299	856	1017	51	59	6	9	31	48
1816	2054	2521	1147	1451	30	48	807	951	29	24	41	47
1817	2011	2688	1155	1579	17	14	770	1000	26	28	43	67
1818	1679	2305	982	1331	8	25	560	744	86	153	43	52
1822	2140	2684	1020	1221	198	169	842	1187	36	65	44	42
SANTA INES DEL ALTAR												
1779	37	28	1	2	18	11	14	8	4	7	0	0
1802	51	53	12	7	9	9	24	30	4	4	2	3
1803	49	54	4	2	9	8	34	42	2	2	0	0
1804	51	53	1	0	16	14	30	37	3	1	1	1

TABLE 1. PARISH POPULATION BY SEX AND RACE (CONTINUED)

YEAR	TOTAL		WHITE		INDIAN		PARDO		NEGRO		SLAVE	
	M	F	M	F	M	F	M	F	M	F	M	F
1805	74	63	3	1	8	6	61	55	2	1	0	0
1806	58	63	4	1	6	9	46	53	1	0	1	0
1810	46	44	0	0	6	5	40	39	0	0	0	0
1811	38	48	0	0	7	8	31	40	0	0	0	0
1818	94	106	0	0	8	10	86	96	0	0	0	0
1819	142	197	9	10	32	36	72	97	29	54	0	0
1820	137	173	10	9	21	27	70	89	35	48	1	0
1829	169	189	7	9	45	47	116	133	0	0	1	0
SANTA LUCIA												
1784	1130	1067	173	135	266	262	143	144	142	148	406	378
1787	1105	1074	195	151	190	192	236	247	59	72	425	412
1802	1335	1543	341	306	141	166	387	548	36	42	430	481
1803	1406	1327	269	218	159	130	542	457	69	55	367	467
1804	1575	1525	326	305	131	152	400	425	120	123	598	520
1805	1401	1287	207	178	232	230	422	418	54	50	486	411
1808	1648	1733	389	318	190	202	455	496	76	145	538	572
1809	1662	1723	389	318	184	202	475	486	76	145	538	572
1811	1704	1816	383	368	160	188	506	566	54	57	601	637
1816	1449	1813	321	365	86	140	428	633	68	48	546	627
1817	1429	1518	486	472	11	10	761	666	21	110	150	260
1818	1381	1477	359	361	15	15	429	471	35	45	543	585
1819	1191	1508	214	256	104	130	359	523	93	121	421	478
SANTA MARIA DE IPIRE												
1783	556	483	170	158	47	48	191	162	32	25	116	90
1798	651	635	185	205	13	13	239	234	111	105	103	78
1803	664	683	176	203	16	17	258	269	97	116	117	78
SANTA ROSA DE LIMA												
1802	1218	1632	454	597	138	178	100	141	466	638	60	78
1803	1260	1759	463	589	151	321	111	142	475	629	60	78
1804	1218	1632	454	597	138	178	100	141	466	638	60	78
1805	1243	1610	464	601	142	169	105	137	471	619	61	84
1807	1272	1654	474	603	148	153	118	152	467	450	65	296
1808	1311	1582	484	612	150	161	143	160	469	353	65	296
1809	2021	2357	589	708	150	171	720	832	499	572	63	74
1810	2137	2426	698	704	160	168	717	907	498	572	64	75
1815	1906	2268	608	711	166	174	562	732	503	573	67	78
1816	2315	2334	621	743	167	188	806	743	655	582	66	78
1817	2158	2525	624	726	118	92	885	1000	449	596	82	111
1819	2086	2488	608	711	86	123	862	969	449	574	81	111
1820	2086	2488	608	711	86	123	862	969	449	574	81	111
SANTA TERESA DE JESUS												
1783	445	409	71	50	67	69	58	46	28	30	221	214
1786	396	418	48	55	71	73	58	63	9	8	210	219

TABLE 1. PARISH POPULATION BY SEX AND RACE (CONTINUED)

YEAR	TOTAL		WHITE		INDIAN		PARDO		NEGRO		SLAVE	
	M	F	M	F	M	F	M	F	M	F	M	F
1787	424	433	49	52	76	78	57	66	34	19	208	218
1788	440	437	49	52	91	72	52	70	32	21	216	222
1802	834	779	176	149	83	83	108	99	109	115	358	333
1803	910	889	208	187	107	98	104	105	110	130	381	369
1804	968	934	206	179	118	106	112	124	123	148	409	377
1805	892	850	193	159	119	111	103	118	119	144	358	318
1810	986	929	230	210	106	109	136	115	163	162	351	333
1811	939	873	223	182	103	96	116	109	144	158	353	328
1815	604	760	80	132	49	81	103	119	111	141	261	287
1816	605	747	116	145	50	83	86	97	89	116	264	306
1817	627	796	123	155	45	65	89	107	97	136	273	333
1820	681	816	156	183	37	38	79	91	99	165	310	339
SARARE												
1779	604	596	106	97	132	165	252	244	83	84	31	6
1802	1183	1327	137	211	187	123	537	625	313	358	9	10
1804	1252	1414	158	232	203	140	563	664	319	368	9	10
1805	1060	1163	170	205	156	151	651	715	67	68	16	24
1807	1169	1270	132	211	178	123	537	618	313	308	9	10
1808	1252	1414	158	232	203	140	563	664	319	368	9	10
1809	1252	1414	158	232	203	140	563	664	319	368	9	10
1810	1350	1509	172	248	209	155	593	680	360	402	16	24
1811	1252	1414	158	232	203	140	563	664	319	368	9	10
1817	1039	1284	203	254	230	248	588	759	8	8	10	15
1818	1233	1545	192	245	260	294	739	961	19	18	23	27
SIQUISIQUE												
1802	1926	2057	163	172	1309	1440	321	294	101	111	32	40
1803	1986	2108	178	184	1324	1450	336	309	116	126	32	39
1804	1580	1730	158	162	990	1155	311	284	85	87	36	42
1805	1596	1811	173	200	990	1180	307	299	88	91	38	41
1807	2166	1917	248	234	1396	1204	449	383	24	27	49	69
TACARIGUA DE MAMPORAL												
1784	316	357	29	32	13	6	16	24	58	44	200	251
1802	360	383	24	16	4	5	17	13	66	53	249	296
1803	337	359	23	15	3	4	14	6	65	54	232	280
1804	355	358	21	15	12	8	16	6	63	48	243	281
1805	292	307	23	13	2	2	19	25	37	34	211	233
1806	296	284	22	15	9	9	9	4	44	34	212	222
1807	280	282	25	16	7	6	14	15	40	28	194	217
1808	280	278	22	12	8	6	31	26	22	18	197	216
1809	261	283	16	11	6	7	36	28	23	18	180	219
1811	234	221	19	11	1	4	27	27	27	15	160	164
1816	240	279	19	17	4	3	43	64	44	49	130	146
1818	233	269	18	10	5	13	28	44	34	51	148	151
1820	285	285	26	12	10	13	40	54	48	60	161	146

TABLE 1. PARISH POPULATION BY SEX AND RACE (CONTINUED)

YEAR	TOTAL M	TOTAL F	WHITE M	WHITE F	INDIAN M	INDIAN F	PARDO M	PARDO F	NEGRO M	NEGRO F	SLAVE M	SLAVE F
TACATA												
1783	370	372	33	18	59	60	112	120	38	66	128	108
1799	569	524	66	49	137	125	175	148	13	16	178	186
1802	714	667	159	143	163	160	150	147	41	34	201	183
1804	716	709	84	62	266	287	162	146	20	24	184	190
1805	726	727	78	65	252	282	177	152	21	25	198	203
1812	747	710	207	187	122	113	236	216	17	17	165	177
1813	839	838	263	234	88	78	258	264	13	17	217	245
1817	609	648	185	172	108	108	200	216	8	11	108	141
1818	841	880	279	260	80	96	305	312	5	7	172	205
1819	871	876	279	230	110	126	319	331	2	5	161	184
1820	1111	1107	293	267	177	181	445	432	4	6	192	221
1821	937	926	310	287	153	151	254	231	10	17	210	240
1822	1011	1043	314	294	149	157	338	331	9	13	201	248
TAGUAI												
1802	988	927	388	364	78	64	339	345	32	19	151	135
1803	896	849	322	300	78	56	323	339	22	19	151	135
1804	844	996	307	362	72	109	116	166	179	208	170	151
1805	844	1024	307	369	72	115	116	170	179	211	170	159
1810	1024	1190	390	462	88	125	151	207	225	245	170	151
TAPIPA												
1803	312	276	24	22	11	20	28	16	2	2	247	216
1804	337	326	24	25	18	26	17	27	10	11	268	237
1805	320	320	29	20	18	24	23	23	13	14	237	239
1806	281	279	14	17	20	17	14	20	13	16	220	209
1807	270	269	14	14	16	11	15	23	10	14	215	207
1808	246	239	17	21	9	6	9	19	11	11	200	182
1811	221	205	21	23	13	8	9	11	9	13	169	150
1812	214	189	19	26	12	9	9	8	7	12	167	134
1816	158	208	10	18	14	26	14	18	9	13	111	133
1817	158	198	12	19	12	15	14	18	9	13	111	133
1818	187	222	19	20	23	30	14	19	15	19	116	134
1819	189	228	16	19	21	30	10	9	24	32	118	138
1820	156	208	9	18	13	26	14	18	9	13	111	133
1829	155	165	15	10	6	9	28	33	18	20	88	93
TARIA												
1803	125	137	4	1	0	0	119	134	0	0	2	2
1808	161	174	1	1	4	4	136	151	14	13	6	5
1810	113	127	2	2	0	0	110	125	0	0	1	0
TARMAS												
1802	260	253	24	20	19	14	62	57	13	13	142	149

TABLE 1. PARISH POPULATION BY SEX AND RACE (CONTINUED)

YEAR	TOTAL M	TOTAL F	WHITE M	WHITE F	INDIAN M	INDIAN F	PARDO M	PARDO F	NEGRO M	NEGRO F	SLAVE M	SLAVE F
1803	245	248	19	12	14	13	63	66	12	13	137	144
1805	235	232	22	19	18	12	58	68	4	4	133	129
1807	262	244	27	21	14	9	76	73	12	10	133	131
1808	249	237	21	22	13	8	76	69	10	9	129	129
1810	270	263	22	23	17	16	75	76	7	5	149	143
1811	276	262	20	23	18	13	81	78	8	5	149	143
1815	238	264	24	15	11	7	62	61	16	19	125	162
1816	243	284	30	16	9	5	66	85	13	16	125	162
1817	259	298	29	19	9	5	70	94	17	12	134	168
1818	274	269	26	21	15	14	74	82	10	6	149	146
1819	262	267	26	13	8	5	74	88	11	16	143	145
1820	244	260	21	11	9	4	63	80	13	12	138	153
1829	251	262	40	32	0	0	157	164	0	0	54	66
TEMERLA												
1802	246	298	7	15	0	0	238	282	0	0	1	1
1803	208	268	8	15	0	0	200	253	0	0	0	0
1804	210	269	6	9	0	0	204	260	0	0	0	0
1805	199	258	6	9	0	0	192	248	0	0	1	1
1806	208	262	6	9	0	0	201	252	0	0	1	1
1807	217	282	5	11	0	0	212	270	0	0	0	1
1808	208	262	6	9	0	0	201	252	0	0	1	1
1810	232	314	0	3	0	0	232	311	0	0	0	0
1817	300	363	15	13	0	0	284	350	0	0	1	0
1818	428	507	20	22	0	0	403	481	0	0	5	4
1819	327	389	15	15	0	0	311	374	0	0	1	0
1820	287	304	13	15	0	0	264	285	0	1	10	3
1821	299	323	13	15	0	0	276	305	0	0	10	3
TINACO												
1771	995	1058	522	579	48	49	345	354	12	7	68	69
1781	922	860	521	518	0	0	336	291	10	6	55	45
1787	873	925	487	543	27	18	303	314	6	5	50	45
1788	793	869	447	509	43	35	255	266	11	13	37	46
1790	749	1562	464	456	42	31	187	1008	14	15	42	52
1791	867	919	464	492	48	55	305	301	7	12	43	59
1794	1132	1162	593	592	47	39	418	451	7	15	67	65
1795	1108	1180	530	563	43	44	458	486	7	20	70	67
1796	1075	1171	519	569	45	40	447	486	8	13	56	63
1798	1110	1217	548	601	32	32	464	500	9	16	57	68
1799	1088	1188	546	573	38	31	426	489	20	23	58	72
1800	1074	1211	542	573	36	28	415	507	26	33	55	70
1801	1059	1199	536	572	34	26	421	506	17	24	51	71
1802	1081	1230	550	583	34	27	348	461	90	84	59	75
1803	1186	1332	574	594	36	27	401	535	98	88	77	88
1804	1203	1374	585	632	35	28	405	522	103	102	75	90
1805	1240	1387	610	639	32	33	430	526	92	96	76	93
1806	1280	1410	623	636	35	34	456	552	88	102	78	86
1807	1258	1437	600	639	34	34	473	576	77	104	74	84

TABLE 1. PARISH POPULATION BY SEX AND RACE (CONTINUED)

YEAR	TOTAL		WHITE		INDIAN		PARDO		NEGRO		SLAVE	
	M	F	M	F	M	F	M	F	M	F	M	F
1808	1204	1404	586	628	32	33	442	583	79	86	65	74
1811	1147	1344	501	536	30	46	485	609	75	89	56	64
1812	1187	1386	567	626	34	41	510	619	9	24	67	76
1816	928	1137	488	599	27	45	344	417	0	0	69	76
1817	838	1143	454	604	23	41	287	415	0	0	74	83
1819	889	1229	454	628	23	41	338	477	0	0	74	83
1820	1290	1223	615	637	52	61	542	427	0	0	81	98
1821	1423	1548	642	698	66	90	634	661	0	0	81	99
1822	1407	1577	644	733	67	80	598	670	9	13	89	81
1823	1631	1742	755	795	118	103	616	686	33	37	109	121
1824	1596	1710	746	786	105	96	609	675	33	37	103	116
1825	1631	1742	755	795	118	103	616	686	33	37	109	121
1826	1802	1804	811	778	110	86	736	760	36	44	109	136
1827	1803	1817	819	803	106	82	733	745	37	49	108	138
1829	1813	1824	830	797	100	79	739	766	34	41	110	141
1830	1685	1839	778	826	89	92	686	737	35	40	97	144
1831	1695	1832	778	844	85	95	692	733	39	42	101	118
1832	1737	1837	798	856	82	86	714	728	41	50	102	117
1834	2045	2111	982	1021	90	96	798	779	103	117	72	98
1835	2279	2307	1023	1134	92	106	966	844	123	119	75	104
1836	2640	3042	1288	1558	91	112	1052	1117	129	142	80	113
1837	3198	3164	1283	1370	126	144	1220	1344	467	188	102	118
TINAJAS												
1781	631	544	47	59	72	59	150	113	157	134	205	179
1801	447	473	43	48	3	1	314	332	15	10	72	82
1802	504	549	34	21	5	9	380	445	23	6	62	68
1803	536	602	56	43	13	15	385	477	10	7	72	60
1804	529	617	31	24	10	10	386	483	28	35	74	65
1805	491	560	34	26	15	8	350	446	26	23	66	57
1807	541	601	19	21	0	0	404	503	65	35	53	42
1808	605	488	20	13	0	0	532	426	0	0	53	49
1809	516	485	20	13	0	0	453	426	0	0	43	46
1810	619	579	21	15	0	0	555	521	0	0	43	43
1811	667	636	26	16	1	8	580	563	0	0	60	49
1813	603	654	44	36	1	1	475	541	32	41	51	35
1818	302	457	11	14	0	0	264	421	0	0	27	22
1819	329	464	9	13	0	0	269	395	26	35	25	21
1820	291	424	9	13	0	0	231	355	26	35	25	21
1821	459	654	19	17	0	0	331	503	26	35	83	99
TINAQUILLO												
1781	422	425	94	97	8	6	300	301	0	0	20	21
1787	558	575	124	130	18	26	406	408	3	1	7	10
1788	470	573	117	126	17	25	323	408	5	4	8	10
1790	508	543	123	145	21	22	343	353	9	3	12	20
1791	520	535	144	144	16	17	348	359	9	3	3	12
1792	574	567	156	143	16	19	387	387	8	4	7	14
1794	571	568	160	148	11	16	384	387	9	7	7	10

TABLE 1. PARISH POPULATION BY SEX AND RACE (CONTINUED)

YEAR	TOTAL M	TOTAL F	WHITE M	WHITE F	INDIAN M	INDIAN F	PARDO M	PARDO F	NEGRO M	NEGRO F	SLAVE M	SLAVE F
1795	571	568	160	148	11	16	384	387	9	7	7	10
1796	571	550	150	138	14	14	388	383	9	2	10	13
1798	579	598	151	151	16	14	396	410	7	6	9	17
1799	514	583	163	147	15	20	316	397	9	4	11	15
1800	515	565	147	143	10	17	336	386	9	4	13	15
1801	531	613	139	147	14	20	359	421	9	7	10	18
1802	541	590	156	147	12	17	359	404	6	6	8	16
1803	535	628	141	140	17	21	361	439	9	7	7	21
1804	596	635	193	171	15	22	369	414	8	8	11	20
1805	563	698	170	168	23	32	352	465	9	13	9	20
1806	582	567	162	175	14	18	395	351	6	6	5	17
1807	621	687	164	182	16	19	426	462	8	6	7	18
1808	628	693	166	185	16	19	429	465	8	6	7	18
1809	619	637	235	221	18	21	353	374	2	0	11	21
1811	670	643	289	257	18	17	356	350	4	6	3	13
1812	676	643	291	257	18	17	358	350	6	6	3	13
1815	666	742	208	217	13	17	441	497	1	1	3	10
1816	779	875	210	218	29	29	524	609	14	12	2	7
1817	672	806	214	223	8	11	440	561	4	1	6	10
1818	889	991	286	286	19	12	576	685	4	4	4	4
1820	1248	1371	347	344	38	36	817	943	18	17	28	31
1822	964	957	431	401	41	45	450	474	13	11	29	26
1823	1240	1512	520	641	50	67	589	706	0	0	81	98
1836	1609	1644	370	380	27	37	1187	1199	4	6	21	22
TOCUYITO												
1803	898	807	246	212	25	16	376	396	20	20	231	163
1804	907	836	242	216	25	16	387	411	20	20	233	173
1805	936	856	248	223	26	19	411	420	18	18	233	176
1812	1599	1696	293	251	7	12	753	891	9	14	537	528
1816	1264	984	165	132	21	24	587	441	41	31	450	356
TUCUPIDO												
1783	221	265	0	0	221	265	0	0	0	0	0	0
1801	926	901	180	161	354	339	288	314	10	12	94	75
1805	987	966	188	172	376	363	14	18	305	326	104	87
1809	1183	1200	216	195	412	430	418	467	11	15	126	93
TUCUPIDO DE GUANARE												
1802	2128	2126	529	477	300	300	811	739	290	420	198	190
1803	1634	1898	554	646	171	218	663	754	152	179	94	101
1804	1985	2251	811	943	159	211	826	851	98	155	91	91
1805	1985	2251	811	943	159	211	826	851	98	155	91	91
1807	2131	2357	898	1103	159	172	916	908	97	93	61	81
1808	1851	2257	691	824	193	255	841	1016	81	98	45	64
1809	2302	2655	811	1018	205	208	1103	1211	128	140	55	78
1810	2444	2848	966	1244	136	119	1194	1301	90	111	58	73
1817	1011	1526	391	611	81	110	450	694	54	71	35	40

TABLE 1. PARISH POPULATION BY SEX AND RACE (CONTINUED)

YEAR	TOTAL M	TOTAL F	WHITE M	WHITE F	INDIAN M	INDIAN F	PARDO M	PARDO F	NEGRO M	NEGRO F	SLAVE M	SLAVE F
TUCURAGUA												
1802	215	220	7	8	1	6	166	170	2	3	39	33
1803	199	226	8	19	0	0	154	171	2	3	35	33
1804	133	130	10	9	0	0	93	98	3	4	27	19
1805	200	209	9	6	0	0	156	170	4	2	31	31
1807	178	173	6	7	0	0	146	138	2	2	24	26
1808	184	222	8	8	0	0	146	182	6	6	24	26
1809	184	221	8	8	0	0	146	182	6	5	24	26
1812	133	160	2	3	0	0	106	130	0	0	25	27
1816	64	89	0	0	0	0	50	76	2	0	12	13
TUREN												
1778	192	226	22	33	113	129	53	58	3	6	1	0
1801	435	569	144	175	98	118	91	141	68	93	34	42
1808	1163	1359	425	498	202	242	511	575	12	19	13	25
1809	361	452	21	24	185	225	116	143	39	57	0	3
1810	1200	1264	413	446	176	214	572	557	24	25	15	22
1811	341	445	89	100	98	112	142	214	12	15	0	4
1812	349	421	93	114	108	121	142	172	5	3	1	11
1816	344	408	102	133	133	157	109	118	0	0	0	0
TURIAMO												
1802	80	101	4	0	0	0	7	12	3	2	66	87
1803	88	86	3	0	0	0	10	9	3	1	72	76
1804	90	114	3	0	0	0	17	16	1	1	69	97
1805	101	111	4	0	0	0	15	16	1	4	81	91
1808	110	129	3	0	0	0	22	17	6	12	79	100
1818	149	177	4	3	0	0	24	27	3	2	118	145
1819	129	135	6	2	0	0	32	39	7	7	84	87
TURMERO												
1781	3431	3487	1542	1433	656	730	969	1021	0	0	264	303
1802	3539	3990	1151	1273	676	739	1002	1129	133	172	577	677
1803	3630	4049	1198	1305	728	790	1026	1173	148	199	530	582
1804	3813	4252	1247	1365	755	833	1079	1228	174	219	558	607
1805	3746	4333	1149	1388	753	854	1084	1228	176	231	584	632
1806	3647	4261	1082	1362	763	886	1000	1128	181	215	621	670
1808	3411	4250	894	1195	715	946	906	1134	201	238	695	737
1809	3315	4044	861	1086	704	936	890	1078	180	214	680	730
1811	3500	4264	970	1154	758	1020	870	1087	190	222	712	781
URACHICHE												
1782	615	735	133	164	201	250	213	251	15	12	53	58
1788	606	739	97	104	195	229	258	356	0	0	56	50
1802	777	886	45	45	200	215	461	543	27	32	44	51

TABLE 1. PARISH POPULATION BY SEX AND RACE (CONTINUED)

YEAR	TOTAL M	TOTAL F	WHITE M	WHITE F	INDIAN M	INDIAN F	PARDO M	PARDO F	NEGRO M	NEGRO F	SLAVE M	SLAVE F
1803	837	905	50	52	204	225	483	541	42	38	58	49
1804	807	912	55	59	207	221	462	533	34	37	49	62
1805	827	982	50	31	223	316	482	547	19	23	53	65
1807	862	1003	54	69	224	220	491	603	36	47	57	64
1808	830	861	82	83	238	228	410	440	40	46	60	64
1809	1079	1196	139	121	232	250	627	735	28	34	53	56
1810	1071	1167	103	102	230	259	654	699	40	46	44	61
1811	1064	1205	92	106	224	271	663	723	40	44	45	61
1815	1071	1171	103	106	230	259	654	699	40	46	44	61
1816	1154	1329	104	144	215	288	778	841	17	15	40	41
1817	988	1111	84	105	212	245	611	695	49	36	32	30
1818	1042	1192	69	94	237	256	597	682	81	81	58	79
1819	1096	1361	86	98	255	294	616	762	80	128	59	79
URAMA												
1802	374	322	12	2	0	0	245	208	85	85	32	27
1804	352	348	12	8	0	0	243	235	68	68	29	37
1806	297	334	9	8	0	0	190	225	75	72	23	29
1807	310	342	14	8	0	0	211	234	63	72	22	28
1808	334	336	12	10	1	0	234	242	65	60	22	24
1810	373	384	11	6	2	2	274	287	65	64	21	25
1818	214	236	3	2	0	0	193	208	0	0	18	26
1819	217	261	1	0	0	0	193	236	0	0	23	25
1820	232	253	16	9	0	0	146	161	45	53	25	30
VALENCIA												
1782	3453	3784	1506	1552	105	100	1390	1606	21	19	431	507
1802	3347	4272	1206	1463	26	42	1591	2018	110	82	414	667
1803	2873	3885	1040	1126	32	54	1373	1896	87	157	341	652
1804	2607	3615	865	1126	32	50	1285	1756	91	131	334	552
1805	2825	3746	910	1203	100	155	1316	1673	143	178	356	537
1808	2828	3746	910	1203	100	155	1316	1673	143	178	359	537
1809	2942	4092	1114	1428	68	83	1220	1809	64	95	476	677
1812	3473	4272	1308	1328	80	95	1434	1954	70	101	581	794
1815	3461	4201	732	903	348	414	1748	2045	79	75	554	764
1816	3592	4367	770	930	366	439	1787	2108	96	105	573	785
1819	4149	4810	904	1045	389	467	2056	2350	115	144	685	804
VALLE DE LA PASCUA												
1804	771	739	259	235	57	49	290	264	0	0	165	191
1805	842	763	266	248	72	58	318	302	0	0	186	155
1806	845	804	225	215	68	70	357	356	0	0	195	163
1808	873	853	238	243	107	125	317	313	0	0	211	172
1809	1021	979	279	275	204	182	336	327	0	0	202	195
VILLA DE CURA												
1780	2218	2235	975	1112	37	48	961	820	69	57	176	198

TABLE 1. PARISH POPULATION BY SEX AND RACE (CONTINUED)

YEAR	TOTAL M	TOTAL F	WHITE M	WHITE F	INDIAN M	INDIAN F	PARDO M	PARDO F	NEGRO M	NEGRO F	SLAVE M	SLAVE F
1796	2567	1693	1870	1087	20	29	312	244	36	25	329	308
1802	2201	2324	966	991	75	76	752	815	67	106	341	336
1803	2079	2544	1045	1170	63	169	447	630	78	64	446	511
1804	2259	2239	1030	1144	255	264	569	488	67	58	338	285
1805	2348	2372	1064	1046	59	66	866	883	14	20	345	357
1806	2386	2501	1056	1054	62	71	904	1013	11	12	353	351
1807	2168	2355	839	906	64	71	917	973	16	20	332	385
1808	2224	2574	893	990	99	130	843	1015	65	91	324	348
1809	2005	2309	663	739	108	106	615	810	47	64	572	590
1811	2507	2852	845	932	95	140	1139	1295	57	77	371	408
1816	1635	1897	516	566	110	204	719	759	0	0	290	368
1817	1461	1953	834	967	89	140	375	621	0	0	163	225
1822	1910	2586	745	1163	91	99	758	954	0	0	316	370
	YARITAGUA											
1782	1336	1408	468	496	99	131	622	677	0	0	147	104
1802	765	1133	188	219	30	103	217	322	251	401	79	88
1803	873	1284	201	230	30	98	246	384	306	467	90	105
1804	880	1284	201	230	30	98	249	384	308	467	92	105
1805	1250	1672	280	358	33	110	306	377	459	633	172	194
1807	1880	2717	387	489	42	83	637	829	715	1140	99	176
1808	2243	3116	452	578	45	85	912	1051	743	1244	91	158
1809	2243	3116	452	578	45	85	912	1051	743	1244	91	158
1810	2243	3116	452	578	45	85	912	1051	743	1244	91	158
1811	2154	2970	443	575	42	76	878	1029	704	1154	87	136
1812	1930	2695	404	536	35	64	734	951	675	1015	82	129
1816	2724	2980	270	326	28	35	2320	2505	48	47	58	67
1817	2282	3126	481	546	55	85	1521	2181	125	171	100	143
1818	2516	3063	570	549	90	132	1673	2135	71	122	112	125
1820	2737	3038	650	804	80	103	1754	1806	138	189	115	136

TABLE 2. PARISH CHILD POPULATION BY SEX AND RACE

YEAR	TOTAL		WHITE		INDIAN		PARDO		NEGRO		SLAVE	
	M	F	M	F	M	F	M	F	M	F	M	F
ACARIGUA												
1778	157	181	0	0	157	181	0	0	0	0	0	0
1802	353	382	56	70	220	228	76	76	0	1	1	7
1803	543	516	62	70	396	362	79	77	2	2	4	5
1804	519	542	64	73	379	384	75	80	0	2	1	3
1805	545	549	70	71	389	395	82	82	0	0	4	1
1808	614	636	98	103	405	412	111	120	0	0	0	1
1809	608	623	99	100	400	401	109	122	0	0	0	0
1810	563	527	95	98	370	317	98	109	0	0	0	3
1812	557	527	98	97	359	317	100	109	0	2	0	2
1829	139	177	34	49	7	7	96	119	2	2	0	0
ACHAGUAS												
1780	29	24	0	2	26	21	2	1	0	0	1	0
1801	169	177	13	24	18	14	135	132	2	5	1	2
1804	174	189	28	24	18	10	88	112	24	25	16	18
1806	109	105	24	20	25	18	48	57	7	6	5	4
1809	205	210	34	38	55	34	82	96	10	12	24	30
1811	373	353	45	53	57	46	212	187	16	19	43	48
AGUA BLANCA												
1779	70	75	5	5	34	36	30	32	0	0	1	2
1801	84	89	12	12	39	27	33	50	0	0	0	0
1802	91	106	12	14	20	33	59	59	0	0	0	0
1803	91	106	12	14	20	33	59	59	0	0	0	0
1804	128	74	28	18	40	24	60	32	0	0	0	0
1805	109	110	7	8	52	50	50	52	0	0	0	0
1808	137	139	11	3	60	70	66	65	0	0	0	1
1812	139	120	10	5	60	43	67	71	2	1	0	0
1815	132	137	27	30	34	40	71	67	0	0	0	0
1830	134	132	36	30	32	46	66	56	0	0	0	0
AGUA CULEBRAS												
1781	276	263	31	21	32	33	180	186	3	1	30	22
1802	143	144	8	15	12	20	116	103	0	0	7	6
1803	145	126	8	8	12	18	118	100	0	0	7	0
1804	114	100	13	5	15	19	82	71	0	0	4	5
1805	133	180	14	8	6	20	110	146	0	0	3	6
1807	96	101	11	5	9	10	76	83	0	0	0	3
1808	124	115	10	5	11	7	99	99	1	1	3	3
1809	125	126	10	15	11	7	99	99	2	2	3	3
1811	124	112	9	5	12	7	99	98	1	1	3	1
1812	141	126	10	5	19	13	107	107	1	1	4	0
1815	114	110	4	2	8	5	101	102	0	0	1	1
1817	34	62	3	5	5	9	24	47	0	0	2	1
1818	82	65	1	1	6	7	74	55	0	0	1	2

TABLE 2. PARISH CHILD POPULATION (CONTINUED)

YEAR	TOTAL		WHITE		INDIAN		PARDO		NEGRO		SLAVE	
	M	F	M	F	M	F	M	F	M	F	M	F
1819	85	140	3	7	7	13	73	119	0	0	2	1
1820	130	140	5	7	0	0	106	106	9	13	10	14
1821	124	158	5	7	9	10	100	100	10	40	0	1
AGUACALIENTE												
1803	86	64	11	6	0	0	69	54	0	0	6	4
1804	88	95	17	9	0	0	64	80	0	0	7	6
1805	52	63	8	10	0	0	30	38	8	8	6	7
1806	81	66	9	10	0	0	62	50	0	0	10	6
1807	80	79	5	6	0	0	61	63	0	0	14	10
1818	77	95	0	0	0	0	70	82	0	0	7	13
1819	85	103	1	0	0	0	78	82	0	0	6	21
ALPARGATON												
1804	40	52	0	0	0	0	30	36	10	16	0	0
1805	33	30	0	0	0	0	24	21	9	9	0	0
1806	31	28	0	0	0	0	24	18	7	10	0	0
1807	40	37	0	0	0	0	24	18	16	19	0	0
1818	37	49	0	0	0	0	37	49	0	0	0	0
1819	31	32	0	0	0	0	31	32	0	0	0	0
1820	86	97	0	0	0	0	70	75	16	22	0	0
ALTAGRACIA DE ORITUCO												
1783	135	117	25	21	55	56	0	2	35	24	20	14
1802	239	227	76	73	81	82	53	51	1	1	28	20
1803	239	229	68	57	91	88	44	55	3	1	33	28
1804	249	256	62	63	39	94	53	63	7	4	88	32
1806	257	282	74	99	89	75	48	66	8	12	38	30
1807	280	270	82	103	92	78	54	41	10	14	42	34
1809	297	275	84	79	97	81	67	72	10	12	39	31
1810	297	277	85	77	94	83	69	75	14	12	35	30
1811	258	277	74	99	88	76	48	57	10	13	38	32
ALTAMIRA												
1783	47	55	0	0	47	55	0	0	0	0	0	0
ANTIMANO												
1811	79	53	8	2	10	6	6	3	5	1	50	41
1819	95	174	15	18	14	20	30	50	1	4	35	82
APARICION												
1802	320	368	60	67	99	111	96	117	50	55	15	18
1803	339	371	98	69	81	109	100	120	48	57	12	16
1804	667	556	196	150	133	125	317	262	0	0	21	19
1805	684	609	65	66	149	131	429	370	20	24	21	18

TABLE 2. PARISH CHILD POPULATION (CONTINUED)

YEAR	TOTAL		WHITE		INDIAN		PARDO		NEGRO		SLAVE	
	M	F	M	F	M	F	M	F	M	F	M	F
1808	587	574	140	93	148	146	282	317	0	0	17	18
1809	214	252	53	63	41	66	113	112	0	0	7	11
1810	654	592	142	127	145	153	349	292	0	0	18	20
1811	642	545	142	127	142	151	340	247	0	0	18	20
1812	413	425	140	96	73	82	189	244	0	0	11	3
APURITO												
1802	62	52	3	1	4	2	20	21	25	20	10	8
1806	14	17	4	5	3	4	5	7	0	0	2	1
1807	72	87	15	20	12	15	39	44	3	4	3	4
ARAGUITA												
1784	96	121	2	3	15	23	16	20	2	4	61	71
1802	106	95	0	2	9	6	2	6	2	1	93	80
1803	98	88	0	2	1	5	0	2	4	0	93	79
1804	101	116	3	4	2	3	2	3	8	8	86	98
1805	81	88	4	2	6	3	2	2	3	0	66	81
1807	83	104	2	3	0	0	3	3	0	4	78	94
1810	67	83	5	4	2	6	20	10	2	6	38	57
1811	44	41	5	3	3	9	14	5	2	3	20	21
1812	54	53	4	4	3	3	20	9	2	3	25	34
1816	56	64	8	8	2	3	6	10	6	4	34	39
1819	65	54	9	11	2	0	7	2	7	2	40	39
ARAURE												
1778	436	478	206	227	43	37	59	61	46	63	82	90
1798	1110	1047	378	331	206	180	482	491	44	45	0	0
1799	1183	1113	400	353	226	199	507	512	50	49	0	0
1800	1256	1128	430	360	246	200	521	515	59	53	0	0
1801	375	361	68	69	9	8	280	260	18	24	0	0
1802	496	459	148	172	24	24	278	231	14	12	32	20
1803	468	451	155	164	18	23	268	243	4	2	23	19
1804	434	415	166	174	21	23	213	181	4	4	30	33
1805	492	893	148	700	1	16	290	135	13	9	40	33
1808	479	442	138	138	64	48	241	217	0	2	36	37
1809	478	512	144	158	65	58	238	256	1	1	30	39
1810	484	520	144	158	65	58	238	266	1	1	36	37
1811	490	521	148	159	65	58	238	266	3	1	36	37
1812	486	531	150	159	60	59	230	270	6	4	40	39
1829	538	625	101	104	68	68	328	405	41	48	0	0
AREGUE												
1802	64	140	13	17	18	81	30	37	0	0	3	5
1803	138	156	11	13	90	100	34	41	0	0	3	2
1804	126	138	12	14	79	98	30	23	0	0	5	3
1805	114	109	21	18	66	56	23	30	0	0	4	5
1809	130	150	17	21	90	103	20	23	0	0	3	3

TABLE 2. PARISH CHILD POPULATION (CONTINUED)

YEAR	TOTAL		WHITE		INDIAN		PARDO		NEGRO		SLAVE	
	M	F	M	F	M	F	M	F	M	F	M	F
1815	109	141	24	30	44	64	34	39	0	0	7	8
ARENALES												
1802	138	127	19	15	15	7	60	58	20	25	24	22
1803	139	125	25	23	16	10	61	59	11	16	26	17
1804	139	124	17	18	13	11	72	59	12	16	25	20
1805	133	124	13	16	22	18	55	46	21	26	22	18
1807	140	119	10	9	17	17	70	62	13	14	30	17
1809	161	151	11	11	32	24	69	74	24	26	25	16
ARICHUNA												
1801	117	115	32	30	66	61	15	18	2	2	2	4
1804	169	179	22	28	110	119	18	15	10	11	9	6
AROA												
1802	389	105	11	14	36	19	300	50	24	12	18	10
1805	200	209	28	23	10	6	92	100	60	65	10	15
1307	206	230	23	20	14	16	100	115	59	70	10	9
1808	219	271	6	20	11	16	122	130	50	80	30	25
1809	154	144	27	16	6	10	100	88	11	16	10	14
1817	147	72	19	16	0	0	125	48	3	4	0	4
1818	180	147	36	29	28	23	77	53	39	42	0	0
ATAMAICA												
1780	28	22	1	2	26	20	0	0	1	0	0	0
1802	41	30	22	11	6	2	12	15	0	0	1	2
AYAMANES												
1802	69	68	6	11	63	57	0	0	0	0	0	0
1803	75	67	8	8	66	59	1	0	0	0	0	0
1804	88	73	7	1	77	71	4	1	0	0	0	0
1805	70	68	8	9	60	59	2	0	0	0	0	0
1807	103	115	17	19	79	93	7	3	0	0	0	0
1808	115	119	21	23	83	92	11	4	0	0	0	0
1815	98	111	17	16	70	82	11	13	0	0	0	0
BANCO LARGO												
1805	279	320	80	93	37	41	62	66	51	64	49	56
1809	184	225	35	39	21	30	109	128	4	8	15	20
BARBACOAS DE LOS LLANOS												
1782	188	203	83	77	22	32	24	32	45	44	14	18
1783	186	205	83	77	22	38	24	38	43	34	14	18
1802	516	477	165	145	93	93	213	188	19	23	26	28

TABLE 2. PARISH CHILD POPULATION (CONTINUED)

YEAR	TOTAL		WHITE		INDIAN		PARDO		NEGRO		SLAVE	
	M	F	M	F	M	F	M	F	M	F	M	F
1803	433	371	152	116	64	61	138	116	66	63	13	15
1804	510	469	177	156	70	54	55	61	171	168	37	30
1805	548	551	147	154	48	47	143	189	189	134	21	27
1809	555	547	192	186	102	111	136	141	98	87	27	22
1810	499	490	179	177	92	76	125	127	86	96	17	14
1811	491	491	187	180	80	70	129	130	80	93	15	18
BARBACOAS DEL TOCUYO												
1802	106	112	25	27	41	42	12	13	25	28	3	2
1803	75	91	12	20	36	44	8	12	14	12	5	3
1804	79	94	14	21	32	36	7	9	19	24	7	4
1805	78	106	11	15	36	49	12	21	13	16	6	5
1806	95	114	8	13	39	45	18	21	26	29	4	6
1807	96	116	9	15	38	46	19	23	27	28	3	4
1808	109	105	19	14	35	34	28	24	23	27	4	6
1809	127	116	22	18	40	36	36	27	24	28	5	7
1810	148	129	23	20	46	40	44	31	26	31	9	7
1812	120	94	44	20	30	32	41	38	5	4	0	0
1815	130	98	15	10	41	35	67	51	1	0	6	2
1816	109	96	17	11	41	36	46	47	2	1	3	1
1817	129	110	13	9	45	36	64	62	2	2	5	1
1818	115	87	9	8	38	27	60	48	1	0	7	4
1819	129	125	13	6	47	41	50	63	11	11	8	4
1820	143	122	17	12	45	35	69	66	5	5	7	4
BARQUISIMETO												
1779	1095	1012	46	56	192	124	450	409	307	330	100	93
1815	1533	1562	72	68	164	195	1171	1191	52	59	74	49
BARQUISIMETO, MITAD DE(1)												
1802	605	720	97	110	97	113	210	260	156	180	45	57
1803	610	722	99	113	98	115	215	261	153	179	45	54
1804	615	732	99	113	99	115	215	261	153	179	49	64
1805	579	702	97	115	79	107	205	255	152	163	46	62
1807	977	920	71	79	199	121	602	599	53	56	52	65
1808	905	1026	76	81	198	195	515	617	58	67	58	66
1809	969	1128	78	89	100	205	615	677	88	77	88	80
1810	977	920	71	79	199	121	602	599	53	56	52	65
1811	970	1140	91	90	112	206	617	677	70	77	80	90
1817	807	716	35	38	193	185	563	485	0	0	16	8
1818	664	583	9	5	199	184	424	369	20	15	12	10
1819	652	671	13	15	200	206	401	406	23	25	15	19
1820	598	623	10	11	154	177	408	409	14	13	12	13
BARQUISIMETO, MITAD DE(2)												
1802	835	668	85	59	38	31	608	464	44	38	60	76
1803	929	260	90	60	36	40	688	40	50	40	65	80

TABLE 2. PARISH CHILD POPULATION (CONTINUED)

YEAR	TOTAL		WHITE		INDIAN		PARDO		NEGRO		SLAVE	
	M	F	M	F	M	F	M	F	M	F	M	F
1804	879	267	96	53	38	48	618	40	58	46	69	80
1805	872	285	94	54	33	42	619	52	56	50	70	87
1807	876	266	98	53	39	44	612	43	58	46	69	80
1808	832	242	90	51	30	40	602	40	50	41	60	70
1809	930	296	104	72	70	50	80	46	606	48	70	80
1810	930	296	104	72	70	50	80	46	606	48	70	80
1811	990	887	146	100	74	60	89	88	604	559	77	80
1817	1047	1055	56	50	41	63	853	852	34	50	63	40
1818	1109	1199	76	92	58	72	861	899	48	78	66	58
1819	1126	1251	78	100	64	93	865	910	50	86	69	62
1820	1139	1224	84	98	63	76	872	906	50	82	70	62
BARUTA												
1802	256	285	118	109	87	118	21	19	6	2	24	37
1803	257	278	96	100	107	121	22	15	11	8	21	34
1804	265	270	96	91	108	114	21	18	8	13	32	34
1805	266	263	92	84	110	110	16	20	8	10	40	39
1811	260	242	100	95	106	87	11	15	6	7	37	38
1816	128	137	34	41	62	64	11	10	4	7	17	15
1817	182	211	66	77	75	78	12	21	3	5	26	30
1819	328	324	66	65	73	74	15	12	0	0	174	173
1820	242	265	108	87	71	103	31	38	4	4	28	33
BAUL												
1781	114	85	33	31	43	26	6	8	31	19	1	1
1802	328	290	110	96	56	41	100	100	52	50	10	3
1805	296	259	131	106	61	44	91	81	13	27	0	1
1811	415	447	180	190	70	76	105	116	0	0	60	65
1812	341	405	126	154	65	81	122	136	0	0	28	34
1815	287	275	103	85	47	59	105	88	6	4	26	39
1816	313	306	126	96	41	55	105	101	8	7	33	47
1817	402	402	199	186	51	58	117	120	13	10	22	28
1825	495	539	162	176	54	62	272	298	2	0	5	3
1829	246	285	59	65	6	8	137	154	28	39	16	19
BOBARE												
1779	34	33	0	0	34	33	0	0	0	0	0	0
1802	92	97	0	0	92	97	0	0	0	0	0	0
1803	92	97	0	0	92	97	0	0	0	0	0	0
1804	111	99	0	0	111	99	0	0	0	0	0	0
1805	111	55	0	0	111	55	0	0	0	0	0	0
1806	111	55	0	0	111	55	0	0	0	0	0	0
1808	102	86	0	0	102	86	0	0	0	0	0	0
1811	195	139	0	0	195	139	0	0	0	0	0	0
1820	90	88	0	0	88	84	2	4	0	0	0	0

TABLE 2. PARISH CHILD POPULATION (CONTINUED)

YEAR	TOTAL		WHITE		INDIAN		PARDO		NEGRO		SLAVE	
	M	F	M	F	M	F	M	F	M	F	M	F
BOCONO												
1778	356	346	161	172	42	45	146	126	0	2	7	1
1795	425	423	188	200	57	44	156	159	7	4	17	16
1796	382	381	176	185	51	41	138	144	6	5	11	6
1798	607	622	392	408	52	44	145	156	4	3	14	11
1799	397	410	174	188	52	43	155	166	4	3	12	10
1800	355	369	167	183	45	36	128	138	4	3	11	9
1802	398	404	64	63	92	95	232	237	6	3	4	6
1803	431	440	67	67	95	98	257	262	7	4	5	9
1804	369	440	76	68	24	97	258	261	6	5	5	9
1805	297	285	121	134	52	26	110	115	6	5	8	5
1806	316	399	82	84	28	39	190	261	10	6	6	9
1807	326	391	78	81	31	29	189	260	19	11	9	10
1808	221	205	69	75	28	26	98	90	18	8	8	6
1810	210	203	72	85	28	28	106	87	0	0	4	3
BORBURATA												
1803	114	101	2	1	3	1	30	32	43	38	36	29
1804	109	105	2	0	1	1	32	24	43	61	31	19
1805	99	113	2	1	0	1	21	24	47	64	29	23
1806	104	117	0	3	0	1	38	39	46	54	20	20
1807	111	128	1	2	0	1	38	47	50	57	22	21
1818	93	76	1	0	0	0	20	17	44	30	28	29
1819	117	99	3	2	0	0	28	19	53	41	33	37
BURERITO												
1802	146	153	0	0	1	0	99	117	37	31	9	5
1803	145	141	0	0	0	0	30	26	106	109	9	6
1804	116	97	0	0	4	6	82	51	20	30	10	10
1807	191	173	0	0	0	0	100	83	78	83	13	7
1809	209	236	0	0	0	0	100	120	96	107	13	9
BURIA												
1779	79	64	3	1	24	22	49	37	3	3	0	1
1802	129	105	0	0	18	13	102	87	7	5	2	0
1803	119	105	0	0	11	13	102	87	6	5	0	0
1804	127	99	0	3	23	7	102	88	0	0	2	1
1805	149	143	1	0	17	16	128	127	0	0	3	0
1807	172	159	5	1	20	17	144	141	0	0	3	0
1809	179	172	3	1	20	14	156	157	0	0	0	0
1810	195	178	4	2	20	14	171	162	0	0	0	0
1811	219	224	4	2	24	18	191	204	0	0	0	0
1817	106	121	5	7	19	23	77	84	5	7	0	0
1818	147	204	20	31	9	16	118	157	0	0	0	0
1819	161	195	8	7	22	22	75	101	54	64	2	1

TABLE 2. PARISH CHILD POPULATION (CONTINUED)

YEAR	TOTAL		WHITE		INDIAN		PARDO		NEGRO		SLAVE	
	M	F	M	F	M	F	M	F	M	F	M	F
CABRIA												
1802	40	18	0	0	0	0	40	18	0	0	0	0
1803	33	42	0	0	0	0	33	42	0	0	0	0
1808	26	20	0	0	0	0	26	20	0	0	0	0
CABRUTA												
1780	57	34	19	18	6	6	21	9	0	0	11	1
1806	21	14	1	0	19	14	1	0	0	0	0	0
1808	33	28	0	2	33	23	0	3	0	0	0	0
1810	81	73	10	6	61	49	10	18	0	0	0	0
CAGUA												
1781	763	762	303	308	44	43	388	377	0	0	28	34
1802	590	580	179	147	17	19	313	338	25	22	56	54
1803	580	582	147	139	20	15	345	367	5	2	63	59
1804	617	600	150	135	39	17	337	385	16	1	75	62
1805	591	555	156	132	13	12	332	337	14	15	76	59
1806	583	555	141	129	15	11	338	323	20	18	69	74
1808	520	508	134	117	18	14	309	314	6	6	53	57
1809	541	545	139	138	14	10	304	329	6	4	78	64
1811	492	419	100	117	6	5	300	225	4	4	82	68
1815	761	674	261	242	156	145	165	182	13	14	166	91
1816	855	725	281	252	176	148	195	200	23	20	180	105
1817	880	750	286	257	181	153	200	205	28	25	185	110
1818	846	747	280	257	170	153	190	202	21	25	185	110
CAICARA DEL ORINOCO												
1802	31	30	6	10	4	3	20	16	0	0	1	1
CALABOZO												
1780	466	374	177	147	10	5	175	154	19	13	85	55
1802	461	616	138	189	13	18	220	285	24	34	66	90
1803	497	608	150	182	17	23	231	280	28	37	71	86
1804	486	579	141	173	16	21	226	262	30	36	73	87
1805	517	603	157	180	22	25	231	264	37	42	70	92
1807	413	453	118	125	16	18	181	197	37	41	61	72
1808	443	505	110	125	12	13	237	259	25	30	59	78
1810	443	414	115	116	4	3	249	206	4	9	71	80
1812	388	385	122	102	6	3	211	196	1	4	48	80
1817	229	224	62	62	0	0	115	115	0	0	52	47
1818	184	222	61	79	0	0	91	94	0	0	32	49
1822	108	163	17	29	0	0	77	113	0	0	14	21

TABLE 2. PARISH CHILD POPULATION (CONTINUED)

YEAR	TOTAL		WHITE		INDIAN		PARDO		NEGRO		SLAVE	
	M	F	M	F	M	F	M	F	M	F	M	F
CAMAGUAN												
1780	89	73	9	4	61	50	3	6	3	4	13	9
1801	144	149	30	26	80	75	26	37	5	6	3	5
1802	140	147	39	26	62	66	31	43	4	6	4	6
1803	197	186	35	27	89	83	63	60	4	9	6	7
1804	196	188	40	29	84	87	64	64	1	4	7	4
1812	158	159	21	27	53	70	82	61	2	1	0	0
1817	70	79	10	12	30	25	15	28	6	8	9	6
CAMATAGUA												
1783	374	348	83	70	101	81	34	36	127	133	29	28
1802	383	581	62	97	184	296	37	54	42	61	58	73
1803	398	599	65	99	186	303	41	57	43	62	63	78
1804	453	569	65	73	120	160	80	119	110	132	78	85
1805	395	585	65	92	186	303	41	57	43	62	60	71
1806	395	585	65	92	186	303	41	57	43	62	60	71
1808	395	585	65	92	186	303	41	57	43	62	60	71
1811	173	255	11	13	38	60	116	168	0	0	8	14
CANOABO												
1781	138	159	10	12	0	0	97	106	0	0	31	41
1788	170	174	3	6	0	0	127	130	0	0	40	38
1802	164	140	5	5	0	0	137	117	0	0	22	18
1803	155	136	6	3	0	0	128	117	0	0	21	16
1804	164	134	9	9	0	0	131	110	0	0	24	15
1805	161	178	5	6	0	0	130	152	0	0	26	20
1806	170	168	12	19	0	0	124	120	5	7	29	22
1807	154	154	19	21	0	0	104	102	8	9	23	22
1808	161	181	18	23	0	0	107	100	10	30	26	28
1809	165	170	25	22	0	0	106	113	11	10	23	25
1810	128	142	7	8	0	0	102	109	2	3	17	22
1815	115	117	5	3	0	0	77	84	3	0	30	30
1817	167	188	14	21	2	3	110	111	7	11	34	42
1819	251	282	11	15	0	10	170	180	20	26	50	51
1820	255	285	12	15	0	10	172	182	21	27	50	51
CAPAYA												
1784	204	202	6	4	31	31	21	22	17	16	129	129
1802	138	160	1	0	40	30	22	32	1	2	74	96
1803	210	172	5	0	34	30	17	15	21	14	133	113
1804	162	130	6	1	36	20	22	18	9	10	89	81
1805	263	281	3	0	35	42	33	35	56	62	136	142
1806	283	211	3	0	16	16	18	14	58	61	188	120
1807	305	198	5	0	16	12	99	83	25	21	160	82
1808	305	198	5	0	16	12	99	83	25	21	160	82
1809	207	221	3	0	29	32	10	8	25	26	140	155

TABLE 2. PARISH CHILD POPULATION (CONTINUED)

YEAR	TOTAL		WHITE		INDIAN		PARDO		NEGRO		SLAVE	
	M	F	M	F	M	F	M	F	M	F	M	F
1811	120	135	4	2	9	21	30	32	10	14	67	66
1812	144	131	4	1	22	19	40	33	6	10	72	68
1817	104	121	1	2	10	13	39	37	1	8	53	61
1818	130	130	1	2	16	13	40	32	7	8	66	75
1819	110	149	3	2	10	14	39	53	7	5	51	75
1820	119	141	4	3	11	12	38	39	8	5	58	82
CARABALLEDA												
1802	159	123	26	18	28	20	36	20	0	0	69	65
1804	154	120	22	15	22	24	22	16	0	0	88	65
CARACAS-ALTAGRACIA												
1796	428	493	139	158	0	0	159	187	38	49	92	99
1802	547	410	164	107	2	5	258	186	36	47	87	65
1803	571	578	169	178	4	3	255	221	44	77	99	99
1804	548	683	180	176	7	12	236	316	47	67	78	112
1805	645	541	162	134	14	8	341	278	40	37	88	84
1807	519	634	161	140	12	3	242	361	26	39	78	91
1808	577	613	164	161	17	11	266	313	32	41	98	87
1810	531	690	173	169	13	7	187	342	51	53	107	119
1811	494	483	157	130	1	0	209	233	44	38	83	82
1815	180	174	60	80	12	8	66	53	21	18	21	15
1816	183	155	75	72	2	0	81	61	10	11	15	11
1817	170	186	73	64	2	1	70	85	13	19	12	17
1818	184	194	83	87	1	5	71	70	6	7	23	25
1819	212	221	99	103	7	8	83	85	6	5	17	20
1820	220	188	80	84	14	10	90	68	12	6	24	20
CARACAS-CANDELARIA												
1800	287	311	61	93	3	3	142	160	13	16	68	39
1802	328	352	118	132	5	2	123	137	13	25	69	56
1803	313	360	115	134	10	11	105	134	18	27	65	54
1804	293	329	108	130	3	5	112	125	14	24	56	45
1805	311	345	107	115	4	3	113	153	25	21	62	53
1806	322	378	113	125	6	10	116	167	22	25	65	51
1808	381	393	103	123	3	8	180	172	18	22	77	68
1809	415	391	133	134	11	2	190	180	14	15	67	60
1811	371	398	135	158	2	2	151	168	30	23	53	47
1815	249	255	84	83	3	4	99	104	29	30	34	34
1816	372	640	91	83	7	5	156	187	13	15	105	350
1817	283	329	66	88	7	6	113	142	52	49	45	44
1818	339	295	89	90	6	4	172	125	22	20	50	56
1819	351	308	75	80	3	4	188	148	29	32	56	44
1820	204	215	66	60	0	0	105	123	6	7	27	25
1821	342	317	87	81	1	0	176	159	26	28	52	49

TABLE 2. PARISH CHILD POPULATION (CONTINUED)

YEAR	TOTAL		WHITE		INDIAN		PARDO		NEGRO		SLAVE	
	M	F	M	F	M	F	M	F	M	F	M	F
CARACAS-CATEDRAL ORIENTE												
1801	324	382	92	126	1	1	105	127	14	11	112	117
1802	373	398	117	101	8	8	103	110	17	19	128	160
1803	336	305	110	105	1	3	82	69	8	14	135	114
1804	295	330	94	114	0	1	87	78	7	8	107	129
1805	312	377	117	128	2	2	87	99	5	11	101	137
1807	315	360	100	116	1	2	100	118	12	8	102	116
1809	361	392	125	131	1	2	113	134	15	13	107	112
1811	380	388	110	123	4	0	136	132	18	12	112	121
1815	193	204	74	69	0	2	68	64	3	4	48	65
1816	323	359	44	62	7	5	168	183	37	25	67	84
1817	226	219	81	73	3	4	76	74	13	13	53	55
1818	252	272	80	61	8	13	82	110	13	18	69	70
1819	264	234	87	82	4	3	93	83	11	5	69	61
CARACAS-CATEDRAL PONIENTE												
1802	274	278	88	76	6	3	87	98	14	11	79	90
1803	320	330	95	88	2	4	109	117	18	16	96	105
1805	307	302	97	83	5	9	87	92	13	12	105	106
1807	294	307	91	90	8	9	96	106	20	17	79	85
1808	325	333	91	102	6	7	117	100	18	16	93	108
1810	297	301	93	95	9	6	106	90	9	18	80	92
1811	341	315	108	93	6	7	114	100	17	29	96	86
1815	161	207	73	85	11	15	56	76	5	8	16	23
1816	495	391	89	77	1	5	165	143	92	73	148	93
1817	271	288	113	104	2	2	83	97	17	20	56	65
1818	273	279	125	116	4	2	69	77	14	13	61	71
1819	277	311	131	128	3	5	70	88	15	11	58	79
1822	207	259	96	99	64	83	1	8	9	12	37	57
CARACAS-CURATO CASTRENSE												
1803	43	57	29	41	0	0	6	2	0	2	8	12
1804	37	47	27	36	0	0	0	1	0	0	10	10
1805	54	55	44	45	1	0	2	2	0	0	7	8
1807	146	129	75	80	0	0	52	31	1	0	18	18
1809	102	108	70	74	1	0	18	24	1	2	12	8
1810	47	51	38	40	0	0	0	0	0	0	9	11
1811	74	55	47	29	0	0	9	7	1	1	17	18
CARACAS-SAN PABLO												
1799	333	514	138	167	1	4	92	220	21	27	81	96
1801	426	469	146	144	0	0	170	187	14	17	96	121
1802	671	698	218	183	13	18	237	339	62	30	141	128
1803	817	1205	266	408	5	4	315	606	2	2	229	185
1804	466	566	189	196	2	5	158	204	12	12	105	149
1805	578	580	262	290	0	5	185	150	66	70	65	65

TABLE 2. PARISH CHILD POPULATION (CONTINUED)

YEAR	TOTAL		WHITE		INDIAN		PARDO		NEGRO		SLAVE	
	M	F	M	F	M	F	M	F	M	F	M	F
1806	417	479	100	190	6	5	185	154	66	70	60	60
1807	451	615	100	190	6	5	185	250	100	70	60	100
1808	1060	563	500	250	10	10	500	264	40	25	10	14
1809	536	523	109	109	109	109	100	118	109	78	109	109
1810	880	1250	205	405	15	25	300	350	155	125	205	345
1811	1184	1310	250	250	44	100	400	450	260	140	230	370
1815	705	714	70	180	55	44	400	250	80	90	100	150
1816	692	632	254	263	2	8	200	213	79	38	157	110
1817	721	763	260	300	2	8	222	213	80	38	157	204
1818	714	840	260	300	2	8	212	200	180	268	60	64
1820	591	649	248	266	12	9	195	219	28	33	108	122

CARACAS-SANTA ROSALIA

YEAR	TOTAL M	TOTAL F	WHITE M	WHITE F	INDIAN M	INDIAN F	PARDO M	PARDO F	NEGRO M	NEGRO F	SLAVE M	SLAVE F
1795	391	353	151	140	0	0	194	148	0	0	46	65
1796	459	552	159	125	0	0	240	337	0	0	60	90
1798	463	437	194	151	0	0	189	182	0	0	80	104
1799	397	448	146	165	0	0	189	198	0	0	62	85
1802	463	515	163	171	12	4	190	203	16	16	82	121
1803	520	736	200	214	16	11	211	249	27	34	66	228
1804	724	621	216	199	17	5	384	215	19	28	88	174
1805	708	593	213	254	8	13	357	194	26	21	104	111
1806	556	562	194	176	7	13	224	257	34	29	97	87
1807	562	582	197	193	13	17	200	209	31	34	121	129
1808	582	588	198	193	10	14	206	209	40	42	128	130
1809	507	545	155	165	23	28	190	208	32	47	107	97
1810	468	535	142	154	12	6	199	229	22	28	93	118
1811	590	620	189	204	12	16	214	218	46	45	129	137
1815	266	260	97	103	1	7	101	99	19	14	48	37
1816	299	364	123	124	3	2	125	138	13	26	35	74
1817	490	641	189	172	2	0	165	306	90	58	44	105
1818	711	707	180	206	2	4	350	338	95	80	84	79
1819	537	510	203	170	5	4	127	161	133	119	69	56
1820	499	427	239	218	4	6	135	123	45	37	76	43
1822	388	411	184	193	6	3	143	150	21	24	34	41

CARAMACATE

YEAR	TOTAL M	TOTAL F	WHITE M	WHITE F	INDIAN M	INDIAN F	PARDO M	PARDO F	NEGRO M	NEGRO F	SLAVE M	SLAVE F
1779	44	35	4	4	35	22	5	9	0	0	0	0
1799	69	63	24	17	15	17	24	28	6	1	0	0
1801	73	63	20	12	11	16	34	32	8	3	0	0
1802	109	88	17	10	11	13	79	63	0	0	2	2
1803	89	94	22	20	19	12	48	60	0	0	0	2
1804	77	91	17	13	11	9	49	66	0	0	0	3
1805	92	96	20	16	12	10	60	70	0	0	0	0
1806	82	96	20	16	12	10	50	70	0	0	0	0
1807	124	118	9	11	20	23	91	82	4	2	0	0
1809	122	109	15	11	20	18	87	80	0	0	0	0
1811	96	82	7	11	17	10	72	61	0	0	0	0
1812	89	85	12	12	18	9	59	64	0	0	0	0
1817	69	52	6	6	10	6	53	40	0	0	0	0

TABLE 2. PARISH CHILD POPULATION (CONTINUED)

YEAR	TOTAL		WHITE		INDIAN		PARDO		NEGRO		SLAVE	
	M	F	M	F	M	F	M	F	M	F	M	F
1818	43	57	8	5	7	9	28	43	0	0	0	0
1819	52	69	8	6	12	6	32	57	0	0	0	0
1822	35	53	5	8	4	4	26	41	0	0	0	0
1823	34	47	4	5	3	2	27	40	0	0	0	0
1828	36	47	6	5	3	2	27	40	0	0	0	0
1829	47	64	4	6	6	12	37	46	0	0	0	0
1831	46	63	4	7	9	12	33	44	0	0	0	0
1832	46	63	4	7	9	12	33	44	0	0	0	0
1833	47	60	0	4	8	11	36	40	3	5	0	0
1834	52	66	5	6	8	11	34	42	5	7	0	0
1835	61	73	5	8	12	15	37	41	7	9	0	0
1836	67	79	5	8	15	16	39	45	8	10	0	0
1837	71	83	8	10	16	18	39	45	8	10	0	0
1838	80	96	8	10	24	28	40	46	8	12	0	0
CARAYACA												
1802	113	97	37	30	1	2	18	12	18	17	39	36
1804	95	79	18	10	12	12	17	11	17	14	31	32
1805	93	88	18	13	2	0	28	33	8	8	37	34
1807	93	88	18	13	2	0	28	33	8	8	37	34
1808	93	88	18	13	2	0	28	33	8	8	37	34
1809	93	88	18	13	2	0	28	33	8	8	37	34
1810	93	88	18	13	2	0	28	33	8	8	37	34
1811	94	85	18	13	2	0	28	31	8	7	38	34
1817	121	106	45	42	0	0	46	43	10	5	20	16
1818	112	110	43	38	1	2	39	40	4	6	25	24
1819	94	120	39	46	2	1	28	38	2	3	23	32
1820	129	126	46	53	3	1	35	42	5	4	40	26
1833	188	245	43	39	9	14	59	82	28	37	49	73
CARORA												
1802	568	576	27	36	6	2	424	451	37	32	74	55
1803	681	682	28	37	6	2	514	535	47	40	86	68
1804	731	744	36	50	6	4	556	584	43	44	90	62
1809	594	630	51	60	6	8	400	440	48	52	89	70
1815	895	795	36	30	1	0	795	726	14	11	49	28
CARUAO												
1811	30	82	0	0	0	0	14	14	0	1	16	67
1815	65	59	0	0	0	1	0	1	10	9	55	48
CASIGUA												
1780	345	380	101	106	3	5	118	133	57	65	66	71
CATA												
1803	35	50	0	0	0	0	0	0	19	19	16	31

TABLE 2. PARISH CHILD POPULATION (CONTINUED)

YEAR	TOTAL		WHITE		INDIAN		PARDO		NEGRO		SLAVE	
	M	F	M	F	M	F	M	F	M	F	M	F
1804	40	56	1	1	0	0	0	0	21	22	18	33
1805	39	58	1	2	0	0	7	9	13	14	18	33
CAUCAGUA												
1794	301	250	18	17	22	15	42	40	24	28	195	150
1802	282	267	7	11	15	27	35	28	28	23	197	178
1803	262	245	4	8	10	15	36	28	24	18	188	176
1804	250	271	5	9	12	18	29	34	26	31	178	179
1805	253	267	5	7	13	20	37	35	28	34	170	171
1806	250	271	1	6	13	18	39	40	30	31	167	176
1807	245	268	2	7	16	19	32	35	34	37	161	170
1808	258	154	2	6	10	8	13	15	10	9	223	116
1809	190	211	1	2	13	19	10	14	6	7	160	169
1811	152	204	6	4	15	11	33	36	2	4	96	149
1812	180	235	8	18	15	21	33	40	4	8	120	148
1816	176	180	13	12	10	11	26	35	7	4	120	118
1817	176	193	9	7	10	16	27	32	7	8	123	130
1818	148	177	7	5	8	23	23	24	4	3	106	122
1819	190	199	10	7	18	20	37	35	6	7	119	130
1820	221	216	10	18	24	20	48	47	5	4	134	127
CERRITO												
1779	432	435	93	96	40	46	288	278	0	0	11	15
CHABASQUEN												
1802	265	378	21	23	204	308	37	43	0	1	3	3
1803	269	385	22	25	203	312	38	44	1	1	5	3
1804	267	394	21	27	201	318	38	45	2	1	5	3
1805	274	394	25	29	204	316	37	43	3	2	5	4
1806	274	400	24	30	205	318	38	45	3	2	4	5
1808	269	364	20	18	208	311	39	35	0	0	2	0
1809	268	367	1	2	215	311	48	53	0	1	4	0
1812	176	152	8	10	115	118	50	20	3	2	0	2
1815	176	160	10	8	106	112	56	35	3	4	1	1
1816	201	169	15	8	120	110	60	38	6	8	0	5
1817	200	160	14	6	120	108	60	36	6	8	0	2
1818	200	160	14	6	120	108	60	36	6	8	0	2
1819	101	172	6	11	60	116	30	37	5	4	0	4
1820	205	302	31	48	123	195	47	59	2	0	2	0
1829	236	194	29	21	112	96	66	50	29	27	0	0
CHACAO												
1802	256	257	71	69	1	5	41	44	54	42	89	97
1803	265	242	66	74	6	5	62	47	41	30	90	86
1804	258	233	72	64	2	4	56	53	42	30	86	82
1805	238	226	63	63	2	2	64	57	33	27	76	77
1808	273	271	41	44	0	0	48	38	81	87	103	102

TABLE 2. PARISH CHILD POPULATION (CONTINUED)

YEAR	TOTAL		WHITE		INDIAN		PARDO		NEGRO		SLAVE	
	M	F	M	F	M	F	M	F	M	F	M	F
1811	242	224	53	42	2	0	51	52	32	32	104	98
1815	212	216	60	62	1	2	45	46	31	32	75	74
1818	278	297	90	112	0	0	140	130	12	15	36	40
1819	294	315	120	134	0	0	119	121	20	24	35	36
CHAGUARAMAL												
1783	277	282	81	76	25	18	124	144	15	10	32	34
1804	226	221	102	111	12	8	94	85	4	6	14	11
1805	293	379	62	81	8	15	118	145	19	29	86	109
CHAGUARAMAS												
1783	246	348	21	106	16	8	71	101	77	61	61	72
1802	380	308	69	55	23	12	180	168	13	7	95	66
1803	387	360	81	48	24	6	189	239	0	0	93	67
1804	376	384	83	52	26	8	192	241	0	0	75	83
1805	404	324	58	52	39	39	203	163	25	16	79	54
1808	415	357	100	86	16	28	179	149	29	38	91	56
1810	532	428	90	74	30	39	300	251	25	10	87	54
CHARALLAVE												
1783	102	88	12	11	62	51	24	24	3	0	1	2
1802	251	242	81	94	125	106	19	23	22	12	4	7
1803	252	227	78	72	126	105	23	27	20	18	5	5
1804	198	171	83	69	62	52	27	29	20	19	6	2
1805	209	217	76	84	79	74	32	34	14	19	8	6
1806	201	202	73	80	80	59	36	40	9	15	3	8
1807	224	192	87	76	92	66	30	36	9	10	6	4
1808	142	171	49	53	43	41	33	50	9	8	8	19
1810	301	256	135	108	82	98	56	35	19	3	9	12
1811	309	312	136	128	89	93	65	74	10	10	9	7
1815	261	276	111	113	91	94	39	46	11	10	9	13
1816	333	323	130	132	115	116	66	50	14	10	8	15
1817	321	313	106	112	128	123	71	58	9	9	7	11
CHIVACOA												
1782	282	316	6	9	153	165	111	129	9	13	3	0
1802	157	173	3	3	76	85	70	72	5	4	3	9
1803	199	203	4	1	80	92	3	4	106	103	6	3
1804	197	216	7	5	85	97	88	89	11	15	6	10
1805	192	188	5	3	105	78	71	92	4	10	7	5
1807	173	195	4	7	97	92	56	79	10	8	6	9
1808	237	240	4	10	112	92	109	115	7	14	5	9
1809	205	241	5	7	92	104	90	108	15	15	3	7
1810	225	258	5	7	89	117	105	110	21	17	5	7
1811	241	255	8	8	98	104	102	110	28	27	5	6
1812	193	259	6	7	63	116	103	105	26	27	1	4
1815	285	287	10	9	99	101	161	163	15	11	0	3

TABLE 2. PARISH CHILD POPULATION (CONTINUED)

YEAR	TOTAL		WHITE		INDIAN		PARDO		NEGRO		SLAVE	
	M	F	M	F	M	F	M	F	M	F	M	F
1816	250	267	11	10	77	122	112	104	48	30	2	1
1817	268	271	10	12	101	121	141	126	16	8	0	4
1818	255	299	32	39	92	114	103	123	26	17	2	6
1819	258	296	30	36	91	108	106	127	28	19	3	6
CHORONI												
1802	228	259	26	15	2	3	155	189	5	6	40	46
1803	222	208	20	18	2	3	154	136	5	7	41	44
1804	202	183	21	18	2	3	164	142	5	7	10	13
1805	282	222	19	18	2	2	201	140	3	2	57	60
1808	338	298	28	24	2	3	244	195	2	3	62	73
1809	316	267	42	25	2	2	200	171	4	5	68	64
1819	125	138	9	3	0	0	91	111	0	0	25	24
CHUAO												
1802	38	47	0	0	0	0	4	3	0	0	34	44
1803	41	52	0	0	0	0	4	3	0	0	37	49
1804	48	47	0	0	0	0	2	2	0	0	46	45
1805	48	42	0	0	0	0	5	3	0	0	43	39
1819	60	50	0	2	0	0	4	1	0	0	56	47
COCOROTE												
1781	310	254	30	19	157	134	82	68	26	17	15	16
1782	310	254	30	19	157	134	82	68	26	17	15	16
1788	266	249	22	21	112	117	82	69	33	24	17	18
1791	241	289	21	33	92	114	93	109	22	26	13	7
1794	288	290	41	34	96	102	113	108	26	38	12	8
1802	278	255	50	52	49	45	165	140	2	2	12	16
1803	281	319	36	41	68	69	163	194	6	5	8	10
1804	258	244	26	27	67	68	109	108	44	25	12	16
1805	251	222	20	17	81	78	113	94	27	15	10	18
1807	274	244	21	21	81	79	113	101	44	31	15	12
1808	245	224	26	27	76	68	83	84	51	36	9	9
1809	264	209	20	23	82	46	101	90	49	42	12	8
1811	223	225	22	23	36	38	126	123	38	34	1	7
1812	234	226	27	38	76	71	83	64	41	46	7	7
1817	193	394	6	12	80	105	70	210	36	64	1	3
1818	298	387	49	68	76	99	166	209	0	0	7	11
1820	193	394	6	12	80	105	70	210	36	64	1	3
1821	352	347	63	68	99	88	187	190	0	0	3	1
COJEDES												
1779	240	237	43	48	139	144	58	45	0	0	0	0
1799	300	276	97	96	91	72	74	78	12	10	26	20
1801	259	268	101	98	53	74	76	81	13	8	16	7
1802	327	304	103	82	91	86	105	112	1	1	27	23
1803	339	274	89	71	109	77	116	108	0	0	25	18

TABLE 2. PARISH CHILD POPULATION (CONTINUED)

YEAR	TOTAL		WHITE		INDIAN		PARDO		NEGRO		SLAVE	
	M	F	M	F	M	F	M	F	M	F	M	F
1804	339	286	69	73	116	79	128	114	0	0	26	20
1805	335	279	81	70	103	69	119	118	0	0	32	22
1806	314	322	65	77	87	93	130	128	0	0	32	24
1807	310	302	81	76	73	81	128	112	0	0	28	33
1808	427	270	93	73	113	68	122	111	0	0	99	18
1809	340	317	80	70	100	88	117	132	0	0	43	27
1811	183	202	23	26	69	84	72	69	0	0	19	23
1812	180	215	27	31	62	86	70	73	0	0	21	25
1816	188	221	28	31	64	87	73	76	0	0	23	27
1817	182	218	28	30	62	87	69	76	0	0	23	25
1818	198	238	26	36	72	85	74	89	0	0	26	28
1819	210	222	28	36	78	82	69	66	7	6	28	32
1820	195	228	33	39	58	67	79	88	6	5	19	29
1822	172	200	23	29	49	59	79	88	6	5	15	19
1823	155	182	20	26	46	57	76	85	6	5	7	9
1824	155	179	25	28	45	56	70	81	8	5	7	9
1829	164	181	27	31	53	60	78	85	6	5	0	0
1831	164	189	20	31	54	62	83	89	7	7	0	0
1833	163	189	22	30	50	65	86	88	5	6	0	0
1834	167	185	20	26	56	65	86	88	5	6	0	0
1835	188	204	24	28	62	69	91	99	11	8	0	0
1836	197	212	26	33	65	69	95	102	11	8	0	0
1837	205	223	28	34	66	72	98	107	13	10	0	0
1838	205	225	28	34	68	75	96	106	13	10	0	0
CUA												
1783	198	165	13	8	6	5	29	22	21	13	129	117
1803	394	386	32	22	35	32	108	79	38	31	181	222
1805	373	365	56	36	22	23	65	67	49	37	181	202
1810	437	415	60	42	38	53	106	85	31	35	202	200
1812	335	277	79	75	15	19	127	112	18	26	96	45
1815	340	303	30	24	20	22	102	93	18	14	170	150
1816	383	400	39	37	29	28	124	138	16	18	175	179
1818	381	324	88	84	23	22	143	136	24	31	103	51
1820	359	299	38	26	57	36	65	49	31	23	168	165
1821	519	599	30	38	15	20	180	216	8	15	286	310
CUBIRO												
1802	105	118	3	0	92	107	5	9	0	0	5	2
1803	96	120	0	4	92	109	1	2	0	0	3	5
1804	79	116	0	4	73	100	4	8	0	0	2	4
1805	89	113	0	0	83	101	2	9	2	1	2	2
1806	106	132	0	0	95	115	5	9	2	1	4	7
1807	115	134	0	0	103	117	6	9	2	1	4	7
1808	117	119	0	0	104	102	6	9	3	1	4	7
1809	131	129	0	0	118	112	6	9	3	1	4	7
1810	133	132	0	0	120	115	6	9	3	1	4	7
1815	113	118	0	0	101	104	8	5	3	1	1	8
1816	133	114	0	0	115	99	11	8	1	0	6	7

TABLE 2. PARISH CHILD POPULATION (CONTINUED)

YEAR	TOTAL		WHITE		INDIAN		PARDO		NEGRO		SLAVE	
	M	F	M	F	M	F	M	F	M	F	M	F
1817	139	125	0	0	119	103	11	12	2	3	7	7
1818	116	111	2	2	91	99	21	6	2	1	0	3
1819	116	111	2	2	91	99	21	6	2	1	0	3
1820	123	128	2	2	97	116	21	6	3	1	0	3
CUNAVICHE												
1780	41	44	0	0	41	44	0	0	0	0	0	0
CUPIRA												
1784	123	104	24	23	5	11	48	29	16	18	30	23
1802	81	67	11	16	2	5	30	23	29	19	9	4
1803	74	69	10	16	2	6	27	23	26	20	9	4
1804	80	65	7	13	3	7	31	23	30	17	9	5
1805	67	53	13	6	3	4	11	18	29	20	11	5
1807	65	57	4	6	5	5	15	17	32	19	9	10
1808	66	66	4	9	5	3	27	31	22	12	8	11
1809	66	60	2	4	4	4	31	25	23	13	6	14
1811	65	77	3	11	13	16	20	18	22	15	7	17
CURARIGUA												
1802	172	156	19	13	3	5	29	31	119	106	2	1
1803	142	159	21	26	3	4	28	32	87	95	3	2
1804	137	142	21	25	6	4	35	37	71	73	4	3
1805	176	187	22	27	5	7	12	19	134	129	3	5
1806	122	110	27	21	14	13	12	15	66	59	3	2
1807	121	111	26	22	15	12	13	16	65	58	2	3
1808	136	139	26	29	15	12	26	32	67	63	2	3
1809	150	148	28	29	19	10	29	39	71	65	3	5
1810	161	150	32	25	12	8	38	45	76	70	3	2
1816	216	227	17	22	0	0	189	195	5	5	5	5
1817	218	228	18	15	0	0	173	183	24	18	3	12
1818	206	200	18	16	0	0	163	164	22	11	3	9
1819	274	245	49	24	14	9	175	182	32	28	4	2
1820	276	257	44	32	13	6	189	179	24	36	6	4
CURIEPE												
1784	228	218	6	4	2	0	64	52	81	92	75	70
1803	184	152	3	4	5	3	86	47	29	31	61	67
1804	251	241	2	6	7	5	67	52	69	81	106	97
1805	239	253	4	7	2	2	48	53	98	102	87	89
1806	226	304	2	7	2	3	50	100	86	100	86	94
1807	256	244	2	4	2	6	75	47	90	100	87	87
1808	258	258	2	4	2	8	79	50	90	106	85	90
1811	248	261	8	5	10	8	70	68	100	140	60	40
1812	280	282	10	7	17	10	76	76	113	143	64	46
1816	226	207	1	6	1	0	65	58	72	59	87	84
1817	195	187	2	5	1	0	84	85	60	46	48	51

TABLE 2. PARISH CHILD POPULATION (CONTINUED)

YEAR	TOTAL		WHITE		INDIAN		PARDO		NEGRO		SLAVE	
	M	F	M	F	M	F	M	F	M	F	M	F
1818	194	187	8	3	3	0	77	76	41	41	65	67
1819	226	218	9	3	3	0	89	88	48	49	77	78
1820	251	222	9	5	3	0	95	86	64	51	80	80
CUYAGUA												
1802	76	67	0	0	4	4	12	19	17	8	43	36
1803	73	70	0	0	2	0	14	15	17	17	40	38
1804	72	70	0	0	0	0	16	13	14	21	42	36
1805	99	92	2	0	0	0	17	17	18	22	62	53
1808	85	56	3	3	2	0	6	12	24	22	50	19
1809	114	91	0	1	1	0	11	14	25	20	77	56
1815	43	32	6	4	2	4	15	6	0	0	20	18
DIVINA PASTORA DEL JOBAL												
1781	285	296	46	60	126	119	93	100	10	12	10	5
1798	476	488	107	102	75	75	173	174	113	132	8	5
1799	480	474	111	101	78	14	172	178	111	174	8	7
1801	339	366	38	45	121	133	180	188	0	0	0	0
1802	360	432	70	98	66	77	160	187	47	60	17	10
1803	367	436	72	99	68	76	163	188	48	62	16	11
1804	396	363	103	104	74	48	190	186	15	15	14	10
1805	441	397	125	130	46	40	208	149	48	70	14	8
1806	440	478	131	166	66	64	233	235	0	0	10	13
1807	372	380	108	116	53	40	186	214	0	3	25	7
1808	430	404	121	115	54	52	245	225	0	0	10	12
1809	441	397	125	130	46	40	208	149	48	70	14	8
1811	361	347	99	90	82	85	173	165	0	0	7	7
1815	425	406	39	37	108	89	220	205	54	61	4	14
1816	472	425	59	39	118	89	226	206	64	75	5	16
1817	499	479	40	37	108	89	293	278	54	62	4	13
1818	562	488	61	79	128	88	277	219	75	86	21	16
1819	582	501	109	72	60	64	408	348	0	2	5	15
1820	630	724	134	125	64	86	428	496	1	8	3	9
1822	276	409	46	82	114	128	109	176	0	0	7	23
1824	396	471	49	47	58	61	284	346	0	0	5	17
1825	419	533	53	82	61	66	300	368	0	0	5	17
1829	307	469	25	34	17	14	256	386	0	0	9	35
1830	303	443	25	34	17	14	256	386	5	9	0	0
1832	303	443	25	34	17	14	256	386	5	9	0	0
1833	326	463	25	38	17	19	266	380	18	26	0	0
1834	326	463	25	38	17	19	266	380	18	26	0	0
DUACA												
1779	60	82	13	8	27	62	16	9	1	1	3	2
1802	51	53	20	10	21	31	10	12	0	0	0	0
1803	40	66	0	0	22	40	18	26	0	0	0	0
1804	40	66	0	0	22	40	18	26	0	0	0	0
1805	55	90	8	13	22	40	25	37	0	0	0	0

TABLE 2. PARISH CHILD POPULATION (CONTINUED)

YEAR	TOTAL		WHITE		INDIAN		PARDO		NEGRO		SLAVE	
	M	F	M	F	M	F	M	F	M	F	M	F
1807	51	47	8	5	21	26	9	6	13	10	0	0
1808	86	104	19	16	47	66	20	20	0	1	0	1
1809	92	102	17	13	48	60	27	28	0	1	0	0
1810	104	102	29	13	48	60	27	28	0	1	0	0
1811	126	63	15	12	92	39	19	12	0	0	0	0
1815	72	78	2	2	27	40	43	36	0	0	0	0
1816	72	78	2	2	27	40	43	36	0	0	0	0
1818	131	92	30	38	48	26	47	20	6	8	0	0
EL CALVARIO												
1783	61	68	18	21	6	10	10	10	5	5	22	22
1802	164	165	53	52	8	8	44	38	19	25	40	42
1803	165	155	52	58	5	6	44	34	20	18	44	39
1804	180	185	60	68	11	13	44	40	22	20	43	44
1805	187	196	58	73	14	13	48	41	18	22	49	47
1808	214	193	66	75	15	11	54	37	18	20	61	50
1812	279	317	92	102	17	21	71	91	34	40	65	63
EL CONSEJO												
1781	259	224	94	58	0	0	50	32	0	0	115	134
1795	313	324	32	42	11	3	129	115	11	12	130	152
1796	323	290	36	38	1	0	128	126	3	2	155	124
1802	402	386	49	60	8	6	109	135	11	11	225	174
1803	486	394	52	64	8	6	190	138	11	12	225	174
1804	431	409	55	68	12	8	119	140	15	13	230	180
1805	439	414	61	64	11	10	119	142	16	18	232	180
1806	363	462	52	63	6	10	111	139	16	21	178	229
1807	412	396	51	62	10	8	111	137	13	13	227	176
1808	418	400	52	63	11	9	112	138	15	13	228	177
1809	377	361	44	55	3	1	104	130	6	6	220	169
1811	389	352	51	54	1	0	109	132	6	8	222	158
1817	363	375	94	95	26	30	125	127	0	0	118	123
1818	374	402	94	104	28	30	129	140	0	0	123	128
1833	291	314	94	95	26	30	83	96	0	0	88	93
EL GUAPO												
1784	63	66	11	8	11	11	30	28	0	7	11	12
1802	174	183	18	21	12	10	23	26	43	39	78	87
1803	190	186	23	19	18	21	44	39	22	26	83	81
1804	192	186	23	19	18	21	44	39	24	26	83	81
1805	239	241	33	35	20	22	46	49	47	49	93	86
1807	179	194	25	29	20	23	40	38	31	34	63	70
1808	177	191	23	27	20	23	40	37	31	34	63	70
1809	177	191	23	27	20	23	40	37	31	34	63	70
1811	217	214	31	27	9	16	40	39	42	33	95	99
1812	193	197	19	21	17	21	39	30	38	31	80	94
1820	143	160	22	32	17	26	50	50	2	6	52	46

TABLE 2. PARISH CHILD POPULATION (CONTINUED)

YEAR	TOTAL		WHITE		INDIAN		PARDO		NEGRO		SLAVE	
	M	F	M	F	M	F	M	F	M	F	M	F
EL HATILLO												
1802	134	125	79	65	4	6	21	14	12	16	18	24
1803	134	125	79	65	4	6	21	14	12	16	18	24
1804	156	140	78	59	5	6	32	27	17	25	24	23
1805	183	171	86	70	6	8	42	36	22	29	27	28
1806	193	198	91	90	11	10	26	21	30	31	35	46
1808	214	198	91	90	11	10	36	21	39	31	37	46
1815	246	241	110	107	0	0	71	53	0	0	65	81
1818	194	223	76	73	0	0	75	86	0	0	43	64
EL PAO												
1781	469	444	70	59	12	11	300	304	24	21	63	49
1791	560	590	62	64	37	36	382	412	70	71	9	7
1792	570	562	67	52	84	71	298	321	106	106	15	12
1794	617	600	67	68	61	49	316	317	159	155	14	11
1796	697	651	69	52	89	71	298	311	226	205	15	12
1798	829	698	72	95	89	71	292	230	274	271	102	31
1801	837	793	120	126	31	34	592	532	71	78	23	23
1802	606	709	34	40	7	9	456	530	71	89	38	41
1803	778	604	120	126	8	13	554	375	54	68	42	22
1804	745	777	117	130	7	9	541	546	45	68	35	24
1805	855	858	117	130	7	9	631	627	65	68	35	24
1808	963	842	109	110	9	12	752	622	68	75	25	23
1809	831	866	85	95	83	87	565	587	54	57	44	40
1811	802	800	86	96	39	37	543	537	85	63	49	67
1812	644	630	84	85	35	32	422	430	76	61	27	22
1815	1032	969	160	130	3	11	834	804	17	11	18	13
1816	1122	1071	182	164	8	14	886	862	28	16	18	15
1817	1004	946	187	190	2	5	753	702	14	14	48	35
1818	840	806	125	122	16	27	652	615	20	17	27	25
1819	848	701	110	28	24	28	657	613	25	6	32	26
1821	664	906	130	120	4	6	460	700	36	50	34	30
1823	1088	1144	160	178	8	6	854	874	45	56	21	30
1824	1040	1173	140	202	7	4	832	884	41	50	20	33
1825	848	844	127	140	7	3	637	627	54	60	23	14
1826	841	863	130	141	6	4	625	641	54	63	26	14
1827	646	789	96	112	8	6	495	611	21	29	26	31
1829	995	1260	16	20	11	13	900	1138	50	67	18	22
1835	1000	936	43	40	0	0	924	864	33	32	0	0
1836	1048	1013	51	52	0	0	956	921	41	40	0	0
1837	1134	1139	55	58	0	0	1069	1070	10	11	0	0
1838	1181	1195	61	65	0	0	1106	1114	14	16	0	0
EL RASTRO												
1807	159	143	81	61	2	3	50	52	5	6	21	21
1810	207	202	104	80	6	4	67	88	4	7	26	23
1811	234	213	121	104	6	5	73	70	8	9	26	25

TABLE 2. PARISH CHILD POPULATION (CONTINUED)

YEAR	TOTAL		WHITE		INDIAN		PARDO		NEGRO		SLAVE	
	M	F	M	F	M	F	M	F	M	F	M	F
1812	197	182	92	83	2	5	72	64	0	0	31	30
1817	146	143	51	52	3	4	58	61	3	2	31	24
1822	158	164	65	72	19	25	69	52	1	1	4	14
EL SOMBRERO												
1781	403	376	102	79	1	0	270	283	0	0	30	14
1783	436	363	138	87	3	1	0	0	264	240	31	35
1802	506	453	119	117	16	13	272	230	62	53	37	40
1803	521	507	118	127	15	15	288	260	59	60	41	45
1804	485	485	111	103	16	11	264	270	50	60	44	41
1805	523	483	129	116	12	7	284	275	55	42	43	43
1809	788	703	181	137	24	21	443	386	92	101	48	58
1810	812	728	186	142	29	26	447	391	97	106	53	63
1811	812	728	186	142	29	26	447	391	97	106	53	63
EL TOCUYO												
1802	1351	1439	181	220	65	55	723	773	152	160	230	231
1803	1423	1519	194	236	74	49	740	820	174	176	241	238
1804	1168	1187	134	137	21	23	639	634	194	218	180	175
1805	1403	1470	200	229	70	61	746	791	159	178	228	211
1806	1363	1533	209	217	71	79	707	794	153	201	223	242
1807	1210	1225	146	129	16	21	668	694	194	218	186	163
1808	1220	1246	155	130	22	27	659	700	199	211	185	178
1809	1228	1249	139	141	23	20	686	699	201	215	179	174
1810	1224	1262	158	139	19	24	664	714	210	200	173	185
1812	1237	1259	144	146	19	26	700	692	211	217	163	178
1815	1637	1737	215	269	23	24	1105	1139	87	87	207	218
1816	1771	1882	251	295	26	28	1142	1187	111	126	241	246
1817	1936	2085	283	326	36	46	1243	1287	113	148	261	278
1818	1197	1206	139	148	20	21	682	664	202	213	154	160
1819	1090	1163	140	139	14	11	794	892	2	2	140	119
1820	1596	1704	199	270	4	4	1249	1269	8	2	136	159
EL VALLE												
1798	161	191	39	45	45	67	35	35	19	15	23	29
1802	136	116	44	32	18	26	28	21	17	12	29	25
1803	157	132	52	32	26	30	30	28	19	14	30	28
1804	173	150	56	42	28	32	35	29	21	18	33	29
1805	212	150	62	41	38	33	36	29	37	14	39	33
1809	234	182	70	53	44	37	40	35	39	23	41	34
1815	174	186	62	61	13	19	39	35	23	22	37	49
1816	236	222	84	79	23	21	52	37	34	27	43	58
1817	307	244	97	83	39	29	79	43	34	27	58	62
1818	181	185	71	78	20	18	49	46	13	20	28	23
1819	191	208	75	86	15	24	48	48	14	19	39	31
1820	221	236	87	93	19	31	56	57	17	22	42	33

TABLE 2. PARISH CHILD POPULATION (CONTINUED)

YEAR	TOTAL		WHITE		INDIAN		PARDO		NEGRO		SLAVE	
	M	F	M	F	M	F	M	F	M	F	M	F
ESPINO												
1804	51	59	14	14	2	2	24	30	3	4	8	9
1807	118	165	20	48	18	50	49	41	1	1	30	25
GUACARA												
1781	477	419	119	139	102	74	141	117	3	4	112	85
1802	901	702	272	204	211	174	365	281	3	2	50	41
1803	984	772	290	232	239	173	393	320	7	4	55	43
1804	1032	911	288	276	198	189	486	380	12	9	48	57
1805	762	728	227	213	205	143	236	325	12	2	82	45
1808	738	628	221	152	117	90	359	332	9	16	32	38
1816	958	925	245	214	140	136	533	532	6	5	34	38
GUADARRAMA												
1820	286	278	70	72	15	12	43	42	157	151	1	1
GUAIGUAZA												
1803	101	72	2	2	0	0	30	22	29	18	40	30
1804	79	79	1	5	0	0	39	46	12	7	27	21
1805	79	78	1	4	0	0	39	46	12	7	27	21
1806	72	68	2	3	0	0	23	34	16	7	31	24
1807	88	79	2	2	0	0	40	35	6	7	40	35
1818	50	66	0	0	0	0	0	0	0	0	50	66
1819	72	83	0	1	0	0	16	15	0	0	56	67
GUAMA												
1781	338	323	66	44	114	88	110	131	35	35	13	25
1794	350	456	38	40	108	180	170	186	20	34	14	16
1803	455	519	12	18	103	139	286	324	14	10	40	28
1804	479	479	15	12	115	133	324	300	6	3	19	31
1805	483	434	28	14	120	91	292	280	13	14	30	35
1807	577	465	33	27	141	98	343	294	33	25	27	21
1808	522	471	45	38	132	108	290	281	35	25	20	19
1809	499	443	40	41	124	100	280	260	39	27	16	15
1810	413	425	26	22	111	96	244	276	22	18	10	13
1811	472	480	31	32	129	113	279	305	26	20	7	10
1812	432	441	25	23	120	101	251	285	24	19	12	13
1817	391	498	30	34	84	81	243	352	24	18	10	13
1818	339	372	30	26	85	81	218	253	2	11	4	1
1819	280	249	40	38	82	58	96	88	53	46	9	19
1820	534	567	45	48	50	61	390	396	40	47	9	15
GUANARE												
1788	1235	1050	543	490	48	55	510	375	40	33	94	97

TABLE 2. PARISH CHILD POPULATION (CONTINUED)

YEAR	TOTAL		WHITE		INDIAN		PARDO		NEGRO		SLAVE	
	M	F	M	F	M	F	M	F	M	F	M	F
1791	1076	1108	343	345	17	21	540	600	32	20	144	122
1792	1337	791	568	150	50	39	550	440	35	40	134	122
1802	2320	1745	784	563	137	118	1235	941	26	11	138	112
1803	1826	1486	686	533	104	81	875	722	28	34	133	116
1804	1510	1264	588	416	94	78	734	682	10	9	84	79
1807	1724	1573	643	544	90	99	847	782	42	40	102	108
1808	1832	1717	652	583	137	144	895	841	23	27	125	122
1809	1783	1792	724	803	76	90	836	757	28	18	119	124
1810	986	991	298	370	139	116	383	346	33	43	133	116
1811	783	893	233	261	120	112	231	290	44	50	155	180
1817	965	925	325	321	32	37	533	498	28	18	47	51
GUANARE VIEJO												
1778	94	76	20	31	28	4	44	40	0	0	2	1
1782	145	160	36	43	53	56	55	59	0	0	1	2
1801	196	177	95	67	55	48	42	58	0	0	4	4
1802	201	165	97	65	54	47	47	51	0	0	3	2
1803	284	257	98	79	71	57	110	116	1	0	4	5
1804	352	272	113	128	22	37	214	102	0	0	3	5
1805	234	197	87	67	76	77	71	53	0	0	0	0
1806	276	283	115	124	31	36	128	122	0	0	2	1
1807	259	267	105	91	52	80	99	94	0	0	3	2
1808	488	596	189	198	100	197	196	199	0	0	3	2
1811	251	273	99	87	44	73	106	112	0	0	2	1
1813	281	258	95	82	99	87	84	88	0	0	3	1
GUANARITO												
1778	163	146	35	32	51	41	76	70	0	0	1	3
1801	236	299	55	74	75	91	59	77	29	35	18	22
1802	252	233	103	98	36	32	82	77	14	12	17	14
1803	499	521	205	239	37	41	193	172	33	42	31	27
1804	377	425	161	152	32	43	168	211	0	0	16	19
1805	247	285	62	75	18	25	81	77	67	81	19	27
1807	749	790	205	190	63	76	457	498	3	1	21	25
1808	699	779	295	300	22	40	364	409	8	16	10	14
1810	709	796	299	306	22	40	368	419	8	16	12	15
1811	761	855	317	330	35	49	377	442	12	17	20	17
GUARDATINAJAS												
1780	77	74	14	8	34	37	20	18	9	11	0	0
1804	398	370	103	77	41	60	92	94	126	107	36	32
1805	395	367	105	76	33	59	94	98	124	99	39	35
1807	379	382	87	66	45	52	77	102	143	140	27	22
1808	417	400	86	68	44	51	84	106	170	141	33	34
1809	412	390	99	85	33	46	87	95	167	128	26	36
1810	401	366	97	77	39	54	214	184	16	9	35	42
1811	435	397	93	82	63	45	220	208	23	16	36	46
1812	448	457	99	90	56	58	228	234	26	27	39	48

TABLE 2. PARISH CHILD POPULATION (CONTINUED)

YEAR	TOTAL		WHITE		INDIAN		PARDO		NEGRO		SLAVE	
	M	F	M	F	M	F	M	F	M	F	M	F
1816	379	364	59	74	62	45	212	208	4	6	42	31
GUARENAS												
1784	205	205	71	71	45	46	38	37	23	23	28	28
1802	353	355	120	104	41	71	28	22	85	71	79	87
1803	373	373	125	110	48	74	30	26	90	75	80	88
1804	339	397	119	116	33	58	13	26	93	98	81	99
1805	350	403	122	118	35	60	15	28	94	99	84	98
1808	207	226	73	65	19	35	26	25	34	43	55	58
1809	317	321	117	99	21	42	48	53	50	52	81	75
1811	389	348	104	81	32	44	118	94	44	36	91	93
1816	305	301	90	86	23	18	101	120	9	1	82	76
GUARICO												
1803	338	297	42	24	142	130	119	112	24	22	11	9
1804	302	302	40	35	112	114	110	113	26	26	14	14
1805	354	330	30	26	154	138	155	153	5	5	10	8
1806	367	362	32	49	158	140	161	157	5	6	11	10
1807	370	366	26	29	166	178	159	146	4	2	15	11
1808	370	360	26	25	166	176	159	146	4	2	15	11
1809	393	391	31	32	177	190	163	149	8	5	14	15
1810	444	449	51	38	182	203	163	149	26	30	22	29
1812	429	416	49	33	145	159	169	152	34	37	32	35
1815	386	401	16	16	123	143	222	210	12	16	13	16
1816	398	422	17	19	127	148	229	220	12	16	13	19
1817	406	443	17	20	133	158	231	230	12	16	13	19
1818	402	443	17	29	127	153	229	230	16	12	13	19
1819	401	504	17	29	120	158	239	280	12	16	13	21
1820	464	543	22	30	136	166	256	291	31	28	19	28
GUASGUAS												
1802	738	634	282	244	147	113	302	269	0	0	7	8
1803	718	533	272	149	140	119	297	258	0	0	9	7
1804	634	543	254	218	118	95	252	222	0	0	10	8
1805	628	527	247	219	130	88	242	213	0	0	9	7
1806	677	585	288	247	143	105	239	225	0	0	7	8
1807	703	603	290	258	143	112	262	225	0	0	8	8
1808	725	645	296	270	149	115	273	254	0	0	7	6
1809	783	699	304	278	172	124	299	293	0	0	8	4
1810	716	695	271	277	174	147	231	223	32	38	8	10
GUATIRE												
1784	236	201	33	18	1	0	45	47	25	33	132	103
1802	273	251	27	31	1	3	71	50	33	37	141	130
1803	265	252	22	21	3	3	55	47	48	45	137	136
1805	242	252	19	21	2	2	47	56	45	41	129	132
1807	194	202	14	12	0	0	63	77	8	2	109	111

TABLE 2. PARISH CHILD POPULATION (CONTINUED)

YEAR	TOTAL		WHITE		INDIAN		PARDO		NEGRO		SLAVE	
	M	F	M	F	M	F	M	F	M	F	M	F
1809	194	202	14	12	0	0	63	77	8	2	109	111
1811	284	263	20	24	4	2	71	77	24	24	165	136
1815	279	265	19	23	2	3	72	75	25	26	161	138
1816	291	232	32	29	5	2	79	96	27	32	148	73
1817	402	352	34	25	8	6	165	153	4	2	191	166
GUAYABAL												
1804	282	331	31	46	18	22	136	154	49	55	48	54
1817	245	211	95	72	21	20	109	96	12	16	8	7
GUIGUE												
1781	407	435	113	120	30	38	124	131	74	72	66	74
1802	533	587	103	107	16	20	316	342	17	20	81	98
1803	547	576	108	112	22	21	318	340	15	11	84	92
1804	553	590	104	114	24	25	320	339	15	13	90	99
1805	567	590	107	112	28	27	324	339	13	13	95	99
1808	591	614	115	125	23	27	340	338	13	26	100	98
1809	616	643	128	132	25	30	342	336	15	36	106	109
1817	499	535	26	36	28	38	285	303	56	76	104	82
GUIRIPA												
1802	182	169	85	90	15	12	65	59	0	0	17	8
1803	182	180	86	104	12	9	67	59	1	0	16	8
1804	170	155	80	67	15	8	63	67	0	0	12	13
1805	176	161	81	67	16	8	67	69	0	0	12	17
1806	129	146	54	57	15	19	46	52	1	3	13	15
1807	137	147	29	44	49	46	51	41	1	2	7	14
1808	150	160	32	38	44	52	61	53	3	2	10	15
1809	160	173	29	35	48	44	72	72	3	2	8	20
1811	143	162	58	65	11	7	63	70	0	0	11	20
HUMOCARO ALTO												
1802	443	394	15	11	370	337	47	41	0	0	11	5
1803	477	411	18	12	395	350	50	43	0	0	14	6
1804	578	444	24	20	490	370	57	47	0	0	7	7
1805	447	360	25	20	354	280	60	51	0	0	8	9
1806	396	487	23	26	307	402	59	50	0	0	7	9
1807	346	441	23	26	257	360	59	49	0	0	7	6
1808	356	448	20	24	270	368	59	50	0	0	7	6
1809	356	472	25	28	272	375	53	61	0	0	6	8
1810	363	302	27	29	278	210	55	61	0	0	3	2
1815	155	186	12	13	117	144	21	26	0	0	5	3
1816	251	201	12	11	213	169	19	15	1	2	6	4
1817	268	235	13	12	228	194	20	23	1	2	6	4
1818	218	238	13	14	175	194	23	26	0	0	7	4
1819	191	224	13	16	145	173	26	29	0	0	7	6
1820	142	228	8	14	90	141	37	64	4	2	3	7

TABLE 2. PARISH CHILD POPULATION (CONTINUED)

YEAR	TOTAL		WHITE		INDIAN		PARDO		NEGRO		SLAVE	
	M	F	M	F	M	F	M	F	M	F	M	F
HUMOCARO BAJO												
1803	227	258	65	76	82	99	37	42	24	26	19	15
1804	227	258	65	76	82	99	37	42	24	26	19	15
1806	202	203	38	46	96	78	56	64	0	0	12	15
1807	209	280	38	47	94	131	63	82	0	0	14	20
1808	319	409	56	63	146	197	98	119	3	2	16	28
1809	347	489	59	71	152	213	111	162	6	5	19	38
1810	367	520	62	75	159	223	115	173	5	7	26	42
1815	215	443	38	79	105	221	44	96	5	8	23	39
1816	253	522	49	94	109	243	65	126	5	7	25	52
1817	270	521	51	96	125	240	67	129	3	7	24	49
1818	296	495	82	93	124	237	65	119	2	5	23	41
1819	316	447	82	93	150	216	63	111	2	4	19	23
1820	310	455	76	91	148	224	65	116	0	0	21	24
IGUANA												
1783	29	27	0	0	28	25	0	0	1	2	0	0
1801	53	40	0	0	48	40	4	0	1	0	0	0
1802	55	40	0	0	50	40	4	0	1	0	0	0
1803	57	49	0	0	54	48	3	1	0	0	0	0
1804	60	42	0	0	57	41	3	1	0	0	0	0
1805	53	38	0	0	51	37	2	1	0	0	0	0
1806	81	54	0	0	79	53	2	1	0	0	0	0
1807	72	58	0	0	72	58	0	0	0	0	0	0
LA GUAIRA												
1802	326	348	92	95	6	1	133	155	45	40	50	57
1804	331	290	94	90	1	3	127	131	71	20	38	46
1805	297	302	82	72	0	0	135	140	48	52	32	38
1807	297	263	102	73	1	2	112	113	47	41	35	34
1809	258	321	65	79	0	2	149	188	28	34	16	18
1810	308	216	113	91	2	0	131	58	34	42	28	25
1811	261	266	73	64	3	1	136	151	25	23	24	27
1815	215	148	85	60	10	5	65	40	25	22	30	21
1816	179	176	69	62	9	5	62	74	15	19	24	16
1817	214	202	60	64	8	6	97	89	29	25	20	18
1818	249	325	81	73	14	6	103	198	23	28	28	20
1819	326	215	65	40	60	39	71	50	68	51	62	35
1820	210	263	53	59	21	18	90	96	27	57	19	33
LA GUAIRA, CURATO CASTRENSE												
1802	6	6	6	5	0	0	0	0	0	0	0	1
1803	3	1	3	0	0	0	0	0	0	0	0	1
1804	8	6	5	3	0	0	3	3	0	0	0	0
1805	23	13	19	8	0	0	3	4	0	0	1	1
1807	18	15	15	11	0	0	2	3	0	0	1	1

TABLE 2. PARISH CHILD POPULATION (CONTINUED)

YEAR	TOTAL		WHITE		INDIAN		PARDO		NEGRO		SLAVE	
	M	F	M	F	M	F	M	F	M	F	M	F
1808	9	6	9	4	0	0	0	1	0	0	0	1
LA SANTISIMA TRINIDAD												
1780	81	95	4	4	56	46	9	18	12	26	0	1
1802	215	208	12	7	11	7	128	111	61	78	3	5
1803	147	89	3	2	11	8	70	18	63	59	0	2
1804	197	196	10	9	24	12	75	107	81	66	7	2
1805	196	180	6	9	10	9	81	66	89	83	10	13
1807	141	129	11	7	9	11	40	29	73	80	8	2
1808	133	142	12	13	23	19	91	101	1	3	6	6
1809	120	140	8	12	19	14	83	104	3	5	7	5
1810	136	150	9	10	23	24	102	111	1	3	1	2
1811	143	174	8	10	25	28	98	124	3	5	9	7
1812	121	130	7	9	20	21	89	92	1	2	4	6
LA VEGA												
1802	298	266	80	79	57	56	66	72	9	8	86	51
1803	364	316	110	84	61	60	78	92	9	8	106	72
1804	222	207	53	46	48	39	39	48	24	19	58	55
1805	269	310	59	53	62	74	46	57	32	43	70	83
1809	128	135	27	36	34	29	41	32	4	5	22	33
1810	118	123	27	29	33	28	38	30	4	5	16	31
1811	106	99	22	25	30	18	43	32	0	4	11	20
1815	64	93	16	30	9	4	21	35	1	1	17	23
1816	84	110	23	33	10	9	22	34	8	10	21	24
1817	80	88	21	20	8	7	24	38	4	1	23	22
1818	76	90	26	35	8	4	22	29	2	2	18	20
1819	76	81	14	19	13	10	28	30	2	2	19	20
1820	69	72	8	13	10	11	38	29	2	2	11	17
1821	62	60	6	10	9	14	25	23	2	1	20	12
1822	58	67	4	16	13	16	30	26	3	2	8	7
1823	54	44	11	16	6	4	27	24	5	0	5	0
LA VICTORIA												
1780	461	539	71	126	124	112	127	148	54	67	85	86
1802	683	685	171	174	81	79	251	271	18	13	162	148
1803	722	725	152	70	112	198	238	259	18	17	202	181
1804	770	677	160	73	116	200	244	204	28	20	222	180
1805	722	772	158	76	114	202	241	262	20	28	189	204
1806	742	786	163	79	117	205	245	266	24	29	193	207
1808	743	660	174	115	110	120	227	214	28	19	204	192
1809	772	816	169	85	123	211	251	272	30	35	199	213
1811	761	1069	91	180	152	195	310	322	26	56	182	316
1816	358	409	122	121	44	50	117	199	0	0	75	39
1817	358	409	122	121	44	50	117	199	0	0	75	39
1818	358	409	122	121	44	50	117	199	0	0	75	39

TABLE 2. PARISH CHILD POPULATION (CONTINUED)

YEAR	TOTAL		WHITE		INDIAN		PARDO		NEGRO		SLAVE	
	M	F	M	F	M	F	M	F	M	F	M	F
LEZAMA												
1783	217	206	33	53	116	97	36	32	19	21	13	3
1802	378	383	115	121	96	87	111	104	15	23	41	48
1803	378	383	115	121	96	87	111	104	15	23	41	48
1804	378	383	115	121	96	87	111	104	15	23	41	48
1805	378	383	115	121	96	87	111	104	15	23	41	48
1806	378	383	115	121	96	87	111	104	15	23	41	48
1807	378	383	115	121	96	87	111	104	15	23	41	48
1808	378	383	115	121	96	87	111	104	15	23	41	48
1809	378	383	115	121	96	87	111	104	15	23	41	48
1810	378	383	115	121	96	87	111	104	15	23	41	48
1811	378	383	115	121	96	87	111	104	15	23	41	48
LOS ANGELES												
1780	64	49	0	3	43	30	17	11	4	5	0	0
1803	50	58	1	5	17	26	31	27	0	0	1	0
1804	51	57	1	5	18	29	31	23	0	0	1	0
1805	48	66	5	6	24	30	18	30	0	0	1	0
1807	54	60	5	5	22	26	27	29	0	0	0	0
1808	53	58	4	2	15	26	34	30	0	0	0	0
1809	121	126	39	38	22	26	56	59	0	0	4	3
1810	120	108	34	28	26	20	55	57	0	0	5	3
1811	135	127	41	36	25	28	62	58	0	0	7	5
1812	111	94	27	22	19	18	61	48	0	0	4	6
1816	147	136	18	31	24	23	97	78	0	0	8	4
1817	162	134	36	41	22	23	98	68	0	0	6	2
LOS ANGELES DE SETENTA												
1801	191	215	123	145	16	18	41	42	0	0	11	10
1805	74	86	32	41	11	11	19	27	0	0	12	7
1806	104	128	48	57	14	9	29	46	0	0	13	16
1807	128	201	49	88	26	46	42	54	0	0	11	13
1809	126	183	51	73	19	36	40	52	0	0	16	22
LOS CANIZOS												
1802	121	96	12	4	0	0	56	47	1	2	52	43
1803	107	93	14	5	0	0	54	47	0	1	39	40
1804	121	93	14	5	0	0	60	49	0	0	47	39
1805	106	76	10	3	0	0	45	32	5	5	46	36
1807	98	76	7	2	0	0	35	36	11	2	45	36
1808	105	92	9	4	0	0	49	55	0	0	47	33
1809	100	95	9	4	0	0	44	55	0	0	47	36
1810	123	130	6	7	0	0	61	81	0	1	56	41
1811	114	123	5	4	0	0	64	74	0	1	45	44
1813	71	85	0	0	0	0	41	59	13	10	17	16
1818	34	45	1	2	0	0	22	30	0	0	11	13

TABLE 2. PARISH CHILD POPULATION (CONTINUED)

YEAR	TOTAL		WHITE		INDIAN		PARDO		NEGRO		SLAVE	
	M	F	M	F	M	F	M	F	M	F	M	F
1819	37	58	2	3	0	0	25	41	0	0	10	14
1820	37	61	2	3	0	0	25	44	0	0	10	14
LOS GUAYOS												
1781	207	193	68	57	97	98	42	37	0	0	0	1
1795	447	428	123	119	136	128	182	172	0	0	6	9
1802	692	692	117	122	219	234	314	310	8	4	34	22
1803	657	657	120	98	399	421	105	113	2	6	31	19
1804	630	632	156	147	163	177	280	282	3	10	28	16
1805	639	658	158	143	161	185	290	309	1	7	29	14
1816	450	456	128	118	80	78	224	252	4	0	14	8
LOS TEQUES												
1796	258	228	145	142	22	16	66	44	6	9	19	17
1799	291	271	160	163	22	16	72	54	12	18	25	20
1800	291	271	160	163	22	16	72	54	12	18	25	20
1801	321	318	168	170	22	18	83	64	18	24	30	42
1805	385	395	138	142	30	45	10	8	9	10	198	190
1811	97	170	21	44	2	7	45	68	19	28	10	23
1816	235	251	126	120	24	26	50	62	1	4	34	39
1817	229	226	121	115	20	21	55	54	2	3	31	33
MACAIRA												
1784	83	76	2	1	23	22	0	0	0	0	58	53
1802	45	40	0	0	6	2	4	3	0	1	35	34
1803	59	39	0	0	7	3	0	1	5	1	47	34
1804	48	45	0	0	5	6	1	3	4	1	38	35
1806	48	46	0	0	6	4	0	0	2	1	40	41
1807	60	46	0	0	3	1	0	0	1	2	56	43
1808	35	35	0	0	5	7	0	0	4	2	26	26
1809	27	36	0	0	2	4	2	2	1	0	22	30
1811	10	9	0	0	3	1	0	0	0	0	7	8
1817	8	13	0	0	0	0	0	0	0	0	8	13
MACAIRITA												
1805	47	39	0	0	5	4	0	0	4	0	38	35
MACARAO												
1802	133	179	50	62	18	26	22	30	7	9	36	52
1803	160	174	35	39	25	23	43	46	12	17	45	49
1804	185	201	85	82	17	17	38	58	4	3	41	41
1805	139	165	67	75	13	17	26	34	3	3	30	36
1807	161	213	66	96	25	32	23	32	4	5	43	48
1808	173	176	81	90	20	21	30	24	7	3	35	38
1809	146	189	76	87	20	27	5	22	5	9	40	44
1810	188	202	86	84	23	29	26	28	3	7	50	54

TABLE 2. PARISH CHILD POPULATION (CONTINUED)

YEAR	TOTAL		WHITE		INDIAN		PARDO		NEGRO		SLAVE	
	M	F	M	F	M	F	M	F	M	F	M	F
1811	158	161	74	77	26	24	21	23	4	7	33	30
1812	146	165	69	94	9	13	18	15	3	2	47	41
1815	188	230	77	94	20	26	26	28	0	9	65	73
1816	200	237	77	96	20	28	32	28	6	10	65	75
1817	134	157	66	89	13	16	16	19	3	0	36	33
1818	130	157	62	89	13	16	16	19	3	0	36	33
1819	142	163	68	90	14	17	18	20	4	2	38	34
1820	142	163	68	90	14	17	18	20	4	2	38	34
1822	179	242	59	78	35	44	24	39	14	22	47	59
1823	209	266	89	98	35	44	24	39	14	26	47	59
MAGDALENO												
1802	334	376	116	97	19	22	173	236	2	1	24	20
1803	441	398	128	114	36	47	247	200	18	23	12	14
1804	431	395	116	117	3	2	292	263	5	0	15	13
1805	410	423	154	144	4	3	225	255	7	0	20	21
1806	504	450	160	156	3	9	292	247	19	13	30	25
1809	210	184	38	27	5	11	129	116	16	11	22	19
1816	408	388	180	115	9	7	186	221	15	25	18	20
MAIQUETIA												
1796	159	176	23	29	6	9	83	113	0	0	47	25
1802	171	188	46	53	5	4	50	42	35	49	35	40
1804	143	183	30	48	9	9	55	67	12	17	37	42
1805	167	205	28	50	7	9	65	70	21	25	46	51
1807	170	206	30	48	7	9	71	72	19	36	43	41
1811	200	227	46	64	16	14	72	73	30	38	36	38
1815	320	359	101	100	5	3	90	112	84	99	40	45
1816	152	166	34	43	21	18	36	39	21	23	40	43
1817	135	158	34	46	11	6	44	54	7	12	39	40
1819	320	359	101	100	5	3	90	112	84	99	40	45
MAMPORAL												
1784	58	64	3	6	5	3	11	11	12	5	27	39
1802	52	65	4	9	3	3	6	6	3	1	36	46
1804	73	66	7	5	4	3	14	15	11	6	37	37
1805	76	62	5	2	11	5	14	14	7	7	39	34
1807	79	64	4	3	6	3	18	19	6	7	45	32
1808	90	69	10	8	9	3	19	7	9	15	43	36
1809	88	65	2	2	9	1	11	12	22	15	44	35
1811	71	76	9	5	6	1	22	22	7	11	27	37
1812	83	77	5	9	14	2	31	26	5	10	28	30
1816	34	34	1	0	1	0	15	10	1	0	16	24
1817	42	35	0	1	9	2	0	0	14	7	19	25
1818	42	38	1	1	0	2	13	9	3	2	25	24
1820	41	50	0	0	0	1	14	15	3	4	24	30

TABLE 2. PARISH CHILD POPULATION (CONTINUED)

YEAR	TOTAL M	TOTAL F	WHITE M	WHITE F	INDIAN M	INDIAN F	PARDO M	PARDO F	NEGRO M	NEGRO F	SLAVE M	SLAVE F
MANAPIRE												
1804	85	57	23	15	10	7	29	22	2	1	21	12
1807	81	64	21	22	6	2	22	23	4	3	28	14
1808	81	64	21	22	6	2	22	23	4	3	28	14
1810	96	78	28	26	5	3	35	28	2	3	26	18
MARACA												
1778	156	132	47	30	65	57	42	42	2	0	0	3
1803	279	247	15	16	160	137	101	93	0	0	3	1
1804	231	218	81	76	60	66	85	72	3	3	2	1
1805	280	296	86	85	91	121	101	86	0	2	2	2
1806	275	279	76	75	106	132	89	67	3	4	1	1
1807	276	314	72	84	123	138	69	74	11	16	1	2
1808	224	267	62	78	94	114	56	59	11	14	1	2
1809	219	245	51	64	99	118	60	50	8	10	1	3
1810	213	249	59	73	87	104	52	56	13	14	2	2
1817	61	64	21	24	17	15	23	22	0	0	0	3
MARACAY												
1782	496	549	146	141	75	89	168	215	15	16	92	88
1796	1123	1055	431	417	0	0	461	445	62	67	169	126
1802	707	851	312	377	12	11	220	312	53	61	110	90
1803	765	878	327	385	13	14	260	326	54	62	111	91
1804	887	950	360	395	11	10	295	370	60	65	161	110
1805	1201	1137	354	309	14	14	541	547	2	0	290	267
1808	1216	1148	357	311	15	16	546	550	5	2	293	269
1809	765	793	327	300	13	14	260	326	54	62	111	91
1811	676	719	300	270	10	10	210	300	50	50	106	89
1816	745	734	87	92	84	90	287	249	22	30	265	273
1817	643	639	180	162	6	5	293	344	12	7	152	121
1818	799	821	242	224	19	29	373	386	68	74	97	108
1819	852	877	258	241	29	39	386	399	73	80	106	118
1820	894	919	267	239	33	39	391	406	84	91	119	144
MARIA												
1803	124	139	46	50	39	40	21	24	16	22	2	3
1804	227	236	103	91	41	44	79	92	0	2	4	7
1805	234	234	100	87	24	29	102	108	3	1	5	9
1806	249	252	114	93	31	29	96	117	2	2	6	11
1807	255	263	102	104	31	27	116	120	2	3	4	9
1811	195	183	87	74	33	34	64	64	4	4	7	7
MARIARA												
1802	315	322	82	65	9	9	145	173	32	36	47	39
1803	327	292	95	62	7	8	137	147	51	43	37	32

TABLE 2. PARISH CHILD POPULATION (CONTINUED)

YEAR	TOTAL		WHITE		INDIAN		PARDO		NEGRO		SLAVE	
	M	F	M	F	M	F	M	F	M	F	M	F
1804	306	305	81	57	9	6	140	171	42	39	34	32
1805	407	366	105	85	8	6	227	216	21	24	46	35
1809	480	483	107	105	48	47	207	201	54	62	64	68
1815	464	414	113	85	17	15	245	238	28	31	61	45
1816	420	435	96	85	6	5	280	299	12	14	26	32
1817	449	454	110	101	5	1	273	280	19	26	42	46
1818	475	472	137	133	9	8	276	273	23	16	30	42
MONTALBAN												
1781	251	208	83	70	9	11	120	80	5	3	34	44
1802	391	363	132	120	0	0	160	144	31	45	68	54
1803	515	386	192	147	0	0	268	191	12	9	43	39
1804	539	399	206	152	0	0	271	197	16	8	46	42
1805	531	399	209	156	0	0	275	201	17	10	30	32
1806	522	516	200	267	0	0	274	205	17	8	31	36
1808	351	304	108	122	0	0	181	126	34	23	28	33
1810	537	426	246	189	1	0	222	166	21	32	47	39
1815	425	495	146	183	4	2	198	232	26	22	51	56
1817	592	541	206	215	6	4	322	239	30	25	28	58
1818	517	595	170	200	3	2	300	319	21	24	23	50
1820	628	688	266	279	4	5	275	315	45	43	38	46
MORON												
1804	55	45	0	0	0	0	27	28	0	0	28	17
1805	66	41	0	0	0	0	35	20	5	2	26	19
1806	52	49	0	0	0	0	28	25	4	4	20	20
1807	55	42	0	0	0	0	28	24	0	0	27	18
1818	57	63	0	0	0	0	42	51	0	0	15	12
1819	44	44	0	0	0	0	30	33	0	0	14	11
1820	147	162	3	2	0	0	89	96	26	29	29	35
MOROTURO												
1802	44	49	3	5	0	0	10	12	29	24	2	8
1804	70	60	7	1	15	19	20	12	24	24	4	4
1805	63	66	4	10	8	16	16	13	33	21	2	6
1807	52	36	4	0	8	8	33	22	4	4	3	2
1808	58	60	7	1	10	19	15	12	24	24	2	4
1809	68	52	10	9	5	1	49	38	1	2	3	2
1815	62	60	1	1	15	19	20	12	24	24	2	4
NAGUANAGUA												
1802	218	192	115	97	0	1	71	70	0	0	32	24
1803	241	219	120	106	0	1	82	90	0	0	39	22
1804	221	174	102	77	3	2	76	73	0	0	40	22
1805	278	211	101	98	3	1	153	81	0	0	21	31
1809	225	218	112	104	0	1	73	83	0	0	40	30
1816	226	227	90	100	23	25	80	40	7	12	26	50

TABLE 2. PARISH CHILD POPULATION (CONTINUED)

YEAR	TOTAL		WHITE		INDIAN		PARDO		NEGRO		SLAVE	
	M	F	M	F	M	F	M	F	M	F	M	F
NAIGUATA												
1801	69	83	4	1	18	20	0	1	1	1	46	60
1802	79	80	3	1	25	20	0	0	1	1	50	58
1804	111	72	3	1	58	18	0	0	0	0	50	53
1805	88	77	4	4	27	14	0	0	0	0	57	59
1809	98	102	5	4	32	21	0	1	0	0	61	76
1810	112	124	7	5	33	22	1	6	1	5	70	86
1811	151	147	11	10	43	36	5	3	6	1	86	97
1816	57	53	5	4	18	7	5	2	1	0	28	40
1817	55	68	5	4	14	12	4	3	1	2	31	47
1822	66	67	4	2	13	14	8	4	3	1	38	46
NIRGUA												
1781	482	503	3	1	0	0	474	498	0	0	5	4
1802	439	374	7	4	0	0	425	360	0	0	7	10
1803	553	531	5	4	0	0	546	522	0	0	2	5
1804	553	531	5	4	0	0	546	522	0	0	2	5
1805	448	421	13	10	0	0	424	401	0	0	11	10
1806	454	428	14	10	0	0	429	408	0	0	11	10
1807	448	421	13	10	0	0	424	401	0	0	11	10
1808	316	307	8	11	0	0	208	174	85	109	15	13
1809	309	355	9	5	1	0	209	237	87	105	3	8
1810	342	430	11	7	5	6	211	293	103	118	12	6
1813	564	546	9	4	0	0	548	534	0	0	7	8
1817	542	536	7	4	0	0	528	524	0	0	7	8
1819	560	574	9	4	0	0	542	562	0	0	9	8
1820	575	583	11	4	0	0	552	573	0	0	12	6
1821	657	624	5	4	0	0	647	612	0	0	5	8
OCUMARE DE LA COSTA												
1802	385	429	5	14	0	0	107	60	0	0	273	355
1803	243	253	6	22	0	2	61	47	37	42	139	140
1804	186	186	10	16	0	0	50	45	43	40	83	85
1805	284	256	8	11	0	0	70	70	6	8	200	167
1809	182	196	10	15	0	0	47	80	2	1	123	100
1815	202	214	6	10	0	0	86	88	6	8	104	108
1816	193	208	4	2	0	0	66	69	10	16	113	121
1817	234	248	8	6	0	0	93	86	7	13	126	143
1819	133	171	7	2	1	1	49	67	5	11	71	90
1820	168	195	12	4	1	1	59	76	15	21	81	93
OCUMARE DEL TUY												
1783	263	227	37	27	5	2	52	50	30	23	139	125
1802	582	594	80	84	56	75	151	143	13	47	282	245
1803	420	499	160	206	90	100	50	60	40	59	80	74
1804	599	566	87	66	54	78	152	139	54	42	252	241

TABLE 2. PARISH CHILD POPULATION (CONTINUED)

YEAR	TOTAL		WHITE		INDIAN		PARDO		NEGRO		SLAVE	
	M	F	M	F	M	F	M	F	M	F	M	F
1805	621	580	104	76	56	79	153	140	55	43	253	242
1810	536	492	52	53	59	49	142	129	24	19	259	242
1811	610	580	67	63	80	57	148	147	31	20	284	293
1815	202	241	22	33	17	21	33	35	10	12	120	140
1820	494	549	57	56	21	37	156	168	86	89	174	199
1821	649	595	113	88	12	17	156	149	46	48	322	293
1822	478	579	64	71	19	38	135	181	78	93	182	196
ORTIZ												
1780	141	155	93	93	14	19	18	18	8	6	8	19
1802	491	178	362	121	4	3	16	33	67	2	42	19
1803	247	203	173	142	5	6	28	33	22	12	19	10
1804	206	182	145	129	8	8	29	26	9	5	15	14
1805	202	196	149	147	9	9	27	23	3	5	14	12
1806	213	219	153	149	8	7	28	39	1	9	23	15
1807	229	267	146	164	11	14	47	58	16	19	9	12
1808	273	286	170	174	13	10	61	68	18	21	11	13
1809	254	289	157	171	10	13	56	62	21	28	10	15
1810	259	292	158	178	9	12	60	62	18	27	14	13
1813	333	314	233	229	9	9	49	46	15	11	27	19
OSPINO												
1802	979	888	281	243	118	129	505	455	25	23	50	38
1803	995	895	285	243	121	123	510	462	22	27	57	40
1804	1040	977	298	251	199	164	474	477	27	41	42	44
1805	1037	1044	313	309	208	214	460	470	6	8	50	43
1806	1082	1060	328	314	218	218	472	474	8	10	56	44
1807	1099	1088	332	318	214	223	485	488	10	13	58	46
1808	1105	1106	331	336	116	251	598	446	16	20	44	53
1809	1292	1068	307	265	240	263	682	472	20	19	43	49
1810	1292	1068	307	265	240	263	682	472	20	19	43	49
1811	1034	893	328	283	122	102	483	434	56	28	45	46
1817	967	793	328	283	122	102	416	334	56	28	45	46
PANAQUIRE												
1784	72	50	4	5	8	2	7	10	0	0	53	33
1802	121	115	4	2	17	12	10	9	0	0	90	92
1803	118	110	7	4	14	7	10	17	0	0	87	82
1804	110	113	2	3	15	10	6	4	0	0	87	96
1805	129	127	4	2	13	16	8	11	2	2	102	96
1807	136	116	3	5	14	5	12	17	0	0	107	89
1808	137	119	3	6	15	6	12	17	0	1	107	89
1809	117	123	2	6	11	15	11	12	0	0	93	90
1811	97	102	1	4	6	6	15	7	1	2	74	83
1812	112	120	2	7	10	13	19	12	2	3	79	85
1816	94	109	5	3	3	3	14	24	6	8	66	71

TABLE 2. PARISH CHILD POPULATION (CONTINUED)

YEAR	TOTAL		WHITE		INDIAN		PARDO		NEGRO		SLAVE	
	M	F	M	F	M	F	M	F	M	F	M	F
PARACOTOS												
1783	211	222	45	55	68	80	80	65	12	7	6	15
1802	292	227	80	56	79	55	88	79	9	7	36	30
1803	324	248	87	56	70	56	108	89	19	9	40	38
1804	274	232	86	80	72	47	81	76	11	6	24	23
1805	289	261	87	82	77	63	83	79	12	8	30	29
1806	278	295	123	143	71	72	58	51	5	4	21	25
1807	285	299	123	143	78	72	58	51	5	8	21	25
1808	297	319	133	153	80	82	58	51	5	8	21	25
1809	264	302	107	117	79	94	30	36	9	12	39	43
1810	270	296	112	122	75	80	34	38	9	12	40	44
1811	323	333	146	148	85	89	36	38	10	14	46	44
1812	281	325	78	89	82	87	50	69	16	26	55	54
1816	261	261	83	60	34	42	61	74	59	65	24	20
1817	262	264	84	63	28	43	66	72	58	62	26	24
1819	274	246	117	89	95	83	24	42	0	0	38	32
1820	278	250	120	90	95	86	24	42	0	0	39	32
PARAPARA												
1780	366	276	91	76	18	30	168	103	63	32	26	35
1781	361	271	90	75	17	29	167	102	62	31	25	34
1782	369	282	87	70	21	31	171	107	64	34	26	40
1788	349	282	87	70	21	31	171	107	35	34	35	40
1802	367	326	88	69	20	18	109	94	129	119	21	26
1803	386	370	98	93	15	16	115	103	135	130	23	28
1805	378	379	99	90	7	9	121	123	128	132	23	25
1807	398	341	74	61	2	3	249	214	55	46	18	17
1809	463	362	89	74	2	3	296	221	60	46	16	18
1810	484	391	87	76	3	3	308	234	62	52	24	26
1811	483	515	97	105	4	7	305	318	60	67	17	18
PATANEMO												
1802	88	79	2	3	0	0	41	31	8	6	37	39
1803	89	85	1	5	0	0	39	36	9	8	40	36
1804	76	52	1	4	1	0	33	26	4	2	37	20
1805	80	64	2	5	2	0	32	30	4	7	40	22
1808	76	68	0	4	0	0	32	35	5	7	39	22
1818	92	83	2	1	1	1	65	61	1	0	23	20
1819	107	95	2	1	1	2	65	69	9	6	30	17
PAYARA												
1780	90	111	5	5	79	103	4	1	0	0	2	2
1802	82	84	6	9	50	42	17	23	4	5	5	5
1804	124	104	15	12	61	43	31	28	7	9	10	12
1805	160	130	20	18	72	50	44	32	10	12	14	18
1806	163	132	23	18	72	50	44	34	10	12	14	18

TABLE 2. PARISH CHILD POPULATION (CONTINUED)

YEAR	TOTAL		WHITE		INDIAN		PARDO		NEGRO		SLAVE	
	M	F	M	F	M	F	M	F	M	F	M	F
1807	155	189	25	33	68	72	41	55	9	12	12	17
1812	130	160	18	20	50	72	32	44	12	10	18	14
PETARE												
1802	523	599	108	129	96	109	67	86	68	77	184	198
1803	537	582	112	123	98	102	70	79	69	78	188	200
1804	463	537	106	129	80	110	65	96	63	83	149	119
1805	460	503	120	117	61	76	116	147	29	26	134	137
1806	490	517	110	123	83	69	120	150	31	33	146	142
1807	473	536	128	137	65	73	128	159	16	16	136	151
1811	522	569	156	190	61	53	108	117	53	59	144	150
1812	441	482	100	106	91	96	82	102	58	61	110	117
1815	380	399	160	163	7	11	73	88	48	47	92	90
1816	568	479	137	96	41	22	83	95	123	157	184	109
1817	533	506	97	90	46	31	73	103	126	162	191	120
1818	410	381	93	79	60	43	103	110	15	12	139	137
1819	466	431	106	90	68	48	125	135	15	12	152	146
1820	517	470	116	100	71	50	146	151	16	13	168	156
1821	563	523	120	105	77	54	163	171	24	19	179	174
1822	560	523	127	111	79	55	164	171	16	15	174	171
PUERTO CABELLO												
1803	497	500	86	86	0	0	272	286	87	77	52	51
1804	501	542	87	102	2	2	306	320	62	57	44	61
1805	472	581	63	133	1	1	315	332	58	43	35	72
1806	441	616	96	110	1	4	207	321	85	107	52	74
1811	434	585	90	101	5	4	200	221	85	231	54	28
1817	500	548	160	202	50	40	150	200	50	50	90	56
1819	311	520	103	195	5	8	123	208	51	73	29	36
1820	149	185	44	85	2	6	65	49	24	23	14	22
PUERTO CABELLO, CASTILLO												
1801	16	24	10	18	0	0	2	1	0	0	4	5
1802	19	5	15	3	0	0	0	0	0	0	4	2
1804	36	25	11	10	0	0	16	8	0	0	9	7
1805	40	39	20	12	0	0	11	13	0	0	9	14
1806	63	51	30	22	0	1	16	10	0	0	17	18
1807	69	56	33	24	0	1	20	16	0	0	16	15
1808	86	68	40	31	0	0	28	23	0	0	18	14
1809	89	77	39	33	0	2	30	26	0	0	20	16
1810	72	74	42	31	0	3	20	33	0	0	10	7
1819	11	16	7	10	0	0	0	0	0	0	4	6
1820	14	14	9	12	0	0	0	0	0	0	5	2
QUARA												
1782	134	152	7	0	122	144	3	5	2	3	0	0
1791	96	83	0	1	92	75	4	7	0	0	0	0

TABLE 2. PARISH CHILD POPULATION (CONTINUED)

YEAR	TOTAL		WHITE		INDIAN		PARDO		NEGRO		SLAVE	
	M	F	M	F	M	F	M	F	M	F	M	F
1802	122	118	6	3	105	107	11	8	0	0	0	0
1803	106	99	7	1	95	91	0	1	4	6	0	0
1804	107	106	3	1	99	99	0	3	5	3	0	0
1805	122	109	4	4	92	89	8	7	18	9	0	0
1807	126	83	6	2	100	67	16	10	4	4	0	0
1808	134	121	9	3	106	105	14	9	5	4	0	0
1809	124	98	6	1	107	88	7	2	4	7	0	0
1810	131	102	2	2	112	89	14	6	3	5	0	0
1811	99	152	6	1	76	136	14	6	3	9	0	0
1815	128	128	2	4	110	107	13	13	3	4	0	0
1816	147	143	4	4	118	116	23	11	2	12	0	0
1817	164	136	4	3	133	112	24	10	3	11	0	0
1818	73	101	4	4	26	36	29	38	11	21	3	2
1819	158	233	4	5	112	166	26	33	13	25	3	4
	QUIBOR											
1802	864	1025	240	298	201	240	210	239	130	152	83	96
1803	864	980	240	298	201	245	210	239	130	102	83	96
1804	956	1045	252	301	204	243	250	251	148	149	102	101
1805	965	1123	264	322	225	264	238	269	145	162	93	106
1806	965	1123	264	322	225	264	238	269	145	162	93	106
1807	965	1141	264	322	225	264	238	287	145	162	93	106
1808	1059	1244	284	345	245	286	267	318	161	182	102	113
1810	1643	1542	465	435	306	332	809	718	11	9	52	48
1812	1378	1680	359	435	137	211	670	779	91	119	121	136
1815	1468	1800	384	475	152	231	720	839	91	119	121	136
1816	1430	1704	372	425	152	225	702	810	89	112	115	132
1817	1586	1859	432	455	177	270	747	856	98	130	132	148
1818	1655	1932	470	496	184	281	759	865	102	138	140	152
1819	1682	1847	492	501	190	285	764	809	102	107	134	145
1820	1824	2021	525	560	231	304	797	866	125	133	146	158
	RIO CHICO											
1802	120	134	5	1	7	6	29	26	10	11	69	90
1803	132	145	5	1	10	8	31	28	12	14	74	94
1804	137	146	5	1	6	2	30	35	16	12	80	96
1805	151	178	4	6	11	10	22	25	16	18	98	119
1806	163	198	4	6	16	14	25	30	18	18	100	130
1807	187	215	4	6	18	16	30	35	25	25	110	133
1808	201	212	4	7	19	18	32	37	27	20	119	130
1809	204	213	7	8	19	18	32	37	27	20	119	130
1810	222	226	12	6	22	21	35	40	31	26	122	133
1811	239	244	14	14	27	24	39	37	33	30	126	139
1812	209	219	10	8	20	18	33	38	28	30	118	125
1816	103	158	5	9	10	16	27	38	4	4	57	91
1817	193	216	10	8	15	16	35	40	18	22	115	130
1819	206	232	12	9	11	14	40	50	14	19	129	140

TABLE 2. PARISH CHILD POPULATION (CONTINUED)

YEAR	TOTAL		WHITE		INDIAN		PARDO		NEGRO		SLAVE	
	M	F	M	F	M	F	M	F	M	F	M	F
RIO DEL TOCUYO												
1802	378	302	58	45	253	220	56	32	0	0	11	5
1803	361	314	54	50	247	202	47	54	0	0	13	8
1804	323	268	29	27	243	206	32	26	0	0	19	9
1805	355	290	36	30	254	222	44	28	0	0	21	10
1808	209	257	22	36	149	183	9	11	0	0	29	27
1809	217	333	41	59	109	199	16	13	0	0	51	62
1815	445	485	86	92	289	298	49	71	0	0	21	24
SABANETA												
1805	422	358	127	123	38	35	244	187	7	8	6	5
1808	445	344	73	43	116	88	245	206	5	4	6	3
1809	589	428	223	211	51	27	300	184	11	5	4	1
1810	743	654	250	255	70	40	380	310	35	45	8	4
1811	808	609	320	280	80	60	366	240	31	23	11	6
1812	471	422	183	108	55	80	185	188	40	40	8	6
1816	414	558	149	167	16	22	249	369	0	0	0	0
SAN ANTONIO DE LAS COCUIZAS												
1780	169	199	16	21	25	30	100	118	25	28	3	2
SAN ANTONIO DE LOS ALTOS												
1796	80	58	74	53	0	0	4	2	0	0	2	3
1802	70	53	64	48	1	0	1	3	0	0	4	2
1803	70	56	59	50	6	3	0	0	0	0	5	3
1804	71	49	63	44	0	1	0	1	0	0	8	3
1805	69	54	62	47	0	1	1	1	0	0	6	5
1808	127	95	87	65	8	2	6	6	0	0	26	22
1809	93	95	70	64	3	0	2	4	0	0	18	27
1810	102	99	56	54	0	3	9	7	0	0	37	35
1811	116	116	75	69	0	1	4	10	0	0	37	36
1812	105	113	69	70	0	0	8	14	0	0	28	29
1815	54	71	28	29	0	1	8	14	1	1	17	26
1816	75	79	36	40	2	2	6	9	0	0	31	28
1817	61	53	39	35	0	0	2	2	0	0	20	16
1818	86	70	37	38	5	3	11	8	0	0	33	21
1819	83	84	39	51	2	0	14	12	0	3	28	18
1820	108	94	46	55	3	4	15	15	2	3	42	17
SAN CARLOS												
1781	921	888	358	319	46	43	210	228	109	114	198	184
1786	937	955	316	311	46	42	270	315	126	119	179	168
1787	916	912	343	322	49	28	251	286	136	119	137	157
1788	925	893	345	327	46	29	255	283	138	122	141	132
1791	1033	1013	371	355	55	37	286	316	157	148	164	157

TABLE 2. PARISH CHILD POPULATION (CONTINUED)

YEAR	TOTAL		WHITE		INDIAN		PARDO		NEGRO		SLAVE	
	M	F	M	F	M	F	M	F	M	F	M	F
1796	1152	1147	397	391	70	53	321	353	175	169	189	181
1798	1053	1025	333	375	41	48	308	281	200	178	171	143
1799	1067	1035	338	380	42	50	310	284	203	176	174	145
1800	1111	1079	347	383	44	53	326	300	219	193	175	150
1801	1127	1100	350	385	47	54	329	302	222	206	179	153
1802	1217	1150	419	377	76	58	377	358	169	176	176	181
1803	1234	1167	422	381	75	60	388	363	170	179	179	184
1804	1408	1373	497	457	88	84	477	421	194	197	152	214
1805	1528	1484	559	504	97	91	520	473	194	197	158	219
1806	1686	1653	601	570	103	98	611	564	206	213	165	208
1808	1529	1484	559	504	98	91	520	473	194	197	158	219
1809	1528	1484	559	504	97	91	520	473	194	197	158	219
1811	782	876	205	257	12	15	354	381	11	15	200	208
1812	794	886	211	259	10	18	360	389	9	15	204	205
1816	1224	1246	359	326	84	93	579	586	32	48	170	193
1817	1111	1639	368	464	15	26	587	896	27	89	114	164
1818	1399	1758	395	499	89	101	698	879	38	96	179	183
1819	1253	1754	383	490	18	33	630	941	36	100	186	190
1820	1285	1724	380	485	17	31	627	933	80	92	181	183
1822	1211	1717	370	477	16	28	613	931	32	93	180	188
1823	1123	1605	323	439	15	20	586	906	29	60	170	180
1824	982	1329	315	400	14	23	501	722	20	37	132	147
SAN DIEGO DE ALCALA												
1781	114	109	31	23	29	26	43	53	0	0	11	7
1802	207	278	31	53	28	42	85	97	60	82	3	4
1803	104	131	22	30	26	29	46	57	8	13	2	2
1804	176	214	49	54	27	35	58	69	40	54	2	2
1805	127	96	29	27	22	14	67	47	5	5	4	3
1809	119	81	26	14	25	10	58	53	8	3	2	1
SAN DIEGO DE LOS ALTOS												
1802	107	107	54	45	23	31	17	21	0	0	13	10
1803	125	146	61	69	33	38	8	11	13	17	10	11
1804	121	107	69	46	28	40	8	9	5	3	11	9
1805	138	122	78	54	30	38	11	13	9	6	10	11
1807	172	140	87	63	45	48	16	13	4	5	20	11
1808	150	149	76	66	43	54	9	10	3	6	19	13
1809	175	181	81	77	52	61	14	18	7	11	21	14
1810	193	208	91	85	50	62	22	29	7	11	23	21
1811	201	221	90	93	50	59	19	21	13	11	29	37
1815	156	186	67	82	47	41	7	14	18	19	17	30
1816	133	152	52	54	38	41	11	17	15	19	17	21
1817	121	164	54	79	29	37	8	10	12	15	18	23
1818	128	145	51	65	35	39	12	14	24	19	6	8
1819	147	149	54	48	49	55	12	16	9	3	23	27
1820	139	141	56	48	41	50	15	22	7	5	20	16

TABLE 2. PARISH CHILD POPULATION (CONTINUED)

YEAR	TOTAL		WHITE		INDIAN		PARDO		NEGRO		SLAVE	
	M	F	M	F	M	F	M	F	M	F	M	F
SAN FELIPE												
1782	681	902	104	308	14	50	430	420	72	82	61	42
1802	700	970	170	220	90	100	220	270	100	110	120	270
1803	650	820	160	210	80	90	210	260	90	100	110	160
1804	496	504	65	64	9	8	349	359	7	5	66	68
1805	567	541	76	73	3	3	402	383	9	6	77	76
1817	353	399	48	54	4	8	260	286	7	10	34	41
1818	556	787	91	193	0	0	428	534	1	1	36	59
1819	396	448	57	64	5	9	284	310	9	13	41	52
1820	355	477	60	68	8	13	231	322	13	17	43	57
1821	325	374	40	50	5	9	230	250	9	13	41	52
SAN FELIPE, MITAD DE (1)												
1807	317	295	37	42	6	0	214	211	1	0	59	42
1808	333	306	47	42	6	0	220	221	1	0	59	43
1809	300	262	37	40	4	2	196	165	3	2	60	53
1810	322	308	43	41	4	0	218	220	1	3	56	44
1811	322	308	43	41	4	0	218	220	1	3	56	44
1812	201	258	18	27	1	0	163	204	1	0	18	27
SAN FELIPE, MITAD DE (2)												
1807	292	301	53	47	3	5	208	212	4	5	24	32
1808	317	309	54	51	10	8	211	210	5	7	37	33
1809	285	296	47	43	13	12	201	188	8	10	16	43
1810	308	304	46	48	14	13	204	186	9	11	35	46
1811	298	336	46	55	12	8	202	230	6	9	32	34
SAN FERNANDO DE APURE												
1801	308	545	113	208	19	29	148	273	9	14	19	21
1805	135	200	60	80	15	25	58	92	0	0	2	3
1806	226	268	93	99	55	77	75	87	0	0	3	5
1816	294	285	118	114	18	25	119	106	20	14	19	26
SAN FERNANDO DE CACHICAMO												
1783	82	69	20	13	2	1	31	22	10	8	19	25
1802	63	54	15	12	6	4	24	29	6	3	12	6
1803	63	51	15	12	6	4	20	24	12	5	10	6
1805	77	87	18	18	3	3	43	53	2	2	11	11
1806	85	92	19	23	7	4	47	51	1	0	11	14
1807	85	79	19	23	7	4	47	51	1	0	11	1
SAN FRANCISCO DE CARA												
1783	190	173	32	36	8	6	138	124	0	0	12	7
1802	136	182	42	37	6	7	35	107	21	14	32	17

TABLE 2. PARISH CHILD POPULATION (CONTINUED)

YEAR	TOTAL		WHITE		INDIAN		PARDO		NEGRO		SLAVE	
	M	F	M	F	M	F	M	F	M	F	M	F
SAN FRANCISCO DE TIZNADOS												
1780	343	302	34	39	17	13	46	38	211	184	35	28
1801	237	310	12	15	3	4	200	264	0	0	22	27
1802	322	329	22	24	6	7	202	138	70	139	22	21
1803	293	311	29	38	1	3	138	142	103	104	22	24
1805	344	330	41	43	1	4	270	257	0	3	32	23
1807	390	378	51	53	1	4	306	295	0	3	32	23
1808	369	358	42	46	1	4	294	282	0	3	32	23
1809	399	388	46	51	4	6	310	302	3	4	36	25
1811	247	249	56	49	21	25	98	100	48	46	24	29
1812	286	323	43	52	28	35	134	163	40	41	41	32
SAN FRANCISCO DE YARE												
1783	195	185	5	2	30	21	19	17	27	27	114	118
1802	291	272	9	14	41	38	7	3	67	76	167	141
1803	255	259	10	10	47	35	7	3	73	79	118	132
1804	252	305	8	12	38	37	4	3	66	84	136	169
1805	224	231	9	9	34	32	4	6	67	72	110	112
1810	300	361	8	7	32	53	61	85	11	10	188	206
1811	300	361	8	7	32	53	61	85	11	10	188	206
1815	96	146	6	4	17	24	19	32	6	10	48	76
1817	454	382	20	10	110	85	115	89	77	21	132	177
1818	251	236	15	5	34	32	74	71	8	8	120	120
1820	307	244	25	9	36	28	55	46	34	26	157	135
1821	275	283	23	13	52	50	72	62	16	23	112	135
1822	368	271	23	13	29	37	58	56	19	24	239	141
SAN JAIME												
1780	312	288	110	101	10	19	142	125	23	19	27	24
SAN JOSE												
1781	148	134	36	25	42	47	66	54	3	2	1	6
1788	275	226	9	10	51	43	199	166	10	5	6	2
1790	270	251	48	61	44	43	162	136	11	11	5	0
1791	270	251	48	61	44	43	162	136	11	11	5	0
1792	327	346	70	87	47	57	205	194	3	1	2	7
1794	327	346	70	87	47	57	205	194	3	1	2	7
1795	217	180	49	30	31	29	65	75	71	45	1	1
1798	260	233	59	59	41	41	75	75	81	55	4	3
1799	260	233	59	59	41	41	75	75	81	55	4	3
1800	277	234	59	59	41	41	95	75	81	55	1	4
1801	282	225	59	44	36	33	101	97	86	51	0	0
1803	414	383	80	79	56	49	270	249	2	2	6	4
1804	415	422	81	77	50	48	280	290	1	3	3	4
1805	323	289	67	47	37	31	214	200	3	7	2	4
1807	171	181	50	53	18	23	100	101	0	0	3	4

TABLE 2. PARISH CHILD POPULATION (CONTINUED)

YEAR	TOTAL		WHITE		INDIAN		PARDO		NEGRO		SLAVE	
	M	F	M	F	M	F	M	F	M	F	M	F
1808	171	181	52	56	16	20	98	100	0	0	5	5
1811	163	174	51	50	20	20	90	100	0	0	2	4
1812	311	361	46	96	13	21	250	243	2	1	0	0
1815	336	305	12	11	33	29	288	260	1	4	2	1
1818	162	198	50	40	24	59	86	96	2	3	0	0
1819	233	193	56	44	89	49	86	96	2	3	0	1
1822	262	439	88	140	86	99	82	186	2	8	4	6
1823	268	427	80	100	80	89	102	226	1	6	5	6
SAN JOSE DE APURE												
1802	69	70	11	12	21	26	25	18	12	14	0	0
1804	118	143	30	37	35	39	28	36	25	31	0	0
1806	107	112	28	30	30	34	28	21	21	27	0	0
1807	63	82	17	26	21	23	14	17	10	16	1	0
1808	64	79	20	25	21	23	11	14	12	17	0	0
1809	64	79	20	25	21	23	11	14	12	17	0	0
SAN JOSE DE TIZNADOS												
1802	249	238	51	29	10	9	167	178	4	3	17	19
1803	298	263	50	34	21	18	196	188	8	3	23	20
1804	304	267	55	41	21	25	197	182	7	3	24	16
1805	268	265	46	38	22	22	179	190	7	3	14	12
1807	382	371	70	47	14	21	207	226	75	64	16	13
1808	394	337	59	42	26	12	263	253	28	18	18	12
1809	426	350	73	52	19	9	275	242	42	33	17	14
1810	440	393	60	50	33	22	294	274	32	31	21	16
1812	483	466	59	53	35	24	333	336	32	31	24	22
1816	361	339	63	49	19	26	186	180	71	68	22	16
1817	485	441	80	64	23	31	277	263	81	64	24	19
SAN JUAN DE LOS MORROS												
1802	182	184	69	67	14	5	35	51	45	49	19	12
1803	178	192	72	75	11	9	38	52	37	39	20	17
1805	216	212	91	92	19	10	49	64	38	28	19	18
1806	219	225	95	88	19	11	33	46	53	61	19	19
1807	251	230	102	96	30	18	43	45	56	49	20	22
1809	267	265	107	115	22	16	54	59	62	51	22	24
1810	260	264	113	114	22	18	58	53	49	58	18	21
1811	252	259	110	112	21	18	53	56	48	46	20	27
SAN MATEO												
1781	281	289	61	56	35	45	124	134	0	0	61	54
1802	289	294	71	65	10	29	127	110	1	1	80	89
1803	332	307	86	70	52	37	112	100	14	16	68	84
1804	299	284	68	56	43	32	103	101	10	13	75	82
1805	303	298	80	71	39	32	100	106	10	7	74	82
1806	286	275	67	63	24	20	120	106	10	10	65	76

TABLE 2. PARISH CHILD POPULATION (CONTINUED)

YEAR	TOTAL		WHITE		INDIAN		PARDO		NEGRO		SLAVE	
	M	F	M	F	M	F	M	F	M	F	M	F
1808	207	244	56	42	30	24	63	113	10	7	48	58
1809	266	323	69	74	38	39	90	122	8	8	61	80
1811	251	323	61	66	23	37	91	136	4	8	72	76
1815	191	270	53	81	17	23	77	111	3	7	41	48
1816	213	256	56	69	20	24	91	115	3	6	43	42
1817	221	249	62	76	26	25	83	105	5	5	45	38
1818	230	253	65	77	25	25	82	101	7	8	51	42
1821	314	331	86	86	41	33	115	154	11	5	61	53
SAN MIGUEL DE TRUJILLO												
1808	504	434	207	155	52	41	210	220	15	18	20	0
SAN NICOLAS DE TOLENTINO												
1803	80	80	0	0	4	0	40	44	20	15	16	21
1808	74	78	16	20	8	4	30	20	10	25	10	9
1818	38	26	0	0	0	0	38	26	0	0	0	0
1820	37	61	2	3	0	0	25	44	0	0	10	14
1821	32	61	0	0	2	3	20	44	10	14	0	0
SAN PEDRO												
1810	135	132	65	58	0	0	55	53	0	0	15	21
1811	161	143	73	62	5	6	60	49	0	0	23	26
1816	96	108	49	60	2	3	41	42	0	0	4	3
1817	86	100	43	56	2	3	37	38	0	0	4	3
SAN RAFAEL DE ONOTO												
1779	80	98	36	40	34	44	8	11	2	3	0	0
1810	213	254	69	82	44	62	99	110	0	0	1	0
1811	196	200	54	47	44	47	98	106	0	0	0	0
1828	124	149	26	28	42	56	52	59	4	6	0	0
1829	131	158	26	28	42	56	59	68	4	6	0	0
SAN RAFAEL DE ORITUCO												
1783	263	246	81	75	6	5	54	56	63	58	59	52
1802	145	143	28	23	0	0	85	87	0	0	32	33
1803	154	136	29	25	0	0	91	82	0	0	34	29
1804	155	140	39	29	0	0	100	91	0	0	16	20
1805	159	159	36	31	0	0	99	96	0	0	24	32
1806	175	190	34	39	0	0	117	116	0	0	24	35
1808	187	198	36	54	0	0	129	105	0	0	22	39
1809	173	173	43	51	7	12	99	81	10	7	14	22
1810	259	339	55	77	6	10	175	222	9	11	14	19
1811	320	473	55	77	6	10	220	175	33	200	6	11

TABLE 2. PARISH CHILD POPULATION (CONTINUED)

YEAR	TOTAL		WHITE		INDIAN		PARDO		NEGRO		SLAVE	
	M	F	M	F	M	F	M	F	M	F	M	F
SAN SEBASTIAN DE LOS REYES												
1783	426	438	76	79	121	101	193	215	11	13	25	30
1802	361	521	93	115	36	32	193	337	5	8	34	29
1803	382	581	102	115	37	95	200	338	7	6	36	27
1804	396	612	110	129	33	99	207	348	8	7	38	29
1805	408	618	107	121	34	105	214	352	13	8	40	32
1806	393	595	111	121	30	88	212	352	15	16	25	18
1809	551	515	140	149	49	36	308	279	17	19	37	32
1810	551	578	147	142	48	50	300	327	17	29	39	30
1811	548	590	147	143	49	51	292	329	19	31	41	36
SANARE												
1803	558	576	82	83	280	302	109	111	75	72	12	8
1804	567	587	83	86	285	310	108	112	77	71	14	8
1805	558	576	82	83	280	302	109	111	75	72	12	8
1806	647	566	77	85	422	309	80	92	57	66	11	14
1807	631	569	67	86	428	309	60	92	57	66	19	16
1808	626	563	68	86	428	309	60	92	51	60	19	16
1809	613	551	68	76	428	309	60	92	41	60	16	14
1810	636	578	78	85	422	316	66	94	47	67	23	16
1812	376	418	49	65	244	257	59	66	17	21	7	9
1815	337	400	42	54	218	253	56	62	14	19	7	12
1816	420	464	45	63	302	310	54	66	14	22	5	3
1817	436	487	45	66	302	310	54	66	24	32	11	13
1818	420	464	45	63	302	310	54	66	14	22	5	3
1819	333	394	42	54	218	253	56	62	14	19	3	6
1820	436	484	45	63	302	310	54	66	24	32	11	13
SANTA CRUZ DE ARAGUA												
1802	986	1064	525	563	8	10	431	478	14	5	8	8
1803	649	905	184	502	10	18	446	379	4	2	5	4
1804	1074	921	568	519	11	10	488	385	4	1	3	6
1805	938	859	519	476	6	10	408	366	0	0	5	7
1808	1018	1084	520	626	5	7	480	423	4	8	9	20
1811	871	881	420	530	4	8	438	335	4	5	5	3
1815	509	522	244	256	236	240	15	16	2	1	12	9
1816	722	705	389	385	11	14	302	292	8	3	12	11
1817	786	816	438	463	5	8	320	322	8	4	15	19
1818	718	705	410	380	4	8	240	248	50	59	14	10
1822	997	684	480	223	18	28	462	403	29	15	8	15
SANTA INES DEL ALTAR												
1779	9	3	0	0	4	0	3	1	2	2	0	0
1802	16	9	1	1	5	4	8	4	1	0	1	0
1803	8	12	0	0	2	3	6	9	0	0	0	0
1804	14	6	0	0	7	3	7	3	0	0	0	0

TABLE 2. PARISH CHILD POPULATION (CONTINUED)

YEAR	TOTAL		WHITE		INDIAN		PARDO		NEGRO		SLAVE	
	M	F	M	F	M	F	M	F	M	F	M	F
1805	25	17	2	0	1	3	22	14	0	0	0	0
1806	20	22	2	0	1	7	17	15	0	0	0	0
1810	20	16	0	0	1	2	19	14	0	0	0	0
1811	10	19	0	0	1	5	9	14	0	0	0	0
1818	27	32	0	0	0	0	27	32	0	0	0	0
1819	47	82	3	4	13	14	19	37	12	27	0	0
1820	51	61	3	4	6	11	27	30	15	16	0	0
1829	62	76	3	5	17	24	42	47	0	0	0	0
SANTA LUCIA												
1784	279	259	34	30	80	73	35	28	45	35	85	93
1787	279	271	35	25	53	54	68	63	19	18	104	111
1802	407	504	91	90	40	60	142	200	4	4	130	150
1803	423	362	74	62	21	36	171	123	14	6	143	135
1804	389	417	74	62	31	48	104	129	32	28	148	150
1805	603	408	75	42	92	81	193	119	17	12	226	154
1808	402	414	83	82	69	59	101	112	19	18	130	143
1809	402	404	83	82	69	59	101	102	19	18	130	143
1811	410	446	93	98	45	50	119	112	10	11	143	175
1816	515	506	93	82	30	52	133	133	25	10	234	229
1817	570	245	206	101	3	2	251	103	10	4	100	35
1818	296	345	95	100	3	4	90	110	8	11	100	120
1819	335	361	48	63	37	38	115	112	30	33	105	115
SANTA MARIA DE IPIRE												
1783	168	158	47	58	13	8	58	48	12	9	38	35
1798	210	249	72	83	5	3	83	92	32	50	18	21
1803	224	260	72	80	4	5	95	101	36	51	17	23
SANTA ROSA DE LIMA												
1802	380	540	145	200	43	61	30	41	148	220	14	18
1803	401	680	150	192	52	201	36	43	150	226	13	18
1804	380	540	145	200	43	61	30	41	148	220	14	18
1805	367	525	132	203	40	51	29	40	150	211	16	20
1807	381	585	130	202	46	44	31	62	156	46	18	231
1808	416	589	136	204	48	44	56	64	158	46	18	231
1809	711	934	198	285	41	47	290	389	176	205	6	8
1810	840	938	308	291	48	40	296	391	178	208	10	8
1815	689	846	218	294	51	45	229	291	179	206	12	10
1816	770	855	218	294	54	54	281	291	207	206	10	10
1817	592	890	214	294	12	17	229	338	119	206	18	35
1819	615	912	218	294	31	39	229	338	119	206	18	35
1820	615	912	218	294	31	39	229	338	119	206	18	35
SANTA TERESA DE JESUS												
1783	137	155	18	18	20	20	20	20	22	22	57	75
1786	109	125	6	10	18	25	23	19	2	1	60	70

TABLE 2. PARISH CHILD POPULATION (CONTINUED)

YEAR	TOTAL		WHITE		INDIAN		PARDO		NEGRO		SLAVE	
	M	F	M	F	M	F	M	F	M	F	M	F
1787	117	137	6	11	21	29	24	21	7	7	59	69
1788	116	145	6	11	23	22	21	32	5	9	61	71
1802	205	202	47	42	15	19	26	32	37	29	80	80
1803	220	248	50	60	24	26	24	31	39	33	83	98
1804	253	264	56	52	29	30	28	39	40	43	100	100
1805	231	238	58	38	30	38	23	40	42	43	78	79
1810	221	201	63	58	21	27	30	28	44	34	63	54
1811	215	200	62	54	20	23	26	28	36	31	71	64
1815	166	165	27	20	16	20	21	28	38	39	64	58
1816	159	154	30	31	13	15	20	20	30	31	66	57
1817	175	176	33	36	13	12	19	25	31	32	79	71
1820	172	173	42	41	11	8	22	20	28	36	69	68
SARARE												
1779	169	180	26	31	33	60	79	62	24	26	7	1
1802	327	354	37	45	47	38	159	169	82	101	2	1
1804	354	396	47	53	57	49	165	189	83	104	2	1
1805	466	394	66	52	80	43	284	267	29	23	7	9
1807	317	354	32	45	42	38	159	169	82	101	2	1
1808	354	396	47	53	57	49	165	189	83	104	2	1
1809	354	396	47	53	57	49	165	189	83	104	2	1
1810	385	420	49	58	60	50	180	190	90	110	6	12
1811	354	396	47	53	57	49	165	189	83	104	2	1
1817	428	431	78	91	113	95	230	235	3	4	4	6
1818	534	522	92	69	111	120	313	320	7	3	11	10
SIQUISIQUE												
1802	634	686	42	31	460	502	87	92	35	49	10	12
1803	654	706	47	36	465	507	92	97	40	54	10	12
1804	490	583	42	38	330	408	81	92	25	32	12	13
1805	483	670	50	64	310	452	82	104	28	36	13	14
1807	919	702	96	99	612	407	186	165	5	3	20	28
TACARIGUA DE MAMPORAL												
1784	83	93	5	8	3	1	5	7	15	17	55	60
1802	122	106	2	1	0	1	5	1	25	13	90	90
1803	112	102	2	0	1	2	4	1	19	12	86	87
1804	119	99	3	1	4	3	5	1	19	12	88	82
1805	102	79	2	1	0	1	1	2	14	5	85	70
1806	100	78	3	2	2	4	2	0	10	4	83	68
1807	87	76	4	3	0	1	3	2	11	4	69	66
1808	92	66	1	1	1	0	7	2	5	1	78	62
1809	80	67	1	1	1	0	7	5	3	0	68	61
1811	74	70	1	1	0	0	7	3	15	7	51	59
1816	68	53	2	5	0	0	14	12	16	3	36	33
1818	72	59	6	3	1	2	10	7	14	10	41	37
1820	91	54	4	2	4	2	10	9	21	13	52	28

TABLE 2. PARISH CHILD POPULATION (CONTINUED)

YEAR	TOTAL		WHITE		INDIAN		PARDO		NEGRO		SLAVE	
	M	F	M	F	M	F	M	F	M	F	M	F
TACATA												
1783	114	97	9	10	19	15	35	23	17	28	34	21
1799	138	129	14	8	25	36	50	34	6	2	43	49
1802	193	199	36	33	48	49	43	52	15	12	51	53
1804	216	222	24	16	87	98	59	44	7	9	39	55
1805	257	243	25	15	102	106	76	55	8	10	46	57
1812	228	199	61	57	47	40	81	61	4	2	35	39
1813	226	210	83	68	24	17	73	78	4	4	42	43
1817	163	191	50	52	42	36	48	68	3	4	20	31
1818	264	249	79	85	28	27	106	98	1	0	50	39
1819	264	250	78	72	38	37	104	102	0	0	44	39
1820	389	346	113	97	53	55	160	140	2	2	61	52
1821	257	225	91	73	38	39	65	58	2	0	61	55
1822	344	314	116	100	53	49	112	107	5	6	58	52
TAGUAI												
1802	344	277	111	78	28	15	137	137	5	1	63	46
1803	305	310	78	111	28	15	131	137	5	1	63	46
1804	278	341	93	118	25	39	40	65	61	75	59	44
1805	278	355	93	120	25	40	40	67	61	78	59	50
1810	375	429	160	180	25	40	50	75	81	90	59	44
TAPIPA												
1803	68	67	2	6	3	9	6	5	0	0	57	47
1804	65	79	3	6	5	14	6	6	0	6	51	47
1805	72	87	4	5	4	13	11	7	4	6	49	56
1806	63	67	1	3	5	5	9	9	2	4	46	46
1807	58	77	1	5	4	4	9	9	1	2	43	57
1808	57	60	3	4	1	3	6	6	3	3	44	44
1811	55	45	5	6	0	0	1	2	3	3	46	34
1812	66	46	6	6	3	3	2	1	3	2	52	34
1816	52	57	4	8	5	9	9	5	2	1	32	34
1817	50	54	5	9	2	5	9	5	2	1	32	34
1818	46	56	4	7	6	6	5	6	5	4	26	33
1819	57	62	6	8	7	6	4	3	15	10	25	35
1820	52	57	4	8	5	9	9	5	2	1	32	34
1829	36	39	1	2	1	2	7	8	8	3	19	24
TARIA												
1803	40	36	0	0	0	0	40	36	0	0	0	0
1808	34	18	0	0	0	0	30	15	2	2	2	1
1810	21	32	0	0	0	0	21	32	0	0	0	0
TARMAS												
1802	70	60	7	2	2	2	17	20	2	0	42	36

TABLE 2. PARISH CHILD POPULATION (CONTINUED)

YEAR	TOTAL		WHITE		INDIAN		PARDO		NEGRO		SLAVE	
	M	F	M	F	M	F	M	F	M	F	M	F
1803	64	57	6	2	3	1	17	24	1	0	37	30
1805	61	62	5	6	5	1	9	21	1	1	41	33
1807	55	67	7	8	3	0	16	23	0	2	29	34
1808	53	66	7	7	2	1	14	18	0	1	30	39
1810	71	82	5	12	2	4	22	18	1	1	41	47
1811	78	81	5	13	3	3	25	18	1	1	44	46
1815	69	69	9	4	1	1	22	16	4	3	33	45
1816	64	82	8	5	0	1	19	25	4	6	33	45
1817	66	90	8	4	0	0	19	31	2	1	37	54
1818	67	79	7	10	0	4	17	18	1	2	42	45
1819	73	84	9	2	1	0	24	30	0	2	39	50
1820	99	104	7	4	1	0	33	41	2	3	56	56
1829	57	81	8	8	0	0	33	51	0	0	16	22
TEMERLA												
1802	91	95	1	4	0	0	90	91	0	0	0	0
1803	81	91	2	4	0	0	79	87	0	0	0	0
1804	80	71	2	1	0	0	78	70	0	0	0	0
1805	74	65	2	1	0	0	72	64	0	0	0	0
1806	94	86	2	1	0	0	92	85	0	0	0	0
1807	97	94	1	2	0	0	96	92	0	0	0	0
1808	94	86	2	1	0	0	92	85	0	0	0	0
1810	93	99	0	1	0	0	93	98	0	0	0	0
1817	99	106	7	6	0	0	92	100	0	0	0	0
1818	111	119	6	7	0	0	103	110	0	0	2	2
1819	128	116	7	7	0	0	121	109	0	0	0	0
1820	114	128	7	9	0	0	105	117	0	0	2	2
1821	126	142	7	9	0	0	117	131	0	0	2	2
TINACO												
1771	260	253	134	124	7	10	101	101	1	1	17	17
1781	271	234	136	145	0	0	114	81	5	0	16	8
1787	287	262	153	159	8	4	110	92	0	0	16	7
1788	200	172	126	129	13	4	49	31	2	0	10	8
1790	140	131	103	90	4	2	17	21	4	3	12	15
1791	246	243	124	123	10	6	99	90	0	5	13	19
1794	275	281	143	131	8	7	113	123	1	1	10	19
1795	276	301	133	127	7	13	124	139	1	4	11	18
1796	270	290	131	118	4	14	124	140	1	1	10	17
1798	282	304	133	134	6	9	131	144	0	4	12	13
1799	270	284	120	117	11	6	120	141	4	8	15	12
1800	271	309	123	123	10	5	118	157	8	9	12	15
1801	249	284	113	112	9	2	112	153	4	8	11	9
1802	259	270	130	101	7	3	89	127	23	26	10	13
1803	318	329	142	114	8	5	122	164	31	28	15	18
1804	301	325	139	128	7	5	116	141	25	35	14	16
1805	304	303	150	116	6	6	116	134	17	28	15	19
1806	346	320	165	129	8	4	134	143	22	28	17	16
1807	351	339	164	128	10	4	145	158	16	35	16	14

TABLE 2. PARISH CHILD POPULATION (CONTINUED)

YEAR	TOTAL		WHITE		INDIAN		PARDO		NEGRO		SLAVE	
	M	F	M	F	M	F	M	F	M	F	M	F
1808	345	334	164	136	9	6	139	153	17	25	16	14
1811	298	326	128	146	6	10	136	135	16	20	12	15
1812	306	327	142	129	6	10	140	167	2	6	16	15
1816	255	252	160	135	17	23	60	79	0	0	18	15
1817	247	250	153	140	16	19	55	73	0	0	23	18
1819	257	292	153	160	16	19	65	95	0	0	23	18
1820	325	375	173	196	25	37	98	111	0	0	29	31
1821	378	380	183	197	26	37	140	115	0	0	29	31
1822	347	400	186	212	26	37	104	124	3	4	28	23
1823	481	494	286	262	36	47	108	128	13	14	38	43
1824	472	486	283	260	35	45	106	126	13	14	35	41
1825	481	494	286	262	36	47	108	128	13	14	38	43
1826	494	475	284	243	31	30	128	139	12	16	39	47
1827	492	499	287	266	32	28	125	138	10	18	38	49
1829	491	481	285	248	27	29	129	142	11	14	39	48
1830	482	510	284	267	25	28	128	153	10	13	35	49
1831	482	517	269	275	23	28	143	165	11	12	36	37
1832	502	524	277	278	26	24	151	173	16	15	32	34
1834	566	691	288	397	25	31	188	196	65	67	0	0
1835	626	761	296	425	26	35	226	228	78	73	0	0
1836	699	1030	325	581	25	39	270	325	79	85	0	0
1837	880	1035	415	456	39	48	327	424	99	107	0	0
TINAJAS												
1781	257	131	12	6	30	15	60	30	52	20	103	60
1801	120	123	7	10	0	0	91	99	2	4	20	10
1802	139	133	5	0	1	4	111	113	1	0	21	16
1803	125	151	11	3	1	5	98	128	2	2	13	13
1804	133	150	5	2	4	0	111	128	3	8	10	12
1805	105	115	6	2	1	0	87	100	1	4	10	9
1807	120	125	3	0	0	0	94	115	16	8	7	2
1808	131	127	4	1	0	0	122	117	0	0	5	9
1809	124	127	4	1	0	0	115	117	0	0	5	9
1810	176	172	5	3	0	0	166	160	0	0	5	9
1811	201	204	11	4	0	7	180	184	0	0	10	9
1813	178	192	13	8	0	0	149	165	8	12	8	7
1818	96	141	2	4	0	0	90	132	0	0	4	5
1819	118	141	2	4	0	0	105	117	9	13	2	7
1820	118	141	2	4	0	0	105	117	9	13	2	7
1821	148	191	2	3	0	0	125	161	9	13	12	14
TINAQUILLO												
1781	123	119	20	25	5	2	91	86	0	0	7	6
1787	188	160	40	31	9	13	138	116	0	0	1	0
1788	105	164	36	27	9	13	58	123	1	0	1	1
1790	175	155	28	30	9	8	135	117	1	0	2	0
1791	168	169	33	39	3	5	127	123	5	0	0	2
1792	156	156	39	32	4	5	110	117	2	1	1	1
1794	200	172	41	38	3	5	149	125	4	2	3	2

TABLE 2. PARISH CHILD POPULATION (CONTINUED)

YEAR	TOTAL		WHITE		INDIAN		PARDO		NEGRO		SLAVE	
	M	F	M	F	M	F	M	F	M	F	M	F
1795	200	172	41	38	3	5	149	125	4	2	3	2
1796	195	151	38	28	3	2	148	117	3	0	3	4
1798	211	174	43	33	5	2	156	130	2	2	5	7
1799	175	163	43	32	4	4	122	121	2	1	4	5
1800	173	171	33	35	3	4	126	126	2	1	9	5
1801	181	177	41	32	4	4	129	132	2	1	5	8
1802	209	164	56	33	3	2	144	119	1	2	5	8
1803	163	196	39	32	6	7	112	142	2	3	4	12
1804	195	176	56	38	4	7	129	122	1	2	5	7
1805	172	194	34	25	8	10	124	146	2	5	4	8
1806	212	195	52	43	4	2	152	144	1	2	3	4
1807	234	201	52	48	4	2	172	144	2	2	4	5
1808	236	201	54	48	4	2	172	144	2	2	4	5
1809	238	217	90	58	6	6	133	147	0	0	9	6
1811	261	240	107	77	6	5	143	147	2	5	3	6
1812	261	240	107	77	6	5	143	147	2	5	3	6
1815	234	223	69	60	5	4	157	155	1	0	2	4
1816	278	269	93	81	5	6	176	172	4	5	0	5
1817	253	276	76	69	2	2	172	202	2	0	1	3
1818	327	298	108	81	6	2	211	214	2	1	0	0
1820	450	453	123	102	13	12	297	324	9	7	8	8
1822	295	283	143	146	16	15	118	113	7	3	11	6
1823	373	454	148	186	23	37	173	200	0	0	29	31
1836	498	518	128	133	9	13	360	370	1	2	0	0
	TUCUYITO											
1803	232	206	71	63	9	6	100	91	8	11	44	35
1804	254	239	75	68	9	6	113	109	8	11	49	45
1805	275	261	80	74	10	7	129	122	7	10	49	48
1812	300	387	52	88	2	4	98	106	6	4	142	185
1816	355	303	43	34	11	8	158	133	18	12	125	116
	TUCUPIDO											
1783	127	161	0	0	127	161	0	0	0	0	0	0
1801	273	278	48	39	104	108	93	107	3	4	25	20
1805	289	297	48	40	110	115	4	6	99	110	28	26
1809	467	454	78	70	172	174	167	172	3	5	47	33
	TUCUPIDO DE GUANARE											
1802	700	589	120	106	160	130	125	104	155	132	140	117
1803	426	514	128	129	91	111	113	118	41	95	53	61
1804	565	686	221	239	83	95	191	211	29	90	41	51
1805	565	686	221	239	83	95	191	211	29	90	41	51
1807	528	641	218	306	51	62	206	213	24	30	29	30
1808	482	666	135	215	61	95	248	297	22	28	16	31
1809	558	738	218	298	48	59	235	291	28	49	29	41
1810	554	680	239	297	35	29	231	290	20	29	29	35
1817	273	463	100	195	21	30	119	191	19	29	14	18

TABLE 2. PARISH CHILD POPULATION (CONTINUED)

YEAR	TOTAL		WHITE		INDIAN		PARDO		NEGRO		SLAVE	
	M	F	M	F	M	F	M	F	M	F	M	F
TUCURAGUA												
1802	55	35	0	0	1	1	45	27	0	0	9	7
1803	80	59	1	12	0	0	64	38	0	0	15	9
1804	65	41	2	0	0	0	51	33	0	0	12	8
1805	64	41	0	0	0	0	52	32	0	0	12	9
1807	43	48	2	1	0	0	34	34	0	0	7	13
1808	56	56	2	1	0	0	47	44	0	1	7	10
1809	56	56	2	1	0	0	47	44	0	1	7	10
1812	34	40	0	0	0	0	26	26	0	0	8	14
1816	23	22	0	0	0	0	22	15	0	0	1	7
TUREN												
1778	66	80	4	9	47	51	14	19	1	1	0	0
1801	213	310	80	96	55	63	38	85	31	59	9	7
1808	350	471	125	170	74	102	141	184	5	9	5	6
1809	87	122	4	5	45	64	23	34	15	18	0	1
1810	485	429	162	142	65	75	243	197	12	10	3	5
1811	97	137	24	20	35	34	34	79	4	2	0	2
1812	126	137	36	37	37	34	52	61	1	0	0	5
1816	126	168	38	56	49	63	39	49	0	0	0	0
TURIAMO												
1802	30	45	0	0	0	0	4	5	1	1	25	39
1803	32	30	0	0	0	0	3	4	2	0	27	26
1804	40	53	0	0	0	0	10	6	0	0	30	47
1805	37	26	0	0	0	0	6	2	0	1	31	23
1808	43	41	0	0	0	0	5	4	2	3	36	34
1818	72	89	0	0	0	0	12	14	0	0	60	75
1819	57	42	2	1	0	0	19	15	3	2	33	24
TURMERO												
1781	1139	1055	590	460	274	287	240	248	0	0	35	60
1802	1011	1174	293	332	138	215	287	346	45	62	198	219
1803	1070	1236	319	345	216	238	294	368	58	81	183	204
1804	1167	1325	356	381	228	255	315	391	69	82	199	216
1805	1228	1421	378	418	237	278	328	407	78	92	207	226
1806	1296	1439	392	437	256	290	335	388	85	89	228	235
1808	1429	1589	407	458	289	326	380	407	91	104	262	294
1809	1510	1658	401	525	285	340	482	415	86	97	256	281
1811	1575	1798	480	595	310	371	433	429	91	100	261	303
URACHICHE												
1782	210	192	42	42	71	67	75	63	3	3	19	17
1788	176	190	24	26	76	62	73	90	0	0	3	12
1802	246	222	5	6	57	43	163	149	5	9	16	15

TABLE 2. PARISH CHILD POPULATION (CONTINUED)

YEAR	TOTAL		WHITE		INDIAN		PARDO		NEGRO		SLAVE	
	M	F	M	F	M	F	M	F	M	F	M	F
1803	271	225	7	9	60	45	171	151	13	8	20	12
1804	263	229	7	9	61	40	171	152	7	10	17	18
1805	263	242	8	10	60	54	170	152	2	7	23	19
1807	274	259	9	14	71	52	172	161	6	17	16	15
1808	296	276	12	20	78	57	180	172	8	7	18	20
1809	332	319	47	31	63	64	203	200	6	5	13	19
1810	339	302	42	28	60	63	217	186	8	7	12	18
1811	312	309	25	29	51	66	220	190	6	4	10	20
1815	339	306	42	32	60	63	217	186	8	7	12	18
1816	389	384	46	42	66	74	261	250	4	4	12	14
1817	311	308	36	42	58	64	196	182	12	8	9	12
1818	320	347	28	35	50	64	193	179	24	38	25	31
1819	418	395	41	37	62	67	265	215	28	46	22	30
URAMA												
1802	115	92	1	0	0	0	71	57	34	27	9	8
1804	135	105	6	3	0	0	86	72	32	20	11	10
1806	94	94	4	3	0	0	52	57	33	24	5	10
1807	91	86	6	4	0	0	67	55	12	18	6	9
1808	133	113	4	4	0	0	94	79	28	20	7	10
1810	175	173	3	0	0	0	140	141	27	27	5	5
1818	87	87	0	0	0	0	84	74	0	0	3	13
1819	83	89	0	0	0	0	77	82	0	0	6	7
1820	116	122	9	3	0	0	82	90	18	20	7	9
VALENCIA												
1782	920	867	368	351	19	20	391	360	7	3	135	133
1802	932	946	300	369	5	7	474	407	16	8	137	155
1803	852	843	275	279	8	9	435	406	24	30	110	119
1804	857	920	211	280	12	9	482	461	37	38	115	132
1805	820	872	196	290	37	26	447	399	43	46	97	111
1808	821	872	196	290	37	26	447	399	43	46	98	111
1809	1005	1005	337	363	17	21	467	446	24	27	160	148
1812	1003	1005	337	363	17	21	467	446	22	27	160	148
1815	1187	1156	252	222	147	152	691	680	11	3	86	99
1816	1246	1208	273	229	159	162	703	695	18	13	93	109
1819	1445	1542	377	412	164	172	771	809	22	30	111	119
VALLE DE LA PASCUA												
1804	289	260	81	85	28	17	115	94	0	0	65	64
1805	206	192	48	49	19	10	94	87	0	0	45	46
1806	230	233	60	63	18	17	101	96	0	0	51	57
1808	257	257	64	72	29	33	98	98	0	0	66	54
1809	305	303	84	84	41	36	119	106	0	0	61	77
VILLA DE CURA												
1780	563	570	210	252	15	23	286	218	16	22	36	55

TABLE 2. PARISH CHILD POPULATION (CONTINUED)

YEAR	TOTAL		WHITE		INDIAN		PARDO		NEGRO		SLAVE	
	M	F	M	F	M	F	M	F	M	F	M	F
1796	622	375	468	274	1	2	64	30	5	3	84	66
1802	606	643	244	249	16	20	238	232	22	45	86	97
1803	763	745	295	458	23	29	145	220	34	25	266	13
1804	631	526	270	196	106	102	143	150	28	18	84	60
1805	577	572	255	228	12	16	222	227	1	3	87	98
1806	659	625	232	204	21	18	310	309	4	2	92	92
1807	611	554	205	174	24	12	274	226	0	3	108	139
1808	617	656	214	229	35	39	257	270	19	20	92	98
1809	413	467	140	148	24	32	128	157	6	10	115	120
1811	947	996	286	290	55	44	442	458	30	37	134	167
1816	364	483	80	120	32	68	142	168	0	0	110	127
1817	416	386	416	386	0	0	0	0	0	0	0	0
1822	628	650	207	293	21	20	282	250	0	0	118	87
	YARITAGUA											
1782	390	376	128	132	35	42	196	183	0	0	31	19
1802	110	184	18	38	9	28	21	39	49	63	13	16
1803	168	268	27	44	10	23	38	85	75	97	18	19
1804	175	268	27	44	10	23	41	85	77	97	20	19
1805	342	465	75	97	7	30	59	87	112	158	89	93
1807	678	876	87	148	21	25	215	313	310	328	45	62
1808	821	1030	117	195	21	25	326	415	325	338	32	57
1809	821	1030	117	195	21	25	326	415	325	338	32	57
1810	821	1030	117	195	21	25	326	415	325	338	32	57
1811	790	1011	120	190	20	22	324	411	295	342	31	46
1812	768	966	112	175	17	20	310	399	300	328	29	44
1816	560	572	67	86	10	10	446	448	23	21	14	7
1817	712	444	142	122	15	21	494	230	35	46	26	25
1818	919	762	162	171	28	33	674	511	19	17	36	30
1820	834	920	232	208	27	30	490	606	49	48	36	28

TABLE 3. MARRIED PERSONS AS A PERCENT OF ADULT POPULATION
(A=ADULTS, PCT=PERCENT MARRIED)

YEAR	TOTAL		WHITE		INDIAN		PARDO		NEGRO		SLAVE	
	A	PCT	A	PCT	A	PCT	A	PCT	A	PCT	A	PCT
ACARIGUA												
1778	597	45.9	0	0.0	597	45.9	0	0.0	0	0.0	0	0.0
1802	1486	42.9	308	35.4	828	45.0	324	45.1	16	62.5	10	0.0
1803	1490	47.7	346	39.6	782	53.6	328	43.9	21	47.6	13	7.7
1804	1509	47.4	346	39.6	810	52.6	333	43.5	9	55.6	11	18.2
1805	1431	47.2	335	40.3	770	53.0	309	40.1	9	66.7	8	25.0
1808	1313	50.9	214	48.6	834	53.0	250	46.4	7	85.7	8	0.0
1809	1352	49.9	217	46.5	874	51.5	250	47.2	6	100.0	5	0.0
1810	1212	51.2	222	46.8	750	53.6	225	48.0	7	85.7	8	12.5
1812	1242	51.5	227	48.5	770	53.8	223	50.2	7	57.1	15	0.0
1829	671	50.2	251	44.6	35	42.9	351	58.4	15	13.3	19	15.8
ACHAGUAS												
1780	103	62.1	12	33.3	87	66.7	2	100.0	0	0.0	2	0.0
1801	758	51.7	83	50.6	74	79.7	568	49.1	19	31.6	14	42.9
1804	2150	53.3	320	56.3	96	58.3	1572	53.6	97	49.5	65	30.8
1806	1024	62.9	156	64.1	272	58.8	480	75.0	34	52.9	82	7.3
1809	1507	56.8	290	58.6	197	67.0	896	57.4	31	45.2	93	28.0
1811	1749	52.8	353	54.4	225	61.3	985	53.6	45	48.9	141	31.2
AGUA BLANCA												
1779	382	42.9	18	44.4	196	48.0	165	37.6	0	0.0	3	0.0
1801	414	44.0	68	41.2	156	43.6	190	45.3	0	0.0	0	0.0
1802	360	52.8	58	62.1	154	51.9	148	50.0	0	0.0	0	0.0
1803	360	52.8	58	62.1	154	51.9	148	50.0	0	0.0	0	0.0
1804	718	59.1	128	53.1	272	58.8	318	61.6	0	0.0	0	0.0
1805	498	50.6	131	64.1	138	58.0	228	38.6	0	0.0	1	0.0
1808	519	42.0	27	44.4	227	43.2	261	40.6	1	100.0	3	33.3
1812	625	40.0	45	48.9	246	41.1	328	38.7	6	0.0	0	0.0
1815	535	42.8	117	47.0	153	44.4	265	40.0	0	0.0	0	0.0
1830	503	41.4	138	50.0	144	38.2	219	38.4	0	0.0	2	0.0
AGUA CULEBRAS												
1781	1367	35.0	229	36.2	150	42.0	823	33.7	11	18.2	154	35.1
1802	926	22.7	114	18.4	140	20.0	625	23.2	16	37.5	31	32.3
1803	792	26.5	97	18.6	106	22.6	558	26.2	15	40.0	16	100.0
1804	532	37.2	86	25.6	68	39.7	341	39.3	13	38.5	24	41.7
1805	896	17.6	111	12.6	80	28.8	629	16.9	13	23.1	63	19.0
1807	684	25.7	73	30.1	87	33.3	491	23.8	14	14.3	19	31.6
1808	755	31.7	83	27.7	95	32.6	536	32.3	15	26.7	26	30.8
1809	756	31.7	83	27.7	95	32.6	536	32.3	16	31.3	26	30.8
1811	619	39.4	80	27.5	71	42.3	428	41.4	13	38.5	27	37.0
1812	521	49.3	55	47.3	61	57.4	367	48.5	8	12.5	30	56.7
1815	437	46.7	29	27.6	40	52.5	349	48.1	5	20.0	14	42.9
1817	312	38.5	23	17.4	63	54.0	219	35.6	0	0.0	7	57.1

TABLE 3. MARRIED PERSONS (CONTINUED)

YEAR	TOTAL		WHITE		INDIAN		PARDO		NEGRO		SLAVE	
	A	PCT	A	PCT	A	PCT	A	PCT	A	PCT	A	PCT
1818	487	41.7	39	25.6	66	53.0	371	41.5	0	0.0	11	36.4
1819	343	49.6	31	25.8	25	40.0	276	54.3	0	0.0	11	18.2
1820	481	44.9	24	50.0	0	0.0	371	49.1	50	28.0	36	22.2
1821	450	48.0	15	80.0	44	31.8	362	50.3	28	28.6	1	0.0
AGUACALIENTE												
1803	357	37.0	59	33.9	0	0.0	288	38.9	0	0.0	10	0.0
1804	326	41.1	54	40.7	0	0.0	259	43.2	0	0.0	13	0.0
1805	421	24.2	97	20.6	0	0.0	266	27.8	15	53.3	43	0.0
1806	337	42.7	53	37.7	0	0.0	236	47.5	0	0.0	48	25.0
1807	389	36.5	51	39.2	0	0.0	280	39.3	0	0.0	58	20.7
1818	207	40.6	6	66.7	0	0.0	172	41.9	0	0.0	29	27.6
1819	206	42.7	6	66.7	0	0.0	176	43.2	0	0.0	24	33.3
ALPARGATON												
1804	147	58.5	0	0.0	0	0.0	108	59.3	39	56.4	0	0.0
1805	164	57.3	0	0.0	0	0.0	115	60.9	49	49.0	0	0.0
1806	124	53.2	0	0.0	0	0.0	91	47.3	33	69.7	0	0.0
1807	139	43.2	0	0.0	0	0.0	74	40.5	65	46.2	0	0.0
1818	105	59.0	0	0.0	0	0.0	105	59.0	0	0.0	0	0.0
1819	93	75.3	0	0.0	0	0.0	93	75.3	0	0.0	0	0.0
1820	163	77.3	0	0.0	0	0.0	120	81.7	43	65.1	0	0.0
ALTAGRACIA DE ORITUCO												
1783	716	50.4	189	48.7	290	49.7	15	73.3	120	55.0	102	47.1
1802	1149	44.2	385	37.4	396	51.5	272	43.4	9	33.3	87	44.8
1803	1184	46.4	353	43.6	397	51.4	293	47.4	22	31.8	119	37.8
1804	1280	47.0	381	44.6	421	52.3	305	46.9	34	26.5	139	42.4
1806	1264	42.1	454	40.1	374	45.7	251	42.6	38	23.7	147	42.9
1807	1315	42.7	463	40.2	385	44.9	262	44.3	46	39.1	159	43.4
1809	1366	42.9	474	39.0	417	43.6	257	45.9	57	31.6	161	51.6
1810	1331	43.4	461	39.3	399	44.6	248	46.8	62	29.0	161	52.8
1811	1365	40.9	454	40.1	431	41.3	267	43.8	53	26.4	160	41.9
ALTAMIRA												
1783	250	59.2	0	0.0	250	59.2	0	0.0	0	0.0	0	0.0
ANTIMANO												
1811	1154	65.0	56	71.4	196	81.6	123	65.0	88	79.5	691	57.9
1819	907	36.9	229	38.9	149	40.3	303	37.0	19	73.7	207	29.0
APARICION												
1802	1685	48.5	490	40.8	437	51.3	505	53.9	188	51.1	65	40.0
1803	1621	48.7	462	39.0	413	52.8	503	55.3	196	53.1	47	21.3
1804	2165	38.2	652	39.3	401	39.4	1043	39.3	0	0.0	69	5.8

TABLE 3. MARRIED PERSONS (CONTINUED)

YEAR	TOTAL A	TOTAL PCT	WHITE A	WHITE PCT	INDIAN A	INDIAN PCT	PARDO A	PARDO PCT	NEGRO A	NEGRO PCT	SLAVE A	SLAVE PCT
1805	1805	44.0	312	48.1	342	45.6	1032	42.8	53	37.7	66	39.4
1808	2136	40.6	510	43.1	481	40.5	1067	41.5	0	0.0	78	12.8
1809	2276	39.1	700	28.6	350	64.0	1140	36.8	0	0.0	86	53.5
1810	1932	36.5	511	32.1	389	39.6	950	40.0	0	0.0	82	9.8
1811	1804	39.1	429	38.9	377	38.7	924	41.6	0	0.0	74	10.8
1812	1616	47.4	483	51.8	402	49.3	701	43.9	0	0.0	30	33.3
APURITO												
1802	332	53.0	23	60.9	31	64.5	225	56.0	30	33.3	23	26.1
1806	376	66.5	76	65.8	40	75.0	245	68.6	0	0.0	15	13.3
1807	386	43.0	87	43.7	77	41.6	191	44.0	16	37.5	15	40.0
ARAGUITA												
1784	667	41.7	27	29.6	64	39.1	99	50.5	16	68.8	461	39.9
1802	460	42.2	18	22.2	40	45.0	15	53.3	21	57.1	366	41.5
1803	395	39.2	21	33.3	11	36.4	2	100.0	24	50.0	337	38.6
1804	359	45.7	14	42.9	6	66.7	9	44.4	18	44.4	312	45.5
1805	335	31.6	12	50.0	5	40.0	5	0.0	6	33.3	307	31.3
1807	424	53.3	13	38.5	8	50.0	58	25.9	12	100.0	333	57.1
1810	358	39.7	31	32.3	22	18.2	58	48.3	23	39.1	224	40.6
1811	394	34.3	30	33.3	18	27.8	89	31.5	22	45.5	235	34.9
1812	284	38.7	29	51.7	18	27.8	44	40.9	16	37.5	177	37.3
1816	335	34.9	42	28.6	27	14.8	38	52.6	28	57.1	200	32.5
1819	334	32.3	48	37.5	11	0.0	41	24.4	23	34.8	211	34.1
ARAURE												
1778	1927	38.0	865	43.4	171	45.6	596	35.2	165	30.3	130	14.6
1798	5371	36.1	1946	36.4	909	41.6	2263	36.2	253	12.6	0	0.0
1799	5408	36.9	2014	35.8	887	43.6	2257	37.8	250	14.4	0	0.0
1800	5451	37.6	1978	37.9	910	43.1	2295	37.8	268	13.8	0	0.0
1801	1932	31.8	424	34.2	63	34.9	1275	33.6	170	11.8	0	0.0
1802	2330	34.2	744	36.8	94	38.3	1268	36.2	46	41.3	178	5.1
1803	2211	31.8	716	36.0	71	39.4	1191	33.2	53	26.4	180	4.4
1804	1755	40.8	625	44.2	87	34.5	873	43.1	28	28.6	142	18.3
1805	1491	44.8	552	45.7	137	21.2	680	50.4	25	24.0	97	39.2
1808	2140	31.6	646	34.5	190	35.3	1117	31.5	13	7.7	174	19.0
1809	2144	33.2	687	35.4	204	35.8	1074	34.0	8	0.0	171	17.5
1810	2163	33.4	698	35.8	204	35.8	1074	34.0	12	0.0	175	19.4
1811	2433	39.1	946	48.4	205	36.1	1079	34.3	24	50.0	179	21.2
1812	2195	33.4	716	36.0	207	35.7	1078	33.4	25	48.0	169	17.8
1829	3066	28.0	1591	10.6	168	64.9	1193	46.6	58	41.4	56	0.0
AREGUE												
1802	500	34.0	74	21.6	252	40.5	160	28.8	0	0.0	14	42.9
1803	558	32.3	51	39.2	331	33.8	162	25.9	0	0.0	14	42.9
1804	489	41.5	52	42.3	324	42.6	104	37.5	0	0.0	9	44.4
1805	475	45.1	70	42.9	258	49.6	129	38.8	0	0.0	18	33.3

TABLE 3. MARRIED PERSONS (CONTINUED)

YEAR	TOTAL A	TOTAL PCT	WHITE A	WHITE PCT	INDIAN A	INDIAN PCT	PARDO A	PARDO PCT	NEGRO A	NEGRO PCT	SLAVE A	SLAVE PCT
1809	700	45.1	82	48.8	441	46.7	153	39.9	2	50.0	22	36.4
1815	688	39.1	124	43.5	355	38.0	184	40.2	0	0.0	25	24.0
	ARENALES											
1802	637	29.2	114	31.6	68	29.4	281	31.0	83	31.3	91	18.7
1803	661	29.8	137	29.9	62	29.0	284	33.8	81	29.6	97	18.6
1804	659	29.1	130	31.5	66	27.3	304	31.9	61	29.5	98	18.4
1805	650	29.8	113	33.6	67	28.4	257	36.6	119	22.7	94	17.0
1807	648	27.2	107	24.3	67	35.8	304	31.6	76	21.1	94	14.9
1809	607	27.3	78	35.9	95	23.2	268	32.1	91	24.2	75	10.7
	ARICHUNA											
1801	357	35.3	79	40.5	165	38.8	82	29.3	26	23.1	5	0.0
1804	507	32.3	102	35.3	226	37.2	101	19.8	43	23.3	35	40.0
	AROA											
1802	1094	26.7	93	28.0	70	28.6	702	22.8	103	48.5	126	28.6
1805	1053	39.0	141	39.7	68	44.1	508	38.6	264	35.2	72	50.0
1807	1032	37.5	150	36.0	68	44.1	497	37.2	265	35.5	52	46.2
1808	1083	41.4	68	44.1	84	54.8	457	40.9	283	37.1	191	41.9
1809	1160	44.2	71	50.7	57	56.1	895	41.9	50	52.0	87	50.6
1817	747	31.6	81	39.5	0	0.0	621	31.2	16	62.5	29	0.0
1818	1062	60.3	153	54.9	68	64.7	741	61.5	100	56.0	0	0.0
	ATAMAICA											
1780	83	77.1	2	100.0	79	75.9	1	100.0	1	100.0	0	0.0
1802	265	67.2	78	64.1	133	75.2	40	70.0	1	0.0	13	0.0
	AYAMANES											
1802	387	46.5	31	38.7	356	47.2	0	0.0	0	0.0	0	0.0
1803	320	52.2	37	43.2	281	53.0	2	100.0	0	0.0	0	0.0
1804	322	58.4	22	45.5	283	59.4	17	58.8	0	0.0	0	0.0
1805	287	52.3	39	35.9	241	54.8	7	57.1	0	0.0	0	0.0
1807	403	50.6	53	45.3	319	52.0	31	45.2	0	0.0	0	0.0
1808	400	52.0	61	52.5	310	52.3	29	48.3	0	0.0	0	0.0
1815	424	49.8	62	35.5	297	53.9	64	43.8	0	0.0	1	100.0
	BANCO LARGO											
1805	705	38.0	203	43.3	102	35.3	168	42.9	115	34.8	117	27.4
1809	755	35.8	118	39.0	68	38.2	480	35.0	29	34.5	60	33.3
	BARBACOAS DE LOS LLANOS											
1782	930	41.4	411	41.1	171	40.4	116	45.7	177	46.9	55	20.0
1783	1323	43.7	411	41.1	171	40.4	316	48.4	370	47.6	55	20.0

TABLE 3. MARRIED PERSONS (CONTINUED)

YEAR	TOTAL A	TOTAL PCT	WHITE A	WHITE PCT	INDIAN A	INDIAN PCT	PARDO A	PARDO PCT	NEGRO A	NEGRO PCT	SLAVE A	SLAVE PCT
1802	1565	43.6	573	48.2	271	40.6	547	43.5	61	55.7	113	21.2
1803	1580	37.3	621	38.3	203	36.5	401	42.9	278	29.5	77	31.2
1804	1737	40.1	635	43.5	185	42.2	197	37.6	576	42.7	144	15.3
1805	2011	43.7	626	49.2	149	48.3	468	51.3	632	36.1	136	22.1
1809	2139	44.5	701	47.6	253	36.4	561	43.9	519	49.3	105	22.9
1810	2067	44.8	714	48.2	220	36.4	561	45.6	490	45.7	82	26.8
1811	2063	45.8	702	50.1	220	38.2	562	46.3	489	45.0	90	31.1
	BARBACOAS DEL TOCUYO											
1802	388	43.6	61	42.6	158	53.2	63	30.2	95	40.0	11	18.2
1803	371	38.8	55	18.2	172	44.2	53	41.5	78	41.0	13	30.8
1804	427	37.2	60	30.0	186	41.9	69	29.0	75	42.7	17	29.4
1805	447	39.8	77	31.2	197	42.6	59	40.7	85	35.3	29	55.2
1806	421	41.8	74	32.4	168	42.9	63	41.3	97	49.5	19	31.6
1807	430	41.9	81	34.6	172	43.0	64	37.5	101	49.5	12	33.3
1808	459	37.0	86	37.2	193	40.4	68	26.5	92	41.3	20	20.0
1809	455	38.2	86	37.2	195	42.1	65	30.8	88	40.9	21	19.0
1810	471	39.3	88	38.6	199	44.2	72	33.3	92	39.1	20	15.0
1812	390	32.6	75	33.3	146	39.7	140	24.3	22	40.9	7	14.3
1815	474	37.1	81	40.7	166	44.0	197	31.0	12	58.3	18	11.1
1816	429	38.9	80	41.3	156	44.2	155	32.9	22	40.9	16	31.3
1817	527	36.6	65	43.1	194	38.7	228	34.2	17	47.1	23	17.4
1818	447	39.6	55	45.5	155	51.6	202	29.2	14	57.1	21	23.8
1819	521	42.2	73	43.8	174	51.7	225	36.9	29	41.4	20	15.0
1820	510	41.0	70	34.3	179	55.9	230	34.3	6	50.0	25	12.0
	BARQUISIMETO											
1779	6669	41.2	712	18.1	344	56.7	4251	49.6	738	15.2	624	33.0
1815	9501	26.4	628	27.4	1083	31.6	6884	26.6	375	28.8	531	10.2
	BARQUISIMETO, MITAD DE(1)											
1802	3842	55.6	652	57.1	444	36.0	1767	61.0	739	56.3	240	45.8
1803	3857	55.2	652	56.9	454	35.7	1770	60.5	738	56.2	243	46.1
1804	4348	50.3	661	56.7	466	36.9	1778	60.3	1162	37.4	281	47.0
1805	4043	57.3	659	57.2	444	38.3	1917	63.0	768	56.8	255	49.4
1807	4095	25.6	282	43.3	247	30.0	2573	25.1	391	25.1	602	18.1
1808	4112	26.3	288	46.5	244	28.7	2573	25.5	408	28.2	599	17.4
1809	4285	26.0	310	43.9	262	28.2	2671	25.3	427	27.9	615	17.6
1810	4096	25.6	282	43.3	247	30.0	2573	25.1	391	25.1	603	18.1
1811	4329	26.3	315	43.8	286	30.8	2686	25.7	427	27.6	615	17.2
1817	4386	32.5	211	26.5	908	34.1	3140	33.3	15	13.3	112	11.6
1818	3297	27.5	116	20.7	711	38.5	2239	25.3	128	20.3	103	17.5
1819	3167	29.5	113	24.8	666	41.4	2170	26.7	115	26.1	103	19.4
1820	3308	30.2	142	22.5	639	36.9	2295	29.6	109	33.0	123	13.0
	BARQUISIMETO, MITAD DE(2)											
1802	3907	30.4	572	30.4	153	31.4	2541	32.7	236	31.4	405	14.8

TABLE 3. MARRIED PERSONS (CONTINUED)

YEAR	TOTAL A	TOTAL PCT	WHITE A	WHITE PCT	INDIAN A	INDIAN PCT	PARDO A	PARDO PCT	NEGRO A	NEGRO PCT	SLAVE A	SLAVE PCT
1803	4783	36.3	1166	13.9	176	31.8	1648	50.2	1370	45.3	423	16.1
1804	4760	36.3	1141	14.7	176	31.8	1636	49.4	1391	45.9	416	14.4
1805	4805	36.5	1148	15.0	184	29.3	1645	49.4	1396	46.0	432	16.7
1807	4788	36.3	1158	14.9	178	31.5	1650	49.2	1384	46.1	418	14.8
1808	4458	37.1	1023	15.6	160	31.3	1505	46.8	1404	48.3	366	16.4
1809	4402	36.3	1025	15.8	160	31.3	1507	46.8	1344	46.0	366	16.4
1810	4402	36.3	1025	15.8	160	31.3	1507	46.8	1344	46.0	366	16.4
1811	4816	33.8	1037	16.2	198	28.3	1724	41.4	1485	42.0	372	17.7
1817	4831	26.9	351	26.2	169	34.3	3795	27.8	198	31.3	318	10.1
1818	4401	30.9	362	30.9	169	33.1	3358	32.3	204	37.3	308	9.7
1819	4420	31.5	377	31.3	176	37.5	3350	32.8	203	39.4	314	8.9
1820	4461	31.3	417	28.8	189	36.0	3336	32.9	210	39.0	309	10.4
BARUTA												
1802	1505	32.5	640	30.8	522	37.2	102	37.3	59	27.1	182	24.2
1803	1574	34.8	615	33.5	570	38.6	119	37.8	77	32.5	193	26.9
1804	1589	33.9	641	33.1	553	38.7	118	33.1	83	28.9	194	25.8
1805	1537	33.8	550	34.5	596	35.6	127	37.0	66	30.3	198	25.8
1811	1527	34.9	614	33.4	512	35.9	106	36.8	58	34.5	237	35.9
1816	890	31.8	365	29.6	268	31.0	45	42.2	68	39.7	144	31.9
1817	1152	33.3	473	34.0	394	36.3	121	25.6	23	34.8	141	29.1
1819	2007	41.8	447	40.3	391	42.7	92	42.4	18	44.4	1059	41.9
1820	1203	44.9	512	45.9	355	49.0	156	46.8	31	38.7	149	30.9
BAUL												
1781	339	53.7	137	46.7	99	65.7	37	70.3	62	41.9	4	25.0
1802	1408	44.2	536	42.2	219	51.6	349	57.3	199	22.1	105	37.1
1805	1205	45.1	490	45.7	238	52.5	407	39.6	51	51.0	19	36.8
1811	1804	51.2	680	54.7	310	38.7	633	55.6	0	0.0	181	44.2
1812	1477	48.1	604	51.0	250	37.6	530	50.2	0	0.0	93	45.2
1815	998	48.3	451	49.2	101	33.7	356	47.8	31	58.1	59	64.4
1816	1378	45.9	579	46.3	125	44.8	551	43.6	41	53.7	82	56.1
1817	1469	48.3	607	48.4	121	38.0	597	47.2	59	50.8	85	68.2
1825	1611	40.8	449	41.6	260	40.4	874	40.4	12	100.0	16	6.3
1829	1144	51.3	466	61.2	19	31.6	445	43.8	195	49.7	19	21.1
BOBARE												
1779	230	55.7	0	0.0	230	55.7	0	0.0	0	0.0	0	0.0
1802	391	55.8	0	0.0	391	55.8	0	0.0	0	0.0	0	0.0
1803	391	55.8	0	0.0	391	55.8	0	0.0	0	0.0	0	0.0
1804	379	53.8	0	0.0	379	53.8	0	0.0	0	0.0	0	0.0
1805	375	54.4	0	0.0	375	54.4	0	0.0	0	0.0	0	0.0
1806	375	54.4	0	0.0	375	54.4	0	0.0	0	0.0	0	0.0
1808	405	57.3	0	0.0	405	57.3	0	0.0	0	0.0	0	0.0
1811	481	44.1	0	0.0	481	44.1	0	0.0	0	0.0	0	0.0
1820	290	64.8	0	0.0	269	64.7	18	77.8	0	0.0	3	0.0

TABLE 3. MARRIED PERSONS (CONTINUED)

YEAR	TOTAL		WHITE		INDIAN		PARDO		NEGRO		SLAVE	
	A	PCT	A	PCT	A	PCT	A	PCT	A	PCT	A	PCT
BOCONO												
1778	1359	43.4	645	44.3	145	52.4	541	41.8	6	33.3	22	0.0
1795	1656	43.0	768	41.1	142	52.8	662	44.6	34	35.3	50	28.0
1796	1423	43.4	690	41.3	95	58.9	597	44.9	16	43.8	25	8.0
1798	1476	45.1	657	46.1	126	54.0	640	44.5	16	25.0	37	16.2
1799	1593	42.1	773	40.4	122	54.1	640	44.4	25	16.0	33	12.1
1800	1338	43.2	631	41.8	109	55.0	550	44.4	16	25.0	32	18.7
1802	925	42.7	356	43.8	88	63.6	439	38.3	26	50.0	16	12.5
1803	1141	37.2	448	35.3	120	56.7	521	34.9	34	44.1	18	11.1
1804	1147	37.1	443	35.2	122	54.1	521	35.3	37	43.2	24	16.7
1805	1701	39.2	1087	39.7	128	50.0	418	34.9	42	52.4	26	7.7
1806	1203	38.1	493	32.9	134	61.2	517	37.1	39	46.2	20	20.0
1807	1424	46.9	717	53.0	121	64.5	510	37.3	40	50.0	36	0.0
1808	1264	49.4	646	58.8	124	58.1	414	36.7	42	47.6	38	0.0
1810	1055	34.5	452	32.3	131	42.7	454	35.7	0	0.0	18	0.0
BORBURATA												
1803	480	39.4	20	35.0	9	11.1	139	43.2	176	44.9	136	30.9
1804	540	37.0	24	45.8	9	22.2	147	45.6	201	37.3	159	28.3
1805	524	36.3	29	37.9	4	0.0	126	43.7	206	37.4	159	29.6
1806	560	34.6	42	19.0	4	0.0	106	41.5	252	34.5	156	35.3
1807	540	35.9	24	41.7	4	0.0	106	41.5	252	34.5	154	34.4
1818	408	39.7	7	28.6	3	0.0	116	50.0	162	37.7	120	34.2
1819	448	43.3	9	66.7	5	0.0	135	50.4	179	43.6	120	35.0
BURERITO												
1802	802	30.3	6	33.3	12	33.3	530	31.7	209	28.2	45	22.2
1803	832	36.1	6	33.3	11	9.1	162	37.0	612	37.1	41	24.4
1804	908	26.4	0	0.0	20	10.0	661	26.6	196	27.6	31	25.8
1807	626	36.3	7	28.6	2	0.0	397	38.3	189	32.8	31	35.5
1809	703	33.3	5	40.0	1	0.0	410	38.3	242	25.6	45	28.9
BURIA												
1779	310	43.5	23	43.5	83	48.2	179	43.6	21	28.6	4	25.0
1802	551	35.4	17	29.4	78	38.5	400	35.5	45	26.7	11	54.5
1803	507	38.9	13	69.2	42	71.4	400	35.5	45	26.7	7	57.1
1804	497	50.9	17	52.9	56	57.1	400	50.2	12	50.0	12	41.7
1805	527	42.5	18	44.4	63	46.0	430	42.1	10	20.0	6	66.7
1807	509	41.1	25	44.0	60	48.3	400	39.2	13	61.5	11	36.4
1809	386	13.2	18	55.6	43	32.6	312	6.7	7	57.1	6	33.3
1810	563	39.1	18	55.6	43	32.6	486	39.5	12	33.3	4	0.0
1811	592	41.7	20	50.0	42	42.9	514	41.6	10	20.0	6	50.0
1817	561	45.1	34	35.3	35	51.4	466	46.8	23	17.4	3	33.3
1818	486	37.0	70	34.3	41	34.1	371	38.3	0	0.0	4	0.0
1819	641	36.2	36	44.4	99	24.2	291	34.4	207	44.4	8	0.0

TABLE 3. MARRIED PERSONS (CONTINUED)

YEAR	TOTAL A	TOTAL PCT	WHITE A	WHITE PCT	INDIAN A	INDIAN PCT	PARDO A	PARDO PCT	NEGRO A	NEGRO PCT	SLAVE A	SLAVE PCT
CABRIA												
1802	142	44.4	0	0.0	0	0.0	141	44.0	0	0.0	1	100.0
1803	137	42.3	0	0.0	0	0.0	137	42.3	0	0.0	0	0.0
1808	131	44.3	0	0.0	0	0.0	127	44.1	4	50.0	0	0.0
CABRUTA												
1780	128	60.9	61	75.4	9	88.9	29	41.4	10	80.0	19	21.1
1806	191	60.7	25	64.0	144	58.3	21	76.2	0	0.0	1	0.0
1808	321	65.4	9	44.4	300	66.7	11	54.5	1	0.0	0	0.0
1810	291	57.0	29	48.3	229	60.3	33	42.4	0	0.0	0	0.0
CAGUA												
1781	3981	34.2	1778	36.4	209	38.8	1796	33.7	0	0.0	198	14.1
1802	3547	27.9	1310	22.7	107	29.9	1715	31.7	100	21.0	315	29.8
1803	3329	28.9	996	29.4	98	24.5	1908	29.1	18	11.1	309	28.2
1804	3446	31.1	1118	26.6	167	35.9	1693	34.1	67	14.9	401	31.9
1805	3350	28.3	1004	26.1	80	33.8	1831	28.6	59	16.9	376	33.5
1806	3530	27.0	1041	26.4	104	28.8	1955	27.1	67	6.0	363	31.7
1808	3471	26.4	1019	26.6	111	25.2	1963	25.8	23	26.1	355	29.3
1809	3495	24.2	1015	21.7	133	23.3	1927	24.2	36	36.1	384	30.5
1811	3385	24.9	964	22.3	120	22.5	1842	25.1	71	29.6	388	30.4
1815	2085	27.0	642	25.1	134	36.6	1018	28.3	12	66.7	279	20.4
1816	1856	36.6	662	27.3	172	40.1	666	49.2	56	51.8	300	24.0
1817	2356	30.9	682	28.0	192	41.1	1086	31.1	76	51.3	320	25.6
1818	2319	30.4	665	27.2	181	39.2	1080	30.9	76	51.3	317	24.9
CAICARA DEL ORINOCO												
1802	189	51.9	49	53.1	28	42.9	90	60.0	0	0.0	22	27.3
CALABOZO												
1780	2608	38.6	1087	42.1	93	40.9	864	41.3	139	36.0	425	24.2
1802	3601	29.9	1162	30.6	130	30.8	1513	36.4	116	25.9	680	14.9
1803	3656	30.5	1188	30.9	121	29.8	1506	37.0	153	30.7	688	15.6
1804	3674	31.3	1188	31.7	119	32.8	1518	37.2	161	34.8	688	16.3
1805	3700	31.4	1212	32.4	119	28.6	1512	37.1	173	38.2	684	15.9
1807	3267	32.7	1042	34.1	105	26.7	1428	35.9	131	42.7	561	20.5
1808	2963	33.9	859	36.3	96	37.5	1340	38.1	167	46.1	501	14.0
1810	2908	31.5	853	37.9	46	34.8	1471	32.2	47	34.0	491	18.1
1812	2166	39.3	721	44.7	40	17.5	1023	42.7	33	30.3	349	21.8
1817	1532	26.2	497	34.2	0	0.0	774	25.2	0	0.0	261	14.2
1818	1148	27.0	424	33.3	0	0.0	539	28.2	0	0.0	185	9.2
1822	1156	21.0	322	25.5	0	0.0	678	22.0	0	0.0	156	7.7

TABLE 3. MARRIED PERSONS (CONTINUED)

YEAR	TOTAL A	TOTAL PCT	WHITE A	WHITE PCT	INDIAN A	INDIAN PCT	PARDO A	PARDO PCT	NEGRO A	NEGRO PCT	SLAVE A	SLAVE PCT
CAMAGUAN												
1780	577	52.3	52	73.1	316	65.8	46	52.2	17	47.1	146	16.4
1801	607	51.1	123	48.8	318	56.0	117	51.3	25	40.0	24	8.3
1802	579	50.8	119	45.4	279	55.9	131	53.4	26	38.5	24	16.7
1803	689	53.1	124	58.1	317	53.6	206	54.4	19	42.1	23	17.4
1804	704	53.7	134	56.7	329	52.3	199	59.3	13	30.8	29	27.6
1812	790	47.1	146	57.5	280	47.1	297	45.1	13	30.8	54	33.3
1817	988	80.6	237	84.4	227	70.5	450	88.9	47	51.1	27	44.4
CAMATAGUA												
1783	1541	41.1	376	40.4	317	53.6	174	37.9	559	40.1	115	19.1
1802	1187	39.4	251	42.2	440	39.1	164	31.7	114	49.1	218	37.6
1803	1131	40.1	251	43.0	409	40.1	151	33.1	105	51.4	215	36.3
1804	1283	33.2	138	32.6	262	36.6	365	25.5	333	30.3	185	49.2
1805	1131	40.1	251	43.0	409	40.1	151	33.1	105	51.4	215	36.3
1806	1131	40.1	251	43.0	409	40.1	151	33.1	105	51.4	215	36.3
1808	1131	40.1	251	43.0	409	40.1	151	33.1	105	51.4	215	36.3
1811	1229	26.9	183	31.7	232	22.4	680	31.8	0	0.0	134	3.0
CANOABO												
1781	825	27.5	75	37.3	0	0.0	618	29.0	0	0.0	132	15.2
1788	748	37.0	56	41.1	0	0.0	531	38.2	0	0.0	161	31.7
1802	777	34.9	45	35.6	0	0.0	603	32.0	0	0.0	129	48.1
1803	750	35.7	40	37.5	0	0.0	589	32.9	0	0.0	121	48.8
1804	765	34.4	50	36.0	0	0.0	595	31.6	0	0.0	120	47.5
1805	795	36.6	30	60.0	0	0.0	604	33.8	0	0.0	161	42.9
1806	882	31.1	53	30.2	0	0.0	672	29.8	13	15.4	144	38.9
1807	842	36.1	59	30.5	0	0.0	630	35.9	13	15.4	140	41.4
1808	852	35.6	62	32.3	0	0.0	626	34.7	13	15.4	151	42.4
1809	879	34.1	68	32.4	0	0.0	617	33.4	17	35.3	177	37.3
1810	767	32.1	49	24.5	7	28.6	548	31.0	44	38.6	119	37.8
1815	607	36.6	45	26.7	0	0.0	429	37.3	12	16.7	121	39.7
1817	641	51.8	35	34.3	7	57.1	444	52.9	46	32.6	109	60.6
1819	754	42.3	80	37.5	18	22.2	428	43.0	42	35.7	186	46.2
1820	770	42.5	84	38.1	18	22.2	436	43.1	46	37.0	186	46.2
CAPAYA												
1784	846	47.3	35	48.6	153	43.8	102	53.9	100	39.0	456	48.7
1802	897	27.9	27	14.8	154	44.2	212	26.4	17	70.6	487	22.6
1803	994	38.1	22	27.3	143	44.1	107	37.4	83	43.4	639	36.6
1804	1064	40.4	15	40.0	141	42.6	121	29.8	71	49.3	716	40.9
1805	811	41.8	21	33.3	128	39.1	92	34.8	122	32.8	448	46.9
1806	948	38.9	7	28.6	124	35.5	156	30.8	180	32.2	481	45.1
1807	991	36.7	17	47.1	78	38.5	231	39.4	80	33.8	585	35.6
1808	953	38.2	17	47.1	80	37.5	231	39.4	80	33.8	545	38.2
1809	676	43.3	18	22.2	89	52.8	65	40.0	85	37.6	419	43.9

TABLE 3. MARRIED PERSONS (CONTINUED)

YEAR	TOTAL A	TOTAL PCT	WHITE A	WHITE PCT	INDIAN A	INDIAN PCT	PARDO A	PARDO PCT	NEGRO A	NEGRO PCT	SLAVE A	SLAVE PCT
1811	918	38.1	28	25.0	127	37.0	225	39.6	70	27.1	468	40.2
1812	860	43.1	22	45.5	244	69.7	204	46.1	40	52.5	350	21.7
1817	678	38.2	17	35.3	57	31.6	213	43.2	31	32.3	360	36.9
1818	753	37.3	22	27.3	69	30.4	202	43.6	47	27.7	413	37.0
1819	782	35.9	15	26.7	81	29.6	230	41.3	56	33.9	400	34.7
1820	800	35.5	17	35.3	81	34.6	238	34.9	50	36.0	414	36.0
CARABALLEDA												
1802	908	37.7	112	42.9	167	36.5	179	39.7	0	0.0	450	36.0
1804	823	36.9	108	35.2	151	42.4	154	39.0	0	0.0	410	34.6
CARACAS-ALTAGRACIA												
1796	5320	23.4	1449	28.8	0	0.0	2634	25.1	351	27.9	886	7.9
1802	4817	21.8	1503	26.9	35	25.7	2084	24.5	454	18.9	741	5.3
1803	4808	22.8	1693	26.8	36	16.7	1874	26.5	498	22.1	707	4.2
1804	5187	22.0	1822	26.4	65	10.8	2092	27.2	465	7.3	743	6.5
1805	5265	20.7	1606	28.4	131	14.5	2046	23.4	445	22.9	1037	3.3
1807	5026	19.7	1548	28.0	98	4.1	1990	22.6	404	19.8	986	2.3
1808	5061	20.2	1504	28.5	69	0.0	2039	23.7	407	18.9	1042	3.4
1810	5172	20.6	1492	27.8	46	4.3	2125	24.8	430	19.3	1079	3.7
1811	4269	22.2	1398	30.6	24	12.5	1846	22.4	301	20.6	700	6.0
1815	1759	33.7	635	31.2	36	33.3	671	32.0	244	54.1	173	20.2
1816	1427	24.3	627	30.0	12	41.7	598	20.2	81	25.9	109	11.0
1817	1727	20.9	726	22.2	7	0.0	697	22.1	113	23.0	184	10.9
1818	1813	20.3	791	26.0	28	35.7	675	16.6	98	17.3	221	10.4
1819	1774	25.5	801	31.1	55	27.3	619	22.6	86	29.1	213	10.8
1820	1547	23.3	538	40.7	40	30.0	656	14.5	86	19.8	227	7.9
CARACAS-CANDELARIA												
1800	2755	27.8	828	32.6	22	22.7	1325	30.3	150	17.3	430	14.9
1802	2858	30.1	1058	33.0	79	11.4	1088	31.4	244	25.8	389	24.7
1803	2676	28.9	981	33.0	94	11.7	942	32.2	279	24.0	380	18.2
1804	2951	28.3	1105	29.5	65	18.5	1094	30.6	284	28.5	403	20.1
1805	2887	29.3	1013	31.7	72	20.8	1072	31.0	331	26.3	399	23.1
1806	3000	29.8	1048	31.5	89	21.3	1108	31.0	322	30.1	433	23.8
1808	3153	29.1	1003	33.1	62	24.2	1400	29.6	267	28.5	421	19.5
1809	3234	27.6	1065	33.5	71	14.1	1462	27.2	214	26.2	422	16.8
1811	2570	30.5	997	35.0	37	21.6	956	30.2	248	30.6	332	18.7
1815	1657	31.1	618	31.4	57	21.1	602	34.7	216	29.6	164	22.0
1816	1713	29.4	591	26.6	27	37.0	800	35.9	88	22.7	207	14.5
1817	2058	34.0	595	38.2	46	39.1	864	31.4	303	42.2	250	22.4
1818	1943	24.4	548	29.4	17	35.3	1000	24.2	152	23.7	226	12.8
1819	1855	25.6	548	29.4	19	36.8	839	23.8	176	26.1	273	22.0
1820	2028	34.2	631	42.3	12	16.7	1068	34.2	95	38.9	222	9.9
1821	1792	28.5	526	43.7	25	24.0	835	21.9	153	25.5	253	20.9

TABLE 3. MARRIED PERSONS (CONTINUED)

YEAR	TOTAL A	TOTAL PCT	WHITE A	WHITE PCT	INDIAN A	INDIAN PCT	PARDO A	PARDO PCT	NEGRO A	NEGRO PCT	SLAVE A	SLAVE PCT
CARACAS-CATEDRAL ORIENTE												
1801	3899	19.6	1244	28.1	58	5.2	1146	20.9	207	20.3	1244	10.5
1802	3921	18.9	1204	28.7	59	11.9	1138	21.2	248	12.5	1272	9.4
1803	3847	19.1	1209	28.7	43	14.0	1100	19.9	227	18.1	1268	9.6
1804	3916	19.8	1116	31.8	49	2.0	1231	20.3	209	16.3	1311	10.2
1805	4185	18.9	1301	27.4	59	6.8	1273	19.6	233	16.3	1319	11.0
1807	3812	17.8	1208	26.9	42	2.4	1109	17.2	216	14.8	1237	10.3
1809	4042	20.0	1284	28.9	51	5.9	1253	20.4	230	19.1	1224	11.0
1811	3830	17.7	1150	27.1	32	0.0	1286	20.0	163	14.1	1199	7.1
1815	1961	19.2	635	28.0	25	24.0	717	18.4	61	23.0	523	9.0
1816	1801	35.3	608	24.3	104	70.2	528	29.4	144	41.0	417	48.0
1817	2440	16.4	821	23.6	39	25.6	727	17.9	150	20.7	703	5.1
1818	2232	20.4	726	30.7	63	14.3	678	22.3	162	9.3	603	9.5
1819	2802	17.2	924	24.9	33	9.1	952	18.1	101	15.8	792	7.8
CARACAS-CATEDRAL PONIENTE												
1802	2923	16.5	872	20.9	80	12.5	986	21.4	125	22.4	860	5.9
1803	3181	18.2	938	24.9	67	17.9	1084	23.2	171	14.6	921	6.3
1805	3182	18.8	1063	23.3	122	19.7	940	22.2	221	26.2	836	6.9
1807	3292	19.1	992	24.6	114	17.5	982	22.1	272	26.8	932	7.9
1808	3223	17.8	979	23.7	96	15.6	1013	20.6	221	22.6	914	7.3
1810	3372	20.0	983	24.7	107	16.8	1094	20.7	222	19.4	966	14.9
1811	3242	21.9	970	27.5	89	27.0	1049	22.5	214	24.3	920	14.2
1815	1993	20.4	748	25.3	62	24.2	627	20.9	124	27.4	432	8.8
1816	2253	29.7	920	26.1	28	28.6	451	35.0	373	50.1	481	15.8
1817	2598	20.2	924	27.4	53	24.5	912	16.0	193	26.4	516	12.2
1818	2674	15.8	1031	22.8	29	20.7	754	17.2	146	19.2	714	3.2
1819	2600	18.9	996	27.0	34	11.8	746	16.8	175	24.6	649	7.7
1822	2186	20.9	819	25.8	750	21.9	33	3.0	128	19.5	456	12.1
CARACAS-CURATO CASTRENSE												
1803	861	23.2	698	25.5	4	0.0	51	35.3	8	0.0	100	4.0
1804	1008	18.8	811	21.0	2	0.0	56	28.6	5	0.0	134	3.0
1805	1150	17.7	950	19.3	8	0.0	67	29.9	4	0.0	121	0.0
1807	2970	20.8	1933	22.3	5	0.0	838	21.7	19	5.3	175	1.7
1809	1823	23.5	1282	26.4	8	0.0	359	25.1	9	0.0	165	0.0
1810	986	20.1	874	22.2	8	0.0	15	13.3	5	0.0	84	2.4
1811	1086	22.7	802	22.6	6	0.0	104	48.1	33	24.2	141	5.7
CARACAS-SAN PABLO												
1799	4977	23.0	1720	28.8	36	11.1	2084	24.9	242	21.1	895	8.6
1801	5052	22.4	1677	29.8	66	3.0	2103	22.8	237	24.1	969	9.4
1802	4918	22.1	1504	29.6	67	0.0	1917	22.9	346	17.1	1084	13.5
1803	3897	26.8	1610	29.2	64	18.7	1334	35.1	97	24.7	792	9.1
1804	4696	26.9	1767	30.4	59	13.6	1897	29.9	137	32.1	836	12.9
1805	5455	56.6	1880	63.8	100	32.0	1835	70.0	990	25.4	650	49.4

TABLE 3. MARRIED PERSONS (CONTINUED)

YEAR	TOTAL		WHITE		INDIAN		PARDO		NEGRO		SLAVE	
	A	PCT	A	PCT	A	PCT	A	PCT	A	PCT	A	PCT
1806	5211	58.5	1840	64.7	96	20.8	1715	74.3	914	26.3	646	50.5
1807	5354	57.0	1840	64.7	96	20.8	1820	70.3	914	26.3	684	47.4
1808	4220	40.8	1300	38.5	50	40.0	1600	43.8	590	71.2	680	11.8
1809	3713	45.0	1100	40.9	70	28.6	810	49.4	860	46.5	873	45.8
1810	3861	23.0	910	33.0	93	53.8	1203	33.5	755	6.0	900	10.0
1811	2836	29.5	850	35.3	95	52.6	1080	37.0	400	12.5	411	8.8
1815	5442	59.8	1228	74.8	190	71.6	1600	37.5	350	28.6	2074	72.4
1816	4893	30.4	1551	31.3	14	28.6	2066	25.6	312	46.8	950	33.9
1817	5385	35.0	1851	37.1	14	28.6	2266	32.1	312	46.8	942	34.0
1818	6661	37.8	2514	35.8	34	70.6	2256	32.3	909	59.7	948	33.8
1820	6334	18.3	2628	23.5	94	10.6	2264	16.1	310	21.0	1038	9.6
CARACAS-SANTA ROSALIA												
1795	3932	22.2	1502	29.1	0	0.0	1852	21.7	0	0.0	578	6.2
1796	4058	22.1	1371	32.1	0	0.0	2107	20.1	0	0.0	580	5.3
1798	3792	24.3	1337	31.0	0	0.0	1918	24.8	0	0.0	537	6.0
1799	3777	24.1	1281	30.8	0	0.0	1938	23.9	0	0.0	558	9.3
1802	4104	23.1	1349	30.5	61	3.3	1861	23.4	222	18.9	611	9.7
1803	3909	25.2	1197	33.4	66	21.2	1805	25.4	206	19.4	635	11.2
1804	3795	28.4	1171	34.6	70	44.3	1717	30.5	178	16.9	659	13.5
1805	3728	34.2	1249	38.6	68	36.8	1473	42.6	182	15.9	756	14.8
1806	4333	22.3	1517	33.0	104	6.7	1901	17.9	269	19.7	542	12.2
1807	4244	20.5	1354	30.1	104	1.0	1792	18.3	263	21.3	731	10.4
1808	4270	20.8	1310	31.0	102	2.0	1813	18.6	268	20.5	777	11.2
1809	4415	23.1	1545	30.5	164	8.5	1705	23.8	325	19.4	676	9.8
1810	4445	22.0	1469	25.9	137	11.7	1880	23.2	295	23.1	664	11.7
1811	5260	17.4	1334	31.2	112	5.4	2729	12.5	286	20.6	799	12.0
1815	2814	21.5	1031	22.6	37	24.3	1118	24.8	159	32.1	469	7.7
1816	3040	18.4	1098	24.3	14	14.3	1195	18.5	163	19.6	570	6.3
1817	2425	29.7	974	32.1	5	20.0	968	34.0	169	28.4	309	9.4
1818	2638	30.3	1057	30.7	11	36.4	972	31.1	280	46.1	318	12.3
1819	2958	19.0	1219	18.5	18	22.2	825	19.0	535	22.6	361	15.2
1820	3163	33.0	1452	33.2	20	30.0	1192	37.2	227	29.5	272	16.5
1822	3496	29.0	1348	35.6	17	23.5	1546	25.7	174	31.0	411	19.2
CARAMACATE												
1779	102	72.5	11	72.7	76	81.6	15	26.7	0	0.0	0	0.0
1799	240	54.2	84	59.5	49	69.4	97	45.4	3	0.0	7	28.6
1801	285	43.5	69	43.5	45	48.9	154	45.5	16	12.5	1	0.0
1802	371	43.4	65	44.6	39	51.3	261	42.9	0	0.0	6	0.0
1803	459	37.9	102	40.2	68	54.4	280	33.2	3	100.0	6	0.0
1804	344	40.4	58	53.4	51	54.9	232	34.5	0	0.0	3	0.0
1805	362	44.8	66	54.5	58	55.2	236	39.8	0	0.0	2	0.0
1806	354	42.1	63	49.2	48	54.2	238	37.8	2	100.0	3	0.0
1807	231	49.8	38	57.9	47	42.6	138	47.8	7	85.7	1	100.0
1809	389	45.0	55	54.5	126	31.7	200	50.0	6	66.7	2	50.0
1811	348	47.7	36	55.6	78	46.2	234	47.0	0	0.0	0	0.0
1812	305	47.9	34	52.9	66	36.4	205	50.7	0	0.0	0	0.0
1817	195	81.0	26	76.9	26	80.8	143	81.8	0	0.0	0	0.0

TABLE 3. MARRIED PERSONS (CONTINUED)

YEAR	TOTAL		WHITE		INDIAN		PARDO		NEGRO		SLAVE	
	A	PCT	A	PCT	A	PCT	A	PCT	A	PCT	A	PCT
1818	192	50.0	19	42.1	41	63.4	132	47.0	0	0.0	0	0.0
1819	206	43.7	31	45.2	39	46.2	136	42.6	0	0.0	0	0.0
1822	164	43.9	15	40.0	22	36.4	126	46.0	1	0.0	0	0.0
1823	128	51.6	11	54.5	17	47.1	99	52.5	0	0.0	1	0.0
1828	138	53.6	19	73.7	17	47.1	99	52.5	1	0.0	2	0.0
1829	161	50.9	13	61.5	39	41.0	108	53.7	1	0.0	0	0.0
1831	180	56.7	26	69.2	47	42.6	103	60.2	3	66.7	1	0.0
1832	178	56.2	24	66.7	47	42.6	101	59.4	5	80.0	1	0.0
1833	172	54.7	19	52.6	45	44.4	104	57.7	4	100.0	0	0.0
1834	184	53.3	19	52.6	45	48.9	108	57.4	12	33.3	0	0.0
1835	221	52.5	26	53.8	57	45.6	122	57.4	16	37.5	0	0.0
1836	234	53.8	28	57.1	64	46.9	124	58.1	18	44.4	0	0.0
1837	251	50.2	26	53.8	70	45.7	135	53.3	20	40.0	0	0.0
1838	263	51.0	26	53.8	79	45.6	137	55.5	21	38.1	0	0.0
CARAYACA												
1802	573	40.0	143	50.3	14	35.7	106	35.8	101	45.5	209	32.5
1804	476	38.2	78	44.9	40	35.0	93	40.9	77	49.4	188	30.3
1805	493	39.6	97	39.2	27	40.7	144	42.4	57	40.4	168	36.9
1807	493	39.6	97	39.2	27	40.7	144	42.4	57	40.4	168	36.9
1808	493	39.6	97	39.2	27	40.7	144	42.4	57	40.4	168	36.9
1809	493	39.6	97	39.2	27	40.7	144	42.4	57	40.4	168	36.9
1810	493	39.6	97	39.2	27	40.7	144	42.4	57	40.4	168	36.9
1811	494	48.8	100	38.0	27	40.7	102	59.8	41	43.9	224	50.4
1817	684	34.2	159	27.7	1	0.0	245	36.7	89	29.2	190	38.9
1818	818	26.4	303	29.0	6	50.0	297	19.9	40	35.0	172	30.2
1819	658	40.1	202	44.6	8	50.0	221	35.7	36	25.0	191	42.9
1820	696	39.8	214	46.7	10	40.0	225	35.1	45	28.9	202	40.1
1833	1259	43.0	265	54.3	66	28.8	344	34.0	180	36.1	404	48.5
CARORA												
1802	3715	19.0	373	22.3	30	16.7	2600	19.6	296	16.9	416	13.9
1803	3955	19.5	381	21.5	34	17.6	2822	20.7	302	14.2	416	13.2
1804	4109	20.2	409	22.2	39	15.4	3000	21.2	276	14.9	385	15.1
1809	4908	20.0	444	28.2	48	20.8	3742	18.2	344	29.4	330	19.4
1815	3905	21.2	314	17.8	10	0.0	3154	19.5	95	37.9	332	36.1
CARUAO												
1811	431	34.3	2	0.0	0	0.0	79	26.6	6	0.0	344	36.9
1815	438	38.8	0	0.0	3	0.0	9	33.3	16	12.5	410	40.2
CASIGUA												
1780	1830	33.1	542	33.4	41	31.7	625	36.6	240	33.3	382	27.0
CATA												
1803	433	36.5	8	25.0	0	0.0	0	0.0	164	32.9	261	39.1

TABLE 3. MARRIED PERSONS (CONTINUED)

YEAR	TOTAL A	TOTAL PCT	WHITE A	WHITE PCT	INDIAN A	INDIAN PCT	PARDO A	PARDO PCT	NEGRO A	NEGRO PCT	SLAVE A	SLAVE PCT
1804	427	37.0	8	87.5	0	0.0	0	0.0	167	32.9	252	38.1
1805	450	35.6	9	44.4	0	0.0	42	42.9	128	29.7	271	36.9
CAUCAGUA												
1784	1871	45.3	106	35.8	97	55.7	224	49.6	98	55.1	1346	43.9
1802	1315	36.7	58	36.2	93	33.3	163	47.2	135	36.3	866	35.2
1803	1293	38.7	61	32.8	85	35.3	140	42.1	144	33.3	863	39.7
1804	1318	38.8	62	30.6	85	37.6	148	40.5	142	34.5	881	39.8
1805	1322	39.3	56	44.6	77	36.4	154	40.9	144	34.7	891	39.7
1806	1329	38.1	61	34.4	78	28.2	153	43.8	141	36.2	896	38.6
1807	1284	37.1	67	34.3	84	29.8	118	33.9	146	34.9	869	38.9
1808	1149	38.5	68	30.9	80	32.5	115	39.1	97	38.1	789	39.7
1809	1234	35.6	62	33.9	118	25.4	120	39.2	109	31.2	825	37.2
1811	1084	37.0	82	31.7	60	28.3	244	25.0	28	35.7	670	42.8
1812	1259	26.4	137	20.4	114	19.3	284	18.7	81	22.2	643	32.8
1816	1149	33.2	76	42.1	61	23.0	165	30.9	74	39.2	773	33.0
1817	988	34.9	57	38.6	53	26.4	170	30.6	37	29.7	671	36.7
1818	980	34.5	51	47.1	79	24.1	178	34.3	21	19.0	651	35.3
1819	1123	33.4	72	41.7	86	20.9	239	31.0	42	21.4	684	35.7
1820	1158	31.8	92	39.1	87	19.5	240	32.9	56	23.2	683	32.7
CERRITO												
1779	2477	37.9	676	36.7	235	39.1	1472	38.9	5	0.0	89	29.2
CHABASQUEN												
1802	1446	55.0	97	33.0	1181	59.3	147	39.5	7	85.7	14	0.0
1803	1449	54.6	92	31.5	1183	59.0	154	39.6	4	75.0	16	0.0
1804	1470	54.1	93	30.1	1193	58.8	162	38.9	5	60.0	17	0.0
1805	1473	54.0	99	28.3	1201	58.9	148	37.8	6	66.7	19	5.3
1806	1480	53.9	105	32.4	1197	58.8	153	35.9	7	57.1	18	5.6
1808	1481	56.8	90	30.0	1217	59.2	157	53.5	14	64.3	3	33.3
1809	1448	54.4	21	19.0	1260	57.4	152	34.9	8	75.0	7	14.3
1812	944	62.5	30	40.0	655	60.3	240	72.5	12	58.3	7	28.6
1815	953	64.2	29	34.5	666	62.2	237	75.1	9	66.7	12	33.3
1816	1028	65.0	58	58.6	686	64.4	233	67.8	40	75.0	11	36.4
1817	1045	64.8	55	65.5	696	64.9	247	62.8	39	76.9	8	50.0
1818	1045	64.8	55	65.5	696	64.9	247	62.8	39	76.9	8	50.0
1819	538	78.1	22	54.5	375	87.5	119	58.8	15	53.3	7	28.6
1820	825	47.0	110	40.0	569	49.9	136	42.6	2	100.0	8	0.0
1829	1217	47.3	151	37.1	601	55.2	334	41.3	128	39.1	3	0.0
CHACAO												
1802	1522	39.4	452	38.9	43	14.0	273	40.3	242	41.3	512	40.6
1803	1596	39.2	480	40.6	35	17.1	363	39.7	207	38.2	511	39.3
1804	1664	38.2	508	39.8	37	5.4	335	39.1	215	42.3	569	36.9
1805	1584	38.3	473	39.5	21	0.0	364	39.6	209	37.3	517	38.1
1808	1470	45.7	557	34.8	4	0.0	190	59.5	364	50.8	355	50.7

TABLE 3. MARRIED PERSONS (CONTINUED)

YEAR	TOTAL A	TOTAL PCT	WHITE A	WHITE PCT	INDIAN A	INDIAN PCT	PARDO A	PARDO PCT	NEGRO A	NEGRO PCT	SLAVE A	SLAVE PCT
1811	1625	35.7	416	38.0	24	16.7	333	34.2	228	34.2	624	36.2
1815	1578	33.3	501	36.1	24	12.5	345	41.4	217	33.2	491	25.9
1818	1663	45.7	705	42.6	2	0.0	586	42.0	76	47.4	294	60.5
1819	1476	51.4	530	54.3	0	0.0	558	43.5	79	48.1	309	61.5
	CHAGUARAMAL											
1783	1048	42.0	294	49.3	84	47.6	425	50.1	45	42.2	200	11.5
1804	1456	41.2	357	47.6	107	48.6	913	35.7	15	80.0	64	62.5
1805	1313	53.0	225	47.1	64	71.9	570	70.4	96	36.5	358	30.2
	CHAGUARAMAS											
1783	1708	36.8	653	39.1	68	57.4	317	32.2	238	46.6	432	28.2
1802	1677	30.8	395	37.5	104	49.0	713	34.9	67	38.8	398	10.6
1803	1672	34.5	412	42.2	64	43.8	737	38.9	0	0.0	459	19.2
1804	1679	32.3	436	41.3	70	45.7	749	38.9	0	0.0	424	9.4
1805	1743	46.5	333	42.6	158	48.1	721	36.1	114	53.5	417	65.2
1808	2046	31.2	446	42.6	121	41.3	936	31.6	164	22.6	379	17.2
1810	1892	37.3	475	38.3	151	43.0	781	40.6	82	48.8	403	25.3
	CHARALLAVE											
1783	628	42.5	102	43.1	342	45.0	148	38.5	21	52.4	15	6.7
1802	1360	39.5	525	37.5	555	45.0	163	37.4	61	23.0	56	26.8
1803	1335	38.2	483	37.5	538	41.1	152	35.5	117	36.8	45	24.4
1804	1085	37.1	497	34.2	335	41.5	106	41.5	107	39.3	40	17.5
1805	1199	40.4	534	37.3	348	45.7	188	37.2	80	46.3	49	38.8
1806	1079	38.7	477	41.5	299	36.5	194	35.1	58	43.1	51	35.3
1807	1122	40.1	453	39.7	367	45.5	180	36.7	56	37.5	66	24.2
1808	1317	52.5	708	58.9	288	55.9	224	33.9	48	41.7	49	36.7
1810	1387	38.0	618	39.2	407	41.0	266	34.2	22	50.0	74	21.6
1811	1522	39.5	703	43.2	374	36.4	305	37.0	52	34.6	88	34.1
1815	1303	37.8	580	37.6	382	36.1	208	42.8	75	34.7	58	37.9
1816	1427	35.5	637	37.2	409	33.5	298	34.9	33	24.2	50	42.0
1817	1436	37.2	600	37.3	418	36.4	321	38.3	42	40.5	55	32.7
	CHIVACOA											
1782	1431	35.2	46	39.1	738	38.2	574	31.9	64	31.3	9	11.1
1802	749	35.8	26	46.2	400	39.5	287	28.6	15	26.7	21	57.1
1803	916	33.5	42	28.6	466	38.4	25	36.0	367	27.8	16	31.3
1804	887	37.3	59	27.1	423	45.6	342	31.0	33	36.4	30	13.3
1805	991	33.3	52	32.7	552	33.0	320	33.4	45	37.8	22	31.8
1807	1040	34.4	61	21.3	557	37.0	349	32.1	37	48.6	36	25.0
1808	1154	34.5	73	21.9	574	33.8	418	36.8	50	48.0	39	25.6
1809	1139	31.8	70	21.4	480	35.2	476	31.1	74	32.4	39	15.4
1810	1277	30.5	61	21.3	699	30.3	417	33.6	69	26.1	31	22.6
1811	1192	34.0	62	25.8	539	36.0	435	33.6	124	34.7	32	18.7
1812	1236	35.4	60	26.7	552	36.6	477	35.8	112	37.5	35	20.0
1815	1357	36.3	67	31.3	580	34.1	613	39.6	65	35.4	32	21.9

TABLE 3. MARRIED PERSONS (CONTINUED)

YEAR	TOTAL A	TOTAL PCT	WHITE A	WHITE PCT	INDIAN A	INDIAN PCT	PARDO A	PARDO PCT	NEGRO A	NEGRO PCT	SLAVE A	SLAVE PCT
1816	1397	38.9	83	34.9	595	41.5	509	39.7	183	32.2	27	25.9
1817	1332	39.6	74	33.8	614	36.8	572	43.0	56	46.4	16	31.3
1818	1310	40.0	98	36.7	535	43.7	539	38.2	124	37.1	14	14.3
1819	1254	41.3	92	41.3	525	43.8	504	39.3	120	41.7	13	15.4
CHORONI												
1802	1059	33.2	123	36.6	12	0.0	664	34.2	24	8.3	236	33.1
1803	1112	30.4	105	39.0	12	0.0	719	29.9	24	8.3	252	31.7
1804	1134	30.7	107	38.3	12	0.0	775	31.4	29	13.8	211	28.4
1805	947	33.1	111	30.6	9	11.1	609	33.5	15	26.7	203	34.5
1808	903	37.5	117	35.9	11	9.1	557	36.1	20	40.0	198	43.9
1809	968	33.4	109	37.6	16	12.5	601	30.1	27	44.4	215	40.5
1819	588	44.7	51	43.1	0	0.0	404	46.5	0	0.0	133	39.8
CHUAO												
1802	240	29.2	1	0.0	0	0.0	8	25.0	0	0.0	231	29.4
1803	236	28.8	0	0.0	0	0.0	4	0.0	1	0.0	231	29.4
1804	253	30.0	2	0.0	0	0.0	4	50.0	1	0.0	246	30.1
1805	266	31.6	1	0.0	0	0.0	12	50.0	1	0.0	252	31.0
1819	274	35.0	7	28.6	0	0.0	14	35.7	2	0.0	251	35.5
COCOROTE												
1781	1548	24.9	184	20.7	760	20.8	345	40.3	151	20.5	108	18.5
1782	1507	25.6	184	20.7	760	20.8	345	40.3	137	22.6	81	24.7
1788	1346	25.0	153	22.9	505	21.4	389	35.0	200	20.5	99	16.2
1791	1251	26.2	174	29.3	415	23.1	402	33.3	181	18.8	79	16.5
1794	1429	24.5	206	31.6	466	17.4	490	30.4	185	23.2	82	14.6
1802	1496	22.1	292	22.3	314	16.9	771	24.6	41	14.6	78	20.5
1803	1532	22.3	287	22.3	306	19.0	797	24.6	56	25.0	86	11.6
1804	1525	21.9	198	18.2	414	19.3	556	29.5	268	17.5	89	7.9
1805	1565	23.7	170	20.6	508	24.8	568	25.7	228	23.7	91	11.0
1807	1600	25.9	168	27.4	451	22.8	629	27.7	278	27.7	74	18.9
1808	1567	24.5	189	24.9	474	23.2	493	25.6	330	27.3	81	13.6
1809	1521	26.4	185	23.2	463	24.2	505	28.1	298	30.5	70	18.6
1811	1564	27.2	190	30.5	241	23.2	814	28.7	278	24.8	41	22.0
1812	1278	31.5	169	40.8	375	24.0	417	33.6	263	32.7	54	31.5
1817	1054	40.8	66	60.6	346	30.1	502	40.2	130	61.5	10	40.0
1818	957	34.9	163	36.8	316	33.5	446	35.4	0	0.0	32	31.3
1820	1054	40.8	66	60.6	346	30.1	502	40.2	130	61.5	10	40.0
1821	1193	40.0	122	50.8	352	30.4	711	43.3	0	0.0	8	0.0
COJEDES												
1779	834	53.0	170	45.9	503	54.5	159	56.6	0	0.0	2	0.0
1799	1161	40.8	421	36.1	313	59.4	282	45.4	30	0.0	115	7.0
1801	1137	42.7	434	35.9	339	55.5	284	46.5	33	12.1	47	12.8
1802	1297	35.9	317	38.8	331	41.7	524	37.6	10	20.0	115	5.2
1803	1167	40.5	372	42.5	308	46.4	390	42.1	2	100.0	95	6.3

TABLE 3. MARRIED PERSONS (CONTINUED)

YEAR	TOTAL		WHITE		INDIAN		PARDO		NEGRO		SLAVE	
	A	PCT	A	PCT	A	PCT	A	PCT	A	PCT	A	PCT
1804	1154	41.6	356	43.0	305	47.5	390	44.6	2	100.0	101	5.9
1805	1201	38.8	381	41.5	326	44.8	391	38.6	5	100.0	98	6.1
1806	1286	40.3	363	45.2	389	41.4	437	41.6	2	100.0	95	9.5
1807	1285	40.4	347	45.8	401	46.6	425	37.4	4	100.0	108	9.3
1808	1198	43.2	352	44.3	362	49.4	391	44.8	2	100.0	91	6.6
1809	1267	44.2	315	48.9	400	45.2	444	45.9	9	100.0	99	12.1
1811	1086	31.5	164	31.7	479	33.0	345	36.5	0	0.0	98	6.1
1812	1117	32.1	183	30.6	474	34.6	356	36.5	0	0.0	104	7.7
1816	1137	31.8	178	33.7	482	34.9	370	34.1	0	0.0	107	7.5
1817	1129	32.2	178	33.7	478	34.3	366	36.1	0	0.0	107	7.5
1818	1119	32.0	173	31.2	475	37.1	366	32.8	0	0.0	105	7.6
1819	1081	30.5	152	30.3	443	35.7	371	31.8	14	0.0	101	7.9
1820	1043	29.8	164	31.7	367	32.2	414	30.2	44	27.3	54	7.4
1822	917	32.2	131	36.6	300	36.7	419	30.3	27	22.2	40	10.0
1823	799	33.0	109	42.2	248	35.5	398	31.2	25	24.0	19	0.0
1824	760	33.2	98	42.9	226	37.2	392	30.6	25	24.0	19	0.0
1829	829	36.1	118	44.1	216	42.6	421	32.1	25	24.0	49	28.6
1831	825	35.9	108	44.4	246	39.8	400	31.7	22	40.9	49	28.6
1833	792	35.4	106	41.5	235	38.3	404	31.7	15	40.0	32	37.5
1834	779	35.0	103	40.8	225	38.2	405	31.4	15	40.0	31	38.7
1835	821	36.8	120	43.3	243	37.9	403	33.7	26	38.5	29	41.4
1836	831	37.2	125	43.2	240	39.2	411	33.8	26	38.5	29	41.4
1837	832	38.7	125	43.2	235	41.7	412	35.4	31	38.7	29	41.4
1838	821	39.0	126	44.4	233	41.2	405	35.6	28	42.9	29	41.4
	CUA											
1783	1168	34.8	80	27.5	27	59.3	158	29.1	111	27.0	792	37.0
1803	1775	43.2	159	47.8	133	32.3	323	45.5	171	42.1	989	43.4
1805	1535	50.9	203	61.1	101	53.5	256	42.2	163	50.3	812	51.0
1810	2232	40.6	274	42.3	199	50.3	473	37.4	215	35.8	1071	40.8
1812	2569	64.0	364	37.9	72	38.9	399	40.4	156	57.7	1578	77.7
1815	2036	33.5	176	33.5	123	33.3	581	30.6	160	30.0	996	35.7
1816	2189	34.0	253	34.8	165	36.4	647	33.2	163	29.4	961	34.8
1818	2585	63.4	372	36.6	76	35.5	421	43.5	140	52.9	1576	77.3
1820	2349	27.8	226	42.0	322	29.8	399	25.3	212	34.4	1190	24.2
1821	2068	61.2	180	55.6	48	41.7	490	65.3	50	52.0	1300	61.5
	CUBIRO											
1802	523	60.8	9	44.4	470	62.6	18	50.0	8	50.0	18	38.9
1803	580	52.6	7	28.6	537	54.2	4	50.0	8	37.5	24	29.2
1804	554	52.7	6	33.3	495	54.9	28	32.1	2	100.0	23	30.4
1805	695	57.3	2	0.0	606	61.1	43	39.5	19	21.1	25	28.0
1806	620	50.3	3	0.0	535	54.2	42	26.2	13	38.5	27	22.2
1807	616	50.3	2	0.0	533	54.0	42	26.2	13	38.5	26	23.1
1808	613	49.8	3	0.0	529	53.7	41	24.4	13	38.5	27	22.2
1809	609	50.7	3	0.0	529	54.1	37	27.0	13	38.5	27	29.6
1810	611	50.2	3	0.0	527	53.9	41	24.4	13	38.5	27	29.6
1815	489	46.6	3	0.0	411	50.6	46	17.4	14	28.6	15	53.3
1816	628	47.5	3	0.0	573	48.5	36	38.9	5	40.0	11	36.4

TABLE 3. MARRIED PERSONS (CONTINUED)

YEAR	TOTAL A	TOTAL PCT	WHITE A	WHITE PCT	INDIAN A	INDIAN PCT	PARDO A	PARDO PCT	NEGRO A	NEGRO PCT	SLAVE A	SLAVE PCT
1817	625	47.7	3	0.0	568	48.8	37	37.8	7	57.1	10	30.0
1818	577	49.4	6	33.3	489	51.9	67	32.8	8	75.0	7	14.3
1819	570	48.9	5	40.0	483	51.3	67	32.8	8	75.0	7	14.3
1820	519	50.3	8	75.0	428	52.8	67	32.8	9	66.7	7	14.3
CUNAVICHE												
1780	308	66.6	1	100.0	305	66.6	1	100.0	1	0.0	0	0.0
CUPIRA												
1784	631	38.8	174	49.4	30	46.7	171	39.2	106	32.1	150	29.3
1802	434	35.3	103	35.9	18	55.6	133	34.6	114	38.6	66	24.2
1803	430	37.7	93	34.4	18	50.0	146	41.1	103	40.8	70	27.1
1804	402	39.6	87	33.3	15	53.3	148	41.9	90	51.1	62	22.6
1805	392	38.8	80	32.5	14	64.3	107	43.9	125	36.0	66	37.9
1807	383	35.5	58	31.0	21	42.9	119	41.2	123	30.1	62	37.1
1808	364	34.3	51	31.4	18	27.8	144	35.4	90	34.4	61	36.1
1809	359	34.8	52	36.5	19	26.3	132	37.1	97	34.0	59	32.2
1811	434	40.6	64	42.2	96	55.2	110	42.7	118	28.0	46	34.8
CURARIGUA												
1802	982	20.7	71	38.0	18	44.4	82	39.0	352	34.1	459	3.5
1803	673	36.4	100	36.0	15	40.0	158	34.2	362	37.6	38	34.2
1804	587	42.2	90	45.6	35	28.6	199	34.2	231	51.1	32	34.4
1805	716	30.4	136	26.5	22	54.5	151	38.4	371	25.9	36	44.4
1806	641	36.7	91	38.5	38	21.1	155	40.0	324	36.4	33	36.4
1807	640	37.3	105	44.8	33	18.2	160	40.0	328	35.4	14	42.9
1808	642	32.9	119	31.9	43	27.9	146	34.2	321	33.6	13	23.1
1809	615	35.3	119	31.9	34	29.4	131	36.6	318	37.1	13	23.1
1810	738	31.7	124	33.9	35	34.3	140	38.6	329	37.7	110	1.8
1816	848	34.2	83	36.1	0	0.0	705	34.3	33	42.4	27	14.8
1817	851	36.4	78	38.5	0	0.0	667	36.6	82	41.5	24	8.3
1818	647	41.4	90	35.6	0	0.0	465	44.3	72	38.9	20	10.0
1819	726	40.9	110	47.3	47	38.3	453	41.5	99	34.3	17	29.4
1820	754	39.8	106	46.2	32	43.8	480	39.8	113	36.3	23	21.7
CURIEPE												
1784	914	41.4	41	48.8	14	50.0	179	46.4	373	48.5	307	28.3
1803	1584	36.5	65	30.8	44	50.0	413	28.1	563	40.9	499	38.1
1804	1371	35.3	53	22.6	41	53.7	263	38.8	537	35.0	477	33.5
1805	1548	36.8	49	40.8	26	23.1	350	45.7	580	32.1	543	36.5
1806	1608	20.5	48	20.8	37	21.6	509	11.8	511	13.7	503	36.2
1807	1629	35.5	43	23.3	61	23.0	461	34.7	562	33.1	502	41.4
1808	1656	35.0	43	23.3	63	25.4	466	34.3	575	32.3	509	40.9
1811	1711	43.0	62	19.4	79	30.4	508	37.0	492	39.0	570	56.1
1812	1758	44.3	68	20.6	90	31.1	531	39.2	509	40.1	560	57.9
1816	1185	30.5	46	32.6	10	20.0	349	27.2	356	25.0	424	38.0
1817	1081	30.2	32	21.9	25	16.0	398	25.4	310	33.2	316	35.1

TABLE 3. MARRIED PERSONS (CONTINUED)

YEAR	TOTAL		WHITE		INDIAN		PARDO		NEGRO		SLAVE	
	A	PCT	A	PCT	A	PCT	A	PCT	A	PCT	A	PCT
1818	1273	31.6	55	43.6	30	16.7	498	23.1	365	36.2	325	38.8
1819	1315	32.0	52	42.3	30	13.3	519	24.1	383	37.1	331	38.7
1820	1422	30.8	48	16.7	42	23.8	552	23.4	424	37.0	356	37.6
CUYAGUA												
1802	328	39.6	16	25.0	31	19.4	79	40.5	56	32.1	146	47.9
1803	313	39.9	9	22.2	8	12.5	58	51.7	102	21.6	136	51.5
1804	310	42.6	7	0.0	10	20.0	79	53.2	79	22.8	135	51.9
1805	302	43.7	14	21.4	9	11.1	69	52.2	60	30.0	150	49.3
1808	312	47.8	12	33.3	8	12.5	53	56.6	91	44.0	148	50.0
1809	292	46.9	10	20.0	6	16.7	57	56.1	81	37.0	138	52.2
1815	386	60.1	36	22.2	7	57.1	95	63.2	2	0.0	246	65.0
DIVINA PASTORA DEL JOBAL												
1781	1455	44.0	241	44.8	554	49.8	522	45.0	54	33.3	84	3.6
1798	1912	35.0	512	35.5	299	46.8	719	40.3	307	15.0	75	16.0
1799	1922	35.4	519	35.5	292	47.9	720	40.3	311	16.1	80	20.0
1801	1902	31.3	470	39.4	209	61.2	1147	24.5	13	15.4	63	0.0
1802	1910	36.8	533	39.0	358	41.3	700	39.1	241	28.2	78	6.4
1803	1938	36.6	538	39.0	362	40.9	710	38.9	248	28.6	80	6.3
1804	1610	43.7	500	48.4	270	47.4	726	43.5	54	33.3	60	0.0
1805	1748	33.2	518	38.8	223	32.7	704	32.8	232	30.6	71	5.6
1806	1762	43.8	558	48.9	263	54.4	873	40.5	4	25.0	64	0.0
1807	1555	34.9	545	42.2	181	33.1	753	33.3	9	22.2	67	0.0
1808	1636	34.3	543	41.3	191	35.6	836	32.2	10	0.0	56	0.0
1809	1748	33.2	518	38.8	223	32.7	704	32.8	232	30.6	71	5.6
1811	1668	33.1	510	35.3	310	34.2	789	33.7	0	0.0	59	0.0
1815	1589	38.5	224	40.2	396	37.1	849	41.9	95	16.8	25	8.0
1816	1589	38.5	224	40.2	396	37.1	849	41.9	95	16.8	25	8.0
1817	1577	38.7	228	39.5	386	38.1	849	41.9	89	16.9	25	8.0
1818	1208	45.6	221	47.5	371	43.9	495	50.9	94	25.5	27	25.9
1819	2916	17.2	435	28.5	421	25.7	1982	13.7	11	0.0	67	0.0
1820	1629	45.5	416	45.7	161	59.0	1017	44.4	13	23.1	22	4.5
1822	2038	30.2	500	16.2	336	20.2	1153	39.9	4	100.0	45	4.4
1824	1112	37.5	169	52.1	139	41.0	776	34.4	9	33.3	19	10.5
1825	1157	37.0	166	53.0	139	41.0	824	33.7	9	33.3	19	10.5
1829	984	37.2	158	45.6	61	47.5	739	34.6	0	0.0	26	34.6
1830	989	36.3	158	45.6	61	47.5	749	34.2	21	9.5	0	0.0
1832	989	36.3	158	45.6	61	47.5	749	34.2	21	9.5	0	0.0
1833	823	43.9	166	43.4	67	43.3	541	45.8	42	28.6	7	0.0
1834	831	44.2	166	43.4	67	43.3	541	45.8	42	28.6	15	40.0
DUACA												
1779	409	39.6	77	28.6	225	46.2	88	38.6	8	0.0	11	18.2
1802	384	36.5	81	32.1	178	43.8	108	29.6	14	28.6	3	0.0
1803	323	34.7	14	28.6	165	38.8	137	29.2	0	0.0	7	57.1
1804	323	34.7	14	28.6	165	38.8	137	29.2	0	0.0	7	57.1
1805	410	31.2	117	20.5	165	38.8	124	29.0	0	0.0	4	100.0

TABLE 3. MARRIED PERSONS (CONTINUED)

YEAR	TOTAL		WHITE		INDIAN		PARDO		NEGRO		SLAVE	
	A	PCT	A	PCT	A	PCT	A	PCT	A	PCT	A	PCT
1807	519	26.6	135	17.8	242	36.4	107	21.5	31	9.7	4	0.0
1808	390	34.9	85	34.1	227	29.1	75	54.7	2	0.0	1	0.0
1809	410	37.6	77	40.3	233	30.9	96	52.1	3	33.3	1	0.0
1810	410	36.1	77	40.3	230	28.7	96	52.1	3	33.3	4	0.0
1811	503	30.8	83	43.4	343	23.0	77	51.9	0	0.0	0	0.0
1815	337	38.6	14	50.0	112	44.6	211	34.6	0	0.0	0	0.0
1816	391	36.3	14	50.0	112	44.6	265	32.1	0	0.0	0	0.0
1818	754	72.3	207	63.8	220	72.7	324	77.2	3	100.0	0	0.0
EL CALVARIO												
1783	524	36.5	183	37.2	40	50.0	47	42.6	48	45.8	206	29.6
1802	933	35.7	312	42.6	40	32.5	202	39.1	120	33.3	259	26.3
1803	944	35.1	310	42.3	41	24.4	211	39.8	116	34.5	266	24.8
1804	977	35.6	329	45.6	58	20.7	203	39.4	121	33.1	266	24.8
1805	1027	36.2	337	44.5	67	22.4	201	39.8	134	36.6	288	27.1
1808	1044	34.6	354	41.5	63	27.0	204	38.2	120	30.8	303	27.1
1812	1256	36.1	379	48.0	85	29.4	284	33.5	188	34.6	320	27.2
EL CONSEJO												
1781	1632	23.7	451	37.5	0	0.0	486	32.1	0	0.0	695	8.8
1795	1866	34.8	271	31.7	25	40.0	764	33.8	39	35.9	767	36.8
1796	1774	29.2	349	26.4	8	50.0	609	35.1	12	33.3	796	25.6
1802	2032	30.1	337	32.6	29	27.6	636	23.3	42	28.6	988	33.8
1803	2045	30.1	342	32.7	29	27.6	644	23.3	42	28.6	988	33.8
1804	2145	31.3	381	36.2	40	30.0	658	24.3	56	32.1	1010	34.1
1805	2154	31.8	376	36.7	38	31.6	658	24.0	54	29.6	1028	35.0
1806	2092	30.6	347	32.9	35	34.3	649	23.7	60	33.3	1001	34.0
1807	2100	31.4	351	34.2	43	41.9	650	24.3	56	39.3	1000	34.2
1808	2120	31.5	355	34.4	47	40.4	654	24.5	60	40.0	1004	34.1
1809	1960	30.1	323	32.8	15	26.7	622	23.2	28	28.6	972	33.7
1811	1999	31.2	336	35.1	17	70.6	618	22.3	38	52.6	990	33.9
1817	2379	31.3	366	23.5	201	18.9	932	46.1	0	0.0	880	21.6
1818	2469	32.6	436	28.9	221	17.2	932	47.4	0	0.0	880	22.5
1833	1998	32.0	373	24.1	175	26.3	705	52.9	0	0.0	745	17.6
EL GUAPO												
1784	353	51.0	124	57.3	50	74.0	30	63.3	36	55.6	113	29.2
1802	875	43.2	112	39.3	62	41.9	122	45.9	202	38.6	377	46.2
1803	1062	39.4	176	29.5	80	37.5	255	29.8	138	46.4	413	47.5
1804	1086	40.3	176	29.5	80	37.5	255	29.8	162	51.9	413	47.5
1805	1051	41.7	154	46.8	76	36.8	236	40.7	201	50.7	384	36.5
1807	1222	39.6	195	34.9	81	37.0	278	34.5	290	38.6	378	47.1
1808	1209	39.5	184	33.7	81	37.0	276	34.8	290	38.6	378	47.1
1809	1209	39.5	184	33.7	81	37.0	276	34.8	290	38.6	378	47.1
1811	1223	44.3	181	49.7	84	23.8	253	39.5	212	50.0	493	45.8
1812	1155	40.7	143	30.8	87	34.5	266	38.3	257	38.9	402	48.3
1820	1022	31.3	182	28.0	128	35.2	370	30.3	66	28.8	276	33.7

TABLE 3. MARRIED PERSONS (CONTINUED)

YEAR	TOTAL		WHITE		INDIAN		PARDO		NEGRO		SLAVE	
	A	PCT	A	PCT	A	PCT	A	PCT	A	PCT	A	PCT
EL HATILLO												
1802	811	36.5	445	34.4	47	57.4	143	34.3	54	33.3	122	40.2
1803	811	36.5	445	34.4	47	57.4	143	34.3	54	33.3	122	40.2
1804	887	37.9	470	37.7	59	49.2	153	34.6	51	39.2	154	37.0
1805	993	36.5	501	35.5	68	52.9	176	33.0	71	45.1	177	32.8
1806	1133	41.0	586	39.6	57	40.4	141	44.0	110	39.1	239	43.5
1808	1233	45.7	686	48.4	57	40.4	141	44.0	110	39.1	239	43.5
1815	1240	38.7	546	41.4	0	0.0	312	42.9	0	0.0	382	31.4
1818	996	39.9	367	43.6	0	0.0	342	40.4	0	0.0	287	34.5
EL PAO												
1781	2414	30.2	331	31.1	31	38.7	1776	31.2	81	22.2	195	21.5
1791	3001	30.2	353	38.5	167	24.0	2020	30.8	318	27.7	143	14.0
1792	2374	29.0	363	35.3	314	26.8	1570	33.4	434	22.1	193	1.0
1794	3229	29.4	385	35.3	228	28.9	1696	34.3	709	21.4	211	6.6
1796	3227	30.2	406	35.5	366	41.0	1683	31.5	518	25.1	254	8.7
1798	3367	30.1	452	35.4	366	41.0	1603	33.1	769	19.5	177	12.4
1801	3085	34.2	498	36.9	156	29.5	1912	36.5	286	32.9	233	14.2
1802	3233	33.3	375	39.2	118	39.8	2136	33.7	325	31.1	279	22.2
1803	3723	30.3	646	35.4	93	24.7	2439	31.5	297	24.2	248	14.9
1804	4042	38.5	621	36.7	50	42.0	2880	41.5	244	33.2	247	13.0
1805	4120	39.7	621	36.7	50	42.0	2952	42.9	244	33.2	253	15.0
1808	4081	31.7	605	30.9	70	11.4	2865	33.9	314	29.3	227	15.9
1809	4123	34.3	446	39.5	294	39.5	3015	33.0	198	32.3	170	35.9
1811	4689	33.1	662	26.1	129	20.2	3064	39.0	506	20.4	328	17.1
1812	4154	31.9	608	26.5	136	19.1	2687	37.1	415	23.1	308	15.3
1815	4507	33.1	747	35.5	35	37.1	3587	32.5	59	37.3	79	32.9
1816	4438	33.7	754	35.9	35	37.1	3501	33.3	65	32.3	83	27.7
1817	4347	34.8	863	37.4	23	39.1	3108	35.3	111	32.4	242	19.4
1818	4136	32.8	650	37.5	126	34.9	2954	33.7	177	26.0	229	12.7
1819	3468	37.6	586	40.8	90	30.0	2468	38.2	118	39.8	206	22.8
1821	4101	34.3	653	36.0	47	27.7	3041	35.2	155	34.8	205	17.1
1823	5473	42.4	749	30.6	46	56.5	4264	46.2	191	28.8	223	19.3
1824	5697	40.8	718	30.4	44	56.8	4523	44.0	147	27.2	265	20.0
1825	4476	38.8	649	31.9	51	43.1	3434	41.8	209	19.6	133	22.6
1826	4622	38.1	783	27.2	53	41.5	3443	42.5	207	19.3	136	18.4
1827	4760	31.4	634	36.0	44	22.7	3138	37.1	551	9.8	393	9.9
1829	5612	74.5	100	60.0	46	65.2	5260	76.0	140	35.7	66	60.6
1835	6485	24.9	266	34.6	0	0.0	5979	25.1	80	20.0	160	6.3
1836	6678	25.3	294	36.1	0	0.0	6114	25.4	97	22.7	173	6.9
1837	6932	24.8	306	35.9	0	0.0	6307	25.0	143	14.0	176	6.8
1838	7010	25.4	322	35.7	0	0.0	6402	25.4	114	22.8	172	6.4
EL RASTRO												
1807	727	40.0	354	46.6	12	33.3	233	39.5	18	72.2	110	15.5
1810	986	38.7	433	45.3	27	14.8	386	38.9	36	50.0	104	13.5
1811	1016	39.2	438	47.5	29	20.7	390	39.0	52	38.5	107	11.2

TABLE 3. MARRIED PERSONS (CONTINUED)

YEAR	TOTAL A	TOTAL PCT	WHITE A	WHITE PCT	INDIAN A	INDIAN PCT	PARDO A	PARDO PCT	NEGRO A	NEGRO PCT	SLAVE A	SLAVE PCT
1812	867	40.8	505	47.9	8	25.0	217	41.5	0	0.0	137	14.6
1817	815	36.8	372	44.6	15	40.0	291	35.7	25	40.0	112	12.5
1822	694	38.2	294	45.2	83	43.4	245	35.1	21	28.6	51	7.8
EL SOMBRERO												
1781	1267	50.8	376	51.3	6	66.7	804	52.1	14	57.1	67	29.9
1783	1380	47.3	376	43.4	16	37.5	3	0.0	883	50.7	102	35.3
1802	2132	32.1	566	39.0	85	40.0	1074	32.2	236	30.5	171	7.0
1803	2232	35.0	568	40.5	78	38.5	1143	37.4	265	28.3	178	10.7
1804	2532	31.7	678	35.1	101	27.7	1269	34.4	275	27.6	209	11.0
1805	2551	33.8	692	39.0	62	38.7	1311	35.1	267	24.3	219	19.6
1809	3094	35.4	753	39.4	101	35.6	1646	36.9	382	32.5	212	13.7
1810	3200	35.1	773	39.7	121	29.8	1676	37.5	392	31.6	238	12.2
1811	3200	35.1	773	39.7	121	29.8	1676	37.5	392	31.6	238	12.2
EL TOCUYO												
1802	6383	36.0	1207	29.7	269	37.9	3192	39.7	638	38.2	1077	30.5
1803	6474	36.2	1221	29.0	259	38.6	3247	40.5	653	38.6	1094	29.7
1804	7114	24.4	1072	21.9	159	22.0	3788	25.9	990	30.6	1105	16.4
1805	6408	36.4	1194	29.1	244	37.3	3254	41.1	648	38.7	1068	28.9
1806	6330	36.5	1204	29.7	261	37.9	3251	40.4	549	44.8	1065	28.0
1807	7092	24.1	1071	21.5	160	19.4	3791	25.3	1006	31.2	1064	16.6
1808	7067	23.7	1066	21.0	157	20.4	3762	24.7	1013	31.3	1069	16.6
1809	7160	24.1	1101	21.3	164	19.5	3818	25.4	1009	30.4	1068	16.8
1810	7127	24.4	1009	23.6	149	20.1	3850	25.5	1015	30.3	1104	16.5
1812	7182	23.9	1096	21.4	165	20.6	3847	25.2	998	30.1	1076	17.0
1815	6050	29.8	940	31.9	73	32.9	4067	30.4	227	34.4	743	21.8
1816	6083	29.8	940	32.4	76	32.9	4082	30.7	235	29.4	750	21.3
1817	5471	36.9	927	36.7	97	42.3	3458	38.4	253	42.7	736	27.3
1818	6928	23.9	1034	21.1	152	20.4	3734	25.5	952	29.6	1056	16.7
1819	8666	38.6	1264	33.2	91	26.4	6307	44.5	24	25.0	980	9.1
1820	6749	24.5	1197	32.0	43	27.9	4719	24.8	63	20.6	727	10.3
EL VALLE												
1798	664	38.6	148	43.2	220	42.7	109	43.1	63	25.4	124	28.2
1802	980	32.2	320	37.5	205	32.2	147	25.9	109	29.4	199	30.2
1803	1008	32.1	330	36.4	211	31.3	146	26.0	111	28.8	210	32.4
1804	1093	31.7	359	35.1	222	32.4	157	25.5	123	29.3	232	31.0
1805	1166	31.6	370	35.1	227	33.5	164	28.0	156	25.6	249	30.5
1809	1166	33.3	370	38.9	227	36.1	158	25.3	162	28.4	249	30.5
1815	1255	29.6	528	29.7	150	30.7	261	32.2	102	26.5	214	27.1
1816	1337	29.8	548	30.5	149	30.9	277	32.5	113	28.3	250	25.6
1817	1652	31.5	634	32.2	255	33.3	338	35.2	130	26.2	295	26.8
1818	1270	34.6	538	34.6	143	42.7	301	34.9	98	28.6	190	31.6
1819	1252	35.1	506	35.4	109	41.3	326	35.9	84	25.0	227	33.9
1820	1375	37.5	516	37.4	127	45.7	352	37.2	118	35.6	262	35.1

TABLE 3. MARRIED PERSONS (CONTINUED)

YEAR	TOTAL A	TOTAL PCT	WHITE A	WHITE PCT	INDIAN A	INDIAN PCT	PARDO A	PARDO PCT	NEGRO A	NEGRO PCT	SLAVE A	SLAVE PCT
ESPINO												
1804	478	36.8	74	37.8	8	25.0	286	42.7	8	50.0	102	19.6
1807	736	38.0	141	22.7	127	17.3	345	58.0	7	28.6	116	20.7
GUACARA												
1781	2184	44.0	666	36.5	393	54.2	663	38.5	29	62.1	433	53.8
1802	2985	39.7	828	39.6	596	43.6	1312	36.6	11	36.4	238	47.1
1803	3259	39.6	928	37.9	626	43.8	1439	37.8	15	26.7	251	47.0
1804	3448	34.2	941	28.1	604	41.1	1589	33.5	24	33.3	290	44.1
1805	3238	33.8	961	24.1	615	40.7	1360	35.4	24	33.3	278	43.9
1808	3559	30.9	1002	29.5	463	38.0	1773	28.1	21	38.1	300	40.0
1816	3176	37.2	821	32.9	450	39.1	1677	38.4	18	33.3	210	40.0
GUADARRAMA												
1820	763	42.7	224	54.5	31	38.7	121	46.3	374	34.2	13	61.5
GUAIGUAZA												
1803	561	42.6	25	56.0	1	0.0	195	50.3	194	39.7	146	34.2
1804	515	36.5	34	47.1	0	0.0	236	39.0	80	40.0	165	29.1
1805	505	37.2	34	47.1	2	100.0	235	38.7	82	41.5	152	29.6
1806	451	36.4	32	59.4	0	0.0	183	38.8	80	31.3	156	31.4
1807	481	39.1	28	42.9	0	0.0	206	38.3	72	40.3	175	38.9
1818	336	50.6	16	25.0	0	0.0	155	64.5	0	0.0	165	40.0
1819	401	49.9	19	21.1	0	0.0	216	59.3	0	0.0	166	41.0
GUAMA												
1781	1596	26.6	256	29.3	505	23.4	603	28.5	133	33.1	99	16.2
1794	1980	37.1	226	30.1	492	28.3	924	42.6	190	42.6	148	35.8
1803	2266	25.0	145	24.8	515	34.2	1440	23.9	37	21.6	129	1.6
1804	2634	26.0	134	20.9	601	29.3	1753	26.0	30	53.3	116	8.6
1805	2346	27.8	152	31.6	573	29.3	1442	27.7	49	40.8	130	12.3
1807	2177	22.6	192	27.6	542	29.0	1196	19.2	157	24.2	90	14.4
1808	2413	28.5	231	27.7	551	29.8	1374	29.5	171	22.8	86	18.6
1809	2350	28.9	203	33.5	558	28.5	1334	29.8	158	25.3	97	15.5
1810	2421	26.9	114	29.8	606	29.0	1433	26.7	173	25.4	95	16.8
1811	2512	28.9	141	34.0	649	28.5	1473	29.9	179	23.5	70	15.7
1812	2398	25.2	126	31.0	570	23.5	1426	26.3	178	23.6	98	15.3
1817	2105	36.1	250	42.4	471	34.6	1155	37.4	147	29.9	82	17.1
1818	2002	26.5	179	36.9	449	33.2	1314	23.3	18	33.3	42	9.5
1819	1600	70.6	164	59.8	273	52.4	962	83.8	136	39.7	65	44.6
1820	1472	34.0	164	31.7	402	42.3	702	31.3	142	26.8	62	32.3
GUANARE												
1788	5997	32.8	2747	35.9	295	46.1	2214	33.6	136	26.5	605	11.1

TABLE 3. MARRIED PERSONS (CONTINUED)

YEAR	TOTAL		WHITE		INDIAN		PARDO		NEGRO		SLAVE	
	A	PCT	A	PCT	A	PCT	A	PCT	A	PCT	A	PCT
1791	5349	30.9	1820	35.2	97	26.8	2644	34.8	157	27.4	631	3.6
1792	5881	36.0	2737	38.4	190	50.0	2220	36.9	135	51.9	599	13.2
1802	9345	33.8	3486	35.3	501	45.1	4554	34.4	114	38.6	690	13.9
1803	7728	32.1	3079	35.8	439	39.9	3324	33.1	135	16.3	751	10.3
1804	7306	34.6	2853	35.2	417	37.4	3302	37.3	128	28.1	606	16.7
1807	7506	34.9	2758	38.7	447	43.2	3508	34.1	172	34.9	621	17.2
1808	7905	34.8	2841	37.8	603	36.5	3626	35.7	183	26.8	652	17.0
1809	7450	30.2	2794	40.2	376	51.3	3115	27.5	95	16.8	1070	5.8
1810	5823	38.4	2362	39.2	558	41.2	2160	41.1	192	60.9	551	14.0
1811	7081	40.3	2535	40.0	494	38.9	3036	43.9	302	37.7	714	28.2
1817	4900	32.1	1446	33.9	334	42.2	2645	32.5	104	19.2	371	16.7
GUANARE VIEJO												
1778	295	38.0	101	46.5	103	53.4	84	11.9	0	0.0	7	0.0
1782	622	49.0	128	22.7	206	61.2	278	53.6	0	0.0	10	10.0
1801	979	42.7	294	55.1	476	32.4	203	50.2	0	0.0	6	0.0
1802	973	43.6	288	56.9	484	31.8	192	55.2	0	0.0	9	0.0
1803	1042	38.4	336	51.8	312	32.7	387	32.0	7	0.0	0	0.0
1804	1596	35.6	616	34.4	304	30.3	668	39.5	0	0.0	8	0.0
1805	1083	36.7	445	34.2	246	41.5	381	37.8	0	0.0	11	0.0
1806	1417	42.9	519	42.0	295	35.3	599	47.7	0	0.0	4	0.0
1807	1183	50.5	479	45.5	279	53.0	420	55.2	0	0.0	5	0.0
1808	1969	48.1	720	45.8	338	51.5	904	49.1	0	0.0	7	0.0
1811	1070	47.5	378	39.2	223	46.6	461	55.5	0	0.0	8	0.0
1813	977	40.1	318	36.5	327	41.0	324	43.8	0	0.0	8	0.0
GUANARITO												
1778	653	50.2	144	48.6	176	60.2	322	46.3	0	0.0	11	27.3
1801	1267	55.4	263	50.2	422	64.0	408	56.4	115	43.5	59	33.9
1802	1331	64.9	501	61.1	134	47.8	621	74.4	35	40.0	40	45.0
1803	2244	48.0	849	47.8	190	35.8	891	55.9	178	43.8	136	19.1
1804	2201	44.6	796	50.3	225	40.9	1070	40.7	0	0.0	110	49.1
1805	2526	46.2	918	50.1	259	47.1	1001	48.8	198	22.2	150	36.0
1807	3620	39.1	1241	40.1	388	38.9	1694	43.8	25	36.0	272	5.5
1808	3023	46.2	1292	45.3	200	48.0	1347	48.9	109	51.4	75	0.0
1810	3069	46.7	1309	45.5	203	48.3	1393	49.7	92	52.2	72	0.0
1811	3176	47.5	1347	45.8	210	49.5	1445	50.7	98	51.0	76	7.9
GUARDATINAJAS												
1780	324	49.4	45	44.4	156	62.2	46	65.2	75	17.3	2	0.0
1804	1460	45.1	346	49.1	176	54.5	374	45.7	436	43.6	128	24.2
1805	1477	44.2	350	49.4	173	53.2	372	45.2	450	41.6	132	25.0
1807	1523	37.6	352	43.2	141	56.0	322	36.3	544	36.0	164	17.7
1808	1546	38.2	362	43.1	162	52.5	321	37.4	544	36.2	157	21.0
1809	1542	40.8	417	38.1	163	49.1	350	46.0	440	41.4	172	27.3
1810	1486	39.9	351	40.5	161	51.6	789	41.1	51	33.3	134	20.1
1811	1702	39.2	365	41.4	212	48.1	850	40.6	66	36.4	209	22.0
1812	1696	41.6	312	49.4	228	50.9	856	41.6	78	41.0	222	21.6

TABLE 3. MARRIED PERSONS (CONTINUED)

YEAR	TOTAL		WHITE		INDIAN		PARDO		NEGRO		SLAVE	
	A	PCT	A	PCT	A	PCT	A	PCT	A	PCT	A	PCT
1816	1717	37.0	336	36.9	218	37.6	951	40.8	28	50.0	184	15.2
GUARENAS												
1784	1923	43.6	765	48.9	484	45.2	198	41.4	247	38.5	229	29.7
1802	2193	33.1	759	36.1	296	31.1	196	34.7	399	22.6	543	37.2
1803	2279	33.8	778	36.0	312	31.4	216	37.0	420	23.8	553	38.3
1804	2263	36.0	769	36.2	306	31.4	187	40.6	464	33.2	537	39.1
1805	2297	36.1	783	36.3	308	29.9	190	42.1	470	33.6	546	39.6
1808	1427	34.8	443	34.5	190	28.9	114	42.1	193	28.5	487	38.2
1809	2028	35.5	718	36.2	216	30.1	284	39.8	265	28.7	545	37.8
1811	2475	34.8	876	33.6	260	38.1	538	34.4	253	38.3	548	33.9
1816	2005	31.4	601	32.9	129	28.7	753	32.1	25	24.0	497	29.6
GUARICO												
1803	1399	42.2	188	26.1	646	46.0	417	48.7	79	39.2	69	14.5
1804	1396	38.3	239	32.6	532	48.5	443	30.2	117	38.5	65	29.2
1805	1148	54.4	154	32.5	553	65.6	341	45.2	47	85.1	48	29.2
1806	1179	53.6	157	31.8	575	64.3	351	44.4	48	83.3	48	33.3
1807	1134	48.6	153	39.2	485	54.4	408	45.1	36	77.8	52	28.8
1808	1108	48.3	149	37.6	466	54.7	408	45.1	36	77.8	49	24.5
1809	1169	48.9	160	37.5	476	54.6	434	46.8	47	74.5	52	26.9
1810	1269	51.4	150	41.3	523	56.8	457	48.6	69	68.1	70	34.3
1812	1269	52.4	161	47.2	481	55.3	469	52.0	80	61.3	78	38.5
1815	1438	24.4	80	37.5	616	21.9	674	24.3	32	37.5	36	27.8
1816	1428	24.6	80	37.5	613	22.0	667	24.6	32	37.5	36	27.8
1817	1502	27.7	130	61.5	622	22.5	682	25.5	32	37.5	36	27.8
1818	1493	27.9	130	61.5	618	22.7	677	25.7	32	37.5	36	27.8
1819	1588	29.4	136	62.5	653	24.5	718	27.0	31	38.7	50	32.0
1820	1697	32.6	136	62.5	711	28.7	766	30.8	32	37.5	52	30.8
GUASGUAS												
1802	2223	37.8	1073	35.2	397	36.8	722	43.6	0	0.0	31	6.5
1803	2193	38.0	1041	37.1	401	37.7	719	41.0	0	0.0	32	6.3
1804	2148	37.6	1009	38.6	386	35.8	723	38.6	0	0.0	30	6.7
1805	2364	36.8	1084	38.7	439	35.8	811	36.0	0	0.0	30	6.7
1806	2541	35.5	1162	37.9	501	31.7	842	35.5	0	0.0	36	11.1
1807	2508	37.3	1148	39.6	455	34.1	871	36.7	0	0.0	34	17.6
1808	2508	37.6	1155	38.5	470	37.2	853	37.3	0	0.0	30	13.3
1809	2617	38.0	1151	39.5	496	38.3	937	36.6	0	0.0	33	18.2
1810	2434	38.9	1221	39.3	422	36.0	637	43.8	124	24.2	30	20.0
GUATIRE												
1784	1505	35.1	218	40.4	21	28.6	324	23.5	180	31.7	762	39.6
1802	1700	35.5	140	48.6	30	16.7	375	26.7	271	31.4	884	39.1
1803	1737	32.6	212	30.2	18	5.6	377	23.9	276	31.9	854	37.8
1805	1683	33.5	219	26.9	16	12.5	365	26.3	282	29.4	801	40.3
1807	1669	33.6	177	32.2	4	0.0	532	28.0	47	40.4	909	37.0

TABLE 3. MARRIED PERSONS (CONTINUED)

YEAR	TOTAL A	TOTAL PCT	WHITE A	WHITE PCT	INDIAN A	INDIAN PCT	PARDO A	PARDO PCT	NEGRO A	NEGRO PCT	SLAVE A	SLAVE PCT
1809	1669	33.6	177	32.2	4	0.0	532	28.0	47	40.4	909	37.0
1811	1782	36.4	205	33.2	53	30.2	461	33.2	169	39.1	894	38.7
1815	1616	34.7	195	32.3	45	31.1	422	33.4	151	38.4	803	35.5
1816	1820	37.4	187	39.6	49	30.6	518	35.3	200	33.0	866	39.5
1817	1738	45.8	158	41.1	33	42.4	715	46.7	69	43.5	763	46.3
	GUAYABAL											
1804	879	26.8	142	29.6	65	33.8	309	39.5	94	31.9	269	7.4
1817	1066	55.7	210	66.7	42	66.7	686	52.5	69	60.9	59	40.7
	GUIGUE											
1781	1590	50.6	522	51.0	40	57.5	454	49.3	280	53.2	294	48.3
1802	1526	41.6	381	37.0	57	36.8	734	42.4	79	26.6	275	51.3
1803	1518	40.8	354	32.8	69	37.7	726	43.1	76	27.6	293	49.1
1804	1512	39.2	357	33.3	70	40.0	740	43.6	77	29.9	268	37.3
1805	1578	41.4	350	34.0	75	40.0	752	43.5	73	28.8	328	47.6
1808	1770	42.0	373	33.0	71	45.1	752	42.8	92	42.4	482	47.1
1809	1824	42.5	388	33.8	88	52.3	758	42.5	86	45.3	504	47.2
1817	1812	48.5	143	50.3	128	50.0	939	48.1	195	44.6	407	49.9
	GUIRIPA											
1802	643	40.9	322	42.9	78	32.1	185	43.2	7	71.4	51	29.4
1803	582	44.3	310	44.5	58	27.6	162	53.1	5	80.0	47	29.8
1804	666	38.4	293	42.0	80	33.8	226	37.6	9	66.7	58	25.9
1805	677	38.8	285	43.5	78	38.5	247	34.8	9	66.7	58	29.3
1806	645	36.6	275	45.8	61	26.2	229	32.3	9	22.2	71	25.4
1807	714	35.4	204	36.3	196	37.2	223	38.6	15	20.0	76	22.4
1808	705	36.0	198	37.9	192	37.0	229	39.7	12	16.7	74	20.3
1809	725	36.7	195	38.5	180	36.1	268	38.4	16	50.0	66	22.7
1811	699	35.6	317	36.0	44	50.0	266	38.7	0	0.0	72	13.9
	HUMOCARO ALTO											
1802	1762	56.0	106	35.8	1447	59.0	158	46.8	8	50.0	43	37.2
1803	1748	55.9	104	34.6	1454	59.4	161	44.7	6	33.3	23	17.4
1804	1890	58.4	90	42.2	1593	61.4	170	47.1	8	50.0	29	13.8
1805	1951	57.3	92	41.3	1646	60.1	172	46.5	8	50.0	33	18.2
1806	1865	60.2	81	44.4	1567	63.2	179	46.9	5	0.0	33	36.4
1807	1927	58.3	81	44.4	1608	61.6	196	42.9	6	0.0	36	38.9
1808	1854	58.4	80	42.5	1536	61.8	196	42.9	6	0.0	36	38.9
1809	1642	51.8	85	44.7	1323	53.7	192	45.8	5	0.0	37	37.8
1810	1543	55.2	78	48.7	1242	57.6	192	46.9	10	40.0	21	19.0
1815	1056	64.0	71	47.9	872	67.9	94	48.9	6	66.7	13	0.0
1816	1361	48.2	146	28.8	973	56.5	205	26.3	10	40.0	27	22.2
1817	1331	50.0	118	33.9	975	57.2	199	28.1	10	40.0	29	27.6
1818	1338	50.4	116	34.5	980	57.1	203	29.6	10	60.0	29	27.6
1819	1197	57.6	70	57.1	886	64.3	200	32.0	10	60.0	31	32.3
1820	1438	77.6	95	56.8	1173	82.5	136	58.8	8	75.0	26	30.8

TABLE 3. MARRIED PERSONS (CONTINUED)

YEAR	TOTAL A	TOTAL PCT	WHITE A	WHITE PCT	INDIAN A	INDIAN PCT	PARDO A	PARDO PCT	NEGRO A	NEGRO PCT	SLAVE A	SLAVE PCT
HUMOCARO BAJO												
1803	1254	32.9	339	49.6	559	21.8	176	36.4	108	33.3	72	30.6
1804	1254	32.9	339	49.6	559	21.8	176	36.4	108	33.3	72	30.6
1806	1017	38.7	157	29.3	443	48.3	327	36.7	6	33.3	84	14.3
1807	1081	38.5	163	28.2	471	48.0	346	36.4	9	22.2	92	17.4
1808	1218	36.1	175	25.1	541	43.6	377	36.6	14	28.6	111	16.2
1809	1316	36.2	175	25.1	616	42.9	379	36.9	16	37.5	130	16.9
1810	1301	36.6	159	23.9	605	44.3	387	36.7	16	25.0	134	17.9
1815	1049	31.5	205	36.1	505	31.3	258	31.8	8	50.0	73	16.4
1816	1013	31.4	189	37.0	461	31.2	276	31.2	7	57.1	80	17.5
1817	989	32.6	181	39.8	449	33.4	269	31.2	8	50.0	82	14.6
1818	938	32.4	173	41.6	423	32.6	255	30.6	7	57.1	80	15.0
1819	717	37.7	151	47.7	311	39.9	207	32.9	5	40.0	43	9.3
1820	748	39.3	154	49.4	318	40.9	226	34.5	4	50.0	46	17.4
IGUANA												
1783	83	67.5	2	100.0	75	69.3	2	100.0	4	0.0	0	0.0
1801	217	57.1	0	0.0	200	58.0	15	40.0	2	100.0	0	0.0
1802	228	56.1	0	0.0	211	56.9	15	40.0	2	100.0	0	0.0
1803	236	53.4	4	50.0	215	54.9	16	37.5	1	0.0	0	0.0
1804	193	59.1	0	0.0	183	60.1	9	44.4	1	0.0	0	0.0
1805	214	53.3	0	0.0	203	54.2	11	36.4	0	0.0	0	0.0
1806	227	54.6	0	0.0	216	55.6	11	36.4	0	0.0	0	0.0
1807	200	56.0	0	0.0	198	56.6	2	0.0	0	0.0	0	0.0
LA GUAIRA												
1802	3381	26.9	946	34.7	59	15.3	1413	28.0	466	27.5	497	10.1
1804	2648	26.4	813	32.5	30	33.3	984	27.5	452	27.7	369	7.9
1805	2927	27.1	713	34.4	6	33.3	1378	29.0	407	28.7	423	6.6
1807	2638	28.4	714	40.1	15	33.3	1074	29.8	473	26.2	362	3.6
1809	2693	27.3	580	34.0	8	0.0	1421	30.6	338	26.3	346	4.0
1810	2743	28.1	618	40.8	7	0.0	1239	30.7	554	20.2	325	8.3
1811	2790	26.9	590	37.5	21	23.8	1432	28.7	364	22.3	383	8.6
1815	1456	18.5	509	23.2	47	25.5	513	17.2	190	21.1	197	6.1
1816	1609	21.9	599	28.2	99	16.2	539	20.8	190	21.1	182	8.2
1817	2298	23.7	636	30.5	88	18.2	1049	26.6	312	11.9	213	8.5
1818	2415	27.9	468	40.6	80	38.7	1280	25.5	279	34.1	308	10.1
1819	2343	30.2	464	28.0	229	41.0	906	27.7	500	27.0	244	40.2
1820	2532	42.7	542	41.9	241	61.0	718	38.6	612	38.7	419	46.3
LA GUAIRA, CURATO CASTRENSE												
1802	298	13.1	269	13.0	0	0.0	4	0.0	3	66.7	22	9.1
1803	276	12.0	257	10.9	0	0.0	2	0.0	3	66.7	14	21.4
1804	443	16.5	382	14.7	0	0.0	46	30.4	2	100.0	13	7.7
1805	629	28.0	457	23.4	0	0.0	148	44.6	5	40.0	19	5.3
1807	749	23.8	402	17.9	0	0.0	325	31.4	5	60.0	17	5.9

TABLE 3. MARRIED PERSONS (CONTINUED)

YEAR	TOTAL		WHITE		INDIAN		PARDO		NEGRO		SLAVE	
	A	PCT	A	PCT	A	PCT	A	PCT	A	PCT	A	PCT
1808	526	18.6	343	15.2	1	0.0	163	27.0	4	50.0	15	0.0
LA SANTISIMA TRINIDAD												
1780	391	40.9	11	54.5	218	44.0	77	33.8	74	35.1	11	54.5
1802	1536	37.6	101	33.7	100	39.0	714	45.1	508	32.1	113	17.7
1803	1714	45.3	64	28.1	87	59.8	932	42.4	576	52.8	55	14.5
1804	1335	34.1	101	42.6	123	47.2	554	29.6	488	36.9	69	14.5
1805	1368	32.7	74	44.6	66	39.4	563	32.9	580	30.7	85	30.6
1807	892	39.0	75	52.0	102	40.2	260	38.1	382	39.3	73	26.0
1808	919	37.9	109	33.0	134	40.3	586	40.6	22	18.2	68	23.5
1809	913	39.2	90	41.1	128	40.6	588	41.3	29	34.5	78	20.5
1810	788	41.4	53	47.2	107	49.5	565	41.4	36	33.3	27	7.4
1811	889	41.7	66	53.0	135	49.6	574	42.3	23	34.8	91	19.8
1812	688	41.7	39	43.6	99	33.3	498	44.4	17	35.3	35	28.6
LA VEGA												
1802	1630	36.4	444	35.1	287	45.3	347	31.1	59	39.0	493	35.9
1803	1645	37.3	446	35.9	289	45.7	344	31.1	59	39.0	507	37.7
1804	1782	27.9	370	31.4	415	35.7	430	27.4	111	41.4	456	15.4
1805	1706	27.3	353	27.2	394	37.1	401	27.9	111	43.2	447	14.3
1809	853	31.5	211	34.1	177	39.5	246	23.6	37	37.8	182	30.2
1810	811	33.4	204	33.8	163	44.8	227	29.5	33	33.3	184	27.7
1811	755	32.8	180	37.2	122	46.7	241	29.9	36	22.2	176	25.0
1815	641	30.7	184	29.3	58	44.8	189	26.5	41	36.6	169	30.8
1816	651	31.3	207	30.9	50	40.0	207	27.5	30	40.0	157	32.5
1817	569	32.5	175	29.7	62	33.9	183	33.3	24	54.2	125	30.4
1818	573	30.0	237	26.6	52	38.5	155	32.3	18	22.2	111	31.5
1819	574	29.3	197	24.4	96	34.4	155	33.5	17	17.6	109	29.4
1820	570	26.8	167	19.2	110	33.6	166	34.3	17	17.6	110	21.8
1821	598	27.8	161	19.9	109	34.9	156	33.3	15	26.7	157	25.5
1822	549	28.6	162	29.0	65	47.7	159	35.8	16	31.3	147	11.6
1823	555	25.9	182	27.5	47	36.2	175	32.0	23	13.0	128	14.1
LA VICTORIA												
1780	4310	28.2	1236	25.6	601	39.1	1559	28.8	286	35.7	628	18.2
1802	4852	23.7	1230	25.3	588	26.9	1856	24.8	140	21.4	1038	18.1
1803	5253	25.2	1363	27.1	656	35.1	1887	24.0	159	25.2	1188	19.7
1804	5180	26.1	1361	27.8	653	35.2	1848	26.0	136	19.1	1182	20.3
1805	5395	25.4	1384	27.3	670	35.2	1900	24.1	181	30.9	1260	19.0
1806	5463	25.7	1398	27.5	683	35.7	1914	24.2	192	32.3	1276	19.6
1808	5714	25.2	1508	26.0	635	34.6	1915	24.5	173	37.0	1483	19.8
1809	5584	26.2	1421	27.9	707	36.2	1938	24.6	216	34.3	1302	20.1
1811	6270	30.2	1388	27.8	726	32.5	2247	22.1	227	33.5	1682	41.6
1816	3888	18.8	921	26.9	427	34.2	2048	11.4	0	0.0	492	21.1
1817	3888	18.8	921	26.9	427	34.2	2048	11.4	0	0.0	492	21.1
1818	3888	18.8	921	26.9	427	34.2	2048	11.4	0	0.0	492	21.1

TABLE 3. MARRIED PERSONS (CONTINUED)

YEAR	TOTAL A	TOTAL PCT	WHITE A	WHITE PCT	INDIAN A	INDIAN PCT	PARDO A	PARDO PCT	NEGRO A	NEGRO PCT	SLAVE A	SLAVE PCT
LEZAMA												
1783	1141	40.0	419	34.4	322	54.7	164	42.7	141	31.2	95	23.2
1802	1627	36.4	577	37.8	390	35.9	445	39.1	79	38.0	136	22.1
1803	1627	36.4	577	37.8	390	35.9	445	39.1	79	38.0	136	22.1
1804	1627	36.4	577	37.8	390	35.9	445	39.1	79	38.0	136	22.1
1805	1627	36.4	577	37.8	390	35.9	445	39.1	79	38.0	136	22.1
1806	1627	36.4	577	37.8	390	35.9	445	39.1	79	38.0	136	22.1
1807	1627	36.4	577	37.8	390	35.9	445	39.1	79	38.0	136	22.1
1808	1627	36.4	577	37.8	390	35.9	445	39.1	79	38.0	136	22.1
1809	1627	36.4	577	37.8	390	35.9	445	39.1	79	38.0	136	22.1
1810	1627	36.4	577	37.8	390	35.9	445	39.1	79	38.0	136	22.1
1811	1627	36.4	577	37.8	390	35.9	445	39.1	79	38.0	136	22.1
LOS ANGELES												
1780	306	44.4	8	50.0	242	43.8	49	44.9	6	66.7	1	0.0
1803	344	36.0	15	40.0	152	32.2	175	39.4	0	0.0	2	0.0
1804	368	37.0	16	25.0	169	37.9	181	37.6	0	0.0	2	0.0
1805	369	38.2	17	47.1	165	38.8	184	37.5	0	0.0	3	0.0
1807	360	38.3	16	37.5	163	36.8	175	41.1	0	0.0	6	0.0
1808	368	39.1	16	37.5	154	36.4	196	41.8	0	0.0	2	0.0
1809	673	36.8	156	43.6	135	43.0	341	33.7	0	0.0	41	17.1
1810	699	36.9	158	42.4	156	37.2	347	36.0	0	0.0	38	21.1
1811	749	39.4	184	48.9	149	41.6	363	37.2	0	0.0	53	15.1
1812	762	38.1	166	44.6	171	36.3	374	38.5	0	0.0	51	19.6
1816	663	39.1	147	46.9	123	40.7	357	35.6	0	0.0	36	36.1
1817	716	36.5	172	44.8	131	42.7	366	32.5	0	0.0	47	19.1
LOS ANGELES DE SETENTA												
1801	708	43.4	454	44.1	51	62.7	165	43.6	0	0.0	38	7.9
1805	618	69.9	283	79.2	86	74.4	182	74.7	0	0.0	67	11.9
1806	647	66.2	284	82.4	107	44.9	192	71.9	0	0.0	64	12.5
1807	767	60.0	293	81.2	192	39.6	241	57.3	0	0.0	41	19.5
1809	672	60.1	274	81.8	142	43.7	203	55.2	0	0.0	53	11.3
LOS CANIZOS												
1802	615	27.8	53	18.9	0	0.0	336	32.1	27	44.4	199	20.6
1803	612	27.3	46	26.1	0	0.0	348	28.7	23	52.2	195	22.1
1804	608	27.5	63	19.0	0	0.0	323	29.1	18	50.0	204	25.5
1805	593	28.7	61	23.0	0	0.0	278	30.2	69	37.7	185	24.9
1807	590	27.1	52	21.2	0	0.0	310	29.4	47	25.5	181	25.4
1808	632	27.5	61	26.2	0	0.0	365	28.5	20	35.0	186	25.3
1809	643	29.5	60	26.7	0	0.0	377	31.6	20	40.0	186	25.3
1810	696	30.7	47	38.3	0	0.0	416	32.7	19	57.9	214	22.9
1811	639	32.7	47	44.7	0	0.0	397	35.0	10	40.0	185	24.3
1813	413	32.7	10	0.0	0	0.0	252	42.1	51	19.6	100	19.0
1818	333	39.6	9	44.4	0	0.0	198	50.5	0	0.0	126	22.2

TABLE 3. MARRIED PERSONS (CONTINUED)

YEAR	TOTAL		WHITE		INDIAN		PARDO		NEGRO		SLAVE	
	A	PCT	A	PCT	A	PCT	A	PCT	A	PCT	A	PCT
1819	357	40.3	15	26.7	0	0.0	217	50.7	0	0.0	125	24.0
1820	344	40.1	15	26.7	0	0.0	210	49.5	0	0.0	119	25.2
LOS GUAYOS												
1781	842	44.1	260	41.2	409	46.5	171	43.3	0	0.0	2	0.0
1795	1717	35.6	473	35.3	593	35.9	615	37.2	0	0.0	36	5.6
1802	2706	37.8	518	37.8	950	39.8	1039	37.3	40	37.5	159	29.6
1803	2298	38.0	434	36.6	1323	38.9	386	38.9	19	10.5	136	34.6
1804	2055	36.0	564	40.1	441	32.7	892	37.0	15	13.3	143	26.6
1805	2110	37.7	541	39.9	513	36.8	926	37.9	13	15.4	117	32.5
1816	2117	37.1	529	37.1	415	38.3	1075	36.7	20	40.0	78	35.9
LOS TEQUES												
1796	1698	31.4	1054	31.5	132	30.3	306	39.2	32	43.8	174	16.1
1799	1747	35.3	1054	36.1	132	30.3	324	45.1	48	29.2	189	19.0
1800	1747	35.3	1054	36.1	132	30.3	324	45.1	48	29.2	189	19.0
1801	1842	35.9	1081	36.6	143	33.6	346	44.5	68	26.5	204	22.5
1805	1993	26.1	1321	24.6	167	39.5	192	35.4	34	17.6	279	20.1
1811	1728	45.6	546	44.0	40	30.0	836	55.5	95	25.3	211	22.7
1816	1869	29.4	1082	30.3	159	31.4	388	29.9	15	33.3	225	22.2
1817	1778	28.8	1054	29.8	139	30.2	370	29.7	17	35.3	198	20.2
MACAIRA												
1784	430	40.9	2	0.0	58	32.8	62	48.4	11	9.1	297	42.4
1802	233	51.9	1	0.0	20	40.0	15	40.0	6	66.7	191	53.9
1803	205	44.4	1	0.0	15	33.3	2	100.0	6	33.3	181	45.3
1804	187	47.6	1	100.0	16	43.8	4	100.0	5	40.0	161	46.6
1806	165	40.6	2	100.0	18	22.2	0	0.0	9	66.7	136	40.4
1807	171	41.5	0	0.0	14	64.3	0	0.0	7	71.4	150	38.0
1808	149	43.6	0	0.0	21	42.9	0	0.0	14	57.1	114	42.1
1809	147	49.0	1	0.0	10	70.0	14	71.4	5	40.0	117	45.3
1811	91	49.5	0	0.0	16	50.0	0	0.0	2	100.0	73	47.9
1817	102	37.3	0	0.0	4	75.0	15	33.3	3	66.7	80	35.0
MACAIRITA												
1805	178	46.1	0	0.0	14	42.9	0	0.0	4	50.0	160	46.3
MACARAO												
1802	857	37.8	348	37.9	82	43.9	168	46.4	43	32.6	216	29.6
1803	779	39.8	253	49.8	73	43.8	195	39.0	35	34.3	223	28.7
1804	868	38.2	365	37.3	89	44.9	191	44.0	36	27.8	187	33.2
1805	871	34.4	355	39.4	77	36.4	187	38.5	32	25.0	220	23.6
1807	886	39.5	372	46.2	84	50.0	156	39.7	28	21.4	246	27.6
1808	891	41.3	412	42.7	80	40.0	178	42.7	36	16.7	185	42.2
1809	915	38.7	402	45.3	81	44.4	141	35.5	26	23.1	265	30.2
1810	998	40.2	422	41.7	91	48.4	189	31.7	38	34.2	258	41.9

TABLE 3. MARRIED PERSONS (CONTINUED)

YEAR	TOTAL		WHITE		INDIAN		PARDO		NEGRO		SLAVE	
	A	PCT	A	PCT	A	PCT	A	PCT	A	PCT	A	PCT
1811	853	39.6	390	41.5	85	47.1	143	36.4	32	31.3	203	36.5
1812	829	37.4	389	44.2	39	41.0	119	26.9	26	23.1	256	32.8
1815	799	36.5	338	41.4	70	37.1	118	33.9	23	34.8	250	31.2
1816	854	36.3	368	41.3	73	35.6	135	32.6	27	29.6	251	31.9
1817	807	36.2	400	38.5	60	46.7	114	29.8	22	18.2	211	34.1
1818	807	36.2	400	38.5	60	46.7	114	29.8	22	18.2	211	34.1
1819	826	36.3	402	38.8	64	46.9	120	30.0	26	23.1	214	33.6
1820	826	36.3	402	38.8	64	46.9	120	30.0	26	23.1	214	33.6
1822	764	40.3	327	42.2	104	42.3	97	35.1	72	38.9	164	39.0
1823	889	46.1	397	49.9	128	50.0	120	45.0	68	29.4	176	42.0
MAGDALENO												
1802	1702	35.7	630	37.8	93	34.4	872	35.8	13	30.8	94	23.4
1803	1871	38.9	492	39.8	207	31.9	963	39.7	126	46.0	83	30.1
1804	1765	40.1	536	40.9	34	17.6	1067	40.7	17	35.3	111	37.8
1805	1685	44.0	586	45.6	28	35.7	920	44.3	13	46.2	138	36.2
1806	1694	42.9	578	44.6	37	32.4	890	43.3	60	25.0	129	44.2
1809	832	35.7	154	26.6	20	40.0	438	37.9	65	33.8	155	38.7
1816	2002	52.0	596	34.6	38	42.1	1180	61.0	83	48.2	105	57.1
MAIQUETIA												
1796	1462	29.4	344	40.7	67	29.9	774	25.3	0	0.0	277	26.7
1802	1295	34.4	355	41.1	46	21.7	388	35.1	226	31.4	280	29.6
1804	1237	32.8	334	38.3	53	30.2	462	31.2	132	31.8	256	29.7
1805	1258	34.7	326	40.5	59	32.2	481	32.8	136	35.3	256	31.3
1807	1394	34.0	397	36.5	57	33.3	475	34.5	195	30.3	270	32.2
1811	1315	38.1	329	38.9	67	44.8	471	35.5	210	36.2	238	42.0
1815	1138	46.7	294	45.9	93	75.3	295	45.8	288	46.9	168	33.9
1816	952	36.7	224	42.0	101	41.6	266	29.7	148	35.8	213	38.0
1817	1034	23.7	275	32.0	46	32.6	363	21.8	101	11.9	249	20.5
1819	1138	46.7	294	45.9	93	75.3	295	45.8	288	46.9	168	33.9
MAMPORAL												
1784	399	36.3	37	37.8	21	42.9	36	38.9	44	36.4	261	35.2
1802	371	50.9	29	62.1	19	52.6	46	56.5	40	47.5	237	48.9
1804	348	45.4	24	58.3	20	60.0	52	53.8	57	36.8	195	42.6
1805	419	43.0	38	57.9	32	59.4	78	53.8	48	39.6	223	35.0
1807	398	37.4	30	40.0	25	44.0	87	42.5	43	34.9	213	34.7
1808	399	34.1	37	35.1	26	53.8	67	23.9	63	25.4	206	37.4
1809	368	35.9	22	36.4	22	59.1	52	25.0	88	39.8	184	34.2
1811	365	35.9	34	35.3	33	42.4	89	37.1	37	32.4	172	34.9
1812	351	39.0	29	34.5	31	54.8	82	52.4	39	23.1	170	34.1
1816	206	34.0	4	50.0	7	85.7	60	31.7	9	22.2	126	32.5
1817	197	37.6	7	28.6	15	40.0	0	0.0	52	44.2	123	35.0
1818	238	33.6	9	44.4	5	80.0	60	26.7	10	30.0	154	34.4
1820	204	39.7	3	0.0	9	55.6	53	39.6	9	55.6	130	38.5

TABLE 3. MARRIED PERSONS (CONTINUED)

YEAR	TOTAL A	TOTAL PCT	WHITE A	WHITE PCT	INDIAN A	INDIAN PCT	PARDO A	PARDO PCT	NEGRO A	NEGRO PCT	SLAVE A	SLAVE PCT
MANAPIRE												
1804	344	39.5	92	43.5	36	33.3	116	39.7	6	66.7	94	36.2
1807	321	42.4	83	45.8	27	44.4	116	40.5	7	100.0	88	36.4
1808	326	42.9	83	45.8	32	50.0	116	40.5	7	100.0	88	36.4
1810	347	49.6	92	52.2	24	58.3	134	53.7	6	100.0	91	35.2
MARACA												
1778	585	41.7	158	39.2	211	48.3	205	38.0	3	66.7	8	0.0
1803	1221	38.4	91	39.6	692	42.6	411	31.1	12	83.3	15	0.0
1804	1187	38.4	452	35.4	310	51.6	382	33.5	28	28.6	15	0.0
1805	1359	37.5	469	39.7	411	38.9	445	35.1	25	32.0	9	0.0
1806	1165	39.1	379	38.0	413	40.2	335	41.8	25	24.0	13	0.0
1807	1158	40.2	370	36.2	448	41.7	274	44.2	41	34.1	25	40.0
1808	973	39.7	322	33.9	379	46.7	209	37.3	40	35.0	23	34.8
1809	1041	38.0	317	36.9	409	37.2	246	39.4	44	40.9	25	48.0
1810	956	37.2	288	32.6	367	39.8	234	38.0	42	40.5	25	40.0
1817	513	26.9	202	30.2	146	21.9	145	26.9	5	40.0	15	26.7
MARACAY												
1782	4519	36.0	1330	36.2	891	27.2	1938	39.8	52	42.3	308	35.1
1796	5755	34.5	2468	31.2	0	0.0	2143	39.5	372	29.8	772	33.7
1802	6652	22.2	1628	25.1	154	19.5	2752	21.9	267	24.3	1851	19.9
1803	6731	22.4	1655	25.1	162	20.4	2772	22.2	274	24.8	1868	20.3
1804	7129	23.4	1780	29.5	167	22.2	2945	21.8	292	26.4	1945	20.0
1805	6036	31.2	2107	29.2	89	25.8	2790	30.5	18	11.1	1032	37.9
1808	6138	31.5	2151	30.1	114	23.7	2802	30.6	27	22.2	1044	38.1
1809	6371	23.7	1655	25.1	102	32.4	2472	24.8	274	24.8	1868	20.3
1811	5943	23.3	1600	25.0	128	21.9	2300	26.1	215	25.6	1700	17.6
1816	4948	39.0	522	51.5	507	52.1	1424	38.1	268	29.9	2227	34.9
1817	3971	27.8	1134	26.4	31	35.5	1889	24.0	59	32.2	858	37.6
1818	4386	48.2	1275	36.6	140	44.3	1625	45.8	235	32.8	1111	68.8
1819	4694	49.4	1439	41.6	180	45.6	1677	46.0	255	34.1	1143	68.1
1820	4729	48.3	1343	37.1	194	44.3	1682	45.8	312	37.5	1198	67.9
MARIA												
1803	582	50.0	302	54.6	111	56.8	122	38.5	37	32.4	10	40.0
1804	906	45.1	445	44.9	154	56.5	277	41.2	10	40.0	20	20.0
1805	960	44.5	446	42.8	156	55.1	324	43.2	12	50.0	22	18.2
1806	972	43.5	444	42.6	159	47.2	333	45.0	14	28.6	22	22.7
1807	1011	43.2	476	42.2	143	49.0	365	43.3	9	33.3	18	27.8
1811	1081	34.9	355	22.5	226	43.4	437	42.3	44	18.2	19	31.6
MARIARA												
1802	1587	40.7	395	42.5	94	41.5	714	42.9	133	33.1	251	35.5
1803	1660	38.9	406	41.9	53	47.2	696	42.4	177	41.8	328	25.0

TABLE 3. MARRIED PERSONS (CONTINUED)

YEAR	TOTAL A	TOTAL PCT	WHITE A	WHITE PCT	INDIAN A	INDIAN PCT	PARDO A	PARDO PCT	NEGRO A	NEGRO PCT	SLAVE A	SLAVE PCT
1804	1577	41.4	392	39.8	42	50.0	729	44.4	160	41.9	254	33.5
1805	1776	43.1	444	43.2	49	53.1	912	46.2	135	37.0	236	32.6
1809	2291	41.2	605	39.3	189	49.2	907	41.6	273	43.6	317	36.9
1815	2054	43.8	492	44.3	87	52.9	1035	45.7	169	39.6	271	35.4
1816	2415	40.6	585	40.2	35	37.1	1431	43.2	105	41.9	259	27.4
1817	2583	42.2	670	36.4	75	72.0	1420	47.2	151	32.5	267	27.7
1818	2449	39.0	719	38.1	31	38.7	1355	42.5	89	27.0	255	27.5
MONTALBAN												
1781	1066	29.5	423	32.6	36	44.4	399	31.8	14	28.6	194	15.5
1802	1519	34.8	577	41.2	0	0.0	605	39.7	74	14.9	263	15.2
1803	1659	33.8	636	39.0	0	0.0	716	34.4	60	33.3	247	19.0
1804	1686	34.3	643	40.0	0	0.0	736	34.6	68	32.4	239	18.4
1805	1665	34.7	653	40.0	0	0.0	738	35.0	69	27.5	205	19.0
1806	1586	36.3	617	43.1	0	0.0	723	35.0	60	25.0	186	22.0
1808	2010	29.2	889	30.3	0	0.0	873	29.9	98	22.4	150	23.3
1810	1755	36.0	641	44.6	9	22.2	855	34.6	120	18.3	130	20.0
1815	2098	43.3	612	45.1	10	40.0	1026	36.8	116	50.0	334	57.5
1817	2239	41.6	661	47.2	12	33.3	1120	33.9	113	44.2	333	55.9
1818	1719	46.4	526	55.5	15	26.7	891	40.4	76	55.3	211	47.4
1820	2430	48.4	825	52.1	18	33.3	1248	52.4	154	26.0	185	24.9
MORON												
1804	197	38.6	0	0.0	0	0.0	108	40.7	7	0.0	82	39.0
1805	195	40.0	0	0.0	0	0.0	101	45.5	19	42.1	75	32.0
1806	201	45.8	0	0.0	0	0.0	98	52.0	25	48.0	78	37.2
1807	240	45.0	0	0.0	0	0.0	114	50.9	37	51.4	89	34.8
1818	227	59.9	0	0.0	0	0.0	146	71.2	0	0.0	81	39.5
1819	246	61.8	0	0.0	0	0.0	152	78.9	0	0.0	94	34.0
1820	278	69.1	4	100.0	0	0.0	161	79.5	42	66.7	71	45.1
MOROTURO												
1802	264	36.0	42	26.2	2	100.0	50	48.0	140	39.3	30	10.0
1804	391	39.1	30	26.7	81	53.1	106	42.5	155	35.5	19	10.5
1805	406	35.5	53	30.2	57	42.1	113	42.5	160	33.8	23	8.7
1807	293	35.5	24	25.0	41	34.1	197	38.6	18	38.9	13	7.7
1808	391	39.1	30	26.7	81	53.1	106	42.5	155	35.5	19	10.5
1809	312	35.3	35	45.7	27	51.9	231	33.8	5	40.0	14	0.0
1815	391	39.1	30	26.7	81	53.1	106	42.5	155	35.5	19	10.5
NAGUANAGUA												
1802	1036	34.9	474	39.7	4	75.0	345	36.5	2	100.0	211	20.4
1803	1140	38.5	544	40.1	4	75.0	373	36.7	2	100.0	217	36.4
1804	945	36.3	425	40.0	3	0.0	325	36.6	2	100.0	190	27.4
1805	1131	36.5	443	37.0	4	50.0	469	34.1	2	100.0	213	39.9
1809	975	36.1	437	35.2	7	42.9	344	36.6	3	100.0	184	35.9
1816	1301	38.4	434	33.9	25	8.0	418	37.3	32	21.9	392	48.0

TABLE 3. MARRIED PERSONS (CONTINUED)

YEAR	TOTAL A	TOTAL PCT	WHITE A	WHITE PCT	INDIAN A	INDIAN PCT	PARDO A	PARDO PCT	NEGRO A	NEGRO PCT	SLAVE A	SLAVE PCT
NAIGUATA												
1801	619	39.3	35	28.6	124	33.9	20	35.0	7	42.9	433	41.8
1802	593	42.2	22	27.3	116	39.7	13	15.4	13	61.5	429	43.8
1804	574	42.2	25	44.0	126	34.9	2	50.0	6	66.7	415	43.9
1805	533	43.9	32	46.9	116	32.8	11	72.7	3	33.3	371	46.4
1809	540	45.2	31	38.7	103	33.0	6	33.3	3	0.0	397	49.4
1810	539	47.1	26	46.2	85	40.0	9	22.2	7	28.6	412	49.5
1811	493	53.5	34	41.2	109	38.5	14	42.9	10	40.0	326	60.7
1816	440	42.3	27	37.0	84	33.3	29	27.6	21	42.9	279	47.0
1817	543	40.5	45	40.0	83	39.8	45	24.4	42	33.3	328	43.9
1822	377	41.6	21	42.9	90	42.2	41	56.1	21	47.6	204	37.7
NIRGUA												
1781	2319	31.7	28	21.4	0	0.0	2280	32.0	0	0.0	11	0.0
1802	2277	20.6	18	88.9	0	0.0	2234	20.3	0	0.0	25	0.0
1803	2090	32.5	26	76.9	0	0.0	2042	32.3	0	0.0	22	0.0
1804	2098	32.7	31	71.0	0	0.0	2045	32.5	0	0.0	22	0.0
1805	1945	33.3	37	59.5	0	0.0	1826	33.7	0	0.0	82	12.2
1806	1974	34.0	44	59.1	0	0.0	1846	34.5	0	0.0	84	11.9
1807	1947	33.4	37	59.5	0	0.0	1828	33.8	0	0.0	82	12.2
1808	3665	39.1	104	39.4	10	30.0	2868	40.8	571	29.1	112	45.5
1809	3405	52.9	68	38.2	2	0.0	2293	51.6	992	57.9	50	36.0
1810	3896	42.0	78	38.5	19	31.6	2553	42.0	1172	42.9	74	33.8
1813	2247	34.8	42	23.8	0	0.0	2175	35.4	0	0.0	30	10.0
1817	2233	34.8	42	23.8	0	0.0	2161	35.4	0	0.0	30	10.0
1819	2124	37.7	42	23.8	0	0.0	2052	38.4	0	0.0	30	10.0
1820	2110	39.3	39	28.2	0	0.0	2028	39.8	0	0.0	43	25.6
1821	1798	42.5	22	27.3	0	0.0	1751	43.2	0	0.0	25	8.0
OCUMARE DE LA COSTA												
1802	1704	39.3	67	32.8	4	0.0	666	26.7	98	12.2	869	52.7
1803	1539	35.1	57	42.1	7	0.0	672	10.7	181	25.4	622	64.0
1804	1142	20.2	71	47.9	5	0.0	231	30.7	150	40.0	685	9.6
1805	1686	38.7	67	47.8	1	100.0	498	27.7	23	52.2	1097	42.8
1809	1284	28.3	73	37.0	0	0.0	484	44.2	51	78.4	676	12.1
1815	1113	29.8	64	32.8	0	0.0	433	25.9	47	25.5	569	32.9
1816	1139	30.5	50	30.0	0	0.0	407	22.1	74	37.8	608	35.2
1817	1067	32.7	51	29.4	0	0.0	423	24.8	63	28.6	530	39.8
1819	850	35.1	47	17.0	1	0.0	296	12.8	61	29.5	445	52.6
1820	964	36.2	94	16.0	1	0.0	336	17.3	105	36.2	428	55.6
OCUMARE DEL TUY												
1783	1651	35.3	289	33.2	52	30.8	354	37.9	161	29.2	795	36.4
1802	2927	39.5	421	32.3	263	39.5	638	39.7	221	27.6	1384	43.4
1803	3222	39.0	1070	39.3	250	52.0	514	35.8	455	26.4	933	43.1
1804	3588	32.4	443	33.4	269	37.2	760	41.6	247	25.1	1869	28.8

TABLE 3. MARRIED PERSONS (CONTINUED)

YEAR	TOTAL A	TOTAL PCT	WHITE A	WHITE PCT	INDIAN A	INDIAN PCT	PARDO A	PARDO PCT	NEGRO A	NEGRO PCT	SLAVE A	SLAVE PCT
1805	3685	33.0	523	35.9	274	38.7	764	41.6	251	25.5	1873	28.8
1810	3663	37.3	433	45.3	241	52.3	782	40.4	150	38.7	2057	32.6
1811	2256	38.7	364	30.8	161	29.8	611	31.4	155	40.0	965	47.5
1815	1001	29.7	155	13.5	67	35.8	169	45.0	54	33.3	556	28.4
1820	2986	35.0	395	32.7	126	31.7	805	28.6	187	9.6	1473	42.6
1821	2581	39.9	459	37.5	55	34.5	594	32.3	210	39.0	1263	44.7
1822	2786	35.1	412	27.4	145	30.3	663	30.3	189	6.9	1377	44.1
ORTIZ												
1780	897	37.9	610	36.6	62	54.8	63	47.6	76	56.6	86	11.6
1802	1031	39.9	654	40.8	37	54.1	77	72.7	147	28.6	116	22.4
1803	1053	42.9	710	44.4	44	40.9	139	54.0	78	35.9	82	19.5
1804	1171	32.7	804	36.3	70	24.3	149	32.2	44	27.3	104	13.5
1805	1172	32.8	804	36.3	71	25.4	149	32.2	44	27.3	104	13.5
1806	1343	44.5	1025	41.6	51	58.8	116	60.3	45	73.3	106	36.8
1807	1400	32.8	727	42.0	29	41.4	445	24.0	67	29.9	132	11.4
1808	1382	35.0	714	43.8	37	43.2	438	27.4	67	29.9	126	11.9
1809	1442	32.6	730	43.0	46	34.8	447	23.0	79	30.4	140	9.3
1810	1468	34.1	745	42.8	53	52.8	448	24.8	79	25.3	143	15.4
1813	1328	38.2	902	43.0	39	38.5	204	43.1	60	18.3	123	4.1
OSPINO												
1802	4154	32.1	1285	29.6	632	37.0	1955	34.6	93	34.4	189	5.3
1803	4177	32.2	1277	30.0	646	36.7	1957	34.6	96	30.2	201	8.0
1804	4358	33.1	1326	33.2	708	36.4	2009	34.9	118	30.5	197	4.6
1805	4338	33.6	1276	34.7	794	35.0	1997	34.8	72	40.3	199	7.0
1806	4625	33.5	1383	34.3	834	35.7	2109	34.3	91	39.6	208	7.7
1807	4675	33.8	1395	34.8	814	35.7	2140	34.7	109	36.7	217	10.1
1808	4891	33.8	1630	34.6	845	33.4	2016	36.5	186	25.8	214	10.3
1809	4917	36.3	1346	37.9	1098	33.3	2085	40.7	192	26.0	196	5.1
1810	4891	36.2	1346	37.9	1096	33.2	2063	40.7	188	23.9	198	6.1
1811	3746	36.9	1364	37.4	467	40.3	1544	40.4	159	23.3	212	10.8
1817	3746	36.9	1364	37.4	467	40.3	1544	40.4	159	23.3	212	10.8
PANAQUIRE												
1784	342	28.1	31	48.4	42	26.2	41	31.7	3	66.7	225	24.4
1802	675	47.1	59	30.5	57	47.4	64	48.4	6	83.3	489	48.5
1803	608	44.1	63	38.1	53	41.5	51	41.2	1	0.0	440	45.7
1804	588	42.0	51	35.3	51	45.1	52	36.5	2	100.0	432	42.8
1805	573	43.3	50	34.0	41	46.3	52	40.4	10	40.0	420	44.5
1807	571	47.3	45	28.9	30	36.7	66	47.0	4	0.0	426	50.5
1808	579	48.2	47	31.9	31	35.5	66	47.0	5	60.0	430	50.9
1809	581	47.5	52	40.4	39	30.8	72	38.9	9	33.3	409	51.8
1811	568	44.2	32	25.0	40	32.5	67	35.8	22	31.8	407	48.9
1812	565	50.1	31	41.9	46	41.3	75	46.7	21	52.4	392	52.3
1816	390	34.4	16	37.5	14	42.9	66	30.3	13	53.8	281	33.8

TABLE 3. MARRIED PERSONS (CONTINUED)

YEAR	TOTAL A	TOTAL PCT	WHITE A	WHITE PCT	INDIAN A	INDIAN PCT	PARDO A	PARDO PCT	NEGRO A	NEGRO PCT	SLAVE A	SLAVE PCT
PARACOTOS												
1783	1415	27.1	296	41.6	450	23.1	267	12.0	121	14.0	281	38.4
1802	1370	36.6	490	38.4	308	35.1	373	36.5	38	31.6	161	36.0
1803	1493	34.5	504	38.7	308	36.4	376	36.7	35	34.3	270	21.5
1804	1258	35.2	549	32.8	275	38.5	291	42.6	29	27.6	114	21.9
1805	1416	36.2	560	32.9	382	41.6	305	43.0	34	32.4	135	20.7
1806	1516	37.9	710	39.0	381	43.0	274	35.0	23	47.8	128	21.1
1807	1546	39.5	691	38.8	376	43.1	274	35.0	27	48.1	178	39.9
1808	1581	39.0	711	39.1	406	44.8	294	36.1	37	62.2	133	20.3
1809	1065	50.9	345	52.8	270	47.4	168	70.2	66	60.6	216	34.3
1810	1191	56.5	424	66.3	299	52.2	180	65.6	66	60.6	222	35.1
1811	1247	56.8	429	65.7	321	55.5	198	62.6	71	56.3	228	36.8
1812	1396	48.4	432	44.4	305	45.2	246	59.3	110	63.6	303	42.9
1816	1289	43.8	383	49.6	215	36.3	287	51.2	269	43.1	135	24.4
1817	1315	45.5	386	51.3	222	37.8	294	52.7	269	43.9	144	29.9
1819	1283	35.8	551	39.2	454	35.9	139	30.2	0	0.0	139	27.3
1820	1284	37.1	551	41.2	454	36.3	138	32.6	0	0.0	141	28.4
PARAPARA												
1780	1366	42.8	380	48.4	62	50.0	623	41.7	162	38.9	139	33.8
1781	1360	43.2	377	48.8	64	53.1	621	41.9	160	39.4	138	34.1
1782	1381	40.6	328	41.2	112	34.8	632	42.7	167	38.9	142	36.6
1788	1347	42.0	329	41.0	72	54.2	632	42.7	172	40.7	142	36.6
1802	1400	35.4	375	29.6	48	29.2	501	42.1	404	36.1	72	18.1
1803	1463	36.0	390	32.8	34	26.5	518	43.1	442	34.6	79	17.7
1805	1474	36.4	409	31.1	24	29.2	534	45.7	430	34.0	77	15.6
1807	1591	38.2	353	41.4	13	0.0	931	39.8	207	37.7	87	14.9
1809	1655	37.7	377	40.1	18	0.0	962	40.1	204	34.8	94	17.0
1810	1710	38.0	383	40.7	20	0.0	995	40.7	213	33.3	99	18.2
1811	1775	37.4	407	39.8	18	0.0	1047	38.9	211	37.0	92	17.4
PATANEMO												
1802	295	47.5	7	85.7	2	0.0	122	49.2	39	25.6	125	51.2
1803	295	48.5	10	80.0	8	25.0	119	48.7	37	27.0	121	53.7
1804	367	37.9	8	75.0	3	66.7	190	34.2	39	38.5	127	40.2
1805	389	38.0	8	100.0	4	50.0	198	35.4	41	39.0	138	37.7
1808	369	36.9	6	66.7	2	0.0	169	33.1	43	27.9	149	43.0
1818	236	61.0	4	25.0	2	50.0	142	69.0	6	50.0	82	50.0
1819	270	67.4	5	40.0	3	66.7	149	77.9	14	42.9	99	56.6
PAYARA												
1780	707	75.8	29	48.3	609	81.1	17	64.7	1	0.0	51	33.3
1802	909	70.0	156	70.5	415	67.5	255	70.6	49	89.8	34	64.7
1804	997	67.6	201	69.7	409	66.0	287	71.1	54	77.8	46	39.1
1805	1135	67.0	248	67.7	430	65.1	334	71.9	66	72.7	57	42.1
1806	1138	66.8	250	67.2	431	65.0	334	71.9	66	72.7	57	42.1

TABLE 3. MARRIED PERSONS (CONTINUED)

YEAR	TOTAL		WHITE		INDIAN		PARDO		NEGRO		SLAVE	
	A	PCT	A	PCT	A	PCT	A	PCT	A	PCT	A	PCT
1807	1151	66.4	256	68.0	430	64.7	352	69.9	61	75.4	52	38.5
1812	1135	67.0	248	67.7	430	65.1	334	71.9	66	72.7	57	42.1
PETARE												
1802	2718	38.2	888	44.4	454	29.3	495	44.4	307	31.3	574	34.1
1803	2756	38.4	904	44.1	458	29.7	509	44.4	309	31.7	576	34.4
1804	2899	36.8	931	42.5	468	31.2	575	41.0	345	28.1	580	32.9
1805	3279	33.6	826	32.7	421	42.3	799	32.3	163	41.1	1070	30.7
1806	3123	35.2	797	35.5	377	43.5	778	34.7	138	31.9	1033	32.6
1807	3548	33.4	878	32.2	402	42.0	894	35.2	142	23.9	1232	31.2
1811	3258	38.9	800	37.5	302	42.4	570	34.6	391	38.9	1195	40.9
1812	3625	65.8	880	70.5	442	53.4	399	53.1	334	55.4	1570	72.1
1815	2665	58.9	649	50.2	327	46.2	315	54.0	272	58.1	1102	69.3
1816	3461	35.0	977	36.5	258	32.2	472	40.3	745	34.1	1009	32.3
1817	3335	34.9	763	35.5	310	32.3	520	40.4	722	32.5	1020	34.1
1818	2609	40.2	658	36.2	263	44.5	656	38.0	168	31.5	864	45.4
1819	2773	39.9	712	36.4	270	44.4	735	37.7	168	31.5	888	44.8
1820	2867	40.3	735	36.7	271	44.6	773	37.5	175	30.9	913	45.9
1821	2876	41.8	729	38.4	272	48.2	777	39.0	175	30.9	923	46.9
1822	2665	44.4	646	42.9	270	44.8	616	50.2	209	26.3	924	45.5
PUERTO CABELLO												
1803	3909	26.0	692	37.1	58	0.0	2115	25.7	496	32.5	548	10.0
1804	4170	26.5	842	33.1	24	8.3	2339	26.3	434	34.6	531	10.9
1805	4178	27.0	730	39.6	23	8.7	2414	26.0	457	31.5	554	11.6
1806	4337	24.9	860	34.5	27	7.4	2246	23.4	614	30.1	590	11.5
1811	4463	24.3	784	32.0	57	15.8	2087	22.1	925	33.8	610	8.2
1817	2594	47.0	910	50.8	210	26.7	626	47.9	364	54.9	484	41.3
1819	2448	60.5	998	52.3	42	61.9	1160	71.9	148	52.7	100	22.0
1820	2778	28.0	615	49.9	33	54.5	1513	16.9	303	51.2	314	13.1
PUERTO CABELLO, CASTILLO												
1801	483	16.1	402	16.2	8	62.5	17	35.3	0	0.0	56	3.6
1802	293	13.3	252	15.1	0	0.0	2	0.0	0	0.0	39	2.6
1804	421	20.4	232	18.1	0	0.0	119	29.4	0	0.0	70	12.9
1805	658	16.1	308	18.8	0	0.0	248	14.1	0	0.0	102	12.7
1806	958	29.2	529	26.1	6	33.3	338	36.1	0	0.0	85	21.2
1807	937	32.6	485	27.0	9	44.4	358	42.7	0	0.0	85	20.0
1808	1044	32.0	556	25.4	16	68.8	380	43.4	0	0.0	92	18.5
1809	973	33.2	502	26.3	24	41.7	348	46.0	0	0.0	99	21.2
1810	1295	21.3	650	19.1	21	28.6	542	24.5	0	0.0	82	15.9
1819	825	41.1	245	33.9	51	41.2	376	50.3	103	44.7	50	0.0
1820	682	38.6	174	20.7	50	24.0	320	53.7	97	38.1	41	14.6
QUARA												
1782	771	35.8	13	61.5	730	35.1	13	46.2	14	42.9	1	0.0
1791	626	40.9	18	44.4	585	40.0	22	63.6	1	0.0	0	0.0

TABLE 3. MARRIED PERSONS (CONTINUED)

YEAR	TOTAL A	TOTAL PCT	WHITE A	WHITE PCT	INDIAN A	INDIAN PCT	PARDO A	PARDO PCT	NEGRO A	NEGRO PCT	SLAVE A	SLAVE PCT
1802	475	45.5	13	61.5	428	45.3	33	42.4	0	0.0	1	0.0
1803	498	41.8	17	47.1	466	42.5	2	0.0	12	16.7	1	0.0
1804	520	51.3	6	33.3	504	51.4	5	40.0	5	80.0	0	0.0
1805	616	40.3	13	61.5	536	41.0	22	27.3	45	31.1	0	0.0
1807	601	41.1	18	44.4	506	42.7	51	25.5	25	40.0	1	0.0
1808	652	39.7	22	36.4	565	40.9	44	22.7	21	47.6	0	0.0
1809	669	36.0	21	38.1	563	37.3	49	22.4	36	33.3	0	0.0
1810	667	38.4	11	36.4	588	39.3	56	23.2	12	66.7	0	0.0
1811	681	39.4	15	53.3	576	40.3	59	27.1	31	38.7	0	0.0
1815	674	32.3	20	45.0	549	32.8	84	27.4	21	28.6	0	0.0
1816	645	39.8	19	31.6	519	41.2	79	32.9	28	39.3	0	0.0
1817	647	40.6	18	44.4	522	42.1	77	32.5	30	33.3	0	0.0
1818	831	30.1	15	26.7	651	31.6	87	29.9	62	16.1	16	25.0
1819	468	52.6	15	13.3	304	67.1	79	35.4	49	16.3	21	19.0
	QUIBOR											
1802	4916	38.1	1734	36.3	887	47.4	1227	38.4	651	34.4	417	31.2
1803	4834	37.1	1732	36.3	807	42.1	1227	38.4	651	34.4	417	31.2
1804	4997	38.4	1754	36.4	902	47.0	1264	38.7	643	34.7	434	33.2
1805	5320	38.8	1821	36.7	976	47.2	1322	39.2	723	36.5	478	31.8
1806	5318	38.8	1819	36.7	976	47.2	1322	39.2	723	36.5	478	31.8
1807	5302	38.9	1821	36.7	976	47.2	1304	39.7	723	36.5	478	31.8
1808	5721	40.4	1891	36.9	995	46.6	1551	45.1	779	35.9	505	33.3
1810	6785	29.8	1930	29.7	1260	32.9	3383	29.8	42	9.5	170	11.2
1812	5388	48.0	1634	45.3	796	57.4	2055	48.3	392	48.2	511	41.1
1815	5638	50.3	1714	47.8	846	59.9	2175	51.1	392	48.2	511	41.1
1816	5572	49.5	1654	47.5	831	59.8	2198	50.1	379	45.9	510	39.2
1817	6559	50.4	1946	49.6	936	58.2	2687	51.7	431	45.0	559	38.1
1818	6193	55.1	1654	59.3	1016	64.6	2604	53.6	406	43.3	513	40.5
1819	5747	54.9	1777	53.1	763	61.1	2310	59.4	371	45.8	526	38.4
1820	6316	55.7	1990	57.3	849	60.3	2494	58.8	420	44.0	563	38.4
	RIO CHICO											
1802	615	42.9	44	27.3	26	46.2	50	40.0	122	41.0	373	45.6
1803	637	44.3	49	30.6	29	48.3	57	47.4	122	42.6	380	45.8
1804	716	49.7	40	45.0	19	63.2	118	62.7	122	42.6	417	48.0
1805	811	49.1	62	29.0	44	54.5	96	62.5	81	59.3	528	47.0
1806	869	47.2	67	29.9	44	54.5	96	62.5	80	57.5	582	44.7
1807	884	46.4	67	29.9	44	54.5	96	62.5	80	57.5	597	43.6
1808	917	47.1	67	26.9	46	52.2	97	63.9	85	56.5	622	45.0
1809	925	47.8	67	29.9	46	52.2	97	63.9	85	56.5	630	45.7
1810	994	47.7	92	39.1	52	50.0	111	59.5	95	54.7	644	45.7
1811	1092	47.8	102	43.1	67	56.7	152	55.3	95	56.8	676	44.7
1812	992	46.9	77	40.3	49	49.0	108	55.6	93	51.6	665	45.4
1816	1164	30.8	98	31.6	99	26.3	263	27.0	69	26.1	635	33.4
1817	970	42.1	90	40.0	69	46.4	148	40.5	73	41.1	590	42.4
1819	979	42.5	86	27.9	68	41.2	174	36.8	73	54.8	578	45.0

TABLE 3. MARRIED PERSONS (CONTINUED)

YEAR	TOTAL A	TOTAL PCT	WHITE A	WHITE PCT	INDIAN A	INDIAN PCT	PARDO A	PARDO PCT	NEGRO A	NEGRO PCT	SLAVE A	SLAVE PCT
RIO DEL TOCUYO												
1802	1207	40.8	279	27.2	705	50.6	172	30.2	0	0.0	51	13.7
1803	1138	41.3	248	33.9	638	50.6	192	29.7	0	0.0	60	10.0
1804	1048	41.4	159	35.2	703	47.2	122	33.6	0	0.0	64	7.8
1805	1070	40.0	158	34.2	714	45.9	131	31.3	0	0.0	67	7.5
1808	1303	40.4	180	43.3	952	41.6	89	36.0	0	0.0	82	24.4
1809	1844	39.3	442	33.9	950	48.4	232	35.3	0	0.0	220	14.5
1815	1456	45.7	257	40.5	988	51.8	170	28.2	0	0.0	41	4.9
SABANETA												
1805	1345	39.9	479	40.5	153	48.4	647	40.2	29	24.1	37	5.4
1808	1594	36.4	283	34.6	433	38.3	822	37.7	27	11.1	29	10.3
1809	1983	36.3	589	41.9	264	37.1	1080	33.4	25	48.0	25	8.0
1810	2123	37.8	600	46.7	305	34.4	1125	34.7	58	39.7	35	11.4
1811	2640	39.9	798	43.5	380	42.1	1278	37.4	116	51.7	68	13.2
1812	1492	42.9	596	47.0	425	34.1	276	50.4	119	48.7	76	23.7
1816	1274	52.4	416	58.2	55	58.2	803	49.1	0	0.0	0	0.0
SAN ANTONIO DE LAS COCUIZAS												
1780	704	52.6	68	35.3	60	66.7	429	55.9	126	47.6	21	28.6
SAN ANTONIO DE LOS ALTOS												
1796	333	34.2	275	38.9	0	0.0	24	29.2	6	0.0	28	0.0
1802	332	41.9	262	46.2	5	0.0	29	27.6	1	0.0	35	28.6
1803	378	38.4	298	40.9	27	29.6	11	0.0	2	0.0	40	37.5
1804	385	36.4	300	39.3	9	22.2	15	13.3	2	0.0	59	30.5
1805	493	33.1	321	42.4	23	17.4	27	11.1	1	0.0	121	16.5
1808	867	34.0	377	44.0	42	19.0	105	13.3	8	25.0	335	31.3
1809	781	33.2	344	43.6	19	10.5	32	12.5	3	0.0	383	26.9
1810	659	39.2	329	42.9	8	12.5	49	22.4	4	50.0	269	38.3
1811	625	43.7	323	45.8	5	40.0	52	28.8	2	0.0	243	44.4
1812	610	43.1	308	49.7	3	33.3	39	17.9	6	66.7	254	38.6
1815	463	38.0	207	38.2	9	33.3	63	30.2	2	50.0	182	40.7
1816	418	41.4	210	40.5	10	30.0	41	36.6	2	0.0	155	45.2
1817	419	40.6	202	40.6	4	25.0	40	20.0	4	0.0	169	46.7
1818	413	38.3	219	38.4	10	30.0	53	30.2	3	0.0	128	43.0
1819	416	43.8	226	44.2	4	0.0	52	36.5	6	16.7	128	48.4
1820	484	36.2	246	38.6	26	42.3	70	24.3	12	0.0	130	40.0
SAN CARLOS												
1781	5537	30.8	2311	39.1	299	35.5	1391	40.5	389	20.6	1147	4.4
1786	5686	31.0	2138	37.8	306	33.3	1603	35.2	513	22.6	1126	15.3
1787	6158	27.2	2294	34.5	321	31.2	1736	30.6	529	23.1	1278	10.2
1788	6293	27.1	2311	34.8	316	32.3	1749	30.6	624	20.2	1293	10.7
1791	6660	27.3	2406	34.8	345	32.5	1870	30.1	696	22.4	1343	11.3

TABLE 3. MARRIED PERSONS (CONTINUED)

YEAR	TOTAL		WHITE		INDIAN		PARDO		NEGRO		SLAVE	
	A	PCT	A	PCT	A	PCT	A	PCT	A	PCT	A	PCT
1796	7074	27.8	2532	35.2	381	32.0	1990	30.8	749	22.4	1422	12.2
1798	5775	26.0	2103	31.3	296	32.4	1574	30.6	815	25.5	987	6.1
1799	5786	26.5	2108	31.7	297	33.0	1588	30.7	795	26.8	998	6.4
1800	6031	25.9	2149	31.5	309	33.0	1638	30.6	935	23.5	1000	6.4
1801	6089	25.9	2161	31.6	316	32.9	1651	30.8	951	23.3	1010	6.1
1802	6438	25.1	2328	32.3	298	32.2	1665	27.3	853	25.3	1294	7.4
1803	6483	25.2	2340	32.4	303	32.3	1685	27.5	856	25.0	1299	7.5
1804	7695	32.9	2603	37.0	510	55.3	2000	33.9	1110	39.1	1472	11.5
1805	7833	32.3	2703	35.7	510	55.3	2000	33.9	1110	39.1	1510	11.4
1806	7886	32.5	2710	35.6	510	55.3	2031	34.6	1115	39.1	1520	11.6
1808	7833	32.3	2703	35.7	510	55.3	2000	33.9	1110	39.1	1510	11.4
1809	7833	32.3	2703	35.7	510	55.3	2000	33.9	1110	39.1	1510	11.4
1811	10470	15.8	3709	16.4	91	59.3	5717	14.1	104	42.3	849	16.5
1812	10355	15.7	3701	16.6	73	56.2	5719	14.2	89	37.1	773	15.8
1816	5256	28.2	1511	32.4	265	32.5	2673	30.2	150	26.0	657	9.6
1817	5440	25.2	1732	27.4	186	19.4	2620	27.6	170	28.2	732	12.3
1818	5543	26.7	1838	30.3	244	28.3	2449	28.7	187	27.8	825	12.0
1819	5382	25.6	1717	27.9	166	17.5	2488	28.9	176	27.3	835	12.6
1820	5339	25.7	1762	27.8	170	18.2	2447	30.2	176	25.0	784	9.1
1822	5426	25.1	1720	27.3	153	20.3	2565	28.2	175	26.9	813	10.9
1823	4945	25.2	1477	28.5	129	18.6	2402	28.4	169	26.6	768	9.9
1824	4630	26.3	1454	30.3	110	20.0	2299	29.2	113	22.1	654	8.9
	SAN DIEGO DE ALCALA											
1781	571	31.7	164	31.1	139	36.0	251	31.1	0	0.0	17	11.8
1802	808	29.1	174	40.2	145	34.5	361	25.5	114	14.0	14	50.0
1803	495	35.2	85	47.1	143	32.2	212	31.1	40	40.0	15	40.0
1804	535	38.7	130	38.5	105	34.3	192	40.6	96	41.7	12	25.0
1805	614	39.3	150	45.3	148	39.2	279	38.4	23	21.7	14	21.4
1809	601	34.6	119	39.5	146	36.3	300	31.3	26	42.3	10	30.0
	SAN DIEGO DE LOS ALTOS											
1802	630	39.2	328	41.2	164	47.6	61	32.8	11	18.2	66	18.2
1803	666	43.5	282	47.5	209	53.6	59	23.7	46	39.1	70	17.1
1804	631	41.7	334	43.4	130	50.8	70	40.0	28	35.7	69	20.3
1805	657	41.9	335	42.7	149	49.7	68	47.1	35	34.3	70	20.0
1807	713	35.9	337	36.2	201	45.8	72	25.0	30	33.3	73	19.2
1808	758	36.9	341	37.2	204	44.6	85	25.9	36	33.3	92	30.4
1809	850	36.9	356	36.8	232	45.3	94	27.7	63	31.7	105	30.5
1810	831	34.9	352	35.8	233	42.1	96	22.9	31	58.1	119	21.8
1811	833	39.9	368	39.1	245	45.7	74	29.7	34	52.9	112	32.1
1815	886	35.4	403	35.2	215	42.8	77	36.4	59	16.9	132	31.8
1816	861	33.7	389	33.9	227	31.7	79	35.4	20	30.0	146	35.6
1817	840	41.4	396	38.4	191	50.8	75	44.0	51	23.5	127	42.5
1818	805	36.3	371	33.7	204	39.7	73	42.5	129	36.4	28	28.6
1819	836	36.2	353	32.6	236	41.5	76	35.5	34	29.4	137	38.7
1820	918	34.7	364	33.5	245	40.8	114	32.5	40	25.0	155	32.3

TABLE 3. MARRIED PERSONS (CONTINUED)

YEAR	TOTAL		WHITE		INDIAN		PARDO		NEGRO		SLAVE	
	A	PCT	A	PCT	A	PCT	A	PCT	A	PCT	A	PCT
SAN FELIPE												
1782	3437	38.9	895	36.1	192	40.6	2175	38.8	78	50.0	97	54.6
1802	4400	34.5	1110	39.6	450	35.6	1680	38.1	430	32.6	730	19.2
1803	4197	33.7	1060	39.6	443	33.9	1637	37.0	377	31.8	680	17.6
1804	3566	20.6	752	21.1	92	23.9	2078	23.1	107	20.6	537	9.7
1805	4019	21.8	762	24.4	55	20.0	2540	23.5	123	17.1	539	11.3
1817	2315	32.7	234	41.0	13	61.5	1887	30.2	33	51.5	148	44.6
1818	1881	23.2	624	13.5	0	0.0	947	33.8	7	57.1	303	9.2
1819	2449	32.8	280	39.3	25	56.0	1932	30.4	54	42.6	158	43.0
1820	2549	33.0	288	38.9	32	46.9	1998	30.8	66	40.9	165	43.6
1821	2057	29.6	245	30.6	25	56.0	1595	27.0	54	42.6	138	47.8
SAN FELIPE, MITAD DE (1)												
1807	2249	21.1	419	23.6	32	18.7	1440	21.3	32	31.3	326	16.3
1808	2250	21.1	419	23.6	32	18.7	1440	21.3	32	31.3	327	16.5
1809	2192	21.1	400	21.3	25	28.0	1373	23.0	23	13.0	371	13.7
1810	2232	20.6	422	23.5	28	25.0	1424	20.4	35	34.3	323	16.1
1811	2232	20.6	422	23.5	28	25.0	1424	20.4	35	34.3	323	16.1
1812	1566	17.9	163	22.1	7	57.1	1203	19.4	9	44.4	184	1.6
SAN FELIPE, MITAD DE (2)												
1807	2249	21.4	377	24.9	37	18.9	1527	23.2	39	7.7	269	8.9
1808	2261	21.3	366	25.4	63	19.0	1487	22.8	86	19.8	259	7.7
1809	2257	26.1	352	35.5	112	21.4	1437	27.6	105	21.0	251	8.4
1810	2266	25.9	350	35.4	111	19.8	1441	27.6	109	22.0	255	8.2
1811	2243	22.5	334	25.7	64	23.4	1544	24.0	83	21.7	218	6.9
SAN FERNANDO DE APURE												
1801	2711	47.8	1007	40.3	210	52.4	1328	56.2	57	24.6	109	18.3
1805	1240	50.8	614	59.6	196	45.9	400	39.0	0	0.0	30	60.0
1806	1970	41.1	832	46.9	364	30.2	724	40.1	0	0.0	50	40.0
1816	1253	52.8	490	51.0	72	55.6	487	55.9	114	70.2	90	22.2
SAN FERNANDO DE CACHICAMO												
1783	269	56.1	72	62.5	11	81.8	86	61.6	29	69.0	71	33.8
1802	307	38.4	70	40.0	23	43.5	126	41.3	33	24.2	55	36.4
1803	301	41.9	65	43.1	25	40.0	125	46.4	32	25.0	54	40.7
1805	275	38.2	49	38.8	16	50.0	159	40.3	7	28.6	44	27.3
1806	336	36.3	79	34.2	21	42.9	178	39.3	9	22.2	49	28.6
1807	339	36.0	81	33.3	21	42.9	178	39.3	9	22.2	50	28.0
SAN FRANCISCO DE CARA												
1783	806	35.7	168	29.8	18	55.6	563	39.1	0	0.0	57	14.0
1802	1190	30.9	291	36.8	26	38.5	710	30.4	37	43.2	126	15.1

TABLE 3. MARRIED PERSONS (CONTINUED)

YEAR	TOTAL A	TOTAL PCT	WHITE A	WHITE PCT	INDIAN A	INDIAN PCT	PARDO A	PARDO PCT	NEGRO A	NEGRO PCT	SLAVE A	SLAVE PCT
SAN FRANCISCO DE TIZNADOS												
1780	1595	33.5	210	47.6	106	35.8	260	45.4	737	34.5	282	8.9
1801	1199	31.9	170	24.7	34	61.8	843	34.4	0	0.0	152	19.7
1802	1336	33.4	165	24.2	5	80.0	612	32.5	423	40.9	131	22.9
1803	1450	31.5	217	25.3	17	58.8	723	27.5	323	51.4	170	15.9
1805	1507	31.9	232	28.4	25	20.0	1082	35.2	14	21.4	154	16.9
1807	1600	33.8	256	28.1	25	20.0	1140	37.1	17	35.3	162	21.0
1808	1634	35.0	248	29.0	25	20.0	1178	38.3	17	35.3	166	22.9
1809	1636	35.0	250	28.8	25	20.0	1178	38.3	17	35.3	166	22.9
1811	1734	24.9	371	36.7	142	18.3	772	21.9	325	23.1	124	21.0
1812	1856	26.3	382	39.8	153	19.6	872	22.5	296	23.6	153	26.1
SAN FRANCISCO DE YARE												
1783	919	45.5	47	38.3	81	50.6	90	38.9	83	31.3	618	48.2
1802	1203	39.0	68	36.8	154	40.9	68	29.4	161	32.3	752	41.1
1803	1226	43.4	59	32.2	158	39.9	82	39.0	202	34.2	725	48.1
1804	1176	40.6	54	29.6	151	44.4	56	37.5	208	31.3	707	43.7
1805	1270	35.5	63	31.7	155	44.5	55	49.1	227	26.9	770	35.6
1810	1484	29.3	73	43.8	200	37.0	347	36.0	78	30.8	786	22.9
1811	1491	29.6	73	43.8	200	37.0	350	36.6	82	34.1	786	22.9
1815	1092	26.6	49	36.7	97	33.0	101	37.6	33	30.3	812	23.6
1817	1260	36.8	60	41.7	196	40.8	208	28.8	60	40.0	736	37.4
1818	1226	38.5	58	44.8	126	41.3	291	37.1	89	23.6	662	40.0
1820	1284	37.9	88	47.7	111	46.8	163	42.3	159	34.0	763	35.3
1821	1448	39.6	93	44.1	184	44.6	254	42.9	89	41.6	828	36.7
1822	1319	39.0	81	46.9	133	49.6	292	34.9	79	49.4	734	36.6
SAN JAIME												
1780	1364	48.5	545	53.2	78	52.6	573	45.7	46	39.1	122	41.8
SAN JOSE												
1781	817	44.6	109	55.0	248	51.6	391	37.9	16	100.0	53	22.6
1788	1015	44.1	67	47.8	186	44.1	693	45.9	36	38.9	33	6.1
1790	1206	44.9	278	45.3	229	52.4	621	42.8	57	52.6	21	0.0
1791	1206	44.9	278	45.3	229	52.4	621	42.8	57	52.6	21	0.0
1792	1429	39.6	336	24.4	275	49.5	764	42.7	29	48.3	25	32.0
1794	1369	41.3	276	29.7	275	49.5	764	42.7	29	48.3	25	32.0
1795	1849	33.7	403	34.2	279	35.8	504	34.9	613	33.0	50	14.0
1798	2024	35.2	443	35.7	319	37.6	544	36.0	656	34.1	62	22.6
1799	2024	35.2	443	35.7	319	37.6	544	36.0	656	34.1	62	22.6
1800	2024	35.2	443	35.7	319	37.6	544	36.0	656	34.1	62	22.6
1801	2065	33.7	434	29.5	342	39.5	594	35.0	677	32.5	18	22.2
1803	1746	43.8	347	36.9	278	32.4	1062	50.1	33	36.4	26	7.7
1804	1723	46.3	358	35.8	182	50.5	1102	50.9	33	36.4	48	8.3
1805	1308	37.3	287	32.8	206	43.7	759	39.0	18	33.3	38	5.3
1807	1272	42.1	304	40.8	125	36.0	813	44.8	0	0.0	30	6.7

TABLE 3. MARRIED PERSONS (CONTINUED)

YEAR	TOTAL		WHITE		INDIAN		PARDO		NEGRO		SLAVE	
	A	PCT	A	PCT	A	PCT	A	PCT	A	PCT	A	PCT
1808	1273	42.0	306	39.5	123	39.0	812	44.7	0	0.0	32	9.4
1811	1260	41.0	284	37.3	135	31.9	809	45.1	0	0.0	32	6.3
1812	893	41.2	173	35.8	61	55.7	642	41.1	17	47.1	0	0.0
1815	1098	39.5	46	30.4	104	57.7	921	38.9	12	0.0	15	13.3
1818	1264	33.9	370	34.9	294	50.3	590	25.1	5	80.0	5	0.0
1819	1243	36.6	281	46.3	380	40.5	568	29.8	7	28.6	7	0.0
1822	1291	41.4	350	48.6	233	39.5	657	39.7	33	24.2	18	22.2
1823	997	41.0	311	48.6	176	36.4	487	38.8	12	33.3	11	9.1
SAN JOSE DE APURE												
1802	420	51.4	52	57.7	168	57.1	139	51.8	53	34.0	8	0.0
1804	458	52.4	91	50.5	138	59.4	138	53.6	89	42.7	2	0.0
1806	437	56.3	85	51.8	148	64.9	122	55.7	78	48.7	4	0.0
1807	470	52.8	85	42.4	161	57.1	129	55.8	93	51.6	2	0.0
1808	450	56.0	82	46.3	152	63.2	128	57.8	85	51.8	3	0.0
1809	450	56.0	82	46.3	152	63.2	128	57.8	85	51.8	3	0.0
SAN JOSE DE TIZNADOS												
1802	1378	37.4	265	38.1	57	43.9	849	39.6	56	35.7	151	21.9
1803	1433	40.1	275	38.5	81	39.5	872	42.9	72	37.5	133	26.3
1804	1367	42.9	262	39.3	95	47.4	831	46.2	74	43.2	105	21.0
1805	1434	39.1	289	33.9	99	36.4	881	42.5	56	55.4	109	19.3
1807	1435	39.7	250	42.0	76	36.8	810	44.1	192	32.3	107	16.8
1808	1278	44.1	198	46.0	44	47.7	840	46.3	95	43.2	101	20.8
1809	1312	44.7	238	43.7	35	34.3	809	48.0	138	41.3	92	27.2
1810	1428	43.7	216	44.0	74	36.5	899	46.2	130	42.3	109	29.4
1812	1322	45.2	174	48.3	73	43.8	860	46.6	121	43.0	94	30.9
1816	1404	36.5	242	41.3	91	38.5	734	39.0	250	30.0	87	19.5
1817	1801	38.0	310	39.7	112	34.8	1002	40.9	275	32.4	102	22.5
SAN JUAN DE LOS MORROS												
1802	866	33.3	405	32.1	81	32.1	173	35.8	135	39.3	72	23.6
1803	857	33.6	424	31.6	75	34.7	178	42.7	120	30.0	60	26.7
1805	961	33.5	480	30.6	90	32.2	239	42.7	84	33.3	68	23.5
1806	986	34.1	474	32.1	86	30.2	168	42.9	192	37.5	66	21.2
1807	1012	35.2	476	33.2	89	38.2	216	42.6	165	35.2	66	21.2
1809	1096	35.9	529	36.3	85	35.3	236	43.2	172	33.7	74	16.2
1810	1098	35.1	527	34.9	90	33.3	226	44.2	183	32.2	72	16.7
1811	1057	35.4	533	34.5	63	34.9	240	43.3	147	34.7	74	17.6
SAN MATEO												
1781	1683	34.1	491	35.2	227	37.0	703	33.7	0	0.0	262	30.5
1802	1693	31.7	505	26.1	170	41.2	611	32.2	11	27.3	396	33.8
1803	1579	31.0	450	28.4	158	41.8	539	29.1	34	29.4	398	32.2
1804	1671	31.4	451	27.7	202	33.2	550	30.9	33	36.4	435	34.7
1805	1685	30.7	483	29.0	194	34.5	556	27.5	35	28.6	417	35.5
1806	1720	30.6	483	25.7	167	40.7	620	28.9	35	22.9	415	35.7

TABLE 3. MARRIED PERSONS (CONTINUED)

YEAR	TOTAL		WHITE		INDIAN		PARDO		NEGRO		SLAVE	
	A	PCT	A	PCT	A	PCT	A	PCT	A	PCT	A	PCT
1808	1673	27.4	516	23.1	171	36.3	510	28.8	64	17.2	412	29.1
1809	1826	30.1	579	27.1	204	33.3	570	27.5	56	25.0	417	36.9
1811	1934	29.5	601	24.0	204	32.8	645	27.3	48	29.2	436	39.0
1815	1425	28.2	520	23.7	120	41.7	488	28.7	49	26.5	248	30.6
1816	1404	27.2	506	25.7	137	35.8	472	26.9	49	28.6	240	25.8
1817	1445	29.0	482	25.3	151	38.4	516	29.3	51	23.5	245	31.0
1818	1447	29.6	475	25.9	161	39.8	511	29.4	53	22.6	247	32.4
1821	1783	31.8	554	29.4	189	32.3	638	32.3	62	25.8	340	35.6
	SAN MIGUEL DE TRUJILLO											
1808	1405	47.3	576	50.3	140	57.1	576	46.9	45	42.2	68	7.4
	SAN NICOLAS DE TOLENTINO											
1803	411	30.4	1	100.0	6	16.7	231	32.0	74	39.2	99	20.2
1808	545	55.8	15	53.3	47	42.6	290	61.4	27	74.1	166	47.0
1818	227	31.7	0	0.0	0	0.0	227	31.7	0	0.0	0	0.0
1820	344	40.1	15	26.7	0	0.0	210	49.5	0	0.0	119	25.2
1821	344	40.1	0	0.0	15	26.7	210	49.5	119	25.2	0	0.0
	SAN PEDRO											
1810	754	31.4	417	37.2	7	0.0	232	25.9	0	0.0	98	22.4
1811	847	36.0	433	40.0	27	51.9	293	32.1	0	0.0	94	25.5
1816	734	35.4	394	39.1	15	40.0	277	34.7	0	0.0	48	8.3
1817	683	35.1	377	38.7	14	42.9	251	33.5	0	0.0	41	9.8
	SAN RAFAEL DE ONOTO											
1779	420	47.9	179	43.6	195	53.8	31	51.6	8	25.0	7	0.0
1810	863	41.8	278	46.0	226	42.0	340	40.0	2	0.0	17	11.8
1811	877	41.5	242	45.5	238	42.9	377	38.7	2	100.0	18	22.2
1828	574	43.6	102	35.3	217	47.5	236	42.8	18	55.6	1	0.0
1829	538	47.2	94	38.3	190	50.5	229	48.0	20	60.0	5	0.0
	SAN RAFAEL DE ORITUCO											
1783	1078	34.0	422	37.0	30	53.3	280	31.1	143	44.8	203	21.7
1802	683	32.8	140	41.4	0	0.0	413	34.4	0	0.0	130	18.5
1803	682	32.8	146	41.1	0	0.0	414	33.8	0	0.0	122	19.7
1804	765	34.0	187	37.4	0	0.0	448	35.7	0	0.0	130	23.1
1805	750	33.6	194	42.3	0	0.0	442	33.9	0	0.0	114	17.5
1806	821	35.3	202	41.6	0	0.0	504	36.5	0	0.0	115	19.1
1808	829	36.9	230	42.6	0	0.0	470	38.3	0	0.0	129	21.7
1809	738	36.0	228	36.8	29	48.3	373	40.2	14	28.6	94	14.9
1810	885	28.2	305	37.7	20	40.0	507	21.1	19	42.1	34	35.3
1811	771	31.3	305	37.7	20	40.0	331	28.7	24	29.2	91	17.6

TABLE 3. MARRIED PERSONS (CONTINUED)

YEAR	TOTAL		WHITE		INDIAN		PARDO		NEGRO		SLAVE	
	A	PCT	A	PCT	A	PCT	A	PCT	A	PCT	A	PCT
SAN SEBASTIAN DE LOS REYES												
1783	2043	33.6	567	34.2	400	39.5	862	34.0	33	39.4	181	15.5
1802	2330	34.5	777	41.4	138	26.1	1172	32.8	44	40.9	199	22.1
1803	2347	34.4	787	41.4	139	25.9	1179	32.5	46	39.1	196	22.4
1804	2376	34.3	797	41.4	144	25.0	1191	32.5	49	36.7	195	22.6
1805	2361	34.3	799	42.1	136	26.5	1197	31.8	48	45.8	181	18.8
1806	2345	33.7	808	39.7	124	32.3	1190	32.2	61	39.3	162	14.2
1809	2022	34.9	686	37.6	117	45.3	994	34.7	61	34.4	164	17.7
1810	2083	35.4	716	38.3	121	45.5	1019	34.9	73	32.9	154	18.2
1811	2107	35.8	724	39.4	118	47.5	1033	35.0	73	32.9	159	17.6
SANARE												
1803	2147	40.1	241	35.7	1360	42.6	339	40.1	183	32.2	24	0.0
1804	2161	41.2	243	37.9	1356	43.5	349	43.0	188	31.4	25	0.0
1805	2147	40.1	241	35.7	1360	42.6	339	40.1	183	32.2	24	0.0
1806	1894	45.1	225	32.0	1187	47.5	298	47.7	131	42.7	53	37.7
1807	1900	44.2	229	29.7	1167	46.6	319	47.6	131	42.7	54	37.0
1808	1903	43.9	233	30.9	1190	46.7	311	47.6	115	34.8	54	37.0
1809	1940	43.9	235	31.5	1190	46.7	352	47.7	115	34.8	48	29.2
1810	1904	43.3	224	30.4	1170	45.8	359	47.9	101	31.7	50	32.0
1812	1757	39.3	257	29.6	1063	41.2	335	46.6	75	18.7	27	22.2
1815	1511	43.5	217	25.8	888	48.2	333	46.8	49	28.6	24	16.7
1816	1780	40.1	256	28.1	1091	41.8	359	47.9	58	20.7	16	12.5
1817	1858	39.4	256	28.1	1091	41.8	359	47.9	111	19.8	41	24.4
1818	1780	40.1	256	28.1	1091	41.8	359	47.9	58	20.7	16	12.5
1819	1505	43.7	217	25.8	888	48.2	333	46.8	49	28.6	18	22.2
1820	1858	39.4	256	28.1	1091	41.8	359	47.9	111	19.8	41	24.4
SANTA CRUZ DE ARAGUA												
1802	4014	33.7	2303	33.6	46	21.7	1541	35.4	48	16.7	76	18.4
1803	4113	34.1	2362	34.1	76	23.7	1561	35.8	45	20.0	69	14.5
1804	4143	33.1	2280	33.5	56	32.1	1741	33.2	12	16.7	54	16.7
1805	3914	31.9	2207	32.9	49	34.7	1609	30.7	3	66.7	46	21.7
1808	3615	36.8	2165	33.2	49	38.8	1317	43.5	28	17.9	56	28.6
1811	2286	38.7	1357	41.9	27	63.0	612	43.5	241	6.6	49	36.7
1815	3285	30.4	1739	28.6	1397	33.6	79	24.1	12	16.7	58	20.7
1816	3148	33.9	1824	31.8	53	24.5	1164	38.3	42	19.0	65	30.8
1817	3097	38.0	1833	35.4	18	44.4	1128	42.6	42	45.2	76	27.6
1818	2561	38.8	1523	37.2	21	19.0	816	46.1	130	23.1	71	23.9
1822	3143	36.1	1538	28.2	321	58.9	1164	42.1	57	22.8	63	15.9
SANTA INES DEL ALTAR												
1779	53	41.5	3	66.7	25	48.0	18	22.2	7	57.1	0	0.0
1802	79	40.5	17	29.4	9	44.4	42	50.0	7	28.6	4	0.0
1803	83	54.2	6	50.0	12	33.3	61	57.4	4	75.0	0	0.0
1804	84	45.2	1	0.0	20	40.0	57	45.6	4	50.0	2	100.0

TABLE 3. MARRIED PERSONS (CONTINUED)

YEAR	TOTAL		WHITE		INDIAN		PARDO		NEGRO		SLAVE	
	A	PCT	A	PCT	A	PCT	A	PCT	A	PCT	A	PCT
1805	95	54.7	2	100.0	10	60.0	80	52.5	3	66.7	0	0.0
1806	79	48.1	3	66.7	7	57.1	67	47.8	1	0.0	1	0.0
1810	54	66.7	0	0.0	8	75.0	46	65.2	0	0.0	0	0.0
1811	57	63.2	0	0.0	9	66.7	48	62.5	0	0.0	0	0.0
1818	141	51.1	0	0.0	18	33.3	123	53.7	0	0.0	0	0.0
1819	210	47.6	12	66.7	41	48.8	113	49.6	44	36.4	0	0.0
1820	198	41.4	12	50.0	31	45.2	102	49.0	52	23.1	1	0.0
1829	220	51.8	8	100.0	51	27.5	160	57.5	0	0.0	1	0.0
	SANTA LUCIA											
1784	1659	42.3	244	31.1	375	42.1	224	36.6	210	43.8	606	48.5
1787	1629	34.8	286	29.0	275	50.2	352	39.8	94	36.2	622	27.7
1802	1967	36.3	466	43.1	207	44.4	593	33.2	70	35.7	631	31.7
1803	1948	36.2	351	41.0	232	36.2	705	36.0	104	30.8	556	34.5
1804	2294	39.7	495	39.6	204	39.2	592	38.9	183	29.5	820	42.7
1805	1677	47.7	268	42.9	289	46.7	528	46.2	75	40.0	517	53.4
1808	2565	38.7	542	33.8	264	41.7	738	35.8	184	46.7	837	41.7
1809	2579	38.5	542	33.8	258	42.6	758	34.8	184	46.7	837	41.7
1811	2664	37.4	560	37.3	253	34.8	841	36.3	90	48.9	920	38.2
1816	2241	36.8	511	33.3	144	31.9	795	33.0	81	56.8	710	42.3
1817	2132	42.8	651	49.9	16	56.3	1073	48.7	117	9.4	275	16.4
1818	2217	31.9	525	40.2	23	60.9	700	32.1	61	24.6	908	26.8
1819	2003	33.0	359	30.6	159	30.2	655	30.8	151	30.5	679	37.4
	SANTA MARIA DE IPIRE											
1783	713	38.8	223	56.5	74	32.4	247	40.1	36	36.1	133	11.3
1798	827	43.9	235	51.1	18	38.9	298	50.0	134	32.1	142	31.0
1803	863	45.7	227	52.0	24	45.8	331	53.2	126	41.3	155	23.9
	SANTA ROSA DE LIMA											
1802	1930	41.3	706	43.1	212	33.0	170	36.5	736	44.3	106	34.0
1803	1938	42.0	710	42.8	219	35.6	174	40.2	728	44.2	107	37.4
1804	1930	41.3	706	43.1	212	33.0	170	36.5	736	44.3	106	34.0
1805	1961	41.7	730	42.5	220	34.5	173	39.3	729	44.2	109	38.5
1807	1960	42.1	745	42.7	211	37.0	177	45.2	715	42.5	112	41.1
1808	1888	44.1	756	42.7	219	36.5	183	43.7	618	49.2	112	41.1
1809	2733	51.7	814	50.5	233	39.1	873	49.0	690	59.4	123	58.5
1810	2785	50.6	803	50.4	240	39.2	937	46.5	684	59.2	121	57.9
1815	2639	53.6	807	50.7	244	39.3	774	55.9	691	58.6	123	58.5
1816	3024	46.9	852	48.0	247	38.1	977	43.4	824	50.6	124	58.9
1817	3201	51.4	842	52.7	181	29.8	1318	50.4	720	57.5	140	50.0
1819	3047	51.5	807	50.7	139	38.8	1264	49.3	698	59.0	139	50.4
1820	3047	51.5	807	50.7	139	38.8	1264	49.3	698	59.0	139	50.4
	SANTA TERESA DE JESUS											
1783	562	40.7	85	50.6	96	47.9	64	32.8	14	42.9	303	37.3
1786	580	36.4	87	37.9	101	41.6	79	30.4	14	35.7	299	35.8

TABLE 3. MARRIED PERSONS (CONTINUED)

YEAR	TOTAL A	TOTAL PCT	WHITE A	WHITE PCT	INDIAN A	INDIAN PCT	PARDO A	PARDO PCT	NEGRO A	NEGRO PCT	SLAVE A	SLAVE PCT
1787	603	35.8	84	40.5	104	38.5	78	32.1	39	25.6	298	35.9
1788	616	34.4	84	40.5	118	33.9	69	29.0	39	25.6	306	35.3
1802	1206	39.1	236	44.9	132	39.4	149	42.3	158	36.7	531	36.2
1803	1331	40.2	285	42.1	155	38.1	154	40.9	168	36.9	569	40.6
1804	1385	38.2	277	41.2	165	35.2	169	40.2	188	35.1	586	38.1
1805	1273	37.5	256	39.5	162	34.0	158	41.8	178	38.8	519	35.8
1810	1493	36.5	319	42.0	167	29.9	193	39.4	247	36.4	567	34.4
1811	1397	37.5	289	43.6	156	29.5	171	41.5	235	36.2	546	35.9
1815	1033	32.5	165	29.1	94	14.9	173	37.0	175	26.9	426	38.3
1816	1039	34.6	200	33.5	105	17.1	143	39.2	144	35.4	447	37.6
1817	1072	37.2	209	39.7	85	21.2	152	36.2	170	35.9	456	39.9
1820	1152	36.8	256	34.0	56	32.1	128	35.9	200	36.0	512	39.3
SARARE												
1779	851	38.9	146	45.9	204	39.7	355	36.6	117	31.6	29	55.2
1802	1829	44.8	266	39.1	225	34.2	834	54.1	488	38.3	16	0.0
1804	1916	44.4	290	38.6	237	34.6	873	53.0	500	38.6	16	0.0
1805	1363	40.9	257	36.6	184	47.8	815	41.5	83	41.0	24	16.7
1807	1768	46.1	266	39.1	221	33.0	827	54.5	438	42.7	16	0.0
1808	1916	44.4	290	38.6	237	34.6	873	53.0	500	38.6	16	0.0
1809	1916	44.4	290	38.6	237	34.6	873	53.0	500	38.6	16	0.0
1810	2054	45.3	313	39.3	254	37.4	903	53.2	562	41.3	22	0.0
1811	1916	44.4	290	38.6	237	34.6	873	53.0	500	38.6	16	0.0
1817	1464	40.9	288	40.6	270	56.3	882	37.0	9	0.0	15	26.7
1818	1722	42.6	276	38.4	323	56.3	1067	40.7	27	22.2	29	20.7
SIQUISIQUE												
1802	2663	43.0	262	35.5	1787	48.4	436	33.9	128	25.0	50	12.0
1803	2734	43.0	279	35.8	1802	48.3	456	34.6	148	28.4	49	12.2
1804	2237	42.3	240	36.2	1407	48.5	422	33.2	115	26.1	53	11.3
1805	2254	40.6	259	37.1	1408	45.5	420	35.7	115	20.9	52	11.5
1807	2462	38.7	287	41.1	1581	40.9	481	32.8	43	55.8	70	8.6
TACARIGUA DE MAMPORAL												
1784	497	40.6	48	39.6	15	86.7	28	46.4	70	41.4	336	38.1
1802	515	34.0	37	16.2	8	25.0	24	37.5	81	42.0	365	34.0
1803	482	35.3	36	11.1	4	0.0	15	33.3	88	42.0	339	36.6
1804	495	36.4	32	18.7	13	30.8	16	25.0	80	50.0	354	35.6
1805	418	38.8	33	18.2	3	66.7	41	46.3	52	46.2	289	38.4
1806	402	30.8	32	18.7	12	50.0	11	54.5	64	15.6	283	33.9
1807	399	34.6	34	23.5	12	41.7	24	41.7	53	39.6	276	34.1
1808	400	33.0	32	25.0	13	23.1	48	41.7	34	41.2	273	31.9
1809	397	33.2	25	16.0	12	8.3	52	42.3	38	50.0	270	31.9
1811	311	33.8	28	14.3	5	20.0	44	40.9	20	35.0	214	35.0
1816	398	28.6	29	24.1	7	14.3	81	22.2	74	31.1	207	31.4
1818	371	26.7	19	10.5	15	13.3	55	21.8	61	27.9	221	29.9
1820	425	27.3	32	25.0	17	11.8	75	37.3	74	21.6	227	27.3

TABLE 3. MARRIED PERSONS (CONTINUED)

YEAR	TOTAL A	TOTAL PCT	WHITE A	WHITE PCT	INDIAN A	INDIAN PCT	PARDO A	PARDO PCT	NEGRO A	NEGRO PCT	SLAVE A	SLAVE PCT
TACATA												
1783	531	43.9	32	43.8	85	55.3	174	48.9	59	27.1	181	39.2
1799	826	43.5	93	35.5	201	38.8	239	46.4	21	38.1	272	47.4
1802	989	39.0	233	36.9	226	38.5	202	46.0	48	33.3	280	37.1
1804	987	42.1	106	30.2	368	42.4	205	43.9	28	28.6	280	46.4
1805	953	31.9	103	35.0	326	27.0	198	26.3	28	42.9	298	38.9
1812	1030	47.4	276	47.1	148	50.0	310	48.4	28	28.6	268	47.0
1813	1241	41.4	346	46.2	125	40.0	371	37.7	22	54.5	377	40.3
1817	903	40.3	255	44.7	138	37.7	300	40.0	12	50.0	198	36.4
1818	1208	40.9	375	44.8	121	38.0	413	38.7	11	36.4	288	40.3
1819	1233	47.0	359	49.6	161	46.0	444	45.9	7	28.6	262	46.6
1820	1483	48.6	350	56.0	250	60.0	577	44.4	6	33.3	300	38.7
1821	1381	43.2	433	50.8	227	39.6	362	43.6	25	24.0	334	36.5
1822	1396	41.3	392	50.0	204	41.2	450	38.2	11	36.4	339	35.4
TAGUAI												
1802	1294	32.1	563	30.7	99	23.2	410	40.2	45	22.2	177	25.4
1803	1130	36.8	433	40.0	91	25.3	394	41.9	35	28.6	177	25.4
1804	1221	30.2	458	37.8	117	23.9	177	33.3	251	31.5	218	13.8
1805	1235	29.9	463	37.4	122	23.0	179	33.0	251	31.5	220	13.6
1810	1410	32.2	512	35.5	148	18.9	233	40.8	299	39.8	218	13.8
TAPIPA												
1803	453	44.6	38	34.2	19	42.1	33	51.5	4	75.0	359	44.8
1804	519	50.1	40	35.0	25	52.0	32	40.6	15	66.7	407	51.6
1805	481	48.9	40	40.0	25	52.0	28	39.3	17	64.7	371	49.6
1806	430	50.0	27	29.6	27	44.4	16	50.0	23	56.5	337	51.6
1807	404	53.5	22	45.5	19	47.4	20	55.0	21	61.9	322	53.7
1808	368	53.8	31	32.3	11	63.6	16	56.3	16	56.3	294	55.4
1811	326	44.2	33	45.5	21	76.2	17	52.9	16	37.5	239	41.0
1812	291	44.7	33	42.4	15	53.3	14	42.9	14	50.0	215	44.2
1816	257	45.1	16	56.3	26	38.5	18	33.3	19	42.1	178	46.6
1817	252	45.6	17	58.8	20	40.0	18	33.3	19	42.1	178	46.6
1818	307	40.4	28	50.0	41	29.3	22	40.9	25	44.0	191	40.8
1819	298	44.0	21	57.1	38	42.1	12	41.7	31	38.7	196	43.9
1820	255	45.1	15	53.3	25	40.0	18	33.3	19	42.1	178	46.6
1829	245	38.8	22	27.3	12	58.3	46	45.7	27	44.4	138	35.5
TARIA												
1803	186	32.3	5	20.0	0	0.0	177	33.3	0	0.0	4	0.0
1808	283	53.0	2	100.0	8	100.0	242	46.3	23	87.0	8	100.0
1810	187	48.1	4	50.0	0	0.0	182	48.4	0	0.0	1	0.0
TARMAS												
1802	383	42.6	35	22.9	29	41.4	82	47.6	24	45.8	213	43.7

TABLE 3. MARRIED PERSONS (CONTINUED)

YEAR	TOTAL		WHITE		INDIAN		PARDO		NEGRO		SLAVE	
	A	PCT	A	PCT	A	PCT	A	PCT	A	PCT	A	PCT
1803	372	44.1	23	39.1	23	39.1	88	47.7	24	37.5	214	44.4
1805	344	44.8	30	33.3	24	37.5	96	44.8	6	50.0	188	47.3
1807	384	43.8	33	36.4	20	35.0	110	40.9	20	45.0	201	47.3
1808	367	45.8	29	51.7	18	33.3	113	41.6	18	55.6	189	47.6
1810	380	41.1	28	46.4	27	29.6	111	38.7	10	40.0	204	43.1
1811	379	39.1	25	44.0	25	28.0	116	35.3	11	27.3	202	42.6
1815	364	42.3	26	53.8	16	43.8	85	38.8	28	35.7	209	43.1
1816	381	42.0	33	45.5	13	46.2	107	40.2	19	31.6	209	43.1
1817	401	42.4	36	47.2	14	35.7	114	40.4	26	46.2	211	42.7
1818	397	41.3	30	43.3	25	36.0	121	38.0	13	30.8	208	44.2
1819	372	41.7	28	39.3	12	50.0	108	39.8	25	40.0	199	42.7
1820	301	54.2	21	52.4	12	58.3	69	56.5	20	55.0	179	53.1
1829	375	38.9	56	37.5	0	0.0	237	38.4	0	0.0	82	41.5
TEMERLA												
1802	358	38.0	17	35.3	0	0.0	339	38.3	0	0.0	2	0.0
1803	304	37.5	17	35.3	0	0.0	287	37.6	0	0.0	0	0.0
1804	328	35.4	12	33.3	0	0.0	316	35.4	0	0.0	0	0.0
1805	318	35.2	12	33.3	0	0.0	304	35.5	0	0.0	2	0.0
1806	290	23.4	12	33.3	0	0.0	276	23.2	0	0.0	2	0.0
1807	308	24.7	13	30.8	0	0.0	294	24.5	0	0.0	1	0.0
1808	290	23.4	12	33.3	0	0.0	276	23.2	0	0.0	2	0.0
1810	354	41.5	2	0.0	0	0.0	352	41.8	0	0.0	0	0.0
1817	458	40.4	15	53.3	0	0.0	442	39.8	0	0.0	1	100.0
1818	705	25.5	29	27.6	0	0.0	671	25.5	0	0.0	5	20.0
1819	472	38.1	16	50.0	0	0.0	455	37.6	0	0.0	1	100.0
1820	349	55.0	12	33.3	0	0.0	327	56.9	1	100.0	9	11.1
1821	354	57.1	12	33.3	0	0.0	333	59.2	0	0.0	9	11.1
TINACO												
1771	1540	32.9	843	33.0	80	40.0	497	36.2	17	47.1	103	8.7
1781	1277	39.6	758	38.3	0	0.0	432	48.1	11	36.4	76	5.3
1787	1249	38.3	718	40.0	33	45.5	415	38.8	11	54.5	72	12.5
1788	1290	35.0	701	36.7	61	44.3	441	36.1	22	27.3	65	3.1
1790	2040	67.6	727	46.6	67	52.2	1157	85.4	22	40.9	67	13.4
1791	1297	34.7	709	35.0	87	43.7	417	36.5	14	28.6	70	11.4
1794	1738	32.6	911	33.0	71	40.8	633	33.8	20	30.0	103	15.5
1795	1711	31.8	833	32.4	67	35.8	681	33.5	22	27.3	108	14.8
1796	1686	31.9	839	31.8	67	31.3	669	33.8	19	36.8	92	17.4
1798	1741	30.6	882	30.3	49	40.8	689	32.5	21	33.3	100	14.0
1799	1722	31.5	882	30.6	52	36.5	654	35.5	31	25.8	103	13.6
1800	1705	30.7	869	29.7	49	40.8	647	35.1	42	14.3	98	13.3
1801	1725	30.7	883	31.3	49	40.8	662	32.8	29	13.8	102	12.7
1802	1782	29.1	902	30.2	51	29.4	593	31.2	125	26.4	111	11.7
1803	1871	29.9	912	30.9	50	32.0	650	32.0	127	30.7	132	11.4
1804	1951	31.2	950	33.6	51	33.3	670	33.0	145	25.5	135	10.4
1805	2020	31.9	983	33.9	53	35.8	706	33.0	143	30.8	135	11.1
1806	2024	32.5	965	35.8	57	36.8	731	32.3	140	30.0	131	10.7
1807	2005	32.4	947	35.0	54	37.0	746	33.6	130	24.6	128	12.5

TABLE 3. MARRIED PERSONS (CONTINUED)

YEAR	TOTAL		WHITE		INDIAN		PARDO		NEGRO		SLAVE	
	A	PCT	A	PCT	A	PCT	A	PCT	A	PCT	A	PCT
1808	1929	32.4	914	34.0	50	32.0	733	34.5	123	24.4	109	13.8
1811	1867	29.7	763	32.4	60	23.3	823	30.1	128	29.7	93	8.6
1812	1940	31.7	922	33.0	59	30.5	822	33.5	25	24.0	112	10.7
1816	1558	35.7	792	38.8	32	46.9	622	35.7	0	0.0	112	10.7
1817	1484	38.8	765	40.7	29	41.4	574	40.9	0	0.0	116	15.5
1819	1569	40.0	769	40.4	29	41.4	655	43.7	0	0.0	116	15.5
1820	1813	52.6	883	55.5	51	54.9	760	55.0	0	0.0	119	15.1
1821	2213	49.6	960	53.9	93	69.9	1040	47.9	0	0.0	120	15.0
1822	2237	49.7	979	53.6	84	66.7	1040	47.9	15	53.3	119	20.2
1823	2398	49.3	1002	52.6	138	55.8	1066	48.6	43	37.2	149	29.5
1824	2348	49.5	989	52.6	121	57.9	1052	48.7	43	37.2	143	30.8
1825	2398	49.3	1002	52.6	138	55.8	1066	48.6	43	37.2	149	29.5
1826	2637	49.7	1062	50.2	135	54.8	1229	51.7	52	38.5	159	30.2
1827	2629	49.4	1069	50.4	128	53.1	1215	51.2	58	41.4	159	28.9
1829	2665	48.7	1094	47.6	123	55.3	1234	51.8	50	42.0	164	29.9
1830	2532	50.3	1053	49.6	128	55.5	1142	53.2	52	44.2	157	31.2
1831	2528	51.0	1078	50.5	129	57.4	1117	53.4	58	46.6	146	32.2
1832	2548	50.7	1099	50.9	118	57.6	1118	52.7	60	51.7	153	30.1
1834	2899	47.1	1318	45.1	130	56.2	1193	51.9	88	31.8	170	30.0
1835	3199	46.1	1436	45.9	137	56.2	1356	48.2	91	35.2	179	30.2
1836	3953	48.3	1940	50.7	139	51.8	1574	48.1	107	37.4	193	30.6
1837	4447	52.5	1782	53.7	183	53.0	1813	46.7	449	81.1	220	31.8
	TINAJAS											
1781	787	46.3	88	34.1	86	69.8	173	46.2	219	41.1	221	47.1
1801	677	36.9	74	27.0	4	100.0	456	39.5	19	57.9	124	28.2
1802	781	29.2	50	24.0	9	44.4	601	29.0	28	57.1	93	23.7
1803	862	28.5	85	20.0	22	27.3	636	30.2	13	69.2	106	20.8
1804	863	29.7	48	20.8	16	18.7	630	32.9	52	34.6	117	15.4
1805	831	28.4	52	26.9	22	22.7	609	31.5	44	25.0	104	13.5
1807	897	29.9	37	21.6	0	0.0	698	30.9	76	28.9	86	25.6
1808	835	37.5	28	35.7	0	0.0	719	37.3	0	0.0	88	39.8
1809	750	38.1	28	35.7	0	0.0	647	39.6	0	0.0	75	26.7
1810	850	33.9	28	35.7	0	0.0	750	34.4	0	0.0	72	27.8
1811	898	34.4	27	40.7	2	100.0	779	35.2	0	0.0	90	24.4
1813	887	38.3	59	37.3	2	100.0	702	40.7	53	26.4	71	22.5
1818	522	45.2	19	52.6	0	0.0	463	44.5	0	0.0	40	50.0
1819	534	44.2	16	50.0	0	0.0	442	44.3	39	35.9	37	48.6
1820	456	39.5	16	50.0	0	0.0	364	38.5	39	35.9	37	48.6
1821	774	38.5	31	38.7	0	0.0	548	40.9	39	35.9	156	30.8
	TINAQUILLO											
1781	605	61.0	146	52.7	7	42.9	424	61.6	0	0.0	28	100.0
1787	785	37.8	183	39.3	22	45.5	560	37.9	4	25.0	16	12.5
1788	774	37.9	180	38.3	20	40.0	550	38.5	8	25.0	16	12.5
1790	721	37.3	210	38.6	26	53.8	444	38.1	11	27.3	30	6.7
1791	718	36.4	216	39.8	25	48.0	457	35.2	7	28.6	13	0.0
1792	829	28.5	228	37.7	26	34.6	547	25.6	9	11.1	19	0.0
1794	767	35.6	229	36.2	19	47.4	497	36.0	10	20.0	12	0.0

TABLE 3. MARRIED PERSONS (CONTINUED)

YEAR	TOTAL		WHITE		INDIAN		PARDO		NEGRO		SLAVE	
	A	PCT	A	PCT	A	PCT	A	PCT	A	PCT	A	PCT
1795	767	35.6	229	36.2	19	47.4	497	36.0	10	20.0	12	0.0
1796	775	32.9	222	37.8	23	30.4	506	31.6	8	25.0	16	12.5
1798	792	37.9	226	43.4	23	52.2	520	36.2	9	22.2	14	0.0
1799	759	37.5	235	46.0	27	37.0	470	34.9	10	30.0	17	0.0
1800	736	39.3	222	44.6	20	35.0	470	38.1	10	40.0	14	0.0
1801	786	36.1	213	39.4	26	42.3	519	35.8	13	23.1	15	0.0
1802	758	37.5	214	43.0	24	37.5	500	35.6	9	55.6	11	0.0
1803	804	35.3	210	43.8	25	48.0	546	32.6	11	18.2	12	0.0
1804	860	34.7	270	43.7	26	38.5	532	31.2	13	30.8	19	0.0
1805	895	36.6	279	41.6	37	21.6	547	36.2	15	40.0	17	0.0
1806	742	41.8	242	44.6	26	30.8	450	42.2	9	44.4	15	0.0
1807	873	36.4	246	45.5	29	34.5	572	33.6	10	40.0	16	0.0
1808	884	37.1	251	46.2	29	34.5	578	34.3	10	40.0	16	0.0
1809	801	36.5	308	40.3	27	37.0	447	35.1	2	50.0	17	0.0
1811	812	40.9	362	37.6	24	45.8	416	44.2	3	33.3	7	0.0
1812	818	41.3	364	37.9	24	45.8	418	44.5	5	60.0	7	0.0
1815	951	34.2	296	39.9	21	28.6	626	32.1	1	0.0	7	0.0
1816	1107	42.2	254	43.7	47	31.9	785	42.7	17	35.3	4	0.0
1817	949	45.0	292	50.3	15	20.0	627	44.2	3	0.0	12	0.0
1818	1255	34.3	383	36.6	23	4.3	836	34.7	5	0.0	8	0.0
1820	1716	38.2	466	44.4	49	16.3	1139	38.4	19	21.1	43	0.0
1822	1343	56.7	543	52.7	55	43.6	693	62.9	14	28.6	38	31.6
1823	1925	61.7	827	64.6	57	59.6	922	65.3	0	0.0	119	15.1
1836	2237	37.1	489	51.1	42	47.6	1656	33.4	7	57.1	43	7.0
TOCUYITO												
1803	1267	37.7	324	34.0	26	46.2	581	36.5	21	28.6	315	43.8
1804	1250	41.6	315	38.7	26	46.2	576	38.9	21	28.6	312	50.0
1805	1256	44.3	317	39.7	28	50.0	580	42.8	19	31.6	312	51.9
1812	2608	30.5	404	37.4	13	30.8	1440	27.0	13	0.0	738	34.0
1816	1590	43.0	220	41.8	26	30.8	737	41.2	42	42.9	565	46.2
TUCUPIDO												
1783	198	87.9	0	0.0	198	87.9	0	0.0	0	0.0	0	0.0
1801	1276	45.8	254	40.9	481	58.2	402	39.8	15	53.3	124	25.8
1805	1367	45.4	272	39.7	514	56.8	22	54.5	422	40.8	137	26.3
1809	1462	51.0	263	40.3	496	67.7	546	46.3	18	33.3	139	32.4
TUCUPIDO DE GUANARE												
1802	2965	39.3	780	40.0	310	32.3	1321	46.3	423	23.6	131	30.5
1803	2592	44.5	943	37.8	187	37.4	1186	54.1	195	31.8	81	29.6
1804	2985	45.7	1294	42.5	192	42.7	1275	51.6	134	38.8	90	24.4
1805	2985	45.7	1294	42.5	192	42.7	1275	51.6	134	38.8	90	24.4
1807	3319	53.9	1477	52.4	218	56.0	1405	56.8	136	50.0	83	31.3
1808	2960	45.5	1165	44.8	292	33.6	1312	50.2	129	48.1	62	12.9
1809	3661	38.6	1313	40.2	306	41.2	1788	36.0	191	54.5	63	15.9
1810	4058	40.1	1674	37.8	191	44.0	1974	40.3	152	67.1	67	17.9
1817	1801	55.5	707	55.7	140	58.6	834	57.3	77	54.5	43	9.3

TABLE 3. MARRIED PERSONS (CONTINUED)

YEAR	TOTAL A	TOTAL PCT	WHITE A	WHITE PCT	INDIAN A	INDIAN PCT	PARDO A	PARDO PCT	NEGRO A	NEGRO PCT	SLAVE A	SLAVE PCT
TUCURAGUA												
1802	345	31.0	15	6.7	5	0.0	264	32.2	5	40.0	56	33.9
1803	286	30.1	14	0.0	0	0.0	223	29.6	5	0.0	44	45.5
1804	157	40.8	17	0.0	0	0.0	107	43.0	7	57.1	26	53.8
1805	304	31.9	15	6.7	0	0.0	242	31.4	6	33.3	41	43.9
1807	260	25.4	10	30.0	0	0.0	216	23.1	4	50.0	30	36.7
1808	294	32.7	13	23.1	0	0.0	237	32.5	11	45.5	33	33.3
1809	293	32.8	13	23.1	0	0.0	237	32.5	10	50.0	33	33.3
1812	219	42.5	5	0.0	0	0.0	184	46.7	0	0.0	30	23.3
1816	108	40.7	0	0.0	0	0.0	89	44.9	2	100.0	17	11.8
TUREN												
1778	272	50.7	42	38.1	144	64.6	78	33.3	7	28.6	1	100.0
1801	481	64.0	143	75.5	98	71.4	109	51.4	71	62.0	60	50.0
1808	1701	30.1	628	33.3	268	29.1	761	27.7	17	47.1	27	22.2
1809	604	32.3	36	61.1	301	26.9	202	41.6	63	12.7	2	0.0
1810	1550	39.0	555	38.2	250	48.8	689	37.2	27	37.0	29	13.8
1811	552	42.0	145	46.9	141	49.6	243	35.4	21	38.1	2	0.0
1812	507	42.6	134	45.5	158	42.4	201	41.8	7	57.1	7	0.0
1816	458	53.3	141	44.0	178	68.5	139	43.2	0	0.0	0	0.0
TURIAMO												
1802	106	61.3	4	25.0	0	0.0	10	40.0	3	66.7	89	65.2
1803	112	76.8	3	100.0	0	0.0	12	50.0	2	100.0	95	78.9
1804	111	68.5	3	0.0	0	0.0	17	47.1	2	50.0	89	75.3
1805	149	56.4	4	0.0	0	0.0	23	43.5	4	50.0	118	61.0
1808	155	48.4	3	0.0	0	0.0	30	40.0	13	30.8	109	54.1
1818	165	48.5	7	28.6	0	0.0	25	68.0	5	100.0	128	43.8
1819	165	33.9	5	0.0	0	0.0	37	54.1	9	44.4	114	28.1
TURMERO												
1781	4724	32.9	1925	35.0	825	37.7	1502	29.8	0	0.0	472	26.3
1802	5344	30.9	1799	31.8	1012	26.0	1498	28.2	198	35.4	837	38.4
1803	5373	31.6	1839	32.4	1064	27.0	1537	29.3	208	35.1	725	40.1
1804	5573	31.4	1875	30.9	1105	27.6	1601	30.0	242	32.6	750	40.7
1805	5430	33.2	1741	33.1	1092	27.4	1577	32.1	237	39.7	783	41.4
1806	5173	35.5	1615	36.3	1103	28.1	1405	35.2	222	41.9	828	42.5
1808	4643	36.3	1224	36.2	1046	30.9	1253	35.9	244	38.1	876	43.2
1809	4191	37.8	1021	39.6	1015	29.1	1071	41.9	211	37.9	873	40.8
1811	4391	38.7	1049	39.9	1097	30.2	1095	44.1	221	36.2	929	41.7
URACHICHE												
1782	948	35.2	213	30.5	313	36.7	326	40.2	21	57.1	75	14.7
1788	979	34.9	151	33.8	286	43.7	451	35.5	0	0.0	91	6.6
1802	1195	36.6	79	43.0	315	34.6	692	38.4	45	44.4	64	12.5

TABLE 3. MARRIED PERSONS (CONTINUED)

YEAR	TOTAL		WHITE		INDIAN		PARDO		NEGRO		SLAVE	
	A	PCT	A	PCT	A	PCT	A	PCT	A	PCT	A	PCT
1803	1246	36.3	86	38.4	324	34.6	702	38.5	59	44.1	75	14.7
1804	1227	37.3	98	40.8	327	33.6	672	40.0	54	48.1	76	17.1
1805	1304	35.7	63	50.8	425	31.1	707	38.9	33	39.4	76	18.4
1807	1332	36.3	100	47.0	321	35.5	761	36.4	60	40.0	90	24.4
1808	1119	43.8	133	43.6	331	33.8	498	55.4	71	31.0	86	25.6
1809	1624	34.9	182	46.7	355	34.1	959	34.4	51	31.4	77	19.5
1810	1597	36.1	135	49.6	366	35.2	950	35.9	71	31.0	75	24.0
1811	1648	35.7	144	51.4	378	33.9	976	35.5	74	27.0	76	26.3
1815	1597	36.1	135	49.6	366	35.2	950	35.9	71	31.0	75	24.0
1816	1710	38.3	160	45.6	363	37.2	1108	37.6	24	66.7	55	25.5
1817	1480	33.6	111	41.4	335	33.7	928	33.0	65	27.7	41	34.1
1818	1567	33.6	100	46.0	379	32.7	907	33.7	100	30.0	81	24.7
1819	1644	32.7	106	47.2	420	31.0	898	35.2	134	19.4	86	18.6
	URAMA											
1802	489	39.7	13	23.1	0	0.0	325	36.9	109	56.0	42	23.8
1804	460	39.6	11	54.5	0	0.0	320	41.3	84	40.5	45	22.2
1806	443	38.8	10	70.0	0	0.0	306	41.8	90	34.4	37	16.2
1807	475	40.0	12	66.7	0	0.0	323	42.7	105	35.2	35	20.0
1808	424	42.5	14	64.3	1	0.0	303	45.2	77	37.7	29	17.2
1810	409	44.7	14	50.0	4	0.0	280	45.7	75	48.0	36	33.3
1818	276	52.9	5	40.0	0	0.0	243	53.5	0	0.0	28	50.0
1819	306	48.4	1	0.0	0	0.0	270	48.9	0	0.0	35	45.7
1820	247	69.2	13	76.9	0	0.0	135	80.0	60	71.7	39	25.6
	VALENCIA											
1782	5450	31.6	2339	35.2	166	36.7	2245	31.7	30	40.0	670	17.5
1802	5741	32.1	2000	38.4	56	17.9	2728	32.8	168	37.5	789	13.2
1803	5063	30.3	1612	37.6	69	26.1	2428	32.8	190	26.3	764	8.6
1804	4445	34.1	1500	37.9	61	21.3	2098	36.7	147	33.3	639	18.3
1805	4879	28.7	1627	33.7	192	21.4	2143	27.5	232	32.3	685	21.5
1808	4881	28.7	1627	33.7	192	21.4	2143	27.5	232	32.3	687	21.4
1809	5024	33.0	1842	36.3	113	41.6	2116	32.2	108	28.7	845	27.2
1812	5737	28.9	1936	34.6	137	34.3	2475	27.5	122	25.4	1067	21.6
1815	5319	38.7	1161	34.9	463	40.6	2422	34.4	140	67.1	1133	47.3
1816	5505	38.3	1198	35.1	484	39.9	2497	34.0	170	61.2	1156	47.1
1819	5972	39.8	1160	38.7	520	38.3	2826	36.6	207	54.6	1259	46.2
	VALLE DE LA PASCUA											
1804	961	33.7	328	42.7	61	39.3	345	29.6	0	0.0	227	25.6
1805	1207	43.6	417	57.6	101	37.6	439	45.6	0	0.0	250	19.2
1806	1186	34.1	317	42.6	103	48.5	516	34.7	0	0.0	250	16.0
1808	1212	38.7	345	40.0	170	51.8	434	42.6	0	0.0	263	22.1
1809	1392	41.6	386	46.1	309	43.7	438	48.4	0	0.0	259	20.8
	VILLA DE CURA											
1780	3320	50.4	1625	54.1	47	66.0	1277	48.1	88	51.1	283	36.4

TABLE 3. MARRIED PERSONS (CONTINUED)

YEAR	TOTAL		WHITE		INDIAN		PARDO		NEGRO		SLAVE	
	A	PCT	A	PCT	A	PCT	A	PCT	A	PCT	A	PCT
1796	3263	24.8	2215	26.2	46	26.1	462	18.4	53	37.7	487	23.0
1802	3276	34.9	1464	34.3	115	28.7	1097	37.3	106	30.2	494	33.6
1803	3115	48.9	1462	49.9	180	47.8	712	48.5	83	47.0	678	47.5
1804	3341	40.4	1708	39.8	311	44.4	764	43.6	79	32.9	479	35.9
1805	3571	35.2	1627	35.3	97	37.1	1300	34.7	30	33.3	517	35.8
1806	3603	30.9	1674	31.4	94	25.5	1298	32.9	17	35.3	520	25.2
1807	3358	30.9	1366	30.2	99	26.3	1390	31.8	33	36.4	470	31.1
1808	3525	30.7	1440	29.2	155	31.0	1331	31.9	117	29.9	482	32.0
1809	3434	25.1	1114	21.4	158	15.2	1140	27.5	95	23.2	927	28.5
1811	3416	34.7	1201	37.3	136	27.9	1534	36.4	67	32.8	478	24.7
1816	2685	27.2	882	35.6	214	24.3	1168	24.8	0	0.0	421	17.6
1817	2612	27.8	999	30.4	229	18.3	996	28.9	0	0.0	388	23.7
1822	3218	33.2	1408	35.6	149	44.3	1180	34.9	0	0.0	481	18.7
YARITAGUA												
1782	1978	32.4	704	35.2	153	36.6	920	33.3	0	0.0	201	14.9
1802	1604	42.8	351	52.4	96	25.0	479	40.5	540	42.6	138	39.1
1803	1721	41.3	360	50.6	95	25.3	507	41.4	601	39.3	158	36.7
1804	1721	41.3	360	50.6	95	25.3	507	41.4	601	39.3	158	36.7
1805	2115	37.3	466	46.4	106	28.3	537	41.7	822	32.6	184	27.2
1807	3043	36.3	641	35.3	79	27.8	938	39.9	1217	35.2	168	33.3
1808	3508	32.8	718	33.4	84	31.0	1222	32.2	1324	33.7	160	28.8
1809	3508	32.8	718	33.4	84	31.0	1222	32.2	1324	33.7	160	28.8
1810	3508	32.8	718	33.4	84	31.0	1222	32.2	1324	33.7	160	28.8
1811	3323	34.7	708	35.3	76	31.6	1172	33.8	1221	36.0	146	30.1
1812	2891	36.5	653	36.8	62	32.3	976	36.5	1062	37.3	138	30.4
1816	4572	27.8	443	47.4	43	55.8	3931	25.3	51	47.1	104	17.3
1817	4252	24.2	763	28.0	104	25.0	2978	23.3	215	32.6	192	12.0
1818	3898	27.7	786	32.6	161	30.4	2623	26.6	157	33.8	171	13.5
1820	4021	48.3	1014	34.0	126	35.7	2464	59.3	230	29.6	187	13.4

TABLE 4. MALE/FEMALE RATIOS BY RACE (M/F)(100)
(* IN LISTING INDICATES A VALUE EXCEEDING 999.9)

YEAR	TOTAL M/F		WHITE M/F		INDIAN M/F		PARDO M/F		NEGRO M/F		SLAVE M/F	
	ADULT	CHILD	ADULT	CHILD	ADULT	CHILD	ADULT	CHILD	ADULT	CHILD	ADULT	CHILD
ACARIGUA												
1778	81.5	86.7	0.0	0.0	81.5	86.7	0.0	0.0	0.0	0.0	0.0	0.0
1802	82.3	92.4	80.1	80.0	82.0	96.5	91.7	100.0	33.3	0.0	25.0	14.3
1803	90.8	105.2	79.3	88.6	98.5	109.4	90.7	102.6	75.0	100.0	30.0	80.0
1804	91.0	95.8	78.4	87.7	97.1	98.7	92.5	93.8	80.0	0.0	57.1	33.3
1805	86.6	99.3	77.2	98.6	89.7	98.5	91.9	100.0	125.0	0.0	14.3	400.0
1808	77.7	96.5	84.5	95.1	75.9	98.3	79.9	92.5	75.0	0.0	33.3	0.0
1809	78.1	97.6	90.4	99.0	75.2	99.8	79.9	89.3	100.0	0.0	25.0	0.0
1810	82.0	106.8	83.5	96.9	82.0	116.7	80.0	89.9	133.3	0.0	60.0	0.0
1812	81.0	105.7	86.1	101.0	82.5	113.2	77.0	91.7	75.0	0.0	25.0	0.0
1829	86.9	78.5	71.9	69.4	45.8	100.0	111.4	80.7	200.0	100.0	5.6	0.0
ACHAGUAS												
1780	134.1	120.8	200.0	0.0	135.1	123.8	100.0	200.0	0.0	0.0	0.0	0.0
1801	103.2	95.5	144.1	54.2	89.7	128.6	102.1	102.3	58.3	40.0	100.0	50.0
1804	99.6	92.1	110.5	116.7	92.0	180.0	99.0	78.6	94.0	96.0	85.7	88.9
1806	112.0	103.8	105.3	120.0	112.5	138.9	95.9	84.2	126.7	116.7	331.6	125.0
1809	100.4	97.6	114.8	89.5	93.1	161.8	98.7	85.4	93.8	83.3	93.8	80.0
1811	96.7	105.7	104.0	84.9	90.7	123.9	97.0	113.4	80.0	84.2	93.2	89.6
AGUA BLANCA												
1779	81.0	93.3	63.6	100.0	76.6	94.4	89.7	93.8	0.0	0.0	50.0	50.0
1801	96.2	94.4	100.0	100.0	119.7	144.4	79.2	66.0	0.0	0.0	0.0	0.0
1802	98.9	85.8	87.1	85.7	97.4	60.6	105.6	100.0	0.0	0.0	0.0	0.0
1803	98.9	85.8	87.1	85.7	97.4	60.6	105.6	100.0	0.0	0.0	0.0	0.0
1804	100.6	173.0	106.5	155.6	100.0	166.7	98.8	187.5	0.0	0.0	0.0	0.0
1805	101.6	99.1	104.7	87.5	109.1	104.0	96.6	96.2	0.0	0.0	0.0	0.0
1808	88.0	98.6	58.8	366.7	83.1	85.7	94.8	101.5	0.0	0.0	200.0	0.0
1812	78.6	115.8	80.0	200.0	74.5	139.5	80.2	94.4	200.0	200.0	0.0	0.0
1815	82.0	96.4	82.8	90.0	93.7	85.0	75.5	106.0	0.0	0.0	0.0	0.0
1830	79.0	101.5	79.2	120.0	75.6	69.6	79.5	117.9	0.0	0.0	0.0	0.0
AGUA CULEBRAS												
1781	80.8	104.9	74.8	147.6	80.7	97.0	81.3	96.8	37.5	300.0	92.5	136.4
1802	84.1	99.3	81.0	53.3	81.8	60.0	82.7	112.6	45.5	0.0	210.0	116.7
1803	59.7	115.1	67.2	100.0	73.8	66.7	55.4	118.0	50.0	0.0	100.0	0.0
1804	62.2	114.0	68.6	260.0	58.1	78.9	59.3	115.5	44.4	0.0	118.2	80.0
1805	87.1	73.9	88.1	175.0	77.8	30.0	83.4	75.3	62.5	0.0	162.5	50.0
1807	82.9	95.0	78.0	220.0	81.3	90.0	83.9	91.6	75.0	0.0	90.0	0.0
1808	82.8	107.8	80.4	200.0	82.7	157.1	81.7	100.0	87.5	100.0	116.7	100.0
1809	83.1	99.2	84.4	66.7	82.7	157.1	81.7	100.0	77.8	100.0	116.7	100.0
1811	84.2	110.7	86.0	180.0	86.8	171.4	79.8	101.0	116.7	100.0	145.5	300.0
1812	72.5	111.9	71.9	200.0	74.3	146.2	73.9	100.0	60.0	100.0	57.9	0.0
1815	76.2	103.6	93.3	200.0	122.2	160.0	70.2	99.0	25.0	0.0	133.3	100.0
1817	78.3	54.8	91.7	60.0	80.0	55.6	76.6	51.1	0.0	0.0	75.0	200.0

TABLE 4. MALE/FEMALE RATIOS (CONTINUED)

YEAR	TOTAL M/F ADULT	TOTAL M/F CHILD	WHITE M/F ADULT	WHITE M/F CHILD	INDIAN M/F ADULT	INDIAN M/F CHILD	PARDO M/F ADULT	PARDO M/F CHILD	NEGRO M/F ADULT	NEGRO M/F CHILD	SLAVE M/F ADULT	SLAVE M/F CHILD
1818	75.8	126.2	85.7	100.0	88.6	85.7	71.8	134.5	0.0	0.0	120.0	50.0
1819	69.8	60.7	106.7	42.9	78.6	53.8	65.3	61.3	0.0	0.0	83.3	200.0
1820	64.2	92.9	60.0	71.4	0.0	0.0	66.4	100.0	51.5	69.2	63.6	71.4
1821	67.3	78.5	150.0	71.4	63.0	90.0	63.8	100.0	100.0	25.0	0.0	0.0
	AGUACALIENTE											
1803	96.2	134.4	110.7	183.3	0.0	0.0	94.6	127.8	0.0	0.0	66.7	150.0
1804	89.5	92.6	145.5	188.9	0.0	0.0	82.4	80.0	0.0	0.0	62.5	116.7
1805	88.8	82.5	86.5	80.0	0.0	0.0	91.4	78.9	87.5	100.0	79.2	85.7
1806	83.2	122.7	120.8	90.0	0.0	0.0	69.8	124.0	0.0	0.0	128.6	166.7
1807	98.5	101.3	155.0	83.3	0.0	0.0	93.1	96.8	0.0	0.0	87.1	140.0
1818	66.9	81.1	0.0	0.0	0.0	0.0	55.0	85.4	0.0	0.0	163.6	53.8
1819	60.9	82.5	0.0	0.0	0.0	0.0	53.0	95.1	0.0	0.0	118.2	28.6
	ALPARGATON											
1804	83.7	76.9	0.0	0.0	0.0	0.0	83.1	83.3	85.7	62.5	0.0	0.0
1805	105.0	110.0	0.0	0.0	0.0	0.0	130.0	114.3	63.3	100.0	0.0	0.0
1806	72.2	110.7	0.0	0.0	0.0	0.0	65.5	133.3	94.1	70.0	0.0	0.0
1807	120.6	108.1	0.0	0.0	0.0	0.0	164.3	133.3	85.7	84.2	0.0	0.0
1818	66.7	75.5	0.0	0.0	0.0	0.0	66.7	75.5	0.0	0.0	0.0	0.0
1819	82.4	96.9	0.0	0.0	0.0	0.0	82.4	96.9	0.0	0.0	0.0	0.0
1820	87.4	88.7	0.0	0.0	0.0	0.0	87.5	93.3	87.0	72.7	0.0	0.0
	ALTAGRACIA DE ORITUCO											
1783	104.0	115.4	92.9	119.0	90.8	98.2	200.0	0.0	130.8	145.8	131.8	142.9
1802	86.5	105.3	87.8	104.1	83.3	98.8	90.2	103.9	80.0	100.0	85.1	140.0
1803	96.7	104.4	88.8	119.3	105.7	103.4	98.0	80.0	100.0	300.0	88.9	117.9
1804	98.4	97.3	87.7	98.4	107.4	41.5	98.1	84.1	100.0	175.0	104.4	275.0
1806	106.5	91.1	105.4	74.7	95.8	118.7	130.3	72.7	100.0	66.7	104.2	126.7
1807	107.4	103.7	104.9	79.6	99.5	117.9	127.8	131.7	109.1	71.4	103.8	123.5
1809	104.5	108.0	106.1	106.3	97.6	119.8	131.5	93.1	96.6	83.3	85.1	125.8
1810	103.5	107.2	104.0	110.4	97.5	113.3	129.6	92.0	93.8	116.7	87.2	116.7
1811	107.4	93.1	105.4	74.7	102.3	115.8	122.5	84.2	96.3	76.9	107.8	118.8
	ALTAMIRA											
1783	103.3	85.5	0.0	0.0	103.3	85.5	0.0	0.0	0.0	0.0	0.0	0.0
	ANTIMANO											
1811	164.7	149.1	133.3	400.0	127.9	166.7	156.3	200.0	131.6	500.0	187.9	122.0
1819	98.5	54.6	118.1	83.3	86.3	70.0	85.9	60.0	111.1	25.0	107.0	42.7
	APARICION											
1802	94.3	87.0	96.0	89.6	94.2	89.2	96.5	82.1	88.0	90.9	85.7	83.3
1803	90.0	91.4	90.9	142.0	84.4	74.3	95.7	83.3	92.2	84.2	67.9	75.0
1804	91.1	120.0	90.6	130.7	89.2	106.4	91.4	121.0	0.0	0.0	102.9	110.5

TABLE 4. MALE/FEMALE RATIOS (CONTINUED)

YEAR	TOTAL M/F ADULT	TOTAL M/F CHILD	WHITE M/F ADULT	WHITE M/F CHILD	INDIAN M/F ADULT	INDIAN M/F CHILD	PARDO M/F ADULT	PARDO M/F CHILD	NEGRO M/F ADULT	NEGRO M/F CHILD	SLAVE M/F ADULT	SLAVE M/F CHILD
1805	84.6	112.3	93.8	98.5	70.1	113.7	87.3	115.9	82.8	83.3	83.3	116.7
1808	87.5	102.3	100.0	150.5	73.0	101.4	90.9	89.0	0.0	0.0	66.0	94.4
1809	95.0	84.9	95.0	84.1	107.1	62.1	90.3	100.9	0.0	0.0	115.0	63.6
1810	79.2	110.5	83.8	111.8	70.6	94.8	81.3	119.5	0.0	0.0	70.8	90.0
1811	80.2	117.8	103.3	111.8	68.3	94.0	75.7	137.7	0.0	0.0	85.0	90.0
1812	86.0	97.2	90.9	145.8	65.4	89.0	95.3	77.5	0.0	0.0	114.3	366.7
	APURITO											
1802	111.5	119.2	76.9	300.0	82.4	200.0	108.3	95.2	130.8	125.0	283.3	125.0
1806	97.9	82.4	85.4	80.0	90.5	75.0	97.6	71.4	0.0	0.0	275.0	200.0
1807	91.1	82.8	93.3	75.0	92.5	80.0	92.9	88.6	77.8	75.0	66.7	75.0
	ARAGUITA											
1784	106.5	79.3	170.0	66.7	120.7	65.2	125.0	80.0	166.7	50.0	97.0	85.9
1802	79.7	111.6	125.0	0.0	110.5	150.0	87.5	33.3	90.9	200.0	74.3	116.2
1803	77.1	111.4	110.0	0.0	120.0	20.0	100.0	0.0	118.2	0.0	71.9	117.7
1804	97.3	87.1	133.3	75.0	100.0	66.7	125.0	66.7	125.0	100.0	93.8	87.8
1805	89.3	92.0	140.0	200.0	25.0	200.0	150.0	100.0	500.0	0.0	86.1	81.5
1807	128.0	79.8	0.0	66.7	300.0	0.0	241.2	100.0	33.3	0.0	114.8	83.0
1810	88.4	80.7	121.4	125.0	120.0	33.3	123.1	200.0	35.3	33.3	82.1	66.7
1811	89.4	107.3	172.7	166.7	80.0	33.3	111.9	280.0	69.2	66.7	78.0	95.2
1812	79.7	101.9	141.7	100.0	80.0	100.0	83.3	222.2	45.5	66.7	75.2	73.5
1816	72.7	87.5	90.9	100.0	125.0	66.7	90.0	60.0	75.0	150.0	61.3	87.2
1819	74.9	120.4	118.2	81.8	83.3	0.0	78.3	350.0	76.9	350.0	66.1	102.6
	ARAURE											
1778	93.9	91.2	100.2	90.7	96.6	116.2	90.4	96.7	96.4	73.0	66.7	91.1
1798	84.6	106.0	84.8	114.2	90.2	114.4	82.9	98.2	78.2	97.8	0.0	0.0
1799	86.5	106.3	89.6	113.3	94.9	113.6	81.7	99.0	77.3	102.0	0.0	0.0
1800	83.7	111.3	82.6	119.4	94.0	123.0	81.7	101.2	76.3	111.3	0.0	0.0
1801	88.3	103.9	83.5	98.6	80.0	112.5	93.2	107.7	70.0	75.0	0.0	0.0
1802	79.9	108.1	86.9	86.0	123.8	100.0	75.6	120.3	130.0	116.7	57.5	160.0
1803	85.2	103.8	96.7	94.5	102.9	78.3	82.7	110.3	71.0	200.0	60.7	121.1
1804	90.8	104.6	89.4	95.4	102.3	91.3	99.8	117.7	55.6	100.0	54.3	90.9
1805	103.7	55.1	119.9	21.1	107.6	6.3	91.5	214.8	150.0	144.4	94.0	121.2
1808	82.3	108.4	88.3	100.0	95.9	133.3	78.1	111.1	44.4	0.0	77.6	97.3
1809	78.4	93.4	88.2	91.1	71.4	112.1	77.2	93.0	60.0	100.0	59.8	76.9
1810	78.8	93.1	89.2	91.1	71.4	112.1	77.2	89.5	140.0	100.0	57.7	97.3
1811	83.6	94.0	98.3	93.1	70.8	112.1	78.1	89.5	118.2	300.0	61.3	97.3
1812	77.6	91.5	85.0	94.3	69.7	101.7	76.7	85.2	108.3	150.0	61.0	102.6
1829	77.2	86.1	75.4	97.1	118.2	100.0	77.3	81.0	70.6	85.4	43.6	0.0
	AREGUE											
1802	90.1	45.7	76.2	76.5	93.8	22.2	88.2	81.1	0.0	0.0	133.3	60.0
1803	79.4	88.5	88.9	84.6	78.0	90.0	78.0	82.9	0.0	0.0	100.0	150.0
1804	80.4	91.3	85.7	85.7	72.3	80.6	112.2	130.4	0.0	0.0	50.0	166.7
1805	86.3	104.6	89.2	116.7	74.3	117.9	108.1	76.7	0.0	0.0	125.0	80.0

TABLE 4. MALE/FEMALE RATIOS (CONTINUED)

YEAR	TOTAL M/F		WHITE M/F		INDIAN M/F		PARDO M/F		NEGRO M/F		SLAVE M/F	
	ADULT	CHILD	ADULT	CHILD	ADULT	CHILD	ADULT	CHILD	ADULT	CHILD	ADULT	CHILD
1809	100.6	86.7	90.7	81.0	107.0	87.4	86.6	87.0	100.0	0.0	120.0	100.0
1815	74.6	77.3	61.0	80.0	83.9	68.8	72.0	87.2	0.0	0.0	47.1	87.5
	ARENALES											
1802	90.7	108.7	93.2	126.7	100.0	214.3	87.3	103.4	97.6	80.0	85.7	109.1
1803	83.6	111.2	73.4	108.7	129.6	160.0	83.2	103.4	80.0	68.8	79.6	152.9
1804	91.0	112.1	85.7	94.4	164.0	118.2	76.7	122.0	110.3	75.0	100.0	125.0
1805	91.2	107.3	82.3	81.3	123.3	122.2	93.2	119.6	70.0	80.8	108.9	122.2
1807	87.3	117.6	81.4	111.1	123.3	100.0	88.8	112.9	81.0	92.9	74.1	176.5
1809	93.9	106.6	169.0	100.0	97.9	133.3	90.1	93.2	85.7	92.3	63.0	156.3
	ARICHUNA											
1801	100.6	101.7	119.4	106.7	89.7	108.2	95.2	83.3	136.4	100.0	150.0	50.0
1804	89.2	94.4	88.9	78.6	85.2	92.4	94.2	120.0	87.0	90.9	105.9	150.0
	AROA											
1802	110.0	370.5	116.3	78.6	55.6	189.5	121.5	600.0	77.6	200.0	117.2	180.0
1805	106.1	95.7	107.4	121.7	112.5	166.7	96.1	92.0	116.4	92.3	140.0	66.7
1807	98.8	89.6	105.5	115.0	94.3	87.5	91.2	87.0	113.7	84.3	92.6	111.1
1808	87.4	80.8	94.3	30.0	75.0	68.8	72.5	93.8	103.6	62.5	109.9	120.0
1809	88.0	106.9	115.2	168.8	90.0	60.0	84.5	113.6	117.4	68.8	89.1	71.4
1817	74.5	204.2	102.5	118.8	0.0	0.0	69.2	260.4	100.0	75.0	123.1	0.0
1818	91.0	122.4	86.6	124.1	126.7	121.7	85.2	145.3	127.3	92.9	0.0	0.0
	ATAMAICA											
1780	97.6	127.3	0.0	50.0	97.5	130.0	0.0	0.0	0.0	0.0	0.0	0.0
1802	103.8	136.7	90.2	200.0	95.6	300.0	122.2	80.0	0.0	0.0	333.3	50.0
	AYAMANES											
1802	95.5	101.5	55.0	54.5	100.0	110.5	0.0	0.0	0.0	0.0	0.0	0.0
1803	73.0	111.9	117.6	100.0	68.3	111.9	100.0	0.0	0.0	0.0	0.0	0.0
1804	83.0	120.5	120.0	700.0	78.0	108.5	142.9	400.0	0.0	0.0	0.0	0.0
1805	73.9	102.9	85.7	88.9	70.9	101.7	133.3	0.0	0.0	0.0	0.0	0.0
1807	79.1	89.6	96.3	89.5	75.3	84.9	93.8	233.3	0.0	0.0	0.0	0.0
1808	82.6	96.6	103.3	91.3	78.2	90.2	93.3	275.0	0.0	0.0	0.0	0.0
1815	57.0	88.3	87.9	106.3	49.2	85.4	73.0	84.6	0.0	0.0	0.0	0.0
	BANCO LARGO											
1805	93.2	87.2	88.0	86.0	88.9	90.2	84.6	93.9	94.9	79.7	120.8	87.5
1809	86.4	81.8	81.5	89.7	78.9	70.0	90.5	85.2	81.3	50.0	76.5	75.0
	BARBACOAS DE LOS LLANOS											
1782	102.6	92.6	129.6	107.8	69.3	68.8	70.6	75.0	113.3	102.3	96.4	77.8
1783	100.8	90.7	129.6	107.8	69.3	57.9	88.1	63.2	102.2	126.5	96.4	77.8

TABLE 4. MALE/FEMALE RATIOS (CONTINUED)

YEAR	TOTAL M/F		WHITE M/F		INDIAN M/F		PARDO M/F		NEGRO M/F		SLAVE M/F	
	ADULT	CHILD	ADULT	CHILD	ADULT	CHILD	ADULT	CHILD	ADULT	CHILD	ADULT	CHILD
1802	92.7	108.2	117.0	113.8	69.4	100.0	78.2	113.3	96.8	82.6	126.0	92.9
1803	99.7	116.7	127.5	131.0	75.0	104.9	76.7	119.0	101.4	104.8	108.1	86.7
1804	94.5	108.7	109.6	113.5	63.7	129.6	97.0	90.2	80.6	101.8	148.3	123.3
1805	97.5	99.5	105.9	95.5	67.4	102.1	101.7	75.7	87.5	141.0	142.9	77.8
1809	115.2	101.5	103.2	103.2	110.8	91.9	109.3	96.5	144.8	112.6	114.3	122.7
1810	112.0	101.8	103.4	101.1	111.5	121.1	110.1	98.4	120.7	89.6	164.5	121.4
1811	110.3	100.0	102.9	103.9	115.7	114.3	106.6	99.2	120.3	86.0	130.8	83.3
	BARBACOAS DEL TOCUYO											
1802	103.1	94.6	110.3	92.6	97.5	97.6	125.0	92.3	97.9	89.3	83.3	150.0
1803	85.5	82.4	77.4	60.0	84.9	81.8	89.3	66.7	90.2	116.7	85.7	166.7
1804	80.2	84.0	81.8	66.7	72.2	88.9	86.5	77.8	92.3	79.2	88.9	175.0
1805	104.1	73.6	67.4	73.3	121.3	73.5	90.3	57.1	107.3	81.3	141.7	120.0
1806	89.6	83.3	89.7	61.5	86.7	86.7	85.3	85.7	90.2	89.7	137.5	66.7
1807	89.4	82.8	92.9	60.0	87.0	82.6	82.9	82.6	90.6	96.4	140.0	75.0
1808	85.1	103.8	79.2	135.7	82.1	102.9	65.9	116.7	109.1	85.2	122.2	66.7
1809	83.5	109.5	83.0	122.2	80.6	111.1	62.5	133.3	104.7	85.7	110.0	71.4
1810	87.6	114.7	83.3	115.0	86.0	115.0	67.4	141.9	104.4	83.9	150.0	128.6
1812	74.1	127.7	78.6	220.0	65.9	93.8	75.0	107.9	83.3	125.0	250.0	0.0
1815	74.3	132.7	97.6	150.0	76.6	117.1	60.2	131.4	200.0	0.0	80.0	300.0
1816	80.3	113.5	105.1	154.5	77.3	113.9	68.5	97.9	100.0	200.0	100.0	300.0
1817	93.8	117.3	97.0	144.4	120.5	125.0	75.4	103.2	70.0	100.0	109.1	500.0
1818	88.6	132.2	103.7	112.5	91.4	140.7	77.2	125.0	180.0	0.0	110.0	175.0
1819	82.8	103.2	92.1	216.7	81.3	114.6	77.2	79.4	81.3	100.0	150.0	200.0
1820	84.1	117.2	118.8	141.7	79.0	128.6	78.3	104.5	20.0	100.0	127.3	175.0
	BARQUISIMETO											
1779	93.4	108.2	79.8	82.1	89.0	154.8	98.8	110.0	80.9	93.0	92.0	107.5
1815	71.4	98.1	89.2	105.9	78.7	84.1	69.5	98.3	56.3	88.1	74.1	151.0
	BARQUISIMETO, MITAD DE(1)											
1802	93.5	84.0	86.3	88.2	92.2	85.8	96.3	80.8	94.5	86.7	92.0	78.9
1803	92.8	84.5	85.8	87.6	90.8	85.2	95.4	82.4	94.7	85.5	91.3	83.3
1804	78.0	84.0	86.2	87.6	91.0	86.1	96.2	82.4	46.5	85.5	93.8	76.6
1805	93.3	82.5	85.6	84.3	96.5	73.8	95.6	80.4	94.4	93.3	87.5	74.2
1807	92.7	106.2	98.6	89.9	85.7	164.5	95.7	100.5	90.7	94.6	82.4	80.0
1808	93.8	88.2	102.8	93.8	90.6	101.5	96.9	83.5	84.6	86.6	84.9	87.9
1809	96.2	85.9	102.6	87.6	94.1	48.8	100.1	90.8	87.3	114.3	84.7	110.0
1810	92.8	106.2	98.6	89.9	85.7	164.5	95.7	100.5	90.7	94.6	82.7	80.0
1811	96.3	85.1	103.2	101.1	91.9	54.4	100.1	91.1	88.1	90.9	85.2	88.9
1817	73.6	112.7	78.8	92.1	76.0	104.3	72.1	116.1	25.0	0.0	103.6	200.0
1818	73.8	113.9	73.1	180.0	92.2	108.2	68.6	114.9	54.2	133.3	110.2	120.0
1819	71.2	97.2	76.6	86.7	97.0	97.1	64.4	98.8	53.3	92.0	94.3	78.9
1820	70.3	96.0	52.7	90.9	80.5	87.0	65.3	99.8	137.0	107.7	98.4	92.3
	BARQUISIMETO, MITAD DE(2)											
1802	73.0	125.0	71.3	144.1	62.8	122.6	72.6	131.0	76.1	115.8	80.0	78.9

TABLE 4. MALE/FEMALE RATIOS (CONTINUED)

YEAR	TOTAL M/F ADULT	TOTAL M/F CHILD	WHITE M/F ADULT	WHITE M/F CHILD	INDIAN M/F ADULT	INDIAN M/F CHILD	PARDO M/F ADULT	PARDO M/F CHILD	NEGRO M/F ADULT	NEGRO M/F CHILD	SLAVE M/F ADULT	SLAVE M/F CHILD
1803	116.5	357.3	25.5	150.0	158.8	90.0	185.1	1720.0	242.5	125.0	80.8	81.3
1804	118.5	329.2	25.8	181.1	158.8	79.2	188.0	1545.0	243.5	126.1	80.9	86.3
1805	118.2	306.0	26.0	174.1	152.1	78.6	187.6	1190.4	242.2	112.0	81.5	80.5
1807	117.2	329.3	25.9	184.9	154.3	88.6	185.5	1423.3	241.7	126.1	81.0	86.3
1808	129.0	343.8	27.4	176.5	171.2	75.0	198.6	1505.0	264.7	122.0	86.7	85.7
1809	125.7	314.2	27.5	144.4	171.2	140.0	197.8	173.9	249.1	1262.5	86.7	87.5
1810	125.7	314.2	27.5	144.4	171.2	140.0	197.8	173.9	249.1	1262.5	86.7	87.5
1811	98.1	111.6	28.0	146.0	112.9	123.3	141.8	101.1	139.5	108.1	90.8	96.2
1817	67.4	99.2	77.3	112.0	83.7	65.1	65.8	100.1	78.4	68.0	62.2	157.5
1818	56.1	92.5	75.7	82.6	76.0	80.6	51.6	95.8	75.9	61.5	64.7	113.8
1819	55.6	90.0	75.3	78.0	70.9	68.8	51.6	95.1	69.2	58.1	63.5	111.3
1820	55.9	93.1	90.4	85.7	75.0	82.9	49.7	96.2	73.6	61.0	66.1	112.9
	BARUTA											
1802	101.2	89.8	98.8	108.3	104.7	73.7	108.2	110.5	103.4	300.0	95.7	64.9
1803	102.8	92.4	101.6	96.0	104.3	88.4	116.4	146.7	92.5	137.5	99.0	61.8
1804	101.6	98.1	103.5	105.5	101.8	94.7	100.0	116.7	112.8	61.5	92.1	94.1
1805	102.5	101.1	100.7	109.5	102.7	100.0	98.4	80.0	88.6	80.0	115.2	102.6
1811	103.6	107.4	104.7	105.3	110.7	121.8	100.0	73.3	107.1	85.7	88.1	97.4
1816	84.6	93.4	76.3	82.9	82.3	96.9	80.0	110.0	126.7	57.1	97.3	113.3
1817	73.5	86.3	81.2	85.7	66.9	96.2	65.8	57.1	91.7	60.0	72.0	86.7
1819	78.1	101.2	96.9	101.5	60.2	98.6	76.9	125.0	63.6	0.0	78.6	100.6
1820	90.0	91.3	100.8	124.1	82.1	68.9	81.4	81.6	82.4	100.0	86.3	84.8
	BAUL											
1781	101.8	134.1	107.6	106.5	110.6	165.4	105.6	75.0	77.1	163.2	100.0	100.0
1802	102.0	113.1	101.5	114.6	110.6	136.6	134.2	100.0	56.7	104.0	105.9	333.3
1805	85.7	114.3	92.9	123.6	90.4	138.6	73.9	112.3	88.9	48.1	111.1	0.0
1811	95.4	92.8	88.9	94.7	97.5	92.1	104.2	90.5	0.0	0.0	88.5	92.3
1812	87.0	84.2	80.3	81.8	90.8	80.2	95.6	89.7	0.0	0.0	75.5	82.4
1815	90.5	104.4	82.6	121.2	74.1	79.7	103.4	119.3	93.8	150.0	110.7	66.7
1816	101.8	102.3	110.5	131.3	101.6	74.5	94.7	104.0	95.2	114.3	95.2	70.2
1817	89.1	100.0	101.0	107.0	75.4	87.9	84.8	97.5	55.3	130.0	88.9	78.6
1825	93.9	91.8	96.9	92.0	92.6	87.1	91.7	91.3	200.0	0.0	100.0	166.7
1829	96.2	86.3	99.1	90.8	72.7	75.0	95.2	89.0	97.0	71.8	72.7	84.2
	BOBARE											
1779	90.1	103.0	0.0	0.0	90.1	103.0	0.0	0.0	0.0	0.0	0.0	0.0
1802	83.6	94.8	0.0	0.0	83.6	94.8	0.0	0.0	0.0	0.0	0.0	0.0
1803	83.6	94.8	0.0	0.0	83.6	94.8	0.0	0.0	0.0	0.0	0.0	0.0
1804	82.2	112.1	0.0	0.0	82.2	112.1	0.0	0.0	0.0	0.0	0.0	0.0
1805	80.3	201.8	0.0	0.0	80.3	201.8	0.0	0.0	0.0	0.0	0.0	0.0
1806	80.3	201.8	0.0	0.0	80.3	201.8	0.0	0.0	0.0	0.0	0.0	0.0
1808	84.1	118.6	0.0	0.0	84.1	118.6	0.0	0.0	0.0	0.0	0.0	0.0
1811	78.1	140.3	0.0	0.0	78.1	140.3	0.0	0.0	0.0	0.0	0.0	0.0
1820	101.4	102.3	0.0	0.0	103.8	104.8	63.6	50.0	0.0	0.0	200.0	0.0

TABLE 4. MALE/FEMALE RATIOS (CONTINUED)

YEAR	TOTAL M/F ADULT	TOTAL M/F CHILD	WHITE M/F ADULT	WHITE M/F CHILD	INDIAN M/F ADULT	INDIAN M/F CHILD	PARDO M/F ADULT	PARDO M/F CHILD	NEGRO M/F ADULT	NEGRO M/F CHILD	SLAVE M/F ADULT	SLAVE M/F CHILD
	BOCONO											
1778	84.1	102.9	89.1	93.6	81.3	93.3	80.3	115.9	50.0	0.0	69.2	700.0
1795	95.1	100.5	102.1	94.0	89.3	129.5	90.2	98.1	142.9	175.0	56.3	106.3
1796	96.8	100.3	102.3	95.1	111.1	124.4	91.3	95.8	60.0	120.0	66.7	183.3
1798	108.8	97.6	138.9	96.1	90.9	118.2	91.0	92.9	128.6	133.3	54.2	127.3
1799	95.9	96.8	100.8	92.6	90.6	120.9	91.0	93.4	257.1	133.3	50.0	120.0
1800	99.4	96.2	106.2	91.3	101.9	125.0	94.3	92.8	128.6	133.3	52.4	122.2
1802	96.8	98.5	119.8	101.6	100.0	96.8	83.7	97.9	100.0	200.0	33.3	66.7
1803	98.8	98.0	120.7	100.0	106.9	96.9	83.5	98.1	112.5	175.0	38.5	55.6
1804	96.4	83.9	116.1	111.8	103.3	24.7	83.5	98.9	131.3	120.0	26.3	55.6
1805	89.8	104.2	93.4	90.3	88.2	200.0	85.8	95.7	75.0	120.0	52.9	160.0
1806	93.1	79.2	102.0	97.6	91.4	71.8	85.3	72.8	116.7	166.7	66.7	66.7
1807	96.7	83.4	103.1	96.3	98.4	106.9	84.8	72.7	110.5	172.7	140.0	90.0
1808	100.3	107.8	103.1	92.0	82.4	107.7	95.3	108.9	110.0	225.0	192.3	133.3
1810	82.5	103.4	83.7	84.7	87.1	100.0	79.4	121.8	0.0	0.0	100.0	133.3
	BORBURATA											
1803	100.8	112.9	185.7	200.0	125.0	300.0	98.6	93.8	89.2	113.2	109.2	124.1
1804	110.9	103.8	242.9	0.0	200.0	100.0	101.4	133.3	111.6	70.5	103.8	163.2
1805	107.9	87.6	163.6	200.0	300.0	0.0	96.9	87.5	106.0	73.4	109.2	126.1
1806	117.1	88.9	162.5	0.0	100.0	0.0	130.4	97.4	113.6	85.2	105.3	100.0
1807	117.7	86.7	166.7	50.0	100.0	0.0	130.4	80.9	113.6	87.7	111.0	104.8
1818	70.7	122.4	0.0	0.0	50.0	0.0	58.9	117.6	67.0	146.7	81.8	96.6
1819	69.1	118.2	0.0	150.0	25.0	0.0	62.7	147.4	62.7	129.3	84.6	89.2
	BURERITO											
1802	100.5	95.4	0.0	0.0	300.0	0.0	79.7	84.6	129.7	119.4	309.1	180.0
1803	99.5	102.8	0.0	0.0	266.7	0.0	84.1	115.4	94.3	97.2	272.7	150.0
1804	73.0	119.6	0.0	0.0	53.8	66.7	69.5	160.8	83.2	66.7	106.7	100.0
1807	95.0	110.4	75.0	0.0	100.0	0.0	78.0	120.5	127.7	94.0	210.0	185.7
1809	84.0	88.6	0.0	0.0	0.0	0.0	83.9	83.3	80.6	89.7	95.7	144.4
	BURIA											
1779	87.9	123.4	130.0	300.0	76.6	109.1	92.5	132.4	61.5	100.0	100.0	0.0
1802	84.9	122.9	88.9	0.0	90.2	138.5	78.6	117.2	114.3	140.0	266.7	0.0
1803	84.4	113.3	85.7	0.0	90.9	84.6	78.6	117.2	114.3	120.0	600.0	0.0
1804	103.7	128.3	142.9	0.0	93.1	328.6	102.0	115.9	71.4	0.0	300.0	200.0
1805	84.3	104.2	125.0	0.0	90.9	106.3	81.4	100.8	100.0	0.0	100.0	0.0
1807	76.7	108.2	108.3	500.0	62.2	117.6	74.7	102.1	116.7	0.0	175.0	0.0
1809	76.3	104.1	100.0	300.0	53.6	142.9	76.3	99.4	75.0	0.0	500.0	0.0
1810	84.0	109.6	100.0	200.0	53.6	142.9	85.5	105.6	71.4	0.0	0.0	0.0
1811	87.3	97.8	100.0	200.0	90.9	133.3	84.9	93.6	100.0	0.0	500.0	0.0
1817	65.0	87.6	126.7	71.4	84.2	82.6	59.6	91.7	64.3	71.4	0.0	0.0
1818	57.3	72.1	55.6	64.5	28.1	56.3	59.9	75.2	0.0	0.0	0.0	0.0
1819	60.7	82.6	56.5	114.3	59.7	100.0	49.2	74.3	78.4	84.4	166.7	200.0

TABLE 4. MALE/FEMALE RATIOS (CONTINUED)

YEAR	TOTAL M/F ADULT	TOTAL M/F CHILD	WHITE M/F ADULT	WHITE M/F CHILD	INDIAN M/F ADULT	INDIAN M/F CHILD	PARDO M/F ADULT	PARDO M/F CHILD	NEGRO M/F ADULT	NEGRO M/F CHILD	SLAVE M/F ADULT	SLAVE M/F CHILD
	CABRIA											
1802	86.8	222.2	0.0	0.0	0.0	0.0	88.0	222.2	0.0	0.0	0.0	0.0
1803	71.2	78.6	0.0	0.0	0.0	0.0	71.2	78.6	0.0	0.0	0.0	0.0
1808	98.5	130.0	0.0	0.0	0.0	0.0	101.6	130.0	33.3	0.0	0.0	0.0
	CABRUTA											
1780	124.6	167.6	125.9	105.6	125.0	100.0	61.1	233.3	100.0	0.0	533.3	1100.0
1806	94.9	150.0	92.3	0.0	94.6	135.7	110.0	0.0	0.0	0.0	0.0	0.0
1808	136.0	117.9	80.0	0.0	140.0	143.5	83.3	0.0	0.0	0.0	0.0	0.0
1810	115.6	111.0	141.7	166.7	108.2	124.5	153.8	55.6	0.0	0.0	0.0	0.0
	CAGUA											
1781	92.9	100.1	96.7	98.4	77.1	102.3	89.9	102.9	0.0	0.0	106.3	82.4
1802	68.4	101.7	52.1	121.8	78.3	89.5	77.5	92.6	75.4	113.6	94.4	103.7
1803	80.6	99.7	89.7	105.8	100.0	133.3	75.7	94.0	38.5	250.0	81.8	106.8
1804	68.7	102.8	73.6	111.1	103.7	229.4	58.4	87.5	67.5	1600.0	92.8	121.0
1805	81.5	106.5	74.3	118.2	100.0	108.3	83.8	98.5	84.4	93.3	86.1	128.8
1806	76.6	105.0	72.6	109.3	79.3	136.4	77.1	104.6	71.8	111.1	86.2	93.2
1808	72.3	102.4	66.5	114.5	91.4	128.6	72.3	98.4	228.6	100.0	79.3	93.0
1809	72.1	99.3	68.3	100.7	121.7	140.0	70.2	92.4	80.0	150.0	77.8	121.9
1811	74.2	117.4	66.5	85.5	110.5	120.0	78.5	133.3	69.0	100.0	66.5	120.6
1815	51.0	112.9	52.1	107.9	69.6	107.6	43.4	90.7	71.4	92.9	71.2	182.4
1816	72.3	117.9	53.2	111.5	73.7	118.9	97.0	97.5	80.6	115.0	69.5	171.4
1817	54.3	117.3	54.3	111.3	76.1	118.3	45.2	97.6	85.4	112.0	71.1	168.2
1818	52.7	113.3	52.2	108.9	66.1	111.1	44.4	94.1	85.4	84.0	72.3	168.2
	CAICARA DEL ORINOCO											
1802	133.3	103.3	157.9	60.0	115.4	133.3	114.3	125.0	0.0	0.0	214.3	100.0
	CALABOZO											
1780	119.9	124.6	119.2	120.4	165.7	200.0	109.7	113.6	124.2	146.2	134.8	154.5
1802	87.2	74.8	86.5	73.0	66.7	72.2	87.7	77.2	93.3	70.6	90.5	73.3
1803	86.9	81.7	86.8	82.4	55.1	73.9	89.4	82.5	84.3	75.7	89.0	82.6
1804	87.7	83.9	87.4	81.5	52.6	76.2	90.0	86.3	85.1	83.3	91.6	83.9
1805	86.9	85.7	87.3	87.2	56.6	88.0	90.7	87.5	73.0	88.1	87.9	76.1
1807	88.6	91.2	87.7	94.4	59.1	88.9	93.2	91.9	87.1	90.2	85.8	84.7
1808	90.1	87.7	93.9	88.0	77.8	92.3	88.5	91.5	106.2	83.3	85.6	75.6
1810	87.9	107.0	97.5	99.1	100.0	133.3	90.8	120.9	95.8	44.4	64.8	88.8
1812	66.9	100.8	78.9	119.6	73.9	200.0	66.3	107.7	57.1	25.0	47.9	60.0
1817	51.4	102.2	72.0	100.0	0.0	0.0	42.3	100.0	0.0	0.0	45.8	110.6
1818	49.9	82.9	69.6	77.2	0.0	0.0	44.5	96.8	0.0	0.0	29.4	65.3
1822	47.6	66.3	77.9	58.6	0.0	0.0	36.4	68.1	0.0	0.0	48.6	66.7

TABLE 4. MALE/FEMALE RATIOS (CONTINUED)

YEAR	TOTAL M/F ADULT	TOTAL M/F CHILD	WHITE M/F ADULT	WHITE M/F CHILD	INDIAN M/F ADULT	INDIAN M/F CHILD	PARDO M/F ADULT	PARDO M/F CHILD	NEGRO M/F ADULT	NEGRO M/F CHILD	SLAVE M/F ADULT	SLAVE M/F CHILD
	CAMAGUAN											
1780	133.6	121.9	108.0	225.0	92.7	122.0	170.6	50.0	142.9	75.0	329.4	144.4
1801	110.8	96.6	105.0	115.4	103.8	106.7	112.7	70.3	127.3	83.3	300.0	60.0
1802	112.9	95.2	108.8	150.0	103.6	93.9	114.8	72.1	136.4	66.7	300.0	66.7
1803	105.7	105.9	103.3	129.6	100.6	107.2	112.4	105.0	72.7	44.4	187.5	85.7
1804	102.9	104.3	100.0	137.9	100.6	96.6	101.0	100.0	85.7	25.0	190.0	175.0
1812	95.1	99.4	124.6	77.8	87.9	75.7	95.4	134.4	85.7	200.0	68.8	0.0
1817	91.1	88.6	94.3	83.3	84.6	120.0	94.0	53.6	74.1	75.0	107.7	150.0
	CAMATAGUA											
1783	84.6	107.5	110.1	118.6	74.2	124.7	93.3	94.4	75.8	95.5	74.2	103.6
1802	80.7	65.9	84.6	63.9	78.1	62.2	84.3	68.5	65.2	68.9	87.9	79.5
1803	79.0	66.4	85.9	65.7	74.8	61.4	79.8	71.9	64.1	69.4	87.0	80.8
1804	76.2	79.6	79.2	89.0	71.2	75.0	80.7	67.2	77.1	83.3	71.3	91.8
1805	79.0	67.5	85.9	70.7	74.8	61.4	79.8	71.9	64.1	69.4	87.0	84.5
1806	79.0	67.5	85.9	70.7	74.8	61.4	79.8	71.9	64.1	69.4	87.0	84.5
1808	79.0	67.5	85.9	70.7	74.8	61.4	79.8	71.9	64.1	69.4	87.0	84.5
1811	131.0	67.8	103.3	84.6	134.3	63.3	125.9	69.0	0.0	0.0	219.0	57.1
	CANOABO											
1781	102.7	86.8	177.8	83.3	0.0	0.0	104.6	91.5	0.0	0.0	69.2	75.6
1788	93.8	97.7	115.4	50.0	0.0	0.0	99.6	97.7	0.0	0.0	71.3	105.3
1802	71.1	117.1	87.5	100.0	0.0	0.0	72.8	117.1	0.0	0.0	59.3	122.2
1803	68.9	114.0	100.0	200.0	0.0	0.0	68.3	109.4	0.0	0.0	63.5	131.3
1804	70.4	122.4	108.3	100.0	0.0	0.0	69.5	119.1	0.0	0.0	62.2	160.0
1805	81.9	90.4	76.5	83.3	0.0	0.0	81.4	85.5	0.0	0.0	85.1	130.0
1806	102.3	101.2	96.3	63.2	0.0	0.0	111.3	103.3	85.7	71.4	71.4	131.8
1807	94.9	100.0	96.7	90.5	0.0	0.0	99.4	102.0	85.7	88.9	77.2	104.5
1808	95.9	89.0	93.8	78.3	0.0	0.0	99.4	107.0	85.7	33.3	84.1	92.9
1809	96.2	97.1	94.3	113.6	0.0	0.0	99.0	93.8	88.9	110.0	88.3	92.0
1810	77.5	90.1	88.5	87.5	133.3	0.0	75.1	93.6	91.3	66.7	77.6	77.3
1815	81.7	98.3	114.3	166.7	0.0	0.0	78.7	91.7	50.0	0.0	86.2	100.0
1817	89.1	88.8	118.8	66.7	40.0	66.7	90.6	99.1	76.9	63.6	84.7	81.0
1819	94.8	89.0	86.0	73.3	125.0	0.0	92.8	94.4	133.3	76.9	93.8	98.0
1820	94.9	89.5	86.7	80.0	125.0	0.0	92.9	94.5	130.0	77.8	93.8	98.0
	CAPAYA											
1784	89.3	101.0	250.0	150.0	80.0	100.0	75.9	95.5	100.0	106.3	86.9	100.0
1802	94.6	86.3	575.0	0.0	85.5	133.3	65.6	68.8	88.9	50.0	105.5	77.1
1803	110.1	122.1	214.3	0.0	83.3	113.3	67.2	113.3	84.4	150.0	129.0	117.7
1804	101.5	124.6	0.0	600.0	88.0	180.0	83.3	122.2	82.1	90.0	106.9	109.9
1805	92.6	93.6	0.0	0.0	91.0	83.3	91.7	94.3	76.8	90.3	90.6	95.8
1806	105.2	134.1	0.0	0.0	93.8	100.0	95.0	128.6	106.9	95.1	109.1	156.7
1807	99.8	154.0	142.9	0.0	100.0	133.3	99.1	119.3	122.2	119.0	96.3	195.1
1808	91.4	154.0	142.9	0.0	95.1	133.3	99.1	119.3	122.2	119.0	82.9	195.1
1809	87.3	93.7	0.0	0.0	64.8	90.6	97.0	125.0	80.9	96.2	87.1	90.3

TABLE 4. MALE/FEMALE RATIOS (CONTINUED)

YEAR	TOTAL M/F		WHITE M/F		INDIAN M/F		PARDO M/F		NEGRO M/F		SLAVE M/F	
	ADULT	CHILD	ADULT	CHILD	ADULT	CHILD	ADULT	CHILD	ADULT	CHILD	ADULT	CHILD
1811	92.9	88.9	154.5	200.0	95.4	42.9	86.0	93.8	66.7	71.4	97.5	101.5
1812	91.1	109.9	450.0	400.0	93.7	115.8	72.9	121.2	73.9	60.0	95.5	105.9
1817	76.6	86.0	142.9	50.0	72.7	76.9	57.8	105.4	47.6	12.5	91.5	86.9
1818	83.7	100.0	175.0	50.0	76.9	123.1	53.0	125.0	74.1	87.5	102.5	88.0
1819	76.9	73.8	114.3	150.0	92.9	71.4	63.1	73.6	43.6	140.0	87.8	68.0
1820	81.0	84.4	142.9	133.3	84.1	91.7	64.1	97.4	92.3	160.0	88.2	70.7
	CARABALLEDA											
1802	99.1	129.3	148.9	144.4	74.0	140.0	65.7	180.0	0.0	0.0	117.4	106.2
1804	103.7	128.3	120.4	146.7	81.9	91.7	85.5	137.5	0.0	0.0	116.9	135.4
	CARACAS-ALTAGRACIA											
1796	59.8	86.8	61.5	88.0	0.0	0.0	60.0	85.0	69.6	77.6	53.0	92.9
1802	53.4	133.4	68.7	153.3	59.1	40.0	51.0	138.7	41.9	76.6	40.6	133.8
1803	55.3	98.8	66.1	94.9	33.3	133.3	53.2	115.4	42.3	57.1	48.5	100.0
1804	55.0	80.2	71.1	102.3	22.6	58.3	51.9	74.7	37.6	70.1	44.6	69.6
1805	53.6	119.2	61.1	120.9	37.9	175.0	57.5	122.7	46.4	108.1	41.7	104.8
1807	52.2	81.9	60.7	115.0	27.3	400.0	56.4	67.0	41.3	66.7	39.9	85.7
1808	51.3	94.1	60.2	101.9	27.8	154.5	55.6	85.0	40.3	78.0	38.6	112.6
1810	53.8	77.0	60.6	102.4	35.3	185.7	58.6	54.7	51.9	96.2	38.9	89.9
1811	47.7	102.3	61.1	120.8	41.2	0.0	42.9	89.7	37.4	115.8	41.7	101.2
1815	54.7	103.4	50.1	75.0	28.6	150.0	42.5	124.5	121.8	116.7	64.8	140.0
1816	46.5	118.1	54.4	104.2	71.4	0.0	41.7	132.8	28.6	90.9	43.4	136.4
1817	44.2	91.4	44.9	114.1	0.0	200.0	44.6	82.4	48.7	68.4	39.4	70.6
1818	40.8	94.8	47.6	95.4	47.4	20.0	30.8	101.4	25.6	85.7	59.0	92.0
1819	47.5	95.9	56.8	96.1	37.5	87.5	39.7	97.6	32.3	120.0	47.9	85.0
1820	47.9	117.0	81.1	95.2	53.8	140.0	31.5	132.4	36.5	200.0	41.0	120.0
	CARACAS-CANDELARIA											
1800	64.8	92.3	79.6	65.6	37.5	100.0	57.4	88.8	59.6	81.3	66.0	174.4
1802	68.1	93.2	74.3	89.4	41.1	250.0	67.1	89.8	60.5	52.0	66.2	123.2
1803	64.8	86.9	72.4	85.8	34.3	90.9	66.7	78.4	51.6	66.7	61.0	120.4
1804	66.8	89.1	72.9	83.1	44.4	60.0	64.0	89.6	58.7	58.3	68.6	124.4
1805	62.8	90.1	72.6	93.0	44.0	133.3	57.4	73.9	47.1	119.0	73.5	117.0
1806	67.3	85.2	73.5	90.4	56.1	60.0	62.9	69.5	51.2	88.0	81.2	127.5
1808	61.1	96.9	70.6	83.7	51.2	37.5	55.6	104.7	65.8	81.8	57.7	113.2
1809	60.8	106.1	73.7	99.3	39.2	550.0	53.9	105.6	52.9	93.3	64.2	111.7
1811	49.5	93.2	55.8	85.4	54.2	100.0	42.9	89.9	43.4	130.4	55.9	112.8
1815	36.8	97.6	35.5	101.2	26.7	75.0	40.7	95.2	39.4	96.7	29.1	100.0
1816	57.3	58.1	48.9	109.6	58.8	140.0	63.3	83.4	63.0	86.7	58.0	30.0
1817	51.7	86.0	54.5	75.0	58.6	116.7	43.3	79.6	57.8	106.1	68.9	102.3
1818	41.9	114.9	54.8	98.9	70.0	150.0	35.3	137.6	36.9	110.0	45.8	89.3
1819	44.9	114.0	50.1	93.8	46.2	75.0	40.1	127.0	41.9	90.6	52.5	127.3
1820	51.7	94.9	60.2	110.0	20.0	0.0	46.7	85.4	37.7	85.7	63.2	108.0
1821	42.9	107.9	50.3	107.4	66.7	0.0	38.0	110.7	36.6	92.9	47.1	106.1

TABLE 4. MALE/FEMALE RATIOS (CONTINUED)

YEAR	TOTAL M/F ADULT	TOTAL M/F CHILD	WHITE M/F ADULT	WHITE M/F CHILD	INDIAN M/F ADULT	INDIAN M/F CHILD	PARDO M/F ADULT	PARDO M/F CHILD	NEGRO M/F ADULT	NEGRO M/F CHILD	SLAVE M/F ADULT	SLAVE M/F CHILD
CARACAS-CATEDRAL ORIENTE												
1801	58.1	84.8	82.4	73.0	28.9	100.0	54.7	82.7	42.8	127.3	45.8	95.7
1802	58.2	93.7	87.0	115.8	37.2	100.0	53.2	93.6	56.0	89.5	42.9	80.0
1803	60.2	110.2	86.3	104.8	79.2	33.3	51.3	118.8	52.3	57.1	48.8	118.4
1804	63.4	89.4	109.8	82.5	22.5	0.0	58.2	111.5	51.4	87.5	44.4	82.9
1805	62.5	82.8	89.4	91.4	25.5	100.0	56.8	87.9	47.5	45.5	51.3	73.7
1807	55.1	87.5	79.8	86.2	31.3	50.0	42.0	84.7	35.8	150.0	52.2	87.9
1809	57.6	92.1	84.7	95.4	27.5	50.0	51.0	84.3	35.3	115.4	47.5	95.5
1811	61.4	97.9	82.5	89.4	53.3	0.0	64.2	103.0	191.1	150.0	36.2	92.6
1815	37.1	94.6	48.4	107.2	31.6	0.0	31.6	106.3	35.6	75.0	33.1	73.8
1816	68.5	90.0	51.2	71.0	73.3	140.0	72.5	91.8	75.6	148.0	90.4	79.8
1817	38.4	103.2	44.8	111.0	39.3	75.0	33.2	102.7	40.2	100.0	36.5	96.4
1818	47.8	92.6	63.9	131.1	50.0	61.5	44.9	74.5	39.7	72.2	36.7	98.6
1819	45.0	112.8	59.6	106.1	65.0	133.3	34.7	112.0	36.5	220.0	43.5	113.1
CARACAS-CATEDRAL PONIENTE												
1802	66.2	98.6	105.2	115.8	50.9	200.0	55.8	88.8	47.1	127.3	52.8	87.8
1803	70.5	97.0	109.4	108.0	67.5	50.0	59.2	93.2	67.6	112.5	54.8	91.4
1805	75.8	101.7	131.1	116.9	40.2	55.6	68.8	94.6	59.0	108.3	47.4	99.1
1807	69.2	95.8	104.5	101.1	46.2	88.9	63.1	90.6	60.0	117.6	52.5	92.9
1808	70.0	97.6	117.6	89.2	50.0	85.7	56.6	117.0	66.2	112.5	51.8	86.1
1810	70.9	98.7	110.9	97.9	75.4	150.0	61.4	117.8	51.0	50.0	55.6	87.0
1811	66.0	108.3	104.6	116.1	56.1	85.7	55.9	114.0	48.6	58.6	52.1	111.6
1815	37.9	77.8	59.5	85.9	37.8	73.3	29.3	73.7	49.4	62.5	19.0	69.6
1816	77.1	126.6	73.3	115.6	55.6	20.0	103.2	115.4	89.3	126.0	58.2	159.1
1817	49.0	94.1	70.8	108.7	43.2	100.0	39.4	85.6	52.0	85.0	34.0	86.2
1818	57.9	97.8	87.5	107.8	26.1	200.0	35.6	89.6	44.6	107.7	53.9	85.9
1819	48.7	89.1	76.9	102.3	21.4	60.0	29.5	79.5	37.8	136.4	43.0	73.4
1822	37.1	79.9	55.1	97.0	25.8	77.1	37.5	12.5	36.2	75.0	29.5	64.9
CARACAS-CURATO CASTRENSE												
1803	295.0	75.4	501.7	70.7	0.0	0.0	142.9	300.0	0.0	0.0	44.9	66.7
1804	318.3	78.7	538.6	75.0	0.0	0.0	180.0	0.0	66.7	0.0	50.6	100.0
1805	365.6	98.2	603.7	97.8	14.3	0.0	252.6	100.0	0.0	0.0	47.6	87.5
1807	412.1	113.2	507.9	93.8	66.7	0.0	559.8	167.7	26.7	0.0	49.6	100.0
1809	327.9	94.4	447.9	94.6	14.3	0.0	348.7	75.0	50.0	50.0	66.7	150.0
1810	369.5	92.2	533.3	95.0	14.3	0.0	50.0	0.0	66.7	0.0	61.5	81.8
1811	260.8	134.5	424.2	162.1	20.0	0.0	181.1	128.6	175.0	100.0	50.0	94.4
CARACAS-SAN PABLO												
1799	62.7	64.8	82.4	82.6	24.1	25.0	56.9	41.8	61.3	77.8	47.0	84.4
1801	59.2	90.8	76.7	101.4	11.9	0.0	54.9	90.9	65.7	82.4	45.7	79.3
1802	61.5	96.1	61.4	119.1	76.3	72.2	67.0	69.9	59.4	206.7	52.7	110.2
1803	81.2	67.8	120.5	65.2	77.8	125.0	55.1	52.0	94.0	100.0	66.7	123.8
1804	69.5	82.3	77.8	96.4	40.5	40.0	62.6	77.5	95.7	100.0	67.9	70.5
1805	102.0	99.7	94.0	90.3	38.9	0.0	118.2	123.3	99.2	94.3	102.5	100.0

TABLE 4. MALE/FEMALE RATIOS (CONTINUED)

YEAR	TOTAL M/F ADULT	TOTAL M/F CHILD	WHITE M/F ADULT	WHITE M/F CHILD	INDIAN M/F ADULT	INDIAN M/F CHILD	PARDO M/F ADULT	PARDO M/F CHILD	NEGRO M/F ADULT	NEGRO M/F CHILD	SLAVE M/F ADULT	SLAVE M/F CHILD
1806	103.6	87.1	95.7	52.6	41.2	120.0	133.3	120.1	85.0	94.3	100.6	100.0
1807	98.1	73.3	95.7	52.6	41.2	120.0	116.7	74.0	85.0	142.9	90.0	60.0
1808	81.9	188.3	85.7	200.0	150.0	100.0	88.2	189.4	90.3	160.0	54.5	71.4
1809	91.1	102.5	83.3	100.0	133.3	100.0	76.1	84.7	100.0	139.7	106.4	100.0
1810	94.4	70.4	64.0	50.6	86.0	60.0	100.2	85.7	128.8	124.0	100.0	59.4
1811	86.2	90.4	112.5	100.0	90.0	44.0	86.2	88.9	45.5	185.7	88.5	62.2
1815	127.1	98.7	82.7	38.9	59.7	125.0	77.8	160.0	75.0	88.9	310.7	66.7
1816	55.9	109.5	55.1	96.6	100.0	25.0	47.6	93.9	93.8	207.9	66.7	142.7
1817	61.5	94.5	67.8	86.7	100.0	25.0	51.1	104.2	93.8	210.5	67.3	77.0
1818	75.2	85.0	98.7	86.7	100.0	25.0	51.4	106.0	97.2	67.2	66.6	93.8
1820	53.1	91.1	51.9	93.2	20.5	133.3	66.7	89.0	31.4	84.8	41.0	88.5
	CARACAS-SANTA ROSALIA											
1795	67.7	110.8	83.4	107.9	0.0	0.0	58.8	131.1	0.0	0.0	61.0	70.8
1796	63.6	83.2	86.8	127.2	0.0	0.0	52.5	71.2	0.0	0.0	58.9	66.7
1798	64.3	105.9	86.7	128.5	0.0	0.0	55.3	103.8	0.0	0.0	50.4	76.9
1799	68.7	88.6	85.9	88.5	0.0	0.0	61.0	95.5	0.0	0.0	61.3	72.9
1802	60.6	89.9	77.5	95.3	19.6	300.0	57.6	93.6	44.2	100.0	49.4	67.8
1803	61.5	70.7	73.0	93.5	26.9	145.5	62.9	84.7	50.4	79.4	47.0	28.9
1804	67.7	116.6	74.3	108.5	55.6	340.0	65.9	178.6	74.5	67.9	61.1	50.6
1805	79.2	119.4	77.9	83.9	30.8	61.5	95.6	184.0	67.0	123.8	62.9	93.7
1806	60.5	98.9	83.7	110.2	23.8	53.8	46.8	87.2	43.1	117.2	77.1	111.5
1807	49.2	96.6	69.2	102.1	28.4	76.5	40.8	95.7	32.2	91.2	48.9	93.8
1808	48.0	99.0	64.2	102.6	27.5	71.4	41.0	98.6	29.5	95.2	50.9	98.5
1809	48.0	93.0	59.6	93.9	30.2	82.1	39.6	91.3	46.4	68.1	51.6	110.3
1810	54.1	87.5	66.2	92.2	48.9	200.0	50.2	86.9	45.3	78.6	46.3	78.8
1811	37.5	95.2	65.5	92.6	30.2	75.0	24.5	98.2	30.0	102.2	53.1	94.2
1815	49.3	102.3	48.8	94.2	32.1	14.3	47.9	102.0	45.9	135.7	56.9	129.7
1816	39.7	82.1	52.5	99.2	27.3	150.0	31.8	90.6	27.3	50.0	39.0	47.3
1817	51.5	76.4	52.0	109.9	25.0	0.0	48.9	53.9	57.9	155.2	55.3	41.9
1818	47.7	100.6	53.4	87.4	10.0	50.0	42.5	103.6	56.4	118.8	40.7	106.3
1819	57.6	105.3	69.8	119.4	38.5	125.0	49.2	78.9	48.6	111.8	54.9	123.2
1820	64.3	116.9	65.4	109.6	81.8	66.7	64.9	109.8	66.9	121.6	53.7	176.7
1822	61.8	94.4	65.8	95.3	30.8	200.0	54.8	95.3	70.6	87.5	75.6	82.9
	CARAMACATE											
1779	92.5	125.7	175.0	100.0	100.0	159.1	36.4	55.6	0.0	0.0	0.0	0.0
1799	114.3	109.5	121.1	141.2	88.5	88.2	120.5	85.7	0.0	600.0	75.0	0.0
1801	103.6	115.9	115.6	166.7	87.5	68.8	111.0	106.3	60.0	266.7	0.0	0.0
1802	100.5	123.9	124.1	170.0	95.0	84.6	97.7	125.4	0.0	0.0	50.0	100.0
1803	99.6	94.7	100.0	110.0	94.3	158.3	98.6	80.0	0.0	0.0	100.0	0.0
1804	85.9	84.6	114.8	130.8	104.0	122.2	77.1	74.2	0.0	0.0	50.0	0.0
1805	95.7	95.8	135.7	125.0	107.1	120.0	84.4	85.7	0.0	0.0	100.0	0.0
1806	93.4	85.4	125.0	125.0	108.7	120.0	83.1	71.4	100.0	0.0	200.0	0.0
1807	113.9	105.1	111.1	81.8	113.6	87.0	112.3	111.0	133.3	200.0	0.0	0.0
1809	98.5	111.9	83.3	136.4	34.0	111.1	185.7	108.7	200.0	0.0	0.0	0.0
1811	94.4	117.1	140.0	63.6	77.3	170.0	95.0	118.0	0.0	0.0	0.0	0.0
1812	95.5	104.7	112.5	100.0	73.7	200.0	101.0	92.2	0.0	0.0	0.0	0.0
1817	74.1	132.7	73.3	100.0	85.7	166.7	72.3	132.5	0.0	0.0	0.0	0.0

TABLE 4. MALE/FEMALE RATIOS (CONTINUED)

YEAR	TOTAL M/F ADULT	TOTAL M/F CHILD	WHITE M/F ADULT	WHITE M/F CHILD	INDIAN M/F ADULT	INDIAN M/F CHILD	PARDO M/F ADULT	PARDO M/F CHILD	NEGRO M/F ADULT	NEGRO M/F CHILD	SLAVE M/F ADULT	SLAVE M/F CHILD
1818	77.8	75.4	72.7	160.0	95.2	77.8	73.7	65.1	0.0	0.0	0.0	0.0
1819	98.1	75.4	82.4	133.3	85.7	200.0	106.1	56.1	0.0	0.0	0.0	0.0
1822	60.8	66.0	66.7	62.5	100.0	100.0	53.7	63.4	0.0	0.0	0.0	0.0
1823	68.4	72.3	83.3	80.0	112.5	150.0	59.7	67.5	0.0	0.0	0.0	0.0
1828	68.3	76.6	90.0	120.0	112.5	150.0	59.7	67.5	0.0	0.0	0.0	0.0
1829	71.3	73.4	85.7	66.7	77.3	50.0	66.2	80.4	0.0	0.0	0.0	0.0
1831	85.6	73.0	85.7	57.1	80.8	75.0	83.9	75.0	200.0	0.0	0.0	0.0
1832	85.4	73.0	84.6	57.1	80.8	75.0	83.6	75.0	150.0	0.0	0.0	0.0
1833	83.0	78.3	90.0	0.0	87.5	72.7	79.3	90.0	100.0	60.0	0.0	0.0
1834	85.9	78.8	90.0	83.3	95.7	72.7	83.1	81.0	71.4	71.4	0.0	0.0
1835	88.9	83.6	85.7	62.5	90.0	80.0	90.6	90.2	77.8	77.8	0.0	0.0
1836	90.2	84.8	86.7	62.5	93.9	93.8	90.8	86.7	80.0	80.0	0.0	0.0
1837	90.2	85.5	85.7	80.0	94.4	88.9	92.9	86.7	66.7	80.0	0.0	0.0
1838	92.0	83.3	85.7	80.0	92.7	85.7	95.7	87.0	75.0	66.7	0.0	0.0
	CARAYACA											
1802	118.7	116.5	130.6	123.3	100.0	50.0	120.8	150.0	134.9	105.9	104.9	108.3
1804	132.2	120.3	129.4	180.0	100.0	100.0	144.7	154.5	156.7	121.4	126.5	96.9
1805	119.1	105.7	115.6	138.5	145.5	0.0	118.2	84.8	103.6	100.0	124.0	108.8
1807	119.1	105.7	115.6	138.5	145.5	0.0	118.2	84.8	103.6	100.0	124.0	108.8
1808	119.1	105.7	115.6	138.5	145.5	0.0	118.2	84.8	103.6	100.0	124.0	108.8
1809	119.1	105.7	115.6	138.5	145.5	0.0	118.2	84.8	103.6	100.0	124.0	108.8
1810	119.1	105.7	115.6	138.5	145.5	0.0	118.2	84.8	103.6	100.0	124.0	108.8
1811	124.5	110.6	108.3	138.5	145.5	0.0	108.2	90.3	115.8	114.3	140.9	111.8
1817	104.2	114.2	120.8	107.1	0.0	0.0	104.2	107.0	78.0	200.0	104.3	125.0
1818	106.0	101.8	93.0	113.2	500.0	50.0	94.1	97.5	207.7	66.7	135.6	104.2
1819	117.9	78.3	108.2	84.8	0.0	200.0	118.8	73.7	111.8	66.7	119.5	71.9
1820	101.2	102.4	84.5	86.8	150.0	300.0	99.1	83.3	125.0	125.0	117.2	153.8
1833	63.5	76.7	68.8	110.3	43.5	64.3	63.0	72.0	66.7	75.7	62.9	67.1
	CARORA											
1802	63.0	98.6	71.9	75.0	25.0	300.0	62.0	94.0	53.4	115.6	73.3	134.5
1803	64.1	99.9	61.4	75.7	47.8	300.0	64.7	96.1	54.9	117.5	71.2	126.5
1804	65.3	98.3	61.0	72.0	39.3	150.0	65.7	95.2	59.5	97.7	75.0	145.2
1809	61.7	94.3	63.2	85.0	45.5	75.0	59.8	90.9	67.0	92.3	80.3	127.1
1815	62.8	112.6	50.2	120.0	42.9	0.0	66.1	109.5	111.1	127.3	39.5	175.0
	CARUAO											
1811	88.2	36.6	0.0	0.0	0.0	0.0	107.9	100.0	50.0	0.0	84.0	23.9
1815	104.7	110.2	0.0	0.0	50.0	0.0	200.0	0.0	14.3	111.1	110.3	114.6
	CASIGUA											
1780	94.7	90.8	89.5	95.3	115.8	60.0	79.1	88.7	114.3	87.7	119.5	93.0
	CATA											
1803	104.2	70.0	0.0	0.0	0.0	0.0	0.0	0.0	90.7	100.0	107.1	51.6

TABLE 4. MALE/FEMALE RATIOS (CONTINUED)

YEAR	TOTAL M/F		WHITE M/F		INDIAN M/F		PARDO M/F		NEGRO M/F		SLAVE M/F	
	ADULT	CHILD	ADULT	CHILD	ADULT	CHILD	ADULT	CHILD	ADULT	CHILD	ADULT	CHILD
1804	101.4	71.4	0.0	100.0	0.0	0.0	0.0	0.0	92.0	95.5	106.6	54.5
1805	98.2	67.2	0.0	50.0	0.0	0.0	90.9	77.8	91.0	92.9	99.3	54.5
	CAUCAGUA											
1784	108.8	120.4	100.0	105.9	76.4	146.7	111.3	105.0	127.9	85.7	110.6	130.0
1802	85.5	105.6	114.8	63.6	82.4	55.6	77.2	125.0	90.1	121.7	85.0	110.7
1803	93.6	106.9	134.6	50.0	70.0	66.7	97.2	128.6	87.0	133.3	94.4	106.8
1804	93.5	92.3	121.4	55.6	77.1	66.7	102.7	85.3	86.8	83.9	93.2	99.4
1805	96.4	94.8	154.5	71.4	79.1	65.0	108.1	105.7	87.0	82.4	95.0	99.4
1806	95.4	92.3	154.2	16.7	69.6	72.2	96.2	97.5	85.5	96.8	96.5	94.9
1807	97.2	91.4	157.7	28.6	90.9	84.2	93.4	91.4	87.2	91.9	96.6	94.7
1808	98.8	167.5	134.5	33.3	56.9	125.0	125.5	86.7	110.9	111.1	96.8	192.2
1809	94.9	90.0	121.4	50.0	90.3	68.4	100.0	71.4	75.8	85.7	96.0	94.7
1811	91.9	74.5	121.6	150.0	62.2	136.4	78.1	91.7	75.0	50.0	98.2	64.4
1812	79.3	76.6	90.3	44.4	72.7	71.4	71.1	82.5	80.0	50.0	82.2	81.1
1816	79.3	97.8	111.1	108.3	56.4	90.9	54.2	74.3	64.4	175.0	86.7	101.7
1817	73.0	91.2	72.7	128.6	51.4	62.5	53.2	84.4	37.0	87.5	83.8	94.6
1818	74.4	83.6	96.2	140.0	41.1	34.8	57.5	95.8	23.5	133.3	86.0	86.9
1819	74.4	95.5	111.8	142.9	56.4	90.0	60.4	105.7	61.5	85.7	80.0	91.5
1820	73.1	102.3	80.4	55.6	50.0	120.0	63.3	102.1	55.6	125.0	81.2	105.5
	CERRITO											
1779	84.6	99.3	95.4	96.9	82.2	87.0	81.5	103.6	66.7	0.0	67.9	73.3
	CHABASQUEN											
1802	80.7	70.1	73.2	91.3	81.4	66.2	81.5	86.0	75.0	0.0	75.0	100.0
1803	81.1	69.9	73.6	88.0	81.4	65.1	83.3	86.4	100.0	100.0	77.8	166.7
1804	81.3	67.8	75.5	77.8	81.3	63.2	84.1	84.4	66.7	200.0	88.9	166.7
1805	81.4	69.5	73.7	86.2	81.7	64.6	85.0	86.0	50.0	150.0	90.0	125.0
1806	81.8	68.5	75.0	80.0	82.2	64.5	84.3	84.4	40.0	150.0	100.0	80.0
1808	81.1	73.9	66.7	111.1	81.6	66.9	84.7	111.4	100.0	0.0	50.0	0.0
1809	81.5	73.0	50.0	50.0	82.3	69.1	76.7	90.6	100.0	0.0	133.3	0.0
1812	107.0	115.8	87.5	80.0	114.8	97.5	90.5	250.0	140.0	150.0	75.0	0.0
1815	101.1	110.0	61.1	125.0	108.8	94.6	88.1	160.0	125.0	75.0	71.4	100.0
1816	87.6	118.9	61.1	187.5	104.8	109.1	60.7	157.9	66.7	75.0	37.5	0.0
1817	87.6	125.0	66.7	233.3	101.2	111.1	64.7	166.7	77.3	75.0	33.3	0.0
1818	87.6	125.0	66.7	233.3	101.2	111.1	64.7	166.7	77.3	75.0	33.3	0.0
1819	77.0	58.7	57.1	54.5	88.4	51.7	58.7	81.1	50.0	125.0	16.7	0.0
1820	77.0	67.9	80.3	64.6	80.1	63.1	65.9	79.7	100.0	0.0	33.3	0.0
1829	86.4	121.6	93.6	138.1	81.6	116.7	104.9	132.0	62.0	107.4	50.0	0.0
	CHACAO											
1802	100.3	99.6	86.0	102.9	115.0	20.0	103.7	93.2	82.0	128.6	122.6	91.8
1803	99.7	109.5	90.5	89.2	66.7	120.0	93.1	131.9	78.4	136.7	130.2	104.7
1804	101.5	110.7	84.7	112.5	85.0	50.0	93.6	105.7	87.0	140.0	134.2	104.9
1805	97.0	105.3	89.2	100.0	90.9	100.0	82.9	112.3	81.7	122.2	125.8	98.7
1808	107.6	100.7	102.5	93.2	300.0	0.0	100.0	126.3	118.0	93.1	108.8	101.0

TABLE 4. MALE/FEMALE RATIOS (CONTINUED)

YEAR	TOTAL M/F ADULT	TOTAL M/F CHILD	WHITE M/F ADULT	WHITE M/F CHILD	INDIAN M/F ADULT	INDIAN M/F CHILD	PARDO M/F ADULT	PARDO M/F CHILD	NEGRO M/F ADULT	NEGRO M/F CHILD	SLAVE M/F ADULT	SLAVE M/F CHILD
1811	92.5	108.0	84.9	126.2	60.0	0.0	90.3	98.1	90.0	100.0	101.9	106.1
1815	66.3	98.1	56.6	96.8	118.2	50.0	62.0	97.8	75.0	96.9	74.7	101.4
1818	90.9	93.6	88.0	80.4	100.0	0.0	87.2	107.7	76.7	80.0	111.5	90.0
1819	91.4	93.3	94.1	89.6	0.0	0.0	92.4	98.3	75.6	83.3	89.6	97.2
	CHAGUARAMAL											
1783	117.4	98.2	131.5	106.6	104.9	138.9	107.3	86.1	73.1	150.0	141.0	94.1
1804	115.1	102.3	141.2	91.9	154.8	150.0	102.0	110.6	150.0	66.7	120.7	127.3
1805	95.1	77.3	73.1	76.5	88.2	53.3	87.5	81.4	118.2	65.5	122.4	78.9
	CHAGUARAMAS											
1783	115.4	70.7	122.9	19.8	83.8	200.0	84.3	70.3	98.3	126.2	152.6	84.7
1802	119.2	123.4	133.7	125.5	131.1	191.7	93.8	107.1	67.5	185.7	178.3	143.9
1803	125.3	107.5	134.1	168.8	106.5	400.0	111.8	79.1	0.0	0.0	145.5	138.8
1804	112.5	97.9	135.7	159.6	105.9	325.0	112.2	79.7	0.0	0.0	94.5	90.4
1805	120.4	124.7	114.8	111.5	113.5	100.0	107.8	124.5	78.1	156.3	176.2	146.3
1808	109.2	116.2	114.4	116.3	98.4	57.1	85.7	120.1	115.8	76.3	193.8	162.5
1810	118.7	124.3	125.1	121.6	98.7	76.9	91.0	119.5	134.3	250.0	200.7	161.1
	CHARALLAVE											
1783	100.6	115.9	92.5	109.1	107.3	121.6	89.7	100.0	133.3	0.0	87.5	50.0
1802	105.7	103.7	101.9	86.2	111.0	117.9	111.7	82.6	117.9	183.3	69.7	57.1
1803	102.6	111.0	94.0	108.3	102.3	120.0	133.8	85.2	125.0	111.1	66.7	100.0
1804	103.6	115.8	105.4	120.3	95.9	119.2	130.4	93.1	94.5	105.3	110.5	300.0
1805	100.2	96.3	86.1	90.5	103.5	106.8	123.8	94.1	142.4	73.7	104.2	133.3
1806	107.1	99.5	92.3	91.3	126.5	135.6	108.6	90.0	132.0	60.0	121.7	37.5
1807	96.8	116.7	83.4	114.5	97.3	139.4	130.8	83.3	107.4	90.0	106.3	150.0
1808	101.1	83.0	92.4	92.5	111.8	104.9	117.5	66.0	118.2	112.5	88.5	42.1
1810	101.9	117.6	93.7	125.0	116.5	83.7	114.5	160.0	69.2	633.3	72.1	75.0
1811	90.5	99.0	85.0	106.3	93.8	95.7	103.3	87.8	62.5	100.0	100.0	128.6
1815	79.5	94.6	78.5	98.2	79.3	96.8	82.5	84.8	87.5	110.0	70.6	69.2
1816	78.6	103.1	73.1	98.5	75.5	99.1	96.1	132.0	106.3	140.0	66.7	53.3
1817	83.6	102.6	81.3	94.6	78.6	104.1	107.1	122.4	55.6	100.0	57.1	63.6
	CHIVACOA											
1782	72.2	89.2	170.6	66.7	69.7	92.7	69.8	86.0	77.8	69.2	80.0	0.0
1802	73.0	90.8	73.3	100.0	75.4	89.4	66.9	97.2	87.5	125.0	110.0	33.3
1803	70.9	98.0	68.0	400.0	75.2	87.0	92.3	75.0	63.8	102.9	100.0	200.0
1804	81.8	91.2	68.6	140.0	93.2	87.6	71.0	98.9	73.7	73.3	100.0	60.0
1805	68.8	102.1	73.3	166.7	64.8	134.6	70.2	77.2	95.7	40.0	100.0	140.0
1807	76.9	88.7	79.4	57.1	81.4	105.4	70.2	70.9	85.0	125.0	63.6	66.7
1808	75.1	98.8	69.8	40.0	79.4	121.7	69.2	94.8	92.3	50.0	69.6	55.6
1809	72.1	85.1	84.2	71.4	64.9	88.5	73.1	83.3	89.7	100.0	105.3	42.9
1810	91.2	87.2	79.4	71.4	108.7	76.1	75.9	95.5	60.5	123.5	63.2	71.4
1811	73.0	94.5	67.6	100.0	75.6	94.2	72.6	92.7	67.6	103.7	68.4	83.3
1812	80.4	76.8	81.8	85.7	91.7	54.3	69.1	98.1	75.0	96.3	94.4	25.0
1815	74.2	99.3	86.1	111.1	73.7	98.0	73.2	98.8	71.1	136.4	88.2	0.0

TABLE 4. MALE/FEMALE RATIOS (CONTINUED)

YEAR	TOTAL M/F		WHITE M/F		INDIAN M/F		PARDO M/F		NEGRO M/F		SLAVE M/F	
	ADULT	CHILD	ADULT	CHILD	ADULT	CHILD	ADULT	CHILD	ADULT	CHILD	ADULT	CHILD
1816	90.6	93.6	72.9	110.0	111.0	63.1	76.1	107.7	84.8	160.0	80.0	200.0
1817	81.5	98.9	94.7	83.3	79.5	83.5	81.6	111.9	86.7	200.0	77.8	0.0
1818	72.8	85.3	78.2	82.1	65.1	80.7	76.7	83.7	87.9	152.9	75.0	33.3
1819	70.1	87.2	73.6	83.3	64.6	84.3	72.6	83.5	81.8	147.4	85.7	50.0
	CHORONI											
1802	91.2	88.0	80.9	173.3	71.4	66.7	87.6	82.0	60.0	83.3	114.5	87.0
1803	83.2	106.7	98.1	111.1	71.4	66.7	75.4	113.2	60.0	71.4	106.6	93.2
1804	82.0	110.4	101.9	116.7	71.4	66.7	74.2	115.5	70.6	71.4	108.9	76.9
1805	77.0	127.0	98.2	105.6	80.0	100.0	69.2	143.6	66.7	150.0	93.3	95.0
1808	75.3	113.4	105.3	116.7	37.5	66.7	65.8	125.1	42.9	66.7	98.0	84.9
1809	86.9	118.4	94.6	168.0	60.0	100.0	86.1	117.0	50.0	80.0	93.7	106.3
1819	53.5	90.6	45.7	300.0	0.0	0.0	62.2	82.0	0.0	0.0	34.3	104.2
	CHUAO											
1802	95.1	80.9	0.0	0.0	0.0	0.0	300.0	133.3	0.0	0.0	90.9	77.3
1803	95.0	78.8	0.0	0.0	0.0	0.0	0.0	133.3	0.0	0.0	90.9	75.5
1804	93.1	102.1	0.0	0.0	0.0	0.0	300.0	100.0	0.0	0.0	89.2	102.2
1805	83.4	114.3	0.0	0.0	0.0	0.0	50.0	166.7	0.0	0.0	83.9	110.3
1819	72.3	120.0	0.0	0.0	0.0	0.0	133.3	400.0	0.0	0.0	69.6	119.1
	COCOROTE											
1781	66.1	122.0	73.6	157.9	54.5	117.2	88.5	120.6	60.6	152.9	89.5	93.8
1782	67.6	122.0	73.6	157.9	54.5	117.2	88.5	120.6	71.2	152.9	113.2	93.8
1788	62.2	106.8	73.9	104.8	52.1	95.7	63.4	118.8	65.3	137.5	94.1	94.4
1791	64.0	83.4	64.2	63.6	60.9	80.7	66.1	85.3	69.2	84.6	58.0	185.7
1794	62.8	99.3	59.7	120.6	55.3	94.1	63.9	104.6	79.6	68.4	74.5	150.0
1802	65.1	109.0	66.9	96.2	60.2	108.9	66.5	117.9	57.7	100.0	69.6	75.0
1803	74.3	88.1	88.8	87.8	94.9	98.6	62.3	84.0	64.7	120.0	91.1	80.0
1804	68.3	105.7	69.2	96.3	64.3	98.5	66.5	100.9	78.7	176.0	67.9	75.0
1805	70.5	113.1	84.8	117.6	72.2	103.8	65.1	120.2	72.7	180.0	65.5	55.6
1807	68.8	112.3	88.8	100.0	61.1	102.5	67.7	111.9	77.1	141.9	57.4	125.0
1808	69.0	109.4	67.3	96.3	66.9	111.8	63.2	98.8	81.3	141.7	76.1	100.0
1809	75.2	126.3	88.8	87.0	73.4	178.3	69.5	112.2	80.6	116.7	75.0	150.0
1811	73.2	99.1	86.3	95.7	66.2	94.7	71.4	102.4	74.8	111.8	86.4	14.3
1812	74.6	103.5	89.9	71.1	63.8	107.0	73.8	129.7	76.5	89.1	116.0	100.0
1817	65.7	49.0	127.6	50.0	54.5	76.2	66.8	33.3	73.3	56.3	42.9	33.3
1818	63.3	77.0	75.3	72.1	45.6	76.8	72.2	79.4	0.0	0.0	88.2	63.6
1820	65.7	49.0	127.6	50.0	54.5	76.2	66.8	33.3	73.3	56.3	42.9	33.3
1821	60.1	101.4	74.3	92.6	55.8	112.5	60.5	98.4	0.0	0.0	33.3	300.0
	COJEDES											
1779	99.5	101.3	107.3	89.6	98.0	96.5	96.3	128.9	0.0	0.0	100.0	0.0
1799	103.3	108.7	99.5	101.0	93.2	126.4	91.8	94.9	87.5	120.0	228.6	130.0
1801	95.0	96.6	101.9	103.1	83.2	71.6	94.5	93.8	65.0	162.5	176.5	228.6
1802	92.1	107.6	93.3	125.6	84.9	105.8	91.2	93.8	150.0	100.0	113.0	117.4
1803	99.8	123.7	95.8	125.4	89.0	141.6	110.8	107.4	100.0	0.0	111.1	138.9

TABLE 4. MALE/FEMALE RATIOS (CONTINUED)

YEAR	TOTAL M/F		WHITE M/F		INDIAN M/F		PARDO M/F		NEGRO M/F		SLAVE M/F	
	ADULT	CHILD	ADULT	CHILD	ADULT	CHILD	ADULT	CHILD	ADULT	CHILD	ADULT	CHILD
1804	99.7	118.5	96.7	94.5	88.3	146.8	110.8	112.3	100.0	0.0	106.1	130.0
1805	108.9	120.1	100.5	115.7	85.2	149.3	137.0	100.8	66.7	0.0	139.0	145.5
1806	109.1	97.5	99.5	84.4	116.1	93.5	110.1	101.6	100.0	0.0	115.9	133.3
1807	108.3	102.6	104.1	106.6	112.2	90.1	103.3	114.3	100.0	0.0	129.8	84.8
1808	98.0	158.1	105.8	127.4	95.7	166.2	97.5	109.9	100.0	0.0	82.0	550.0
1809	97.7	107.3	83.1	114.3	100.0	113.6	101.8	88.6	50.0	0.0	130.2	159.3
1811	86.6	90.6	97.6	88.5	80.8	82.1	89.6	104.3	0.0	0.0	88.5	82.6
1812	86.5	83.7	96.8	87.1	78.2	72.1	91.4	95.9	0.0	0.0	92.6	84.0
1816	85.8	85.1	97.8	90.3	76.6	73.6	90.7	96.1	0.0	0.0	94.5	85.2
1817	84.2	83.5	97.8	93.3	76.4	71.3	85.8	90.8	0.0	0.0	94.5	92.0
1818	83.4	83.2	90.1	72.2	77.9	84.7	86.7	83.1	0.0	0.0	87.5	92.9
1819	83.8	94.6	83.1	77.8	77.2	95.1	93.2	104.5	55.6	116.7	87.0	87.5
1820	86.3	85.5	84.3	84.6	77.3	86.6	94.4	89.8	69.2	120.0	116.0	65.5
1822	95.9	86.0	92.6	79.3	93.5	83.1	95.8	89.8	107.7	120.0	122.2	78.9
1823	92.1	85.2	91.2	76.9	86.5	80.7	95.1	89.4	127.3	120.0	72.7	77.8
1824	84.5	86.6	71.9	89.3	82.3	80.4	88.5	86.4	108.3	160.0	72.7	77.8
1829	83.4	90.6	90.3	87.1	63.6	88.3	92.2	91.8	127.3	120.0	75.0	0.0
1831	87.5	86.8	92.9	64.5	89.2	87.1	85.2	93.3	120.0	100.0	75.0	0.0
1833	87.2	86.2	92.7	73.3	92.6	76.9	80.4	97.7	150.0	83.3	100.0	0.0
1834	88.6	90.3	90.7	76.9	97.4	86.2	80.8	97.7	150.0	83.3	106.7	0.0
1835	91.8	92.2	90.5	85.7	94.4	89.9	90.1	91.9	85.7	137.5	107.1	0.0
1836	91.0	92.9	89.4	78.8	93.5	94.2	89.4	93.1	85.7	137.5	107.1	0.0
1837	95.8	91.9	89.4	82.4	99.2	91.7	95.3	91.6	93.8	130.0	107.1	0.0
1838	94.5	91.1	88.1	82.4	99.1	90.7	94.7	90.6	75.0	130.0	107.1	0.0
	CUA											
1783	102.4	120.0	175.9	162.5	80.0	120.0	77.5	131.8	109.4	161.5	102.6	110.3
1803	100.1	102.1	148.4	145.5	118.0	109.4	81.5	136.7	108.5	122.6	97.0	81.5
1805	87.0	102.2	123.1	155.6	98.0	95.7	69.5	97.0	68.0	132.4	88.4	89.6
1810	93.6	105.3	132.2	142.9	87.7	71.7	87.0	124.7	106.7	88.6	87.2	101.0
1812	90.0	120.9	89.6	105.3	71.4	78.9	86.4	113.4	38.1	69.2	99.5	213.3
1815	78.3	112.2	114.6	125.0	51.9	90.9	72.4	109.7	86.0	128.6	79.1	113.3
1816	74.8	95.7	99.2	105.4	55.7	103.6	74.4	89.9	61.4	88.9	75.7	97.8
1818	94.1	117.6	91.8	104.8	85.4	104.5	86.3	105.1	45.8	77.4	103.4	202.0
1820	65.7	120.1	89.9	146.2	70.4	158.3	65.6	132.7	76.7	134.8	58.9	101.8
1821	111.7	86.6	80.0	78.9	92.0	75.0	113.0	83.3	127.3	53.3	116.7	92.3
	CUBIRO											
1802	97.4	89.0	125.0	0.0	91.8	86.0	100.0	55.6	166.7	0.0	350.0	250.0
1803	104.2	80.0	0.0	0.0	100.4	84.4	100.0	50.0	60.0	0.0	242.9	60.0
1804	105.2	68.1	0.0	0.0	98.8	73.0	100.0	50.0	0.0	0.0	360.0	50.0
1805	106.8	78.8	0.0	0.0	99.3	82.2	87.0	22.2	533.3	200.0	316.7	100.0
1806	103.3	80.3	0.0	0.0	97.4	82.6	82.6	55.6	225.0	200.0	285.7	57.1
1807	103.3	85.8	0.0	0.0	97.4	88.0	82.6	66.7	225.0	200.0	333.3	57.1
1808	103.0	98.3	0.0	0.0	97.4	102.0	78.3	66.7	225.0	300.0	285.7	57.1
1809	101.7	101.6	0.0	0.0	97.4	105.4	60.9	66.7	225.0	300.0	285.7	57.1
1810	103.0	100.8	0.0	0.0	97.4	104.3	78.3	66.7	225.0	300.0	285.7	57.1
1815	102.1	95.8	0.0	0.0	98.6	97.1	91.7	160.0	250.0	300.0	114.3	12.5
1816	119.6	116.7	0.0	0.0	122.1	116.2	89.5	137.5	66.7	0.0	83.3	85.7

TABLE 4. MALE/FEMALE RATIOS (CONTINUED)

YEAR	TOTAL M/F ADULT	TOTAL M/F CHILD	WHITE M/F ADULT	WHITE M/F CHILD	INDIAN M/F ADULT	INDIAN M/F CHILD	PARDO M/F ADULT	PARDO M/F CHILD	NEGRO M/F ADULT	NEGRO M/F CHILD	SLAVE M/F ADULT	SLAVE M/F CHILD
1817	120.8	111.2	0.0	0.0	123.6	115.5	85.0	91.7	75.0	66.7	100.0	100.0
1818	94.3	104.5	0.0	100.0	94.8	91.9	76.3	350.0	100.0	200.0	133.3	0.0
1819	93.2	104.5	0.0	100.0	94.0	91.9	76.3	350.0	100.0	200.0	133.3	0.0
1820	96.6	96.1	0.0	100.0	98.1	83.6	76.3	350.0	125.0	300.0	133.3	0.0
	CUNAVICHE											
1780	97.4	93.2	0.0	0.0	96.8	93.2	0.0	0.0	0.0	0.0	0.0	0.0
	CUPIRA											
1784	106.2	118.3	128.9	104.3	87.5	45.5	94.3	165.5	82.8	88.9	120.6	130.4
1802	90.4	120.9	110.2	68.8	200.0	40.0	64.2	130.4	83.9	152.6	120.0	225.0
1803	102.8	107.2	106.7	62.5	260.0	33.3	82.5	117.4	106.0	130.0	118.8	225.0
1804	94.2	123.1	97.7	53.8	275.0	42.9	94.7	134.8	69.8	176.5	106.7	180.0
1805	89.4	126.4	95.1	216.7	133.3	75.0	75.4	61.1	78.6	145.0	127.6	220.0
1807	88.7	114.0	100.0	66.7	75.0	100.0	80.3	88.2	80.9	168.4	121.4	90.0
1808	85.7	100.0	88.9	44.4	50.0	166.7	80.0	87.1	83.7	183.3	117.9	72.7
1809	93.0	110.0	100.0	50.0	90.0	100.0	76.0	124.0	102.1	176.9	118.5	42.9
1811	95.5	84.4	88.2	27.3	100.0	81.3	86.4	111.1	103.4	146.7	100.0	41.2
	CURARIGUA											
1802	43.1	110.3	115.2	146.2	100.0	60.0	86.4	93.5	108.3	112.3	6.5	200.0
1803	91.2	89.3	85.2	80.8	87.5	75.0	90.4	87.5	84.7	91.6	245.5	150.0
1804	96.3	96.5	100.0	84.0	66.7	150.0	93.2	94.6	90.9	97.3	255.6	133.3
1805	94.0	94.1	94.3	81.5	83.3	71.4	86.4	63.2	91.2	103.9	200.0	60.0
1806	99.7	110.9	93.6	128.6	72.7	107.7	96.2	80.0	98.8	111.9	230.0	150.0
1807	96.9	109.0	87.5	118.2	73.7	125.0	97.5	81.3	98.8	112.1	250.0	66.7
1808	98.1	97.8	88.9	89.7	87.0	125.0	102.8	81.3	96.9	106.3	333.3	66.7
1809	98.4	101.4	88.9	96.6	78.9	190.0	98.5	74.4	100.0	109.2	333.3	60.0
1810	129.2	107.3	87.9	128.0	84.2	150.0	102.9	84.4	99.4	108.6	3566.7	150.0
1816	96.8	95.2	80.4	77.3	0.0	0.0	98.6	96.9	120.0	100.0	80.0	100.0
1817	86.2	95.6	100.0	120.0	0.0	0.0	82.7	94.5	90.7	133.3	140.0	25.0
1818	78.7	103.0	76.5	112.5	0.0	0.0	81.6	99.4	60.0	200.0	100.0	33.3
1819	79.7	111.8	93.0	204.2	135.0	155.6	70.3	96.2	76.8	114.3	240.0	200.0
1820	74.9	107.4	79.7	137.5	128.6	216.7	72.7	105.6	59.2	66.7	155.6	150.0
	CURIEPE											
1784	93.6	104.6	215.4	150.0	366.7	0.0	72.1	123.1	86.5	88.0	102.0	107.1
1803	90.6	121.1	225.0	75.0	131.6	166.7	91.2	183.0	72.7	93.5	99.6	91.0
1804	83.8	104.1	211.8	33.3	141.2	140.0	42.9	128.8	83.9	85.2	102.1	109.3
1805	104.5	94.5	188.2	57.1	420.0	100.0	94.4	90.6	95.3	96.1	110.5	97.8
1806	98.5	74.3	336.4	28.6	236.4	66.7	92.1	50.0	85.1	86.0	103.6	91.5
1807	102.4	104.9	290.9	50.0	221.1	33.3	84.4	159.6	94.5	90.0	112.7	100.0
1808	101.7	100.0	290.9	50.0	215.0	25.0	82.0	158.0	96.2	84.9	111.2	94.4
1811	119.6	95.0	244.4	160.0	113.5	125.0	92.4	102.9	146.0	71.4	119.2	150.0
1812	121.1	99.3	223.8	142.9	125.0	170.0	93.1	100.0	145.9	79.0	122.2	139.1
1816	67.6	109.2	119.0	16.7	233.3	0.0	62.3	112.1	52.8	122.0	80.4	103.6
1817	63.3	104.3	220.0	40.0	78.6	0.0	48.0	98.8	52.0	130.4	91.5	94.1

TABLE 4. MALE/FEMALE RATIOS (CONTINUED)

YEAR	TOTAL M/F ADULT	TOTAL M/F CHILD	WHITE M/F ADULT	WHITE M/F CHILD	INDIAN M/F ADULT	INDIAN M/F CHILD	PARDO M/F ADULT	PARDO M/F CHILD	NEGRO M/F ADULT	NEGRO M/F CHILD	SLAVE M/F ADULT	SLAVE M/F CHILD
1818	67.5	103.7	96.4	266.7	150.0	0.0	60.6	101.3	61.5	100.0	76.6	97.0
1819	70.6	103.7	92.6	300.0	150.0	0.0	63.7	101.1	64.4	98.0	81.9	98.7
1820	69.1	113.1	65.5	180.0	162.5	0.0	66.8	110.5	63.7	125.5	72.8	100.0
CUYAGUA												
1802	86.4	113.4	220.0	0.0	55.0	100.0	79.5	63.2	69.7	212.5	97.3	119.4
1803	92.0	104.3	0.0	0.0	60.0	0.0	93.3	93.3	72.9	100.0	106.1	105.3
1804	83.4	102.9	0.0	0.0	42.9	0.0	97.5	123.1	49.1	66.7	98.5	116.7
1805	81.9	107.6	0.0	0.0	50.0	0.0	81.6	100.0	57.9	81.8	85.2	117.0
1808	90.2	151.8	200.0	100.0	60.0	0.0	120.8	50.0	68.5	109.1	92.2	263.2
1809	86.0	125.3	0.0	0.0	100.0	0.0	103.6	78.6	65.3	125.0	86.5	137.5
1815	100.0	134.4	200.0	150.0	40.0	50.0	90.0	250.0	0.0	0.0	95.2	111.1
DIVINA PASTORA DEL JOBAL												
1781	103.8	96.3	109.6	76.7	113.1	105.9	87.1	93.0	92.9	83.3	162.5	200.0
1798	93.7	97.5	108.1	104.9	83.4	100.0	83.9	99.4	113.2	85.6	74.4	160.0
1799	93.9	101.3	111.8	109.9	82.5	557.1	82.3	96.6	114.5	63.8	73.9	114.3
1801	97.1	92.6	101.7	84.4	99.0	91.0	95.4	95.7	116.7	0.0	85.3	0.0
1802	79.8	83.3	96.0	71.4	66.5	85.7	83.2	85.6	60.7	78.3	81.4	170.0
1803	81.5	84.2	97.8	72.7	68.4	89.5	84.4	86.7	62.1	77.4	86.0	145.5
1804	93.7	109.1	83.8	99.0	95.7	154.2	98.9	102.2	125.0	100.0	87.5	140.0
1805	96.6	111.1	115.8	96.2	77.0	115.0	102.3	139.6	69.3	68.6	86.8	175.0
1806	93.6	92.1	96.5	78.9	90.6	103.1	93.1	99.1	100.0	0.0	88.2	76.9
1807	93.4	97.9	102.6	93.1	81.0	132.5	91.1	86.9	125.0	0.0	81.1	357.1
1808	81.2	106.4	87.2	105.2	87.3	103.8	76.0	108.9	233.3	0.0	69.7	83.3
1809	96.6	111.1	115.8	96.2	77.0	115.0	102.3	139.6	69.3	68.6	86.8	175.0
1811	87.2	104.0	96.9	110.0	87.9	96.5	84.3	104.8	0.0	0.0	51.3	100.0
1815	88.0	104.7	80.6	105.4	120.0	121.3	78.7	107.3	102.1	88.5	31.6	28.6
1816	88.0	111.1	80.6	151.3	120.0	132.6	78.7	109.7	102.1	85.3	31.6	31.3
1817	89.3	104.2	83.9	108.1	127.1	121.3	78.7	105.4	97.8	87.1	31.6	30.8
1818	56.3	115.2	63.7	77.2	85.5	145.5	41.8	126.5	38.2	87.2	28.6	131.3
1819	105.8	116.2	95.9	151.4	95.8	93.8	114.7	117.2	83.3	0.0	31.4	33.3
1820	100.9	87.0	87.4	107.2	101.2	74.4	108.4	86.3	116.7	12.5	46.7	33.3
1822	74.9	67.5	61.8	56.1	59.2	89.1	88.1	61.9	0.0	0.0	40.6	30.4
1824	87.2	84.1	98.8	104.3	73.8	95.1	87.4	82.1	200.0	0.0	58.3	29.4
1825	88.1	78.6	102.4	64.6	65.5	92.4	89.9	81.5	200.0	0.0	58.3	29.4
1829	87.8	65.5	92.7	73.5	74.3	121.4	87.1	66.3	0.0	0.0	116.7	25.7
1830	84.5	68.4	92.7	73.5	74.3	121.4	84.9	66.3	50.0	55.6	0.0	0.0
1832	84.5	68.4	92.7	73.5	74.3	121.4	84.9	66.3	50.0	55.6	0.0	0.0
1833	72.5	70.4	76.6	65.8	63.4	89.5	76.8	70.0	40.0	69.2	16.7	0.0
1834	72.0	70.4	76.6	65.8	63.4	89.5	76.8	70.0	40.0	69.2	25.0	0.0
DUACA												
1779	96.6	73.2	83.3	162.5	114.3	43.5	83.3	177.8	100.0	100.0	22.2	150.0
1802	78.6	96.2	68.8	200.0	79.8	67.7	80.0	83.3	75.0	0.0	0.0	0.0
1803	61.5	60.6	55.6	0.0	47.3	55.0	80.3	69.2	0.0	0.0	133.3	0.0
1804	61.5	60.6	55.6	0.0	47.3	55.0	80.3	69.2	0.0	0.0	133.3	0.0
1805	79.0	61.1	80.0	61.5	79.3	55.0	77.1	67.6	0.0	0.0	100.0	0.0

TABLE 4. MALE/FEMALE RATIOS (CONTINUED)

YEAR	TOTAL M/F		WHITE M/F		INDIAN M/F		PARDO M/F		NEGRO M/F		SLAVE M/F	
	ADULT	CHILD	ADULT	CHILD	ADULT	CHILD	ADULT	CHILD	ADULT	CHILD	ADULT	CHILD
1807	93.7	108.5	92.9	160.0	98.4	80.8	91.1	150.0	55.0	130.0	0.0	0.0
1808	99.0	82.7	93.2	118.8	106.4	71.2	87.5	100.0	100.0	0.0	0.0	0.0
1809	96.2	90.2	79.1	130.8	111.8	80.0	77.8	96.4	200.0	0.0	0.0	0.0
1810	96.2	102.0	79.1	223.1	109.1	80.0	77.8	96.4	200.0	0.0	300.0	0.0
1811	74.7	200.0	80.4	125.0	68.1	235.9	102.6	158.3	0.0	0.0	0.0	0.0
1815	78.3	92.3	100.0	100.0	69.7	67.5	81.9	119.4	0.0	0.0	0.0	0.0
1816	85.3	92.3	100.0	100.0	69.7	67.5	92.0	119.4	0.0	0.0	0.0	0.0
1818	106.0	142.4	105.0	78.9	109.5	184.6	103.8	235.0	200.0	75.0	0.0	0.0
	EL CALVARIO											
1783	159.4	89.7	165.2	85.7	81.8	60.0	80.8	100.0	128.6	100.0	221.9	100.0
1802	119.0	99.4	108.0	101.9	110.5	100.0	112.6	115.8	90.5	76.0	161.6	95.2
1803	119.0	106.5	105.3	89.7	86.4	83.3	117.5	129.4	87.1	111.1	168.7	112.8
1804	113.8	97.3	101.8	88.2	75.8	84.6	99.0	110.0	98.4	110.0	171.4	97.7
1805	115.3	95.4	109.3	79.5	86.1	107.7	105.1	117.1	91.4	81.8	157.1	104.3
1808	115.7	110.9	108.2	88.0	85.3	136.4	92.5	145.9	103.4	90.0	163.5	122.0
1812	102.9	88.0	100.5	90.2	73.5	81.0	94.5	78.0	80.8	85.0	144.3	103.2
	EL CONSEJO											
1781	107.6	115.6	136.1	162.1	0.0	0.0	98.4	156.3	0.0	0.0	98.6	85.8
1795	103.5	96.6	111.7	76.2	92.3	366.7	96.9	112.2	77.3	91.7	109.6	85.5
1796	99.6	111.4	115.4	94.7	100.0	0.0	99.7	101.6	100.0	150.0	93.2	125.0
1802	121.4	104.1	111.9	81.7	81.3	133.3	144.6	80.7	110.0	100.0	113.4	129.3
1803	121.1	123.4	111.1	81.3	81.3	133.3	143.9	137.7	110.0	91.7	113.4	129.3
1804	120.5	105.4	110.5	80.9	81.8	150.0	141.9	85.0	115.4	115.4	114.0	127.8
1805	120.9	106.0	111.2	95.3	81.0	110.0	145.5	83.8	107.7	88.9	113.3	128.9
1806	84.8	78.6	110.3	82.5	84.2	60.0	69.0	79.9	87.5	76.2	88.2	77.7
1807	120.6	104.0	111.4	82.3	87.0	125.0	143.4	81.0	107.4	100.0	113.2	129.0
1808	120.8	104.5	111.3	82.5	95.8	122.2	144.0	81.2	100.0	115.4	113.6	128.8
1809	122.2	104.4	112.5	80.0	66.7	300.0	145.8	80.0	115.4	100.0	113.6	130.2
1811	122.1	110.5	112.7	94.4	70.0	0.0	149.2	82.6	111.1	75.0	112.4	140.5
1817	92.5	96.8	111.6	98.9	87.9	86.7	81.0	98.4	0.0	0.0	99.5	95.9
1818	90.5	93.0	95.5	90.4	88.9	93.3	81.0	92.1	0.0	0.0	99.5	96.1
1833	103.7	92.7	110.7	98.9	124.4	86.7	98.6	86.5	0.0	0.0	100.8	94.6
	EL GUAPO											
1784	122.0	95.5	158.3	137.5	66.7	100.0	172.7	107.1	80.0	0.0	126.0	91.7
1802	103.5	95.1	115.4	85.7	87.9	120.0	96.8	88.5	88.8	110.3	114.2	89.7
1803	103.8	102.2	109.5	121.1	105.1	85.7	107.3	112.8	94.4	84.6	102.5	102.5
1804	104.1	103.2	109.5	121.1	105.1	85.7	107.3	112.8	97.6	92.3	102.5	102.5
1805	96.4	99.2	92.5	94.3	90.0	90.9	96.7	93.9	99.0	95.9	97.9	108.1
1807	99.7	92.3	89.3	86.2	107.7	87.0	104.4	105.3	98.6	91.2	101.1	90.0
1808	98.8	92.7	85.9	85.2	107.7	87.0	102.9	108.1	98.6	91.2	101.1	90.0
1809	98.8	92.7	85.9	85.2	107.7	87.0	102.9	108.1	98.6	91.2	101.1	90.0
1811	103.5	101.4	110.5	114.8	133.3	56.3	93.1	102.6	78.2	127.3	115.3	96.0
1812	92.5	98.0	93.2	90.5	89.1	81.0	87.3	130.0	77.2	122.6	108.3	85.1
1820	79.3	89.4	82.0	68.8	62.0	65.4	81.4	100.0	127.6	33.3	74.7	113.0

TABLE 4. MALE/FEMALE RATIOS (CONTINUED)

YEAR	TOTAL M/F ADULT	TOTAL M/F CHILD	WHITE M/F ADULT	WHITE M/F CHILD	INDIAN M/F ADULT	INDIAN M/F CHILD	PARDO M/F ADULT	PARDO M/F CHILD	NEGRO M/F ADULT	NEGRO M/F CHILD	SLAVE M/F ADULT	SLAVE M/F CHILD
EL HATILLO												
1802	122.8	107.2	119.2	121.5	176.5	66.7	155.4	150.0	74.2	75.0	114.0	75.0
1803	122.8	107.2	119.2	121.5	176.5	66.7	155.4	150.0	74.2	75.0	114.0	75.0
1804	114.3	111.4	109.8	132.2	156.5	83.3	128.4	118.5	112.5	68.0	102.6	104.3
1805	116.8	107.0	118.8	122.9	134.5	75.0	125.6	116.7	102.9	75.9	103.4	96.4
1806	117.5	97.5	113.9	101.1	159.1	110.0	107.4	123.8	115.7	96.8	125.5	76.1
1808	98.6	108.1	83.4	101.1	159.1	110.0	107.4	171.4	115.7	125.8	125.5	80.4
1815	117.5	102.1	109.2	102.8	0.0	0.0	118.2	134.0	0.0	0.0	130.1	80.2
1818	84.4	87.0	90.2	104.1	0.0	0.0	81.0	87.2	0.0	0.0	81.6	67.2
EL PAO												
1781	100.8	105.6	103.1	118.6	106.7	109.1	93.5	98.7	84.1	114.3	214.5	128.6
1791	88.3	94.9	86.8	96.9	59.0	102.8	91.1	92.7	62.2	98.6	204.3	128.6
1792	81.7	101.4	77.9	128.8	51.7	118.3	81.7	92.8	61.3	100.0	407.9	125.0
1794	86.6	102.8	89.7	98.5	67.6	124.5	85.4	99.7	61.9	102.6	455.3	127.3
1796	82.3	107.1	75.0	132.7	69.4	125.4	80.2	95.8	62.4	110.2	268.1	125.0
1798	89.8	118.8	88.3	75.8	69.4	125.4	87.7	127.0	78.8	101.1	420.6	329.0
1801	102.0	105.5	86.5	95.2	143.8	91.2	100.6	111.3	66.3	91.0	228.2	100.0
1802	83.6	85.5	72.0	85.0	84.4	77.8	79.8	86.0	65.0	79.8	196.8	92.7
1803	88.9	128.8	82.0	95.2	181.8	61.5	80.5	147.7	75.7	79.4	293.7	190.9
1804	89.7	95.9	81.0	90.0	85.2	77.8	88.0	99.1	48.8	66.2	280.0	145.8
1805	89.9	99.7	81.0	90.0	85.2	77.8	87.9	100.6	48.8	95.6	289.2	145.8
1808	79.9	114.4	86.7	99.1	59.1	75.0	73.4	120.9	73.5	90.7	238.8	108.7
1809	118.7	96.0	112.4	89.5	114.6	95.4	122.0	96.3	92.2	94.7	120.8	110.0
1811	83.3	100.2	87.5	89.6	76.7	105.4	74.4	101.1	81.4	134.9	241.7	73.1
1812	77.7	102.2	84.2	98.8	65.9	109.4	70.6	98.1	58.4	124.6	250.0	122.7
1815	75.7	106.5	83.5	123.1	66.7	27.3	72.5	103.7	63.9	154.5	276.2	138.5
1816	73.2	104.8	86.2	111.0	52.2	57.1	69.1	102.8	66.7	175.0	219.2	120.0
1817	74.9	106.1	72.6	98.4	155.6	40.0	70.8	107.3	56.3	100.0	181.4	137.1
1818	75.6	104.2	85.7	102.5	55.6	59.3	70.6	106.0	67.0	117.6	166.3	108.0
1819	68.6	121.0	72.4	392.9	87.5	85.7	65.1	107.2	57.3	416.7	108.1	123.1
1821	71.6	73.3	69.2	108.3	74.1	66.7	71.6	65.7	61.5	72.0	88.1	113.3
1823	93.9	95.1	64.3	89.9	109.1	133.3	98.2	97.7	87.3	80.4	142.4	70.0
1824	88.3	88.7	62.1	69.3	100.0	175.0	90.0	94.1	96.0	82.0	154.8	60.6
1825	92.9	100.5	131.0	90.7	75.9	233.3	89.0	101.6	48.2	90.0	155.8	164.3
1826	90.6	97.5	95.7	92.2	71.0	150.0	91.8	97.5	42.8	85.7	151.9	185.7
1827	113.8	81.9	81.1	85.7	100.0	133.3	88.7	81.0	512.2	72.4	289.1	83.9
1829	94.9	79.0	81.8	80.0	91.7	84.6	95.5	79.1	86.7	74.6	83.3	81.8
1835	89.7	106.8	90.0	107.5	0.0	0.0	90.3	106.9	86.0	103.1	72.0	0.0
1836	90.4	103.5	89.7	98.1	0.0	0.0	91.0	103.8	90.2	102.5	73.0	0.0
1837	91.2	99.6	90.1	94.8	0.0	0.0	93.2	99.9	44.4	90.9	74.3	0.0
1838	93.6	98.8	90.5	93.8	0.0	0.0	94.6	99.3	86.9	87.5	72.0	0.0
EL RASTRO												
1807	98.1	111.2	105.8	132.8	200.0	66.7	100.9	96.2	100.0	83.3	66.7	100.0
1810	103.7	102.5	123.2	130.0	200.0	150.0	104.2	76.1	125.0	57.1	36.8	113.0
1811	104.8	109.9	120.1	116.3	190.0	120.0	108.6	104.3	126.1	88.9	39.0	104.0

TABLE 4. MALE/FEMALE RATIOS (CONTINUED)

YEAR	TOTAL M/F ADULT	TOTAL M/F CHILD	WHITE M/F ADULT	WHITE M/F CHILD	INDIAN M/F ADULT	INDIAN M/F CHILD	PARDO M/F ADULT	PARDO M/F CHILD	NEGRO M/F ADULT	NEGRO M/F CHILD	SLAVE M/F ADULT	SLAVE M/F CHILD
1812	101.2	108.2	120.5	110.8	60.0	40.0	110.7	112.5	0.0	0.0	45.7	103.3
1817	84.8	102.1	105.5	98.1	87.5	75.0	86.5	95.1	78.6	150.0	36.6	129.2
1822	72.2	96.3	87.3	90.3	59.6	76.0	71.3	132.7	110.0	100.0	24.4	28.6
	EL SOMBRERO											
1781	99.2	107.2	145.8	129.1	500.0	0.0	80.7	95.4	55.6	0.0	139.3	214.3
1783	98.3	120.1	135.0	158.6	166.7	300.0	0.0	0.0	82.8	110.0	117.0	88.6
1802	85.1	111.7	105.1	101.7	60.4	123.1	78.4	118.3	73.5	117.0	101.2	92.5
1803	85.8	102.8	106.5	92.9	81.4	100.0	80.3	110.8	66.7	98.3	97.8	91.1
1804	90.4	100.0	112.5	107.8	77.2	145.5	85.5	97.8	67.7	83.3	97.2	107.3
1805	88.8	108.3	106.0	111.2	77.1	171.4	87.6	103.3	72.3	131.0	73.8	100.0
1809	93.6	112.1	108.0	132.1	90.6	114.3	91.2	114.8	86.3	91.1	81.2	82.8
1810	94.8	111.5	107.8	131.0	92.1	111.5	91.3	114.3	86.7	91.5	95.1	84.1
1811	94.8	111.5	107.8	131.0	92.1	111.5	91.3	114.3	86.7	91.5	95.1	84.1
	EL TOCUYO											
1802	94.4	93.9	90.4	82.3	96.4	118.2	102.0	93.5	79.7	95.0	86.7	99.6
1803	92.7	93.7	90.8	82.2	77.4	151.0	99.3	90.2	85.0	98.9	85.1	101.3
1804	80.5	98.4	79.6	97.8	72.8	91.3	77.8	100.8	80.0	89.0	92.8	102.9
1805	90.9	95.4	91.3	87.3	92.1	114.8	96.1	94.3	79.0	89.3	82.9	108.1
1806	93.0	88.9	90.2	96.3	105.5	89.9	97.5	89.0	99.6	76.1	78.1	92.1
1807	81.6	98.8	82.1	113.2	81.8	76.2	78.9	96.3	84.2	89.0	88.7	114.1
1808	83.4	97.9	82.8	119.2	101.3	81.5	80.6	94.1	82.5	94.3	93.0	103.9
1809	81.8	98.3	79.6	98.6	90.7	115.0	80.9	98.1	84.8	93.5	83.2	102.9
1810	85.2	97.0	97.8	113.7	88.6	79.2	81.9	93.0	90.4	105.0	80.7	93.5
1812	82.2	98.3	79.1	98.6	89.7	73.1	81.4	101.2	84.5	97.2	85.2	91.6
1815	67.8	94.2	65.8	79.9	58.7	95.8	65.4	97.0	72.0	100.0	85.3	95.0
1816	70.0	94.1	68.8	85.1	52.0	92.9	68.3	96.2	67.9	88.1	84.3	98.0
1817	71.2	92.9	54.0	86.8	49.2	78.3	77.8	96.6	38.3	76.4	84.0	93.9
1818	78.8	99.3	73.5	93.9	83.1	95.2	78.8	102.7	77.3	94.8	84.9	96.2
1819	77.6	93.7	102.2	100.7	93.6	127.3	70.1	89.0	118.2	100.0	100.0	117.6
1820	72.6	93.7	87.3	73.7	87.0	100.0	66.4	98.4	110.0	400.0	90.3	85.5
	EL VALLE											
1798	78.5	84.3	85.0	86.7	76.0	67.2	75.8	100.0	70.3	126.7	82.4	79.3
1802	84.6	117.2	98.8	137.5	73.7	69.2	75.0	133.3	87.9	141.7	80.9	116.0
1803	82.9	118.9	94.1	162.5	73.0	86.7	75.9	107.1	85.0	135.7	81.0	107.1
1804	83.7	115.3	94.1	133.3	74.8	87.5	72.5	120.7	80.9	116.7	87.1	113.8
1805	83.6	141.3	91.7	151.2	76.0	115.2	76.3	124.1	73.3	264.3	91.5	118.2
1809	83.6	128.6	91.7	132.1	76.0	118.9	75.6	114.3	74.2	169.6	91.5	120.6
1815	63.0	93.5	64.0	101.6	89.9	68.4	57.2	111.4	70.0	104.5	49.7	75.5
1816	65.9	106.3	68.1	106.3	91.0	109.5	59.2	140.5	76.6	125.9	52.4	74.1
1817	73.9	125.8	74.2	116.9	80.9	134.5	69.8	183.7	97.0	125.9	63.9	93.5
1818	68.4	97.8	77.6	91.0	62.5	111.1	62.7	106.5	55.6	65.0	65.2	121.7
1819	75.6	91.8	81.4	87.2	75.8	62.5	76.2	100.0	61.5	73.7	68.1	125.8
1820	73.0	93.6	75.5	93.5	69.3	61.3	71.7	98.2	87.3	77.3	65.8	127.3

TABLE 4. MALE/FEMALE RATIOS (CONTINUED)

YEAR	TOTAL M/F ADULT	TOTAL M/F CHILD	WHITE M/F ADULT	WHITE M/F CHILD	INDIAN M/F ADULT	INDIAN M/F CHILD	PARDO M/F ADULT	PARDO M/F CHILD	NEGRO M/F ADULT	NEGRO M/F CHILD	SLAVE M/F ADULT	SLAVE M/F CHILD
	ESPINO											
1804	103.4	86.4	111.4	100.0	100.0	100.0	93.2	80.0	100.0	75.0	131.8	88.9
1807	84.9	71.5	64.0	41.7	39.6	36.0	97.1	119.5	250.0	100.0	163.6	120.0
	GUACARA											
1781	87.6	113.8	88.7	85.6	88.9	137.8	83.7	120.5	107.1	75.0	89.9	131.8
1802	79.4	128.3	54.5	133.3	80.6	121.3	95.5	129.9	120.0	150.0	95.1	122.0
1803	79.8	127.5	57.6	125.0	79.4	138.2	94.5	122.8	114.3	175.0	96.1	127.9
1804	76.4	113.3	77.9	104.3	92.4	104.8	67.1	127.9	118.2	133.3	93.3	84.2
1805	76.7	104.7	70.7	106.6	82.0	143.4	78.0	72.6	71.4	600.0	81.7	182.2
1808	94.0	117.5	79.6	145.4	83.0	130.0	104.0	108.1	162.5	56.3	104.1	84.2
1816	71.9	103.6	65.5	114.5	92.3	102.9	69.7	100.2	80.0	120.0	75.0	89.5
	GUADARRAMA											
1820	53.5	102.9	56.6	97.2	40.9	125.0	65.8	102.4	48.4	104.0	85.7	100.0
	GUAIGUAZA											
1803	73.1	140.3	92.3	100.0	0.0	0.0	80.6	136.4	39.6	161.1	128.1	133.3
1804	99.6	100.0	126.7	20.0	0.0	0.0	107.0	84.8	77.8	171.4	96.4	128.6
1805	101.2	101.3	126.7	25.0	100.0	0.0	108.0	84.8	74.5	171.4	102.7	128.6
1806	98.7	105.9	128.6	66.7	0.0	0.0	92.6	67.6	73.9	228.6	116.7	129.2
1807	90.9	111.4	180.0	100.0	0.0	0.0	79.1	114.3	125.0	85.7	84.2	114.3
1818	122.5	75.8	300.0	0.0	0.0	0.0	121.4	0.0	0.0	0.0	114.3	75.8
1819	98.5	86.7	216.7	0.0	0.0	0.0	81.5	106.7	0.0	0.0	115.6	83.6
	GUAMA											
1781	72.5	104.6	84.2	150.0	55.9	129.5	78.4	84.0	98.5	100.0	73.7	52.0
1794	75.8	76.8	76.6	95.0	39.8	60.0	89.3	91.4	128.9	58.8	97.3	87.5
1803	76.9	87.7	81.3	66.7	67.2	74.1	78.4	88.3	146.7	140.0	81.7	142.9
1804	82.9	100.0	69.6	125.0	97.0	86.5	79.4	108.0	76.5	200.0	87.1	61.3
1805	70.6	111.3	76.7	200.0	64.2	131.9	73.3	104.3	63.3	92.9	66.7	85.7
1807	67.5	124.1	76.1	122.2	62.8	143.9	65.9	116.7	80.5	132.0	80.0	128.6
1808	73.0	110.8	75.0	118.4	73.8	122.2	73.9	103.2	69.3	140.0	56.4	105.3
1809	72.8	112.6	73.5	97.6	68.1	124.0	74.8	107.7	69.9	144.4	76.4	106.7
1810	78.9	97.2	90.0	118.2	73.1	115.6	80.3	88.4	78.4	122.2	86.3	76.9
1811	77.5	93.3	93.2	96.9	74.0	114.2	77.0	91.5	80.8	130.0	84.2	70.0
1812	76.2	98.0	90.9	108.7	70.1	118.8	76.0	88.1	78.0	126.3	96.0	92.3
1817	72.8	78.5	81.2	88.2	64.7	103.7	73.9	69.0	83.7	133.3	64.0	76.9
1818	73.5	91.1	79.0	115.4	60.9	104.9	77.3	86.2	28.6	18.2	110.0	400.0
1819	61.6	112.4	92.9	105.3	62.5	141.4	58.7	109.1	51.1	115.2	58.5	47.4
1820	46.6	94.2	54.7	93.8	52.9	82.0	37.6	98.5	67.1	85.1	55.0	60.0
	GUANARE											
1788	85.0	117.6	87.3	110.8	95.4	87.3	81.5	136.0	97.1	121.2	80.6	96.9

TABLE 4. MALE/FEMALE RATIOS (CONTINUED)

YEAR	TOTAL M/F ADULT	TOTAL M/F CHILD	WHITE M/F ADULT	WHITE M/F CHILD	INDIAN M/F ADULT	INDIAN M/F CHILD	PARDO M/F ADULT	PARDO M/F CHILD	NEGRO M/F ADULT	NEGRO M/F CHILD	SLAVE M/F ADULT	SLAVE M/F CHILD
1791	85.3	97.1	89.6	99.4	56.5	81.0	84.0	90.0	86.9	160.0	83.4	118.0
1792	84.5	169.0	88.9	378.7	63.8	128.2	82.0	125.0	107.7	87.5	77.7	109.8
1802	88.6	133.0	90.8	139.3	86.9	116.1	87.1	131.2	119.2	236.4	85.0	123.2
1803	88.6	122.9	85.7	128.7	96.9	128.4	87.6	121.2	101.5	82.4	98.7	114.7
1804	86.2	119.5	91.0	141.3	75.9	120.5	87.7	107.6	66.2	111.1	70.2	106.3
1807	81.7	109.6	84.5	118.2	83.2	90.9	79.6	108.3	84.9	105.0	79.5	94.4
1808	81.7	106.7	86.5	111.8	72.3	95.1	80.0	106.4	74.3	85.2	82.6	102.5
1809	87.8	99.5	95.1	90.2	80.8	84.4	90.2	110.4	55.7	155.6	70.4	96.0
1810	90.5	99.5	81.6	80.5	90.4	119.8	98.9	110.7	93.9	76.7	98.2	114.7
1811	79.0	87.7	77.9	89.3	65.8	107.1	84.0	79.7	80.8	88.0	72.0	86.1
1817	77.5	104.3	74.2	101.2	118.3	86.5	71.1	107.0	55.2	155.6	126.2	92.2
GUANARE VIEJO												
1778	107.7	123.7	119.6	64.5	90.7	700.0	121.1	110.0	0.0	0.0	75.0	200.0
1782	90.8	90.6	96.9	83.7	89.0	94.6	89.1	93.2	0.0	0.0	100.0	50.0
1801	104.0	110.7	110.0	141.8	97.5	114.6	116.0	72.4	0.0	0.0	20.0	100.0
1802	101.4	121.8	113.3	149.2	94.4	114.9	104.3	92.2	0.0	0.0	80.0	150.0
1803	94.4	110.5	90.9	124.1	97.5	124.6	96.4	94.8	40.0	0.0	0.0	80.0
1804	96.1	129.4	111.0	88.3	58.3	59.5	105.5	209.8	0.0	0.0	60.0	60.0
1805	105.1	118.8	130.6	129.9	74.5	98.7	102.7	134.0	0.0	0.0	83.3	0.0
1806	70.9	97.5	77.7	92.7	52.8	86.1	75.7	104.9	0.0	0.0	33.3	200.0
1807	97.5	97.0	110.1	115.4	75.5	65.0	101.0	105.3	0.0	0.0	66.7	150.0
1808	96.9	81.9	98.3	95.5	93.1	50.8	96.9	98.5	0.0	0.0	133.3	150.0
1811	83.5	91.9	90.9	113.8	72.9	60.3	84.4	94.6	0.0	0.0	33.3	200.0
1813	91.9	108.9	86.0	115.9	99.4	113.8	90.6	95.5	0.0	0.0	100.0	300.0
GUANARITO												
1778	110.0	111.6	114.9	109.4	107.1	124.4	109.1	108.6	0.0	0.0	120.0	33.3
1801	98.9	78.9	93.4	74.3	93.6	82.4	102.0	76.6	117.0	82.9	110.7	81.8
1802	99.3	108.2	102.8	105.1	97.1	112.5	97.8	106.5	105.9	116.7	81.8	121.4
1803	96.0	95.8	107.6	85.8	47.3	90.2	96.3	112.2	95.6	78.6	119.4	114.8
1804	95.0	88.7	96.1	105.9	108.3	74.4	90.1	79.6	0.0	0.0	111.5	84.2
1805	99.7	86.7	100.9	82.7	110.6	72.0	97.8	105.2	96.0	82.7	92.3	70.4
1807	108.8	94.8	99.8	107.9	83.9	82.9	113.4	91.8	212.5	300.0	172.0	84.0
1808	86.7	89.7	88.6	98.3	77.0	55.0	87.6	89.0	70.3	50.0	92.3	71.4
1810	90.1	89.1	91.4	97.7	78.1	55.0	92.7	87.8	67.3	50.0	89.5	80.0
1811	90.3	89.0	92.7	96.1	78.0	71.4	91.6	85.3	71.9	70.6	85.4	117.6
GUARDATINAJAS												
1780	145.5	104.1	66.7	175.0	113.7	91.9	142.1	111.1	525.0	81.8	100.0	0.0
1804	109.8	107.6	126.1	133.8	89.2	68.3	114.9	97.9	104.7	117.8	103.2	112.5
1805	111.0	107.6	124.4	138.2	82.1	55.9	117.5	95.9	108.3	125.3	112.9	111.4
1807	107.2	99.2	142.8	131.8	80.8	86.5	113.2	75.5	94.3	102.1	102.5	122.7
1808	108.4	104.2	143.0	126.5	68.8	86.3	109.8	79.2	96.4	120.6	134.3	97.1
1809	116.0	105.6	146.7	116.5	87.4	71.7	103.5	91.6	105.6	130.5	138.9	72.2
1810	102.7	109.6	110.2	126.0	67.7	72.2	106.0	116.3	96.2	177.8	119.7	83.3
1811	116.8	109.6	137.0	113.4	79.7	140.0	117.4	105.8	127.6	143.8	124.7	78.3
1812	109.1	98.0	96.2	110.0	90.0	96.6	116.2	97.4	129.4	96.3	117.6	81.3

TABLE 4. MALE/FEMALE RATIOS (CONTINUED)

YEAR	TOTAL M/F ADULT	TOTAL M/F CHILD	WHITE M/F ADULT	WHITE M/F CHILD	INDIAN M/F ADULT	INDIAN M/F CHILD	PARDO M/F ADULT	PARDO M/F CHILD	NEGRO M/F ADULT	NEGRO M/F CHILD	SLAVE M/F ADULT	SLAVE M/F CHILD
1816	94.5	104.1	106.1	79.7	73.0	137.8	94.9	101.9	64.7	66.7	106.7	135.5
GUARENAS												
1784	89.6	100.0	95.2	100.0	99.2	97.8	100.0	102.7	102.5	100.0	44.9	100.0
1802	92.0	99.4	94.6	115.4	83.9	57.7	71.9	127.3	79.7	119.7	112.9	90.8
1803	92.0	100.0	94.5	113.6	84.6	64.9	71.4	115.4	82.6	120.0	111.1	90.9
1804	88.7	85.4	89.4	102.6	81.1	56.9	87.0	50.0	77.8	94.9	104.2	81.8
1805	88.0	86.8	90.5	103.4	81.2	58.3	82.7	53.6	74.7	94.9	103.7	85.7
1808	93.6	91.6	95.2	112.3	91.9	54.3	123.5	104.0	78.7	79.1	93.3	94.8
1809	97.1	98.8	101.1	118.2	98.2	50.0	98.6	90.6	85.3	96.2	96.8	108.0
1811	97.8	111.8	104.2	128.4	91.2	72.7	94.2	125.5	86.0	122.2	100.7	97.8
1816	72.3	101.3	72.2	104.7	44.9	127.8	68.1	84.2	127.3	900.0	86.1	107.9
GUARICO												
1803	109.4	113.8	91.8	175.0	94.6	109.2	126.6	106.3	229.2	109.1	130.0	122.2
1804	87.6	100.0	89.7	114.3	89.3	98.2	86.9	97.3	67.1	100.0	116.7	100.0
1805	88.2	107.3	79.1	115.4	96.5	111.6	73.1	101.3	104.3	100.0	140.0	125.0
1806	86.8	101.4	76.4	65.3	94.9	112.9	72.9	102.5	100.0	83.3	140.0	110.0
1807	82.3	101.1	84.3	89.7	79.6	93.3	73.6	108.9	227.3	200.0	126.1	136.4
1808	82.8	102.8	86.3	104.0	81.3	94.3	73.6	108.9	227.3	200.0	113.0	136.4
1809	85.6	100.5	86.0	96.9	85.2	93.2	77.9	109.4	135.0	160.0	126.1	93.3
1810	86.1	98.9	105.5	134.2	78.5	89.7	80.6	109.4	109.1	86.7	133.3	75.9
1812	83.6	103.1	91.7	148.5	77.5	91.2	79.7	111.2	105.1	91.9	116.7	91.4
1815	95.9	96.3	77.8	100.0	98.1	86.0	96.5	105.7	100.0	75.0	89.5	81.3
1816	94.6	94.3	77.8	89.5	97.1	85.8	94.5	104.1	100.0	75.0	89.5	68.4
1817	96.9	91.6	100.0	85.0	97.5	84.2	96.0	100.4	100.0	75.0	89.5	68.4
1818	98.0	90.7	100.0	58.6	98.7	83.0	97.4	99.6	100.0	133.3	89.5	68.4
1819	98.0	79.6	94.3	58.6	100.3	75.9	97.3	85.4	93.8	75.0	92.3	61.9
1820	95.5	85.5	94.3	73.3	98.1	81.9	93.9	88.0	100.0	110.7	85.7	67.9
GUASGUAS												
1802	74.8	116.4	76.8	115.6	70.4	130.1	76.1	112.3	0.0	0.0	40.9	87.5
1803	72.9	134.7	76.7	182.6	66.4	117.6	73.7	115.1	0.0	0.0	33.3	128.6
1804	73.4	116.8	74.6	116.5	66.4	124.2	77.2	113.5	0.0	0.0	42.9	125.0
1805	72.1	119.2	75.7	112.8	63.2	147.7	73.7	113.6	0.0	0.0	42.9	128.6
1806	75.5	115.7	76.9	116.6	75.8	136.2	75.1	106.2	0.0	0.0	44.0	87.5
1807	73.2	116.6	79.4	112.4	63.7	127.7	71.8	116.4	0.0	0.0	47.8	100.0
1808	74.0	112.4	78.0	109.6	70.9	129.6	72.0	107.5	0.0	0.0	42.9	116.7
1809	76.7	112.0	86.9	109.4	67.6	138.7	71.6	102.0	0.0	0.0	43.5	200.0
1810	75.7	103.0	77.0	97.8	62.9	118.4	85.2	103.6	74.6	84.2	42.9	80.0
GUATIRE												
1784	93.7	117.4	111.7	183.3	250.0	0.0	76.1	95.7	76.5	75.8	99.5	128.2
1802	98.1	108.8	86.7	87.1	233.3	33.3	83.8	142.0	77.1	89.2	112.0	108.5
1803	100.3	105.2	125.5	104.8	157.1	100.0	90.4	117.0	75.8	106.7	107.8	100.7
1805	86.4	96.0	123.5	90.5	433.3	100.0	84.3	83.9	69.9	109.8	82.9	97.7
1807	91.6	96.0	75.2	116.7	100.0	0.0	77.9	81.8	74.1	400.0	105.7	98.2

TABLE 4. MALE/FEMALE RATIOS (CONTINUED)

YEAR	TOTAL M/F		WHITE M/F		INDIAN M/F		PARDO M/F		NEGRO M/F		SLAVE M/F	
	ADULT	CHILD	ADULT	CHILD	ADULT	CHILD	ADULT	CHILD	ADULT	CHILD	ADULT	CHILD
1809	91.6	96.0	75.2	116.7	100.0	0.0	77.9	81.8	74.1	400.0	105.7	98.2
1811	98.7	108.0	111.3	83.3	130.4	200.0	88.9	92.2	83.7	100.0	102.7	121.3
1815	92.6	105.3	121.6	82.6	114.3	66.7	81.1	96.0	79.8	96.2	94.4	116.7
1816	98.7	125.4	120.0	110.3	133.3	250.0	89.1	82.3	81.8	84.4	103.3	202.7
1817	76.8	114.2	107.9	136.0	73.7	133.3	58.2	107.8	97.1	200.0	90.3	115.1
	GUAYABAL											
1804	136.3	85.2	89.3	67.4	85.7	81.8	90.7	88.3	84.3	89.1	449.0	88.9
1817	88.0	116.1	68.0	131.9	75.0	105.0	94.9	113.5	91.7	75.0	96.7	114.3
	GUIGUE											
1781	108.7	93.6	105.5	94.2	122.2	78.9	104.5	94.7	112.1	102.8	116.2	89.2
1802	95.1	90.8	105.9	96.3	67.6	80.0	97.8	92.4	92.7	85.0	82.1	82.7
1803	92.9	95.0	98.9	96.4	76.9	104.8	92.6	93.5	94.9	136.4	90.3	91.3
1804	83.9	93.7	88.9	91.2	75.0	96.0	90.7	94.4	87.8	115.4	63.4	90.9
1805	91.0	96.1	89.2	95.5	82.9	103.7	91.3	95.6	78.0	100.0	97.6	96.0
1808	88.9	96.3	93.3	92.0	73.2	85.2	89.4	100.6	87.8	50.0	87.5	102.0
1809	90.8	95.8	97.0	97.0	72.5	83.3	91.4	101.8	79.2	41.7	90.9	97.2
1817	85.1	93.3	107.2	72.2	73.0	73.7	80.9	94.1	68.1	73.7	102.5	126.8
	GUIRIPA											
1802	110.1	107.7	106.4	94.4	136.4	125.0	105.6	110.2	0.0	0.0	88.9	212.5
1803	112.4	101.1	109.5	82.7	163.6	133.3	100.0	113.6	0.0	0.0	104.3	200.0
1804	104.3	109.7	103.5	119.4	116.2	187.5	98.2	94.0	800.0	0.0	93.3	92.3
1805	109.6	109.3	108.0	120.9	129.4	200.0	104.1	97.1	800.0	0.0	93.3	70.6
1806	104.8	88.4	95.0	94.7	90.6	78.9	118.1	88.5	200.0	33.3	108.8	86.7
1807	108.8	93.2	121.7	65.9	113.0	106.5	95.6	124.4	150.0	50.0	100.0	50.0
1808	110.4	93.8	125.0	84.2	104.3	84.6	102.7	115.1	200.0	150.0	105.6	66.7
1809	104.8	92.5	109.7	82.9	104.5	109.1	95.6	100.0	100.0	150.0	135.7	40.0
1811	111.2	88.3	109.9	89.2	144.4	157.1	104.6	90.0	0.0	0.0	125.0	55.0
	HUMOCARO ALTO											
1802	83.0	112.4	71.0	136.4	83.4	109.8	92.7	114.6	60.0	0.0	72.0	220.0
1803	81.9	116.1	67.7	150.0	82.4	112.9	91.7	116.3	50.0	0.0	64.3	233.3
1804	85.7	130.2	83.7	120.0	85.4	132.4	86.8	121.3	60.0	0.0	107.1	100.0
1805	86.9	124.2	84.0	125.0	86.8	126.4	87.0	117.6	60.0	0.0	106.3	88.9
1806	80.9	81.3	76.1	88.5	79.9	76.4	92.5	118.0	66.7	0.0	83.3	77.8
1807	81.1	78.5	76.1	88.5	80.3	71.4	86.7	120.4	50.0	0.0	111.8	116.7
1808	78.6	79.5	70.2	83.3	77.6	73.4	86.7	118.0	50.0	0.0	111.8	116.7
1809	72.5	75.4	70.0	89.3	71.2	72.5	76.1	86.9	66.7	0.0	117.6	75.0
1810	66.8	120.2	66.0	93.1	64.7	132.4	76.1	90.2	150.0	0.0	90.9	150.0
1815	89.6	83.3	54.3	92.3	95.1	81.3	77.4	80.8	100.0	0.0	62.5	166.7
1816	72.1	124.9	62.2	109.1	89.3	126.0	23.5	126.7	100.0	50.0	68.8	150.0
1817	69.8	114.0	34.1	108.3	91.6	117.5	20.6	87.0	100.0	50.0	70.6	150.0
1818	68.7	91.6	31.8	92.9	90.3	90.2	21.6	88.5	66.7	0.0	70.6	175.0
1819	74.0	85.3	55.6	81.3	93.9	83.8	23.5	89.7	66.7	0.0	72.2	116.7
1820	88.5	62.3	69.6	57.1	93.6	63.8	65.9	57.8	166.7	200.0	62.5	42.9

TABLE 4. MALE/FEMALE RATIOS (CONTINUED)

YEAR	TOTAL M/F ADULT	TOTAL M/F CHILD	WHITE M/F ADULT	WHITE M/F CHILD	INDIAN M/F ADULT	INDIAN M/F CHILD	PARDO M/F ADULT	PARDO M/F CHILD	NEGRO M/F ADULT	NEGRO M/F CHILD	SLAVE M/F ADULT	SLAVE M/F CHILD
	HUMOCARO BAJO											
1803	77.9	88.0	71.2	85.5	80.9	82.8	77.8	88.1	77.0	92.3	89.5	126.7
1804	77.9	88.0	71.2	85.5	80.9	82.8	77.8	88.1	77.0	92.3	89.5	126.7
1806	91.2	99.5	76.4	82.6	88.5	123.1	97.0	87.5	50.0	0.0	121.1	80.0
1807	76.9	74.6	71.6	80.9	73.2	71.8	76.5	76.8	125.0	0.0	109.1	70.0
1808	73.0	78.0	73.3	88.9	73.4	74.1	70.6	82.4	75.0	150.0	79.0	57.1
1809	64.1	71.0	66.7	83.1	72.5	71.4	54.1	68.5	45.5	120.0	56.6	50.0
1810	62.6	70.6	63.9	82.7	69.5	71.3	54.8	66.5	45.5	71.4	57.6	61.9
1815	46.3	48.5	43.4	48.1	47.7	47.5	44.9	45.8	33.3	62.5	52.1	59.0
1816	50.5	48.5	44.3	52.1	52.1	44.9	52.5	51.6	40.0	71.4	50.9	48.1
1817	50.1	51.8	44.8	53.1	54.3	52.1	46.2	51.9	33.3	42.9	54.7	49.0
1818	51.3	59.8	50.4	88.2	55.5	52.3	45.7	54.6	40.0	40.0	50.9	56.1
1819	62.6	70.7	55.7	88.2	78.7	69.4	51.1	56.8	25.0	50.0	48.3	82.6
1820	63.0	68.1	62.1	83.5	76.7	66.1	48.7	56.0	33.3	0.0	58.6	87.5
	IGUANA											
1783	124.3	107.4	0.0	0.0	114.3	112.0	0.0	0.0	100.0	50.0	0.0	0.0
1801	133.3	132.5	0.0	0.0	138.1	120.0	87.5	0.0	100.0	0.0	0.0	0.0
1802	130.3	137.5	0.0	0.0	134.4	125.0	87.5	0.0	100.0	0.0	0.0	0.0
1803	129.1	116.3	0.0	0.0	133.7	112.5	100.0	300.0	0.0	0.0	0.0	0.0
1804	124.4	142.9	0.0	0.0	128.7	139.0	80.0	300.0	0.0	0.0	0.0	0.0
1805	132.6	139.5	0.0	0.0	133.3	137.8	120.0	200.0	0.0	0.0	0.0	0.0
1806	134.0	150.0	0.0	0.0	134.8	149.1	120.0	200.0	0.0	0.0	0.0	0.0
1807	124.7	124.1	0.0	0.0	122.5	124.1	0.0	0.0	0.0	0.0	0.0	0.0
	LA GUAIRA											
1802	73.9	93.7	109.3	96.8	68.6	600.0	57.2	85.8	56.9	112.5	90.4	87.7
1804	82.5	114.1	92.7	104.4	114.3	33.3	85.3	96.9	66.8	355.0	73.2	82.6
1805	68.7	98.3	114.1	113.9	100.0	0.0	55.5	96.4	50.2	92.3	74.8	84.2
1807	65.0	112.9	105.8	139.7	87.5	50.0	51.5	99.1	48.3	114.6	67.6	102.9
1809	52.1	80.4	110.9	82.3	60.0	0.0	37.7	79.3	43.2	82.4	55.9	88.9
1810	65.3	142.6	100.6	124.2	75.0	0.0	46.5	225.9	77.0	81.0	72.9	112.0
1811	58.5	98.1	111.5	114.1	75.0	300.0	44.6	90.1	51.7	108.7	60.3	88.9
1815	44.4	145.3	63.1	141.7	51.6	200.0	31.9	162.5	31.0	113.6	50.4	142.9
1816	70.3	101.7	77.2	111.3	62.3	180.0	85.2	83.8	32.9	78.9	62.5	150.0
1817	55.3	105.9	82.2	93.8	63.0	133.3	42.1	109.0	44.4	116.0	73.2	111.1
1818	48.7	76.6	64.8	111.0	86.0	233.3	36.5	52.0	69.1	82.1	58.8	140.0
1819	64.4	151.6	70.6	162.5	86.2	153.8	40.2	142.0	100.0	133.3	82.1	177.1
1820	72.7	79.8	71.5	89.8	45.2	116.7	80.4	93.8	72.4	47.4	81.4	57.6
	LA GUAIRA, CURATO CASTRENSE											
1802	626.8	100.0	860.7	120.0	0.0	0.0	300.0	0.0	50.0	0.0	120.0	0.0
1803	1154.5	0.0	1876.9	0.0	0.0	0.0	100.0	0.0	200.0	0.0	100.0	0.0
1804	980.5	133.3	1810.0	166.7	0.0	0.0	283.3	100.0	100.0	0.0	62.5	0.0
1805	1086.8	176.9	1475.9	237.5	0.0	0.0	1245.5	75.0	150.0	0.0	72.7	100.0
1807	1148.3	120.0	1388.9	136.4	0.0	0.0	1377.3	66.7	400.0	0.0	70.0	100.0

TABLE 4. MALE/FEMALE RATIOS (CONTINUED)

YEAR	TOTAL M/F ADULT	TOTAL M/F CHILD	WHITE M/F ADULT	WHITE M/F CHILD	INDIAN M/F ADULT	INDIAN M/F CHILD	PARDO M/F ADULT	PARDO M/F CHILD	NEGRO M/F ADULT	NEGRO M/F CHILD	SLAVE M/F ADULT	SLAVE M/F CHILD
1808	1284.2	150.0	1272.0	225.0	0.0	0.0	*200.0	0.0	300.0	0.0	50.0	0.0
	LA SANTISIMA TRINIDAD											
1780	99.5	85.3	120.0	100.0	96.4	121.7	102.6	50.0	100.0	46.2	120.0	0.0
1802	127.9	103.4	206.1	171.4	92.3	157.1	119.0	115.3	114.3	78.2	334.6	60.0
1803	109.5	165.2	106.5	150.0	55.4	137.5	111.3	388.9	105.0	106.8	511.1	0.0
1804	99.9	100.5	65.6	111.1	70.8	200.0	99.3	70.1	110.3	122.7	176.0	350.0
1805	96.8	108.9	124.2	66.7	127.6	111.1	100.4	122.7	92.7	107.2	66.7	76.9
1807	97.3	109.3	97.4	157.1	100.0	81.8	109.7	137.9	83.7	91.3	135.5	400.0
1808	114.2	93.7	78.7	92.3	103.0	121.1	113.9	90.1	144.4	33.3	257.9	100.0
1809	109.4	85.7	80.0	66.7	100.0	135.7	103.5	79.8	141.7	60.0	271.4	140.0
1810	98.5	90.7	103.8	90.0	81.4	95.8	94.2	91.9	140.0	33.3	350.0	50.0
1811	112.7	82.2	94.1	80.0	87.5	89.3	100.7	79.0	130.0	60.0	468.8	128.6
1812	102.4	93.1	143.8	77.8	86.8	95.2	98.4	96.7	88.9	50.0	218.2	66.7
	LA VEGA											
1802	101.5	112.0	95.6	101.3	88.8	101.8	97.2	91.7	103.4	112.5	119.1	168.6
1803	102.1	115.2	96.5	131.0	90.1	101.7	96.6	84.8	103.4	112.5	119.5	147.2
1804	113.7	107.2	110.2	115.2	94.8	123.1	93.7	81.3	113.5	126.3	166.7	105.5
1805	117.0	86.8	116.6	111.3	94.1	83.8	92.8	80.7	109.4	74.4	181.1	84.3
1809	88.7	94.8	90.1	75.0	94.5	117.2	78.3	128.1	85.0	80.0	97.8	66.7
1810	88.2	95.9	85.5	93.1	89.5	117.9	69.4	126.7	94.1	80.0	119.0	51.6
1811	83.7	107.1	73.1	88.0	100.0	166.7	62.8	134.4	89.5	0.0	122.8	55.0
1815	61.9	68.8	60.0	53.3	48.7	225.0	58.8	60.0	51.9	100.0	76.0	73.9
1816	65.6	76.4	68.3	69.7	35.1	111.1	54.5	64.7	66.7	80.0	93.8	87.5
1817	80.1	90.9	84.2	105.0	106.7	114.3	56.4	63.2	84.6	400.0	104.9	104.5
1818	63.2	84.4	65.7	74.3	57.6	200.0	56.6	75.9	28.6	100.0	79.0	90.0
1819	65.9	93.8	82.4	73.7	62.7	130.0	47.6	93.3	21.4	100.0	81.7	95.0
1820	69.6	95.8	79.6	61.5	52.8	90.9	53.7	131.0	41.7	100.0	115.7	64.7
1821	79.0	103.3	76.9	60.0	75.8	64.3	54.5	108.7	36.4	200.0	127.5	166.7
1822	89.3	86.6	74.2	25.0	124.1	81.3	74.7	115.4	45.5	150.0	122.7	114.3
1823	83.8	122.7	71.7	68.8	88.0	150.0	82.3	112.5	64.3	0.0	109.8	0.0
	LA VICTORIA											
1780	82.9	85.5	86.1	56.3	77.8	110.7	81.9	85.8	93.2	80.6	79.9	98.8
1802	79.5	99.7	81.1	98.3	74.0	102.5	71.4	92.6	89.2	138.5	96.2	109.5
1803	88.6	99.6	85.4	217.1	95.8	56.6	79.2	91.9	91.6	105.9	105.2	111.6
1804	85.5	113.7	85.4	219.2	87.6	58.0	74.7	119.6	86.3	140.0	103.8	123.3
1805	87.3	93.5	84.8	207.9	95.9	56.4	79.4	92.0	94.6	71.4	97.5	92.6
1806	87.3	94.4	84.4	206.3	96.3	57.1	79.5	92.1	93.9	82.8	97.5	93.2
1808	87.3	112.6	82.3	151.3	95.4	91.7	80.3	106.1	88.0	147.4	99.1	106.3
1809	87.4	94.6	84.5	198.8	96.4	58.3	79.8	92.3	94.6	85.7	97.3	93.4
1811	94.5	71.2	85.1	50.6	122.0	77.9	89.1	96.3	87.6	46.4	101.0	57.6
1816	86.0	87.5	50.0	100.8	59.9	88.0	133.8	58.8	0.0	0.0	47.7	192.3
1817	86.0	87.5	50.0	100.8	59.9	88.0	133.8	58.8	0.0	0.0	47.7	192.3
1818	86.0	87.5	50.0	100.8	59.9	88.0	133.8	58.8	0.0	0.0	47.7	192.3

TABLE 4. MALE/FEMALE RATIOS (CONTINUED)

YEAR	TOTAL M/F ADULT	TOTAL M/F CHILD	WHITE M/F ADULT	WHITE M/F CHILD	INDIAN M/F ADULT	INDIAN M/F CHILD	PARDO M/F ADULT	PARDO M/F CHILD	NEGRO M/F ADULT	NEGRO M/F CHILD	SLAVE M/F ADULT	SLAVE M/F CHILD
	LEZAMA											
1783	99.8	105.3	98.6	62.3	98.8	119.6	88.5	112.5	110.4	90.5	115.9	433.3
1802	86.8	98.7	94.3	95.0	75.7	110.3	81.6	106.7	79.5	65.2	115.9	85.4
1803	86.8	98.7	94.3	95.0	75.7	110.3	81.6	106.7	79.5	65.2	115.9	85.4
1804	86.8	98.7	94.3	95.0	75.7	110.3	81.6	106.7	79.5	65.2	115.9	85.4
1805	86.8	98.7	94.3	95.0	75.7	110.3	81.6	106.7	79.5	65.2	115.9	85.4
1806	86.8	98.7	94.3	95.0	75.7	110.3	81.6	106.7	79.5	65.2	115.9	85.4
1807	86.8	98.7	94.3	95.0	75.7	110.3	81.6	106.7	79.5	65.2	115.9	85.4
1808	86.8	98.7	94.3	95.0	75.7	110.3	81.6	106.7	79.5	65.2	115.9	85.4
1809	86.8	98.7	94.3	95.0	75.7	110.3	81.6	106.7	79.5	65.2	115.9	85.4
1810	86.8	98.7	94.3	95.0	75.7	110.3	81.6	106.7	79.5	65.2	115.9	85.4
1811	86.8	98.7	94.3	95.0	75.7	110.3	81.6	106.7	79.5	65.2	115.9	85.4
	LOS ANGELES											
1780	102.6	130.6	14.3	0.0	110.4	143.3	75.0	154.5	500.0	80.0	0.0	0.0
1803	92.2	86.2	87.5	20.0	92.4	65.4	92.3	114.8	0.0	0.0	100.0	0.0
1804	100.0	89.5	100.0	20.0	106.1	62.1	94.6	134.8	0.0	0.0	100.0	0.0
1805	90.2	72.7	142.9	83.3	81.3	80.0	95.7	60.0	0.0	0.0	50.0	0.0
1807	82.7	90.0	128.6	100.0	83.1	84.6	76.8	93.1	0.0	0.0	200.0	0.0
1808	89.7	91.4	128.6	200.0	79.1	57.7	96.0	113.3	0.0	0.0	100.0	0.0
1809	121.4	96.0	113.7	102.6	101.5	84.6	120.0	94.9	0.0	0.0	355.6	133.3
1810	115.1	111.1	110.7	121.4	81.4	130.0	122.4	96.5	0.0	0.0	375.0	166.7
1811	112.8	106.3	97.8	113.9	79.5	89.3	120.0	106.9	0.0	0.0	381.8	140.0
1812	115.9	118.1	104.9	122.7	85.9	105.6	124.0	127.1	0.0	0.0	292.3	66.7
1816	87.3	108.1	90.9	58.1	80.9	104.3	80.3	124.4	0.0	0.0	227.3	200.0
1817	77.2	120.9	87.0	87.8	70.1	95.7	67.9	144.1	0.0	0.0	176.5	300.0
	LOS ANGELES DE SETENTA											
1801	87.3	88.8	84.6	84.8	88.9	88.9	94.1	97.6	0.0	0.0	90.0	110.0
1805	98.1	86.0	95.2	78.0	91.1	100.0	87.6	70.4	0.0	0.0	168.0	171.4
1806	105.4	81.3	94.5	84.2	137.8	155.6	92.0	63.0	0.0	0.0	166.7	81.3
1807	90.8	63.7	95.3	55.7	95.9	56.5	81.2	77.8	0.0	0.0	95.2	84.6
1809	87.7	68.9	91.6	69.9	94.5	52.8	84.5	76.9	0.0	0.0	65.6	72.7
	LOS CANIZOS											
1802	101.0	126.0	112.0	300.0	0.0	0.0	89.8	119.1	125.0	50.0	116.3	120.9
1803	81.6	115.1	70.4	280.0	0.0	0.0	83.2	114.9	130.0	0.0	77.3	97.5
1804	90.6	130.1	96.9	280.0	0.0	0.0	93.4	122.4	157.1	0.0	80.5	120.5
1805	80.8	139.5	103.3	333.3	0.0	0.0	75.9	140.6	97.1	100.0	76.2	127.8
1807	94.1	128.9	100.0	350.0	0.0	0.0	95.0	97.2	104.3	550.0	88.5	125.0
1808	90.9	114.1	103.3	225.0	0.0	0.0	92.1	89.1	122.2	0.0	82.4	142.4
1809	92.5	105.3	100.0	225.0	0.0	0.0	95.3	80.0	122.2	0.0	82.4	130.6
1810	74.4	94.6	135.0	85.7	0.0	0.0	69.8	75.3	111.1	0.0	71.2	136.6
1811	82.1	92.7	123.8	125.0	0.0	0.0	81.3	86.5	100.0	0.0	74.5	102.3
1813	78.8	83.5	150.0	0.0	0.0	0.0	93.8	69.5	45.7	130.0	61.3	106.3
1818	79.0	75.6	0.0	50.0	0.0	0.0	78.4	73.3	0.0	0.0	72.6	84.6

TABLE 4. MALE/FEMALE RATIOS (CONTINUED)

YEAR	TOTAL M/F		WHITE M/F		INDIAN M/F		PARDO M/F		NEGRO M/F		SLAVE M/F	
	ADULT	CHILD	ADULT	CHILD	ADULT	CHILD	ADULT	CHILD	ADULT	CHILD	ADULT	CHILD
1819	84.0	63.8	200.0	66.7	0.0	0.0	83.9	61.0	0.0	0.0	76.1	71.4
1820	81.1	60.7	200.0	66.7	0.0	0.0	84.2	56.8	0.0	0.0	67.6	71.4
LOS GUAYOS												
1781	100.5	107.3	116.7	119.3	89.4	99.0	106.0	113.5	0.0	0.0	100.0	0.0
1795	98.3	104.4	110.2	103.4	96.4	106.3	89.8	105.8	0.0	0.0	140.0	66.7
1802	100.7	100.0	125.2	95.9	89.2	93.6	93.1	101.3	150.0	200.0	156.5	154.5
1803	93.3	100.0	118.1	122.4	86.3	94.8	75.5	92.9	216.7	33.3	151.9	163.2
1804	92.8	99.7	103.6	106.1	86.1	92.1	81.7	99.3	200.0	30.0	155.4	175.0
1805	84.3	97.1	89.2	110.5	72.7	87.0	83.7	93.9	116.7	14.3	125.0	207.1
1816	91.9	98.7	81.8	108.5	86.1	102.6	98.7	88.9	100.0	0.0	105.3	175.0
LOS TEQUES												
1796	98.4	113.2	98.5	102.1	85.9	137.5	106.8	150.0	88.2	66.7	95.5	111.8
1799	98.1	107.4	98.5	98.2	85.9	137.5	106.4	133.3	77.8	66.7	96.9	125.0
1800	98.1	107.4	98.5	98.2	85.9	137.5	106.4	133.3	77.8	66.7	96.9	125.0
1801	98.3	100.9	98.3	98.8	85.7	122.2	107.2	129.7	88.9	75.0	96.2	71.4
1805	120.7	97.5	116.2	97.2	145.6	66.7	220.0	125.0	61.9	90.0	95.1	104.2
1811	71.3	57.1	68.5	47.7	81.8	28.6	68.2	66.2	69.6	67.9	91.8	43.5
1816	92.5	93.6	92.5	105.0	91.6	92.3	98.0	80.6	66.7	25.0	86.0	87.2
1817	92.2	101.3	92.7	105.2	90.4	95.2	97.9	101.9	70.0	66.7	83.3	93.9
MACAIRA												
1784	112.9	109.2	0.0	200.0	132.0	104.5	113.8	0.0	266.7	0.0	104.8	109.4
1802	113.8	112.5	0.0	0.0	122.2	300.0	275.0	133.3	100.0	0.0	105.4	102.9
1803	105.0	151.3	0.0	0.0	200.0	233.3	100.0	0.0	200.0	500.0	96.7	138.2
1804	105.5	106.7	0.0	0.0	166.7	83.3	100.0	33.3	150.0	400.0	98.8	108.6
1806	98.8	104.3	0.0	0.0	80.0	150.0	0.0	0.0	200.0	200.0	97.1	97.6
1807	98.8	130.4	0.0	0.0	100.0	300.0	0.0	0.0	250.0	50.0	94.8	130.2
1808	79.5	100.0	0.0	0.0	133.3	71.4	0.0	0.0	133.3	200.0	67.6	100.0
1809	98.6	75.0	0.0	0.0	150.0	50.0	100.0	100.0	400.0	0.0	88.7	73.3
1811	106.8	111.1	0.0	0.0	77.8	300.0	0.0	0.0	100.0	0.0	114.7	87.5
1817	137.2	61.5	0.0	0.0	300.0	0.0	114.3	0.0	50.0	0.0	142.4	61.5
MACAIRITA												
1805	100.0	120.5	0.0	0.0	133.3	125.0	0.0	0.0	100.0	0.0	97.5	108.6
MACARAO												
1802	81.2	74.3	87.1	80.6	78.3	69.2	69.7	73.3	59.3	77.8	87.8	69.2
1803	101.3	92.0	60.1	89.7	92.1	108.7	143.8	93.5	66.7	70.6	147.8	91.8
1804	102.8	92.0	98.4	103.7	93.5	100.0	101.1	65.5	50.0	133.3	136.7	100.0
1805	97.1	84.2	92.9	89.3	87.8	76.5	92.8	76.5	68.4	100.0	117.8	83.3
1807	92.2	75.6	95.8	68.8	78.7	78.1	83.5	71.9	86.7	80.0	98.4	89.6
1808	86.8	98.3	90.7	90.0	81.8	95.2	81.6	125.0	63.6	233.3	90.7	92.1
1809	82.6	77.2	88.7	87.4	84.1	74.1	74.1	22.7	52.9	55.6	81.5	90.9
1810	113.2	93.1	97.2	102.4	133.3	79.3	110.0	92.9	90.0	42.9	145.7	92.6

TABLE 4. MALE/FEMALE RATIOS (CONTINUED)

YEAR	TOTAL M/F		WHITE M/F		INDIAN M/F		PARDO M/F		NEGRO M/F		SLAVE M/F	
	ADULT	CHILD	ADULT	CHILD	ADULT	CHILD	ADULT	CHILD	ADULT	CHILD	ADULT	CHILD
1811	85.0	98.1	89.3	96.1	80.9	108.3	83.3	91.3	68.4	57.1	82.9	110.0
1812	88.8	88.5	87.9	73.4	95.0	69.2	85.9	120.0	73.3	150.0	92.5	114.6
1815	82.0	81.7	81.7	81.9	70.7	76.9	63.9	92.9	91.7	0.0	95.3	89.0
1816	84.1	84.4	87.8	80.2	69.8	71.4	64.6	114.3	80.0	60.0	96.1	86.7
1817	78.5	85.4	81.8	74.2	81.8	81.3	62.9	84.2	37.5	0.0	86.7	109.1
1818	78.5	82.8	81.8	69.7	81.8	81.3	62.9	84.2	37.5	0.0	86.7	109.1
1819	79.6	87.1	82.7	75.6	82.9	82.4	64.4	90.0	44.4	200.0	87.7	111.8
1820	79.6	87.1	82.7	75.6	82.9	82.4	64.4	90.0	44.4	200.0	87.7	111.8
1822	82.8	74.0	78.7	75.6	89.1	79.5	86.5	61.5	80.0	63.6	86.4	79.7
1823	84.8	78.6	86.4	90.8	88.2	79.5	84.6	61.5	70.0	53.8	85.3	79.7
	MAGDALENO											
1802	93.6	88.8	88.1	119.6	86.0	86.4	96.8	73.3	62.5	200.0	118.6	120.0
1803	94.3	110.8	94.5	112.3	65.6	76.6	98.1	123.5	121.1	78.3	97.6	85.7
1804	92.1	109.1	92.8	99.1	78.9	150.0	87.2	111.0	142.9	0.0	146.7	115.4
1805	98.0	96.9	87.8	106.9	115.4	133.3	96.2	88.2	225.0	0.0	160.4	95.2
1806	95.8	112.0	92.7	102.5	164.3	33.3	95.2	118.2	50.0	146.2	134.5	120.0
1809	93.9	114.1	136.9	140.7	100.0	45.5	85.6	111.2	75.7	145.5	91.4	115.8
1816	92.5	105.2	73.8	156.5	90.0	128.6	103.4	84.2	76.6	60.0	110.0	90.0
	MAIQUETIA											
1796	92.4	90.3	89.0	79.3	148.1	66.7	86.5	73.5	0.0	0.0	103.7	188.0
1802	86.3	91.0	80.2	86.8	130.0	125.0	72.4	119.0	86.8	71.4	112.1	87.5
1804	89.1	78.1	95.3	62.5	89.3	100.0	73.7	82.1	78.4	70.6	122.6	88.1
1805	93.8	81.5	102.5	56.0	73.5	77.8	80.1	92.9	91.5	84.0	120.7	90.2
1807	77.4	82.5	71.9	62.5	96.6	77.8	78.6	98.6	57.3	52.8	98.5	104.9
1811	80.6	88.1	75.9	71.9	103.0	114.3	75.7	98.6	62.8	78.9	114.4	94.7
1815	73.7	89.1	98.6	101.0	57.6	166.7	60.3	80.4	67.4	84.8	82.6	88.9
1816	64.7	91.6	61.2	79.1	94.2	116.7	43.8	92.3	60.9	91.3	93.6	93.0
1817	44.6	85.4	48.6	73.9	48.4	183.3	34.4	81.5	38.4	58.3	59.6	97.5
1819	73.7	89.1	98.6	101.0	57.6	166.7	60.3	80.4	67.4	84.8	82.6	88.9
	MAMPORAL											
1784	95.6	90.6	94.7	50.0	133.3	166.7	71.4	100.0	69.2	240.0	102.3	69.2
1802	97.3	80.0	141.7	44.4	58.3	100.0	91.7	100.0	81.8	300.0	100.8	78.3
1804	95.5	110.6	140.0	140.0	185.7	133.3	67.7	93.3	67.6	183.3	103.1	100.0
1805	94.0	122.6	111.1	250.0	113.3	220.0	85.7	100.0	50.0	100.0	104.6	114.7
1807	91.3	123.4	200.0	133.3	66.7	200.0	85.1	94.7	48.3	85.7	99.1	140.6
1808	85.6	130.4	164.3	125.0	73.3	300.0	86.1	271.4	57.5	60.0	87.3	119.4
1809	76.9	135.4	214.3	100.0	100.0	900.0	52.9	91.7	66.0	146.7	78.6	125.7
1811	92.1	93.4	161.5	180.0	65.0	600.0	74.5	100.0	131.3	63.6	91.1	73.0
1812	79.1	107.8	163.6	55.6	121.4	700.0	121.6	119.2	56.0	50.0	56.0	93.3
1816	80.7	100.0	0.0	0.0	75.0	0.0	87.5	150.0	200.0	0.0	75.0	66.7
1817	97.0	120.0	0.0	0.0	87.5	450.0	0.0	0.0	147.6	200.0	80.9	76.0
1818	114.4	110.5	0.0	100.0	25.0	0.0	81.8	144.4	150.0	150.0	129.9	104.2
1820	88.9	82.0	0.0	0.0	80.0	0.0	65.6	93.3	50.0	75.0	100.0	80.0

TABLE 4. MALE/FEMALE RATIOS (CONTINUED)

YEAR	TOTAL M/F ADULT	TOTAL M/F CHILD	WHITE M/F ADULT	WHITE M/F CHILD	INDIAN M/F ADULT	INDIAN M/F CHILD	PARDO M/F ADULT	PARDO M/F CHILD	NEGRO M/F ADULT	NEGRO M/F CHILD	SLAVE M/F ADULT	SLAVE M/F CHILD
	MANAPIRE											
1804	149.3	149.1	130.0	153.3	111.8	142.9	118.9	131.8	100.0	200.0	276.0	175.0
1807	126.1	126.6	112.8	95.5	107.7	300.0	93.3	95.7	133.3	133.3	225.9	200.0
1808	126.4	126.6	112.8	95.5	113.3	300.0	93.3	95.7	133.3	133.3	225.9	200.0
1810	139.3	123.1	119.0	107.7	118.2	166.7	119.7	125.0	100.0	66.7	225.0	144.4
	MARACA											
1778	86.3	118.2	81.6	156.7	90.1	114.0	89.8	100.0	200.0	0.0	14.3	0.0
1803	77.2	113.0	62.5	93.8	74.7	116.8	83.5	108.6	140.0	0.0	87.5	300.0
1804	77.7	106.0	71.9	106.6	86.7	90.9	75.2	118.1	100.0	100.0	114.3	200.0
1805	80.0	94.6	66.9	101.2	94.8	75.2	78.7	117.4	108.3	0.0	350.0	100.0
1806	77.9	98.6	64.8	101.3	96.7	80.3	71.8	132.8	66.7	75.0	160.0	100.0
1807	89.2	87.9	74.5	85.7	98.2	89.1	94.3	93.2	95.2	68.8	108.3	50.0
1808	85.0	83.9	77.9	79.5	84.9	82.5	91.7	94.9	100.0	78.6	109.1	50.0
1809	90.7	89.4	87.6	79.7	94.8	83.9	82.2	120.0	120.0	80.0	108.3	33.3
1810	87.5	85.5	87.0	80.8	80.8	83.7	90.2	92.9	121.1	92.9	127.3	100.0
1817	87.2	95.3	74.1	87.5	102.8	113.3	83.5	104.5	150.0	0.0	200.0	0.0
	MARACAY											
1782	112.2	90.3	118.4	103.5	146.1	84.3	99.0	78.1	92.6	93.8	94.9	104.5
1796	92.5	106.4	104.0	103.4	0.0	0.0	82.4	103.6	78.0	92.5	94.9	134.1
1802	125.9	83.1	127.1	82.8	208.0	109.1	141.8	70.5	102.3	86.9	103.9	122.2
1803	125.3	87.1	127.3	84.9	200.0	92.9	140.0	79.8	103.0	87.1	103.9	122.0
1804	121.3	93.4	112.4	91.1	183.1	110.0	140.4	79.7	97.3	92.3	104.5	146.4
1805	84.2	105.6	82.3	114.6	102.3	100.0	80.5	98.9	200.0	0.0	96.9	108.6
1808	84.9	105.9	83.1	114.8	103.6	93.8	80.7	99.3	170.0	250.0	97.7	108.9
1809	113.2	96.5	127.3	109.0	88.9	92.9	114.0	79.8	103.0	87.1	103.9	122.0
1811	112.9	94.0	128.6	111.1	300.0	100.0	109.1	70.0	115.0	100.0	97.7	119.1
1816	80.3	101.5	51.3	94.6	50.0	93.3	89.9	115.3	78.7	73.3	91.7	97.1
1817	60.5	100.6	51.6	111.1	55.0	120.0	51.6	85.2	51.3	171.4	103.8	125.6
1818	96.3	97.3	91.2	108.0	150.0	65.5	93.2	96.6	126.0	91.9	96.3	89.8
1819	100.6	97.1	105.9	107.1	136.8	74.4	93.4	96.7	123.7	91.3	95.7	89.8
1820	96.4	97.3	91.0	111.7	131.0	84.6	93.3	96.3	126.1	92.3	95.4	82.6
	MARIA											
1803	86.5	89.2	91.1	92.0	73.4	97.5	90.6	87.5	76.2	72.7	100.0	66.7
1804	81.9	96.2	83.1	113.2	75.0	93.2	81.0	85.9	150.0	0.0	100.0	57.1
1805	87.9	100.0	89.0	114.9	81.4	82.8	87.3	94.4	100.0	300.0	120.0	55.6
1806	86.2	98.8	83.5	122.6	80.7	106.9	89.2	82.1	133.3	100.0	120.0	54.5
1807	84.8	97.0	84.5	98.1	83.3	114.8	81.6	96.7	200.0	66.7	157.1	44.4
1811	85.7	106.6	81.1	117.6	91.5	97.1	82.1	100.0	144.4	100.0	90.0	100.0
	MARIARA											
1802	101.4	97.8	128.3	126.2	80.8	100.0	100.6	83.8	79.7	88.9	88.7	120.5
1803	107.5	112.0	116.0	153.2	120.8	87.5	105.9	93.2	94.5	118.6	106.3	115.6

TABLE 4. MALE/FEMALE RATIOS (CONTINUED)

YEAR	TOTAL M/F ADULT	TOTAL M/F CHILD	WHITE M/F ADULT	WHITE M/F CHILD	INDIAN M/F ADULT	INDIAN M/F CHILD	PARDO M/F ADULT	PARDO M/F CHILD	NEGRO M/F ADULT	NEGRO M/F CHILD	SLAVE M/F ADULT	SLAVE M/F CHILD
1804	108.3	100.3	125.3	142.1	100.0	150.0	108.3	81.9	107.8	107.7	88.1	106.3
1805	103.4	111.2	115.5	123.5	96.0	133.3	95.7	105.1	154.7	87.5	91.9	131.4
1809	97.0	99.4	105.1	101.9	105.4	102.1	91.4	103.0	102.2	87.1	89.8	94.1
1815	93.2	112.1	100.0	132.9	107.1	113.3	84.2	102.9	148.5	90.3	86.9	135.6
1816	91.7	96.6	87.5	112.9	133.3	120.0	85.6	93.6	110.0	85.7	131.3	81.3
1817	98.8	98.9	99.4	108.9	120.6	500.0	100.6	97.5	77.6	73.1	96.3	91.3
1818	87.7	100.6	92.8	103.0	93.8	112.5	82.1	101.1	102.3	143.8	99.2	71.4
	MONTALBAN											
1781	89.0	120.7	94.0	118.6	89.5	81.8	86.4	150.0	180.0	166.7	79.6	77.3
1802	86.8	107.7	100.3	110.0	0.0	0.0	85.6	111.1	60.9	68.9	71.9	125.9
1803	84.3	133.4	89.3	130.6	0.0	0.0	81.3	140.3	252.9	133.3	62.5	110.3
1804	83.7	135.1	88.0	135.5	0.0	0.0	81.7	137.6	195.7	200.0	61.5	109.5
1805	81.2	133.1	87.1	134.0	0.0	0.0	80.0	136.8	176.0	170.0	51.9	93.8
1806	79.0	101.2	84.2	74.9	0.0	0.0	78.5	133.7	160.9	212.5	51.2	86.1
1808	74.6	115.5	66.5	88.5	0.0	0.0	82.6	143.7	145.0	147.8	51.5	84.8
1810	85.7	126.1	99.1	130.2	125.0	0.0	79.6	133.7	64.4	65.6	85.7	120.5
1815	105.9	85.9	106.1	79.8	100.0	200.0	113.3	85.3	93.3	118.2	89.8	91.1
1817	96.6	109.4	103.4	95.8	140.0	150.0	93.8	134.7	91.5	120.0	93.6	48.3
1818	85.2	86.9	83.9	85.0	87.5	150.0	85.2	94.0	76.7	87.5	91.8	46.0
1820	95.8	91.3	95.0	95.3	80.0	80.0	97.5	87.3	97.4	104.7	88.8	82.6
	MORON											
1804	116.5	122.2	0.0	0.0	0.0	0.0	120.4	96.4	0.0	0.0	95.2	164.7
1805	103.1	161.0	0.0	0.0	0.0	0.0	94.2	175.0	90.0	250.0	120.6	136.8
1806	93.3	106.1	0.0	0.0	0.0	0.0	100.0	112.0	92.3	100.0	85.7	100.0
1807	100.0	131.0	0.0	0.0	0.0	0.0	96.6	116.7	85.0	0.0	111.9	150.0
1818	87.6	90.5	0.0	0.0	0.0	0.0	73.8	82.4	0.0	0.0	118.9	125.0
1819	98.4	100.0	0.0	0.0	0.0	0.0	90.0	90.9	0.0	0.0	113.6	127.3
1820	95.8	90.7	0.0	150.0	0.0	0.0	98.8	92.7	90.9	89.7	91.9	82.9
	MOROTURO											
1802	84.6	89.8	75.0	60.0	100.0	0.0	100.0	83.3	86.7	120.8	66.7	25.0
1804	81.9	116.7	76.5	700.0	92.9	78.9	86.0	166.7	78.2	100.0	58.3	100.0
1805	87.1	95.5	65.6	40.0	90.0	50.0	91.5	123.1	83.9	157.1	155.6	33.3
1807	75.4	144.4	100.0	0.0	70.8	100.0	66.9	150.0	125.0	100.0	160.0	150.0
1808	81.9	96.7	76.5	700.0	92.9	52.6	86.0	125.0	78.2	100.0	58.3	50.0
1809	81.4	130.8	94.4	111.1	145.5	500.0	72.4	128.9	150.0	50.0	100.0	150.0
1815	81.9	103.3	76.5	100.0	92.9	78.9	86.0	166.7	78.2	100.0	58.3	50.0
	NAGUANAGUA											
1802	109.7	113.5	90.4	118.6	100.0	0.0	104.1	101.4	100.0	0.0	189.0	133.3
1803	101.1	110.0	85.7	113.2	100.0	0.0	87.4	91.1	100.0	0.0	201.4	177.3
1804	102.8	127.0	81.6	132.5	50.0	150.0	103.1	104.1	100.0	0.0	175.4	181.8
1805	98.1	131.8	78.6	103.1	33.3	300.0	101.3	188.9	0.0	0.0	144.8	67.7
1809	93.5	103.2	82.8	107.7	75.0	0.0	90.1	88.0	0.0	0.0	130.0	133.3
1816	104.6	99.6	98.2	90.0	78.6	92.0	90.0	200.0	146.2	58.3	130.6	52.0

TABLE 4. MALE/FEMALE RATIOS (CONTINUED)

YEAR	TOTAL M/F		WHITE M/F		INDIAN M/F		PARDO M/F		NEGRO M/F		SLAVE M/F	
	ADULT	CHILD	ADULT	CHILD	ADULT	CHILD	ADULT	CHILD	ADULT	CHILD	ADULT	CHILD
	NAIGUATA											
1801	114.9	83.1	191.7	400.0	85.1	90.0	185.7	0.0	250.0	100.0	116.5	76.7
1802	118.8	98.8	144.4	300.0	87.1	125.0	160.0	0.0	160.0	100.0	125.8	86.2
1804	111.0	154.2	108.3	300.0	85.3	322.2	100.0	0.0	100.0	0.0	120.7	94.3
1805	95.2	114.3	128.6	100.0	65.7	192.9	175.0	0.0	50.0	0.0	102.7	96.6
1809	98.5	96.1	138.5	125.0	68.9	152.4	50.0	0.0	50.0	0.0	106.8	80.3
1810	109.7	90.3	188.9	140.0	84.8	150.0	50.0	16.7	75.0	20.0	114.6	81.4
1811	94.1	102.7	240.0	110.0	67.7	119.4	100.0	166.7	100.0	600.0	95.2	88.7
1816	82.6	107.5	68.8	125.0	100.0	257.1	38.1	250.0	75.0	0.0	86.0	70.0
1817	88.5	80.9	114.3	125.0	88.6	116.7	50.0	133.3	110.0	50.0	89.6	66.0
1822	69.8	98.5	200.0	200.0	63.6	92.9	57.7	200.0	90.9	300.0	65.9	82.6
	NIRGUA											
1781	87.8	95.8	250.0	300.0	0.0	0.0	86.9	95.2	0.0	0.0	57.1	125.0
1802	79.2	117.4	100.0	175.0	0.0	0.0	79.1	118.1	0.0	0.0	66.7	70.0
1803	98.5	104.1	73.3	125.0	0.0	0.0	98.8	104.6	0.0	0.0	100.0	40.0
1804	99.1	104.1	93.8	125.0	0.0	0.0	99.1	104.6	0.0	0.0	100.0	40.0
1805	67.7	106.4	94.7	130.0	0.0	0.0	66.2	105.7	0.0	0.0	95.2	110.0
1806	68.0	106.1	100.0	140.0	0.0	0.0	66.5	105.1	0.0	0.0	90.9	110.0
1807	67.7	106.4	94.7	130.0	0.0	0.0	66.2	105.7	0.0	0.0	95.2	110.0
1808	91.2	102.9	89.1	72.7	25.0	0.0	96.2	119.5	77.3	78.0	60.0	115.4
1809	65.0	87.0	54.5	180.0	0.0	0.0	57.2	88.2	86.8	82.9	78.6	37.5
1810	96.1	79.5	77.3	157.1	72.7	83.3	100.9	72.0	91.5	87.3	51.0	200.0
1813	71.3	103.3	121.1	225.0	0.0	0.0	70.6	102.6	0.0	0.0	66.7	87.5
1817	70.5	101.1	121.1	175.0	0.0	0.0	69.8	100.8	0.0	0.0	66.7	87.5
1819	59.6	97.6	121.1	225.0	0.0	0.0	58.6	96.4	0.0	0.0	66.7	112.5
1820	55.6	98.6	77.3	275.0	0.0	0.0	54.8	96.3	0.0	0.0	79.2	200.0
1821	55.7	105.3	144.4	125.0	0.0	0.0	55.0	105.7	0.0	0.0	56.3	62.5
	OCUMARE DE LA COSTA											
1802	83.2	89.7	148.1	35.7	100.0	0.0	79.0	178.3	113.0	0.0	79.9	76.9
1803	93.3	96.0	147.8	27.3	250.0	0.0	89.3	129.8	86.6	88.1	95.0	99.3
1804	75.7	100.0	129.0	62.5	150.0	0.0	68.6	111.1	66.7	107.5	75.6	97.6
1805	97.0	110.9	123.3	72.7	0.0	0.0	77.2	100.0	91.7	75.0	106.2	119.8
1809	106.4	92.9	151.7	66.7	0.0	0.0	106.0	58.7	112.5	200.0	102.4	123.0
1815	72.8	94.4	93.9	60.0	0.0	0.0	64.0	97.7	42.4	75.0	81.2	96.3
1816	69.7	92.8	78.6	200.0	0.0	0.0	59.0	95.7	39.6	62.5	82.0	93.4
1817	76.7	94.4	64.5	133.3	0.0	0.0	60.2	108.1	37.0	53.8	101.5	88.1
1819	84.4	77.8	161.1	350.0	0.0	100.0	96.0	73.1	32.6	45.5	81.6	78.9
1820	82.9	86.2	80.8	300.0	0.0	100.0	96.5	77.6	59.1	71.4	80.6	87.1
	OCUMARE DEL TUY											
1783	92.0	115.9	86.5	137.0	136.4	250.0	85.3	104.0	50.5	130.4	106.5	111.2
1802	96.7	98.0	96.7	95.2	100.8	74.7	74.3	105.6	76.8	27.7	112.3	115.1
1803	80.3	84.2	89.7	77.7	85.2	90.0	59.6	83.3	59.6	67.8	94.0	108.1
1804	93.7	105.8	78.6	131.8	100.7	69.2	80.1	109.4	71.5	128.6	106.7	104.6

TABLE 4. MALE/FEMALE RATIOS (CONTINUED)

YEAR	TOTAL M/F		WHITE M/F		INDIAN M/F		PARDO M/F		NEGRO M/F		SLAVE M/F	
	ADULT	CHILD	ADULT	CHILD	ADULT	CHILD	ADULT	CHILD	ADULT	CHILD	ADULT	CHILD
1805	93.7	107.1	81.6	136.8	98.6	70.9	80.2	109.3	71.9	127.9	106.7	104.5
1810	92.8	108.9	98.6	98.1	94.4	120.4	76.1	110.1	87.5	126.3	98.9	107.0
1811	80.6	105.2	97.8	106.3	85.1	140.4	69.3	100.7	80.2	155.0	81.7	96.9
1815	91.8	83.8	74.2	66.7	81.1	81.0	94.3	94.3	80.0	83.3	99.3	85.7
1820	79.3	90.0	103.6	101.8	65.8	56.8	60.4	92.9	73.1	96.6	87.6	87.4
1821	66.2	109.1	69.4	128.4	37.5	70.6	57.6	104.7	50.0	95.8	74.2	109.9
1822	64.0	82.6	78.4	90.1	66.7	50.0	36.4	74.6	56.2	83.9	77.9	92.9
	ORTIZ											
1780	117.2	91.0	109.6	100.0	113.8	73.7	80.0	100.0	162.1	133.3	196.6	42.1
1802	98.7	275.8	83.2	299.2	76.2	133.3	87.8	48.5	126.2	3350.0	231.4	221.1
1803	88.7	121.7	78.8	121.8	144.4	83.3	90.4	84.8	105.3	183.3	156.3	190.0
1804	99.5	113.2	95.1	112.4	79.5	100.0	106.9	111.5	100.0	180.0	147.6	107.1
1805	99.3	103.1	95.1	101.4	77.5	100.0	106.9	117.4	100.0	60.0	147.6	116.7
1806	131.6	97.3	139.5	102.7	96.2	114.3	114.8	71.8	73.1	11.1	130.4	153.3
1807	99.7	85.8	96.5	89.0	93.3	78.6	91.8	81.0	116.1	84.2	149.1	75.0
1808	98.3	95.5	96.2	97.7	117.6	130.0	88.0	89.7	91.4	85.7	162.5	84.6
1809	98.6	87.9	95.2	91.8	109.1	76.9	93.5	90.3	92.7	75.0	141.4	66.7
1810	98.6	88.7	96.6	88.8	89.3	75.0	95.6	96.8	92.7	66.7	130.6	107.7
1813	97.0	106.1	94.0	101.7	69.6	100.0	102.0	106.5	81.8	136.4	136.5	142.1
	OSPINO											
1802	76.5	110.2	77.5	115.6	67.2	91.5	80.7	111.0	89.8	108.7	57.5	131.6
1803	75.9	111.2	77.6	117.3	67.4	98.4	79.2	110.4	88.2	81.5	58.3	142.5
1804	80.4	106.4	72.0	118.7	94.5	121.3	82.3	99.4	81.5	65.9	72.8	95.5
1805	83.3	99.3	82.3	101.3	85.5	97.2	85.3	97.9	89.5	75.0	61.8	116.3
1806	83.4	102.1	82.5	104.5	87.0	100.0	84.5	99.6	93.6	80.0	62.5	127.3
1807	84.3	101.0	81.4	104.4	87.6	96.0	86.9	99.4	91.2	76.9	65.6	126.1
1808	88.4	99.9	92.9	98.5	77.5	46.2	93.5	134.1	84.2	80.0	62.1	83.0
1809	75.1	121.0	83.4	115.8	66.1	91.3	74.9	144.5	82.9	105.3	69.0	87.8
1810	74.2	121.0	83.4	115.8	65.8	91.3	73.1	144.5	79.0	105.3	70.7	87.8
1811	75.9	115.8	80.7	115.9	66.2	119.6	78.1	111.3	71.0	200.0	58.2	97.8
1817	75.9	121.9	80.7	115.9	66.2	119.6	78.1	124.6	71.0	200.0	58.2	97.8
	PANAQUIRE											
1784	117.8	144.0	121.4	80.0	147.1	400.0	173.3	70.0	50.0	0.0	106.4	160.6
1802	123.5	105.2	195.0	200.0	137.5	141.7	137.0	111.1	100.0	0.0	114.5	97.8
1803	116.4	107.3	152.0	175.0	140.9	200.0	155.0	58.8	0.0	0.0	106.6	106.1
1804	130.6	97.3	200.0	66.7	168.4	150.0	188.9	150.0	100.0	0.0	116.0	90.6
1805	130.1	101.6	177.8	200.0	127.8	81.3	147.6	72.7	233.3	100.0	122.2	106.3
1807	128.4	117.2	181.3	60.0	130.8	280.0	187.0	70.6	0.0	0.0	115.2	120.2
1808	125.3	115.1	147.4	50.0	138.5	250.0	187.0	70.6	150.0	0.0	115.0	120.2
1809	116.0	95.1	188.9	33.3	160.0	73.3	140.0	91.7	200.0	0.0	101.5	103.3
1811	114.3	95.1	300.0	25.0	207.7	100.0	91.4	214.3	46.7	50.0	109.8	89.2
1812	113.2	93.3	210.0	28.6	130.0	76.9	92.3	158.3	61.5	66.7	114.2	92.9
1816	85.7	86.2	220.0	166.7	100.0	100.0	61.0	58.3	62.5	75.0	88.6	93.0

TABLE 4. MALE/FEMALE RATIOS (CONTINUED)

YEAR	TOTAL M/F ADULT	TOTAL M/F CHILD	WHITE M/F ADULT	WHITE M/F CHILD	INDIAN M/F ADULT	INDIAN M/F CHILD	PARDO M/F ADULT	PARDO M/F CHILD	NEGRO M/F ADULT	NEGRO M/F CHILD	SLAVE M/F ADULT	SLAVE M/F CHILD
	PARACOTOS											
1783	131.2	95.0	150.8	81.8	161.6	85.0	130.2	123.1	92.1	171.4	96.5	40.0
1802	109.5	128.6	110.3	142.9	94.9	143.6	113.1	111.4	100.0	128.6	133.3	120.0
1803	121.2	130.6	105.7	155.4	90.1	125.0	112.4	121.3	118.8	211.1	260.0	105.3
1804	105.9	118.1	108.0	107.5	97.8	153.2	114.0	106.6	141.7	183.3	90.0	104.3
1805	104.9	110.7	108.2	106.1	100.0	122.2	111.8	105.1	142.9	150.0	84.9	103.4
1806	103.8	94.2	99.4	86.0	105.9	98.6	104.5	113.7	130.0	125.0	116.9	84.0
1807	95.0	95.3	94.1	86.0	106.6	108.3	104.5	113.7	92.9	62.5	66.4	84.0
1808	100.4	93.1	94.3	86.9	106.1	97.6	104.2	113.7	94.7	62.5	111.1	84.0
1809	90.2	87.4	93.8	91.5	78.8	84.0	97.6	83.3	106.3	75.0	89.5	90.7
1810	97.5	91.2	94.5	91.8	107.6	93.8	97.8	89.5	106.3	75.0	88.1	90.9
1811	97.9	97.0	95.9	98.6	107.1	95.5	102.0	94.7	91.9	71.4	88.4	104.5
1812	95.5	86.5	101.9	87.6	93.0	94.3	92.2	72.5	93.0	61.5	93.0	101.9
1816	92.4	100.0	93.4	138.3	93.7	81.0	79.4	82.4	89.4	90.8	128.8	120.0
1817	90.9	99.2	93.0	133.3	88.1	65.1	81.5	91.7	89.4	93.5	114.9	108.3
1819	81.0	111.4	80.7	131.5	78.0	114.5	98.6	57.1	0.0	0.0	75.9	118.8
1820	80.8	111.2	80.7	133.3	78.0	110.5	97.1	57.1	0.0	0.0	76.3	121.9
	PARAPARA											
1780	96.3	132.6	104.3	119.7	82.4	60.0	94.7	163.1	74.2	196.9	120.6	74.3
1781	96.2	133.2	103.8	120.0	88.2	58.6	94.7	163.7	73.9	200.0	119.0	73.5
1782	98.1	130.9	152.3	124.3	40.0	67.7	95.1	159.8	75.8	188.2	108.8	65.0
1788	105.0	123.8	153.1	124.3	80.0	67.7	95.1	159.8	81.1	102.9	108.8	87.5
1802	93.6	112.6	99.5	127.5	118.2	111.1	77.7	116.0	98.0	108.4	166.7	80.8
1803	94.8	104.3	99.0	105.4	88.9	93.8	86.3	111.7	94.7	103.8	146.9	82.1
1805	96.5	99.7	98.5	110.0	84.6	77.8	89.4	98.4	97.2	97.0	148.4	92.0
1807	88.1	116.7	88.8	121.3	44.4	66.7	88.1	116.4	83.2	119.6	107.1	105.9
1809	87.9	127.9	91.4	120.3	50.0	66.7	87.9	133.9	78.9	130.4	104.3	88.9
1810	87.5	123.8	92.5	114.5	42.9	100.0	87.0	131.6	79.0	119.2	106.3	92.3
1811	88.2	93.8	87.6	92.4	50.0	57.1	88.0	95.9	90.1	89.6	100.0	94.4
	PATANEMO											
1802	78.8	111.4	0.0	66.7	100.0	0.0	87.7	132.3	39.3	133.3	83.8	94.9
1803	83.2	104.7	150.0	20.0	100.0	0.0	88.9	108.3	42.3	112.5	89.1	111.1
1804	88.2	146.2	0.0	25.0	200.0	0.0	74.3	126.9	77.3	200.0	108.2	185.0
1805	89.8	125.0	0.0	40.0	100.0	0.0	75.2	106.7	70.8	57.1	119.0	181.8
1808	85.4	111.8	0.0	0.0	0.0	0.0	72.4	91.4	87.0	71.4	93.5	177.3
1818	91.9	110.8	0.0	200.0	0.0	100.0	79.7	106.6	200.0	0.0	105.0	115.0
1819	103.0	112.6	0.0	200.0	200.0	50.0	96.1	94.2	75.0	150.0	115.2	176.5
	PAYARA											
1780	103.7	81.1	190.0	100.0	92.7	76.7	142.9	400.0	0.0	0.0	264.3	100.0
1802	100.2	97.6	92.6	66.7	102.4	119.0	104.0	73.9	96.0	80.0	88.9	100.0
1804	99.4	119.2	97.1	125.0	102.5	141.9	96.6	110.7	92.9	77.8	109.1	83.3
1805	99.5	123.1	96.8	111.1	104.8	144.0	94.2	137.5	94.1	83.3	111.1	77.8
1806	99.0	123.5	95.3	127.8	104.3	144.0	94.2	129.4	94.1	83.3	111.1	77.8

TABLE 4. MALE/FEMALE RATIOS (CONTINUED)

YEAR	TOTAL M/F ADULT	TOTAL M/F CHILD	WHITE M/F ADULT	WHITE M/F CHILD	INDIAN M/F ADULT	INDIAN M/F CHILD	PARDO M/F ADULT	PARDO M/F CHILD	NEGRO M/F ADULT	NEGRO M/F CHILD	SLAVE M/F ADULT	SLAVE M/F CHILD
1807	96.4	82.0	88.2	75.8	99.1	94.4	95.6	74.5	90.6	75.0	136.4	70.6
1812	99.5	81.3	96.8	90.0	104.8	69.4	94.2	72.7	94.1	120.0	111.1	128.6
	PETARE											
1802	96.5	87.3	89.3	83.7	84.6	88.1	133.5	77.9	89.5	88.3	95.2	92.9
1803	97.6	92.3	88.7	91.1	83.9	96.1	137.9	88.6	90.7	88.5	97.9	94.0
1804	103.3	86.2	101.5	82.2	88.0	72.7	122.0	67.7	106.6	75.9	100.7	125.2
1805	109.7	91.5	102.9	102.6	92.2	80.3	92.1	78.9	77.2	111.5	148.8	97.8
1806	101.9	94.8	96.3	89.4	83.9	120.3	95.5	80.0	62.4	93.9	128.0	102.8
1807	107.9	88.2	96.4	93.4	96.1	89.0	100.0	80.5	97.2	100.0	129.9	90.1
1811	99.5	91.7	98.0	82.1	106.8	115.1	100.0	92.3	100.5	89.8	98.2	96.0
1812	98.6	91.5	106.6	94.3	99.1	94.8	100.5	80.4	82.5	95.1	97.5	94.0
1815	98.6	95.2	97.3	98.2	101.9	63.6	99.4	83.0	95.7	102.1	98.9	102.2
1816	77.1	118.6	67.6	142.7	72.0	186.4	77.4	87.4	72.1	78.3	93.3	168.8
1817	81.3	105.3	83.9	107.8	67.6	148.4	75.7	70.9	75.2	77.8	92.1	159.2
1818	78.5	107.6	70.5	117.7	67.5	139.5	63.6	93.6	73.2	125.0	105.2	101.5
1819	78.0	108.1	70.7	117.8	64.6	141.7	65.2	92.6	73.2	125.0	104.1	104.1
1820	79.3	110.0	72.1	116.0	65.2	142.0	67.3	96.7	73.3	123.1	105.2	107.7
1821	79.9	107.6	71.5	114.3	64.8	142.6	68.9	95.3	73.3	126.3	106.0	102.9
1822	99.0	107.1	92.3	114.4	65.6	143.6	112.4	95.9	104.9	106.7	106.3	101.8
	PUERTO CABELLO											
1803	71.1	99.4	107.2	100.0	31.8	0.0	63.4	95.1	64.8	113.0	76.2	102.0
1804	71.3	92.4	98.1	85.3	41.2	100.0	61.0	95.6	70.9	108.8	85.7	72.1
1805	66.9	81.2	85.8	47.4	53.3	100.0	57.7	94.9	75.8	134.9	82.2	48.6
1806	65.0	71.6	93.3	87.3	28.6	25.0	50.6	64.5	74.9	79.4	83.8	70.3
1811	63.1	74.2	77.8	89.1	58.3	125.0	67.9	90.5	56.0	36.8	43.9	192.9
1817	72.6	91.2	98.3	79.2	59.1	125.0	67.4	75.0	78.4	100.0	44.9	160.7
1819	80.9	59.8	84.8	52.8	90.9	62.5	78.2	59.1	80.5	69.9	72.4	80.6
1820	48.2	80.5	107.1	51.8	175.0	33.3	28.1	132.7	62.0	104.3	58.6	63.6
	PUERTO CABELLO, CASTILLO											
1801	339.1	66.7	402.5	55.6	0.0	0.0	466.7	200.0	0.0	0.0	107.4	80.0
1802	380.3	380.0	641.2	500.0	0.0	0.0	0.0	0.0	0.0	0.0	56.0	200.0
1804	242.3	144.0	480.0	110.0	0.0	0.0	164.4	200.0	0.0	0.0	84.2	128.6
1805	301.2	102.6	366.7	166.7	0.0	0.0	367.9	84.6	0.0	0.0	126.7	64.3
1806	502.5	123.5	545.1	136.4	20.0	0.0	686.0	160.0	0.0	0.0	193.1	94.4
1807	432.4	123.2	491.5	137.5	125.0	0.0	539.3	125.0	0.0	0.0	150.0	106.7
1808	414.3	126.5	456.0	129.0	128.6	0.0	533.3	121.7	0.0	0.0	155.6	128.6
1809	370.0	115.6	457.8	118.2	242.9	0.0	364.0	115.4	0.0	0.0	182.9	125.0
1810	611.5	97.3	1103.7	135.5	425.0	0.0	530.2	60.6	0.0	0.0	115.8	142.9
1819	1962.5	68.8	1013.6	70.0	0.0	0.0	0.0	0.0	0.0	0.0	177.8	66.7
1820	2100.0	100.0	728.6	75.0	0.0	0.0	0.0	0.0	0.0	0.0	310.0	250.0
	QUARA											
1782	81.4	88.2	44.4	0.0	83.0	84.7	85.7	60.0	55.6	66.7	0.0	0.0
1791	79.9	115.7	125.0	0.0	78.4	122.7	100.0	57.1	0.0	0.0	0.0	0.0

TABLE 4. MALE/FEMALE RATIOS (CONTINUED)

YEAR	TOTAL M/F		WHITE M/F		INDIAN M/F		PARDO M/F		NEGRO M/F		SLAVE M/F	
	ADULT	CHILD	ADULT	CHILD	ADULT	CHILD	ADULT	CHILD	ADULT	CHILD	ADULT	CHILD
1802	74.6	103.4	62.5	200.0	75.4	98.1	65.0	137.5	0.0	0.0	0.0	0.0
1803	71.7	107.1	54.5	700.0	73.9	104.4	0.0	0.0	33.3	66.7	0.0	0.0
1804	89.8	100.9	50.0	300.0	90.9	100.0	66.7	0.0	66.7	166.7	0.0	0.0
1805	75.0	111.9	116.7	100.0	71.2	103.4	175.0	114.3	80.0	200.0	0.0	0.0
1807	90.2	151.8	100.0	300.0	88.1	149.3	96.2	160.0	108.3	100.0	0.0	0.0
1808	79.6	110.7	83.3	300.0	77.1	101.0	109.5	155.6	90.9	125.0	0.0	0.0
1809	79.4	126.5	133.3	600.0	78.2	121.6	75.0	350.0	80.0	57.1	0.0	0.0
1810	77.9	128.4	120.0	100.0	76.0	125.8	86.7	233.3	100.0	60.0	0.0	0.0
1811	74.2	65.1	150.0	600.0	70.4	55.9	84.4	233.3	106.7	33.3	0.0	0.0
1815	68.1	100.0	185.7	50.0	65.9	102.8	71.4	100.0	50.0	75.0	0.0	0.0
1816	75.3	102.8	216.7	100.0	74.2	101.7	75.6	209.1	47.4	16.7	0.0	0.0
1817	72.5	120.6	157.1	133.3	70.0	118.8	71.1	240.0	87.5	27.3	0.0	0.0
1818	90.2	72.3	150.0	100.0	92.0	72.2	77.6	76.3	82.4	52.4	77.8	150.0
1819	82.1	67.8	150.0	80.0	83.1	67.5	71.7	78.8	75.0	52.0	90.9	75.0
	QUIBOR											
1802	89.2	84.3	88.3	80.5	82.9	83.7	94.8	87.9	91.5	85.5	87.8	86.5
1803	86.2	88.2	88.5	80.5	66.4	82.0	94.8	87.9	91.5	127.5	87.8	86.5
1804	89.6	91.5	88.6	83.7	83.7	84.0	94.5	99.6	91.9	99.3	88.7	101.0
1805	90.9	85.9	89.7	82.0	85.6	85.2	95.3	88.5	94.4	89.5	89.7	87.7
1806	90.9	85.9	89.7	82.0	85.6	85.2	95.3	88.5	94.4	89.5	89.7	87.7
1807	90.2	84.6	89.7	82.0	85.6	85.2	92.6	82.9	94.4	89.5	89.7	87.7
1808	91.5	85.1	90.6	82.3	87.0	85.7	92.7	84.0	97.2	88.5	91.3	90.3
1810	81.4	106.5	81.6	106.9	79.7	92.2	82.0	112.7	82.6	122.2	78.9	108.3
1812	88.0	82.0	85.7	82.5	76.9	64.9	94.1	86.0	94.1	76.5	85.8	89.0
1815	88.5	81.6	86.3	80.8	78.1	65.8	94.4	85.8	94.1	76.5	85.8	89.0
1816	90.2	83.9	85.8	87.5	74.9	67.6	98.2	86.7	93.4	79.5	96.2	87.1
1817	86.7	85.3	85.0	94.9	75.6	65.6	89.8	87.3	89.0	75.4	96.1	89.2
1818	69.9	85.7	55.6	94.8	57.8	65.5	82.7	87.7	80.4	73.9	77.5	92.1
1819	71.4	91.1	69.9	98.2	71.1	66.7	70.4	94.4	54.6	95.3	98.5	92.4
1820	73.3	90.3	71.6	93.8	75.4	76.0	72.2	92.0	56.1	94.0	98.2	92.4
	RIO CHICO											
1802	101.0	89.6	388.9	500.0	136.4	116.7	127.3	111.5	84.8	90.9	88.4	76.7
1803	99.1	91.0	345.5	500.0	93.3	125.0	119.2	110.7	84.8	85.7	88.1	78.7
1804	97.8	93.8	185.7	500.0	90.0	300.0	103.4	85.7	84.8	133.3	94.9	83.3
1805	145.8	84.8	463.6	66.7	83.3	110.0	174.3	88.0	118.9	88.9	136.8	82.4
1806	163.3	82.3	509.1	66.7	83.3	114.3	174.3	83.3	116.2	100.0	161.0	76.9
1807	162.3	87.0	509.1	66.7	83.3	112.5	174.3	85.7	116.2	100.0	159.6	82.7
1808	157.6	94.8	509.1	57.1	84.0	105.6	162.2	86.5	112.5	135.0	156.0	91.5
1809	156.9	95.8	509.1	87.5	84.0	105.6	162.2	86.5	112.5	135.0	155.1	91.5
1810	152.3	98.2	338.1	200.0	85.7	104.8	141.3	87.5	111.1	119.2	153.5	91.7
1811	140.0	98.0	277.8	100.0	91.4	112.5	102.7	105.4	126.2	110.0	144.9	90.6
1812	142.5	95.4	305.3	125.0	81.5	111.1	125.0	86.8	89.8	93.3	150.0	94.4
1816	89.3	65.2	133.3	55.6	65.0	62.5	85.2	71.1	81.6	100.0	90.7	62.6
1817	96.0	89.4	181.3	125.0	109.1	93.8	64.4	87.5	108.6	81.8	93.4	88.5
1819	107.0	88.8	120.5	133.3	112.5	78.6	67.3	80.0	108.6	73.7	119.8	92.1

TABLE 4. MALE/FEMALE RATIOS (CONTINUED)

YEAR	TOTAL M/F		WHITE M/F		INDIAN M/F		PARDO M/F		NEGRO M/F		SLAVE M/F	
	ADULT	CHILD	ADULT	CHILD	ADULT	CHILD	ADULT	CHILD	ADULT	CHILD	ADULT	CHILD
	RIO DEL TOCUYO											
1802	89.2	125.2	89.8	128.9	94.8	115.0	79.2	175.0	0.0	0.0	54.5	220.0
1803	84.1	115.0	92.2	108.0	82.8	122.3	82.9	87.0	0.0	0.0	71.4	162.5
1804	85.5	120.5	89.3	107.4	85.5	118.0	90.6	123.1	0.0	0.0	68.4	211.1
1805	85.8	122.4	88.1	120.0	86.4	114.4	89.9	157.1	0.0	0.0	67.5	210.0
1808	106.8	81.3	89.5	61.1	116.4	81.4	71.2	81.8	0.0	0.0	90.7	107.4
1809	82.9	65.2	90.5	69.5	72.7	54.8	107.1	123.1	0.0	0.0	93.0	82.3
1815	81.5	91.8	87.6	93.5	83.3	97.0	73.5	69.0	0.0	0.0	46.4	87.5
	SABANETA											
1805	88.1	117.9	86.4	103.3	75.9	108.6	89.7	130.5	107.1	87.5	131.3	120.0
1808	84.5	129.4	119.4	169.8	68.5	131.8	83.1	118.9	50.0	125.0	163.6	200.0
1809	114.8	137.6	138.5	105.7	164.0	188.9	93.5	163.0	78.6	220.0	525.0	400.0
1810	110.0	113.6	140.0	98.0	144.0	175.0	86.0	122.6	152.2	77.8	337.5	200.0
1811	108.5	132.7	112.2	114.3	137.5	133.3	95.7	152.5	87.1	134.8	353.3	183.3
1812	86.3	111.6	112.9	169.4	63.5	68.8	81.6	98.4	63.0	100.0	111.1	133.3
1816	89.6	74.2	80.9	89.2	89.7	72.7	94.4	67.5	0.0	0.0	0.0	0.0
	SAN ANTONIO DE LAS COCUIZAS											
1780	89.8	84.9	78.9	76.2	114.3	83.3	87.3	84.7	85.3	89.3	162.5	150.0
	SAN ANTONIO DE LOS ALTOS											
1796	101.8	137.9	96.4	139.6	0.0	0.0	166.7	200.0	100.0	0.0	115.4	66.7
1802	125.9	132.1	118.3	133.3	150.0	0.0	93.3	33.3	0.0	0.0	288.9	200.0
1803	129.1	125.0	129.2	118.0	107.7	200.0	57.1	0.0	100.0	0.0	185.7	166.7
1804	129.2	144.9	127.3	143.2	350.0	0.0	114.3	0.0	0.0	0.0	136.0	266.7
1805	162.2	127.8	136.0	131.9	187.5	0.0	237.5	100.0	0.0	0.0	245.7	120.0
1808	191.9	133.7	144.8	133.8	500.0	400.0	275.0	100.0	300.0	0.0	216.0	118.2
1809	119.4	97.9	142.3	109.4	216.7	0.0	113.3	50.0	0.0	0.0	101.6	66.7
1810	156.4	103.0	138.4	103.7	33.3	0.0	122.7	128.6	100.0	0.0	202.2	105.7
1811	134.1	100.0	122.8	108.7	66.7	0.0	126.1	40.0	100.0	0.0	155.8	102.8
1812	127.6	92.9	105.3	98.6	200.0	0.0	62.5	57.1	100.0	0.0	182.2	96.6
1815	97.9	76.1	95.3	96.6	80.0	0.0	61.5	57.1	100.0	100.0	119.3	65.4
1816	100.0	94.9	96.3	90.0	42.9	100.0	57.7	66.7	100.0	0.0	127.9	110.7
1817	94.9	115.1	96.1	111.4	300.0	0.0	48.1	100.0	100.0	0.0	106.1	125.0
1818	83.6	122.9	100.9	97.4	66.7	166.7	35.9	137.5	50.0	0.0	85.5	157.1
1819	91.7	98.8	101.8	76.5	0.0	0.0	67.7	116.7	100.0	0.0	91.0	155.6
1820	89.1	114.9	96.8	83.6	73.3	75.0	66.7	100.0	200.0	66.7	85.7	247.1
	SAN CARLOS											
1781	101.2	103.7	98.4	112.2	116.7	107.0	117.3	92.1	80.9	95.6	93.1	107.6
1786	96.5	98.1	99.8	101.6	85.5	109.5	95.0	85.7	76.9	105.9	105.9	106.5
1787	89.6	100.4	91.6	106.5	99.4	175.0	87.3	87.8	79.9	114.3	91.0	87.3
1788	86.7	103.6	91.6	105.5	101.3	158.6	87.1	90.1	58.4	113.1	90.4	106.8
1791	87.3	102.0	92.5	104.5	98.3	148.6	88.3	90.5	62.2	106.1	89.2	104.5

TABLE 4. MALE/FEMALE RATIOS (CONTINUED)

YEAR	TOTAL M/F ADULT	TOTAL M/F CHILD	WHITE M/F ADULT	WHITE M/F CHILD	INDIAN M/F ADULT	INDIAN M/F CHILD	PARDO M/F ADULT	PARDO M/F CHILD	NEGRO M/F ADULT	NEGRO M/F CHILD	SLAVE M/F ADULT	SLAVE M/F CHILD
1796	87.4	100.4	93.3	101.5	95.4	132.1	88.4	90.9	63.2	103.6	88.6	104.4
1798	80.0	102.7	81.9	88.8	76.2	85.4	96.7	109.6	77.6	112.4	57.7	119.6
1799	79.1	103.1	82.8	88.9	74.7	84.0	96.3	109.2	71.0	115.3	57.7	120.0
1800	82.4	103.0	82.1	90.6	75.6	83.0	96.2	108.7	93.6	113.5	58.0	116.7
1801	82.4	102.5	82.4	90.9	75.6	87.0	96.3	108.9	93.7	107.8	57.6	117.0
1802	83.5	105.8	82.0	111.1	93.5	131.0	76.4	105.3	72.0	96.0	103.5	97.2
1803	83.7	105.7	82.2	110.8	94.2	125.0	76.6	106.9	72.2	95.0	103.6	97.3
1804	93.8	102.5	100.7	108.8	97.7	104.8	76.5	113.3	82.3	98.5	118.7	71.0
1805	91.7	103.0	93.5	110.9	97.7	106.6	76.5	109.9	82.3	98.5	118.8	72.1
1806	91.6	102.0	93.4	105.4	97.7	105.1	76.8	108.3	82.5	96.7	118.4	79.3
1808	91.7	103.0	93.5	110.9	98.4	107.7	76.5	109.9	82.3	98.5	118.8	72.1
1809	91.7	103.0	93.5	110.9	97.7	106.6	76.5	109.9	82.3	98.5	118.8	72.1
1811	90.2	89.3	84.7	79.8	93.6	80.0	96.0	92.9	92.6	73.3	77.2	96.2
1812	90.9	89.6	85.1	81.5	92.1	55.6	96.5	92.5	102.3	60.0	78.5	99.5
1816	68.9	98.2	67.7	110.1	102.3	90.3	67.4	98.8	145.9	66.7	55.7	88.1
1817	64.7	67.8	63.8	79.3	73.8	57.7	64.3	65.5	61.9	30.3	55.7	69.5
1818	63.1	79.6	67.4	79.2	62.7	88.1	60.0	79.4	59.8	39.6	64.3	97.8
1819	56.2	71.4	62.7	78.2	44.3	54.5	51.2	67.0	47.9	36.0	63.7	97.9
1820	59.6	74.5	67.3	78.4	60.4	54.8	49.9	67.2	117.3	87.0	65.4	98.9
1822	62.4	70.5	67.0	77.6	96.2	57.1	57.9	65.8	59.1	34.4	62.6	95.7
1823	57.2	70.0	59.7	73.6	95.5	75.0	53.7	64.7	59.4	48.3	58.0	94.4
1824	60.0	73.9	73.7	78.7	86.4	60.9	53.5	69.4	68.7	54.1	51.4	89.8
SAN DIEGO DE ALCALA												
1781	81.3	104.6	84.3	134.8	80.5	111.5	84.6	81.1	0.0	0.0	30.8	157.1
1802	58.7	74.5	59.6	58.5	59.3	66.7	63.3	87.6	40.7	73.2	100.0	75.0
1803	64.5	79.4	63.5	73.3	55.4	89.7	65.6	80.7	90.5	61.5	87.5	100.0
1804	82.0	82.2	73.3	90.7	81.0	77.1	86.4	84.1	84.6	74.1	100.0	100.0
1805	82.7	132.3	80.7	107.4	92.2	157.1	73.3	142.6	187.5	100.0	100.0	133.3
1809	83.2	146.9	83.1	185.7	117.9	250.0	68.5	109.4	116.7	266.7	66.7	200.0
SAN DIEGO DE LOS ALTOS												
1802	97.5	100.0	98.8	120.0	92.9	74.2	84.8	81.0	120.0	0.0	112.9	130.0
1803	91.9	85.6	95.8	88.4	97.2	86.8	68.6	72.7	84.0	76.5	89.2	90.9
1804	108.9	113.1	104.9	150.0	116.7	70.0	112.1	88.9	75.0	166.7	130.0	122.2
1805	107.9	113.1	101.8	144.4	112.9	78.9	112.5	84.6	75.0	150.0	150.0	90.9
1807	94.8	122.9	87.2	138.1	97.1	93.8	94.6	123.1	76.5	80.0	143.3	181.8
1808	104.9	100.7	96.0	115.2	102.0	79.6	129.7	90.0	100.0	50.0	130.0	146.2
1809	108.8	96.7	97.8	105.2	107.1	85.2	168.6	77.8	90.9	63.6	123.4	150.0
1810	90.2	92.8	90.3	107.1	91.0	80.6	84.6	75.9	158.3	63.6	80.3	109.5
1811	96.5	91.0	90.7	96.8	92.9	84.7	111.4	90.5	126.7	118.2	107.4	78.4
1815	98.2	83.9	91.0	81.7	90.3	114.6	126.5	50.0	84.4	94.7	131.6	56.7
1816	95.2	87.5	90.7	96.3	84.6	92.7	107.9	64.7	66.7	78.9	128.1	81.0
1817	95.8	73.8	91.3	68.4	87.3	78.4	108.3	80.0	82.1	80.0	126.8	78.3
1818	96.8	88.3	103.8	78.5	74.4	89.7	87.2	85.7	130.4	126.3	86.7	75.0
1819	96.2	98.7	96.1	112.5	78.8	89.1	117.1	75.0	78.9	300.0	128.3	85.2
1820	95.3	98.6	89.6	116.7	91.4	82.0	86.9	68.2	81.8	140.0	131.3	125.0

TABLE 4. MALE/FEMALE RATIOS (CONTINUED)

YEAR	TOTAL M/F ADULT	TOTAL M/F CHILD	WHITE M/F ADULT	WHITE M/F CHILD	INDIAN M/F ADULT	INDIAN M/F CHILD	PARDO M/F ADULT	PARDO M/F CHILD	NEGRO M/F ADULT	NEGRO M/F CHILD	SLAVE M/F ADULT	SLAVE M/F CHILD
	SAN FELIPE											
1782	104.9	75.5	74.1	33.8	291.8	28.0	111.4	102.4	105.3	87.8	106.4	145.2
1802	79.6	72.2	91.4	77.3	80.0	90.0	78.7	81.5	79.2	90.9	65.9	44.4
1803	81.3	79.3	92.7	76.2	94.3	88.9	78.9	80.8	82.1	90.0	63.9	68.8
1804	59.6	98.4	61.0	101.6	46.0	112.5	61.2	97.2	44.6	140.0	57.0	97.1
1805	60.6	104.8	62.1	104.1	44.7	100.0	60.1	105.0	59.7	150.0	62.8	101.3
1817	77.9	88.5	67.1	88.9	116.7	50.0	78.9	90.9	120.0	70.0	74.1	82.9
1818	41.9	70.6	29.5	47.2	0.0	0.0	52.7	80.1	40.0	100.0	38.4	61.0
1819	78.1	88.4	65.7	89.1	108.3	55.6	79.9	91.6	92.9	69.2	71.7	78.8
1820	77.9	74.4	65.5	88.2	100.0	61.5	79.8	71.7	83.3	76.5	71.9	75.4
1821	73.0	86.9	66.7	80.0	108.3	55.6	71.5	92.0	92.9	69.2	91.7	78.8
	SAN FELIPE, MITAD DE (1)											
1807	74.9	107.5	64.3	88.1	68.4	0.0	75.8	101.4	113.3	0.0	83.1	140.5
1808	75.0	108.8	64.3	111.9	68.4	0.0	75.8	99.5	113.3	0.0	83.7	137.2
1809	74.2	114.5	59.4	92.5	66.7	200.0	77.6	118.8	64.3	150.0	81.0	113.2
1810	74.8	104.5	64.8	104.9	55.6	0.0	75.8	99.1	94.4	33.3	84.6	127.3
1811	74.8	104.5	64.8	104.9	55.6	0.0	75.8	99.1	94.4	33.3	84.6	127.3
1812	113.1	77.9	87.4	66.7	133.3	0.0	122.4	79.9	80.0	0.0	85.9	66.7
	SAN FELIPE, MITAD DE (2)											
1807	60.9	97.0	66.1	112.8	60.9	60.0	58.9	98.1	95.0	80.0	61.1	75.0
1808	62.9	102.6	68.7	105.9	40.0	125.0	63.8	100.5	72.0	71.4	54.2	112.1
1809	63.9	96.3	69.2	109.3	57.7	108.3	65.0	106.9	61.5	80.0	54.9	37.2
1810	63.7	101.3	65.9	95.8	60.9	107.7	65.3	109.7	58.0	81.8	56.4	76.1
1811	57.2	88.7	61.4	83.6	73.0	150.0	56.3	87.8	69.4	66.7	49.3	94.1
	SAN FERNANDO DE APURE											
1801	81.8	56.5	78.2	54.3	82.6	65.5	87.0	54.2	78.1	64.3	58.0	90.5
1805	93.4	67.5	97.4	75.0	90.3	60.0	88.7	63.0	0.0	0.0	100.0	66.7
1806	87.1	84.3	92.6	93.9	76.7	71.4	86.6	86.2	0.0	0.0	85.2	60.0
1816	81.9	103.2	71.9	103.5	63.6	72.0	86.6	112.3	93.2	142.9	125.0	73.1
	SAN FERNANDO DE CACHICAMO											
1783	126.1	118.8	140.0	153.8	37.5	200.0	120.5	140.9	93.3	125.0	163.0	76.0
1802	108.8	116.7	84.2	125.0	155.6	150.0	100.0	82.8	94.1	200.0	175.0	200.0
1803	106.2	123.5	97.0	125.0	150.0	150.0	89.4	83.3	88.2	240.0	170.0	166.7
1805	96.4	88.5	104.2	100.0	220.0	100.0	87.1	81.1	40.0	100.0	109.5	100.0
1806	114.0	92.4	139.4	82.6	133.3	175.0	97.8	92.2	125.0	0.0	133.3	78.6
1807	113.2	107.6	138.2	82.6	133.3	175.0	97.8	92.2	125.0	0.0	127.3	1100.0
	SAN FRANCISCO DE CARA											
1783	91.0	109.8	86.7	88.9	80.0	133.3	96.9	111.3	0.0	0.0	58.3	171.4
1802	96.7	74.7	95.3	113.5	73.3	85.7	100.0	32.7	131.3	150.0	80.0	188.2

TABLE 4. MALE/FEMALE RATIOS (CONTINUED)

YEAR	TOTAL M/F ADULT	TOTAL M/F CHILD	WHITE M/F ADULT	WHITE M/F CHILD	INDIAN M/F ADULT	INDIAN M/F CHILD	PARDO M/F ADULT	PARDO M/F CHILD	NEGRO M/F ADULT	NEGRO M/F CHILD	SLAVE M/F ADULT	SLAVE M/F CHILD
	SAN FRANCISCO DE TIZNADOS											
1780	124.6	113.6	169.2	87.2	112.0	130.8	94.0	121.1	116.1	114.7	163.6	125.0
1801	104.6	76.5	115.2	80.0	88.9	75.0	91.2	75.8	0.0	0.0	216.7	81.5
1802	106.2	97.9	117.1	91.7	150.0	85.7	98.1	146.4	92.3	50.4	219.5	104.8
1803	108.9	94.2	114.9	76.3	112.5	33.3	93.8	97.2	97.0	99.0	254.2	91.7
1805	102.8	104.2	116.8	95.3	66.7	25.0	92.2	105.1	180.0	0.0	190.6	139.1
1807	102.3	103.2	115.1	96.2	66.7	25.0	92.6	103.7	112.5	0.0	184.2	139.1
1808	101.7	103.1	112.0	91.3	66.7	25.0	92.8	104.3	112.5	0.0	181.4	139.1
1809	102.0	102.8	113.7	90.2	66.7	66.7	92.8	102.6	112.5	75.0	181.4	144.0
1811	97.5	99.2	98.4	114.3	105.8	84.0	99.0	98.0	86.8	104.3	106.7	82.8
1812	92.1	88.5	101.1	82.7	84.3	80.0	85.5	82.2	94.7	97.6	115.5	128.1
	SAN FRANCISCO DE YARE											
1783	108.4	105.4	95.8	250.0	88.4	142.9	157.1	111.8	102.4	100.0	107.4	96.6
1802	103.6	107.0	134.5	64.3	90.1	107.9	106.1	233.3	75.0	88.2	111.2	118.4
1803	86.6	98.5	145.8	100.0	71.7	134.3	100.0	233.3	72.6	92.4	89.3	89.4
1804	93.1	82.6	107.7	66.7	84.1	102.7	100.0	133.3	74.8	78.6	99.7	80.5
1805	91.0	97.0	162.5	100.0	78.2	106.3	129.2	66.7	69.4	93.1	94.4	98.2
1810	108.1	83.1	121.2	114.3	110.5	60.4	93.9	71.8	81.4	110.0	116.5	91.3
1811	109.1	83.1	121.2	114.3	110.5	60.4	95.5	71.8	90.7	110.0	116.5	91.3
1815	64.7	65.8	88.5	150.0	86.5	70.8	80.4	59.4	73.7	60.0	59.2	63.2
1817	71.9	118.8	100.0	200.0	46.3	129.4	25.3	129.2	81.8	366.7	98.9	74.6
1818	71.2	106.4	123.1	300.0	100.0	106.3	56.5	104.2	58.9	100.0	71.9	100.0
1820	73.0	125.8	95.6	277.8	76.2	128.6	66.3	119.6	51.4	130.8	77.0	116.3
1821	88.5	97.2	138.5	176.9	65.8	104.0	68.2	116.1	67.9	69.6	100.0	83.0
1822	87.4	135.8	92.9	176.9	90.0	78.4	83.6	103.6	102.6	79.2	86.3	169.5
	SAN JAIME											
1780	131.6	108.3	128.0	108.9	200.0	52.6	136.8	113.6	318.2	121.1	71.8	112.5
	SAN JOSE											
1781	102.2	110.4	105.7	144.0	90.8	89.4	111.4	122.2	100.0	150.0	89.3	16.7
1788	91.5	121.7	86.1	90.0	86.0	118.6	95.8	119.9	71.4	200.0	73.7	300.0
1790	106.2	107.6	98.6	78.7	80.3	102.3	116.4	119.1	83.9	100.0	0.0	0.0
1791	106.2	107.6	98.6	78.7	80.3	102.3	116.4	119.1	83.9	100.0	0.0	0.0
1792	88.3	94.5	60.8	80.5	83.3	82.5	106.5	105.7	93.3	300.0	66.7	28.6
1794	95.9	94.5	85.2	80.5	83.3	82.5	106.5	105.7	93.3	300.0	66.7	28.6
1795	96.9	120.6	96.6	163.3	80.0	106.9	100.8	86.7	103.7	157.8	85.2	100.0
1798	96.9	111.6	96.9	100.0	82.3	100.0	100.7	100.0	103.7	147.3	77.1	133.3
1799	96.9	111.6	96.9	100.0	82.3	100.0	100.7	100.0	103.7	147.3	77.1	133.3
1800	96.9	118.4	96.9	100.0	82.3	100.0	100.7	126.7	103.7	147.3	77.1	25.0
1801	91.6	125.3	88.7	134.1	82.9	109.1	94.8	104.1	95.7	168.6	80.0	0.0
1803	90.4	108.1	88.6	101.3	90.4	114.3	91.0	108.4	106.3	100.0	73.3	150.0
1804	97.6	98.3	84.5	105.2	225.0	104.2	91.0	96.6	106.3	33.3	65.5	75.0
1805	92.6	111.8	87.6	142.6	89.0	119.4	96.1	107.0	80.0	42.9	90.0	50.0
1807	88.4	94.5	76.7	94.3	71.2	78.3	95.9	99.0	0.0	0.0	100.0	75.0

TABLE 4. MALE/FEMALE RATIOS (CONTINUED)

YEAR	TOTAL M/F		WHITE M/F		INDIAN M/F		PARDO M/F		NEGRO M/F		SLAVE M/F	
	ADULT	CHILD	ADULT	CHILD	ADULT	CHILD	ADULT	CHILD	ADULT	CHILD	ADULT	CHILD
1808	88.3	94.5	75.9	92.9	73.2	80.0	94.7	98.0	0.0	0.0	128.6	100.0
1811	86.9	93.7	71.1	102.0	75.3	100.0	95.4	90.0	0.0	0.0	88.2	50.0
1812	76.5	86.1	90.1	47.9	64.9	61.9	75.9	102.9	30.8	200.0	0.0	0.0
1815	71.0	110.2	53.3	109.1	96.2	113.8	69.0	110.8	71.4	25.0	114.3	200.0
1818	43.3	81.8	37.0	125.0	65.2	40.7	37.9	89.6	66.7	66.7	66.7	0.0
1819	52.5	120.7	80.1	127.3	53.2	181.6	40.6	89.6	133.3	66.7	75.0	0.0
1822	51.3	59.7	66.7	62.9	76.5	86.9	39.2	44.1	26.9	25.0	38.5	66.7
1823	61.1	62.8	72.8	80.0	79.6	89.9	50.8	45.1	20.0	16.7	37.5	83.3
	SAN JOSE DE APURE											
1802	98.1	98.6	116.7	91.7	97.6	80.8	87.8	138.9	103.8	85.7	166.7	0.0
1804	90.0	82.5	82.0	81.1	94.4	89.7	91.7	77.8	85.4	80.6	0.0	0.0
1806	95.1	95.5	80.9	93.3	94.7	88.2	106.8	133.3	85.7	77.8	0.0	0.0
1807	92.6	76.8	80.9	65.4	98.8	91.3	101.6	82.4	78.8	62.5	0.0	0.0
1808	92.3	81.0	82.2	80.0	94.9	91.3	93.9	78.6	88.9	70.6	0.0	0.0
1809	92.3	81.0	82.2	80.0	94.9	91.3	93.9	78.6	88.9	70.6	0.0	0.0
	SAN JOSE DE TIZNADOS											
1802	103.2	104.6	115.4	175.9	103.6	111.1	92.5	93.8	93.1	133.3	164.9	89.5
1803	98.5	113.3	111.5	147.1	102.5	116.7	84.0	104.3	148.3	266.7	171.4	115.0
1804	92.8	113.9	116.5	134.1	79.2	84.0	79.5	108.2	174.1	233.3	133.3	150.0
1805	90.4	101.1	99.3	121.1	73.7	100.0	83.5	94.2	154.5	233.3	122.4	116.7
1807	87.6	103.0	117.4	148.9	61.7	66.7	83.3	91.6	74.5	117.2	109.8	123.1
1808	86.0	116.9	117.6	140.5	76.0	216.7	75.4	104.0	63.8	155.6	197.1	150.0
1809	87.4	121.7	118.3	140.4	75.0	211.1	80.6	113.6	66.3	127.3	130.0	121.4
1810	79.8	112.0	120.4	120.0	54.2	150.0	82.0	107.3	88.4	103.2	28.2	131.3
1812	87.3	103.6	112.2	111.3	52.1	145.8	82.2	99.1	80.6	103.2	154.1	109.1
1816	66.7	106.5	71.6	128.6	71.7	73.1	62.4	103.3	58.2	104.4	128.9	137.5
1817	68.8	110.0	71.3	125.0	72.3	74.2	66.4	105.3	60.8	126.6	112.5	126.3
	SAN JUAN DE LOS MORROS											
1802	88.3	98.9	89.3	103.0	102.5	280.0	90.1	68.6	70.9	91.8	100.0	158.3
1803	91.3	92.7	91.9	96.0	114.3	122.2	89.4	73.1	87.5	94.9	76.5	117.6
1805	84.5	101.9	95.1	98.9	100.0	190.0	77.0	76.6	55.6	135.7	65.9	105.6
1806	82.6	97.3	94.3	108.0	65.4	172.7	82.6	71.7	69.9	86.9	69.2	100.0
1807	84.0	109.1	92.7	106.3	71.2	166.7	94.6	95.6	61.8	114.3	73.7	90.9
1809	81.2	100.8	91.7	93.0	66.7	137.5	78.8	91.5	65.4	121.6	76.2	91.7
1810	81.5	98.5	93.0	99.1	69.8	122.2	79.4	109.4	64.9	84.5	71.4	85.7
1811	83.8	97.3	89.7	98.2	125.0	116.7	77.8	94.6	63.3	104.3	80.5	74.1
	SAN MATEO											
1781	82.9	97.2	75.4	108.9	70.7	77.8	93.1	92.5	0.0	0.0	83.2	113.0
1802	92.4	98.3	87.0	109.2	73.5	34.5	86.9	115.5	83.3	100.0	121.2	89.9
1803	89.8	108.1	73.7	122.9	83.7	140.5	89.8	112.0	88.9	87.5	115.1	81.0
1804	87.8	105.3	77.6	121.4	68.3	134.4	84.6	102.0	73.7	76.9	118.6	91.5
1805	88.7	101.7	78.9	112.7	81.3	121.9	84.7	94.3	75.0	142.9	113.8	90.2
1806	88.4	104.0	70.1	106.3	85.6	120.0	86.2	113.2	66.7	100.0	124.3	85.5

TABLE 4. MALE/FEMALE RATIOS (CONTINUED)

YEAR	TOTAL M/F ADULT	TOTAL M/F CHILD	WHITE M/F ADULT	WHITE M/F CHILD	INDIAN M/F ADULT	INDIAN M/F CHILD	PARDO M/F ADULT	PARDO M/F CHILD	NEGRO M/F ADULT	NEGRO M/F CHILD	SLAVE M/F ADULT	SLAVE M/F CHILD
1808	101.8	84.8	81.7	133.3	131.1	125.0	106.5	55.8	82.9	142.9	118.0	82.8
1809	92.4	82.4	82.1	93.2	90.7	97.4	88.1	73.8	86.7	100.0	118.3	76.3
1811	94.4	77.7	90.8	92.4	96.2	62.2	87.5	66.9	128.6	50.0	106.6	94.7
1815	60.7	70.7	57.1	65.4	71.4	73.9	58.4	69.4	75.0	42.9	65.3	85.4
1816	64.6	83.2	60.1	81.2	69.1	83.3	69.2	79.1	75.0	50.0	61.1	102.4
1817	64.8	88.8	59.6	81.6	71.6	104.0	67.0	79.0	70.0	100.0	65.5	118.4
1818	65.4	90.9	63.2	84.4	76.9	100.0	63.8	81.2	76.7	87.5	63.6	121.4
1821	64.0	94.9	66.9	100.0	60.2	124.2	59.9	74.7	82.4	220.0	66.7	115.1
SAN MIGUEL DE TRUJILLO												
1808	102.7	116.1	101.4	133.5	102.9	126.8	90.7	95.5	95.7	83.3	423.1	0.0
SAN NICOLAS DE TOLENTINO												
1803	96.7	100.0	0.0	0.0	200.0	0.0	104.4	90.9	64.4	133.3	102.0	76.2
1808	76.4	94.9	114.3	80.0	113.6	200.0	53.4	150.0	107.7	40.0	112.8	111.1
1818	73.3	146.2	0.0	0.0	0.0	0.0	73.3	146.2	0.0	0.0	0.0	0.0
1820	81.1	60.7	200.0	66.7	0.0	0.0	84.2	56.8	0.0	0.0	67.6	71.4
1821	81.1	52.5	0.0	0.0	200.0	66.7	84.2	45.5	67.6	71.4	0.0	0.0
SAN PEDRO												
1810	98.4	102.3	92.2	112.1	133.3	0.0	109.0	103.8	0.0	0.0	100.0	71.4
1811	100.7	112.6	95.9	117.7	92.9	83.3	120.3	122.4	0.0	0.0	74.1	88.5
1816	90.2	88.9	96.0	81.7	87.5	66.7	88.4	97.6	0.0	0.0	60.0	133.3
1817	90.3	86.0	94.3	76.8	133.3	66.7	88.7	97.4	0.0	0.0	57.7	133.3
SAN RAFAEL DE ONOTO												
1779	115.4	81.6	118.3	90.0	107.4	77.3	138.5	72.7	100.0	66.7	250.0	0.0
1810	103.1	83.9	102.9	84.1	109.3	71.0	94.3	90.0	0.0	0.0	240.0	0.0
1811	97.1	98.0	90.6	114.9	108.8	93.6	87.6	92.5	0.0	0.0	500.0	0.0
1828	84.6	83.2	85.5	92.9	85.5	75.0	82.9	88.1	80.0	66.7	0.0	0.0
1829	94.9	82.9	95.8	92.9	88.1	75.0	99.1	86.8	81.8	66.7	400.0	0.0
SAN RAFAEL DE ORITUCO												
1783	100.4	106.9	108.9	108.0	87.5	120.0	113.7	96.4	70.2	108.6	93.3	113.5
1802	92.4	101.4	137.3	121.7	0.0	0.0	83.6	97.7	0.0	0.0	83.1	97.0
1803	85.8	113.2	111.6	116.0	0.0	0.0	80.0	111.0	0.0	0.0	79.4	117.2
1804	87.0	110.7	96.8	134.5	0.0	0.0	84.4	109.9	0.0	0.0	83.1	80.0
1805	82.5	100.0	120.5	116.1	0.0	0.0	72.0	103.1	0.0	0.0	72.7	75.0
1806	91.4	92.1	117.2	87.2	0.0	0.0	81.3	100.9	0.0	0.0	98.3	68.6
1808	86.3	94.4	113.0	66.7	0.0	0.0	75.4	122.9	0.0	0.0	87.0	56.4
1809	85.9	100.0	93.2	84.3	70.6	58.3	79.3	122.2	133.3	142.9	95.8	63.6
1810	89.5	76.4	89.4	71.4	233.3	60.0	86.4	78.8	58.3	81.8	112.5	73.7
1811	65.5	67.7	89.4	71.4	233.3	60.0	40.9	125.7	84.6	16.5	78.4	54.5

TABLE 4. MALE/FEMALE RATIOS (CONTINUED)

YEAR	TOTAL M/F ADULT	TOTAL M/F CHILD	WHITE M/F ADULT	WHITE M/F CHILD	INDIAN M/F ADULT	INDIAN M/F CHILD	PARDO M/F ADULT	PARDO M/F CHILD	NEGRO M/F ADULT	NEGRO M/F CHILD	SLAVE M/F ADULT	SLAVE M/F CHILD
SAN SEBASTIAN DE LOS REYES												
1783	83.6	97.3	78.3	96.2	86.9	119.8	92.4	89.8	106.3	84.6	54.7	83.3
1802	89.3	69.3	86.3	80.9	81.6	112.5	94.4	57.3	109.5	62.5	74.6	117.2
1803	89.0	65.7	87.4	88.7	80.5	38.9	93.6	59.2	109.1	116.7	71.9	133.3
1804	88.6	64.7	87.1	85.3	80.0	33.3	93.7	59.5	96.0	114.3	71.1	131.0
1805	89.9	66.0	86.2	88.4	74.4	32.4	96.6	60.8	100.0	162.5	75.7	125.0
1806	91.4	66.1	89.7	91.7	69.9	34.1	95.7	60.2	110.3	93.8	82.0	138.9
1809	80.1	107.0	80.1	94.0	88.7	136.1	77.5	110.4	110.3	89.5	80.2	115.6
1810	81.1	95.3	86.0	103.5	77.9	96.0	79.4	91.7	82.5	58.6	73.0	130.0
1811	79.9	92.9	83.8	102.8	76.1	96.1	79.0	88.8	82.5	61.3	71.0	113.9
SANARE												
1803	82.4	96.9	85.4	98.8	81.1	92.7	84.2	98.2	84.8	104.2	84.6	150.0
1804	83.4	96.6	85.5	96.5	82.3	91.9	84.7	96.4	86.1	108.5	92.3	175.0
1805	82.4	96.9	85.4	98.8	81.1	92.7	84.2	98.2	84.8	104.2	84.6	150.0
1806	95.7	114.3	92.3	90.6	97.8	136.6	96.1	87.0	81.9	86.4	96.3	78.6
1807	95.7	110.9	95.7	77.9	97.8	138.5	94.5	65.2	81.9	86.4	92.9	118.8
1808	94.4	111.2	95.8	79.1	96.4	138.5	92.0	65.2	79.7	85.0	92.9	118.8
1809	94.4	111.3	95.8	89.5	96.4	138.5	92.3	65.2	79.7	68.3	92.0	114.3
1810	94.3	110.0	96.5	91.8	96.3	133.5	94.1	70.2	62.9	70.1	117.4	143.8
1812	98.8	90.0	93.2	75.4	100.6	94.9	94.8	89.4	108.3	81.0	107.7	77.8
1815	94.0	84.2	92.0	77.8	94.7	86.2	92.5	90.3	88.5	73.7	118.2	58.3
1816	94.3	90.5	93.9	71.4	95.9	97.4	94.1	81.8	75.8	63.6	77.8	166.7
1817	95.0	89.5	93.9	68.2	95.9	97.4	94.1	81.8	88.1	75.0	105.0	84.6
1818	94.3	90.5	93.9	71.4	95.9	97.4	94.1	81.8	75.8	63.6	77.8	166.7
1819	93.9	84.5	92.0	77.8	94.7	86.2	92.5	90.3	88.5	73.7	125.0	50.0
1820	95.0	90.1	93.9	71.4	95.9	97.4	94.1	81.8	88.1	75.0	105.0	84.6
SANTA CRUZ DE ARAGUA												
1802	93.8	92.7	92.9	93.3	187.5	80.0	94.6	90.2	65.5	280.0	90.0	100.0
1803	91.6	71.7	86.1	36.7	145.2	55.6	97.8	117.7	45.2	200.0	155.6	125.0
1804	95.4	116.6	93.1	109.4	180.0	110.0	96.9	126.8	33.3	400.0	107.7	50.0
1805	83.3	109.2	77.4	109.0	69.0	60.0	91.5	111.5	50.0	0.0	130.0	71.4
1808	86.3	93.9	92.4	83.1	133.3	71.4	77.0	113.5	27.3	50.0	100.0	45.0
1811	156.3	98.9	268.8	79.2	92.9	50.0	27.5	130.7	1621.4	80.0	206.3	166.7
1815	72.0	97.5	66.7	95.3	79.8	98.3	83.7	93.8	50.0	200.0	48.7	133.3
1816	73.3	102.4	71.1	101.0	55.9	78.6	76.6	103.4	100.0	266.7	80.6	109.1
1817	65.4	96.3	64.2	94.6	200.0	62.5	66.4	99.4	75.0	200.0	58.3	78.9
1818	60.1	101.8	60.1	107.9	23.5	50.0	64.5	96.8	38.3	84.7	69.0	140.0
1822	57.2	145.8	54.1	215.2	127.7	64.3	48.5	114.6	14.0	193.3	133.3	53.3
SANTA INES DEL ALTAR												
1779	112.0	300.0	0.0	0.0	127.3	0.0	157.1	300.0	40.0	100.0	0.0	0.0
1802	79.5	177.8	183.3	100.0	80.0	125.0	61.5	200.0	75.0	0.0	33.3	0.0
1803	97.6	66.7	0.0	0.0	140.0	66.7	84.8	66.7	100.0	0.0	0.0	0.0
1804	78.7	233.3	0.0	0.0	81.8	233.3	67.6	233.3	300.0	0.0	100.0	0.0

TABLE 4. MALE/FEMALE RATIOS (CONTINUED)

YEAR	TOTAL M/F ADULT	TOTAL M/F CHILD	WHITE M/F ADULT	WHITE M/F CHILD	INDIAN M/F ADULT	INDIAN M/F CHILD	PARDO M/F ADULT	PARDO M/F CHILD	NEGRO M/F ADULT	NEGRO M/F CHILD	SLAVE M/F ADULT	SLAVE M/F CHILD
1805	106.5	147.1	0.0	0.0	233.3	33.3	95.1	157.1	200.0	0.0	0.0	0.0
1806	92.7	90.9	0.0	0.0	250.0	14.3	76.3	113.3	0.0	0.0	0.0	0.0
1810	92.9	125.0	0.0	0.0	166.7	50.0	84.0	135.7	0.0	0.0	0.0	0.0
1811	96.6	52.6	0.0	0.0	200.0	20.0	84.6	64.3	0.0	0.0	0.0	0.0
1818	90.5	84.4	0.0	0.0	80.0	0.0	92.2	84.4	0.0	0.0	0.0	0.0
1819	82.6	57.3	100.0	75.0	86.4	92.9	88.3	51.4	63.0	44.4	0.0	0.0
1820	76.8	83.6	140.0	75.0	93.8	54.5	72.9	90.0	62.5	93.8	0.0	0.0
1829	94.7	81.6	100.0	60.0	121.7	70.8	86.0	89.4	0.0	0.0	0.0	0.0
	SANTA LUCIA											
1784	105.3	107.7	132.4	113.3	98.4	109.6	93.1	125.0	85.8	128.6	112.6	91.4
1787	102.9	103.0	127.0	140.0	99.3	98.1	91.3	107.9	74.1	105.6	106.6	93.7
1802	89.3	80.8	115.7	101.1	95.3	66.7	70.4	71.0	84.2	100.0	90.6	86.7
1803	101.9	116.9	125.0	119.4	146.8	58.3	111.1	139.0	112.2	233.3	67.5	105.9
1804	107.0	93.3	103.7	119.4	96.2	64.6	100.0	80.6	92.6	114.3	121.6	98.7
1805	90.8	147.8	97.1	178.6	94.0	113.6	76.6	162.2	97.4	141.7	101.2	146.8
1808	94.5	97.1	129.7	101.2	84.6	116.9	92.2	90.2	44.9	105.6	95.1	90.9
1809	95.5	99.5	129.7	101.2	80.4	116.9	97.4	99.0	44.9	105.6	95.1	90.9
1811	94.5	91.9	107.4	94.9	83.3	90.0	85.2	106.3	95.7	90.9	99.1	81.7
1816	71.5	101.8	80.6	113.4	63.6	57.7	59.0	100.0	113.2	250.0	78.4	102.2
1817	67.5	232.7	75.5	204.0	100.0	150.0	90.6	243.7	10.4	250.0	22.2	285.7
1818	95.8	85.8	101.1	95.0	109.1	75.0	93.9	81.8	79.4	72.7	95.3	83.3
1819	74.6	92.8	86.0	76.2	72.8	97.4	59.4	102.7	71.6	90.9	87.1	91.3
	SANTA MARIA DE IPIRE											
1783	119.4	106.3	123.0	81.0	85.0	162.5	116.7	120.8	125.0	133.3	141.8	108.6
1798	114.2	84.3	92.6	86.7	80.0	166.7	109.9	90.2	143.6	64.0	149.1	85.7
1803	104.0	86.2	84.6	90.0	100.0	80.0	97.0	94.1	93.8	70.6	181.8	73.9
	SANTA ROSA DE LIMA											
1802	76.7	70.4	77.8	72.5	81.2	70.5	70.0	73.2	76.1	67.3	76.7	77.8
1803	79.6	59.0	78.8	78.1	82.5	25.9	75.8	83.7	80.6	66.4	78.3	72.2
1804	76.7	70.4	77.8	72.5	81.2	70.5	70.0	73.2	76.1	67.3	76.7	77.8
1805	80.7	69.9	83.4	65.0	86.4	78.4	78.4	72.5	78.7	71.1	70.3	80.0
1807	83.3	65.1	85.8	64.4	93.6	104.5	96.7	50.0	77.0	339.1	72.3	7.8
1808	90.1	70.6	85.3	66.7	87.2	109.1	90.6	87.5	101.3	343.5	72.3	7.8
1809	92.1	76.1	92.4	69.5	87.9	87.2	97.1	74.6	88.0	85.9	86.4	75.0
1810	87.2	89.6	94.4	105.8	87.5	120.0	81.6	75.7	87.9	85.6	80.6	125.0
1815	85.6	81.4	93.5	74.1	89.1	113.3	75.5	78.7	88.3	86.9	80.9	120.0
1816	104.5	90.1	89.8	74.1	84.3	100.0	116.2	96.6	119.1	100.5	82.4	100.0
1817	95.8	66.5	94.9	72.8	141.3	70.6	99.1	67.8	84.6	57.8	84.2	51.4
1819	93.3	67.4	93.5	74.1	65.5	79.5	100.3	67.8	89.7	57.8	82.9	51.4
1820	93.3	67.4	93.5	74.1	65.5	79.5	100.3	67.8	89.7	57.8	82.9	51.4
	SANTA TERESA DE JESUS											
1783	121.3	88.4	165.6	100.0	95.9	100.0	146.2	100.0	75.0	100.0	118.0	76.0
1786	98.0	87.2	93.3	60.0	110.4	72.0	79.5	121.1	100.0	200.0	100.7	85.7

TABLE 4. MALE/FEMALE RATIOS (CONTINUED)

YEAR	TOTAL M/F ADULT	TOTAL M/F CHILD	WHITE M/F ADULT	WHITE M/F CHILD	INDIAN M/F ADULT	INDIAN M/F CHILD	PARDO M/F ADULT	PARDO M/F CHILD	NEGRO M/F ADULT	NEGRO M/F CHILD	SLAVE M/F ADULT	SLAVE M/F CHILD
1787	103.7	85.4	104.9	54.5	112.2	72.4	73.3	114.3	225.0	100.0	100.0	85.5
1788	111.0	80.0	104.9	54.5	136.0	104.5	81.6	65.6	225.0	55.6	102.6	85.9
1802	109.0	101.5	120.6	111.9	106.3	78.9	122.4	81.3	83.7	127.6	109.9	100.0
1803	107.6	88.7	124.4	83.3	115.3	92.3	108.1	77.4	73.2	118.2	110.0	84.7
1804	106.7	95.8	118.1	107.7	117.1	96.7	98.8	71.8	79.0	93.0	111.6	100.0
1805	108.0	97.1	111.6	152.6	121.9	78.9	102.6	57.5	76.2	97.7	117.2	98.7
1810	105.1	110.0	109.9	108.6	103.7	77.8	121.8	107.1	93.0	129.4	103.2	116.7
1811	107.6	107.5	125.8	114.8	113.7	87.0	111.1	92.9	85.0	116.1	106.8	110.9
1815	73.6	100.6	47.3	135.0	54.1	80.0	90.1	75.0	71.6	97.4	86.0	110.3
1816	75.2	103.2	75.4	96.8	54.4	86.7	85.7	100.0	69.4	96.8	79.5	115.8
1817	72.9	99.4	75.6	91.7	60.4	108.3	85.4	76.0	63.5	96.9	74.0	111.3
1820	79.2	99.4	80.3	102.4	86.7	137.5	80.3	110.0	55.0	77.8	88.9	101.5
	SARARE											
1779	104.6	93.9	121.2	83.9	94.3	55.0	95.1	127.4	101.7	92.3	480.0	700.0
1802	88.0	92.4	60.2	82.2	164.7	123.7	82.9	94.1	89.9	81.2	77.8	200.0
1804	88.2	89.4	62.0	88.7	160.4	116.3	83.8	87.3	89.4	79.8	77.8	200.0
1805	77.2	118.3	68.0	126.9	70.4	186.0	81.9	106.4	84.4	126.1	60.0	77.8
1807	93.0	89.5	60.2	71.1	160.0	110.5	84.2	94.1	111.6	81.2	77.8	200.0
1808	88.2	89.4	62.0	88.7	160.4	116.3	83.8	87.3	89.4	79.8	77.8	200.0
1809	88.2	89.4	62.0	88.7	160.4	116.3	83.8	87.3	89.4	79.8	77.8	200.0
1810	88.6	91.7	64.7	84.5	141.9	120.0	84.3	94.7	92.5	81.8	83.3	50.0
1811	88.2	89.4	62.0	88.7	160.4	116.3	83.8	87.3	89.4	79.8	77.8	200.0
1817	71.6	99.3	76.7	85.7	76.5	118.9	68.3	97.9	125.0	75.0	66.7	66.7
1818	68.3	102.3	56.8	133.3	85.6	92.5	66.5	97.8	80.0	233.3	70.6	110.0
	SIQUISIQUE											
1802	94.2	92.4	85.8	135.5	90.5	91.6	115.8	94.6	106.5	71.4	78.6	83.3
1803	95.0	92.6	88.5	130.6	91.1	91.7	115.1	94.8	105.6	74.1	81.5	83.3
1804	95.0	84.0	93.5	110.5	88.4	80.9	119.8	88.0	109.1	78.1	82.8	92.3
1805	97.5	72.1	90.4	78.1	93.4	68.6	115.4	78.8	109.1	77.8	92.6	92.9
1807	102.6	130.9	112.6	97.0	98.4	150.4	120.6	112.7	79.2	166.7	70.7	71.4
	TACARIGUA DE MAMPORAL											
1784	88.3	89.2	100.0	62.5	200.0	300.0	64.7	71.4	159.3	88.2	75.9	91.7
1802	85.9	115.1	146.7	200.0	100.0	0.0	100.0	500.0	102.5	192.3	77.2	100.0
1803	87.5	109.8	140.0	0.0	100.0	50.0	200.0	400.0	109.5	158.3	75.6	98.9
1804	91.1	120.2	128.6	300.0	160.0	133.3	220.0	500.0	122.2	158.3	77.9	107.3
1805	83.3	129.1	175.0	200.0	200.0	0.0	78.3	50.0	79.3	280.0	77.3	121.4
1806	95.1	128.2	146.2	150.0	140.0	50.0	175.0	0.0	113.3	250.0	83.8	122.1
1807	93.7	114.5	161.5	133.3	140.0	0.0	84.6	150.0	120.8	275.0	82.8	104.5
1808	88.7	139.4	190.9	100.0	116.7	0.0	100.0	350.0	100.0	500.0	77.3	125.8
1809	83.8	119.4	150.0	100.0	71.4	0.0	126.1	140.0	111.1	0.0	70.9	111.5
1811	106.0	105.7	180.0	100.0	25.0	0.0	83.3	233.3	150.0	214.3	103.8	86.4
1816	76.1	128.3	141.7	40.0	133.3	0.0	55.8	116.7	60.9	533.3	83.2	109.1
1818	76.7	122.0	171.4	200.0	36.4	50.0	48.6	142.9	48.8	140.0	93.9	110.8
1820	84.0	168.5	220.0	200.0	54.5	200.0	66.7	111.1	57.4	161.5	92.4	185.7

TABLE 4. MALE/FEMALE RATIOS (CONTINUED)

YEAR	TOTAL M/F ADULT	TOTAL M/F CHILD	WHITE M/F ADULT	WHITE M/F CHILD	INDIAN M/F ADULT	INDIAN M/F CHILD	PARDO M/F ADULT	PARDO M/F CHILD	NEGRO M/F ADULT	NEGRO M/F CHILD	SLAVE M/F ADULT	SLAVE M/F CHILD
	TACATA											
1783	93.1	117.5	300.0	90.0	88.9	126.7	79.4	152.2	55.3	60.7	108.0	161.9
1799	109.1	107.0	126.8	175.0	125.8	69.4	109.6	147.1	50.0	300.0	98.5	87.8
1802	111.3	97.0	111.8	109.1	103.6	98.0	112.6	82.7	118.2	125.0	115.4	96.2
1804	102.7	97.3	130.4	150.0	94.7	88.8	101.0	134.1	86.7	77.8	107.4	70.9
1805	96.9	105.8	106.0	166.7	85.2	96.2	104.1	138.2	86.7	80.0	104.1	80.7
1812	101.6	114.6	112.3	107.0	102.7	117.5	100.0	132.8	86.7	200.0	94.2	89.7
1813	97.6	107.6	108.4	122.1	104.9	141.2	99.5	93.6	69.2	100.0	86.6	97.7
1817	97.6	85.3	112.5	96.2	91.7	116.7	102.7	70.6	71.4	75.0	80.0	64.5
1818	91.4	106.0	114.3	92.9	75.4	103.7	93.0	108.2	57.1	0.0	73.5	128.2
1819	97.0	105.6	127.2	108.3	80.9	102.7	93.9	102.0	40.0	0.0	80.7	112.8
1820	94.9	112.4	105.9	116.5	98.4	96.4	97.6	114.3	50.0	100.0	77.5	117.3
1821	97.0	114.2	102.3	124.7	102.7	97.4	109.2	112.1	47.1	0.0	80.5	110.9
1822	91.5	109.6	102.1	116.0	88.9	108.2	100.9	104.7	57.1	83.3	73.0	111.5
	TAGUAI											
1802	99.1	124.2	96.9	142.3	102.0	186.7	97.1	100.0	150.0	500.0	98.9	137.0
1803	109.6	98.4	129.1	70.3	122.0	186.7	95.0	95.6	94.4	500.0	98.9	137.0
1804	86.4	81.5	87.7	78.8	67.1	64.1	75.2	61.5	88.7	81.3	103.7	134.1
1805	84.6	78.3	85.9	77.5	62.7	62.5	73.8	59.7	88.7	78.2	101.8	118.0
1810	85.3	87.4	81.6	88.9	74.1	62.5	76.5	66.7	92.9	90.0	103.7	134.1
	TAPIPA											
1803	116.7	101.5	137.5	33.3	72.7	33.3	200.0	120.0	100.0	0.0	112.4	121.3
1804	110.1	82.3	110.5	50.0	108.3	35.7	52.4	100.0	200.0	0.0	114.2	108.5
1805	106.4	82.8	166.7	80.0	127.3	30.8	75.0	157.1	112.5	66.7	102.7	87.5
1806	102.8	94.0	92.9	33.3	125.0	100.0	45.5	100.0	91.7	50.0	106.7	100.0
1807	110.4	75.3	144.4	20.0	171.4	100.0	42.9	100.0	75.0	50.0	114.7	75.4
1808	105.6	95.0	82.4	75.0	266.7	33.3	23.1	100.0	100.0	100.0	113.0	100.0
1811	103.7	122.2	94.1	83.3	162.5	0.0	88.9	50.0	60.0	100.0	106.0	135.3
1812	103.5	143.5	65.0	100.0	150.0	100.0	100.0	200.0	40.0	150.0	115.0	152.9
1816	70.2	91.2	60.0	50.0	52.9	55.6	38.5	180.0	58.3	200.0	79.8	94.1
1817	75.0	92.6	70.0	55.6	100.0	40.0	38.5	180.0	58.3	200.0	79.8	94.1
1818	84.9	82.1	115.4	57.1	70.8	100.0	69.2	83.3	66.7	125.0	89.1	78.8
1819	79.5	91.9	90.9	75.0	58.3	116.7	100.0	133.3	40.9	150.0	90.3	71.4
1820	68.9	91.2	50.0	50.0	47.1	55.6	38.5	180.0	58.3	200.0	79.8	94.1
1829	94.4	92.3	175.0	50.0	71.4	50.0	84.0	87.5	58.8	266.7	100.0	79.2
	TARIA											
1803	84.2	111.1	0.0	0.0	0.0	0.0	80.6	111.1	0.0	0.0	100.0	0.0
1808	81.4	188.9	0.0	0.0	100.0	0.0	77.9	200.0	109.1	100.0	100.0	200.0
1810	96.8	65.6	0.0	0.0	0.0	0.0	95.7	65.6	0.0	0.0	0.0	0.0
	TARMAS											
1802	98.4	116.7	94.4	350.0	141.7	100.0	121.6	85.0	84.6	0.0	88.5	116.7

TABLE 4. MALE/FEMALE RATIOS (CONTINUED)

YEAR	TOTAL M/F		WHITE M/F		INDIAN M/F		PARDO M/F		NEGRO M/F		SLAVE M/F	
	ADULT	CHILD	ADULT	CHILD	ADULT	CHILD	ADULT	CHILD	ADULT	CHILD	ADULT	CHILD
1803	94.8	112.3	130.0	300.0	91.7	300.0	109.5	70.8	84.6	0.0	87.7	123.3
1805	102.4	98.4	130.8	83.3	118.2	500.0	104.3	42.9	100.0	100.0	95.8	124.2
1807	116.9	82.1	153.8	87.5	122.2	0.0	120.0	69.6	150.0	0.0	107.2	85.3
1808	114.6	80.3	93.3	100.0	157.1	200.0	121.6	77.8	125.0	0.0	110.0	76.9
1810	109.9	86.6	154.5	41.7	125.0	50.0	91.4	122.2	150.0	100.0	112.5	87.2
1811	109.4	96.3	150.0	38.5	150.0	100.0	93.3	138.9	175.0	100.0	108.2	95.7
1815	86.7	100.0	136.4	225.0	166.7	100.0	88.9	137.5	75.0	133.3	78.6	73.3
1816	88.6	78.0	200.0	160.0	225.0	0.0	78.3	76.0	90.0	66.7	78.6	73.3
1817	92.8	73.3	140.0	200.0	130.0	0.0	81.0	61.3	136.4	200.0	85.1	68.5
1818	108.9	84.8	172.7	70.0	150.0	0.0	89.1	94.4	225.0	50.0	105.9	93.3
1819	103.3	86.9	154.5	450.0	140.0	0.0	86.2	80.0	78.6	0.0	109.5	78.0
1820	92.9	95.2	200.0	175.0	200.0	0.0	76.9	80.5	122.2	66.7	84.5	100.0
1829	107.2	70.4	133.3	100.0	0.0	0.0	109.7	64.7	0.0	0.0	86.4	72.7
	TEMERLA											
1802	76.4	95.8	54.5	25.0	0.0	0.0	77.5	98.9	0.0	0.0	100.0	0.0
1803	71.8	89.0	54.5	50.0	0.0	0.0	72.9	90.8	0.0	0.0	0.0	0.0
1804	65.7	112.7	50.0	200.0	0.0	0.0	66.3	111.4	0.0	0.0	0.0	0.0
1805	64.8	113.8	50.0	200.0	0.0	0.0	65.2	112.5	0.0	0.0	100.0	0.0
1806	64.8	109.3	50.0	200.0	0.0	0.0	65.3	108.2	0.0	0.0	100.0	0.0
1807	63.8	103.2	44.4	50.0	0.0	0.0	65.2	104.3	0.0	0.0	0.0	0.0
1808	64.8	109.3	50.0	200.0	0.0	0.0	65.3	108.2	0.0	0.0	100.0	0.0
1810	64.7	93.9	0.0	0.0	0.0	0.0	65.3	94.9	0.0	0.0	0.0	0.0
1817	78.2	93.4	114.3	116.7	0.0	0.0	76.8	92.0	0.0	0.0	0.0	0.0
1818	81.7	93.3	93.3	85.7	0.0	0.0	80.9	93.6	0.0	0.0	150.0	100.0
1819	72.9	110.3	100.0	100.0	0.0	0.0	71.7	111.0	0.0	0.0	0.0	0.0
1820	98.3	89.1	100.0	77.8	0.0	0.0	94.6	89.7	0.0	0.0	800.0	100.0
1821	95.6	88.7	100.0	77.8	0.0	0.0	91.4	89.3	0.0	0.0	800.0	100.0
	TINACO											
1771	91.3	102.8	85.3	108.1	105.1	70.0	96.4	100.0	183.3	100.0	98.1	100.0
1781	104.0	115.8	103.2	93.8	0.0	0.0	105.7	140.7	83.3	0.0	105.4	200.0
1787	88.4	109.5	87.0	96.2	135.7	200.0	86.9	119.6	120.0	0.0	89.5	228.6
1788	85.1	116.3	84.5	97.7	96.8	325.0	87.7	158.1	69.2	0.0	71.1	125.0
1790	42.6	106.9	98.6	114.4	131.0	200.0	17.2	81.0	83.3	133.3	81.1	80.0
1791	91.9	101.2	92.1	100.8	77.6	166.7	97.6	110.0	100.0	0.0	75.0	68.4
1794	97.3	97.9	97.6	109.2	121.9	114.3	93.0	91.9	42.9	100.0	123.9	52.6
1795	94.7	91.7	91.1	104.7	116.1	53.8	96.3	89.2	37.5	25.0	120.4	61.1
1796	91.4	93.1	86.0	111.0	157.7	28.6	93.4	88.6	58.3	100.0	100.0	58.8
1798	90.7	92.8	88.9	99.3	113.0	66.7	93.5	91.0	75.0	0.0	81.8	92.3
1799	90.5	95.1	93.4	102.6	108.0	183.3	87.9	85.1	106.7	50.0	71.7	125.0
1800	89.0	87.7	93.1	100.0	113.0	200.0	84.9	75.2	75.0	88.9	78.2	80.0
1801	88.5	87.7	92.0	100.9	104.2	450.0	87.5	73.2	81.3	50.0	64.5	122.2
1802	85.6	95.9	87.1	128.7	112.5	233.3	77.5	70.1	115.5	88.5	79.0	76.9
1803	86.5	96.7	90.0	124.6	127.3	160.0	75.2	74.4	111.7	110.7	88.6	83.3
1804	86.0	92.6	88.5	108.6	121.7	140.0	75.9	82.3	116.4	71.4	82.4	87.5
1805	86.3	100.3	88.0	129.3	96.3	100.0	80.1	86.6	110.3	60.7	82.4	78.9
1806	85.7	108.1	90.3	127.9	90.0	200.0	78.7	93.7	89.2	78.6	87.1	106.3
1807	82.6	103.5	85.3	128.1	80.0	250.0	78.5	91.8	88.4	45.7	82.9	114.3

TABLE 4. MALE/FEMALE RATIOS (CONTINUED)

YEAR	TOTAL M/F		WHITE M/F		INDIAN M/F		PARDO M/F		NEGRO M/F		SLAVE M/F	
	ADULT	CHILD	ADULT	CHILD	ADULT	CHILD	ADULT	CHILD	ADULT	CHILD	ADULT	CHILD
1808	80.3	103.3	85.8	120.6	85.2	150.0	70.5	90.8	101.6	68.0	81.7	114.3
1811	83.4	91.4	95.6	87.7	66.7	60.0	73.6	100.7	85.5	80.0	89.8	80.0
1812	83.2	93.6	85.5	110.1	90.3	60.0	81.9	83.8	38.9	33.3	83.6	106.7
1816	76.0	101.2	70.7	118.5	45.5	73.9	84.0	75.9	0.0	0.0	83.6	120.0
1817	66.2	98.8	64.9	109.3	31.8	84.2	67.8	75.3	0.0	0.0	78.5	127.8
1819	67.4	88.0	64.3	95.6	31.8	84.2	71.5	68.4	0.0	0.0	78.5	127.8
1820	113.8	86.7	100.2	88.3	112.5	67.6	140.5	88.3	0.0	0.0	77.6	93.5
1821	89.5	99.5	91.6	92.9	75.5	70.3	90.5	121.7	0.0	0.0	76.5	93.5
1822	90.1	86.7	87.9	87.7	95.3	70.3	90.5	83.9	66.7	75.0	105.2	121.7
1823	92.1	97.4	88.0	109.2	146.4	76.6	91.0	84.4	87.0	92.9	91.0	88.4
1824	91.8	97.1	88.0	108.8	137.3	77.8	91.6	84.1	87.0	92.9	90.7	85.4
1825	92.1	97.4	88.0	109.2	146.4	76.6	91.0	84.4	87.0	92.9	91.0	88.4
1826	98.4	104.0	98.5	116.9	141.1	103.3	97.9	92.1	85.7	75.0	78.7	83.0
1827	99.5	98.6	99.1	107.9	137.0	114.3	100.2	90.6	87.1	55.6	78.7	77.6
1829	98.4	102.1	99.3	114.9	146.0	93.1	97.8	90.8	85.2	78.6	76.3	81.3
1830	90.5	94.5	88.4	106.4	100.0	89.3	95.5	83.7	92.6	76.9	65.3	71.4
1831	92.2	93.2	89.5	97.8	92.5	82.1	96.7	86.7	93.3	91.7	80.2	97.3
1832	94.1	95.8	90.1	99.6	90.3	108.3	101.4	87.3	71.4	106.7	84.3	94.1
1834	104.2	81.9	111.2	72.5	100.0	80.6	104.6	95.9	76.0	97.0	73.5	0.0
1835	106.9	82.3	102.5	69.6	93.0	74.3	120.1	99.1	97.8	106.8	72.1	0.0
1836	96.5	67.9	98.6	55.9	90.4	64.1	98.7	83.1	87.7	92.9	70.8	0.0
1837	108.9	85.0	95.0	91.0	90.6	81.3	97.1	77.1	454.3	92.5	86.4	0.0
TINAJAS												
1781	90.6	196.2	66.0	200.0	95.5	200.0	108.4	200.0	92.1	260.0	85.7	171.7
1801	93.4	97.6	94.7	70.0	300.0	0.0	95.7	91.9	216.7	50.0	72.2	200.0
1802	87.7	104.5	138.1	0.0	80.0	25.0	81.0	98.2	366.7	0.0	78.8	131.3
1803	91.1	82.8	112.5	366.7	120.0	20.0	82.2	76.6	160.0	100.0	125.5	100.0
1804	84.8	88.7	118.2	250.0	60.0	0.0	77.5	86.7	92.6	37.5	120.8	83.3
1805	86.7	91.3	116.7	300.0	175.0	0.0	76.0	87.0	131.6	25.0	116.7	111.1
1807	88.4	96.0	76.2	0.0	0.0	0.0	79.9	81.7	181.5	200.0	115.0	350.0
1808	131.3	103.1	133.3	400.0	0.0	0.0	132.7	104.3	0.0	0.0	120.0	55.6
1809	109.5	97.6	133.3	400.0	0.0	0.0	109.4	98.3	0.0	0.0	102.7	55.6
1810	108.8	102.3	133.3	166.7	0.0	0.0	107.8	103.7	0.0	0.0	111.8	55.6
1811	107.9	98.5	125.0	275.0	100.0	0.0	105.5	97.8	0.0	0.0	125.0	111.1
1813	92.0	92.7	110.7	162.5	100.0	0.0	86.7	90.3	82.8	66.7	153.6	114.3
1818	65.2	68.1	90.0	50.0	0.0	0.0	60.2	68.2	0.0	0.0	135.3	80.0
1819	65.3	83.7	77.8	50.0	0.0	0.0	59.0	89.7	77.3	69.2	164.3	28.6
1820	61.1	83.7	77.8	50.0	0.0	0.0	52.9	89.7	77.3	69.2	164.3	28.6
1821	67.2	77.5	121.4	66.7	0.0	0.0	60.2	77.6	77.3	69.2	83.5	85.7
TINAQUILLO												
1781	97.7	103.4	102.8	80.0	75.0	250.0	97.2	105.8	0.0	0.0	86.7	116.7
1787	89.2	117.5	84.8	129.0	69.2	69.2	91.8	119.0	300.0	0.0	60.0	0.0
1788	89.2	64.0	81.8	133.3	66.7	69.2	93.0	47.2	100.0	0.0	77.8	100.0
1790	85.8	112.9	82.6	93.3	85.7	112.5	88.1	115.4	266.7	0.0	50.0	0.0
1791	96.2	99.4	105.7	84.6	108.3	60.0	93.6	103.3	133.3	0.0	30.0	0.0
1792	101.7	100.0	105.4	121.9	85.7	80.0	102.6	94.0	200.0	200.0	46.2	100.0
1794	93.7	116.3	108.2	107.9	72.7	60.0	89.7	119.2	100.0	200.0	50.0	150.0

TABLE 4. MALE/FEMALE RATIOS (CONTINUED)

YEAR	TOTAL M/F		WHITE M/F		INDIAN M/F		PARDO M/F		NEGRO M/F		SLAVE M/F	
	ADULT	CHILD	ADULT	CHILD	ADULT	CHILD	ADULT	CHILD	ADULT	CHILD	ADULT	CHILD
1795	93.7	116.3	108.2	107.9	72.7	60.0	89.7	119.2	100.0	200.0	50.0	150.0
1796	94.2	129.1	101.8	135.7	91.7	150.0	90.2	126.5	300.0	0.0	77.8	75.0
1798	86.8	121.3	91.5	130.3	91.7	250.0	85.7	120.0	125.0	100.0	40.0	71.4
1799	80.7	107.4	104.3	134.4	68.8	100.0	70.3	100.8	233.3	200.0	70.0	80.0
1800	86.8	101.2	105.6	94.3	53.8	75.0	80.8	100.0	233.3	200.0	40.0	180.0
1801	80.3	102.3	85.2	128.1	62.5	100.0	79.6	97.7	116.7	200.0	50.0	62.5
1802	77.9	127.4	87.7	169.7	60.0	150.0	75.4	121.0	125.0	50.0	37.5	62.5
1803	86.1	83.2	94.4	121.9	78.6	85.7	83.8	78.9	175.0	66.7	33.3	33.3
1804	87.4	110.8	103.0	147.4	73.3	57.1	82.2	105.7	116.7	50.0	46.2	71.4
1805	77.6	88.7	95.1	136.0	68.2	80.0	71.5	84.9	87.5	40.0	41.7	50.0
1806	99.5	108.7	83.3	120.9	62.5	200.0	117.4	105.6	125.0	50.0	15.4	75.0
1807	79.6	116.4	83.6	108.3	70.6	200.0	79.9	119.4	150.0	100.0	23.1	80.0
1808	79.7	117.4	83.2	112.5	70.6	200.0	80.1	119.4	150.0	100.0	23.1	80.0
1809	90.7	109.7	89.0	155.2	80.0	100.0	96.9	90.5	0.0	0.0	13.3	150.0
1811	101.5	108.7	101.1	139.0	100.0	120.0	104.9	97.3	200.0	40.0	0.0	50.0
1812	103.0	108.7	102.2	139.0	100.0	120.0	105.9	97.3	400.0	40.0	0.0	50.0
1815	83.2	104.9	88.5	115.0	61.5	125.0	83.0	101.3	0.0	0.0	16.7	50.0
1816	82.7	103.3	85.4	114.8	104.3	83.3	79.6	102.3	142.9	80.0	100.0	0.0
1817	79.1	91.7	89.6	110.1	66.7	100.0	74.7	85.1	200.0	0.0	71.4	33.3
1818	81.1	109.7	86.8	133.3	130.0	300.0	77.5	98.6	66.7	200.0	100.0	0.0
1820	86.9	99.3	92.6	120.6	104.2	108.3	84.0	91.7	90.0	128.6	87.0	100.0
1822	99.3	104.2	112.9	97.9	83.3	106.7	92.0	104.4	75.0	233.3	90.0	183.3
1823	81.9	82.2	81.8	79.6	90.0	62.2	82.2	86.5	0.0	0.0	77.6	93.5
1836	98.7	96.1	98.0	96.2	75.0	69.2	99.8	97.3	75.0	50.0	95.5	0.0

TOCUYITO

YEAR	TOTAL ADULT	TOTAL CHILD	WHITE ADULT	WHITE CHILD	INDIAN ADULT	INDIAN CHILD	PARDO ADULT	PARDO CHILD	NEGRO ADULT	NEGRO CHILD	SLAVE ADULT	SLAVE CHILD
1803	110.8	112.6	117.4	112.7	160.0	150.0	90.5	109.9	133.3	72.7	146.1	125.7
1804	109.4	106.3	112.8	110.3	160.0	150.0	90.7	103.7	133.3	72.7	143.8	108.9
1805	111.1	105.4	112.8	108.1	133.3	142.9	94.6	105.7	137.5	70.0	143.8	102.1
1812	99.2	77.5	147.9	59.1	62.5	50.0	83.4	92.5	30.0	150.0	115.2	76.8
1816	133.5	117.2	124.5	126.5	62.5	137.5	139.3	118.8	121.1	150.0	135.4	107.8

TUCUPIDO

YEAR	TOTAL ADULT	TOTAL CHILD	WHITE ADULT	WHITE CHILD	INDIAN ADULT	INDIAN CHILD	PARDO ADULT	PARDO CHILD	NEGRO ADULT	NEGRO CHILD	SLAVE ADULT	SLAVE CHILD
1783	90.4	78.9	0.0	0.0	90.4	78.9	0.0	0.0	0.0	0.0	0.0	0.0
1801	104.8	98.2	108.2	123.1	108.2	96.3	94.2	86.9	87.5	75.0	125.5	125.0
1805	104.3	97.3	106.1	120.0	107.3	95.7	83.3	66.7	95.4	90.0	124.6	107.7
1809	96.0	102.9	110.4	111.4	93.8	98.9	85.1	97.1	80.0	60.0	131.7	142.4

TUCUPIDO DE GUANARE

YEAR	TOTAL ADULT	TOTAL CHILD	WHITE ADULT	WHITE CHILD	INDIAN ADULT	INDIAN CHILD	PARDO ADULT	PARDO CHILD	NEGRO ADULT	NEGRO CHILD	SLAVE ADULT	SLAVE CHILD
1802	92.9	118.8	110.2	113.2	82.4	123.1	108.0	120.2	46.9	117.4	79.5	119.7
1803	87.3	82.9	82.4	99.2	74.8	82.0	86.5	95.8	132.1	43.2	102.5	86.9
1804	90.7	82.4	83.8	92.5	65.5	87.4	99.2	90.5	106.2	32.2	125.0	80.4
1805	90.7	82.4	83.8	92.5	65.5	87.4	99.2	90.5	106.2	32.2	125.0	80.4
1807	93.4	82.4	85.3	71.2	98.2	82.3	102.2	96.7	115.9	80.0	62.7	96.7
1808	86.0	72.4	91.3	62.8	82.5	64.2	82.5	83.5	84.3	78.6	87.9	51.6
1809	91.0	75.6	82.4	73.2	105.4	81.4	94.3	80.8	109.9	57.1	70.3	70.7
1810	87.2	81.5	76.8	80.5	112.2	120.7	95.3	79.7	85.4	69.0	76.3	82.9
1817	69.4	59.0	70.0	51.3	75.0	70.0	65.8	62.3	83.3	65.5	95.5	77.8

TABLE 4. MALE/FEMALE RATIOS (CONTINUED)

YEAR	TOTAL M/F		WHITE M/F		INDIAN M/F		PARDO M/F		NEGRO M/F		SLAVE M/F	
	ADULT	CHILD	ADULT	CHILD	ADULT	CHILD	ADULT	CHILD	ADULT	CHILD	ADULT	CHILD
	TUCURAGUA											
1802	86.5	157.1	87.5	0.0	0.0	100.0	84.6	166.7	66.7	0.0	115.4	128.6
1803	71.3	135.6	100.0	8.3	0.0	0.0	67.7	168.4	66.7	0.0	83.3	166.7
1804	76.4	158.5	88.9	0.0	0.0	0.0	64.6	154.5	75.0	0.0	136.4	150.0
1805	81.0	156.1	150.0	0.0	0.0	0.0	75.4	162.5	200.0	0.0	86.4	133.3
1807	108.0	89.6	66.7	200.0	0.0	0.0	107.7	100.0	100.0	0.0	130.8	53.8
1808	77.1	100.0	85.7	200.0	0.0	0.0	71.7	106.8	120.0	0.0	106.3	70.0
1809	77.6	100.0	85.7	200.0	0.0	0.0	71.7	106.8	150.0	0.0	106.3	70.0
1812	82.5	85.0	0.0	0.0	0.0	0.0	76.9	100.0	0.0	0.0	130.8	57.1
1816	61.2	104.5	0.0	0.0	0.0	0.0	45.9	146.7	0.0	0.0	183.3	14.3
	TUREN											
1778	86.3	82.5	75.0	44.4	84.6	92.2	100.0	73.7	40.0	100.0	0.0	0.0
1801	85.7	68.7	81.0	83.3	78.2	87.3	94.6	44.7	108.8	52.5	71.4	128.6
1808	91.6	74.3	91.5	73.5	91.4	72.5	94.6	76.6	70.0	55.6	42.1	83.3
1809	83.0	71.3	89.5	80.0	87.0	70.3	85.3	67.6	61.5	83.3	0.0	0.0
1810	85.6	113.1	82.6	114.1	79.9	86.7	91.4	123.4	80.0	120.0	70.6	60.0
1811	79.2	70.8	81.3	120.0	80.8	102.9	80.0	43.0	61.5	200.0	0.0	0.0
1812	78.5	92.0	74.0	97.3	81.6	108.8	81.1	85.2	133.3	0.0	16.7	0.0
1816	90.8	75.0	83.1	67.9	89.4	77.8	101.4	79.6	0.0	0.0	0.0	0.0
	TURIAMO											
1802	89.3	66.7	0.0	0.0	0.0	0.0	42.9	80.0	200.0	100.0	85.4	64.1
1803	100.0	106.7	0.0	0.0	0.0	0.0	140.0	75.0	100.0	0.0	90.0	103.8
1804	82.0	75.5	0.0	0.0	0.0	0.0	70.0	166.7	100.0	0.0	78.0	63.8
1805	75.3	142.3	0.0	0.0	0.0	0.0	64.3	300.0	33.3	0.0	73.5	134.8
1808	76.1	104.9	0.0	0.0	0.0	0.0	130.8	125.0	44.4	66.7	65.2	105.9
1818	87.5	80.9	0.0	0.0	0.0	0.0	92.3	85.7	150.0	0.0	82.9	80.0
1819	77.4	135.7	0.0	200.0	0.0	0.0	54.2	126.7	80.0	150.0	81.0	137.5
	TURMERO											
1781	94.2	108.0	97.8	128.3	86.2	95.5	94.3	96.8	0.0	0.0	94.2	58.3
1802	89.8	86.1	91.2	88.3	93.1	87.4	91.3	82.9	80.0	72.6	82.8	90.4
1803	91.0	86.6	91.6	92.5	92.8	90.8	90.9	79.9	76.3	71.6	91.8	89.7
1804	90.4	88.1	90.5	93.4	91.2	89.4	91.3	80.6	76.6	84.1	91.8	92.1
1805	86.5	86.4	79.5	90.4	89.6	85.3	92.1	80.6	70.5	84.8	92.9	91.6
1806	83.3	90.1	74.6	89.7	85.1	88.3	89.9	86.3	76.2	95.5	90.3	97.0
1808	74.5	89.9	66.1	88.9	68.7	88.7	72.4	93.4	82.1	87.5	97.7	89.1
1809	75.6	91.1	82.0	76.4	70.3	83.8	61.5	116.1	80.3	88.7	94.4	91.1
1811	78.1	87.6	87.7	80.7	69.0	83.6	66.4	100.9	81.1	91.0	94.4	86.1
	URACHICHE											
1782	74.6	109.4	74.6	100.0	71.0	106.0	73.4	119.0	133.3	100.0	82.9	111.8
1788	78.3	92.6	93.6	92.3	71.3	122.6	69.5	81.1	0.0	0.0	139.5	25.0
1802	80.0	110.8	102.6	83.3	83.1	132.6	75.6	109.4	95.7	55.6	77.8	106.7

TABLE 4. MALE/FEMALE RATIOS (CONTINUED)

YEAR	TOTAL M/F		WHITE M/F		INDIAN M/F		PARDO M/F		NEGRO M/F		SLAVE M/F	
	ADULT	CHILD	ADULT	CHILD	ADULT	CHILD	ADULT	CHILD	ADULT	CHILD	ADULT	CHILD
1803	83.2	120.4	100.0	77.8	80.0	133.3	80.0	113.2	96.7	162.5	102.7	166.7
1804	79.6	114.8	96.0	77.8	80.7	152.5	76.4	112.5	100.0	70.0	72.7	94.4
1805	76.2	108.7	200.0	80.0	62.2	111.1	79.0	111.8	106.3	28.6	65.2	121.1
1807	79.0	105.8	81.8	64.3	91.1	136.5	72.2	106.8	100.0	35.3	83.7	106.7
1808	91.3	107.2	111.1	60.0	93.6	136.8	85.8	104.7	82.1	114.3	95.5	90.0
1809	85.2	104.1	102.2	151.6	90.9	98.4	79.3	101.5	75.9	120.0	108.1	68.4
1810	84.6	112.3	82.4	150.0	86.7	95.2	85.2	116.7	82.1	114.3	74.4	66.7
1811	83.9	101.0	87.0	86.2	84.4	77.3	83.1	115.8	85.0	150.0	85.4	50.0
1815	84.6	110.8	82.4	131.3	86.7	95.2	85.2	116.7	82.1	114.3	74.4	66.7
1816	81.0	101.3	56.9	109.5	69.6	89.2	87.5	104.4	118.2	100.0	103.7	85.7
1817	84.3	101.0	76.2	85.7	85.1	90.6	80.9	107.7	132.1	150.0	127.8	75.0
1818	85.4	92.2	69.5	80.0	97.4	78.1	80.3	107.8	132.6	63.2	68.8	80.6
1819	70.2	105.8	73.8	110.8	85.0	92.5	64.2	123.3	63.4	60.9	75.5	73.3
	URAMA											
1802	112.6	125.0	0.0	0.0	0.0	0.0	115.2	124.6	87.9	125.9	121.1	112.5
1804	89.3	128.6	120.0	200.0	0.0	0.0	96.3	119.4	75.0	160.0	66.7	110.0
1806	84.6	100.0	100.0	133.3	0.0	0.0	82.1	91.2	87.5	137.5	94.7	50.0
1807	85.5	105.8	200.0	150.0	0.0	0.0	80.4	121.8	94.4	66.7	84.2	66.7
1808	90.1	117.7	133.3	100.0	0.0	0.0	85.9	119.0	92.5	140.0	107.1	70.0
1810	93.8	101.2	133.3	0.0	100.0	0.0	91.8	99.3	102.7	100.0	80.0	100.0
1818	85.2	100.0	0.0	0.0	0.0	0.0	81.3	113.5	0.0	0.0	115.4	23.1
1819	77.9	93.3	0.0	0.0	0.0	0.0	75.3	93.9	0.0	0.0	94.4	85.7
1820	88.5	95.1	116.7	300.0	0.0	0.0	90.1	91.1	81.8	90.0	85.7	77.8
	VALENCIA											
1782	86.8	106.1	94.8	104.8	107.5	95.0	80.2	108.6	87.5	233.3	79.1	101.5
1802	72.6	98.5	82.8	81.3	60.0	71.4	69.3	116.5	127.0	200.0	54.1	88.4
1803	66.4	101.1	90.3	98.6	53.3	88.9	63.0	107.1	49.6	80.0	43.3	92.4
1804	64.9	93.2	77.3	75.4	48.8	133.3	62.0	104.6	58.1	97.4	52.1	87.1
1805	69.8	94.0	78.2	67.6	48.8	142.3	68.2	112.0	75.8	93.5	60.8	87.4
1808	69.8	94.2	78.2	67.6	48.8	142.3	68.2	112.0	75.8	93.5	61.3	88.3
1809	62.7	100.0	73.0	92.8	82.3	81.0	55.2	104.7	58.8	88.9	59.7	108.1
1812	75.6	99.8	100.6	92.8	85.1	81.0	64.1	104.7	64.9	81.5	65.2	108.1
1815	74.7	102.7	70.5	113.5	76.7	96.7	77.4	101.6	94.4	366.7	70.4	86.9
1816	74.3	103.1	70.9	119.2	74.7	98.1	76.7	101.2	84.8	138.5	71.0	85.3
1819	82.7	93.7	83.3	91.5	76.3	95.3	83.4	95.3	81.6	73.3	83.8	93.3
	VALLE DE LA PASCUA											
1804	100.6	111.2	118.7	95.3	90.6	164.7	102.9	122.3	0.0	0.0	78.7	101.6
1805	111.4	107.3	109.5	98.0	110.4	190.0	104.2	108.0	0.0	0.0	129.4	97.8
1806	107.7	98.7	108.6	95.2	94.3	105.9	98.5	105.2	0.0	0.0	135.8	89.5
1808	103.4	100.0	101.8	88.9	84.8	87.9	101.9	100.0	0.0	0.0	122.9	122.2
1809	105.9	100.7	102.1	100.0	111.6	113.9	98.2	112.3	0.0	0.0	119.5	79.2
	VILLA DE CURA											
1780	99.4	98.8	89.0	83.3	88.0	65.2	112.1	131.2	151.4	72.7	97.9	65.5

TABLE 4. MALE/FEMALE RATIOS (CONTINUED)

YEAR	TOTAL M/F		WHITE M/F		INDIAN M/F		PARDO M/F		NEGRO M/F		SLAVE M/F	
	ADULT	CHILD	ADULT	CHILD	ADULT	CHILD	ADULT	CHILD	ADULT	CHILD	ADULT	CHILD
1796	147.6	165.9	172.4	170.8	70.4	50.0	115.9	213.3	140.9	166.7	101.2	127.3
1802	94.9	94.2	97.3	98.0	105.4	80.0	88.2	102.6	73.8	48.9	106.7	88.7
1803	73.2	102.4	105.3	64.4	28.6	79.3	73.7	65.9	112.8	136.0	36.1	2046.2
1804	95.0	120.0	80.2	137.8	92.0	103.9	126.0	95.3	97.5	155.6	112.9	140.0
1805	98.4	100.9	98.9	111.8	94.0	75.0	98.2	97.8	76.5	33.3	99.6	88.8
1806	92.1	105.4	96.9	113.7	77.4	116.7	84.4	100.3	70.0	200.0	100.8	100.0
1807	86.5	110.3	86.6	117.8	67.8	200.0	86.1	121.2	94.1	0.0	91.1	77.7
1808	83.8	94.1	89.2	93.4	70.3	89.7	78.7	95.2	64.8	95.0	92.8	93.9
1809	86.4	88.4	88.5	94.6	113.5	75.0	74.6	81.5	75.9	60.0	97.2	95.8
1811	84.1	95.1	87.1	98.6	41.7	125.0	83.3	96.5	67.5	81.1	98.3	80.2
1816	89.9	75.4	97.8	66.7	57.4	47.1	97.6	84.5	0.0	0.0	74.7	86.6
1817	66.7	107.8	71.9	107.8	63.6	0.0	60.4	0.0	0.0	0.0	72.4	0.0
1822	66.2	96.6	61.8	70.6	88.6	105.0	67.6	112.8	0.0	0.0	70.0	135.6
	YARITAGUA											
1782	91.7	103.7	93.4	97.0	71.9	83.3	86.2	107.1	0.0	0.0	136.5	163.2
1802	69.0	59.8	93.9	47.4	28.0	32.1	69.3	53.8	59.8	77.8	91.7	81.3
1803	69.4	62.7	93.5	61.4	26.7	43.5	69.6	44.7	62.4	77.3	83.7	94.7
1804	69.4	65.3	93.5	61.4	26.7	43.5	69.6	48.2	62.4	79.4	83.7	105.3
1805	75.2	73.5	78.5	77.3	32.5	23.3	85.2	67.8	73.1	70.9	82.2	95.7
1807	65.3	77.4	88.0	58.8	36.2	84.0	81.8	68.7	49.9	94.5	47.4	72.6
1808	68.2	79.7	87.5	60.0	40.0	84.0	92.1	78.6	46.1	96.2	58.4	56.1
1809	68.2	79.7	87.5	60.0	40.0	84.0	92.1	78.6	46.1	96.2	58.4	56.1
1810	68.2	79.7	87.5	60.0	40.0	84.0	92.1	78.6	46.1	96.2	58.4	56.1
1811	69.6	78.1	83.9	63.2	40.7	90.9	89.6	78.8	50.4	86.3	62.2	67.4
1812	67.2	79.5	80.9	64.0	40.9	85.0	76.8	77.7	54.6	91.5	62.4	65.9
1816	89.9	97.9	84.6	77.9	72.0	100.0	91.1	99.6	96.2	109.5	73.3	200.0
1817	58.5	160.4	80.0	116.4	62.5	71.4	52.6	214.8	72.0	76.1	62.7	104.0
1818	69.4	120.6	107.9	94.7	62.6	84.8	61.5	131.9	49.5	111.8	80.0	120.0
1820	89.8	90.7	70.1	111.5	72.6	90.0	105.3	80.9	63.1	102.1	73.1	128.6

TABLE 5. POPULATION BY RACE (PERCENT)

YEAR	TOTAL	WHITE	INDIAN	PARDO	NEGRO	SLAVE	BLACK
		ACARIGUA					
1778	935	0.00	100.00	0.00	0.00	0.00	0.00
1802	2221	19.54	57.45	21.43	.77	.81	23.01
1803	2549	18.75	60.42	18.99	.98	.86	20.83
1804	2570	18.79	61.21	18.99	.43	.58	20.00
1805	2525	18.85	61.54	13.73	.36	.51	19.60
1808	2563	16.19	64.42	18.77	.27	.35	19.39
1809	2583	16.11	64.85	18.62	.23	.19	19.05
1810	2302	18.03	62.42	18.77	.30	.48	19.55
1812	2326	18.14	62.17	18.57	.39	.73	19.69
1829	987	33.84	4.96	57.35	1.93	1.93	61.20
		ACHAGUAS					
1780	156	8.97	85.90	3.21	0.00	1.92	5.13
1801	1104	10.87	9.60	75.63	2.36	1.54	79.53
1804	2513	14.80	4.93	70.51	5.81	3.94	80.26
1806	1238	16.16	25.44	47.25	3.80	7.35	58.40
1809	1922	18.83	14.88	55.88	2.76	7.65	66.29
1811	2475	18.22	13.25	55.92	3.23	9.37	68.53
		AGUA BLANCA					
1779	527	5.31	50.47	43.07	0.00	1.14	44.21
1801	587	15.67	37.82	46.51	0.00	0.00	46.51
1802	557	15.08	37.16	47.76	0.00	0.00	47.76
1803	557	15.08	37.16	47.76	0.00	0.00	47.76
1804	920	18.91	36.52	44.57	0.00	0.00	44.57
1805	717	20.36	33.47	46.03	0.00	.14	46.16
1808	795	5.16	44.91	49.31	.13	.50	49.94
1812	884	6.79	39.48	52.71	1.02	0.00	53.73
1815	804	21.64	28.23	50.12	0.00	0.00	50.12
1830	769	26.53	28.87	44.34	0.00	.26	44.60
		AGUA CULEBRAS					
1781	1906	14.74	11.28	62.38	.79	10.81	73.98
1802	1213	11.29	14.18	69.58	1.32	3.63	74.53
1803	1063	10.63	12.79	73.00	1.41	2.16	76.58
1804	746	13.94	13.67	66.22	1.74	4.42	72.39
1805	1209	11.00	8.77	73.20	1.08	5.96	80.23
1807	881	10.10	12.03	73.78	1.59	2.50	77.87
1808	994	9.86	11.37	73.84	1.71	3.22	78.77
1809	1007	10.72	11.22	72.89	1.99	3.18	78.05
1811	855	10.99	10.53	73.10	1.75	3.63	78.48
1812	788	8.88	11.80	73.73	1.27	4.31	79.31
1815	661	5.30	8.02	83.51	.76	2.42	86.69
1817	408	7.60	18.87	71.08	0.00	2.45	73.53
1818	634	6.47	12.46	78.86	0.00	2.21	81.07
1819	568	7.22	7.92	82.39	0.00	2.46	84.86
1820	751	4.79	0.00	77.63	9.59	7.99	95.21

TABLE 5. POPULATION BY RACE (CONTINUED)

YEAR	TOTAL	WHITE	INDIAN	PARDO	NEGRO	SLAVE	BLACK
1821	732	3.69	8.61	76.78	10.66	.27	87.70
		AGUACALIENTE					
1803	507	14.99	0.00	81.07	0.00	3.94	85.01
1804	509	15.72	0.00	79.17	0.00	5.11	84.28
1805	536	21.46	0.00	62.31	5.78	10.45	78.54
1806	484	14.88	0.00	71.90	0.00	13.22	85.12
1807	548	11.31	0.00	73.72	0.00	14.96	88.69
1818	379	1.58	0.00	85.49	0.00	12.93	98.42
1819	394	1.78	0.00	85.28	0.00	12.94	98.22
		ALPARGATON					
1804	239	0.00	0.00	72.80	27.20	0.00	100.00
1805	227	0.00	0.00	70.48	29.52	0.00	100.00
1806	183	0.00	0.00	72.68	27.32	0.00	100.00
1807	216	0.00	0.00	53.70	46.30	0.00	100.00
1818	191	0.00	0.00	100.00	0.00	0.00	100.00
1819	156	0.00	0.00	100.00	0.00	0.00	100.00
1820	346	0.00	0.00	76.59	23.41	0.00	100.00
		ALTAGRACIA DE ORITUCO					
1783	968	24.28	41.43	1.76	18.49	14.05	34.30
1802	1615	33.07	34.61	23.28	.68	8.36	32.32
1803	1652	28.93	34.87	23.73	1.57	10.90	36.20
1804	1785	28.35	31.04	23.59	2.52	14.51	40.62
1806	1803	34.78	29.84	20.24	3.22	11.92	35.39
1807	1865	34.75	29.76	19.14	3.75	12.60	35.50
1809	1938	32.87	30.70	20.43	4.08	11.92	36.43
1810	1905	32.70	30.24	20.58	4.62	11.86	37.06
1811	1900	33.00	31.32	19.58	4.00	12.11	35.68
		ALTAMIRA					
1783	352	0.00	100.00	0.00	0.00	0.00	0.00
		ANTIMANO					
1811	1286	5.13	16.49	10.26	7.31	60.81	78.38
1819	1176	22.28	15.56	32.57	2.04	27.55	62.16
		APARICION					
1802	2373	26.00	27.27	30.26	12.35	4.13	46.73
1803	2331	26.98	25.87	31.02	12.91	3.22	47.15
1804	3388	29.46	19.45	47.87	0.00	3.22	51.09
1805	3098	14.30	20.08	59.10	3.13	3.39	65.62
1808	3297	22.54	23.51	50.53	0.00	3.43	53.96
1809	2742	29.76	16.67	49.78	0.00	3.79	53.57
1810	3178	24.54	21.62	50.06	0.00	3.78	53.84
1811	2991	23.34	22.40	50.52	0.00	3.74	54.26

TABLE 5. POPULATION BY RACE (CONTINUED)

YEAR	TOTAL	WHITE	INDIAN	PARDO	NEGRO	SLAVE	BLACK
1812	2454	29.30	22.70	46.21	0.00	1.79	48.00
		APURITO					
1802	446	6.05	8.30	59.64	16.82	9.19	85.65
1806	407	20.88	11.55	63.14	0.00	4.42	67.57
1807	545	22.39	19.08	50.28	4.22	4.04	58.53
		ARAGUITA					
1784	884	3.62	11.54	15.27	2.49	67.08	84.84
1802	661	3.03	8.32	3.48	3.63	81.54	88.65
1803	581	3.96	2.93	.69	4.82	87.61	93.12
1804	576	3.65	1.91	2.43	5.90	86.11	94.44
1805	504	3.57	2.78	1.79	1.79	90.08	93.65
1807	611	2.95	1.31	10.47	2.62	82.65	95.74
1810	508	7.87	5.91	17.32	6.10	62.80	86.22
1811	479	7.93	6.26	22.55	5.64	57.62	85.80
1812	391	9.46	6.14	18.67	5.37	60.36	84.40
1816	455	12.75	7.03	11.87	8.35	60.00	80.22
1819	453	15.01	2.87	11.04	7.06	64.02	82.12
		ARAURE					
1778	2841	45.69	8.83	25.20	9.64	10.63	45.48
1798	7528	35.27	17.20	42.99	4.54	0.00	47.53
1799	7704	35.92	17.03	42.52	4.53	0.00	47.05
1800	7835	35.33	17.31	42.51	4.85	0.00	47.36
1801	2668	21.03	3.00	68.03	7.95	0.00	75.97
1802	3285	32.39	4.32	54.09	2.19	7.00	63.29
1803	3130	33.07	3.58	54.38	1.88	7.09	63.35
1804	2604	37.06	5.03	48.66	1.38	7.87	57.91
1805	2876	48.68	5.35	38.42	1.63	5.91	45.97
1808	3061	30.12	9.87	51.45	.49	8.07	60.01
1809	3134	31.56	10.43	50.03	.32	7.66	58.01
1810	3167	31.58	10.33	49.83	.44	7.83	58.10
1811	3444	36.38	9.52	45.96	.81	7.32	54.09
1812	3212	31.91	10.15	49.13	1.09	7.72	57.94
1829	4229	42.47	7.19	45.54	3.48	1.32	50.34
		AREGUE					
1802	704	14.77	49.86	32.24	0.00	3.13	35.37
1803	852	8.80	61.15	27.82	0.00	2.23	30.05
1804	753	10.36	66.53	20.85	0.00	2.26	23.11
1805	698	15.62	54.44	26.07	0.00	3.87	29.94
1809	980	12.24	64.69	20.00	.20	2.86	23.06
1815	938	18.98	49.36	27.40	0.00	4.26	31.66
		ARENALES					
1802	902	16.41	9.98	44.24	14.19	15.19	73.61
1803	925	20.00	9.51	43.68	11.68	15.14	70.49

TABLE 5. POPULATION BY RACE (CONTINUED)

YEAR	TOTAL	WHITE	INDIAN	PARDO	NEGRO	SLAVE	BLACK
1804	922	17.90	9.76	47.18	9.65	15.51	72.34
1805	907	15.66	11.80	39.47	18.30	14.77	72.55
1807	907	13.89	11.14	48.07	11.36	15.55	74.97
1809	919	10.88	16.43	44.72	15.34	12.62	72.69
		ARICHUNA					
1801	589	23.94	49.58	19.52	5.09	1.87	26.49
1804	855	17.78	53.22	15.67	7.49	5.85	29.01
		AROA					
1802	1588	7.43	7.87	66.25	8.75	9.70	84.70
1805	1462	13.13	5.75	47.88	26.61	6.63	81.12
1807	1468	13.15	6.68	48.50	26.84	4.84	80.18
1808	1573	5.98	7.06	45.07	26.26	15.64	86.97
1809	1458	7.82	5.01	74.28	5.28	7.61	87.17
1817	966	12.01	0.00	82.19	2.38	3.42	87.99
1818	1389	15.69	8.57	62.71	13.03	0.00	75.74
		ATAMAICA					
1780	133	3.76	93.98	.75	1.50	0.00	2.26
1802	336	33.04	41.96	19.94	.30	4.76	25.00
		AYAMANES					
1802	524	9.16	90.84	0.00	0.00	0.00	0.00
1803	462	11.47	87.88	.65	0.00	0.00	.65
1804	483	6.21	89.23	4.55	0.00	0.00	4.55
1805	425	13.18	84.71	2.12	0.00	0.00	2.12
1807	621	14.33	79.07	6.60	0.00	0.00	6.60
1808	634	16.56	76.50	6.94	0.00	0.00	6.94
1815	633	15.01	70.93	13.90	0.00	.16	14.06
		BANCO LARGO					
1805	1304	28.83	13.80	22.70	17.64	17.02	57.36
1809	1164	16.49	10.22	61.60	3.52	8.16	73.28
		BARBACOAS DE LOS LLANOS					
1782	1321	43.22	17.03	13.02	20.14	6.59	39.74
1783	1714	33.31	13.48	22.05	26.08	5.08	53.21
1802	2558	34.52	17.87	37.06	4.03	6.53	47.62
1803	2384	37.29	13.76	27.47	17.07	4.40	48.95
1804	2716	35.64	11.38	11.52	33.69	7.77	52.98
1805	3110	29.81	7.85	25.72	30.71	5.92	62.35
1809	3241	33.29	14.38	25.86	21.72	4.75	52.33
1810	3056	35.01	12.70	26.60	21.99	3.70	52.29
1811	3045	35.11	12.15	26.96	21.74	4.04	52.74

TABLE 5. POPULATION BY RACE (CONTINUED)

YEAR	TOTAL	WHITE	INDIAN	PARDO	NEGRO	SLAVE	BLACK
			BARBACOAS DEL TOCUYO				
1802	606	18.65	39.77	14.52	24.42	2.64	41.58
1803	537	16.20	46.93	13.59	19.37	3.91	36.87
1804	600	19.17	42.33	14.17	19.67	4.67	38.50
1805	631	16.32	44.69	14.58	18.07	6.34	38.99
1806	630	15.08	40.00	16.19	24.13	4.60	44.92
1807	642	16.36	39.88	16.51	24.30	2.96	43.77
1808	673	17.68	38.93	17.83	21.10	4.46	43.39
1809	698	18.05	38.83	18.34	20.06	4.73	43.12
1810	748	17.51	38.10	19.65	19.92	4.81	44.39
1812	604	23.01	34.44	36.26	5.13	1.16	42.55
1815	702	15.10	34.47	44.87	1.85	3.70	50.43
1816	634	17.03	36.75	39.12	3.94	3.15	46.21
1817	766	11.36	35.90	46.21	2.74	3.79	52.74
1818	649	11.09	33.90	47.77	2.31	4.93	55.01
1819	775	11.87	33.81	43.61	6.58	4.13	54.32
1820	775	12.77	33.42	47.10	2.06	4.65	53.81
			BARQUISIMETO				
1779	8776	9.28	7.52	58.23	15.67	9.31	83.20
1815	12596	6.10	11.45	73.40	3.86	5.19	82.45
			BARQUISIMETO, MITAD DE(1)				
1802	5167	16.62	12.66	43.29	20.81	6.62	70.72
1803	5189	16.65	12.85	43.28	20.62	6.59	70.50
1804	5695	15.33	11.94	39.58	26.23	6.92	72.73
1805	5324	16.36	11.83	44.65	20.34	6.82	71.81
1807	5992	7.21	9.46	62.98	8.34	12.00	83.33
1808	6043	7.36	10.54	61.31	8.82	11.96	82.09
1809	6382	7.47	8.88	62.10	9.28	12.27	83.64
1810	5993	7.21	9.46	62.97	8.34	12.01	83.33
1811	6439	7.70	9.38	61.81	8.91	12.19	82.92
1817	5909	4.81	21.76	70.87	.25	2.30	73.43
1818	4544	2.86	24.08	66.73	3.59	2.75	73.06
1819	4490	3.14	23.88	66.30	3.63	3.05	72.98
1820	4529	3.60	21.42	68.71	3.00	3.27	74.98
			BARQUISIMETO, MITAD DE(2)				
1802	5410	13.23	4.10	66.78	5.88	10.00	82.66
1803	5972	22.04	4.22	39.79	24.45	9.51	73.74
1804	5906	21.84	4.44	38.84	25.31	9.57	73.72
1805	5962	21.74	4.34	38.85	25.19	9.88	73.92
1807	5930	22.07	4.40	38.87	25.09	9.56	73.52
1808	5532	21.04	4.16	38.81	27.02	8.97	74.80
1809	5628	21.34	4.98	29.02	35.50	9.17	73.69
1810	5628	21.34	4.98	29.02	35.50	9.17	73.69
1811	6693	19.17	4.96	28.40	39.56	7.90	75.87
1817	6933	6.59	3.94	79.33	4.07	6.07	89.47

TABLE 5. POPULATION BY RACE (CONTINUED)

YEAR	TOTAL	WHITE	INDIAN	PARDO	NEGRO	SLAVE	BLACK
1818	6709	7.90	4.46	76.29	4.92	6.44	87.64
1819	6797	8.17	4.90	75.40	4.99	6.55	86.94
1820	6824	8.78	4.81	74.94	5.01	6.46	86.42
		BARUTA					
1802	2046	42.38	35.53	6.94	3.27	11.88	22.09
1803	2109	38.45	37.84	7.40	4.55	11.76	23.71
1804	2124	38.98	36.49	7.39	4.90	12.24	24.53
1805	2066	35.14	39.50	7.89	4.07	13.41	25.36
1811	2029	39.87	34.75	6.51	3.50	15.38	25.38
1816	1155	38.10	34.11	5.71	6.84	15.24	27.79
1817	1545	39.87	35.40	9.97	2.01	12.75	24.72
1819	2659	21.74	20.23	4.48	.68	52.88	58.03
1820	1710	41.35	30.94	13.16	2.28	12.28	27.72
		BAUL					
1781	538	37.36	31.23	9.48	20.82	1.12	31.41
1802	2026	36.62	15.60	27.10	14.86	5.82	47.78
1805	1760	41.31	19.49	32.90	5.17	1.14	39.20
1811	2666	39.38	17.10	32.03	0.00	11.48	43.51
1812	2223	39.77	17.81	35.45	0.00	6.97	42.42
1815	1560	40.96	13.27	35.19	2.63	7.95	45.77
1816	1997	40.11	11.07	37.91	2.80	8.11	48.82
1817	2273	43.64	10.12	36.69	3.61	5.94	46.24
1825	2645	29.75	14.22	54.59	.53	.91	56.03
1829	1675	35.22	1.97	43.94	15.64	3.22	62.81
		BOBARE					
1779	297	0.00	100.00	0.00	0.00	0.00	0.00
1802	580	0.00	100.00	0.00	0.00	0.00	0.00
1803	580	0.00	100.00	0.00	0.00	0.00	0.00
1804	589	0.00	100.00	0.00	0.00	0.00	0.00
1805	541	0.00	100.00	0.00	0.00	0.00	0.00
1806	541	0.00	100.00	0.00	0.00	0.00	0.00
1808	593	0.00	100.00	0.00	0.00	0.00	0.00
1811	815	0.00	100.00	0.00	0.00	0.00	0.00
1820	468	0.00	94.23	5.13	0.00	.64	5.77
		BOCONO					
1778	2061	47.45	11.26	39.45	.39	1.46	41.29
1795	2504	46.17	9.70	39.02	1.80	3.31	44.13
1796	2106	48.08	8.55	40.21	1.24	1.92	43.37
1798	2705	53.86	8.21	34.79	.85	2.29	37.93
1799	2400	47.29	9.04	40.04	1.33	2.29	43.67
1800	2062	47.58	9.21	39.57	1.12	2.52	43.21
1802	1727	27.97	15.92	52.58	2.03	1.51	56.11
1803	2012	28.93	15.56	51.69	2.24	1.59	55.52
1804	1956	30.01	12.42	53.17	2.45	1.94	57.57
1805	2283	58.78	9.02	28.16	2.32	1.71	32.19

TABLE 5. POPULATION BY RACE (CONTINUED)

YEAR	TOTAL	WHITE	INDIAN	PARDO	NEGRO	SLAVE	BLACK
1806	1918	34.36	10.48	50.47	2.87	1.82	55.16
1807	2141	40.92	8.45	44.79	3.27	2.57	50.63
1808	1690	46.75	10.53	35.62	4.02	3.08	42.72
1810	1468	41.49	12.74	44.07	0.00	1.70	45.78
		BORBURATA					
1803	695	3.31	1.87	28.92	36.98	28.92	94.82
1804	754	3.45	1.46	26.92	40.45	27.72	95.09
1805	736	4.35	.68	23.23	43.07	28.67	94.97
1806	781	5.76	.64	23.43	45.07	25.10	93.60
1807	779	3.47	.64	24.52	46.08	25.29	95.89
1818	577	1.39	.52	26.52	40.90	30.68	98.09
1819	664	2.11	.75	27.41	41.11	28.61	97.14
		BURERITO					
1802	1101	.54	1.18	67.76	25.16	5.36	98.27
1803	1118	.54	.98	19.50	73.97	5.01	98.48
1804	1121	0.00	2.68	70.83	21.94	4.55	97.32
1807	990	.71	.20	58.59	35.35	5.15	99.09
1809	1148	.44	.09	54.88	38.76	5.84	99.48
		BURIA					
1779	453	5.96	28.48	58.50	5.96	1.10	65.56
1802	785	2.17	13.89	75.03	7.26	1.66	83.95
1803	731	1.78	9.03	80.57	7.66	.96	89.19
1804	723	2.77	11.89	81.60	1.66	2.07	85.34
1805	819	2.32	11.72	83.64	1.22	1.10	85.96
1807	840	3.69	11.55	81.55	1.55	1.67	84.76
1809	737	2.99	10.45	84.80	.95	.81	86.57
1810	936	2.56	8.23	87.50	1.28	.43	89.21
1811	1035	2.51	8.12	87.83	.97	.58	89.37
1817	788	5.84	9.77	79.57	4.44	.38	84.39
1818	837	14.46	7.89	77.18	0.00	.48	77.66
1819	997	5.12	14.34	46.84	32.60	1.10	80.54
		CABRIA					
1802	200	0.00	0.00	99.50	0.00	.50	100.00
1803	212	0.00	0.00	100.00	0.00	0.00	100.00
1808	177	0.00	0.00	97.74	2.26	0.00	100.00
		CABRUTA					
1780	219	44.75	9.59	26.94	4.57	14.16	45.66
1806	226	11.50	78.32	9.73	0.00	.44	10.18
1808	382	2.88	93.19	3.66	.26	0.00	3.93
1810	445	10.11	76.18	13.71	0.00	0.00	13.71

TABLE 5. POPULATION BY RACE (CONTINUED)

YEAR	TOTAL	WHITE	INDIAN	PARDO	NEGRO	SLAVE	BLACK
		CAGUA					
1781	5506	43.39	5.38	46.51	0.00	4.72	51.24
1802	4717	34.68	3.03	50.16	3.12	9.01	62.29
1803	4491	28.55	2.96	58.34	.56	9.60	68.49
1804	4663	30.09	4.78	51.79	1.80	11.54	65.13
1805	4496	28.74	2.34	55.60	1.96	11.37	68.93
1806	4668	28.08	2.78	56.04	2.25	10.84	69.13
1808	4499	28.23	3.18	57.48	.78	10.34	68.59
1809	4581	28.20	3.43	55.88	1.00	11.48	68.37
1811	4296	27.49	3.05	55.10	1.84	12.52	69.46
1815	3520	32.53	12.36	38.78	1.11	15.23	55.11
1816	3436	34.78	14.44	30.88	2.88	17.03	50.79
1817	3986	30.73	13.20	37.41	3.24	15.43	56.07
1818	3912	30.73	12.88	37.63	3.12	15.64	56.39
		CAICARA DEL ORINOCO					
1802	250	26.00	14.00	50.40	0.00	9.60	60.00
		CALABOZO					
1780	3448	40.92	3.13	34.60	4.96	16.39	55.95
1802	4678	31.83	3.44	43.14	3.72	17.87	64.73
1803	4761	31.93	3.38	42.37	4.58	17.75	64.69
1804	4739	31.69	3.29	42.33	4.79	17.89	65.01
1805	4820	32.14	3.44	41.64	5.23	17.55	64.42
1807	4133	31.09	3.36	43.70	5.06	16.79	65.55
1808	3911	27.97	3.09	46.94	5.68	16.31	68.93
1810	3765	28.79	1.41	51.16	1.59	17.05	69.80
1812	2939	32.15	1.67	48.66	1.29	16.23	66.18
1817	1985	31.28	0.00	50.58	0.00	18.14	68.72
1818	1554	36.29	0.00	46.59	0.00	17.12	63.71
1822	1427	25.79	0.00	60.83	0.00	13.38	74.21
		CAMAGUAN					
1780	739	8.80	57.78	7.44	3.25	22.73	33.42
1801	900	19.89	52.56	20.00	4.00	3.56	27.56
1802	866	21.25	47.00	23.67	4.16	3.93	31.76
1803	1072	17.35	45.62	30.69	2.99	3.36	37.03
1804	1088	18.66	45.96	30.06	1.65	3.68	35.39
1812	1107	17.52	36.40	39.75	1.45	4.88	46.07
1817	1137	22.78	24.80	43.36	5.36	3.69	52.42
		CAMATAGUA					
1783	2263	23.38	22.05	10.78	36.19	7.60	54.57
1802	2151	19.06	42.77	11.85	10.09	16.23	38.17
1803	2128	19.50	42.20	11.70	9.87	16.73	38.30
1804	2305	11.97	23.51	24.47	24.95	15.10	64.51
1805	2111	19.33	42.54	11.80	9.95	16.39	38.13

TABLE 5. POPULATION BY RACE (CONTINUED)

YEAR	TOTAL	WHITE	INDIAN	PARDO	NEGRO	SLAVE	BLACK
1806	2111	19.33	42.54	11.80	9.95	16.39	38.13
1808	2111	19.33	42.54	11.80	9.95	16.39	38.13
1811	1657	12.49	19.92	58.18	0.00	9.41	67.59
		CANOABO					
1781	1122	8.65	0.00	73.17	0.00	18.18	91.35
1788	1092	5.95	0.00	72.16	0.00	21.89	94.05
1802	1081	5.09	0.00	79.28	0.00	15.63	94.91
1803	1041	4.71	0.00	80.12	0.00	15.18	95.29
1804	1063	6.40	0.00	78.65	0.00	14.96	93.60
1805	1134	3.62	0.00	78.13	0.00	18.25	96.38
1806	1220	6.89	0.00	75.08	2.05	15.98	93.11
1807	1150	8.61	0.00	72.70	2.61	16.09	91.39
1808	1194	8.63	0.00	69.77	4.44	17.17	91.37
1809	1214	9.47	0.00	68.86	3.13	18.53	90.53
1810	1037	6.17	.68	73.19	4.73	15.24	93.15
1815	839	6.32	0.00	70.32	1.79	21.57	93.68
1817	996	7.03	1.20	66.77	6.43	18.57	91.77
1819	1287	8.24	2.18	60.45	6.84	22.30	89.59
1820	1310	8.47	2.14	60.31	7.18	21.91	89.39
		CAPAYA					
1784	1252	3.59	17.17	11.58	10.62	57.03	79.23
1802	1195	2.34	18.74	22.26	1.67	54.98	78.91
1803	1376	1.96	15.04	10.10	8.58	64.32	82.99
1804	1356	1.62	14.53	11.87	6.64	65.34	83.85
1805	1355	1.77	15.13	11.81	17.71	53.58	83.10
1806	1442	.69	10.82	13.04	20.74	54.72	88.49
1807	1494	1.47	7.10	27.64	8.43	55.35	91.43
1808	1456	1.51	7.42	28.37	8.65	54.05	91.07
1809	1104	1.90	13.59	7.52	12.32	64.67	84.51
1811	1173	2.90	13.38	24.47	8.01	51.24	83.72
1812	1135	2.38	25.11	24.41	4.93	43.17	72.51
1817	903	2.21	8.86	32.00	4.43	52.49	88.93
1818	1013	2.47	9.67	27.05	6.12	54.69	87.86
1819	1041	1.92	10.09	30.93	6.53	50.53	87.99
1820	1060	2.26	9.81	29.72	5.94	52.26	87.92
		CARABALLECA					
1802	1190	13.11	18.07	19.75	0.00	49.08	68.82
1804	1097	13.22	17.96	17.50	0.00	51.32	68.82
		CARACAS-ALTAGRACIA					
1796	6241	27.98	0.00	47.75	7.02	17.26	72.02
1802	5774	30.72	.73	43.78	9.30	15.47	68.55
1803	5957	34.25	.72	39.45	10.39	15.19	65.03
1804	6418	33.94	1.31	41.20	9.02	14.54	64.76
1805	6451	29.48	2.37	41.31	8.09	18.74	68.14
1807	6179	29.92	1.83	41.96	7.59	18.69	68.25

TABLE 5. POPULATION BY RACE (CONTINUED)

YEAR	TOTAL	WHITE	INDIAN	PARDO	NEGRO	SLAVE	BLACK
1808	6251	29.26	1.55	41.88	7.68	19.63	69.19
1810	6393	28.69	1.03	41.51	8.35	20.41	70.28
1811	5246	32.12	.48	43.61	7.30	16.49	67.40
1815	2113	36.68	2.65	37.39	13.39	9.89	60.67
1816	1765	43.85	.79	41.93	5.78	7.65	55.35
1817	2083	41.43	.48	40.90	6.96	10.23	58.09
1818	2191	43.86	1.55	37.24	5.07	12.28	54.59
1819	2207	45.45	3.17	35.66	4.40	11.33	51.38
1820	1955	35.91	3.27	41.64	5.32	13.86	60.82
			CARACAS-CANDELARIA				
1800	3353	29.29	.84	48.52	5.34	16.02	69.88
1802	3538	36.97	2.43	38.10	7.97	14.53	60.60
1803	3349	36.73	3.43	35.26	9.67	14.90	59.84
1804	3573	37.59	2.04	37.25	9.01	14.11	60.37
1805	3543	34.86	2.23	37.76	10.64	14.51	62.91
1806	3700	34.76	2.84	37.59	9.97	14.84	62.41
1808	3927	31.30	1.86	44.61	7.82	14.41	66.84
1809	4040	32.97	2.08	45.35	6.01	13.59	64.95
1811	3339	38.63	1.23	38.19	9.01	12.94	60.14
1815	2161	36.33	2.96	37.25	12.73	10.74	60.71
1816	2725	28.07	1.43	41.94	4.26	24.29	70.50
1817	2670	28.05	2.21	41.91	15.13	12.70	69.74
1818	2577	28.21	1.05	50.33	7.53	12.88	70.74
1819	2514	27.96	1.03	46.74	9.43	14.84	71.00
1820	2447	30.94	.49	52.96	4.41	11.20	68.57
1821	2451	28.31	1.06	47.74	8.45	14.44	70.62
			CARACAS-CATEDRAL ORIENTE				
1801	4605	31.75	1.30	29.92	5.04	31.99	66.95
1802	4692	30.31	1.60	28.79	6.05	33.25	68.09
1803	4488	31.73	1.05	27.87	5.55	33.80	67.22
1804	4541	29.16	1.10	30.74	4.93	34.07	69.74
1805	4874	31.72	1.29	29.93	5.11	31.95	66.99
1807	4487	31.74	1.00	29.57	5.26	32.43	67.26
1809	4795	32.12	1.13	31.28	5.38	30.09	66.76
1811	4598	30.08	.78	33.80	4.20	31.14	69.14
1815	2358	32.99	1.15	36.01	2.88	26.97	65.86
1816	2483	28.76	4.67	35.40	8.30	22.88	66.57
1817	2885	33.80	1.59	30.40	6.10	28.11	64.61
1818	2756	31.46	3.05	31.57	7.00	26.92	65.49
1819	3300	33.12	1.21	34.18	3.55	27.94	65.67
			CARACAS-CATEDRAL PONIENTE				
1802	3475	29.81	2.56	33.70	4.32	29.61	67.63
1803	3831	29.26	1.91	34.19	5.35	29.29	68.83
1805	3791	32.79	3.59	29.52	6.49	27.62	63.62
1807	3893	30.13	3.37	30.41	7.94	28.15	66.50
1808	3881	30.20	2.81	31.69	6.57	28.73	66.99
1810	3970	29.50	3.07	32.49	6.27	28.66	67.43

TABLE 5. POPULATION BY RACE (CONTINUED)

YEAR	TOTAL	WHITE	INDIAN	PARDO	NEGRO	SLAVE	BLACK
1811	3898	30.04	2.62	32.40	6.67	28.27	67.34
1815	2361	38.37	3.73	32.15	5.80	19.95	57.90
1816	3139	34.60	1.08	24.18	17.14	23.00	64.32
1817	3157	36.14	1.81	34.59	7.29	20.18	62.05
1818	3226	39.43	1.08	27.90	5.36	26.22	59.49
1819	3188	39.37	1.32	28.36	6.30	24.65	59.32
1822	2652	38.24	33.82	1.58	5.62	20.74	27.94
CARACAS-CURATO CASTRENSE							
1803	961	79.92	.42	6.14	1.04	12.49	19.67
1804	1092	80.04	.18	5.22	.46	14.10	19.78
1805	1259	82.53	.71	5.64	.32	10.80	16.76
1807	3245	64.35	.15	28.38	.62	6.50	35.50
1809	2033	70.14	.44	19.72	.59	9.10	29.41
1810	1084	87.82	.74	1.38	.46	9.59	11.44
1811	1215	72.26	.49	9.88	2.88	14.49	27.24
CARACAS-SAN PABLO							
1799	5824	34.77	.70	41.14	4.98	18.41	64.53
1801	5947	33.08	1.11	41.37	4.51	19.94	65.81
1802	6287	30.30	1.56	39.65	6.97	21.52	68.14
1803	5919	38.59	1.23	38.10	1.71	20.38	60.18
1804	5728	37.57	1.15	39.44	2.81	19.03	61.28
1805	6613	36.78	1.59	32.81	17.03	11.79	61.64
1806	6107	34.88	1.75	33.63	17.19	12.54	63.37
1807	6420	33.18	1.67	35.12	16.88	13.15	65.16
1808	5843	35.08	1.20	40.46	11.21	12.05	63.72
1809	4772	27.62	6.04	21.54	21.94	22.86	66.35
1810	5991	25.37	2.22	30.93	17.28	24.20	72.41
1811	5330	25.33	4.48	36.21	15.01	18.97	70.19
1815	6861	21.54	4.21	32.79	7.58	33.87	74.25
1816	6217	33.26	.39	39.87	6.90	19.58	66.35
1817	6869	35.10	.35	39.32	6.26	18.97	64.55
1818	8215	37.42	.54	32.48	16.52	13.05	62.05
1820	7574	41.48	1.52	35.36	4.90	16.74	57.00
CARACAS-SANTA ROSALIA							
1795	4676	38.34	0.00	46.92	0.00	14.73	61.66
1796	5069	32.65	0.00	52.95	0.00	14.40	67.35
1798	4692	35.85	0.00	48.79	0.00	15.37	64.15
1799	4622	34.44	0.00	50.30	0.00	15.25	65.56
1802	5082	33.12	1.52	44.35	5.00	16.02	65.37
1803	5165	31.19	1.80	43.85	5.17	17.99	67.01
1804	5140	30.86	1.79	45.06	4.38	17.92	67.35
1805	5029	34.12	1.77	40.25	4.55	19.31	64.11
1806	5451	34.62	2.27	43.70	6.09	13.32	63.11
1807	5388	32.37	2.49	40.85	6.09	18.21	65.14
1808	5440	31.27	2.32	40.96	6.43	19.03	66.42
1809	5467	34.11	3.93	38.47	7.39	16.10	61.95
1810	5448	32.40	2.65	42.36	6.33	16.06	64.76

TABLE 5. POPULATION BY RACE (CONTINUED)

YEAR	TOTAL	WHITE	INDIAN	PARDO	NEGRO	SLAVE	BLACK
1811	6470	26.69	2.16	48.86	5.83	16.46	71.14
1815	3340	36.86	1.35	39.46	5.75	16.59	61.80
1816	3703	36.32	.51	39.37	5.46	18.34	63.17
1817	3556	37.54	.20	40.47	8.91	12.88	62.26
1818	4056	35.58	.42	40.93	11.22	11.86	64.00
1819	4005	39.75	.67	27.79	19.65	12.13	59.58
1820	4089	46.69	.73	35.46	7.56	9.56	52.58
1822	4295	40.16	.61	42.82	5.10	11.32	59.23
		CARAMACATE					
1779	181	10.50	73.48	16.02	0.00	0.00	16.02
1799	372	33.60	21.77	40.05	2.69	1.88	44.62
1801	421	23.99	17.10	52.26	6.41	.24	58.91
1802	568	16.20	11.09	70.95	0.00	1.76	72.71
1803	642	22.43	15.42	60.44	.47	1.25	62.15
1804	512	17.19	13.87	67.77	0.00	1.17	68.95
1805	550	18.55	14.55	66.55	0.00	.36	66.91
1806	532	18.61	13.16	67.29	.38	.56	68.23
1807	473	12.26	19.03	65.75	2.75	.21	68.71
1809	620	13.06	26.45	59.19	.97	.32	60.48
1811	526	10.27	19.96	69.77	0.00	0.00	69.77
1812	479	12.11	19.42	68.48	0.00	0.00	68.48
1817	316	12.03	13.29	74.68	0.00	0.00	74.68
1818	292	10.96	19.52	69.52	0.00	0.00	69.52
1819	327	13.76	17.43	68.81	0.00	0.00	68.81
1822	252	11.11	11.90	76.59	.40	0.00	76.98
1823	209	9.57	10.53	79.43	0.00	.48	79.90
1828	221	13.57	9.95	75.11	.45	.90	76.47
1829	272	8.46	20.96	70.22	.37	0.00	70.59
1831	289	12.80	23.53	62.28	1.04	.35	63.67
1832	287	12.20	23.69	62.02	1.74	.35	64.11
1833	279	8.24	22.94	64.52	4.30	0.00	68.82
1834	302	9.93	21.19	60.93	7.95	0.00	68.87
1835	355	10.99	23.66	56.34	9.01	0.00	65.35
1836	380	10.79	25.00	54.74	9.47	0.00	64.21
1837	405	10.86	25.68	54.07	9.38	0.00	63.46
1838	439	10.02	29.84	50.80	9.34	0.00	60.14
		CARAYACA					
1802	783	26.82	2.17	17.37	17.37	36.27	71.01
1804	650	16.31	9.85	18.62	16.62	38.62	73.85
1805	674	18.99	4.30	30.42	10.83	35.46	76.71
1807	674	18.99	4.30	30.42	10.83	35.46	76.71
1808	674	18.99	4.30	30.42	10.83	35.46	76.71
1809	674	18.99	4.30	30.42	10.83	35.46	76.71
1810	674	18.99	4.30	30.42	10.83	35.46	76.71
1811	673	19.47	4.31	23.92	8.32	43.98	76.23
1817	911	27.00	.11	36.66	11.42	24.81	72.89
1818	1040	36.92	.87	36.15	4.81	21.25	62.21
1819	872	32.91	1.26	32.91	4.70	28.21	65.83
1820	951	32.91	1.47	31.76	5.68	28.18	65.62

TABLE 5. POPULATION BY RACE (CONTINUED)

YEAR	TOTAL	WHITE	INDIAN	PARDO	NEGRO	SLAVE	BLACK
1833	1692	20.51	5.26	28.66	14.48	31.09	74.23
		CARORA					
1802	4859	8.97	.78	71.52	7.51	11.22	90.24
1803	5318	8.39	.79	72.79	7.31	10.72	90.82
1804	5584	8.86	.88	74.14	6.50	9.62	90.26
1809	6132	9.05	1.01	74.72	7.24	7.97	89.94
1815	5595	6.79	.20	83.56	2.14	7.31	93.01
		CARUAO					
1811	543	.37	0.00	19.71	1.29	78.64	99.63
1815	562	0.00	.71	1.78	6.23	91.28	99.29
		CASIGUA					
1780	2555	29.32	1.92	34.29	14.17	20.31	68.77
		CATA					
1803	518	1.54	0.00	0.00	39.00	59.46	98.46
1804	523	1.91	0.00	0.00	40.15	57.93	98.09
1805	547	2.19	0.00	10.60	28.34	58.87	97.81
		CAUCAGUA					
1784	2422	5.82	5.53	12.63	6.19	69.82	88.65
1802	1864	4.08	7.24	12.12	9.98	66.58	88.68
1803	1800	4.06	6.11	11.33	10.33	68.17	89.83
1804	1839	4.13	6.25	11.47	10.82	67.32	89.61
1805	1842	3.69	5.97	12.27	11.18	66.88	90.34
1806	1850	3.68	5.89	12.54	10.92	66.97	90.43
1807	1797	4.23	6.62	10.29	12.08	66.78	89.15
1808	1561	4.87	6.28	9.16	7.43	72.26	88.85
1809	1635	3.98	9.17	8.81	7.46	70.58	86.85
1811	1440	6.39	5.97	21.74	2.36	63.54	87.64
1812	1674	9.74	8.96	21.33	5.56	54.42	81.30
1816	1505	6.71	5.45	15.02	5.65	67.18	87.84
1817	1357	5.38	5.82	16.88	3.83	68.09	88.80
1818	1305	4.83	8.43	17.24	2.15	67.36	86.74
1819	1512	5.89	8.20	20.57	3.64	61.71	85.91
1820	1595	7.52	8.21	21.00	4.08	59.18	84.26
		CERRITO					
1779	3344	25.87	9.60	60.94	.15	3.44	64.53
		CHABASQUEN					
1802	2089	6.75	81.04	10.87	.38	.96	12.21
1803	2103	6.61	80.74	11.22	.29	1.14	12.65
1804	2131	6.62	80.34	11.50	.38	1.17	13.05

TABLE 5. POPULATION BY RACE (CONTINUED)

YEAR	TOTAL	WHITE	INDIAN	PARDO	NEGRO	SLAVE	BLACK
1805	2141	7.15	80.38	10.65	.51	1.31	12.47
1806	2154	7.38	79.85	10.96	.56	1.25	12.77
1808	2114	6.05	82.12	10.93	.66	.24	11.83
1809	2083	1.15	85.74	12.15	.43	.53	13.11
1812	1272	3.77	69.81	24.37	1.34	.71	26.42
1815	1289	3.65	68.58	25.45	1.24	1.09	27.77
1816	1398	5.79	65.52	23.68	3.86	1.14	28.68
1817	1405	5.34	65.77	24.41	3.77	.71	28.90
1818	1405	5.34	65.77	24.41	3.77	.71	28.90
1819	811	4.81	67.94	22.93	2.96	1.36	27.25
1820	1332	14.19	66.59	18.17	.30	.75	19.22
1829	1647	12.20	49.12	27.32	11.17	.18	38.68
		CHACAO					
1802	2035	29.09	2.41	17.59	16.61	34.30	68.50
1803	2103	29.48	2.19	22.44	13.22	32.67	68.33
1804	2155	29.88	2.00	20.60	13.32	34.20	68.12
1805	2048	29.25	1.22	23.68	13.13	32.71	69.53
1808	2014	31.88	.20	13.70	26.42	27.81	67.92
1811	2091	24.44	1.24	20.85	13.96	39.50	74.32
1815	2006	31.06	1.35	21.73	13.96	31.90	67.60
1818	2238	40.53	.09	38.25	4.60	16.53	59.38
1819	2085	37.60	0.00	38.27	5.90	18.23	62.40
		CHAGUARAMAL					
1783	1607	28.06	7.90	43.12	4.36	16.55	64.03
1804	1903	29.95	6.67	57.38	1.31	4.68	63.37
1805	1985	13.54	4.38	41.96	7.25	27.86	77.08
		CHAGUARAMAS					
1783	2302	33.88	4.00	21.24	16.33	24.54	62.12
1802	2365	21.95	5.88	44.86	3.68	23.64	72.18
1803	2419	22.36	3.89	48.16	0.00	25.59	73.75
1804	2439	23.41	4.26	48.46	0.00	23.86	72.32
1805	2471	17.93	9.55	43.99	6.27	22.26	72.52
1808	2818	22.43	5.86	44.85	8.20	18.67	71.72
1810	2852	22.41	7.71	46.70	4.10	19.07	69.88
		CHARALLAVE					
1783	818	15.28	55.62	23.96	2.93	2.20	29.10
1802	1853	37.78	42.42	11.06	5.13	3.62	19.81
1803	1814	34.90	42.39	11.14	8.54	3.03	22.71
1804	1454	44.64	30.88	11.14	10.04	3.30	24.48
1805	1625	42.71	30.83	15.63	6.95	3.88	26.46
1806	1482	42.51	29.55	18.22	5.53	4.18	27.94
1807	1538	40.05	34.14	15.99	4.88	4.94	25.81
1808	1630	49.69	22.82	18.83	3.99	4.66	27.48
1810	1944	44.29	30.20	18.36	2.26	4.89	25.51
1811	2143	45.12	25.94	20.72	3.36	4.85	28.93

TABLE 5. POPULATION BY RACE (CONTINUED)

YEAR	TOTAL	WHITE	INDIAN	PARDO	NEGRO	SLAVE	BLACK
1815	1840	43.70	30.82	15.92	5.22	4.35	25.49
1816	2083	43.16	30.72	19.88	2.74	3.50	26.12
1817	2070	39.52	32.32	21.74	2.90	3.53	28.16
		CHIVACOA					
1782	2029	3.01	52.05	40.12	4.24	.59	44.95
1802	1079	2.97	51.99	39.76	2.22	3.06	45.04
1803	1318	3.57	48.41	2.43	43.70	1.90	48.03
1804	1300	5.46	46.54	39.92	4.54	3.54	48.00
1805	1371	4.33	53.61	35.23	4.30	2.48	42.01
1807	1408	5.11	52.98	34.38	3.91	3.62	41.90
1808	1631	5.33	47.70	39.36	4.35	3.25	46.97
1809	1585	5.17	42.65	42.52	6.56	3.09	52.18
1810	1760	4.15	51.42	35.91	6.08	2.44	44.43
1811	1688	4.62	43.90	38.33	10.60	2.55	51.48
1812	1694	4.31	43.15	40.44	9.74	2.36	52.54
1815	1929	4.46	40.44	48.57	4.72	1.81	55.11
1816	1914	5.43	41.48	37.88	13.64	1.57	53.08
1817	1871	5.13	44.68	44.84	4.28	1.07	50.19
1818	1864	9.07	39.75	41.04	8.96	1.18	51.18
1819	1808	8.74	40.04	40.76	9.24	1.22	51.22
		CHORONI					
1802	1546	10.61	1.10	65.20	2.26	20.83	88.29
1803	1542	9.27	1.10	65.43	2.33	21.85	89.62
1804	1519	9.61	1.12	71.17	2.70	15.40	89.27
1805	1451	10.20	.90	65.47	1.38	22.05	88.90
1808	1539	10.98	1.04	64.72	1.62	21.64	87.98
1809	1551	11.35	1.29	62.67	2.32	22.37	87.36
1819	851	7.40	0.00	71.21	0.00	21.39	92.60
		CHUAO					
1802	325	.31	0.00	4.62	0.00	95.08	99.69
1803	329	0.00	0.00	3.34	.30	96.35	100.00
1804	348	.57	0.00	2.30	.29	96.84	99.43
1805	356	.28	0.00	5.62	.28	93.82	99.72
1819	384	2.34	0.00	4.95	.52	92.19	97.66
		COCOROTE					
1781	2112	11.03	49.76	23.44	9.19	6.58	39.20
1782	2071	11.25	50.75	23.90	8.69	5.41	38.00
1788	1861	10.53	39.44	29.02	13.81	7.20	50.03
1791	1781	12.80	34.87	33.91	12.86	5.56	52.33
1794	2007	14.00	33.08	35.43	12.41	5.08	52.91
1802	2029	19.42	20.11	53.03	2.22	5.22	60.47
1803	2132	17.07	20.78	54.13	3.14	4.88	62.15
1804	2027	12.38	27.08	38.14	16.63	5.77	60.53
1805	2038	10.16	32.73	38.03	13.25	5.84	57.11
1807	2118	9.92	28.85	39.30	16.67	4.77	61.24

TABLE 5. POPULATION BY RACE (CONTINUED)

YEAR	TOTAL	WHITE	INDIAN	PARDO	NEGRO	SLAVE	BLACK
1808	2036	11.89	30.35	32.42	20.48	4.86	57.76
1809	1994	11.43	29.64	34.90	19.51	4.51	58.93
1811	2012	11.68	15.66	52.83	17.40	2.44	72.66
1812	1738	13.46	30.03	32.45	20.14	3.91	56.50
1817	1641	5.12	32.36	47.65	14.02	.85	62.52
1818	1642	17.05	29.90	50.00	0.00	3.05	53.05
1820	1641	5.12	32.36	47.65	14.02	.85	62.52
1821	1892	13.37	28.49	57.51	0.00	.63	58.14
		COJEDES					
1779	1311	19.91	59.95	19.98	0.00	.15	20.14
1799	1737	35.35	27.40	24.99	2.99	9.27	37.25
1801	1664	38.04	28.00	26.50	3.25	4.21	33.95
1802	1928	26.04	26.35	38.43	.62	8.56	47.61
1803	1780	29.89	27.75	34.49	.11	7.75	42.36
1804	1779	27.99	28.11	35.53	.11	8.26	43.90
1805	1815	29.31	27.44	34.60	.28	8.37	43.25
1806	1922	26.27	29.60	36.16	.10	7.86	44.12
1807	1897	26.57	29.26	35.06	.21	8.91	44.18
1808	1895	27.34	28.65	32.93	.11	10.98	44.01
1809	1924	24.17	30.56	36.02	.47	8.78	45.27
1811	1471	14.48	42.96	33.04	0.00	9.52	42.56
1812	1512	15.94	41.14	33.00	0.00	9.92	42.92
1816	1546	15.33	40.94	33.57	0.00	10.16	43.73
1817	1529	15.43	41.01	33.42	0.00	10.14	43.56
1818	1555	15.11	40.64	34.02	0.00	10.23	44.24
1819	1513	14.28	39.85	33.44	1.78	10.64	45.87
1820	1466	16.10	33.56	39.63	3.75	6.96	50.34
1822	1289	14.20	31.65	45.46	2.95	5.74	54.15
1823	1136	13.64	30.90	49.21	3.17	3.08	55.46
1824	1094	13.80	29.89	49.63	3.47	3.20	56.31
1829	1174	14.99	28.02	49.74	3.07	4.17	56.98
1831	1178	13.50	30.73	48.56	3.06	4.16	55.77
1833	1144	13.81	30.59	50.52	2.27	2.80	55.59
1834	1131	13.17	30.59	51.19	2.30	2.74	56.23
1835	1213	14.18	30.83	48.89	3.71	2.39	54.99
1836	1240	14.84	30.16	49.03	3.63	2.34	55.00
1837	1260	14.84	29.60	48.97	4.29	2.30	55.56
1838	1251	15.03	30.06	48.52	4.08	2.32	54.92
		CUA					
1783	1531	6.60	2.48	13.65	9.47	67.80	90.92
1803	2555	8.34	7.83	19.96	9.39	54.48	83.84
1805	2273	12.98	6.42	17.07	10.95	52.57	80.60
1810	3084	12.19	9.40	21.53	9.11	47.76	78.40
1812	3181	16.28	3.33	20.06	6.29	54.04	80.38
1815	2679	8.59	6.16	28.97	7.17	49.12	85.26
1816	2972	11.07	7.47	30.59	6.63	44.25	81.46
1818	3290	16.53	3.68	21.28	5.93	52.58	79.79
1820	3007	9.64	13.80	17.06	8.85	50.65	76.55
1821	3186	7.78	2.61	27.81	2.29	59.51	89.61

TABLE 5. POPULATION BY RACE (CONTINUED)

YEAR	TOTAL	WHITE	INDIAN	PARDO	NEGRO	SLAVE	BLACK
		CUBIRO					
1802	746	1.61	89.68	4.29	1.07	3.35	8.71
1803	796	1.38	92.71	.88	1.01	4.02	5.90
1804	749	1.34	89.19	5.34	.27	3.87	9.48
1805	897	.22	88.07	6.02	2.45	3.23	11.71
1806	858	.35	86.83	6.53	1.86	4.43	12.82
1807	865	.23	87.05	6.59	1.85	4.28	12.72
1808	849	.35	86.57	6.60	2.00	4.48	13.07
1809	869	.35	87.34	5.98	1.96	4.37	12.31
1810	876	.34	86.99	6.39	1.94	4.34	12.67
1815	720	.42	85.56	8.19	2.50	3.33	14.03
1816	875	.34	89.94	6.29	.69	2.74	9.71
1817	889	.34	88.86	6.75	1.35	2.70	10.80
1818	804	1.24	84.45	11.69	1.37	1.24	14.30
1819	797	1.13	84.44	11.79	1.38	1.25	14.43
1820	770	1.56	83.25	12.21	1.69	1.30	15.19
		CUNAVICHE					
1780	393	.25	99.24	.25	.25	0.00	.51
		CUPIRA					
1784	858	25.76	5.36	28.90	16.32	23.66	68.88
1802	582	22.34	4.30	31.96	27.84	13.57	73.37
1803	573	20.77	4.54	34.21	26.00	14.49	74.69
1804	547	19.56	4.57	36.93	25.05	13.89	75.87
1805	512	19.34	4.10	26.56	33.98	16.02	76.56
1807	505	13.47	6.14	29.90	34.46	16.04	80.40
1808	496	12.90	5.24	40.73	25.00	16.13	81.85
1809	485	11.96	5.57	38.76	27.42	16.29	82.47
1811	576	13.54	21.70	25.69	26.91	12.15	64.76
		CURARIGUA					
1802	1310	7.86	1.98	10.84	44.05	35.27	90.15
1803	974	15.09	2.26	22.38	55.85	4.41	82.65
1804	866	15.70	5.20	31.29	43.30	4.50	79.10
1805	1079	17.15	3.15	16.87	58.76	4.08	79.70
1806	873	15.92	7.45	20.85	51.43	4.35	76.63
1807	872	17.55	6.88	21.67	51.72	2.18	75.57
1808	917	18.97	7.63	22.25	49.18	1.96	73.39
1809	913	19.28	6.90	21.80	49.73	2.30	73.82
1810	1049	17.25	5.24	21.26	45.28	10.96	77.50
1816	1291	9.45	0.00	84.35	3.33	2.87	90.55
1817	1297	8.56	0.00	78.87	9.56	3.01	91.44
1818	1053	11.78	0.00	75.21	9.97	3.04	88.22
1819	1245	14.70	5.62	65.06	12.77	1.85	79.68
1820	1287	14.14	3.96	65.89	13.44	2.56	81.90

TABLE 5. POPULATION BY RACE (CONTINUED)

YEAR	TOTAL	WHITE	INDIAN	PARDO	NEGRO	SLAVE	BLACK
		CURIEPE					
1784	1360	3.75	1.18	21.69	40.15	33.24	95.07
1803	1920	3.75	2.71	28.44	32.45	32.66	93.54
1804	1863	3.27	2.84	20.50	36.88	36.50	93.88
1805	2040	2.94	1.47	22.11	38.24	35.25	95.59
1806	2138	2.67	1.96	30.82	32.60	31.95	95.37
1807	2129	2.30	3.24	27.38	35.32	31.75	94.46
1808	2172	2.26	3.36	27.39	35.50	31.49	94.38
1811	2220	3.38	4.37	29.10	32.97	30.18	92.25
1812	2320	3.66	5.04	29.44	32.97	28.88	91.29
1816	1618	3.28	.68	29.17	30.10	36.77	96.04
1817	1463	2.67	1.78	38.76	28.43	28.37	95.56
1818	1654	3.99	2.00	39.36	27.03	27.63	94.01
1819	1759	3.64	1.88	39.57	27.29	27.63	94.49
1820	1895	3.27	2.37	38.68	28.44	27.23	94.35
		CUYAGUA					
1802	471	3.40	8.28	23.35	17.20	47.77	88.32
1803	456	1.97	2.19	19.08	29.82	46.93	95.83
1804	452	1.55	2.21	23.89	25.22	47.12	96.24
1805	493	3.25	1.83	20.89	20.28	53.75	94.93
1808	453	3.97	2.21	15.67	30.24	47.90	93.82
1809	497	2.21	1.41	16.50	25.35	54.53	96.38
1815	461	9.98	2.82	25.16	.43	61.61	87.20
		DIVINA PASTORA DEL JOBAL					
1781	2036	17.04	39.24	35.12	3.73	4.86	43.71
1798	2876	25.07	15.61	37.07	19.19	3.06	59.32
1799	2876	25.42	13.35	37.20	20.72	3.30	61.23
1801	2607	21.21	17.76	58.11	.50	2.42	61.03
1802	2702	25.94	18.54	38.75	12.88	3.89	55.51
1803	2741	25.87	18.46	38.71	13.06	3.90	55.67
1804	2369	29.84	16.55	46.52	3.55	3.55	53.61
1805	2586	29.89	11.95	41.03	13.53	3.60	58.16
1806	2680	31.90	14.66	50.04	.15	3.25	53.43
1807	2307	33.33	11.88	49.98	.52	4.29	54.79
1808	2470	31.54	12.02	52.87	.40	3.16	56.44
1809	2586	29.89	11.95	41.03	13.53	3.60	58.16
1811	2376	29.42	20.08	47.43	0.00	3.07	50.51
1815	2420	12.40	24.50	52.64	8.68	1.78	63.10
1816	2486	12.95	24.26	51.53	9.41	1.85	62.79
1817	2555	11.94	22.82	55.58	8.02	1.64	65.24
1818	2258	15.99	26.00	43.89	11.29	2.83	58.02
1819	3999	15.40	13.63	68.47	.33	2.18	70.97
1820	2983	22.63	10.43	65.07	.74	1.14	66.95
1822	2723	23.06	21.23	52.81	.15	2.75	55.71
1824	1979	13.39	13.04	71.05	.45	2.07	73.57
1825	2109	14.27	12.61	70.74	.43	1.94	73.12
1829	1760	12.33	5.23	78.47	0.00	3.98	82.44

TABLE 5. POPULATION BY RACE (CONTINUED)

YEAR	TOTAL	WHITE	INDIAN	PARDO	NEGRO	SLAVE	BLACK
1830	1735	12.51	5.30	80.17	2.02	0.00	82.19
1832	1735	12.51	5.30	80.17	2.02	0.00	82.19
1833	1612	14.21	6.39	73.64	5.33	.43	79.40
1834	1620	14.14	6.36	73.27	5.31	.93	79.51
		DUACA					
1779	551	17.79	56.99	20.51	1.81	2.90	25.23
1802	488	22.75	47.13	26.64	2.87	.61	30.12
1803	429	3.26	52.91	42.19	0.00	1.63	43.82
1804	429	3.26	52.91	42.19	0.00	1.63	43.82
1805	555	24.86	40.90	33.51	0.00	.72	34.23
1807	617	23.99	46.84	19.77	8.75	.65	29.17
1808	580	20.69	58.62	19.83	.52	.34	20.69
1809	604	17.72	56.46	25.00	.66	.17	25.83
1810	616	19.32	54.87	24.51	.65	.65	25.81
1811	692	15.90	68.50	15.61	0.00	0.00	15.61
1815	487	3.70	36.76	59.55	0.00	0.00	59.55
1816	541	3.33	33.09	63.59	0.00	0.00	63.59
1818	977	28.15	30.09	40.02	1.74	0.00	41.76
		EL CALVARIO					
1783	653	34.00	8.58	10.26	8.88	38.28	57.43
1802	1262	33.04	4.44	22.50	13.00	27.02	62.52
1803	1264	33.23	4.11	22.86	12.18	27.61	62.66
1804	1342	34.05	6.11	21.39	12.15	26.30	59.84
1805	1410	33.19	6.67	20.57	12.34	27.23	60.14
1808	1451	34.11	6.13	20.33	10.89	28.53	59.75
1812	1852	30.94	6.64	24.08	14.15	24.19	62.42
		EL CONSEJO					
1781	2115	28.51	0.00	26.86	0.00	44.63	71.49
1795	2503	13.78	1.56	40.27	2.48	41.91	84.66
1796	2387	17.72	.38	36.15	.71	45.04	81.90
1802	2820	15.82	1.52	31.21	2.27	49.18	82.66
1803	2925	15.66	1.47	33.23	2.22	47.42	82.87
1804	2985	16.88	2.01	30.72	2.81	47.57	81.11
1805	3007	16.66	1.96	30.56	2.93	47.89	81.38
1806	2917	15.84	1.75	30.82	3.33	48.27	82.41
1807	2908	15.96	2.10	30.88	2.82	48.25	81.95
1808	2938	16.00	2.28	30.77	3.00	47.96	81.72
1809	2698	15.64	.70	31.73	1.48	50.44	83.65
1811	2740	16.09	.66	31.35	1.90	50.00	83.25
1817	3117	17.81	8.25	37.99	0.00	35.96	73.95
1818	3245	19.54	8.60	37.01	0.00	34.85	71.86
1833	2603	21.59	8.87	33.96	0.00	35.57	69.54
		EL GUAPO					
1784	482	29.67	14.94	18.26	8.92	28.22	55.39
1802	1232	12.26	6.82	13.88	23.05	43.99	80.93

TABLE 5. POPULATION BY RACE (CONTINUED)

YEAR	TOTAL	WHITE	INDIAN	PARDO	NEGRO	SLAVE	BLACK
1803	1438	15.16	8.28	23.50	12.93	40.13	76.56
1804	1464	14.89	8.13	23.09	14.48	39.41	76.98
1805	1531	14.50	7.71	21.62	19.40	36.77	77.79
1807	1595	15.61	7.77	22.32	22.26	32.04	76.61
1808	1577	14.84	7.86	22.38	22.51	32.40	77.30
1809	1577	14.84	7.86	22.38	22.51	32.40	77.30
1811	1654	14.45	6.59	20.07	17.35	41.54	78.96
1812	1545	11.84	8.09	21.68	21.10	37.28	80.06
1820	1325	17.81	12.91	35.47	5.58	28.23	69.28
		EL HATILLO					
1802	1070	55.05	5.33	16.64	7.66	15.33	39.63
1803	1070	55.05	5.33	16.64	7.66	15.33	39.63
1804	1183	51.31	5.92	17.92	7.86	16.99	42.77
1805	1347	48.78	6.09	18.86	9.06	17.22	45.14
1806	1524	50.33	5.12	12.34	11.22	21.00	44.55
1808	1645	52.71	4.74	12.04	10.94	19.57	42.55
1815	1727	44.18	0.00	25.25	0.00	30.57	55.82
1818	1413	36.52	0.00	35.60	0.00	27.88	63.48
		EL PAO					
1781	3327	13.83	1.62	71.54	3.79	9.23	84.55
1791	4151	11.54	5.78	67.79	11.06	3.83	82.68
1792	4006	12.03	11.71	54.64	16.13	5.49	76.26
1794	4446	11.70	7.60	52.38	23.01	5.31	80.70
1796	4575	11.52	11.50	50.10	20.74	6.14	76.98
1798	4894	12.65	10.75	43.42	26.85	6.33	76.60
1801	4715	15.78	4.69	64.39	9.23	5.92	79.53
1802	4548	9.87	2.95	68.65	10.66	7.87	87.18
1803	5105	17.47	2.23	65.97	8.21	6.11	80.29
1804	5564	15.60	1.19	71.30	6.42	5.50	83.21
1805	5833	14.88	1.13	72.18	6.46	5.35	83.99
1808	5886	14.00	1.55	72.02	7.76	4.67	84.45
1809	5820	10.76	7.97	71.60	5.31	4.36	81.27
1811	6291	13.42	3.26	65.87	10.40	7.06	83.33
1812	5428	14.31	3.74	65.20	10.17	6.58	81.95
1815	6508	15.93	.75	80.29	1.34	1.69	83.31
1816	6631	16.59	.86	79.16	1.64	1.75	82.55
1817	6297	19.69	.48	72.46	2.21	5.16	79.83
1818	5782	15.51	2.92	73.00	3.70	4.86	81.56
1819	5017	14.43	2.83	74.51	2.97	5.26	82.74
1821	5671	15.92	1.01	74.08	4.25	4.74	83.07
1823	7705	14.11	.78	77.77	3.79	3.56	85.11
1824	7910	13.40	.70	78.87	3.01	4.02	85.90
1825	6168	14.85	.99	76.17	5.24	2.76	84.16
1826	6326	16.66	1.00	74.44	5.12	2.78	82.34
1827	6195	13.59	.94	68.51	9.70	7.26	85.47
1829	7867	1.73	.89	92.77	3.27	1.35	97.38
1835	8421	4.14	0.00	92.23	1.72	1.90	95.86
1836	8739	4.54	0.00	91.44	2.04	1.98	95.46
1837	9205	4.55	0.00	91.75	1.78	1.91	95.45

TABLE 5. POPULATION BY RACE (CONTINUED)

YEAR	TOTAL	WHITE	INDIAN	PARDO	NEGRO	SLAVE	BLACK
1838	9386	4.77	0.00	91.86	1.53	1.83	95.23
		EL RASTRO					
1807	1029	48.20	1.65	32.56	2.82	14.77	50.15
1810	1395	44.23	2.65	38.78	3.37	10.97	53.12
1811	1463	45.32	2.73	36.43	4.72	10.80	51.95
1812	1246	54.57	1.20	28.33	0.00	15.89	44.22
1817	1104	43.03	1.99	37.14	2.72	15.13	54.98
1822	1016	42.42	12.50	36.02	2.26	6.79	45.08
		EL SOMBRERO					
1781	2046	27.22	.34	66.32	.68	5.43	72.43
1783	2179	27.58	.92	.14	63.65	7.71	71.50
1802	3091	25.95	3.69	50.99	11.36	8.02	70.37
1803	3260	24.94	3.31	51.87	11.78	8.10	71.75
1804	3502	25.47	3.66	51.48	10.99	8.40	70.87
1805	3557	26.34	2.28	52.57	10.23	8.57	71.38
1809	4585	23.36	3.18	53.98	12.54	6.94	73.46
1810	4740	23.23	3.71	53.04	12.55	7.47	73.06
1811	4740	23.23	3.71	53.04	12.55	7.47	73.06
		EL TOCUYO					
1802	9173	17.53	4.24	51.11	10.36	16.77	78.23
1803	9416	17.53	4.06	51.05	10.65	16.71	78.41
1804	9469	14.18	2.14	53.45	14.81	15.42	83.67
1805	9281	17.49	4.04	51.62	10.61	16.24	78.47
1806	9226	17.67	4.45	51.51	9.79	16.58	77.88
1807	9527	14.13	2.07	54.09	14.88	14.83	83.80
1808	9533	14.17	2.16	53.72	14.93	15.02	83.67
1809	9637	14.33	2.15	53.99	14.79	14.75	83.52
1810	9613	13.59	2.00	54.38	14.82	15.21	84.42
1812	9678	14.32	2.17	54.13	14.73	14.64	83.51
1815	9424	15.11	1.27	66.97	4.26	12.39	83.62
1816	9736	15.26	1.34	65.85	4.85	12.71	83.40
1817	9492	16.18	1.89	63.08	5.42	13.43	81.93
1818	9331	14.16	2.07	54.44	14.65	14.68	83.77
1819	10919	14.13	1.06	73.20	.26	11.35	84.81
1820	10049	16.58	.51	72.02	.73	10.17	82.91
		EL VALLE					
1798	1016	22.83	32.68	17.62	9.55	17.32	44.49
1802	1232	32.14	20.21	15.91	11.20	20.54	47.65
1803	1297	31.92	20.59	15.73	11.10	20.66	47.49
1804	1416	32.27	19.92	15.61	11.44	20.76	47.81
1805	1528	30.96	19.50	14.99	13.55	21.01	49.54
1809	1582	31.16	19.47	14.73	14.16	20.48	49.37
1815	1615	40.31	11.27	20.74	9.10	18.58	48.42
1816	1795	39.61	10.75	20.39	9.69	19.55	49.64
1817	2203	36.95	14.66	20.88	8.67	18.84	48.39

TABLE 5. POPULATION BY RACE (CONTINUED)

YEAR	TOTAL	WHITE	INDIAN	PARDO	NEGRO	SLAVE	BLACK
1818	1636	41.99	11.06	24.21	8.01	14.73	46.94
1819	1651	40.40	8.96	25.56	7.09	17.99	50.64
1820	1832	37.99	9.66	25.38	8.57	18.40	52.35
		ESPINO					
1804	588	17.35	2.04	57.82	2.55	20.24	80.61
1807	1019	20.51	19.14	42.69	.88	16.78	60.35
		GUACARA					
1781	3080	30.00	18.47	29.90	1.17	20.45	51.53
1802	4588	28.42	21.38	42.68	.35	7.17	50.20
1803	5015	28.91	20.70	42.91	.52	6.96	50.39
1804	5391	27.92	18.38	45.54	.83	7.33	53.70
1805	4728	29.63	20.37	40.63	.80	8.57	50.00
1808	4925	27.92	13.60	50.03	.93	7.51	58.48
1816	5059	25.30	14.35	54.20	.57	5.57	60.35
		GUADARRAMA					
1820	1327	27.58	4.37	15.52	51.39	1.13	68.05
		GUAIGUAZA					
1803	734	3.95	.14	33.65	32.83	29.43	95.91
1804	673	5.94	0.00	47.70	14.71	31.65	94.06
1805	662	5.89	.30	48.34	15.26	30.21	93.81
1806	591	6.26	0.00	40.61	17.43	35.70	93.74
1807	648	4.94	0.00	43.36	13.12	38.58	95.06
1818	452	3.54	0.00	34.29	0.00	62.17	96.46
1819	556	3.60	0.00	44.42	0.00	51.98	96.40
		GUAMA					
1781	2257	16.22	31.32	37.39	8.99	6.07	52.46
1794	2786	10.91	28.00	45.94	8.76	6.39	61.09
1803	3240	5.40	23.36	63.27	1.88	6.08	71.23
1804	3592	4.48	23.64	66.17	1.09	4.62	71.88
1805	3263	5.95	24.03	61.72	2.33	5.98	70.03
1807	3219	7.83	24.26	56.94	6.68	4.29	67.91
1808	3406	9.22	23.22	57.11	6.78	3.67	67.56
1809	3292	8.63	23.75	56.93	6.80	3.89	67.62
1810	3259	4.97	24.95	59.93	6.54	3.62	70.08
1811	3464	5.89	25.72	59.38	6.50	2.51	68.39
1812	3271	5.32	24.18	59.98	6.76	3.76	70.50
1817	2994	10.49	21.24	58.45	6.31	3.51	68.27
1818	2713	8.66	22.67	65.79	1.14	1.73	68.67
1819	2129	11.37	19.40	53.83	11.04	4.37	69.23
1820	2573	9.99	19.94	57.83	8.90	3.34	70.07

TABLE 5. POPULATION BY RACE (CONTINUED)

YEAR	TOTAL	WHITE	INDIAN	PARDO	NEGRO	SLAVE	BLACK
			GUANARE				
1788	8282	45.64	4.81	37.42	2.52	9.61	49.55
1791	7533	33.29	1.79	50.23	2.77	11.91	64.91
1792	8009	43.14	3.48	40.08	2.62	10.68	53.38
1802	13410	36.04	5.64	50.19	1.13	7.01	58.32
1803	11040	38.93	5.65	44.57	1.78	9.06	55.42
1804	10080	38.26	5.84	46.81	1.46	7.63	55.89
1807	10803	36.52	5.89	47.55	2.35	7.69	57.60
1808	11454	35.59	7.72	46.81	2.03	7.85	56.70
1809	11025	39.19	4.92	42.70	1.28	11.91	55.89
1810	7800	38.85	10.42	37.04	3.44	10.26	50.73
1811	8757	34.59	8.29	40.62	4.52	11.98	57.12
1817	6790	30.81	5.94	54.14	2.21	6.91	63.25
			GUANARE VIEJO				
1778	465	32.69	29.03	36.13	0.00	2.15	38.28
1782	927	22.33	33.98	42.29	0.00	1.40	43.69
1801	1352	33.73	42.83	22.41	0.00	1.04	23.45
1802	1339	33.61	43.69	21.66	0.00	1.05	22.70
1803	1583	32.41	27.80	38.72	.51	.57	39.80
1804	2220	38.60	16.35	44.32	0.00	.72	45.05
1805	1514	39.56	26.35	33.36	0.00	.73	34.08
1806	1976	38.36	18.32	42.97	0.00	.35	43.32
1807	1709	39.50	24.05	35.87	0.00	.59	36.45
1808	3053	36.26	20.80	42.55	0.00	.39	42.94
1811	1594	35.38	21.33	42.60	0.00	.69	43.29
1813	1516	32.65	33.84	32.72	0.00	.79	33.51
			GUANARITO				
1778	962	21.93	27.86	48.65	0.00	1.56	50.21
1801	1802	21.75	32.63	30.19	9.93	5.49	45.62
1802	1816	38.66	11.12	42.95	3.36	3.91	50.22
1803	3264	39.61	8.21	38.48	7.75	5.94	52.18
1804	3003	36.93	9.99	48.25	0.00	4.83	53.08
1805	3058	34.50	9.88	37.90	11.31	6.41	55.62
1807	5159	31.71	10.22	51.35	.56	6.16	58.07
1808	4501	41.92	5.82	47.10	2.95	2.20	52.26
1810	4574	41.85	5.79	47.66	2.54	2.16	52.36
1811	4792	41.61	6.14	47.25	2.65	2.36	52.25
			GUARDATINAJAS				
1780	475	14.11	47.79	17.68	20.00	.42	38.11
1804	2228	23.61	12.43	25.13	30.03	8.80	63.96
1805	2239	23.72	11.84	25.19	30.06	9.20	64.45
1807	2284	22.11	10.42	21.94	36.21	9.33	67.47
1808	2363	21.84	10.88	21.63	36.18	9.48	67.29
1809	2344	25.64	10.32	22.70	31.36	9.98	64.04
1810	2253	23.30	11.27	52.69	3.37	9.37	65.42

TABLE 5. POPULATION BY RACE (CONTINUED)

YEAR	TOTAL	WHITE	INDIAN	PARDO	NEGRO	SLAVE	BLACK
1811	2534	21.31	12.63	50.43	4.14	11.48	66.06
1812	2601	19.26	13.15	50.67	5.04	11.88	67.59
1816	2460	19.07	13.21	55.73	1.54	10.45	67.72
		GUARENAS					
1784	2333	38.88	24.65	11.70	12.56	12.22	36.48
1802	2901	33.88	14.06	8.48	19.13	24.44	52.05
1803	3025	33.49	14.35	8.99	19.34	23.83	52.17
1804	2999	33.48	13.24	7.54	21.84	23.91	53.28
1805	3050	33.54	13.21	7.64	21.74	23.87	53.25
1808	1860	31.24	13.12	8.87	14.52	32.26	55.65
1809	2666	35.03	10.47	14.44	13.77	26.29	54.50
1811	3212	33.03	10.46	23.35	10.37	22.79	56.51
1816	2611	29.76	6.51	37.30	1.34	25.09	63.73
		GUARICO					
1803	2034	12.49	45.13	31.86	6.15	4.38	42.38
1804	2000	15.70	37.90	33.30	8.45	4.65	46.40
1805	1832	11.46	46.40	35.43	3.11	3.60	42.14
1806	1908	12.47	45.75	35.06	3.09	3.62	41.77
1807	1870	11.12	44.33	38.13	2.25	4.17	44.55
1808	1838	10.88	43.96	38.79	2.29	4.08	45.16
1809	1953	11.42	43.16	38.20	3.07	4.15	45.42
1810	2162	11.05	42.00	35.57	5.78	5.60	46.95
1812	2114	11.49	37.13	37.37	7.14	6.86	51.37
1815	2225	5.03	39.64	49.71	2.70	2.92	55.33
1816	2248	5.16	39.50	49.64	2.67	3.02	55.34
1817	2351	7.10	38.83	48.62	2.55	2.89	54.06
1818	2338	7.53	38.41	48.59	2.57	2.91	54.06
1819	2493	7.30	37.34	49.62	2.37	3.37	55.35
1820	2704	6.95	37.46	48.56	3.37	3.66	55.58
		GUASGUAS					
1802	3595	44.48	18.28	35.97	0.00	1.28	37.25
1803	3444	42.45	19.16	36.99	0.00	1.39	38.39
1804	3325	44.54	18.02	36.00	0.00	1.44	37.44
1805	3519	44.05	18.67	35.98	0.00	1.31	37.28
1806	3803	44.62	19.69	34.34	0.00	1.34	35.68
1807	3814	44.47	18.62	35.61	0.00	1.31	36.92
1808	3878	44.38	18.93	35.59	0.00	1.11	36.69
1809	4099	42.28	19.32	37.30	0.00	1.10	38.40
1810	3845	46.01	19.32	28.37	5.05	1.25	34.67
		GUATIRE					
1784	1942	13.85	1.13	21.42	12.26	51.34	85.02
1802	2224	8.90	1.53	22.30	15.33	51.93	89.57
1803	2254	11.31	1.06	21.25	16.37	50.00	87.62
1805	2177	11.90	.92	21.50	16.90	48.78	87.18
1807	2065	9.83	.19	32.54	2.76	54.67	89.98

TABLE 5. POPULATION BY RACE (CONTINUED)

YEAR	TOTAL	WHITE	INDIAN	PARDO	NEGRO	SLAVE	BLACK
1809	2065	9.83	.19	32.54	2.76	54.67	89.98
1811	2329	10.69	2.53	26.15	9.32	51.31	86.78
1815	2160	10.97	2.31	26.34	9.35	51.02	86.71
1816	2343	10.58	2.39	29.58	11.05	46.39	87.03
1817	2492	8.71	1.89	41.45	3.01	44.94	89.41
		GUAYABAL					
1804	1492	14.68	7.04	40.15	13.27	24.87	78.28
1817	1522	24.77	5.45	58.54	6.37	4.86	69.78
		GUIGUE					
1781	2432	31.04	4.44	29.15	17.52	17.85	64.51
1802	2646	22.34	3.51	52.61	4.38	17.16	74.15
1803	2641	21.73	4.24	52.40	3.86	17.76	74.02
1804	2655	21.66	4.48	52.69	3.95	17.21	73.86
1805	2735	20.80	4.75	51.74	3.62	19.09	74.44
1808	2975	20.61	4.07	48.07	4.40	22.86	75.33
1809	3083	21.02	4.64	46.58	4.44	23.32	74.34
1817	2846	7.20	6.82	53.65	11.49	20.84	85.98
		GUIRIPA					
1802	994	50.00	10.56	31.09	.70	7.65	39.44
1803	944	52.97	8.37	30.51	.64	7.52	38.67
1804	991	44.40	10.39	35.92	.91	8.38	45.21
1805	1014	42.70	10.06	37.77	.89	8.58	47.24
1806	920	41.96	10.33	35.54	1.41	10.76	47.72
1807	998	27.76	29.16	31.56	1.80	9.72	43.09
1808	1015	26.40	28.37	33.79	1.67	9.75	45.22
1809	1058	24.48	25.71	38.94	1.98	8.88	49.81
1811	1004	43.82	6.18	39.74	0.00	10.26	50.00
		HUMOCARO ALTO					
1802	2599	5.08	82.88	9.47	.31	2.27	12.04
1803	2636	5.08	83.42	9.64	.23	1.63	11.49
1804	2912	4.60	84.24	9.41	.27	1.48	11.16
1805	2758	4.97	82.67	10.26	.29	1.81	12.36
1806	2748	4.73	82.82	10.48	.18	1.78	12.45
1807	2714	4.79	81.98	11.20	.22	1.81	13.23
1808	2658	4.67	81.79	11.47	.23	1.84	13.54
1809	2470	5.59	79.76	12.39	.20	2.06	14.66
1810	2208	6.07	78.35	13.95	.45	1.18	15.58
1815	1397	6.87	81.10	10.09	.43	1.50	12.03
1816	1813	9.32	74.74	13.18	.72	2.04	15.94
1817	1834	7.80	76.17	13.20	.71	2.13	16.03
1818	1794	7.97	75.20	14.05	.56	2.23	16.83
1819	1612	6.14	74.69	15.82	.62	2.73	19.17
1820	1808	6.47	77.65	13.11	.77	1.99	15.87

TABLE 5. POPULATION BY RACE (CONTINUED)

YEAR	TOTAL	WHITE	INDIAN	PARDO	NEGRO	SLAVE	BLACK
		HUMOCARO BAJO					
1803	1739	27.60	42.55	14.66	9.09	6.10	29.84
1804	1739	27.60	42.55	14.66	9.09	6.10	29.84
1806	1422	16.95	43.39	31.43	.42	7.81	39.66
1807	1570	15.80	44.33	31.27	.57	8.03	39.87
1808	1946	15.11	45.43	30.52	.98	7.97	39.47
1809	2152	14.17	45.59	30.30	1.25	8.69	40.24
1810	2188	13.53	45.11	30.85	1.28	9.23	41.36
1815	1707	18.86	48.68	23.32	1.23	7.91	32.45
1816	1788	18.57	45.47	26.12	1.06	8.78	35.96
1817	1780	18.43	45.73	26.12	1.01	8.71	35.84
1818	1729	20.13	45.34	25.39	.81	8.33	34.53
1819	1480	22.03	45.74	25.74	.74	5.74	32.23
1820	1513	21.22	45.60	26.90	.26	6.01	33.18
		IGUANA					
1783	139	1.44	92.09	1.44	5.04	0.00	6.47
1801	310	0.00	92.90	6.13	.97	0.00	7.10
1802	323	0.00	93.19	5.88	.93	0.00	6.81
1803	342	1.17	92.69	5.85	.29	0.00	6.14
1804	295	0.00	95.25	4.41	.34	0.00	4.75
1805	305	0.00	95.41	4.59	0.00	0.00	4.59
1806	362	0.00	96.13	3.87	0.00	0.00	3.87
1807	330	0.00	99.39	.61	0.00	0.00	.61
		LA GUAIRA					
1802	4055	27.94	1.63	41.95	13.59	14.90	70.43
1804	3269	30.50	1.04	37.99	16.61	13.86	68.46
1805	3526	24.59	.17	46.88	14.38	13.98	75.24
1807	3198	27.80	.56	40.62	17.54	13.48	71.64
1809	3272	22.13	.31	53.73	12.22	11.61	77.57
1810	3267	25.16	.28	43.71	19.28	11.57	74.56
1811	3317	21.92	.75	51.82	12.42	13.08	77.33
1815	1819	35.95	3.41	33.97	13.03	13.63	60.64
1816	1964	37.17	5.75	34.37	11.41	11.30	57.08
1817	2714	28.00	3.76	45.50	13.49	9.25	68.24
1818	2989	20.81	3.35	52.89	11.04	11.91	75.84
1819	2884	19.73	11.37	35.61	21.46	11.82	68.90
1820	3005	21.76	9.32	30.08	23.16	15.67	68.92
		LA GUAIRA, CURATO CASTRENSE					
1802	310	90.32	0.00	1.29	.97	7.42	9.68
1803	280	92.86	0.00	.71	1.07	5.36	7.14
1804	457	85.34	0.00	11.38	.44	2.84	14.66
1805	665	72.78	0.00	23.31	.75	3.16	27.22
1807	782	54.73	0.00	42.20	.64	2.43	45.27
1808	541	65.80	.18	30.31	.74	2.96	34.01

TABLE 5. POPULATION BY RACE (CONTINUED)

YEAR	TOTAL	WHITE	INDIAN	PARDO	NEGRO	SLAVE	BLACK
			LA SANTISIMA TRINIDAD				
1780	567	3.35	56.44	18.34	19.75	2.12	40.21
1802	1959	6.13	6.02	48.65	33.03	6.18	87.85
1803	1950	3.54	5.44	52.31	35.79	2.92	91.03
1804	1728	6.94	9.20	42.59	36.75	4.51	83.85
1805	1744	5.10	4.87	40.71	43.12	6.19	90.02
1807	1162	8.00	10.50	28.31	46.04	7.14	81.50
1808	1194	11.22	14.74	65.16	2.18	6.70	74.04
1809	1173	9.38	13.73	66.07	3.15	7.67	76.90
1810	1074	6.70	14.34	72.44	3.72	2.79	78.96
1811	1206	6.97	15.59	66.00	2.57	8.87	77.45
1812	939	5.86	14.91	72.31	2.13	4.79	79.23
			LA VEGA				
1802	2194	27.48	18.23	22.11	3.46	28.71	54.28
1803	2325	27.53	17.63	22.11	3.27	29.46	54.84
1804	2211	21.21	22.70	23.38	6.97	25.73	56.08
1805	2285	20.35	23.19	22.06	8.14	26.26	56.46
1809	1116	24.55	21.51	28.58	4.12	21.24	53.94
1810	1052	24.71	21.29	28.04	3.99	21.96	53.99
1811	960	23.65	17.71	32.92	4.17	21.56	58.65
1815	798	28.82	8.90	30.70	5.39	26.19	62.28
1816	845	31.12	8.17	31.12	5.68	23.91	60.71
1817	737	29.31	10.45	33.24	3.93	23.07	60.24
1818	739	40.32	8.66	27.88	2.98	20.16	51.01
1819	731	31.46	16.28	29.14	2.87	20.25	52.26
1820	711	26.44	18.42	32.77	2.95	19.41	55.13
1821	720	24.58	18.33	28.33	2.50	26.25	57.08
1822	674	27.00	13.95	31.90	3.12	24.04	59.05
1823	653	32.01	8.73	34.61	4.29	20.37	59.26
			LA VICTORIA				
1780	5310	26.99	15.76	34.54	7.66	15.05	57.25
1802	6220	25.32	12.03	38.23	2.75	21.67	62.65
1803	6700	23.66	14.42	35.58	2.90	23.45	61.93
1804	6627	24.05	14.62	34.65	2.78	23.90	61.32
1805	6889	23.49	14.31	34.88	3.32	23.99	62.20
1806	6991	23.46	14.38	34.69	3.50	23.97	62.17
1808	7117	25.25	12.15	33.10	3.09	26.40	62.60
1809	7172	23.35	14.51	34.31	3.92	23.90	62.13
1811	8100	20.48	13.25	35.54	3.81	26.91	66.27
1816	4655	25.01	11.19	50.78	0.00	13.02	63.80
1817	4655	25.01	11.19	50.78	0.00	13.02	63.80
1818	4655	25.01	11.19	50.78	0.00	13.02	63.80
			LEZAMA				
1783	1564	32.29	34.21	14.83	11.57	7.10	33.50
1802	2388	34.05	23.99	27.64	4.90	9.42	41.96

TABLE 5. POPULATION BY RACE (CONTINUED)

YEAR	TOTAL	WHITE	INDIAN	PARDO	NEGRO	SLAVE	BLACK
1803	2388	34.05	23.99	27.64	4.90	9.42	41.96
1804	2388	34.05	23.99	27.64	4.90	9.42	41.96
1805	2388	34.05	23.99	27.64	4.90	9.42	41.96
1806	2388	34.05	23.99	27.64	4.90	9.42	41.96
1807	2388	34.05	23.99	27.64	4.90	9.42	41.96
1808	2388	34.05	23.99	27.64	4.90	9.42	41.96
1809	2388	34.05	23.99	27.64	4.90	9.42	41.96
1810	2388	34.05	23.99	27.64	4.90	9.42	41.96
1811	2388	34.05	23.99	27.64	4.90	9.42	41.96
		LOS ANGELES					
1780	419	2.63	75.18	18.38	3.58	.24	22.20
1803	452	4.65	43.14	51.55	0.00	.66	52.21
1804	476	4.62	45.38	49.37	0.00	.63	50.00
1805	483	5.80	45.34	48.03	0.00	.83	48.86
1807	474	5.49	44.51	48.73	0.00	1.27	50.00
1808	479	4.59	40.71	54.28	0.00	.42	54.70
1809	920	25.33	19.89	49.57	0.00	5.22	54.78
1810	927	23.73	21.79	49.51	0.00	4.96	54.48
1811	1011	25.82	19.98	47.77	0.00	6.43	54.20
1812	967	22.23	21.51	49.95	0.00	6.31	56.26
1816	946	20.72	17.97	56.24	0.00	5.07	61.31
1817	1012	24.60	17.39	52.57	0.00	5.43	58.00
		LOS ANGELES DE SETENTA					
1801	1114	64.81	7.63	22.26	0.00	5.30	27.56
1805	778	45.76	13.88	29.31	0.00	11.05	40.36
1806	879	44.25	14.79	30.38	0.00	10.58	40.96
1807	1096	39.23	24.09	30.75	0.00	5.93	36.68
1809	981	40.57	20.08	30.07	0.00	9.28	39.35
		LOS CANIZOS					
1802	832	8.29	0.00	52.76	3.61	35.34	91.71
1803	812	8.00	0.00	55.30	2.96	33.74	92.00
1804	822	9.98	0.00	52.55	2.19	35.28	90.02
1805	775	9.55	0.00	45.81	10.19	34.45	90.45
1807	764	7.98	0.00	49.87	7.85	34.29	92.02
1808	829	8.93	0.00	56.57	2.41	32.09	91.07
1809	838	8.71	0.00	56.80	2.39	32.10	91.29
1810	949	6.32	0.00	58.80	2.11	32.77	93.68
1811	876	6.39	0.00	61.07	1.26	31.28	93.61
1813	569	1.76	0.00	61.86	13.01	23.37	98.24
1818	412	2.91	0.00	60.68	0.00	36.41	97.09
1819	452	4.42	0.00	62.61	0.00	32.96	95.58
1820	442	4.52	0.00	63.12	0.00	32.35	95.48
		LOS GUAYOS					
1781	1242	31.00	48.63	20.13	0.00	.24	20.37
1795	2592	27.58	33.06	37.38	0.00	1.97	39.35

TABLE 5. POPULATION BY RACE (CONTINUED)

YEAR	TOTAL	WHITE	INDIAN	PARDO	NEGRO	SLAVE	BLACK
1802	4090	18.51	34.30	40.66	1.27	5.26	47.19
1803	3612	18.05	59.33	16.72	.75	5.15	22.62
1804	3317	26.14	23.55	43.83	.84	5.64	50.32
1805	3407	24.71	25.21	44.76	.62	4.70	50.07
1816	3023	25.64	18.95	51.31	.79	3.31	55.41
LOS TEQUES							
1796	2184	61.40	7.78	19.05	2.15	9.62	30.82
1799	2309	59.64	7.36	19.49	3.38	10.13	33.00
1800	2309	59.64	7.36	19.49	3.38	10.13	33.00
1801	2481	57.19	7.38	19.87	4.43	11.12	35.43
1805	2773	57.74	8.73	7.57	1.91	24.05	33.54
1811	1995	30.63	2.46	47.57	7.12	12.23	66.92
1816	2355	56.39	8.87	21.23	.85	12.65	34.73
1817	2233	57.77	8.06	21.45	.99	11.73	34.17
MACAIRA							
1784	589	.85	17.49	10.53	1.87	69.27	81.66
1802	318	.31	8.81	6.92	2.20	81.76	90.88
1803	303	.33	8.25	.99	3.96	86.47	91.42
1804	280	.36	9.64	2.86	3.57	83.57	90.00
1806	259	.77	10.81	0.00	4.63	83.78	88.42
1807	277	0.00	6.50	0.00	3.61	89.89	93.50
1808	219	0.00	15.07	0.00	9.13	75.80	84.93
1809	210	.48	7.62	8.57	2.86	80.48	91.90
1811	110	0.00	18.18	0.00	1.82	80.00	81.82
1817	123	0.00	3.25	12.20	2.44	82.11	96.75
MACAIRITA							
1805	264	0.00	8.71	0.00	3.03	88.26	91.29
MACARAO							
1802	1169	39.35	10.78	18.82	5.05	26.01	49.87
1803	1113	29.38	10.87	25.52	5.75	28.48	59.75
1804	1254	42.42	9.81	22.89	3.43	21.45	47.77
1805	1175	42.30	9.11	21.02	3.23	24.34	48.60
1807	1260	42.38	11.19	16.75	2.94	26.75	46.43
1808	1240	47.02	9.76	18.71	3.71	20.81	43.23
1809	1250	45.20	10.24	13.44	3.20	27.92	44.56
1810	1388	42.65	10.30	17.51	3.46	26.08	47.05
1811	1172	46.16	11.52	15.96	3.67	22.70	42.32
1812	1140	48.42	5.35	13.33	2.72	30.18	46.23
1815	1217	41.82	9.53	14.13	2.63	31.88	48.64
1816	1291	41.91	9.37	15.10	3.33	30.29	48.72
1817	1098	50.55	8.11	13.57	2.28	25.50	41.35
1818	1094	50.37	8.14	13.62	2.29	25.59	41.50
1819	1131	49.51	8.40	13.97	2.83	25.29	42.09
1820	1131	49.51	8.40	13.97	2.83	25.29	42.09
1822	1185	39.16	15.44	13.50	9.11	22.78	45.40

TABLE 5. POPULATION BY RACE (CONTINUED)

YEAR	TOTAL	WHITE	INDIAN	PARDO	NEGRO	SLAVE	BLACK
1823	1364	42.82	15.18	13.42	7.92	20.67	42.01
		MAGDALENO					
1802	2412	34.95	5.56	53.11	.66	5.72	59.49
1803	2710	27.08	10.70	52.03	6.16	4.02	62.21
1804	2591	29.68	1.51	62.60	.85	5.36	68.82
1805	2518	35.11	1.39	55.60	.79	7.11	63.50
1806	2648	33.76	1.85	53.97	3.47	6.95	64.39
1809	1226	17.86	2.94	55.71	7.50	15.99	79.20
1816	2798	31.84	1.93	56.72	4.40	5.11	66.23
		MAIQUETIA					
1796	1797	22.04	4.56	53.98	0.00	19.42	73.40
1802	1654	27.45	3.33	29.02	18.74	21.46	69.23
1804	1563	26.36	4.54	37.36	10.30	21.43	69.10
1805	1630	24.79	4.60	37.79	11.17	21.66	70.61
1807	1770	26.84	4.12	34.92	14.12	20.00	69.04
1811	1742	25.20	5.57	35.36	15.96	17.91	69.23
1815	1817	27.24	5.56	27.35	25.92	13.92	67.20
1816	1270	23.70	11.02	26.85	15.12	23.31	65.28
1817	1327	26.75	4.75	34.74	9.04	24.72	68.50
1819	1817	27.24	5.56	27.35	25.92	13.92	67.20
		MAMPORAL					
1784	521	8.83	5.57	11.13	11.71	62.76	85.60
1802	488	8.61	5.12	11.89	9.02	65.37	86.27
1804	487	7.39	5.54	16.63	15.20	55.24	87.06
1805	557	8.08	8.62	19.03	11.13	53.14	83.30
1807	541	6.84	6.28	22.92	10.35	53.60	86.88
1808	558	9.86	6.81	16.67	15.59	51.08	83.33
1809	521	4.99	6.14	14.40	23.99	50.48	88.87
1811	512	9.38	7.81	25.98	10.74	46.09	82.81
1812	511	8.41	9.20	27.20	10.57	44.62	82.39
1816	274	1.82	2.92	31.02	3.65	60.58	95.26
1817	274	2.92	9.49	0.00	26.64	60.95	87.59
1818	318	3.46	2.20	25.79	4.72	63.84	94.34
1820	295	1.02	3.39	27.80	5.42	62.37	95.59
		MANAPIRE					
1804	486	26.75	10.91	34.36	1.85	26.13	62.35
1807	466	27.04	7.51	34.55	3.00	27.90	65.45
1808	471	26.75	8.49	34.18	2.97	27.60	64.76
1810	521	28.02	6.14	37.81	2.11	25.91	65.83
		MARACA					
1778	873	26.92	38.14	33.10	.57	1.26	34.94
1803	1747	6.98	56.61	34.63	.69	1.09	36.41
1804	1636	37.22	26.65	32.95	2.08	1.10	36.12

TABLE 5. POPULATION BY RACE (CONTINUED)

YEAR	TOTAL	WHITE	INDIAN	PARDO	NEGRO	SLAVE	BLACK
1805	1935	33.07	32.20	32.66	1.40	.67	34.73
1806	1719	30.83	37.87	28.56	1.86	.87	31.30
1807	1748	30.09	40.56	23.86	3.89	1.60	29.35
1808	1464	31.56	40.10	22.13	4.44	1.78	28.35
1809	1505	28.70	41.59	23.65	4.12	1.93	29.70
1810	1418	29.62	39.35	24.12	4.87	2.05	31.03
1817	638	38.71	27.90	29.78	.78	2.82	33.39
		MARACAY					
1782	5564	29.06	18.96	41.71	1.49	8.77	51.98
1796	7933	41.80	0.00	38.43	6.32	13.45	58.20
1802	8210	28.22	2.16	40.00	4.64	24.98	69.62
1803	8374	28.27	2.26	40.10	4.66	24.72	69.48
1804	8966	28.27	2.10	40.26	4.65	24.72	69.63
1805	8374	33.08	1.40	46.31	.24	18.98	65.52
1808	8502	33.16	1.71	45.85	.40	18.89	65.14
1809	7929	28.78	1.63	38.57	4.92	26.11	69.59
1811	7338	29.57	2.02	38.29	4.29	25.82	68.41
1816	6427	10.91	10.60	30.50	4.98	43.02	78.50
1817	5253	28.10	.80	48.09	1.48	21.53	71.10
1818	6006	28.99	3.13	39.69	6.28	21.91	67.88
1819	6423	30.17	3.86	38.33	6.35	21.28	65.97
1820	6542	28.26	4.07	37.89	7.44	22.33	67.67
		MARIA					
1803	845	47.10	22.49	19.76	8.88	1.78	30.41
1804	1369	46.68	17.46	32.72	.88	2.26	35.87
1805	1428	44.33	14.64	37.39	1.12	2.52	41.04
1806	1473	44.20	14.87	37.07	1.22	2.65	40.94
1807	1529	44.60	13.15	39.31	.92	2.03	42.25
1811	1459	35.37	20.08	38.73	3.56	2.26	44.55
		MARIARA					
1802	2224	24.37	5.04	46.40	9.04	15.15	70.59
1803	2279	24.70	2.98	43.00	11.89	17.42	72.31
1804	2188	24.22	2.61	47.53	11.01	14.63	73.17
1805	2549	24.87	2.47	53.16	7.06	12.44	72.66
1809	3254	25.11	8.73	40.41	11.95	13.80	66.16
1815	2932	23.53	4.06	51.77	7.78	12.86	72.41
1816	3270	23.43	1.41	61.47	4.01	9.69	75.17
1817	3486	25.27	2.32	56.60	5.62	10.18	72.40
1818	3396	29.12	1.41	56.07	3.77	9.63	69.46
		MONTALBAN					
1781	1525	37.77	3.67	39.28	1.44	17.84	58.56
1802	2273	36.47	0.00	39.99	6.60	16.94	63.53
1803	2560	38.09	0.00	45.90	3.16	12.85	61.91
1804	2624	38.15	0.00	45.88	3.51	12.46	61.85
1805	2595	39.23	0.00	46.78	3.70	10.29	60.77

TABLE 5. POPULATION BY RACE (CONTINUED)

YEAR	TOTAL	WHITE	INDIAN	PARDO	NEGRO	SLAVE	BLACK
1806	2624	41.31	0.00	45.81	3.24	9.64	58.69
1808	2665	41.99	0.00	44.28	5.82	7.92	58.01
1810	2718	39.59	.37	45.73	6.36	7.95	60.04
1815	3018	31.18	.53	48.24	5.43	14.61	68.29
1817	3372	32.09	.65	49.85	4.98	12.43	67.26
1818	2831	31.65	.71	53.34	4.27	10.03	67.64
1820	3746	36.57	.72	49.07	6.46	7.18	62.71
		MORON					
1804	297	0.00	0.00	54.88	2.36	42.76	100.00
1805	302	0.00	0.00	51.66	8.61	39.74	100.00
1806	302	0.00	0.00	50.00	10.93	39.07	100.00
1807	337	0.00	0.00	49.26	10.98	39.76	100.00
1818	347	0.00	0.00	68.88	0.00	31.12	100.00
1819	334	0.00	0.00	64.37	0.00	35.63	100.00
1820	587	1.53	0.00	58.94	16.52	23.00	98.47
		MOROTURO					
1802	357	14.01	.56	20.17	54.06	11.20	85.43
1804	521	7.29	22.07	26.49	38.96	5.18	70.63
1805	535	12.52	15.14	26.54	40.00	5.79	72.34
1807	381	7.35	14.96	66.14	6.82	4.72	77.69
1808	509	7.47	21.61	26.13	39.88	4.91	70.92
1809	432	12.50	7.64	73.61	1.85	4.40	79.86
1815	513	6.24	22.42	26.90	39.57	4.87	71.35
		NAGUANAGUA					
1802	1446	47.44	.35	33.61	.14	18.46	52.21
1803	1600	48.12	.31	34.06	.13	17.37	51.56
1804	1340	45.07	.60	35.37	.15	18.81	54.33
1805	1620	39.63	.49	43.40	.12	16.36	59.88
1809	1418	46.05	.56	35.26	.21	17.91	53.39
1816	1754	35.58	4.16	30.67	2.91	26.68	60.26
		NAIGUATA					
1801	771	5.19	21.01	2.72	1.17	69.91	73.80
1802	752	3.46	21.41	1.73	1.99	71.41	75.13
1804	757	3.83	26.68	.26	.79	68.43	69.48
1805	698	5.73	22.49	1.58	.43	69.77	71.78
1809	740	5.41	21.08	.95	.41	72.16	73.51
1810	775	4.90	18.06	2.06	1.68	73.29	77.03
1811	791	6.95	23.77	2.78	2.15	64.35	69.28
1816	550	6.55	19.82	6.55	4.00	63.09	73.64
1817	666	8.11	16.37	7.81	6.76	60.96	75.53
1822	510	5.29	22.94	10.39	4.90	56.47	71.76
		NIRGUA					
1781	3304	.97	0.00	98.43	0.00	.61	99.03

TABLE 5. POPULATION BY RACE (CONTINUED)

YEAR	TOTAL	WHITE	INDIAN	PARDO	NEGRO	SLAVE	BLACK
1802	3090	.94	0.00	97.70	0.00	1.36	99.06
1803	3174	1.10	0.00	97.98	0.00	.91	98.90
1804	3182	1.26	0.00	97.83	0.00	.91	98.74
1805	2814	2.13	0.00	94.21	0.00	3.66	97.87
1806	2856	2.38	0.00	93.94	0.00	3.68	97.62
1807	2816	2.13	0.00	94.21	0.00	3.66	97.87
1808	4288	2.87	.23	75.79	17.84	3.26	96.90
1809	4069	2.02	.07	67.31	29.10	1.50	97.91
1810	4668	2.06	.64	65.49	29.84	1.97	97.30
1813	3357	1.64	0.00	97.02	0.00	1.34	98.36
1817	3311	1.60	0.00	97.04	0.00	1.36	98.40
1819	3258	1.69	0.00	96.87	0.00	1.44	98.31
1820	3268	1.65	0.00	96.48	0.00	1.87	98.35
1821	3079	1.01	0.00	97.76	0.00	1.23	98.99

OCUMARE DE LA COSTA

YEAR	TOTAL	WHITE	INDIAN	PARDO	NEGRO	SLAVE	BLACK
1802	2518	3.42	.16	33.08	3.89	59.45	96.43
1803	2035	4.18	.44	38.33	12.78	44.28	95.38
1804	1514	6.41	.33	21.53	15.39	56.34	93.26
1805	2226	3.86	.04	28.66	1.66	65.77	96.09
1809	1662	5.90	0.00	36.76	3.25	54.09	94.10
1815	1529	5.23	0.00	39.70	3.99	51.08	94.77
1816	1540	3.64	0.00	35.19	6.49	54.68	96.36
1817	1549	4.20	0.00	38.86	5.36	51.58	95.80
1819	1154	4.85	.26	35.70	6.67	52.51	94.89
1820	1327	8.29	.23	35.49	10.63	45.37	91.48

OCUMARE DEL TUY

YEAR	TOTAL	WHITE	INDIAN	PARDO	NEGRO	SLAVE	BLACK
1783	2141	16.49	2.76	21.30	10.00	49.46	80.76
1802	4103	14.26	9.60	22.72	6.85	46.58	76.14
1803	4141	34.68	10.63	15.07	13.38	26.25	54.70
1804	4753	12.54	8.44	22.11	7.22	49.69	79.02
1805	4886	14.39	8.37	21.63	7.14	48.47	77.24
1810	4691	11.47	7.44	22.45	4.11	54.53	81.09
1811	3446	14.34	8.65	26.29	5.98	44.75	77.02
1815	1444	14.54	7.27	16.41	5.26	56.51	78.19
1820	4029	12.61	4.57	28.02	8.98	45.82	82.82
1821	3825	17.25	2.20	23.50	7.95	49.10	80.55
1822	3843	14.23	5.26	25.47	9.37	45.67	80.51

ORTIZ

YEAR	TOTAL	WHITE	INDIAN	PARDO	NEGRO	SLAVE	BLACK
1780	1193	66.72	7.96	8.30	7.54	9.47	25.31
1802	1700	66.88	2.59	7.41	12.71	10.41	30.53
1803	1503	68.20	3.66	13.31	7.45	7.39	28.14
1804	1559	69.15	5.52	13.09	3.72	8.53	25.34
1805	1570	70.06	5.67	12.68	3.31	8.28	24.27
1806	1775	74.76	3.72	10.31	3.10	8.11	21.52
1807	1896	54.69	2.85	29.01	5.38	8.07	42.46
1808	1941	54.51	3.09	29.21	5.46	7.73	42.40
1809	1985	53.30	3.48	28.46	6.45	8.31	43.22

TABLE 5. POPULATION BY RACE (CONTINUED)

YEAR	TOTAL	WHITE	INDIAN	PARDO	NEGRO	SLAVE	BLACK
1810	2019	53.54	3.67	28.23	6.14	8.42	42.79
1813	1975	69.06	2.89	15.14	4.35	8.56	28.05
		OSPINO					
1802	6021	30.04	14.60	48.41	2.34	4.60	55.36
1803	6067	29.75	14.67	48.28	2.39	4.91	55.58
1804	6375	29.41	16.80	46.43	2.92	4.44	53.79
1805	6419	29.57	18.94	45.60	1.34	4.55	51.49
1806	6767	29.92	18.77	45.15	1.61	4.55	51.31
1807	6862	29.80	18.23	45.37	1.92	4.68	51.97
1808	7102	32.34	17.07	43.09	3.13	4.38	50.59
1809	7277	26.36	22.00	44.51	3.17	3.96	51.64
1810	7251	26.45	22.05	44.37	3.13	4.00	51.50
1811	5673	34.81	12.18	43.38	4.28	5.34	53.01
1817	5506	35.87	12.55	41.66	4.41	5.50	51.58
		PANAQUIRE					
1784	464	8.62	11.21	12.50	.65	67.03	80.17
1802	911	7.14	9.44	9.11	.66	73.66	83.42
1803	836	8.85	8.85	9.33	.12	72.85	82.30
1804	811	6.91	9.37	7.64	.25	75.83	83.72
1805	829	6.76	8.44	8.56	1.69	74.55	84.80
1807	823	6.44	5.95	11.54	.49	75.58	87.61
1808	835	6.71	6.23	11.38	.72	74.97	87.07
1809	821	7.31	7.92	11.57	1.10	72.11	84.77
1811	767	4.82	6.78	11.60	3.26	73.53	88.40
1812	797	5.02	8.66	13.30	3.26	69.76	86.32
1816	593	4.05	3.37	17.54	4.55	70.49	92.58
		PARACOTOS					
1783	1848	21.43	32.36	22.29	7.58	16.34	46.21
1802	1889	33.14	23.40	28.59	2.86	12.02	43.46
1803	2065	31.33	21.02	27.75	3.05	16.85	47.65
1804	1764	40.53	22.34	25.40	2.61	9.13	37.13
1805	1966	37.08	26.55	23.75	2.75	9.87	36.37
1806	2089	46.72	25.08	18.33	1.53	8.33	28.20
1807	2130	44.93	24.69	17.98	1.88	10.52	30.38
1808	2197	45.38	25.85	18.34	2.28	8.15	28.77
1809	1631	34.89	27.16	14.35	5.33	18.27	37.95
1810	1757	37.45	25.84	14.34	4.95	17.42	36.71
1811	1903	37.99	26.01	14.29	4.99	16.71	36.00
1812	2002	29.92	23.68	18.23	7.59	20.58	46.40
1816	1311	29.04	16.07	23.30	21.70	9.88	54.89
1817	1841	28.95	15.92	23.47	21.13	10.54	55.13
1819	1803	41.99	35.05	11.37	0.00	11.59	22.96
1820	1812	42.00	35.04	11.26	0.00	11.70	22.96
		PARAPARA					
1780	2008	27.24	5.48	44.52	12.80	9.96	67.28

TABLE 5. POPULATION BY RACE (CONTINUED)

YEAR	TOTAL	WHITE	INDIAN	PARDO	NEGRO	SLAVE	BLACK
1781	1992	27.21	5.52	44.68	12.70	9.89	67.27
1782	2032	23.87	8.07	44.78	13.04	10.24	68.06
1788	1978	24.57	6.27	46.01	12.18	10.97	69.16
1802	2093	25.42	4.11	33.64	31.15	5.69	70.47
1803	2219	26.18	2.93	33.17	31.86	5.86	70.89
1805	2231	26.80	1.79	34.87	30.93	5.60	71.40
1807	2330	20.94	.77	59.83	13.22	5.24	78.28
1809	2480	21.77	.93	59.64	12.50	5.16	77.30
1810	2585	21.12	1.01	59.46	12.65	5.76	77.87
1811	2773	21.96	1.05	60.22	12.19	4.58	76.99
		PATANEMO					
1802	462	2.60	.43	41.99	11.47	43.51	96.97
1803	469	3.41	1.71	41.36	11.51	42.00	94.88
1804	495	2.63	.81	50.30	9.09	37.17	96.57
1805	533	2.81	1.13	48.78	9.76	37.52	96.06
1808	513	1.95	.39	46.00	10.72	40.94	97.66
1818	411	1.70	.97	65.21	1.70	30.41	97.32
1819	472	1.69	1.27	59.96	6.14	30.93	97.03
		PAYARA					
1780	908	4.30	87.11	2.42	.11	6.06	8.59
1802	1075	15.91	47.16	27.44	5.40	4.09	36.93
1804	1225	18.61	41.88	28.24	5.71	5.55	39.51
1805	1425	20.07	38.74	28.77	6.18	6.25	41.19
1806	1433	20.31	38.59	28.75	6.14	6.21	41.10
1807	1495	21.00	38.13	29.97	5.48	5.42	40.87
1812	1425	20.07	38.74	28.77	6.18	6.25	41.19
		PETARE					
1802	3840	29.30	17.16	16.88	11.77	24.90	53.54
1803	3875	29.39	16.98	16.98	11.77	24.88	53.63
1804	3899	29.91	16.88	18.88	12.59	21.75	53.22
1805	4242	25.06	13.15	25.04	5.14	31.61	61.79
1806	4130	24.94	12.81	25.38	4.89	31.99	62.25
1807	4557	25.08	11.85	25.92	3.82	33.33	63.07
1811	4349	26.35	9.57	18.28	11.57	34.24	64.08
1812	4548	23.88	13.83	12.82	9.96	39.51	62.29
1815	3444	28.22	10.02	13.82	10.66	37.28	61.76
1816	4508	26.84	7.12	14.42	22.74	28.88	66.04
1817	4374	21.72	8.85	15.91	23.09	30.43	69.43
1818	3400	24.41	10.76	25.56	5.74	33.53	64.82
1819	3670	24.74	10.52	27.11	5.31	32.32	64.74
1820	3854	24.68	10.17	27.76	5.29	32.10	65.15
1821	3962	24.08	10.17	28.04	5.50	32.21	65.75
1822	3748	23.59	10.78	25.37	6.40	33.86	65.64
		PUERTO CABELLO					
1803	4906	17.61	1.18	54.48	13.45	13.27	81.21

TABLE 5. POPULATION BY RACE (CONTINUED)

YEAR	TOTAL	WHITE	INDIAN	PARDO	NEGRO	SLAVE	BLACK
1804	5213	19.78	.54	56.88	10.61	12.20	79.69
1805	5231	17.70	.48	58.52	10.67	12.64	81.82
1806	5394	19.76	.59	51.43	14.94	13.27	79.64
1811	5482	17.79	1.20	45.75	22.64	12.62	81.01
1817	3642	34.93	8.24	26.80	12.74	17.30	56.84
1819	3279	39.52	1.68	45.47	8.30	5.03	58.80
1820	3112	23.91	1.32	52.28	11.25	11.25	74.78
		PUERTO CABELLO, CASTILLO					
1801	523	82.22	1.53	3.82	0.00	12.43	16.25
1802	317	85.17	0.00	.63	0.00	14.20	14.83
1804	482	52.49	0.00	29.67	0.00	17.84	47.51
1805	737	46.13	0.00	36.91	0.00	16.96	53.87
1806	1072	54.20	.65	33.96	0.00	11.19	45.15
1807	1062	51.04	.94	37.10	0.00	10.92	48.02
1808	1198	52.34	1.34	35.98	0.00	10.35	46.33
1809	1139	50.40	2.28	35.47	0.00	11.85	47.32
1810	1441	50.17	1.67	41.29	0.00	6.87	48.16
1819	852	30.75	5.99	44.13	12.09	7.04	63.26
1820	710	27.46	7.04	45.07	13.66	6.76	65.49
		QUARA					
1782	1057	1.89	94.23	1.99	1.80	.09	3.88
1791	805	2.36	93.42	4.10	.12	0.00	4.22
1802	715	3.08	89.51	7.27	0.00	.14	7.41
1803	703	3.56	92.75	.43	3.13	.14	3.70
1804	733	1.36	95.77	1.09	1.77	0.00	2.86
1805	847	2.48	84.65	4.37	8.50	0.00	12.87
1807	810	3.21	83.09	9.51	4.07	.12	13.70
1808	907	3.75	85.56	7.39	3.31	0.00	10.69
1809	891	3.14	85.07	6.51	5.27	0.00	11.78
1810	900	1.67	87.67	8.44	2.22	0.00	10.67
1811	932	2.36	84.55	8.48	4.61	0.00	13.09
1815	930	2.80	82.37	11.83	3.01	0.00	14.84
1816	935	2.89	80.53	12.09	4.49	0.00	16.58
1817	947	2.64	80.99	11.72	4.65	0.00	16.37
1818	1005	2.29	70.95	15.32	9.35	2.09	26.77
1819	859	2.79	67.75	16.07	10.13	3.26	29.45
		QUIBOR					
1802	6805	33.39	19.52	24.63	13.71	8.76	47.10
1803	6678	33.99	18.76	25.10	13.22	8.92	47.24
1804	6998	32.97	19.28	25.22	13.43	9.10	47.76
1805	7408	32.49	19.78	24.69	13.90	9.14	47.73
1806	7406	32.47	19.78	24.70	13.91	9.14	47.75
1807	7408	32.49	19.78	24.69	13.90	9.14	47.73
1808	8024	31.41	19.02	26.62	13.98	8.97	49.58
1810	9970	28.39	19.04	49.25	.62	2.71	52.58
1812	8446	28.75	13.54	41.49	7.13	9.09	57.71
1815	8906	28.89	13.80	41.93	6.76	8.62	57.31

TABLE 5. POPULATION BY RACE (CONTINUED)

YEAR	TOTAL	WHITE	INDIAN	PARDO	NEGRO	SLAVE	BLACK
1816	8706	28.15	13.88	42.61	6.66	8.70	57.97
1817	10004	28.32	13.82	42.88	6.59	8.39	57.86
1818	9780	26.79	15.14	43.23	6.61	8.23	58.07
1819	9276	29.86	13.35	41.86	6.25	8.68	56.79
1820	10161	30.26	13.62	40.91	6.67	8.53	56.12
		RIO CHICO					
1802	869	5.75	4.49	12.08	16.46	61.22	89.76
1803	914	6.02	5.14	12.69	16.19	59.96	88.84
1804	999	4.60	2.70	18.32	15.02	59.36	92.69
1805	1140	6.32	5.70	12.54	10.09	65.35	87.98
1806	1230	6.26	6.02	12.28	9.43	66.02	87.72
1807	1286	5.99	6.07	12.52	10.11	65.32	87.95
1808	1330	5.86	6.24	12.48	9.92	65.49	87.89
1809	1342	6.11	6.18	12.37	9.84	65.50	87.70
1810	1442	7.63	6.59	12.90	10.54	62.34	85.78
1811	1575	8.25	7.49	14.48	10.03	59.75	84.25
1812	1420	6.69	6.13	12.61	10.63	63.94	87.18
1816	1425	7.86	8.77	23.02	5.40	54.95	83.37
1817	1379	7.83	7.25	16.17	8.19	60.55	84.92
1819	1417	7.55	6.56	18.63	7.48	59.77	85.89
		RIO DEL TOCUYO					
1802	1887	20.24	62.43	13.78	0.00	3.55	17.33
1803	1813	19.42	59.96	16.16	0.00	4.47	20.63
1804	1639	13.12	70.29	10.98	0.00	5.61	16.60
1805	1715	13.06	69.39	11.84	0.00	5.71	17.55
1808	1769	13.45	72.58	6.16	0.00	7.80	13.96
1809	2394	22.64	52.55	10.90	0.00	13.91	24.81
1815	2386	18.23	66.01	12.15	0.00	3.60	15.76
		SABANETA					
1805	2125	34.31	10.64	50.73	2.07	2.26	55.06
1808	2383	16.74	26.73	53.42	1.51	1.59	56.53
1809	3000	34.10	11.40	52.13	1.37	1.00	54.50
1810	3520	31.39	11.79	51.56	3.92	1.34	56.82
1811	4057	34.46	12.82	46.44	4.19	2.10	52.72
1812	2385	37.19	23.48	27.21	8.34	3.77	39.33
1816	2246	32.59	4.14	63.27	0.00	0.00	63.27
		SAN ANTONIO DE LAS COCUIZAS					
1780	1072	9.79	10.73	60.35	16.70	2.43	79.48
		SAN ANTONIO DE LOS ALTOS					
1796	471	85.35	0.00	6.37	1.27	7.01	14.65
1802	455	82.20	1.32	7.25	.22	9.01	16.48
1803	504	80.75	7.14	2.18	.40	9.52	12.10
1804	505	80.59	1.98	3.17	.40	13.86	17.43

TABLE 5. POPULATION BY RACE (CONTINUED)

YEAR	TOTAL	WHITE	INDIAN	PARDO	NEGRO	SLAVE	BLACK
1805	616	69.81	3.90	4.71	.16	21.43	26.30
1808	1089	48.58	4.78	10.74	.73	35.17	46.65
1809	969	49.33	2.27	3.92	.31	44.17	48.40
1810	860	51.05	1.28	7.56	.47	39.65	47.67
1811	857	54.49	.70	7.70	.23	36.87	44.81
1812	828	53.99	.36	7.37	.72	37.56	45.65
1815	588	44.90	1.70	14.46	.68	38.27	53.40
1816	572	50.00	2.45	9.79	.35	37.41	47.55
1817	533	51.78	.75	8.26	.75	38.46	47.47
1818	569	51.67	3.16	12.65	.53	31.99	45.17
1819	583	54.20	1.03	13.38	1.54	29.85	44.77
1820	686	50.58	4.81	14.58	2.48	27.55	44.61
			SAN CARLOS				
1781	7346	40.68	5.28	24.90	8.33	20.81	54.04
1786	7578	36.49	5.20	28.87	10.00	19.44	58.31
1787	7986	37.05	4.98	28.46	9.82	19.68	57.96
1788	8111	36.78	4.82	28.20	10.90	19.31	58.40
1791	8706	35.98	5.02	28.39	11.50	19.11	59.01
1796	9373	35.42	5.38	28.42	11.66	19.12	59.20
1798	7853	35.80	4.90	27.54	15.19	16.57	59.30
1799	7888	35.83	4.93	27.66	14.88	16.70	59.24
1800	8221	35.02	4.94	27.54	16.38	16.12	60.04
1801	8316	34.82	5.01	27.44	16.58	16.14	60.16
1802	8805	35.48	4.91	27.26	13.61	18.75	59.61
1803	8884	35.38	4.93	27.42	13.56	18.71	59.69
1804	10476	33.95	6.51	27.66	14.33	17.54	59.54
1805	10845	34.73	6.44	27.60	13.84	17.40	58.84
1806	11225	34.57	6.33	28.56	13.67	16.86	59.09
1808	10846	34.72	6.44	27.60	13.84	17.40	58.83
1809	10845	34.73	6.44	27.60	13.84	17.40	58.84
1811	12128	34.39	.97	53.20	1.07	10.36	64.64
1812	12035	34.66	.84	53.74	.94	9.82	64.50
1816	7726	28.42	5.72	49.68	2.98	13.20	65.86
1817	8190	31.31	2.77	50.10	3.49	12.33	65.92
1818	8700	31.40	4.99	46.28	3.69	13.64	63.61
1819	8389	30.87	2.59	48.38	3.72	14.44	66.54
1820	8348	31.47	2.61	48.00	4.17	13.75	65.92
1822	8354	30.73	2.36	49.19	3.59	14.14	66.91
1823	7673	29.18	2.14	50.75	3.36	14.57	68.68
1824	6941	31.25	2.12	50.74	2.45	13.44	66.63
			SAN DIEGO DE ALCALA				
1781	794	27.46	24.43	43.70	0.00	4.41	48.11
1802	1293	19.95	16.63	42.00	19.80	1.62	63.42
1803	730	18.77	27.12	43.15	8.36	2.60	54.11
1804	925	25.19	18.05	34.49	20.54	1.73	56.76
1805	837	24.61	21.98	46.95	3.94	2.51	53.41
1809	801	19.85	22.60	51.31	4.62	1.62	57.55

TABLE 5. POPULATION BY RACE (CONTINUED)

YEAR	TOTAL	WHITE	INDIAN	PARDO	NEGRO	SLAVE	BLACK
			SAN DIEGO DE LOS ALTOS				
1802	844	50.59	25.83	11.73	1.30	10.55	23.58
1803	937	43.97	29.88	8.32	8.11	9.71	26.15
1804	859	52.27	23.05	10.13	4.19	10.36	24.68
1805	917	50.93	23.66	10.03	5.45	9.92	25.41
1807	1025	47.51	28.68	9.85	3.80	10.15	23.80
1808	1057	45.70	28.48	9.84	4.26	11.73	25.83
1809	1206	42.62	28.61	10.45	6.72	11.61	28.77
1810	1232	42.86	28.00	11.93	3.98	13.23	29.14
1811	1255	43.90	28.21	9.08	4.62	14.18	27.89
1815	1228	44.95	24.67	7.98	7.82	14.58	30.37
1816	1146	43.19	26.70	9.34	4.71	16.06	30.10
1817	1125	47.02	22.84	8.27	6.93	14.93	30.13
1818	1078	45.18	25.79	9.18	15.96	3.90	29.04
1819	1132	40.19	30.04	9.19	4.06	16.52	29.77
1820	1198	39.07	28.05	12.60	4.34	15.94	32.89
			SAN FELIPE				
1782	5020	26.04	5.10	60.26	4.62	3.98	68.86
1802	6070	24.71	10.54	35.75	10.54	18.45	64.74
1803	5667	25.23	10.82	37.18	10.01	16.76	63.95
1804	4566	19.29	2.39	61.02	2.61	14.70	78.32
1805	5127	17.77	1.19	64.85	2.69	13.50	81.04
1817	3067	10.96	.82	79.33	1.63	7.27	88.23
1818	3224	28.16	0.00	59.21	.28	12.34	71.84
1819	3293	12.18	1.18	76.71	2.31	7.62	86.64
1820	3381	12.30	1.57	75.45	2.84	7.84	86.13
1821	2756	12.16	1.42	75.29	2.76	8.38	86.43
			SAN FELIPE, MITAD DE (1)				
1807	2861	17.41	1.33	65.19	1.15	14.92	81.27
1808	2889	17.58	1.32	65.11	1.14	14.85	81.10
1809	2754	17.32	1.13	62.96	1.02	17.57	81.55
1810	2862	17.68	1.12	65.06	1.36	14.78	81.20
1811	2862	17.68	1.12	65.06	1.36	14.78	81.20
1812	2025	10.27	.40	77.53	.49	11.31	89.33
			SAN FELIPE, MITAD DE (2)				
1807	2842	16.78	1.58	68.51	1.69	11.44	81.63
1808	2887	16.31	2.81	66.09	3.39	11.40	80.88
1809	2838	15.57	4.83	64.34	4.33	10.92	79.60
1810	2878	15.43	4.79	63.62	4.48	11.67	79.78
1811	2877	15.12	2.92	68.68	3.41	9.87	81.96
			SAN FERNANDO DE APURE				
1801	3564	37.26	7.24	49.07	2.24	4.18	55.50
1805	1575	47.87	14.98	34.92	0.00	2.22	37.14

TABLE 5. POPULATION BY RACE (CONTINUED)

YEAR	TOTAL	WHITE	INDIAN	PARDO	NEGRO	SLAVE	BLACK
1806	2464	41.56	20.13	35.96	0.00	2.35	38.31
1816	1832	39.41	6.28	38.86	8.08	7.37	54.31
		SAN FERNANDO DE CACHICAMO					
1783	420	25.00	3.33	33.10	11.19	27.38	71.67
1802	424	22.88	7.78	42.22	9.91	17.22	69.34
1803	415	22.17	8.43	40.72	11.81	16.87	69.40
1805	439	19.36	5.01	58.09	2.51	15.03	75.63
1806	513	23.59	6.24	53.30	1.95	14.42	70.18
1807	503	24.45	6.36	54.87	1.99	12.33	69.18
		SAN FRANCISCO DE CARA					
1783	1169	20.19	2.74	70.57	0.00	6.50	77.07
1802	1508	24.54	2.59	56.50	4.77	11.60	72.88
		SAN FRANCISCO DE TIZNADOS					
1780	2240	12.63	6.07	15.36	50.54	15.40	81.29
1801	1746	11.28	2.35	74.86	0.00	11.51	86.37
1802	1987	10.62	.91	47.91	31.81	8.76	88.48
1803	2054	13.83	1.02	48.83	25.80	10.52	85.15
1805	2181	14.49	1.38	73.77	.78	9.58	84.14
1807	2368	15.20	1.27	73.52	.84	9.16	83.53
1808	2361	14.23	1.27	74.29	.85	9.36	84.50
1809	2423	14.32	1.44	73.88	.99	9.37	84.23
1811	2230	21.35	8.43	43.50	18.79	7.94	70.22
1812	2465	19.35	8.76	47.42	15.29	9.17	71.89
		SAN FRANCISCO DE YARE					
1783	1299	4.16	10.16	9.70	10.55	65.43	85.68
1802	1766	5.15	13.19	4.42	17.21	60.02	81.65
1803	1740	4.54	13.79	5.29	20.34	56.03	81.67
1804	1733	4.27	13.04	3.64	20.66	58.40	82.69
1805	1725	4.70	12.81	3.77	21.22	57.51	82.49
1810	2145	4.10	13.29	22.98	4.62	55.01	82.61
1811	2152	4.09	13.24	23.05	4.79	54.83	82.67
1815	1334	4.42	10.34	11.39	3.67	70.16	85.23
1817	2096	4.29	18.65	19.66	7.54	49.86	77.05
1818	1713	4.55	11.21	25.45	6.13	52.66	84.24
1820	1835	6.65	9.54	14.39	11.93	57.49	83.81
1821	2006	6.43	14.26	19.34	6.38	53.59	79.31
1822	1958	5.98	10.16	20.74	6.23	56.89	83.86
		SAN JAIME					
1780	1964	38.49	5.45	42.77	4.48	8.81	56.06
		SAN JOSE					
1781	1099	15.47	30.66	46.50	1.91	5.46	53.87

TABLE 5. POPULATION BY RACE (CONTINUED)

YEAR	TOTAL	WHITE	INDIAN	PARDO	NEGRO	SLAVE	BLACK
1788	1516	5.67	18.47	69.79	3.36	2.70	75.86
1790	1727	22.41	18.30	53.21	4.57	1.51	59.29
1791	1727	22.41	18.30	53.21	4.57	1.51	59.29
1792	2102	23.45	18.03	55.33	1.57	1.62	58.52
1794	2042	21.20	18.56	56.95	1.62	1.67	60.24
1795	2246	21.46	15.09	28.67	32.46	2.32	63.45
1798	2517	22.29	15.93	27.57	31.47	2.74	61.78
1799	2517	22.29	15.93	27.57	31.47	2.74	61.78
1800	2535	22.13	15.82	28.17	31.24	2.64	62.05
1801	2572	20.88	15.98	30.79	31.65	.70	63.14
1803	2543	19.90	15.06	62.17	1.45	1.42	65.04
1804	2560	20.16	10.94	65.31	1.45	2.15	68.91
1805	1920	20.89	14.27	61.09	1.46	2.29	64.84
1807	1624	25.06	10.22	62.44	0.00	2.28	64.72
1808	1625	25.48	9.78	62.15	0.00	2.58	64.74
1811	1597	24.11	10.96	62.55	0.00	2.38	64.93
1812	1565	20.13	6.07	72.52	1.28	0.00	73.80
1815	1739	3.97	9.55	84.47	.98	1.04	86.49
1818	1624	28.33	23.21	47.54	.62	.31	48.46
1819	1669	22.83	31.04	44.94	.72	.48	46.14
1822	1992	29.02	20.98	46.44	2.16	1.41	50.00
1823	1692	29.02	20.39	48.17	1.12	1.30	50.59
			SAN JOSE DE APURE				
1802	559	13.42	38.46	32.56	14.13	1.43	48.12
1804	719	21.97	29.49	28.09	20.17	.28	48.54
1806	656	21.80	32.32	26.07	19.21	.61	45.88
1807	615	20.81	33.33	26.02	19.35	.49	45.85
1808	593	21.42	33.05	25.80	19.22	.51	45.53
1809	593	21.42	33.05	25.80	19.22	.51	45.53
			SAN JOSE DE TIZNADOS				
1802	1865	18.50	4.08	64.02	3.38	10.03	77.43
1803	1994	18.00	6.02	62.99	4.16	8.83	75.98
1804	1938	18.47	7.28	62.44	4.33	7.48	74.25
1805	1967	18.96	7.27	63.55	3.36	6.86	73.77
1807	2188	16.77	5.07	56.81	15.13	6.22	78.15
1808	2009	14.88	4.08	67.50	7.02	6.52	81.04
1809	2088	17.39	3.02	63.51	10.20	5.89	79.60
1810	2261	14.42	5.71	64.88	8.54	6.46	79.88
1812	2271	12.59	5.81	67.33	8.10	6.16	81.59
1816	2104	16.83	6.46	52.28	18.49	5.94	76.71
1817	2727	16.65	6.09	56.55	15.40	5.32	77.26
			SAN JUAN DE LOS MORROS				
1802	1232	43.91	8.12	21.02	18.59	8.36	47.97
1803	1227	46.54	7.74	21.84	15.97	7.91	45.72
1805	1389	47.73	8.57	25.34	10.80	7.56	43.70
1806	1430	45.94	8.11	17.27	21.40	7.27	45.94
1807	1493	45.14	9.18	20.36	18.08	7.23	45.68

TABLE 5. POPULATION BY RACE (CONTINUED)

YEAR	TOTAL	WHITE	INDIAN	PARDO	NEGRO	SLAVE	BLACK
1809	1628	46.13	7.56	21.44	17.51	7.37	46.31
1810	1622	46.49	8.01	20.78	17.88	6.84	45.50
1811	1568	48.15	6.51	22.26	15.37	7.72	45.34
		SAN MATEO					
1781	2253	26.99	13.63	42.65	0.00	16.73	59.39
1802	2276	28.16	9.18	37.26	.57	24.82	62.65
1803	2218	27.32	11.14	33.86	2.89	24.80	61.54
1804	2254	25.51	12.29	33.45	2.48	26.26	62.20
1805	2286	27.73	11.59	33.33	2.27	25.07	60.67
1806	2281	26.87	9.25	37.09	2.41	24.38	63.88
1808	2124	28.91	10.59	32.30	3.81	24.39	60.50
1809	2415	29.90	11.64	32.38	2.98	23.11	58.47
1811	2508	29.03	10.53	34.77	2.39	23.29	60.45
1815	1886	34.68	8.48	35.84	3.13	17.87	56.84
1816	1873	33.69	9.66	36.20	3.10	17.35	56.65
1817	1915	32.38	10.55	36.76	3.19	17.13	57.08
1818	1930	31.97	10.93	35.96	3.52	17.62	57.10
1821	2428	29.90	10.83	37.36	3.21	18.70	59.27
		SAN MIGUEL DE TRUJILLO					
1808	2343	40.03	9.94	42.94	3.33	3.76	50.02
		SAN NICOLAS DE TOLENTINO					
1803	571	.18	1.75	55.17	19.09	23.82	98.07
1808	697	7.32	8.46	48.78	8.90	26.54	84.22
1818	291	0.00	0.00	100.00	0.00	0.00	100.00
1820	442	4.52	0.00	63.12	0.00	32.35	95.48
1821	437	0.00	4.58	62.70	32.72	0.00	95.42
		SAN PEDRO					
1810	1021	52.89	.69	33.30	0.00	13.12	46.43
1811	1151	49.35	3.30	34.93	0.00	12.42	47.35
1816	938	53.62	2.13	38.38	0.00	5.86	44.24
1817	869	54.78	2.19	37.51	0.00	5.52	43.04
		SAN RAFAEL DE ONOTO					
1779	598	42.64	45.65	8.36	2.17	1.17	11.71
1810	1330	32.26	24.96	41.28	.15	1.35	42.78
1811	1273	26.94	25.84	45.64	.16	1.41	47.21
1828	847	18.42	37.19	40.97	3.31	.12	44.39
1829	827	17.90	34.82	43.05	3.63	.60	47.28
		SAN RAFAEL DE ORITUCO					
1783	1587	36.42	2.58	24.57	16.64	19.79	61.00
1802	971	19.67	0.00	60.25	0.00	20.08	80.33
1803	972	20.58	0.00	60.39	0.00	19.03	79.42

TABLE 5. POPULATION BY RACE (CONTINUED)

YEAR	TOTAL	WHITE	INDIAN	PARDO	NEGRO	SLAVE	BLACK
1804	1060	24.06	0.00	60.28	0.00	15.66	75.94
1805	1068	24.44	0.00	59.64	0.00	15.92	75.56
1806	1186	23.19	0.00	62.14	0.00	14.67	76.81
1808	1214	26.36	0.00	57.99	0.00	15.65	73.64
1809	1084	29.70	4.43	51.01	2.86	11.99	65.87
1810	1483	29.47	2.43	60.96	2.63	4.52	68.11
1811	1564	27.94	2.30	46.42	16.43	6.91	69.76
SAN SEBASTIAN DE LOS REYES							
1783	2907	24.84	21.40	43.69	1.96	8.12	53.77
1802	3212	30.67	6.41	52.99	1.77	3.16	62.92
1803	3310	30.33	8.19	51.87	1.78	7.82	61.48
1804	3384	30.61	8.16	51.60	1.89	7.74	61.23
1805	3387	30.32	8.12	52.05	2.04	7.47	61.56
1806	3333	31.20	7.26	52.63	2.76	6.15	61.54
1809	3088	31.57	6.54	51.20	3.14	7.55	61.88
1810	3212	31.29	6.82	51.25	3.70	6.94	61.89
1811	3245	31.25	6.72	50.97	3.79	7.27	62.03
SANARE							
1803	3281	12.37	59.19	17.04	10.06	1.34	28.44
1804	3315	12.43	58.85	17.16	10.14	1.42	28.72
1805	3281	12.37	59.19	17.04	10.06	1.34	28.44
1806	3107	12.46	61.73	15.13	8.18	2.51	25.81
1807	3100	12.32	61.42	15.19	8.19	2.87	26.26
1808	3092	12.52	62.32	14.97	7.31	2.88	25.16
1809	3104	12.21	62.08	16.24	6.96	2.51	25.71
1810	3118	12.41	61.19	16.65	6.90	2.85	26.40
1812	2551	14.54	61.31	13.03	4.43	1.69	24.15
1815	2248	13.92	60.45	20.06	3.65	1.91	25.62
1816	2664	13.66	63.93	17.98	3.53	.90	22.41
1817	2781	13.20	61.24	17.22	6.01	2.34	25.57
1818	2664	13.66	63.93	17.98	3.53	.90	22.41
1819	2232	14.02	60.89	20.21	3.67	1.21	25.09
1820	2778	13.10	61.30	17.24	6.01	2.34	25.59
SANTA CRUZ DE ARAGUA							
1802	6064	55.92	1.06	40.40	1.10	1.52	43.02
1803	5667	53.79	1.84	42.10	.90	1.38	44.38
1804	6138	54.86	1.25	42.59	.28	1.03	43.89
1805	5711	56.07	1.14	41.73	.05	1.02	42.79
1808	5717	57.91	1.07	38.83	.70	1.49	41.02
1811	4038	57.13	.97	34.30	6.19	1.41	41.90
1815	4316	51.88	43.40	2.55	.35	1.83	4.73
1816	4575	56.79	1.70	38.43	1.16	1.92	41.51
1817	4699	58.18	.66	37.67	1.15	2.34	41.16
1818	3984	58.06	.83	32.73	6.00	2.38	41.11
1822	4824	46.46	7.61	42.06	2.09	1.78	45.94

TABLE 5. POPULATION BY RACE (CONTINUED)

YEAR	TOTAL	WHITE	INDIAN	PARDO	NEGRO	SLAVE	BLACK
		SANTA INES DEL ALTAR					
1779	65	4.62	44.62	33.85	16.92	0.00	50.77
1802	104	18.27	17.31	51.92	7.69	4.81	64.42
1803	103	5.83	16.50	73.79	3.88	0.00	77.67
1804	104	.96	28.85	64.42	3.85	1.92	70.19
1805	137	2.92	10.22	84.67	2.19	0.00	86.86
1806	121	4.13	12.40	81.82	.83	.83	83.47
1810	90	0.00	12.22	87.78	0.00	0.00	87.78
1811	86	0.00	17.44	82.56	0.00	0.00	82.56
1818	200	0.00	9.00	91.00	0.00	0.00	91.00
1819	339	5.60	20.06	49.85	24.48	0.00	74.34
1820	310	6.13	15.48	51.29	26.77	.32	78.39
1829	358	4.47	25.70	69.55	0.00	.28	69.83
		SANTA LUCIA					
1784	2197	14.02	24.03	13.06	13.20	35.69	61.95
1787	2179	15.88	17.53	22.17	6.01	38.41	66.59
1802	2878	22.48	10.67	32.49	2.71	31.65	66.85
1803	2733	17.82	10.57	36.55	4.54	30.52	71.61
1804	3100	20.35	9.13	26.61	7.84	36.06	70.52
1805	2688	14.32	17.19	31.25	3.87	33.37	68.49
1808	3381	20.91	11.59	28.13	6.54	32.83	67.49
1809	3385	20.89	11.40	28.39	6.53	32.79	67.71
1811	3520	21.34	9.89	30.45	3.15	35.17	68.78
1816	3262	21.03	6.93	32.53	3.56	35.96	72.04
1817	2947	32.51	.71	48.42	4.45	13.91	66.78
1818	2858	25.19	1.05	31.49	2.80	39.47	73.76
1819	2699	17.41	8.67	32.68	7.93	33.31	73.92
		SANTA MARIA DE IPIRE					
1783	1039	31.57	9.14	33.97	5.49	19.83	59.29
1798	1286	30.33	2.02	36.78	16.80	14.07	67.65
1803	1347	28.14	2.45	39.12	15.81	14.48	69.41
		SANTA ROSA DE LIMA					
1802	2850	36.38	11.09	8.46	38.74	4.84	52.04
1803	3019	34.85	15.63	8.38	36.57	4.57	49.52
1804	2850	36.88	11.09	8.46	38.74	4.84	52.04
1805	2853	37.33	10.90	8.48	38.21	5.08	51.77
1807	2926	36.81	10.29	9.23	31.34	12.34	52.90
1808	2893	37.88	10.75	10.47	28.41	12.48	51.37
1809	4378	29.63	7.33	35.45	24.46	3.13	63.04
1810	4563	30.73	7.19	35.59	23.45	3.05	62.09
1815	4174	31.60	8.15	31.00	25.78	3.47	60.25
1816	4649	29.34	7.64	33.32	26.61	3.10	63.02
1817	4683	28.83	4.48	40.25	22.31	4.12	66.69
1819	4574	28.84	4.57	40.03	22.37	4.20	66.59
1820	4574	28.84	4.57	40.03	22.37	4.20	66.59

TABLE 5. POPULATION BY RACE (CONTINUED)

YEAR	TOTAL	WHITE	INDIAN	PARDO	NEGRO	SLAVE	BLACK
			SANTA TERESA DE JESUS				
1783	854	14.17	15.93	12.18	6.79	50.94	69.91
1786	814	12.65	17.69	14.86	2.09	52.70	69.66
1787	857	11.79	17.97	14.35	6.18	49.71	70.25
1788	877	11.52	18.59	13.91	6.04	49.94	69.90
1802	1613	20.15	10.29	12.83	13.89	42.84	69.56
1803	1799	21.96	11.40	11.62	13.34	41.69	66.65
1804	1902	20.24	11.78	12.41	14.25	41.32	67.98
1805	1742	20.21	13.20	12.69	15.10	38.81	66.59
1810	1915	22.98	11.23	13.11	16.97	35.72	65.80
1811	1812	22.35	10.98	12.42	16.67	37.58	66.67
1815	1364	15.54	9.53	16.28	18.48	40.18	74.93
1816	1352	19.30	9.84	13.54	15.16	42.16	70.86
1817	1423	19.54	7.73	13.77	16.37	42.59	72.73
1820	1497	22.65	5.01	11.36	17.64	43.35	72.34
			SARARE				
1779	1200	16.92	24.75	41.33	13.92	3.08	58.33
1802	2510	13.86	12.35	46.29	26.73	.76	73.78
1804	2666	14.63	12.87	46.02	25.77	.71	72.51
1805	2223	16.87	13.81	61.45	6.07	1.80	69.32
1807	2439	14.06	12.34	47.36	25.46	.78	73.60
1808	2666	14.63	12.87	46.02	25.77	.71	72.51
1809	2666	14.63	12.87	46.02	25.77	.71	72.51
1810	2859	14.69	12.73	44.53	26.65	1.40	72.58
1811	2666	14.63	12.87	46.02	25.77	.71	72.51
1817	2323	19.67	20.58	57.99	.69	1.08	59.75
1818	2778	15.73	19.94	61.20	1.33	1.80	64.33
			SIQUISIQUE				
1802	3983	8.41	69.02	15.44	5.32	1.81	22.57
1803	4094	8.84	67.76	15.75	5.91	1.73	23.40
1804	3310	9.67	64.80	17.98	5.20	2.36	25.53
1805	3407	10.95	63.69	17.79	5.25	2.32	25.36
1807	4083	11.81	63.68	20.38	1.25	2.89	24.52
			TACARIGUA DE MAMPORAL				
1784	673	9.06	2.82	5.94	15.16	67.01	88.11
1802	743	5.38	1.21	4.04	16.02	73.35	93.41
1803	696	5.46	1.01	2.87	17.10	73.56	93.53
1804	713	5.05	2.81	3.09	15.57	73.49	92.15
1805	599	6.01	.67	7.35	11.85	74.12	93.32
1806	580	6.38	3.10	2.24	13.45	74.83	90.52
1807	562	7.30	2.31	5.16	12.10	73.13	90.39
1808	558	6.09	2.51	10.22	7.17	74.01	91.40
1809	544	4.96	2.39	11.76	7.54	73.35	92.65
1811	455	6.59	1.10	11.87	9.23	71.21	92.31
1816	519	6.94	1.35	20.62	17.92	53.18	91.71

TABLE 5. POPULATION BY RACE (CONTINUED)

YEAR	TOTAL	WHITE	INDIAN	PARDO	NEGRO	SLAVE	BLACK
1818	502	5.58	3.59	14.34	16.93	59.56	90.84
1820	570	6.67	4.04	16.49	18.95	53.86	89.30
		TACATA					
1783	742	6.87	16.04	31.27	14.02	31.81	77.09
1799	1093	10.52	23.97	29.55	2.65	33.30	65.51
1802	1381	21.87	23.39	21.51	5.43	27.81	54.74
1804	1425	10.25	38.81	21.61	3.09	26.25	50.95
1805	1453	9.84	36.75	22.64	3.17	27.60	53.41
1812	1457	27.04	16.13	31.02	2.33	23.47	56.83
1813	1677	29.64	9.90	31.13	1.79	27.55	60.47
1817	1257	28.40	17.18	33.09	1.51	19.81	54.42
1818	1721	31.32	10.23	35.85	.70	21.91	58.45
1819	1747	29.14	13.51	37.21	.40	19.75	57.36
1820	2218	25.25	16.14	39.54	.45	18.62	58.61
1821	1863	32.05	16.32	26.03	1.45	24.15	51.64
1822	2054	29.60	14.90	32.57	1.07	21.86	55.50
		TAGUAI					
1802	1915	39.27	7.42	35.72	2.66	14.93	53.32
1803	1745	35.64	7.68	37.94	2.35	16.39	56.68
1804	1840	36.36	9.84	15.33	21.03	17.45	53.80
1805	1868	36.19	10.01	15.31	20.88	17.61	53.80
1810	2214	38.48	9.62	16.17	21.23	14.50	51.90
		TAPIPA					
1803	588	7.82	5.27	7.48	.68	78.74	86.90
1804	663	7.39	6.64	5.64	3.17	76.17	85.97
1805	640	7.66	6.56	7.19	4.22	74.37	85.78
1806	560	5.54	6.61	6.07	5.18	76.61	87.86
1807	539	5.19	5.01	7.05	4.45	78.29	89.80
1808	485	7.84	3.09	5.77	4.54	78.76	89.07
1811	426	10.33	4.93	4.69	5.16	74.88	84.74
1812	403	11.17	5.21	4.22	4.71	74.69	83.62
1816	366	7.65	10.93	8.74	6.01	66.67	81.42
1817	356	8.71	7.58	8.99	6.18	68.54	83.71
1818	409	9.54	12.96	8.07	8.31	61.12	77.51
1819	417	8.39	12.23	4.56	13.43	61.39	79.38
1820	364	7.42	10.71	8.79	6.04	67.03	81.87
1829	320	7.81	4.69	19.06	11.88	56.56	87.50
		TARIA					
1803	262	1.91	0.00	96.56	0.00	1.53	98.09
1808	335	.60	2.39	85.67	8.06	3.28	97.01
1810	240	1.67	0.00	97.92	0.00	.42	98.33
		TARMAS					
1802	513	8.58	6.43	23.20	5.07	56.73	84.99

TABLE 5. POPULATION BY RACE (CONTINUED)

YEAR	TOTAL	WHITE	INDIAN	PARDO	NEGRO	SLAVE	BLACK
1803	493	6.29	5.48	26.17	5.07	57.00	88.24
1805	467	8.78	6.42	26.98	1.71	56.10	84.80
1807	506	9.49	4.55	29.45	4.35	52.17	85.97
1808	486	8.85	4.32	29.84	3.91	53.09	86.83
1810	533	8.44	6.19	28.33	2.25	54.78	85.37
1811	538	7.99	5.76	29.55	2.42	54.28	86.25
1815	502	7.77	3.59	24.50	6.97	57.17	88.65
1816	527	8.73	2.66	28.65	5.50	54.46	88.61
1817	557	8.62	2.51	29.44	5.21	54.22	88.87
1818	543	8.66	5.34	28.73	2.95	54.33	86.00
1819	529	7.37	2.46	30.62	5.10	54.44	90.17
1820	504	6.35	2.58	28.37	4.96	57.74	91.07
1829	513	14.04	0.00	62.57	0.00	23.39	85.96
		TEMERLA					
1802	544	4.04	0.00	95.59	0.00	.37	95.96
1803	476	4.83	0.00	95.17	0.00	0.00	95.17
1804	479	3.13	0.00	96.87	0.00	0.00	96.87
1805	457	3.28	0.00	96.28	0.00	.44	96.72
1806	470	3.19	0.00	96.38	0.00	.43	96.81
1807	499	3.21	0.00	96.59	0.00	.20	96.79
1808	470	3.19	0.00	96.38	0.00	.43	96.81
1810	546	.55	0.00	99.45	0.00	0.00	99.45
1817	663	4.22	0.00	95.63	0.00	.15	95.78
1818	935	4.49	0.00	94.55	0.00	.96	95.51
1819	716	4.19	0.00	95.67	0.00	.14	95.81
1820	591	4.74	0.00	92.89	.17	2.20	95.26
1821	622	4.50	0.00	93.41	0.00	2.09	95.50
		TINACO					
1771	2053	53.63	4.72	34.05	.93	6.67	41.65
1781	1782	58.31	0.00	35.19	.90	5.61	41.69
1787	1798	57.29	2.50	34.32	.61	5.28	40.21
1788	1662	57.52	4.69	31.35	1.44	4.99	37.79
1790	2311	39.81	3.16	51.71	1.25	4.07	57.03
1791	1786	53.53	5.77	33.93	1.06	5.71	40.71
1794	2294	51.66	3.75	37.88	.96	5.75	44.59
1795	2288	47.77	3.80	41.26	1.18	5.99	48.43
1796	2246	48.44	3.78	41.54	.93	5.30	47.77
1798	2327	49.38	2.75	41.43	1.07	5.37	47.87
1799	2276	49.17	3.03	40.20	1.89	5.71	47.80
1800	2285	48.80	2.80	40.35	2.58	5.47	48.40
1801	2258	49.07	2.66	41.05	1.82	5.40	48.27
1802	2311	49.03	2.64	35.01	7.53	5.80	48.33
1803	2518	46.39	2.50	37.17	7.39	6.55	51.11
1804	2577	47.23	2.44	35.97	7.95	6.40	50.33
1805	2627	47.54	2.47	36.39	7.16	6.43	49.98
1806	2690	46.80	2.57	37.47	7.06	6.10	50.63
1807	2695	45.97	2.52	38.92	6.72	5.86	51.50
1808	2608	46.55	2.49	39.30	6.33	5.33	50.96
1811	2491	41.63	3.05	43.92	6.58	4.82	55.32

TABLE 5. POPULATION BY RACE (CONTINUED)

YEAR	TOTAL	WHITE	INDIAN	PARDO	NEGRO	SLAVE	BLACK
1812	2573	46.37	2.91	43.88	1.28	5.56	50.72
1816	2065	52.64	3.49	36.85	0.00	7.02	43.87
1817	1981	53.41	3.23	35.44	0.00	7.93	43.36
1819	2118	51.09	3.02	38.48	0.00	7.41	45.89
1820	2513	49.82	4.50	38.56	0.00	7.12	45.68
1821	2971	45.10	5.25	43.59	0.00	6.06	49.65
1822	2984	46.15	4.93	42.49	.74	5.70	48.93
1823	3373	45.95	6.55	38.60	2.08	6.82	47.49
1824	3306	46.34	6.08	38.84	2.12	6.62	47.58
1825	3373	45.95	6.55	38.60	2.08	6.82	47.49
1826	3606	44.07	5.44	41.49	2.22	6.79	50.50
1827	3620	44.81	5.19	40.83	2.38	6.80	50.00
1829	3637	44.73	4.92	41.38	2.06	6.90	50.34
1830	3524	45.52	5.14	40.38	2.13	6.84	49.35
1831	3527	45.99	5.10	40.40	2.30	6.21	48.91
1832	3574	46.28	4.70	40.35	2.55	6.13	49.02
1834	4156	48.20	4.48	37.95	5.29	4.09	47.33
1835	4586	47.03	4.32	39.47	5.28	3.90	48.65
1836	5682	50.09	3.57	38.17	4.77	3.40	46.34
1837	6362	41.70	4.24	40.30	10.30	3.46	54.06
		TINAJAS					
1781	1175	9.02	11.15	22.38	24.77	32.68	79.83
1801	920	9.89	.43	70.22	2.72	16.74	89.67
1802	1053	5.22	1.33	78.35	2.75	12.35	93.45
1803	1138	8.70	2.46	75.75	1.49	11.60	88.84
1804	1146	4.80	1.75	75.83	5.50	12.13	93.46
1805	1051	5.71	2.19	75.74	4.66	11.70	92.10
1807	1142	3.50	0.00	79.42	8.76	8.32	96.50
1808	1093	3.02	0.00	87.65	0.00	9.33	96.98
1809	1001	3.30	0.00	87.81	0.00	8.89	96.70
1810	1198	3.01	0.00	89.82	0.00	7.18	96.99
1811	1303	3.22	.69	87.72	0.00	8.37	96.09
1813	1257	6.36	.16	80.83	5.81	6.84	93.48
1818	759	3.29	0.00	90.25	0.00	6.46	96.71
1819	793	2.77	0.00	83.73	7.69	5.80	97.23
1820	715	3.08	0.00	81.96	8.53	6.43	96.92
1821	1113	3.23	0.00	74.93	5.48	16.35	96.77
		TINAQUILLO					
1781	847	22.55	1.65	70.96	0.00	4.84	75.80
1787	1133	22.42	3.88	71.34	.35	1.50	73.70
1788	1043	23.30	4.03	70.09	.86	1.73	72.67
1790	1051	25.50	4.09	66.22	1.14	3.04	70.41
1791	1055	27.30	3.13	67.01	1.14	1.42	69.57
1792	1141	26.21	3.07	67.84	1.05	1.84	70.73
1794	1139	27.04	2.37	67.69	1.40	1.49	70.59
1795	1139	27.04	2.37	67.69	1.40	1.49	70.59
1796	1121	25.69	2.50	68.78	.98	2.05	71.81
1798	1177	25.66	2.55	68.48	1.10	2.21	71.79
1799	1097	28.26	3.19	65.00	1.19	2.37	68.55

TABLE 5. POPULATION BY RACE (CONTINUED)

YEAR	TOTAL	WHITE	INDIAN	PARDO	NEGRO	SLAVE	BLACK
1800	1080	26.85	2.50	66.85	1.20	2.59	70.65
1801	1144	25.00	2.97	68.18	1.40	2.45	72.03
1802	1131	26.79	2.56	67.46	1.06	2.12	70.65
1803	1163	24.16	3.27	68.79	1.38	2.41	72.57
1804	1231	29.57	3.01	63.61	1.30	2.52	67.42
1805	1261	26.80	4.36	64.79	1.74	2.30	68.83
1806	1149	29.33	2.79	64.93	1.04	1.91	67.89
1807	1308	26.45	2.68	67.89	1.07	1.91	70.87
1808	1321	26.72	2.65	67.68	1.06	1.89	70.63
1809	1256	36.31	3.11	57.88	.16	2.55	60.59
1811	1313	41.58	2.67	53.77	.76	1.22	55.75
1812	1319	41.55	2.65	53.68	.91	1.21	55.80
1815	1408	30.18	2.13	66.62	.14	.92	67.68
1816	1654	25.88	3.51	68.50	1.57	.54	70.62
1817	1478	29.57	1.29	67.73	.34	1.08	69.15
1818	1880	30.43	1.65	67.07	.43	.43	67.93
1820	2619	26.38	2.83	67.20	1.34	2.25	70.79
1822	1921	43.31	4.48	48.10	1.25	2.86	52.21
1823	2752	42.19	4.25	47.06	0.00	6.50	53.56
1836	3253	23.06	1.97	73.35	.31	1.32	74.98
		TOCUYITO					
1803	1705	26.86	2.40	45.28	2.35	23.11	70.73
1804	1743	26.28	2.35	45.78	2.29	23.29	71.37
1805	1792	26.28	2.51	46.37	2.01	22.82	71.21
1812	3295	16.51	.58	49.89	.70	32.32	82.91
1816	2248	13.21	2.00	45.73	3.20	35.85	84.79
		TUCUPIDO					
1783	486	0.00	100.00	0.00	0.00	0.00	0.00
1801	1827	18.66	37.93	32.95	1.20	9.25	43.40
1805	1953	18.43	37.84	1.64	32.31	9.78	43.73
1809	2383	17.25	35.33	37.14	1.09	9.19	47.42
		TUCUPIDO DE GUANARE					
1802	4254	23.65	14.10	36.44	16.69	9.12	62.25
1803	3532	33.98	11.01	40.12	9.37	5.52	55.01
1804	4236	41.41	8.73	39.59	5.97	4.30	49.86
1805	4236	41.41	8.73	39.59	5.97	4.30	49.86
1807	4488	44.59	7.38	40.64	4.23	3.16	48.04
1808	4108	36.88	10.91	45.20	4.36	2.65	52.22
1809	4957	36.90	8.33	46.68	5.41	2.68	54.77
1810	5292	41.76	4.82	47.15	3.80	2.48	53.42
1817	2537	39.50	7.53	45.09	4.93	2.96	52.98
		TUCURAGUA					
1802	435	3.45	1.61	77.24	1.15	16.55	94.94
1803	425	6.35	0.00	76.47	1.18	16.00	93.65
1804	263	7.22	0.00	72.62	2.66	17.49	92.78

TABLE 5. POPULATION BY RACE (CONTINUED)

YEAR	TOTAL	WHITE	INDIAN	PARDO	NEGRO	SLAVE	BLACK
1805	409	3.67	0.00	79.71	1.47	15.16	96.33
1807	351	3.70	0.00	80.91	1.14	14.25	96.30
1808	406	3.94	0.00	80.79	2.96	12.32	96.06
1809	405	3.95	0.00	80.99	2.72	12.35	96.05
1812	293	1.71	0.00	80.55	0.00	17.75	98.29
1816	153	0.00	0.00	82.35	1.31	16.34	100.00
		TUREN					
1778	418	13.16	57.89	26.56	2.15	.24	28.95
1801	1004	31.77	21.51	23.11	16.04	7.57	46.71
1808	2522	36.60	17.61	43.06	1.23	1.51	45.80
1809	813	5.54	50.43	31.86	11.81	.37	44.03
1810	2464	34.86	15.83	45.82	1.99	1.50	49.31
1811	786	24.05	26.72	45.29	3.44	.51	49.24
1812	770	26.88	29.74	40.78	1.04	1.56	43.38
1816	752	31.25	38.56	30.19	0.00	0.00	30.19
		TURIAMO					
1802	181	2.21	0.00	10.50	2.76	84.53	97.79
1803	174	1.72	0.00	10.92	2.30	85.06	98.28
1804	204	1.47	0.00	16.18	.98	81.37	98.53
1805	212	1.89	0.00	14.62	2.36	81.13	98.11
1808	239	1.26	0.00	16.32	7.53	74.90	98.74
1818	326	2.15	0.00	15.64	1.53	80.67	97.85
1819	264	3.03	0.00	26.89	5.30	64.77	96.97
		TURMERO					
1781	6918	43.00	20.03	28.77	0.00	8.20	36.96
1802	7529	32.20	18.79	28.30	4.05	16.66	49.01
1803	7679	32.60	19.77	28.64	4.52	14.48	47.64
1804	8065	32.39	19.69	28.61	4.87	14.45	47.92
1805	8079	31.40	19.89	28.62	5.04	15.05	48.71
1806	7908	30.91	20.85	26.91	5.01	16.33	48.24
1808	7661	27.27	21.68	26.63	5.73	18.69	51.05
1809	7359	26.46	22.29	26.74	5.35	19.16	51.26
1811	7764	27.36	22.90	25.21	5.31	19.23	49.74
		URACHICHE					
1782	1350	22.00	33.41	34.37	2.00	8.22	44.59
1788	1345	14.94	31.52	45.65	0.00	7.88	53.53
1802	1663	5.41	24.95	60.37	3.55	5.71	69.63
1803	1742	5.86	24.63	58.78	4.59	6.14	69.52
1804	1719	6.63	24.90	57.88	4.13	6.46	68.47
1805	1809	4.48	29.80	56.88	2.32	6.52	65.73
1807	1865	6.60	23.81	58.66	4.45	6.49	69.60
1808	1691	9.76	27.56	50.27	5.09	7.33	62.68
1809	2275	11.43	21.19	59.87	2.73	4.79	67.38
1810	2238	9.16	21.85	60.46	3.84	4.69	68.99
1811	2269	8.73	21.82	61.08	3.70	4.67	69.46

TABLE 5. POPULATION BY RACE (CONTINUED)

YEAR	TOTAL	WHITE	INDIAN	PARDO	NEGRO	SLAVE	BLACK
1815	2242	9.32	21.81	60.35	3.84	4.68	68.87
1816	2483	9.99	20.26	65.20	1.29	3.26	69.75
1817	2099	9.00	21.77	62.22	4.05	2.95	69.22
1818	2234	7.30	22.07	57.25	7.25	6.13	70.64
1819	2457	7.49	22.34	56.08	8.47	5.62	70.17
		URAMA					
1802	696	2.01	0.00	65.09	24.43	8.48	97.99
1804	700	2.86	0.00	68.29	19.43	9.43	97.14
1806	631	2.69	0.00	65.77	23.30	8.24	97.31
1807	652	3.37	0.00	68.25	20.71	7.67	96.63
1808	670	3.28	.15	71.04	18.66	6.87	96.57
1810	757	2.25	.53	74.11	17.04	6.08	97.23
1818	450	1.11	0.00	89.11	0.00	9.78	98.89
1819	478	.21	0.00	89.75	0.00	10.04	99.79
1820	485	5.15	0.00	63.30	20.21	11.34	94.85
		VALENCIA					
1782	7237	42.26	2.83	41.40	.55	12.96	54.91
1802	7619	35.03	.89	47.37	2.52	14.19	64.08
1803	6758	32.05	1.27	48.37	3.61	14.69	66.68
1804	6222	32.00	1.32	48.87	3.57	14.24	66.68
1805	6571	32.16	3.88	45.49	4.89	13.59	63.96
1808	6574	32.14	3.88	45.47	4.88	13.63	63.98
1809	7034	36.14	2.15	43.06	2.26	16.39	61.71
1812	7745	34.03	2.26	43.74	2.21	17.75	63.71
1815	7662	21.34	9.95	49.50	2.01	17.20	68.72
1816	7959	21.36	10.11	48.94	2.53	17.06	68.53
1819	8959	21.75	9.55	49.18	2.89	16.62	68.69
		VALLE DE LA PASCUA					
1804	1510	32.72	7.02	36.69	0.00	23.58	60.26
1805	1605	32.02	8.10	38.63	0.00	21.25	59.88
1806	1649	26.68	8.37	43.24	0.00	21.71	64.95
1808	1726	27.87	13.44	36.50	0.00	22.19	58.69
1809	2000	27.70	19.30	33.15	0.00	19.85	53.00
		VILLA DE CURA					
1780	4453	46.87	1.91	40.00	2.83	8.40	51.22
1796	4260	69.41	1.15	13.05	1.43	14.95	29.44
1802	4525	43.25	3.34	34.63	3.82	14.96	53.41
1803	4623	47.91	5.02	23.30	3.07	20.70	47.07
1804	4498	48.33	11.54	23.50	2.78	13.85	40.13
1805	4720	44.70	2.65	37.06	.72	14.87	52.65
1806	4887	43.18	2.72	39.23	.47	14.41	54.10
1807	4523	38.58	2.98	41.79	.80	15.85	58.43
1808	4798	39.25	4.77	38.72	3.25	14.01	55.98
1809	4314	32.50	4.96	33.03	2.57	26.94	62.54
1811	5359	33.16	4.39	45.42	2.50	14.54	62.46

TABLE 5. POPULATION BY RACE (CONTINUED)

YEAR	TOTAL	WHITE	INDIAN	PARDO	NEGRO	SLAVE	BLACK
1816	3532	30.63	8.89	41.85	0.00	18.63	60.48
1817	3414	52.75	6.71	29.17	0.00	11.36	40.54
1822	4496	42.44	4.23	38.08	0.00	15.26	53.34
		YARITAGUA					
1782	2744	35.13	8.38	47.34	0.00	9.15	56.49
1802	1898	21.44	7.01	28.40	34.35	8.80	71.55
1803	2157	19.98	5.93	29.21	35.84	9.04	74.08
1804	2164	19.92	5.91	29.25	35.81	9.10	74.17
1805	2922	21.83	4.89	23.37	37.37	12.53	73.27
1807	4597	19.06	2.72	31.89	40.35	5.98	78.22
1808	5359	19.22	2.43	36.63	37.08	4.65	78.35
1809	5359	19.22	2.43	36.63	37.08	4.65	78.35
1810	5359	19.22	2.43	36.63	37.08	4.65	78.35
1811	5124	19.87	2.30	37.22	36.26	4.35	77.83
1812	4625	20.32	2.14	36.43	36.54	4.56	77.54
1816	5704	10.45	1.10	84.59	1.67	2.19	88.45
1817	5408	18.99	2.59	68.45	5.47	4.49	78.42
1818	5579	20.06	3.98	68.26	3.46	4.25	75.96
1820	5775	25.18	3.17	61.65	5.66	4.35	71.65

TABLE 6. POPULATION/ECCLESIASTIC

YEAR	ECCLESIASTICS	POPULATION	POP/ECC
ACARIGUA			
1778	0	935	0.00
1802	1	2221	2221.00
1803	1	2549	2549.00
1804	1	2570	2570.00
1805	1	2525	2525.00
1808	1	2563	2563.00
1809	1	2583	2583.00
1810	1	2302	2302.00
1812	1	2326	2326.00
1829	0	987	0.00
ACHAGUAS			
1780	1	156	156.00
1801	0	1104	0.00
1804	0	2513	0.00
1806	0	1238	0.00
1809	0	1922	0.00
1811	0	2475	0.00
AGUA BLANCA			
1779	1	527	527.00
1801	0	587	0.00
1802	0	557	0.00
1803	0	557	0.00
1804	0	920	0.00
1805	0	717	0.00
1808	1	795	795.00
1812	1	884	884.00
1815	0	804	0.00
1830	0	769	0.00
AGUA CULEBRAS			
1781	1	1906	1906.00
1802	0	1213	0.00
1803	0	1063	0.00
1804	0	746	0.00
1805	0	1209	0.00
1807	0	881	0.00
1808	0	994	0.00
1809	0	1007	0.00
1811	0	855	0.00
1812	0	788	0.00
1815	0	661	0.00
1817	0	408	0.00
1818	0	634	0.00
1819	1	568	568.00
1820	1	751	751.00
1821	0	732	0.00
AGUACALIENTE			
1803	1	507	507.00
1804	0	509	0.00
1805	0	536	0.00
1806	0	484	0.00
1807	0	548	0.00
1818	1	379	379.00
1819	0	394	0.00
ALPARGATON			
1804	0	239	0.00
1805	0	227	0.00
1806	0	183	0.00
1807	0	216	0.00
1818	0	191	0.00
1819	0	156	0.00
1820	0	346	0.00
ALTAGRACIA DE ORITUCO			
1783	1	968	968.00
1802	2	1615	807.50
1803	3	1652	550.67
1804	4	1785	446.25
1806	2	1803	901.50
1807	3	1865	621.67
1809	2	1938	969.00
1810	2	1905	952.50
1811	2	1900	950.00
ALTAMIRA			
1783	1	352	352.00
ANTIMANO			
1811	0	1286	0.00
1819	2	1176	588.00
APARICION			
1802	1	2373	2373.00
1803	1	2331	2331.00
1804	1	3388	3388.00
1805	1	3098	3098.00
1808	1	3297	3297.00
1809	1	2742	2742.00
1810	1	3178	3178.00

TABLE 6. POPULATION/ECCLESIASTIC (CONTINUED)

YEAR	ECCLESIASTICS	POPULATION	POP/ECC
1811	1	2991	2991.00
1812	1	2454	2454.00
APURITO			
1802	0	446	0.00
1806	0	407	0.00
1807	0	545	0.00
ARAGUITA			
1784	1	884	884.00
1802	0	661	0.00
1803	0	581	0.00
1804	0	576	0.00
1805	0	504	0.00
1807	1	611	611.00
1810	0	508	0.00
1811	1	479	479.00
1812	1	391	391.00
1816	0	455	0.00
1819	1	453	453.00
ARAURE			
1778	1	2841	2841.00
1798	0	7528	0.00
1799	0	7704	0.00
1800	0	7835	0.00
1801	0	2668	0.00
1802	1	3285	3285.00
1803	1	3130	3130.00
1804	1	2604	2604.00
1805	1	2876	2876.00
1808	1	3061	3061.00
1809	0	3134	0.00
1810	0	3167	0.00
1811	0	3444	0.00
1812	2	3212	1606.00
1829	3	4229	1409.67
AREGUE			
1802	1	704	704.00
1803	1	852	852.00
1804	1	753	753.00
1805	1	698	698.00
1809	0	980	0.00
1815	1	938	938.00
ARENALES			
1802	0	902	0.00
1803	0	925	0.00
1804	0	922	0.00
1805	0	907	0.00
1807	0	907	0.00
1809	0	919	0.00
ARICHUNA			
1801	0	589	0.00
1804	0	855	0.00
AROA			
1802	1	1588	1588.00
1805	1	1462	1462.00
1807	1	1468	1468.00
1808	1	1573	1573.00
1809	1	1458	1458.00
1817	0	966	0.00
1818	1	1389	1389.00
ATAMAICA			
1780	1	133	133.00
1802	0	336	0.00
AYAMANES			
1802	0	524	0.00
1803	0	462	0.00
1804	0	483	0.00
1805	0	425	0.00
1807	0	621	0.00
1808	0	634	0.00
1815	1	633	633.00
BANCO LARGO			
1805	0	1304	0.00
1809	0	1164	0.00
BARBACOAS DE LOS LLANOS			
1782	0	1321	0.00
1783	1	1714	1714.00
1802	1	2558	2558.00
1803	0	2384	0.00
1804	0	2716	0.00
1805	1	3110	3110.00
1809	0	3241	0.00
1810	0	3056	0.00
1811	1	3045	3045.00

TABLE 6. POPULATION/ECCLESIASTIC (CONTINUED)

BARBACOAS DEL TOCUYO

YEAR	ECCLESIASTICS	POPULATION	POP/ECC
1802	1	606	606.00
1803	0	537	0.00
1804	1	600	600.00
1805	1	631	631.00
1806	1	630	630.00
1807	1	642	642.00
1808	1	673	673.00
1809	1	698	698.00
1810	1	748	748.00
1812	1	604	604.00
1815	1	702	702.00
1816	1	634	634.00
1817	1	766	766.00
1818	1	649	649.00
1819	1	775	775.00
1820	1	775	775.00

BARQUISIMETO

YEAR	ECCLESIASTICS	POPULATION	POP/ECC
1779	54	8776	162.52
1815	6	12596	2099.33

BARQUISIMETO, MITAD DE(1)

YEAR	ECCLESIASTICS	POPULATION	POP/ECC
1802	3	5167	1722.33
1803	2	5189	2594.50
1804	2	5695	2847.50
1805	1	5324	5324.00
1807	2	5992	2996.00
1808	1	6043	6043.00
1809	2	6382	3191.00
1810	2	5993	2996.50
1811	1	6439	6439.00
1817	1	5909	5909.00
1818	2	4544	2272.00
1819	1	4490	4490.00
1820	1	4529	4529.00

BARQUISIMETO, MITAD DE(2)

YEAR	ECCLESIASTICS	POPULATION	POP/ECC
1802	4	5410	1352.50
1803	4	5972	1493.00
1804	4	5906	1476.50
1805	5	5962	1192.40
1807	3	5930	1976.67
1808	4	5532	1383.00
1809	3	5628	1876.00
1810	3	5628	1876.00
1811	4	6693	1673.25
1817	2	6933	3466.50
1818	0	6709	0.00
1819	1	6797	6797.00
1820	0	6824	0.00

BARUTA

YEAR	ECCLESIASTICS	POPULATION	POP/ECC
1802	1	2046	2046.00
1803	1	2109	2109.00
1804	1	2124	2124.00
1805	1	2066	2066.00
1811	1	2029	2029.00
1816	0	1155	0.00
1817	1	1545	1545.00
1819	2	2659	1329.50
1820	2	1710	855.00

BAUL

YEAR	ECCLESIASTICS	POPULATION	POP/ECC
1781	1	538	538.00
1802	1	2026	2026.00
1805	1	1760	1760.00
1811	2	2666	1333.00
1812	1	2223	2223.00
1815	1	1560	1560.00
1816	1	1997	1997.00
1817	1	2273	2273.00
1825	1	2645	2645.00
1829	1	1675	1675.00

BOBARE

YEAR	ECCLESIASTICS	POPULATION	POP/ECC
1779	1	297	297.00
1802	0	580	0.00
1803	0	580	0.00
1804	0	589	0.00
1805	0	541	0.00
1806	0	541	0.00
1808	0	593	0.00
1811	0	815	0.00
1820	0	468	0.00

BOCONO

YEAR	ECCLESIASTICS	POPULATION	POP/ECC
1778	1	2061	2061.00
1795	1	2504	2504.00
1796	0	2186	0.00
1798	0	2705	0.00
1799	1	2400	2400.00
1800	1	2062	2062.00
1802	1	1727	1727.00
1803	1	2012	2012.00
1804	2	1956	978.00
1805	2	2283	1141.50

TABLE 6. POPULATION/ECCLESIASTIC (CONTINUED)

YEAR	ECCLESIASTICS	POPULATION	POP/ECC
1806	2	1918	959.00
1807	1	2141	2141.00
1808	2	1690	845.00
1810	1	1468	1468.00
BORBURATA			
1803	0	695	0.00
1804	0	754	0.00
1805	0	736	0.00
1806	0	781	0.00
1807	0	779	0.00
1818	1	577	577.00
1819	1	664	664.00
BURESITO			
1802	1	1101	1101.00
1803	1	1118	1118.00
1804	1	1121	1121.00
1807	1	990	990.00
1809	1	1148	1148.00
BURIA			
1779	1	453	453.00
1802	1	785	785.00
1803	1	731	731.00
1804	1	723	723.00
1805	1	819	819.00
1807	1	840	840.00
1809	1	737	737.00
1810	1	936	936.00
1811	1	1035	1035.00
1817	1	788	788.00
1818	1	837	837.00
1819	0	997	0.00
CABRIA			
1802	0	200	0.00
1803	0	212	0.00
1808	1	177	177.00
CABRUTA			
1780	1	219	219.00
1806	1	226	226.00
1808	0	382	0.00
1810	1	445	445.00
CAGUA			
1781	1	5506	5506.00
1802	2	4717	2358.50
1803	2	4491	2245.50
1804	2	4663	2331.50
1805	2	4496	2248.00
1806	2	4668	2334.00
1808	2	4499	2249.50
1809	1	4581	4581.00
1811	2	4296	2148.00
1815	1	3520	3520.00
1816	1	3436	3436.00
1817	2	3986	1993.00
1818	2	3912	1956.00
CAICARA DEL ORINOCO			
1802	0	250	0.00
CALABOZO			
1780	2	3448	1724.00
1802	7	4678	668.29
1803	10	4761	476.10
1804	10	4739	473.90
1805	10	4820	482.00
1807	7	4133	590.43
1808	8	3911	488.87
1810	5	3765	753.00
1812	5	2939	587.80
1817	3	1985	661.67
1818	2	1554	777.00
1822	2	1427	713.50
CAMAGUAN			
1780	1	739	739.00
1801	0	900	0.00
1802	0	866	0.00
1803	0	1072	0.00
1804	0	1088	0.00
1812	1	1107	1107.00
1817	0	1137	0.00
CAMATAGUA			
1783	1	2263	2263.00
1802	1	2151	2151.00
1803	1	2128	2128.00
1804	1	2305	2305.00
1805	1	2111	2111.00

TABLE 6. POPULATION/ECCLESIASTIC (CONTINUED)

YEAR	ECCLESIASTICS	POPULATION	POP/ECC
1806	1	2111	2111.00
1808	1	2111	2111.00
1811	1	1657	1657.00
CANOABO			
1781	1	1122	1122.00
1788	0	1092	0.00
1802	1	1081	1081.00
1803	1	1041	1041.00
1804	1	1063	1063.00
1805	0	1134	0.00
1806	0	1220	0.00
1807	0	1150	0.00
1808	1	1194	1194.00
1809	0	1214	0.00
1810	1	1037	1037.00
1815	0	839	0.00
1817	0	996	0.00
1819	1	1287	1287.00
1820	1	1310	1310.00
CAPAYA			
1784	1	1252	1252.00
1802	0	1195	0.00
1803	0	1376	0.00
1804	0	1356	0.00
1805	1	1355	1355.00
1806	1	1442	1442.00
1807	1	1494	1494.00
1808	1	1456	1456.00
1809	1	1104	1104.00
1811	0	1173	0.00
1812	0	1135	0.00
1817	0	903	0.00
1818	1	1013	1013.00
1819	1	1041	1041.00
1820	1	1060	1060.00
CARABALLEDA			
1802	0	1190	0.00
1804	0	1097	0.00
CARACAS-ALTAGRACIA			
1796	39	6241	160.03
1802	37	5774	156.05
1803	37	5957	161.00
1804	40	6418	160.45
1805	35	6451	184.31
1807	45	6179	137.31
1808	30	6251	208.37
1810	30	6393	213.10
1811	33	5246	158.97
1815	8	2113	264.12
1816	12	1765	147.08
1817	11	2083	189.36
1818	11	2191	199.18
1819	10	2207	220.70
1820	11	1955	177.73
CARACAS-CANDELARIA			
1800	0	3353	0.00
1802	17	3538	208.12
1803	17	3349	197.00
1804	18	3573	198.50
1805	20	3543	177.15
1806	19	3700	194.74
1808	20	3927	196.35
1809	21	4040	192.38
1811	20	3339	166.95
1815	11	2161	196.45
1816	9	2725	302.78
1817	10	2670	267.00
1818	9	2577	286.33
1819	8	2514	314.25
1820	10	2447	244.70
1821	8	2451	306.37
CARACAS-CATEDRAL ORIENTE			
1801	43	4605	107.09
1802	54	4692	86.89
1803	59	4488	76.07
1804	51	4541	89.04
1805	50	4874	97.48
1807	47	4487	95.47
1809	43	4795	111.51
1811	52	4598	88.42
1815	21	2358	112.29
1816	28	2483	88.68
1817	21	2885	137.38
1818	32	2756	86.12
1819	37	3300	89.19
CARACAS-CATEDRAL PONIENTE			
1802	48	3475	72.40
1803	38	3831	100.82
1805	48	3791	78.98
1807	111	3893	35.07
1808	107	3881	36.27
1810	108	3970	36.76

TABLE 6. POPULATION/ECCLESIASTIC (CONTINUED)

YEAR	ECCLESIASTICS	POPULATION	POP/ECC
1811	105	3898	37.12
1815	18	2361	131.17
1816	38	3139	82.61
1817	23	3157	137.26
1818	13	3226	248.15
1819	21	3188	151.81
1822	17	2652	156.00

CARACAS-CURATO CASTRENSE

YEAR	ECCLESIASTICS	POPULATION	POP/ECC
1803	3	961	320.33
1804	2	1092	546.00
1805	2	1259	629.50
1807	3	3245	1081.67
1809	2	2033	1016.50
1810	3	1084	361.33
1811	4	1215	303.75

CARACAS-SAN PABLO

YEAR	ECCLESIASTICS	POPULATION	POP/ECC
1799	28	5824	208.00
1801	26	5947	228.73
1802	45	6287	139.71
1803	32	5919	184.97
1804	34	5728	168.47
1805	31	6613	213.32
1806	36	6107	169.64
1807	36	6420	178.33
1808	24	5843	243.46
1809	24	4772	198.83
1810	32	5991	187.22
1811	29	5330	183.79
1815	21	6861	326.71
1816	40	6217	155.43
1817	28	6869	245.32
1818	21	8215	391.19
1820	25	7574	302.96

CARACAS-SANTA ROSALIA

YEAR	ECCLESIASTICS	POPULATION	POP/ECC
1795	11	4676	425.09
1796	10	5069	506.90
1798	12	4692	391.00
1799	12	4622	385.17
1802	24	5082	211.75
1803	32	5165	161.41
1804	29	5140	177.24
1805	21	5029	239.48
1806	24	5451	227.12
1807	24	5388	224.50
1808	19	5440	286.32
1809	25	5467	218.68
1810	20	5448	272.40

YEAR	ECCLESIASTICS	POPULATION	POP/ECC
1811	22	6470	294.09
1815	19	3340	175.79
1816	14	3703	264.50
1817	18	3556	197.56
1818	16	4056	253.50
1819	19	4005	210.79
1820	20	4089	204.45
1822	14	4295	306.79

CARAMACATE

YEAR	ECCLESIASTICS	POPULATION	POP/ECC
1779	0	181	0.00
1799	1	372	372.00
1801	0	421	0.00
1802	0	568	0.00
1803	1	642	642.00
1804	0	512	0.00
1805	0	550	0.00
1806	0	532	0.00
1807	0	473	0.00
1809	0	620	0.00
1811	0	526	0.00
1812	0	479	0.00
1817	0	316	0.00
1818	0	292	0.00
1819	1	327	327.00
1822	0	252	0.00
1823	0	209	0.00
1828	0	221	0.00
1829	0	272	0.00
1831	0	289	0.00
1832	0	287	0.00
1833	0	279	0.00
1834	0	302	0.00
1835	0	355	0.00
1836	0	380	0.00
1837	0	405	0.00
1838	0	439	0.00

CARAYACA

YEAR	ECCLESIASTICS	POPULATION	POP/ECC
1802	1	783	783.00
1804	1	650	650.00
1805	1	674	674.00
1807	1	674	674.00
1808	1	674	674.00
1809	1	674	674.00
1810	1	674	674.00
1811	1	673	673.00
1817	1	911	911.00
1818	1	1040	1040.00
1819	1	872	872.00
1820	1	951	951.00

TABLE 6. POPULATION/ECCLESIASTIC (CONTINUED)

YEAR	ECCLESIASTICS	POPULATION	POP/ECC
1833	0	1692	0.00
CARORA			
1802	4	4859	1214.75
1803	6	5318	886.33
1804	5	5584	1116.80
1809	6	6132	1022.00
1815	6	5595	932.50
CARUAO			
1811	0	543	0.00
1815	0	562	0.00
CASIGUA			
1780	0	2555	0.00
CATA			
1803	0	518	0.00
1804	0	523	0.00
1805	0	547	0.00
CAUCAGUA			
1784	1	2422	2422.00
1802	0	1864	0.00
1803	1	1800	1800.00
1804	1	1839	1839.00
1805	1	1842	1842.00
1806	1	1850	1850.00
1807	1	1797	1797.00
1808	0	1561	0.00
1809	0	1635	0.00
1811	0	1440	0.00
1812	0	1674	0.00
1816	0	1505	0.00
1817	0	1357	0.00
1818	0	1305	0.00
1819	1	1512	1512.00
1820	0	1595	0.00
CERRITO			
1779	1	3344	3344.00
CHABASQUEN			
1802	1	2089	2089.00
1803	1	2103	2103.00
1804	1	2131	2131.00

YEAR	ECCLESIASTICS	POPULATION	POP/ECC
1805	1	2141	2141.00
1806	1	2154	2154.00
1808	1	2114	2114.00
1809	1	2083	2083.00
1812	0	1272	0.00
1815	1	1289	1289.00
1816	0	1398	0.00
1817	1	1405	1405.00
1818	1	1405	1405.00
1819	1	811	811.00
1820	1	1332	1332.00
1829	1	1647	1647.00
CHACAO			
1802	4	2035	508.75
1803	5	2103	420.60
1804	5	2155	431.00
1805	3	2048	682.67
1808	2	2014	1007.00
1811	4	2091	522.75
1815	5	2006	401.20
1818	1	2238	2238.00
1819	2	2085	1042.50
CHAGUARAMAL			
1783	0	1607	0.00
1804	1	1903	1903.00
1805	1	1985	1985.00
CHAGUARAMAS			
1783	2	2302	1151.00
1802	1	2365	2365.00
1803	3	2419	806.33
1804	2	2439	1219.50
1805	1	2471	2471.00
1808	1	2818	2818.00
1810	1	2852	2852.00
CHARALLAVE			
1783	1	818	818.00
1802	0	1853	0.00
1803	0	1814	0.00
1804	0	1454	0.00
1805	0	1625	0.00
1806	0	1482	0.00
1807	1	1538	1538.00
1808	0	1630	0.00
1810	0	1944	0.00
1811	0	2143	0.00

TABLE 6. POPULATION/ECCLESIASTIC (CONTINUED)

YEAR	ECCLESIASTICS	POPULATION	POP/ECC
1815	1	1840	1840.00
1816	1	2083	2083.00
1817	1	2070	2070.00
	CHIVACOA		
1782	1	2029	2029.00
1802	1	1079	1079.00
1803	1	1318	1318.00
1804	0	1300	0.00
1805	1	1371	1371.00
1807	0	1408	0.00
1808	0	1631	0.00
1809	0	1585	0.00
1810	1	1760	1760.00
1811	1	1688	1688.00
1812	1	1694	1694.00
1815	1	1929	1929.00
1816	1	1914	1914.00
1817	1	1871	1871.00
1818	1	1864	1864.00
1819	1	1808	1808.00
	CHORONI		
1802	1	1546	1546.00
1803	1	1542	1542.00
1804	1	1519	1519.00
1805	1	1451	1451.00
1808	1	1539	1539.00
1809	1	1551	1551.00
1819	0	851	0.00
	CHUAO		
1802	0	325	0.00
1803	1	329	329.00
1804	1	348	348.00
1805	1	356	356.00
1819	0	384	0.00
	COCOROTE		
1781	1	2112	2112.00
1782	0	2071	0.00
1788	1	1861	1861.00
1791	1	1781	1781.00
1794	0	2007	0.00
1802	0	2029	0.00
1803	0	2132	0.00
1804	1	2027	2027.00
1805	1	2038	2038.00
1807	1	2118	2118.00

YEAR	ECCLESIASTICS	POPULATION	POP/ECC
1808	1	2036	2036.00
1809	1	1994	1994.00
1811	1	2012	2012.00
1812	1	1738	1738.00
1817	0	1641	0.00
1818	0	1642	0.00
1820	0	1641	0.00
1821	0	1892	0.00
	COJEDES		
1779	1	1311	1311.00
1799	1	1737	1737.00
1801	1	1664	1664.00
1802	0	1928	0.00
1803	1	1780	1780.00
1804	1	1779	1779.00
1805	1	1815	1815.00
1806	1	1922	1922.00
1807	1	1897	1897.00
1808	1	1895	1895.00
1809	1	1924	1924.00
1811	0	1471	0.00
1812	0	1512	0.00
1816	0	1546	0.00
1817	0	1529	0.00
1818	0	1555	0.00
1819	0	1513	0.00
1820	0	1466	0.00
1822	0	1289	0.00
1823	0	1136	0.00
1824	0	1094	0.00
1829	0	1174	0.00
1831	0	1178	0.00
1833	0	1144	0.00
1834	0	1131	0.00
1835	0	1213	0.00
1836	0	1240	0.00
1837	0	1260	0.00
1838	0	1251	0.00
	CUA		
1783	1	1531	1531.00
1803	2	2555	1277.50
1805	1	2273	2273.00
1810	2	3084	1542.00
1812	1	3181	3181.00
1815	0	2679	0.00
1816	0	2972	0.00
1818	1	3290	3290.00
1820	1	3007	3007.00
1821	1	3186	3186.00

TABLE 6. POPULATION/ECCLESIASTIC (CONTINUED)

YEAR	ECCLESIASTICS	POPULATION	POP/ECC
	CUBIRO		
1802	0	746	0.00
1803	0	796	0.00
1804	0	749	0.00
1805	0	897	0.00
1806	0	858	0.00
1807	0	865	0.00
1808	0	849	0.00
1809	0	869	0.00
1810	0	876	0.00
1815	0	720	0.00
1816	0	875	0.00
1817	0	889	0.00
1818	0	804	0.00
1819	0	797	0.00
1820	0	770	0.00
	CUNAVICHE		
1780	1	393	393.00
	CUPIRA		
1784	1	858	858.00
1802	0	582	0.00
1803	0	573	0.00
1804	0	547	0.00
1805	0	512	0.00
1807	0	505	0.00
1808	0	496	0.00
1809	0	485	0.00
1811	0	576	0.00
	CURARIGUA		
1802	0	1310	0.00
1803	1	974	974.00
1804	0	866	0.00
1805	0	1079	0.00
1806	0	873	0.00
1807	0	872	0.00
1808	0	917	0.00
1809	1	913	913.00
1810	0	1049	0.00
1816	0	1291	0.00
1817	0	1297	0.00
1818	0	1053	0.00
1819	0	1245	0.00
1820	0	1287	0.00
	CURIEPE		
1784	1	1360	1360.00
1803	0	1920	0.00
1804	0	1863	0.00
1805	0	2040	0.00
1806	1	2138	2138.00
1807	0	2129	0.00
1808	0	2172	0.00
1811	0	2220	0.00
1812	0	2320	0.00
1816	0	1618	0.00
1817	0	1463	0.00
1818	0	1654	0.00
1819	0	1759	0.00
1820	0	1895	0.00
	CUYAGUA		
1802	1	471	471.00
1803	1	456	456.00
1804	1	452	452.00
1805	1	493	493.00
1808	1	453	453.00
1809	1	497	497.00
1815	3	461	153.67
	DIVINA PASTORA DEL JOBAL		
1781	1	2036	2036.00
1798	1	2876	2876.00
1799	1	2876	2876.00
1801	0	2607	0.00
1802	2	2702	1351.00
1803	1	2741	2741.00
1804	1	2369	2369.00
1805	1	2586	2586.00
1806	1	2680	2680.00
1807	1	2307	2307.00
1808	1	2470	2470.00
1809	0	2586	0.00
1811	0	2376	0.00
1815	1	2420	2420.00
1816	0	2486	0.00
1817	1	2555	2555.00
1818	1	2258	2258.00
1819	0	3999	0.00
1820	1	2983	2983.00
1822	1	2723	2723.00
1824	1	1979	1979.00
1825	1	2109	2109.00
1829	1	1760	1760.00

TABLE 6. POPULATION/ECCLESIASTIC (CONTINUED)

YEAR	ECCLESIASTICS	POPULATION	POP/ECC
1830	0	1735	0.00
1832	1	1735	1735.00
1833	1	1612	1612.00
1834	1	1620	1620.00

DUACA

YEAR	ECCLESIASTICS	POPULATION	POP/ECC
1779	1	551	551.00
1802	0	488	0.00
1803	0	429	0.00
1804	0	429	0.00
1805	0	555	0.00
1807	0	617	0.00
1808	0	580	0.00
1809	0	604	0.00
1810	0	616	0.00
1811	1	692	692.00
1815	1	487	487.00
1816	1	541	541.00
1818	0	977	0.00

EL CALVARIO

YEAR	ECCLESIASTICS	POPULATION	POP/ECC
1783	1	653	653.00
1802	1	1262	1262.00
1803	1	1264	1264.00
1804	1	1342	1342.00
1805	1	1410	1410.00
1808	2	1451	725.50
1812	2	1852	926.00

EL CONSEJO

YEAR	ECCLESIASTICS	POPULATION	POP/ECC
1781	1	2115	2115.00
1795	1	2503	2503.00
1796	1	2387	2387.00
1802	0	2820	0.00
1803	0	2925	0.00
1804	0	2985	0.00
1805	0	3007	0.00
1806	0	2917	0.00
1807	0	2908	0.00
1808	0	2938	0.00
1809	0	2698	0.00
1811	0	2740	0.00
1817	0	3117	0.00
1818	0	3245	0.00
1833	0	2603	0.00

EL GUAPO

YEAR	ECCLESIASTICS	POPULATION	POP/ECC
1784	2	482	241.00
1802	1	1232	1232.00
1803	1	1438	1438.00
1804	1	1464	1464.00
1805	1	1531	1531.00
1807	1	1595	1595.00
1808	1	1577	1577.00
1809	1	1577	1577.00
1811	1	1654	1654.00
1812	1	1545	1545.00
1820	0	1325	0.00

EL HATILLO

YEAR	ECCLESIASTICS	POPULATION	POP/ECC
1802	1	1070	1070.00
1803	1	1070	1070.00
1804	0	1183	0.00
1805	0	1347	0.00
1806	0	1524	0.00
1808	1	1645	1645.00
1815	0	1727	0.00
1818	0	1413	0.00

EL PAO

YEAR	ECCLESIASTICS	POPULATION	POP/ECC
1781	1	3327	3327.00
1791	1	4151	4151.00
1792	1	4006	4006.00
1794	1	4446	4446.00
1796	1	4575	4575.00
1798	1	4894	4894.00
1801	0	4715	0.00
1802	1	4548	4548.00
1803	1	5105	5105.00
1804	1	5564	5564.00
1805	1	5833	5833.00
1808	1	5886	5886.00
1809	2	5820	2910.00
1811	2	6291	3145.50
1812	2	5428	2714.00
1815	2	6508	3254.00
1816	1	6631	6631.00
1817	2	6297	3148.50
1818	2	5782	2891.00
1819	1	5017	5017.00
1821	1	5671	5671.00
1823	1	7705	7705.00
1824	1	7910	7910.00
1825	1	6168	6168.00
1826	1	6326	6326.00
1827	1	6195	6195.00
1829	1	7867	7867.00
1835	1	8421	8421.00
1836	1	8739	8739.00
1837	1	9205	9205.00

TABLE 6. POPULATION/ECCLESIASTIC (CONTINUED)

YEAR	ECCLESIASTICS	POPULATION	POP/ECC
1838	1	9386	9386.00

EL RASTRO

YEAR	ECCLESIASTICS	POPULATION	POP/ECC
1807	1	1029	1029.00
1810	1	1395	1395.00
1811	1	1463	1463.00
1812	1	1246	1246.00
1817	2	1104	552.00
1822	1	1016	1016.00

EL SOMBRERO

YEAR	ECCLESIASTICS	POPULATION	POP/ECC
1781	0	2046	0.00
1783	1	2179	2179.00
1802	1	3091	3091.00
1803	3	3260	1086.67
1804	1	3502	3502.00
1805	1	3557	3557.00
1809	2	4585	2292.50
1810	2	4740	2370.00
1811	3	4740	1580.00

EL TOCUYO

YEAR	ECCLESIASTICS	POPULATION	POP/ECC
1802	5	9173	1834.60
1803	5	9416	1883.20
1804	5	9469	1893.80
1805	5	9281	1856.20
1806	7	9226	1318.00
1807	6	9527	1587.83
1808	6	9533	1588.83
1809	5	9637	1927.40
1810	6	9613	1602.17
1812	6	9678	1613.00
1815	9	9424	1047.11
1816	10	9736	973.60
1817	9	9492	1054.67
1818	7	9331	1333.00
1819	4	10919	2729.75
1820	12	10049	837.42

EL VALLE

YEAR	ECCLESIASTICS	POPULATION	POP/ECC
1798	0	1016	0.00
1802	3	1232	410.67
1803	2	1297	648.50
1804	3	1416	472.00
1805	2	1528	764.00
1809	3	1582	527.33
1815	3	1615	538.33
1816	1	1795	1795.00
1817	2	2203	1101.50

YEAR	ECCLESIASTICS	POPULATION	POP/ECC
1818	2	1636	818.00
1819	2	1651	825.50
1820	2	1832	916.00

ESPINO

YEAR	ECCLESIASTICS	POPULATION	POP/ECC
1804	0	588	0.00
1807	1	1019	1019.00

GUACARA

YEAR	ECCLESIASTICS	POPULATION	POP/ECC
1781	1	3080	3080.00
1802	0	4588	0.00
1803	1	5015	5015.00
1804	1	5391	5391.00
1805	1	4728	4728.00
1808	1	4925	4925.00
1816	2	5059	2529.50

GUADARRAMA

YEAR	ECCLESIASTICS	POPULATION	POP/ECC
1820	0	1327	0.00

GUAIGUAZA

YEAR	ECCLESIASTICS	POPULATION	POP/ECC
1803	0	734	0.00
1804	0	673	0.00
1805	0	662	0.00
1806	1	591	591.00
1807	0	648	0.00
1818	0	452	0.00
1819	0	556	0.00

GUAMA

YEAR	ECCLESIASTICS	POPULATION	POP/ECC
1781	1	2257	2257.00
1794	1	2786	2786.00
1803	0	3240	0.00
1804	0	3592	0.00
1805	0	3263	0.00
1807	1	3219	3219.00
1808	1	3406	3406.00
1809	1	3292	3292.00
1810	1	3259	3259.00
1811	1	3464	3464.00
1812	1	3271	3271.00
1817	0	2994	0.00
1818	0	2713	0.00
1819	0	2129	0.00
1820	0	2573	0.00

TABLE 6. POPULATION/ECCLESIASTIC (CONTINUED)

YEAR	ECCLESIASTICS	POPULATION	POP/ECC
GUANARE			
1788	0	8282	0.00
1791	0	7533	0.00
1792	0	8009	0.00
1802	12	13410	1117.50
1803	16	11040	690.00
1804	11	10080	916.36
1807	5	10803	2160.60
1808	9	11454	1272.67
1809	4	11025	2756.25
1810	5	7800	1560.00
1811	6	8757	1459.50
1817	2	6790	3395.00
GUANARE VIEJO			
1778	1	465	465.00
1782	0	927	0.00
1801	0	1352	0.00
1802	0	1339	0.00
1803	0	1583	0.00
1804	0	2220	0.00
1805	0	1514	0.00
1806	0	1976	0.00
1807	0	1709	0.00
1808	0	3053	0.00
1811	0	1594	0.00
1813	0	1516	0.00
GUANARITO			
1778	1	962	962.00
1801	0	1802	0.00
1802	0	1816	0.00
1803	0	3264	0.00
1804	0	3003	0.00
1805	0	3058	0.00
1807	0	5159	0.00
1808	0	4501	0.00
1810	0	4574	0.00
1811	0	4792	0.00
GUARDATINAJAS			
1780	1	475	475.00
1804	1	2228	2228.00
1805	1	2239	2239.00
1807	1	2284	2284.00
1808	1	2363	2363.00
1809	1	2344	2344.00
1810	1	2253	2253.00
1811	1	2534	2534.00
1812	1	2601	2601.00
1816	1	2460	2460.00
GUARENAS			
1784	1	2333	2333.00
1802	2	2901	1450.50
1803	2	3025	1512.50
1804	2	2999	1499.50
1805	2	3050	1525.00
1808	3	1860	620.00
1809	3	2666	888.67
1811	3	3212	1070.67
1816	3	2611	870.33
GUARICO			
1803	1	2034	2034.00
1804	1	2000	2000.00
1805	0	1832	0.00
1806	0	1908	0.00
1807	0	1870	0.00
1808	0	1838	0.00
1809	0	1953	0.00
1810	0	2162	0.00
1812	0	2114	0.00
1815	0	2225	0.00
1816	0	2248	0.00
1817	0	2351	0.00
1818	0	2338	0.00
1819	0	2493	0.00
1820	0	2704	0.00
GUASGUAS			
1802	2	3595	1797.50
1803	2	3444	1722.00
1804	2	3325	1662.50
1805	2	3519	1759.50
1806	1	3803	3803.00
1807	1	3814	3814.00
1808	1	3878	3878.00
1809	1	4099	4099.00
1810	1	3845	3845.00
GUATIRE			
1784	1	1942	1942.00
1802	2	2224	1112.00
1803	1	2254	2254.00
1805	1	2177	2177.00
1807	2	2065	1032.50

TABLE 6. POPULATION/ECCLESIASTIC (CONTINUED)

YEAR	ECCLESIASTICS	POPULATION	POP/ECC
1809	1	2065	2065.00
1811	1	2329	2329.00
1815	2	2160	1080.00
1816	0	2343	0.00
1817	0	2492	0.00

GUAYABAL

YEAR	ECCLESIASTICS	POPULATION	POP/ECC
1804	0	1492	0.00
1817	0	1522	0.00

GUIGUE

YEAR	ECCLESIASTICS	POPULATION	POP/ECC
1781	1	2432	2432.00
1802	1	2646	2646.00
1803	2	2641	1320.50
1804	2	2655	1327.50
1805	2	2735	1367.50
1808	2	2975	1487.50
1809	2	3083	1541.50
1817	2	2846	1423.00

GUIRIPA

YEAR	ECCLESIASTICS	POPULATION	POP/ECC
1802	1	994	994.00
1803	1	944	944.00
1804	1	991	991.00
1805	1	1014	1014.00
1806	0	920	0.00
1807	1	998	998.00
1808	1	1015	1015.00
1809	1	1058	1058.00
1811	0	1004	0.00

HUMOCARO ALTO

YEAR	ECCLESIASTICS	POPULATION	POP/ECC
1802	1	2599	2599.00
1803	1	2636	2636.00
1804	1	2912	2912.00
1805	1	2758	2758.00
1806	1	2748	2748.00
1807	1	2714	2714.00
1808	1	2658	2658.00
1809	1	2470	2470.00
1810	1	2208	2208.00
1815	1	1397	1397.00
1816	1	1813	1813.00
1817	1	1834	1834.00
1818	1	1794	1794.00
1819	1	1612	1612.00
1820	1	1808	1808.00

HUMOCARO BAJO

YEAR	ECCLESIASTICS	POPULATION	POP/ECC
1803	2	1739	869.50
1804	2	1739	869.50
1806	1	1422	1422.00
1807	1	1570	1570.00
1808	1	1946	1946.00
1809	1	2152	2152.00
1810	1	2188	2188.00
1815	1	1707	1707.00
1816	1	1788	1788.00
1817	1	1780	1780.00
1818	1	1729	1729.00
1819	1	1480	1480.00
1820	1	1513	1513.00

IGUANA

YEAR	ECCLESIASTICS	POPULATION	POP/ECC
1783	1	139	139.00
1801	0	310	0.00
1802	0	323	0.00
1803	0	342	0.00
1804	0	295	0.00
1805	0	305	0.00
1806	0	362	0.00
1807	0	330	0.00

LA GUAIRA

YEAR	ECCLESIASTICS	POPULATION	POP/ECC
1802	8	4055	506.87
1804	7	3269	467.00
1805	7	3526	503.71
1807	5	3198	639.60
1809	6	3272	545.33
1810	6	3267	544.50
1811	12	3317	276.42
1815	7	1819	259.86
1816	6	1964	327.33
1817	5	2714	542.80
1818	5	2989	597.80
1819	4	2884	721.00
1820	6	3005	500.83

LA GUAIRA, CURATO CASTRENSE

YEAR	ECCLESIASTICS	POPULATION	POP/ECC
1802	1	310	310.00
1803	1	280	280.00
1804	1	457	457.00
1805	1	665	665.00
1807	1	782	782.00
1808	1	541	541.00

TABLE 6. POPULATION/ECCLESIASTIC (CONTINUED)

YEAR	ECCLESIASTICS	POPULATION	POP/ECC
LA SANTISIMA TRINIDAD			
1780	0	567	0.00
1802	1	1959	1959.00
1803	1	1950	1950.00
1804	1	1728	1728.00
1805	1	1744	1744.00
1807	1	1162	1162.00
1808	1	1194	1194.00
1809	1	1173	1173.00
1810	1	1074	1074.00
1811	1	1206	1206.00
1812	1	939	939.00
LA VEGA			
1802	2	2194	1097.00
1803	2	2325	1162.50
1804	1	2211	2211.00
1805	1	2285	2285.00
1809	2	1116	558.00
1810	2	1052	526.00
1811	1	960	960.00
1815	1	798	798.00
1816	1	845	845.00
1817	1	737	737.00
1818	1	739	739.00
1819	1	731	731.00
1820	1	711	711.00
1821	1	720	720.00
1822	1	674	674.00
1823	1	653	653.00
LA VICTORIA			
1780	0	5310	0.00
1802	7	6220	888.57
1803	9	6700	744.44
1804	9	6627	736.33
1805	8	6889	861.12
1806	11	6991	635.55
1808	7	7117	1016.71
1809	8	7172	896.50
1811	0	8100	0.00
1816	7	4655	665.00
1817	7	4655	665.00
1818	5	4655	931.00
LEZAMA			
1783	1	1564	1564.00
1802	1	2388	2388.00
1803	1	2388	2388.00
1804	1	2388	2388.00
1805	1	2388	2388.00
1806	1	2388	2388.00
1807	1	2388	2388.00
1808	1	2388	2388.00
1809	1	2388	2388.00
1810	1	2388	2388.00
1811	1	2388	2388.00
LOS ANGELES			
1780	1	419	419.00
1803	1	452	452.00
1804	1	476	476.00
1805	1	483	483.00
1807	1	474	474.00
1808	1	479	479.00
1809	1	920	920.00
1810	1	927	927.00
1811	1	1011	1011.00
1812	1	967	967.00
1816	0	946	0.00
1817	1	1012	1012.00
LOS ANGELES DE SETENTA			
1801	0	1114	0.00
1805	0	778	0.00
1806	0	879	0.00
1807	0	1096	0.00
1809	0	981	0.00
LOS CANIZOS			
1802	0	832	0.00
1803	0	812	0.00
1804	0	822	0.00
1805	0	775	0.00
1807	0	764	0.00
1808	0	829	0.00
1809	0	838	0.00
1810	1	949	949.00
1811	0	876	0.00
1813	0	569	0.00
1818	0	412	0.00
1819	0	452	0.00
1820	0	442	0.00
LOS GUAYOS			
1781	0	1242	0.00
1795	1	2592	2592.00

TABLE 6. POPULATION/ECCLESIASTIC (CONTINUED)

YEAR	ECCLESIASTICS	POPULATION	POP/ECC
1802	1	4090	4090.00
1803	1	3612	3612.00
1804	1	3317	3317.00
1805	2	3407	1703.50
1816	0	3023	0.00
	LOS TEQUES		
1796	0	2184	0.00
1799	0	2309	0.00
1800	1	2309	2309.00
1801	1	2481	2481.00
1805	0	2773	0.00
1811	2	1995	997.50
1816	0	2355	0.00
1817	0	2233	0.00
	MACAIRA		
1784	1	589	589.00
1802	0	318	0.00
1803	0	303	0.00
1804	0	280	0.00
1806	0	259	0.00
1807	1	277	277.00
1808	0	219	0.00
1809	0	210	0.00
1811	1	110	110.00
1817	0	123	0.00
	MACAIRITA		
1805	0	264	0.00
	MACARAO		
1802	1	1169	1169.00
1803	1	1113	1113.00
1804	1	1254	1254.00
1805	1	1175	1175.00
1807	1	1260	1260.00
1808	1	1240	1240.00
1809	1	1250	1250.00
1810	1	1388	1388.00
1811	1	1172	1172.00
1812	1	1140	1140.00
1815	1	1217	1217.00
1816	1	1291	1291.00
1817	2	1098	549.00
1818	2	1094	547.00
1819	2	1131	565.50
1820	2	1131	565.50
1822	2	1185	592.50
1823	2	1364	682.00
	MAGDALENO		
1802	0	2412	0.00
1803	0	2710	0.00
1804	0	2591	0.00
1805	0	2518	0.00
1806	0	2648	0.00
1809	0	1226	0.00
1816	1	2798	2798.00
	MAIQUETIA		
1796	1	1797	1797.00
1802	1	1654	1654.00
1804	2	1563	781.50
1805	1	1630	1630.00
1807	2	1770	885.00
1811	1	1742	1742.00
1815	3	1817	605.67
1816	1	1270	1270.00
1817	1	1327	1327.00
1819	1	1817	1817.00
	MAMPORAL		
1784	1	521	521.00
1802	0	488	0.00
1804	0	487	0.00
1805	0	557	0.00
1807	0	541	0.00
1808	0	558	0.00
1809	0	521	0.00
1811	0	512	0.00
1812	0	511	0.00
1816	0	274	0.00
1817	0	274	0.00
1818	0	318	0.00
1820	0	295	0.00
	MANAPIRE		
1804	0	486	0.00
1807	1	466	466.00
1808	1	471	471.00
1810	1	521	521.00
	MARACA		
1778	1	873	873.00
1803	1	1747	1747.00
1804	1	1636	1636.00

TABLE 6. POPULATION/ECCLESIASTIC (CONTINUED)

YEAR	ECCLESIASTICS	POPULATION	POP/ECC
1805	0	1935	0.00
1806	0	1719	0.00
1807	1	1748	1748.00
1808	0	1464	0.00
1809	0	1505	0.00
1810	0	1418	0.00
1817	0	638	0.00

MARACAY

YEAR	ECCLESIASTICS	POPULATION	POP/ECC
1782	1	5564	5564.00
1796	1	7933	7933.00
1802	6	8210	1368.33
1803	5	8374	1674.80
1804	5	8966	1793.20
1805	6	8374	1395.67
1808	8	8502	1062.75
1809	7	7929	1132.71
1811	7	7338	1048.29
1816	2	6427	3213.50
1817	4	5253	1313.25
1818	4	6006	1501.50
1819	7	6423	917.57
1820	8	6542	817.75

MARIA

YEAR	ECCLESIASTICS	POPULATION	POP/ECC
1803	1	845	845.00
1804	1	1369	1369.00
1805	1	1428	1428.00
1806	1	1473	1473.00
1807	1	1529	1529.00
1811	0	1459	0.00

MARIARA

YEAR	ECCLESIASTICS	POPULATION	POP/ECC
1802	1	2224	2224.00
1803	1	2279	2279.00
1804	1	2188	2188.00
1805	1	2549	2549.00
1809	1	3254	3254.00
1815	1	2932	2932.00
1816	1	3270	3270.00
1817	1	3486	3486.00
1818	2	3396	1698.00

MONTALBAN

YEAR	ECCLESIASTICS	POPULATION	POP/ECC
1781	1	1525	1525.00
1802	1	2273	2273.00
1803	1	2560	2560.00
1804	1	2624	2624.00
1805	1	2595	2595.00

YEAR	ECCLESIASTICS	POPULATION	POP/ECC
1806	1	2624	2624.00
1808	0	2665	0.00
1810	0	2718	0.00
1815	0	3018	0.00
1817	0	3372	0.00
1818	0	2831	0.00
1820	0	3746	0.00

MORON

YEAR	ECCLESIASTICS	POPULATION	POP/ECC
1804	0	297	0.00
1805	0	302	0.00
1806	0	302	0.00
1807	0	337	0.00
1818	0	347	0.00
1819	0	334	0.00
1820	0	587	0.00

MOROTURO

YEAR	ECCLESIASTICS	POPULATION	POP/ECC
1802	1	357	357.00
1804	1	521	521.00
1805	1	535	535.00
1807	1	381	381.00
1808	1	509	509.00
1809	1	432	432.00
1815	1	513	513.00

NAGUANAGUA

YEAR	ECCLESIASTICS	POPULATION	POP/ECC
1802	2	1446	723.00
1803	2	1600	800.00
1804	1	1340	1340.00
1805	1	1620	1620.00
1809	1	1418	1418.00
1816	0	1754	0.00

NAIGUATA

YEAR	ECCLESIASTICS	POPULATION	POP/ECC
1801	0	771	0.00
1802	1	752	752.00
1804	0	757	0.00
1805	0	698	0.00
1809	0	740	0.00
1810	0	775	0.00
1811	0	791	0.00
1816	1	550	550.00
1817	1	666	666.00
1822	0	510	0.00

NIRGUA

YEAR	ECCLESIASTICS	POPULATION	POP/ECC
1781	2	3304	1652.00

TABLE 6. POPULATION/ECCLESIASTIC (CONTINUED)

YEAR	ECCLESIASTICS	POPULATION	POP/ECC
1802	0	3090	0.00
1803	1	3174	3174.00
1804	2	3182	1591.00
1805	2	2814	1407.00
1806	2	2856	1428.00
1807	1	2816	2816.00
1808	1	4288	4288.00
1809	1	4069	4069.00
1810	1	4668	4668.00
1813	1	3357	3357.00
1817	1	3311	3311.00
1819	1	3258	3258.00
1820	1	3268	3268.00
1821	1	3079	3079.00
	OCUMARE DE LA COSTA		
1802	1	2518	2518.00
1803	1	2035	2035.00
1804	1	1514	1514.00
1805	1	2226	2226.00
1809	0	1662	0.00
1815	1	1529	1529.00
1816	1	1540	1540.00
1817	1	1549	1549.00
1819	1	1154	1154.00
1820	1	1327	1327.00
	OCUMARE DEL TUY		
1783	2	2141	1070.50
1802	2	4103	2051.50
1803	2	4141	2070.50
1804	1	4753	4753.00
1805	1	4886	4886.00
1810	1	4691	4691.00
1811	4	3446	861.50
1815	2	1444	722.00
1820	2	4029	2014.50
1821	2	3825	1912.50
1822	2	3843	1921.50
	ORTIZ		
1780	1	1193	1193.00
1802	0	1700	0.00
1803	1	1503	1503.00
1804	1	1559	1559.00
1805	1	1570	1570.00
1806	1	1775	1775.00
1807	1	1896	1896.00
1808	1	1941	1941.00
1809	0	1985	0.00
1810	1	2019	2019.00
1813	1	1975	1975.00
	OSPINO		
1802	2	6021	3010.50
1803	2	6067	3033.50
1804	2	6375	3187.50
1805	3	6419	2139.67
1806	2	6767	3383.50
1807	2	6862	3431.00
1808	2	7102	3551.00
1809	2	7277	3638.50
1810	2	7251	3625.50
1811	3	5673	1891.00
1817	2	5506	2753.00
	PANAQUIRE		
1784	2	464	232.00
1802	1	911	911.00
1803	1	836	836.00
1804	1	811	811.00
1805	1	829	829.00
1807	1	823	823.00
1808	1	835	835.00
1809	1	821	821.00
1811	1	767	767.00
1812	1	797	797.00
1816	0	593	0.00
	PARACOTOS		
1783	1	1848	1848.00
1802	1	1889	1889.00
1803	1	2065	2065.00
1804	1	1764	1764.00
1805	1	1966	1966.00
1806	1	2089	2089.00
1807	1	2130	2130.00
1808	0	2197	0.00
1809	1	1631	1631.00
1810	0	1757	0.00
1811	0	1903	0.00
1812	0	2002	0.00
1816	0	1811	0.00
1817	0	1841	0.00
1819	1	1803	1803.00
1820	1	1812	1812.00
	PARAPARA		
1780	1	2008	2008.00

TABLE 6. POPULATION/ECCLESIASTIC (CONTINUED)

YEAR	ECCLESIASTICS	POPULATION	POP/ECC
1781	1	1992	1992.00
1782	1	2032	2032.00
1788	1	1978	1978.00
1802	1	2093	2093.00
1803	1	2219	2219.00
1805	1	2231	2231.00
1807	1	2330	2330.00
1809	1	2480	2480.00
1810	1	2585	2585.00
1811	1	2773	2773.00
PATANEMO			
1802	0	462	0.00
1803	0	469	0.00
1804	0	495	0.00
1805	0	533	0.00
1808	0	513	0.00
1818	0	411	0.00
1819	0	472	0.00
PAYARA			
1780	1	908	908.00
1802	0	1075	0.00
1804	0	1225	0.00
1805	0	1425	0.00
1806	0	1433	0.00
1807	1	1495	1495.00
1812	0	1425	0.00
PETARE			
1802	3	3840	1280.00
1803	2	3875	1937.50
1804	1	3899	3899.00
1805	1	4242	4242.00
1806	1	4130	4130.00
1807	2	4557	2278.50
1811	3	4349	1449.67
1812	5	4548	909.60
1815	2	3444	1722.00
1816	3	4508	1502.67
1817	3	4374	1458.00
1818	3	3400	1133.33
1819	3	3670	1223.33
1820	3	3854	1284.67
1821	3	3962	1320.67
1822	3	3748	1249.33
PUERTO CABELLO			
1803	1	4906	4906.00
1804	4	5213	1303.25
1805	3	5231	1743.67
1806	3	5394	1798.00
1811	4	5482	1370.50
1817	4	3642	910.50
1819	6	3279	546.50
1820	4	3112	778.00
PUERTO CABELLO, CASTILLO			
1801	0	523	0.00
1802	0	317	0.00
1804	0	482	0.00
1805	0	737	0.00
1806	0	1072	0.00
1807	1	1062	1062.00
1808	3	1198	399.33
1809	3	1139	379.67
1810	1	1441	1441.00
1819	1	852	852.00
1820	0	710	0.00
QUARA			
1782	0	1057	0.00
1791	1	805	805.00
1802	0	715	0.00
1803	0	703	0.00
1804	0	733	0.00
1805	0	847	0.00
1807	0	810	0.00
1808	0	907	0.00
1809	0	891	0.00
1810	0	900	0.00
1811	0	932	0.00
1815	0	930	0.00
1816	0	935	0.00
1817	1	947	947.00
1818	1	1005	1005.00
1819	0	859	0.00
QUIBOR			
1802	0	6805	0.00
1803	1	6678	6678.00
1804	1	6998	6998.00
1805	1	7408	7408.00
1806	0	7406	0.00
1807	1	7408	7408.00
1808	0	8024	0.00
1810	1	9970	9970.00
1812	0	8446	0.00
1815	0	8906	0.00

TABLE 6. POPULATION/ECCLESIASTIC (CONTINUED)

YEAR	ECCLESIASTICS	POPULATION	POP/ECC
1816	0	8706	0.00
1817	0	10004	0.00
1818	0	9780	0.00
1819	0	9276	0.00
1820	0	10161	0.00
RIO CHICO			
1802	1	869	869.00
1803	1	914	914.00
1804	1	999	999.00
1805	1	1140	1140.00
1806	1	1230	1230.00
1807	1	1286	1286.00
1808	0	1330	0.00
1809	1	1342	1342.00
1810	1	1442	1442.00
1811	1	1575	1575.00
1812	0	1420	0.00
1816	0	1425	0.00
1817	0	1379	0.00
1819	0	1417	0.00
RIO DEL TOCUYO			
1802	1	1887	1887.00
1803	1	1813	1813.00
1804	1	1639	1639.00
1805	1	1715	1715.00
1808	0	1769	0.00
1809	0	2394	0.00
1815	1	2386	2386.00
SABANETA			
1805	0	2125	0.00
1808	0	2383	0.00
1809	1	3000	3000.00
1810	1	3520	3520.00
1811	1	4057	4057.00
1812	1	2385	2385.00
1816	0	2246	0.00
SAN ANTONIO DE LAS COCUIZAS			
1780	1	1072	1072.00
SAN ANTONIO DE LOS ALTOS			
1796	2	471	235.50
1802	0	455	0.00
1803	1	504	504.00
1804	1	505	505.00

YEAR	ECCLESIASTICS	POPULATION	POP/ECC
1805	2	616	308.00
1808	2	1089	544.50
1809	1	969	969.00
1810	1	860	860.00
1811	1	857	857.00
1812	2	828	414.00
1815	1	588	588.00
1816	1	572	572.00
1817	1	533	533.00
1818	1	569	569.00
1819	3	583	194.33
1820	2	686	343.00
SAN CARLOS			
1781	13	7346	565.08
1786	11	7578	688.91
1787	12	7986	665.50
1788	11	8111	737.36
1791	13	8706	669.69
1796	9	9373	1041.44
1798	10	7853	785.30
1799	10	7888	788.80
1800	10	8221	822.10
1801	1	8316	8316.00
1802	12	8805	733.75
1803	13	8884	683.38
1804	12	10476	873.00
1805	11	10845	985.91
1806	10	11225	1122.50
1808	13	10846	834.31
1809	10	10845	1084.50
1811	8	12128	1516.00
1812	7	12035	1719.29
1816	6	7726	1287.67
1817	5	8190	1638.00
1818	9	8700	966.67
1819	8	8389	1048.62
1820	7	8348	1192.57
1822	7	8354	1193.43
1823	7	7673	1096.14
1824	7	6941	991.57
SAN DIEGO DE ALCALA			
1781	1	794	794.00
1802	0	1293	0.00
1803	0	730	0.00
1804	0	925	0.00
1805	0	837	0.00
1809	0	801	0.00

TABLE 6. POPULATION/ECCLESIASTIC (CONTINUED)

YEAR	ECCLESIASTICS	POPULATION	POP/ECC
SAN DIEGO DE LOS ALTOS			
1802	1	844	844.00
1803	1	937	937.00
1804	1	859	859.00
1805	1	917	917.00
1807	1	1025	1025.00
1808	1	1057	1057.00
1809	1	1206	1206.00
1810	1	1232	1232.00
1811	0	1255	0.00
1815	1	1228	1228.00
1816	0	1146	0.00
1817	1	1125	1125.00
1818	1	1078	1078.00
1819	1	1132	1132.00
1820	2	1198	599.00
SAN FELIPE			
1782	14	5020	358.57
1802	7	6070	867.14
1803	5	5667	1133.40
1804	5	4566	913.20
1805	6	5127	854.50
1817	3	3067	1022.33
1818	3	3224	1074.67
1819	3	3293	1097.67
1820	3	3381	1127.00
1821	3	2756	918.67
SAN FELIPE, MITAD DE (1)			
1807	3	2861	953.67
1808	3	2889	963.00
1809	4	2754	688.50
1810	3	2862	954.00
1811	3	2862	954.00
1812	3	2025	675.00
SAN FELIPE, MITAD DE (2)			
1807	1	2842	2842.00
1808	1	2887	2887.00
1809	1	2838	2838.00
1810	1	2878	2878.00
1811	0	2877	0.00
SAN FERNANDO DE APURE			
1801	0	3564	0.00
1805	0	1575	0.00
1806	0	2464	0.00
1816	0	1832	0.00
SAN FERNANDO DE CACHICAMO			
1783	1	420	420.00
1802	0	424	0.00
1803	1	415	415.00
1805	1	439	439.00
1806	1	513	513.00
1807	1	503	503.00
SAN FRANCISCO DE CARA			
1783	1	1169	1169.00
1802	1	1508	1508.00
SAN FRANCISCO DE TIZNADOS			
1780	1	2240	2240.00
1801	1	1746	1746.00
1802	1	1987	1987.00
1803	1	2054	2054.00
1805	1	2181	2181.00
1807	1	2368	2368.00
1808	1	2361	2361.00
1809	1	2423	2423.00
1811	0	2230	0.00
1812	1	2465	2465.00
SAN FRANCISCO DE YARE			
1783	1	1299	1299.00
1802	1	1766	1766.00
1803	0	1740	0.00
1804	0	1733	0.00
1805	0	1725	0.00
1810	1	2145	2145.00
1811	1	2152	2152.00
1815	0	1334	0.00
1817	0	2096	0.00
1818	0	1713	0.00
1820	1	1835	1835.00
1821	0	2006	0.00
1822	0	1958	0.00
SAN JAIME			
1780	1	1964	1964.00
SAN JOSE			
1781	1	1099	1099.00

TABLE 6. POPULATION/ECCLESIASTIC (CONTINUED)

YEAR	ECCLESIASTICS	POPULATION	POP/ECC
1788	1	1516	1516.00
1790	1	1727	1727.00
1791	1	1727	1727.00
1792	1	2102	2102.00
1794	1	2042	2042.00
1795	0	2246	0.00
1798	0	2517	0.00
1799	0	2517	0.00
1800	0	2535	0.00
1801	0	2572	0.00
1803	0	2543	0.00
1804	0	2560	0.00
1805	0	1920	0.00
1807	1	1624	1624.00
1808	1	1625	1625.00
1811	1	1597	1597.00
1812	1	1565	1565.00
1815	1	1739	1739.00
1818	1	1624	1624.00
1819	0	1669	0.00
1822	1	1992	1992.00
1823	1	1692	1692.00

SAN JOSE DE APURE

YEAR	ECCLESIASTICS	POPULATION	POP/ECC
1802	0	559	0.00
1804	1	719	719.00
1806	1	656	656.00
1807	1	615	615.00
1808	1	593	593.00
1809	1	593	593.00

SAN JOSE DE TIZNADOS

YEAR	ECCLESIASTICS	POPULATION	POP/ECC
1802	0	1865	0.00
1803	0	1994	0.00
1804	0	1938	0.00
1805	1	1967	1967.00
1807	1	2188	2188.00
1808	1	2009	2009.00
1809	1	2088	2088.00
1810	1	2261	2261.00
1812	1	2271	2271.00
1816	1	2104	2104.00
1817	1	2727	2727.00

SAN JUAN DE LOS MORROS

YEAR	ECCLESIASTICS	POPULATION	POP/ECC
1802	1	1232	1232.00
1803	1	1227	1227.00
1805	1	1389	1389.00
1806	1	1430	1430.00
1807	1	1493	1493.00
1809	1	1628	1628.00
1810	1	1622	1622.00
1811	1	1568	1568.00

SAN MATEO

YEAR	ECCLESIASTICS	POPULATION	POP/ECC
1781	1	2253	2253.00
1802	1	2276	2276.00
1803	1	2218	2218.00
1804	0	2254	0.00
1805	1	2286	2286.00
1806	1	2281	2281.00
1808	0	2124	0.00
1809	0	2415	0.00
1811	1	2508	2508.00
1815	1	1886	1886.00
1816	1	1873	1873.00
1817	1	1915	1915.00
1818	1	1930	1930.00
1821	1	2428	2428.00

SAN MIGUEL DE TRUJILLO

YEAR	ECCLESIASTICS	POPULATION	POP/ECC
1808	0	2343	0.00

SAN NICOLAS DE TOLENTINO

YEAR	ECCLESIASTICS	POPULATION	POP/ECC
1803	0	571	0.00
1808	1	697	697.00
1818	1	291	291.00
1820	1	442	442.00
1821	0	437	0.00

SAN PEDRO

YEAR	ECCLESIASTICS	POPULATION	POP/ECC
1810	0	1021	0.00
1811	0	1151	0.00
1816	0	938	0.00
1817	0	869	0.00

SAN RAFAEL DE ONOTO

YEAR	ECCLESIASTICS	POPULATION	POP/ECC
1779	1	598	598.00
1810	0	1330	0.00
1811	0	1273	0.00
1828	0	847	0.00
1829	0	827	0.00

SAN RAFAEL DE ORITUCO

YEAR	ECCLESIASTICS	POPULATION	POP/ECC
1783	1	1587	1587.00
1802	1	971	971.00
1803	1	972	972.00

TABLE 6. POPULATION/ECCLESIASTIC (CONTINUED)

YEAR	ECCLESIASTICS	POPULATION	POP/ECC
1804	1	1060	1060.00
1805	1	1068	1068.00
1806	1	1186	1186.00
1808	2	1214	607.00
1809	2	1084	542.00
1810	4	1483	370.75
1811	2	1564	782.00

SAN SEBASTIAN DE LOS REYES

YEAR	ECCLESIASTICS	POPULATION	POP/ECC
1783	4	2907	726.75
1802	3	3212	1070.67
1803	3	3310	1103.33
1804	3	3384	1128.00
1805	3	3387	1129.00
1806	3	3333	1111.00
1809	3	3088	1029.33
1810	2	3212	1606.00
1811	3	3245	1081.67

SANARE

YEAR	ECCLESIASTICS	POPULATION	POP/ECC
1803	1	3281	3281.00
1804	1	3315	3315.00
1805	1	3281	3281.00
1806	1	3107	3107.00
1807	1	3100	3100.00
1808	1	3092	3092.00
1809	1	3104	3104.00
1810	1	3118	3118.00
1812	1	2551	2551.00
1815	1	2248	2248.00
1816	1	2664	2664.00
1817	1	2781	2781.00
1818	1	2664	2664.00
1819	1	2232	2232.00
1820	1	2778	2778.00

SANTA CRUZ DE ARAGUA

YEAR	ECCLESIASTICS	POPULATION	POP/ECC
1802	0	6064	0.00
1803	1	5667	5667.00
1804	1	6138	6138.00
1805	2	5711	2855.50
1808	2	5717	2858.50
1811	2	4038	2019.00
1815	2	4316	2158.00
1816	2	4575	2287.50
1817	2	4699	2349.50
1818	2	3984	1992.00
1822	1	4824	4824.00

SANTA INES DEL ALTAR

YEAR	ECCLESIASTICS	POPULATION	POP/ECC
1779	1	65	65.00
1802	1	104	104.00
1803	1	103	103.00
1804	1	104	104.00
1805	1	137	137.00
1806	1	121	121.00
1810	1	90	90.00
1811	1	86	86.00
1818	0	200	0.00
1819	0	339	0.00
1820	0	310	0.00
1829	0	358	0.00

SANTA LUCIA

YEAR	ECCLESIASTICS	POPULATION	POP/ECC
1784	1	2197	2197.00
1787	1	2179	2179.00
1802	0	2878	0.00
1803	0	2733	0.00
1804	0	3100	0.00
1805	0	2688	0.00
1808	0	3381	0.00
1809	0	3385	0.00
1811	0	3520	0.00
1816	0	3262	0.00
1817	1	2947	2947.00
1818	2	2858	1429.00
1819	3	2699	899.67

SANTA MARIA DE IPIRE

YEAR	ECCLESIASTICS	POPULATION	POP/ECC
1783	1	1039	1039.00
1798	1	1286	1286.00
1803	1	1347	1347.00

SANTA ROSA DE LIMA

YEAR	ECCLESIASTICS	POPULATION	POP/ECC
1802	0	2850	0.00
1803	0	3019	0.00
1804	0	2850	0.00
1805	0	2853	0.00
1807	0	2926	0.00
1808	0	2893	0.00
1809	0	4378	0.00
1810	0	4563	0.00
1815	0	4174	0.00
1816	0	4649	0.00
1817	0	4683	0.00
1819	0	4574	0.00
1820	0	4574	0.00

TABLE 6. POPULATION/ECCLESIASTIC (CONTINUED)

SANTA TERESA DE JESUS

YEAR	ECCLESIASTICS	POPULATION	POP/ECC
1783	1	854	854.00
1786	1	814	814.00
1787	1	857	857.00
1788	1	877	877.00
1802	0	1613	0.00
1803	0	1799	0.00
1804	0	1902	0.00
1805	0	1742	0.00
1810	0	1915	0.00
1811	0	1812	0.00
1815	0	1364	0.00
1816	0	1352	0.00
1817	0	1423	0.00
1820	0	1497	0.00

SARARE

YEAR	ECCLESIASTICS	POPULATION	POP/ECC
1779	1	1200	1200.00
1802	1	2510	2510.00
1804	0	2666	0.00
1805	0	2223	0.00
1807	1	2439	2439.00
1808	1	2666	2666.00
1809	1	2666	2666.00
1810	1	2859	2859.00
1811	1	2666	2666.00
1817	1	2323	2323.00
1818	1	2778	2778.00

SIQUISIQUE

YEAR	ECCLESIASTICS	POPULATION	POP/ECC
1802	1	3983	3983.00
1803	1	4094	4094.00
1804	1	3310	3310.00
1805	1	3407	3407.00
1807	1	4083	4083.00

TACARIGUA DE MAMPORAL

YEAR	ECCLESIASTICS	POPULATION	POP/ECC
1784	1	673	673.00
1802	1	743	743.00
1803	1	696	696.00
1804	1	713	713.00
1805	0	599	0.00
1806	0	580	0.00
1807	1	562	562.00
1808	0	558	0.00
1809	0	544	0.00
1811	0	455	0.00
1816	0	519	0.00
1818	0	502	0.00
1820	1	570	570.00

TACATA

YEAR	ECCLESIASTICS	POPULATION	POP/ECC
1783	1	742	742.00
1799	1	1093	1093.00
1802	0	1381	0.00
1804	0	1425	0.00
1805	0	1453	0.00
1812	1	1457	1457.00
1813	1	1677	1677.00
1817	1	1257	1257.00
1818	2	1721	860.50
1819	2	1747	873.50
1820	2	2218	1109.00
1821	2	1863	931.50
1822	2	2054	1027.00

TAGUAI

YEAR	ECCLESIASTICS	POPULATION	POP/ECC
1802	2	1915	957.50
1803	2	1745	872.50
1804	2	1840	920.00
1805	2	1868	934.00
1810	1	2214	2214.00

TAPIPA

YEAR	ECCLESIASTICS	POPULATION	POP/ECC
1803	1	588	588.00
1804	1	663	663.00
1805	1	640	640.00
1806	1	560	560.00
1807	1	539	539.00
1808	1	485	485.00
1811	0	426	0.00
1812	0	403	0.00
1816	0	366	0.00
1817	0	356	0.00
1818	0	409	0.00
1819	0	417	0.00
1820	0	364	0.00
1829	0	320	0.00

TARIA

YEAR	ECCLESIASTICS	POPULATION	POP/ECC
1803	0	262	0.00
1808	1	335	335.00
1810	0	240	0.00

TARMAS

YEAR	ECCLESIASTICS	POPULATION	POP/ECC
1802	1	513	513.00

TABLE 6. POPULATION/ECCLESIASTIC (CONTINUED)

YEAR	ECCLESIASTICS	POPULATION	POP/ECC
1803	1	493	493.00
1805	1	467	467.00
1807	1	506	506.00
1808	0	486	0.00
1810	1	533	533.00
1811	1	538	538.00
1815	1	502	502.00
1816	1	527	527.00
1817	1	557	557.00
1818	1	543	543.00
1819	1	529	529.00
1820	1	504	504.00
1829	1	513	513.00
TEMERLA			
1802	1	544	544.00
1803	1	476	476.00
1804	1	479	479.00
1805	1	457	457.00
1806	1	470	470.00
1807	1	499	499.00
1808	1	470	470.00
1810	1	546	546.00
1817	1	663	663.00
1818	1	935	935.00
1819	1	716	716.00
1820	1	591	591.00
1821	1	622	622.00
TINACO			
1771	0	2053	0.00
1781	1	1782	1782.00
1787	1	1798	1798.00
1788	1	1662	1662.00
1790	0	2311	0.00
1791	1	1786	1786.00
1794	1	2294	2294.00
1795	1	2288	2288.00
1796	1	2246	2246.00
1798	1	2327	2327.00
1799	1	2276	2276.00
1800	0	2285	0.00
1801	0	2258	0.00
1802	0	2311	0.00
1803	0	2518	0.00
1804	0	2577	0.00
1805	0	2627	0.00
1806	0	2690	0.00
1807	0	2695	0.00
1808	0	2608	0.00
1811	1	2491	2491.00
1812	1	2573	2573.00
1816	2	2065	1032.50
1817	2	1981	990.50
1819	2	2118	1059.00
1820	2	2513	1256.50
1821	1	2971	2971.00
1822	1	2984	2984.00
1823	1	3373	3373.00
1824	1	3306	3306.00
1825	1	3373	3373.00
1826	1	3606	3606.00
1827	1	3620	3620.00
1829	1	3637	3637.00
1830	1	3524	3524.00
1831	1	3527	3527.00
1832	1	3574	3574.00
1834	1	4156	4156.00
1835	1	4586	4586.00
1836	1	5682	5682.00
1837	1	6362	6362.00
TINAJAS			
1781	1	1175	1175.00
1801	1	920	920.00
1802	0	1053	0.00
1803	1	1138	1138.00
1804	1	1146	1146.00
1805	1	1051	1051.00
1807	1	1142	1142.00
1808	1	1093	1093.00
1809	1	1001	1001.00
1810	1	1198	1198.00
1811	1	1303	1303.00
1813	0	1257	0.00
1818	0	759	0.00
1819	0	793	0.00
1820	0	715	0.00
1821	0	1113	0.00
TINAQUILLO			
1781	1	847	847.00
1787	1	1133	1133.00
1788	1	1043	1043.00
1790	1	1051	1051.00
1791	1	1055	1055.00
1792	1	1141	1141.00
1794	1	1139	1139.00
1795	1	1139	1139.00
1796	1	1121	1121.00
1798	1	1177	1177.00
1799	1	1097	1097.00

TABLE 6. POPULATION/ECCLESIASTIC (CONTINUED)

YEAR	ECCLESIASTICS	POPULATION	POP/ECC
1800	1	1080	1080.00
1801	1	1144	1144.00
1802	1	1131	1131.00
1803	1	1163	1163.00
1804	1	1231	1231.00
1805	1	1261	1261.00
1806	1	1149	1149.00
1807	1	1308	1308.00
1808	1	1321	1321.00
1809	0	1256	0.00
1811	1	1313	1313.00
1812	1	1319	1319.00
1815	1	1408	1408.00
1816	0	1654	0.00
1817	0	1478	0.00
1818	0	1880	0.00
1820	1	2619	2619.00
1822	1	1921	1921.00
1823	0	2752	0.00
1836	1	3253	3253.00
TOCUYITO			
1803	1	1705	1705.00
1804	0	1743	0.00
1805	0	1792	0.00
1812	1	3295	3295.00
1816	2	2248	1124.00
TUCUPIDO			
1783	1	486	486.00
1801	0	1827	0.00
1805	0	1953	0.00
1809	1	2383	2383.00
TUCUPIDO DE GUANARE			
1802	1	4254	4254.00
1803	1	3532	3532.00
1804	1	4236	4236.00
1805	1	4236	4236.00
1807	1	4488	4488.00
1808	0	4108	0.00
1809	1	4957	4957.00
1810	1	5292	5292.00
1817	1	2537	2537.00
TUCURAGUA			
1802	0	435	0.00
1803	0	425	0.00
1804	0	263	0.00
1805	0	409	0.00
1807	0	351	0.00
1808	0	406	0.00
1809	0	405	0.00
1812	0	293	0.00
1816	0	153	0.00
TUREN			
1778	1	418	418.00
1801	0	1004	0.00
1808	0	2522	0.00
1809	1	813	813.00
1810	1	2464	2464.00
1811	1	786	786.00
1812	1	770	770.00
1816	0	752	0.00
TURIAMO			
1802	0	181	0.00
1803	0	174	0.00
1804	0	204	0.00
1805	0	212	0.00
1808	0	239	0.00
1818	0	326	0.00
1819	0	264	0.00
TURMERO			
1781	2	6918	3459.00
1802	1	7529	7529.00
1803	1	7679	7679.00
1804	1	8065	8065.00
1805	1	8079	8079.00
1806	1	7908	7908.00
1808	2	7661	3830.50
1809	2	7359	3679.50
1811	2	7764	3882.00
URACHICHE			
1782	1	1350	1350.00
1788	1	1345	1345.00
1802	1	1663	1663.00
1803	1	1742	1742.00
1804	1	1719	1719.00
1805	1	1809	1809.00
1807	1	1865	1865.00
1808	1	1691	1691.00
1809	1	2275	2275.00
1810	1	2238	2238.00
1811	1	2269	2269.00

TABLE 6. POPULATION/ECCLESIASTIC (CONTINUED)

YEAR	ECCLESIASTICS	POPULATION	POP/ECC
1815	1	2242	2242.00
1816	1	2483	2483.00
1817	1	2099	2099.00
1818	1	2234	2234.00
1819	1	2457	2457.00

URAMA

YEAR	ECCLESIASTICS	POPULATION	POP/ECC
1802	0	696	0.00
1804	0	700	0.00
1806	0	631	0.00
1807	0	652	0.00
1808	0	670	0.00
1810	0	757	0.00
1818	0	450	0.00
1819	0	478	0.00
1820	0	485	0.00

VALENCIA

YEAR	ECCLESIASTICS	POPULATION	POP/ECC
1782	26	7237	278.35
1802	16	7619	476.19
1803	17	6758	397.53
1804	15	6222	414.80
1805	16	6571	410.69
1808	18	6574	365.22
1809	18	7034	390.78
1812	19	7745	407.63
1815	16	7662	478.87
1816	18	7959	442.17
1819	16	8959	559.94

VALLE DE LA PASCUA

YEAR	ECCLESIASTICS	POPULATION	POP/ECC
1804	1	1510	1510.00
1805	1	1605	1605.00
1806	1	1649	1649.00
1808	1	1726	1726.00
1809	1	2000	2000.00

VILLA DE CURA

YEAR	ECCLESIASTICS	POPULATION	POP/ECC
1780	2	4453	2226.50
1796	0	4260	0.00
1802	4	4525	1131.25
1803	7	4623	660.43
1804	7	4498	642.57
1805	5	4720	944.00
1806	5	4887	977.40
1807	5	4523	904.60
1808	5	4798	959.60
1809	5	4314	862.80
1811	4	5359	1339.75

YEAR	ECCLESIASTICS	POPULATION	POP/ECC
1816	1	3532	3532.00
1817	1	3414	3414.00
1822	2	4496	2248.00

YARITAGUA

YEAR	ECCLESIASTICS	POPULATION	POP/ECC
1782	1	2744	2744.00
1802	1	1898	1898.00
1803	1	2157	2157.00
1804	1	2164	2164.00
1805	1	2922	2922.00
1807	1	4597	4597.00
1808	1	5359	5359.00
1809	1	5359	5359.00
1810	3	5359	1786.33
1811	2	5124	2562.00
1812	2	4625	2312.50
1816	1	5704	5704.00
1817	1	5408	5408.00
1818	0	5579	0.00
1820	1	5775	5775.00

TABLE 7. CENSUS RETURNS BY YEAR

YEAR	NUMBER OF RETURNS	YEAR	NUMBER OF RETURNS
1771	1	1805	165
1772	0	1806	75
1773	0	1807	110
1774	0	1808	123
1775	0	1809	116
1776	0	1810	86
1777	0	1811	105
1778	7	1812	54
1779	11	1813	6
1780	18	1814	0
1781	24	1815	60
1782	11	1816	78
1783	23	1817	91
1784	13	1818	80
1785	0	1819	75
1786	2	1820	67
1787	5	1821	17
1788	10	1822	20
1789	0	1823	9
1790	3	1824	5
1791	8	1825	4
1792	4	1826	2
1793	0	1827	2
1794	6	1828	2
1795	7	1829	13
1796	13	1830	3
1797	0	1831	3
1798	11	1832	3
1799	13	1833	5
1800	8	1834	4
1801	27	1835	4
1802	150	1836	5
1803	152	1837	4
1804	163	1838	3
		TOTAL NUMBER OF RETURNS	2089

INDEX FOR PARTS I AND II